McGraw-Hill Education

IELTS

McGraw-Hill Education
IELTS

Monica Sorrenson

Second Edition

New York | Chicago | San Francisco | Athens | London | Madrid

Mexico City | Milan | New Delhi | Singapore | Sydney | Toronto

Monica Sorrenson has been an IELTS examiner in nine countries and a teacher in fifteen. She has qualifications from Australia and the United Kingdom.

2 3 4 5 6 7 8 9   LHS   21 20 19 18 17

ISBN   978-1-259-85956-4 (book and CD set)
MHID   1-259-85956-8

ISBN   978-1-259-85958-8 (book for set)
MHID   1-259-85958-4

e-ISBN   978-1-259-85957-1
e-MHID   1-259-85957-6

IELTS is a trademark of IELTS Partners, defined as the British Council, IELTS Australia Pty Ltd (solely owned by IDP Education Pty Ltd), and the University of Cambridge: Cambridge English: Language Assessment. These organizations were not involved in the production of, and do not endorse, this product.

McGraw-Hill Education products are available at special quantity discounts to use as premiums and sales promotions, or for use in corporate training programs. To contact a representative, please visit the Contact Us pages at www.mhprofessional.com.

CONTENTS

PART III   IELTS Practice Tests

ON CD-ROM: Audio Recordings 1-75

PART I

Getting Started

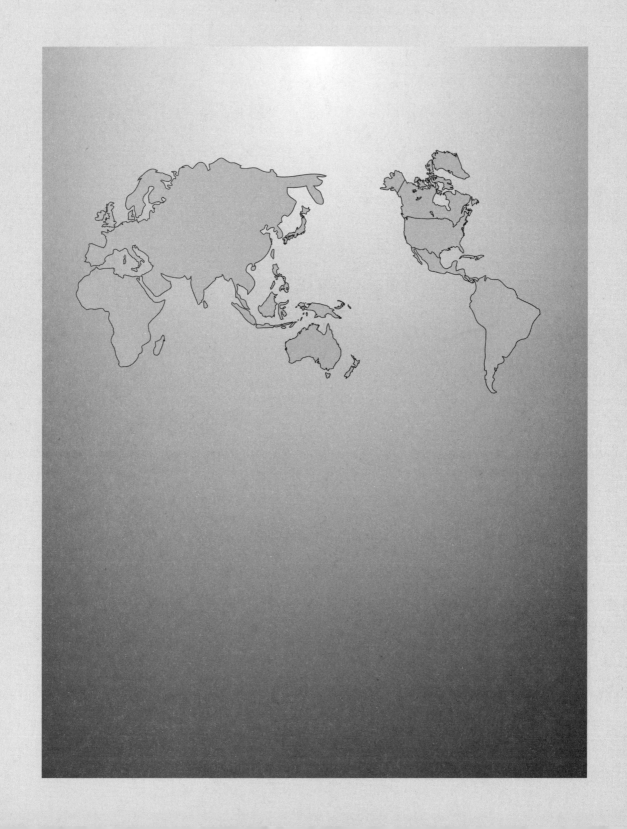

CHAPTER 1 Introducing IELTS

What is the IELTS exam?

The International English Language Testing System (IELTS) is the world's largest exam, and as its name suggests, it is used to test English language for college and university entrance, as well as for immigration or registration with professional bodies.

There are two kinds of IELTS tests: the Academic test for further study and the General Training (GT) test for immigration.

There is no pass or fail with IELTS. Instead, there are bands that show a person's level. These bands range from 0-9. A Zero is a candidate who didn't come for the test; and a Nine is a native speaker – someone whose English is perfect. A Five is a person who makes a lot of mistakes but can generally be understood. A Six is still an intermediate speaker, whereas a Seven is starting to get good. An Eight has perhaps only five or six errors in his or her 650 words of writing, and in the Speaking test, makes only very occasional errors. A Six is not that hard to score, but a Seven takes years of intensive study and usually residence in an English-speaking country.

The bands are used by different institutions or authorities. If you want to attend university in many English-speaking countries, you need at least IELTS 5.5 – the more famous the university, or the course, the higher the score you need. If you want permanent residence in Canada, you need a Seven. If you're a nurse and you want to continue nursing in Australia, then you also need a Seven overall, including a Seven in Speaking.

IELTS has full and half bands, meaning that a person who gets 6.5 is better than a Six, but not yet a Seven. One thing to note about these scores is that it's rather easy to go from a Four to a 4.5, or even a Five to a 5.5, but to progress beyond Six takes much longer. There are also candidates who never reach Six. You can't just take the test, take it again, and again and again, and hope on the fifth attempt you'll be handed a 6.5. No. You've got to fit the description of 6.5 in order to get it.

If you'd like to know which nationalities or first languages currently achieve which scores, go to the IELTS website: **www.ielts.org**. There's plenty of interesting data there as well as free practice materials.

What are the four parts of the test?

IELTS is made up of four sub-tests. Candidates do all of them on one or two days. They are, in the order that they take place: Listening, Reading, Writing, and Speaking.

The four tests are equally weighted, or if you think of it another way: worth 25% each. A band is given for each one, and there is also an average or Overall Band. A candidate receives a report within two weeks of taking the test with five scores on it like this:

Listening	Reading	Writing	Speaking
7	6.5	6	6.5

Overall Band = 6.5

You can see that the candidate above was best at Listening and worst at Writing. Reading and Speaking were the same. The majority of candidates receive a report like this. It's very rare for one skill to be much better than another.

But what was the Listening test? What did the candidate need to do for Writing?

Read the table below about the IELTS Academic test to understand exactly what happens. GT is the same as Academic for Listening and Speaking, but a little different for Reading and Writing.

ACADEMIC

Test	How long does the test take?	What is its format?	What question types are there?
Listening	40 minutes A recording lasts for 30 minutes. There are 10 extra minutes to transfer answers from a question booklet onto an answer sheet after the recording has finished.	Around 40 questions in four sections. Each section has 10 questions. Each question is worth one mark. Questions are easy at the start and become more difficult as the test progresses. On a test day, all candidates listen to the same recording and have the same questions, but these recordings and questions differ from test to test. There are different versions of all IELTS tests.	The following may be used: Multi-choice (choosing one answer from three possibilities) Multiple matching (choosing more than one answer from a list of up to seven possibilities) Choosing a graphic Note / Table / Sentence / Summary completion (filling in gaps) Labelling maps or plans Providing one- to three-word answers
Reading	60 minutes Candidates transfer their answers as they read. There is no extra time.	Around 40 questions in three passages. **Passage 1**: (13 or 14 questions) **Passage 2**: (13 or 14 questions) **Passage 3**: (13 questions) Each question is worth one mark. Questions are easy at the start and become more difficult as the test progresses. Words to be read in the passages: 2500-2750. (With questions, there are around 3500 words.)	The following may be used: Multi-choice (choosing one answer from four possibilities) Multiple matching (choosing more than one answer from a list of up to seven possibilities) Choosing a graphic Note / Table / Sentence / Summary completion (filling in gaps) Labelling maps or plans Providing one- to three-word answers Completing a summary by choosing words that are given in a long list Indicating which paragraph contains information Choosing True / False / Not Given for facts Choosing Yes / No / Not Given for views or opinions Choosing headings Labelling a diagram or a flowchart

Writing	60 minutes	Two short pieces of writing called tasks. **Task 1**: A report or description of a table, chart, process, or other visual input. Words to be written: at least 150 **Task 2**: An essay on a social or academic topic that is given. Words to be written: at least 250 Task 1 is easier than Task 2. Task 2 is worth twice as much as Task 1. On a test day, every candidate gets the same two tasks, but these differ from test to test.	Task 1: Describing a visual input that could be one, two, or three graphs, tables, or charts; two plans or maps; or a process. Task 2: Essays that discuss one or both sides of an issue, or offer solutions to a problem are the most common.
Speaking	11-14 minutes	There are three parts. **Part 1**: (4-5 minutes) The candidate is asked one set of questions on personal information, and two sets of questions on simple topics. **Part 2**: (3-4 minutes) The candidate is given a random specific topic, has one minute to think, then two minutes to talk about it. There may be one or two short questions at the end. **Part 3**: (4-5 minutes) The candidate is asked more general questions connected to the topic of Part 2. A single band is given at the end of this. In Part 1, candidates may be asked the same questions, but in Parts 2 and 3, each candidate gets different questions. These will be similar from test to test. Part 1 is easy; Part 2, more difficult; and Part 3 is rather challenging.	Questions in Parts 1 and 2 are personal; in Part 3, they are more general or abstract. Any topic of general interest may be discussed. Candidates need to: agree or disagree; assess; compare; describe; explain; express possibility and probability; justify an opinion; narrate; speculate; suggest; and summarise. Additional skills include: the ability to self-correct; to circumlocute; to paraphrase; and to ask for clarification.

GENERAL TRAINING

Test	How long does it take?	What is its format?	What question types are there?
Reading	60 minutes Candidates transfer their answers while they read. There is no extra time.	Around 40 questions in three sections. The first two sections are divided into two parts, so there are five different texts to read in total. Each question is worth one mark. Questions are easy at the start and become more difficult as the test progresses. Words to be read in the passages: 2000-2300. (With questions, there are around 3000 words.) Note: There are fewer words in the GT than the Academic test, but candidates need to get more correct answers to be awarded the same band. See page 7.	See Academic Reading above.
Writing	60 minutes	Two short pieces of writing called tasks. **Task 1**: A formal or semi-formal letter. Words to be written: at least 150 **Task 2**: An essay on a social topic that is given. Words to be written: at least 250	Task 1: Letters of: request, advice, offer, complaint, congratulation, or opinion are the most common. Task 2: Essays that discuss one or both sides of an issue, or offer solutions to a problem are the most common.

How is IELTS marked?

On the day of the test, the Speaking is marked by the examiner who interviewed the candidate. Task 1 writing is marked by one examiner; Task 2, by another. Listening and Reading are calculated by a clerk who is not a Speaking or Writing examiner. Therefore four different people evaluate one candidate's performance. Among other things, this reduces corruption as the examiners and clerical markers seldom know each other.

As we have just learnt, IELTS uses bands. Do you remember this candidate?

Listening	Reading	Writing	Speaking
7	6.5	6	6.5

Overall Band = 6.5

Another candidate might get:

Listening	Reading	Writing	Speaking
5.5	5	5	5

Overall Band = 5

The *majority* of candidates have most skills in the same band. If a candidate has one test that is two bands different from another, his or her paper is marked again, and the higher of the two marks becomes the new score.

For example: a candidate gets:

Listening	Reading	Writing	Speaking
6	6	4	6

Overall Band = 5.5

If his or her Writing is marked again and is still a Four or becomes a 4.5, then the Overall Band remains a 5.5. If a Four goes up to a Five, then the new Overall Band is a Six. All this happens before the final report is sent out.

Listening and Reading

These two tests are made up of 40 questions each that are either right or wrong. There are no half marks. The marking of these is fairly easy, but they are marked twice for accuracy.

There are multiple versions of the Listening and Reading tests. Each version differs slightly in its degree of difficulty. They are all pre-tested. As you already know, Academic and GT Reading tests are also different. Here's a guide to the scores needed for some bands for Listening and Reading. Since there are so many versions of these tests, this table is approximate.

Band	Listening /40	Academic Reading /40	GT Reading /40
4	9	8	15
4.5	12	12	19
5	16	15	23
5.5	19	19	27
6	23	23	30
6.5	27	27	32
7	30	30	34
7.5	33	33	36
8	35	35	37

Writing and Speaking

As you can imagine, Writing and Speaking are harder to mark than Listening and Reading since each candidate will give different answers. Candidates will, however, have common features, which determine their level.

For Writing and Speaking, these common features are described by special criteria at each band. (Look up 'criteria' in your dictionary now.)

This book, the second edition of *McGraw-Hill Education's IELTS*, is based on criterion marking, so it's important to understand how it works. A great many candidates prepare for IELTS without having any idea what they're being judged on, and so can't improve their performance effectively. Here, the criteria will be described and analysed. For example, Pronunciation is a Speaking criterion, but it's likely you've got only a vague idea what pronunciation means. Once you've understood what many things really make up pronunciation, then you can start learning how to pronounce English well.

Remember this?

Listening	Reading	Writing	Speaking
7	6.5	6	6.5

Overall Band = 6.5

There's nothing about criteria on this report – nothing to tell you how the examiners reached their conclusions. A candidate knows only in a general sense that his Listening is stronger than everything else. He probably has no idea why his Writing got a Six.

So what are the Writing and Speaking criteria?

Writing and Speaking criteria are similar: both include a judgment on a candidate's vocabulary and grammar. In Writing, candidates must also describe, analyse, and argue well. In Speaking, pronunciation plays a major role. To achieve a high band in IELTS, it's important to understand exactly what marking criteria are.

Writing criteria

There are four criteria for Writing. They're the same for Task 1 and Task 2.
In brief, the criteria are:

1 Task Fulfilment (Also called Task Achievement or Task Response: Answering the question fully)

2 Coherence and Cohesion (Words, sentences, paragraphs joined smoothly; a logical order throughout)

3 Lexical Resource (Vocabulary)

4 Grammatical Range and Accuracy (Grammar)

Each criterion carries the same weight. This is significant because, when asked, most candidates believe grammar is the most important thing in writing.

While each criterion is worth the same, a large amount of research has shown that one criterion – Lexical Resource, called Vocabulary in the book – is most difficult. This is because English vocabulary is vast. The most common problem IELTS candidates have is that their vocabulary is limited. It is boring, repetitive, childish, or inaccurate. Perhaps the tone of their language is also inappropriate. Usually this is because they do not read much in English. Reading exposes you to vocabulary most quickly. Probably, learners need to do *three times* the amount of work on vocabulary that they do on *any* of the other criteria to improve. This book reflects this necessity with a large number of activities on Vocabulary.

As previously mentioned, candidates don't have a breakdown of criteria on their report form. But let's look at a typical score sheet an examiner has. This is for Writing for Task 1:

Task Fulfilment	Coherence & Cohesion	Vocabulary	Grammar
6	6	5	6

The candidate gets 5.5 for this task.
(By the way: there are no half bands within criteria.)

Here is a Writing score sheet for Task 2:

Task Fulfilment	Coherence & Cohesion	Vocabulary	Grammar
7	6	5	7

The candidate gets Six for this task.
Task 2 is worth twice as much as Task 1. The candidate above ends up with a Six as a Writing band.

Basically, Vocabulary was this candidate's weak point, and if it had been a Six, he or she would have ended up with 6.5 for Writing. Now perhaps it's a small difference between Six and 6.5, but let's say you want to do an MA in Canada. The university you've applied for asks for 6.5 for IELTS Writing for direct admission. If you get a Six, then you need to do a ten-week English-language course first. That's another two months of your life you have to pay for and live through before starting your MA.

Speaking criteria

There are also four criteria for Speaking. Unlike Writing, where the tasks are rated separately, there is only one score given for the candidate's whole Speaking test.

In brief, the criteria are:

1 Fluency and Coherence (The ability to keep speaking; accurate use of linkers; sound logic)

2 Lexical Resource (Vocabulary)

3 Grammatical Range and Accuracy (Grammar)

4 Pronunciation

You can see that there's no Task Fulfilment criterion. This means the examiner doesn't judge the *content* of the candidate's answers – the candidate can say pretty much anything he or she likes. If you want to say your mother's an astronaut on the International Space Station and your father's Bill Gates' best mate, that's fine, as long as your English is correct.

Like Writing, each criterion is worth 25%.

Generally, candidates still find Vocabulary problematic. Fluency is also a challenge because it's possible the candidate has never spoken for so long in English. Also, almost no teachers or textbooks focus on Fluency. (Is it anywhere in the Table of Contents of your best mate's IELTS book?) Depending on what your first language is, pronunciation may be difficult. If you're German, it's not so hard; if you're Vietnamese, it's hell. Let's say you're from Ho Chi Minh City, and you want permanent residence in Australia. For residence, you may need a Seven for Speaking. Frankly, that's going to be extremely tough because time and time again even if you're really good, you'll get:

Fluency & Coherence	Grammar	Vocabulary	Pronunciation
7	7	7	6

Overall Band = 6.5

Hopefully this book will give your pronunciation a boost.

If you've read this far, you've realised that IELTS is not just a matter of learning the question types (any old book deals with those), but more importantly understanding the marking criteria for Writing and Speaking. If you look at the Table of Contents of this book, you'll see how each criterion is pulled apart and practised here. Then we put them all together for the practice tests.

How should I prepare for IELTS?

The simplest answer to this question is: *put in the effort*. If this means setting your alarm for 5 AM, and studying for an hour each day before you go to work, that's what you have to do.

Here are six days in a week. Write in time you can spend each day on IELTS prep. Be realistic, but also don't be lazy.

Day						
AM Activity						
PM Activity						

For most candidates, reading needs to be a priority. Not only is reading tested in IELTS, but as mentioned previously, vocabulary is learnt most effectively through reading. Twenty minutes' reading in English every day will dramatically improve your IELTS score. It doesn't matter what kinds of things you read: football, Indian cookery, the lives of insects, as long as you're practising. Use a dictionary only once or twice a day. Just absorb and enjoy. (Use the Reading Log on page 444.)

It's a good idea to take IELTS as soon as you can. This lets you see what your level is. You may be pleasantly surprised and discover you only need to work on one skill for your 'real' test, but it's more likely you'll be shocked, and panic.

You may also need to buy some more books, perhaps for grammar or vocabulary. There are plenty to choose from.

Some IELTS candidates like to find a buddy, a friend who is also taking the test, to work with. It's fun to compete, testing each other on new vocabulary, for instance; or doing the practice tests together under exam conditions. Learning needs feedback, which means you don't learn until someone tells you what your mistakes are, so if your buddy can also do this – in the nicest way possible – then that's excellent.

Of course IELTS is a major exam, but there is life after IELTS whether you get the band you need or not. You won't stop learning English just because you get a Six. It's likely your new job, or the course you're doing in another country, will prove more challenging than this one exam.

Characteristics of different bands

There are ten IELTS bands. The creators of the IELTS exam describe them in this way:

9	Expert user	Has fully operational command of the language: appropriate, accurate and fluent with complete understanding.
8	Very good user	Has fully operational command of the language with only occasional unsystematic inaccuracies and inappropriacies. Misunderstandings may occur in unfamiliar situations. Handles complex detailed argumentation well.
7	Good user	Has operational command of the language, though with occasional inaccuracies and misunderstandings in some situations. Generally handles complex language well and understands detailed reasoning.
6	Competent user	Has generally effective command of the language despite some inaccuracies, inappropriacies and misunderstandings. Can use fairly complex language, particularly in familiar situations.
5	Modest user	Has partial command of the language, coping with overall meaning in most situations, though is likely to make many mistakes. Should be able to handle basic communication in own field.
4	Limited user	Basic competence is limited to familiar situations. Has frequent problems in understanding and expression. Is not able to use complex language.
3	Extremely limited user	Conveys and understands only general meaning in very familiar situations. Frequent breakdowns in communication occur.
2	Intermittent user	No real communication is possible except for the most basic information using isolated words or short formulae in familiar situations and to meet immediate needs. Has great difficulty understanding spoken and written English.
1	Non user	Essentially has no ability to use the language beyond possibly a few isolated words.
0	Did not attempt the test	No assessable information provided.

What does all this mean?

Choose words from the box to fill in the numbered gaps below. There is an example.

accent	answers	assuming	going	Mandarin
	~~no~~	operational	residency	

Clearly, a Nine makes (eg) *no* mistakes at all. An Eight has 'occasional' mistakes, meaning four of five wrong (1) _____ in a Listening or Reading test (35-36/40) and five or six mistakes in a Writing or Speaking test. Considering an Eight writes around 650 words and says about 1350, that's 1988/2000 correct words. While an adult Eight may have an (2) _____ from his or her first language, there will be no noticeable errors in pronunciation. Bearing this in mind, not a lot of candidates are (3) _____ to be Eights.

The vast majority of people who learn English can never expect to reach Eight. Furthermore, a Seven is not easy to achieve either – it has to be earned with years of study, practice, and perhaps living in an English-speaking environment. A Six can't just keep taking the IELTS exam week after week (4) _____ he or she will automatically be given a Seven.

For many candidates, the difference between a Six and a Seven is important, and this book aims to define it, as well as to develop some higher-level skills. Having '(5) _____ command', which a Seven has, means a person can easily work in English in an English-speaking country. For that reason, Australia, Britain, Canada, and New Zealand require Sevens for (6) _____.

The good news is that many people reach Five or 5.5 after a couple of years' study. English is not hard to learn in comparison to Arabic, (7) _____, or Russian.

If you've already taken the IELTS exam and not got the score you wanted . . .
Here are ten questions to ask yourself:

• Which skill was my weakest?

• Do I accept that this is not a matter of luck but an indication of my level?

• Which qualified person can I ask about why this is my weakest skill?

• Can I seriously devote time to improving this skill?

• Can I find an IELTS buddy?

• Can I take an English course or private lessons?

• Do I accept that improving all my skills is not a matter of doing ever more practice tests (especially many online ones that resemble actual exams only in appearance)?

• Do I accept that I need to understand skills more deeply and practise more meaningfully? (*See the Appendices at the back of this book.*)

• Can I work on my vocabulary, grammar, and pronunciation consistently?

• If I don't get the score I need within one year, what is Plan B?

PART II

Building IELTS Skills

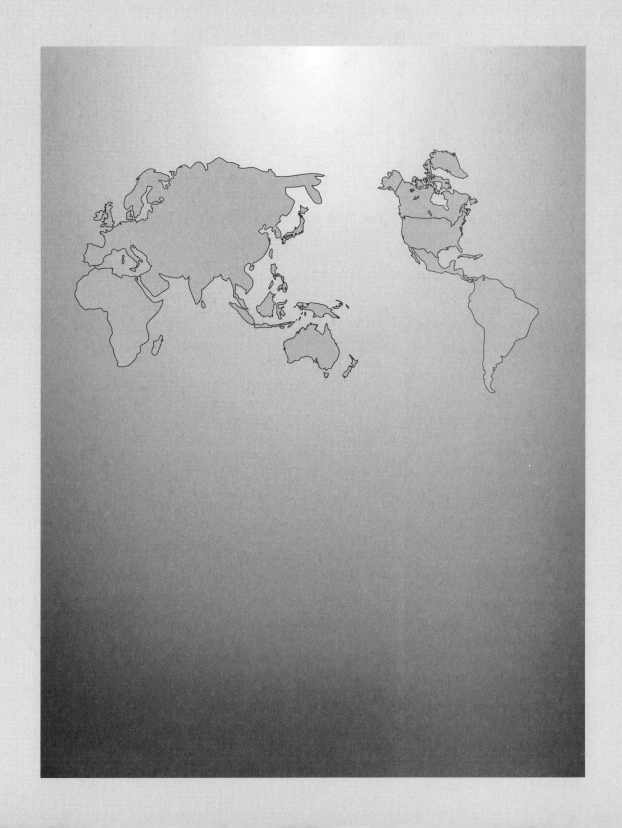

CHAPTER **2** IELTS Listening

Introduction to the Listening test

The Listening test is the first part of the IELTS exam. <u>It is the same test for both Academic and General Training candidates.</u> (eg)

Test centres worldwide have different rules about pens or pencils – check what you can bring, or what's provided. Candidates can't use dictionaries in the test, nor ask anyone for help. Candidates who copy from others are warned to stop, and if they don't, are asked to leave the exam.

Each candidate is given a question booklet and an answer sheet, which are collected at the end of the test. The booklet contains the instructions and questions, and candidates can write on it. The answer sheet is for the final answers, which must be written neatly. Any answer that can't be read easily is marked wrong. Candidates are not penalised for writing in capitals, and punctuation is not counted.

A woman, on a recording, introduces the Listening test. She says something like: 'The Listening test takes around 40 minutes. There are four different recordings. You answer questions about what you hear. You have time to read the instructions and questions before each recording, and time to check your answers afterwards. Listen carefully as the recordings are only played <u>once</u>. You write your answers on the Listening test booklet while you listen. After the last recording, there are ten minutes to transfer your answers to your answer sheet. Now, open your booklet to Section 1.'

The woman does <u>not</u> tell candidates that each recording, or section, lasts between five to six minutes. (Pretty short, huh?) The rest of the time is for reading questions or checking answers. The sections are divided into two parts as well.

There are usually two question types per section. Sometimes there are three; occasionally, there is one. Question types are:

- **gapfill** – Fill in a gap with the missing word(s). In forms and tables, this is in note form. In sentences and summaries, this is in grammatically correct English. (This is also called form filling, note completion, table completion, sentence completion, and summary completion in some IELTS books.)

- **short-answer** – Provide answers, usually to 'Wh-' questions.

- **multi-choice (MCQs)** – Choose answers from A, B, or C. These could be single-word answers, whole-sentence answers, or choosing the correct graphic. (There are seldom more than ten MCQs in a test.)

- **multiple matching** – Choose two or more answers from a list that relates to a single question. There are never more than seven items in a list (A, B, C, D, E, F, or G). If the instructions say so, candidates may use any letter more than once. In a Listening test, there is only likely to be one multiple matching question. (This is also called matching lists or classification.)

- **labelling** of maps, plans, diagrams, or flowcharts.

No answer in the IELTS Listening test is more than three words. Sixty percent of the answers are just one word. There are usually only three or four three-word answers in any test. (Look at the proportion of answer types in the Practice Tests.) Occasionally, two letters are needed for one answer.

Listening questions are all in order. That is, the answer to question 1 comes on the recording before the answer to question 2. Often answers are repeated. Questions become more difficult as the test progresses.

YOUR TURN *The following statements refer to the text that you have just read. For each statement, write T (True), F (False), or NG (Not Given) in the space provided. Underline your evidence in the text. There is an example.*

Eg Academic and General Training candidates take different Listening tests. <u>F</u>

1   Cheating is a problem worldwide in IELTS. ____

2   Messy handwriting means Listening answers may be disregarded. ____

3   The Listening test lasts for 40 minutes. ____

4   Some Listening sections are five minutes long. ____

5   Labelling questions are generally the most difficult. ____

6   Up to 25% of the Listening test could be multi-choice questions. ____

7   IELTS answers in the Listening test may be any length. ____

8   The answer to question 7 always comes before the answer to question 8 in the recording of the Listening test. ____

What are the four different sections of the Listening test?

Match the words in the box with the numbers in the text below. Write the numbers in the spaces provided. There is an example.

				eg	
academic	challenging	programme	refute	social	talking about

Section 1 is an *informal dialogue* (two speakers) about a(n) —**eg**— or semi-official situation. This could be someone buying tickets, or asking for information, or reporting lost property. It might be people —**1**— a house to rent or a holiday to go on.

Section 2 is an *informal monologue* (one speaker), like a guided tour, or a person giving a short talk on a topic of general interest. It could be part of a radio —**2**—, where the interviewer doesn't speak much. The language and the question types are slightly more difficult than in Section 1.

Section 3 is a *more formal discussion* in a(n) —**3**— setting: perhaps a group of students discussing their assignment, or a student and lecturer resolving a problem. There may be up to four speakers.

Section 4 is a *mini-lecture*. In this section, not only are the language of the speaker and the question types more —**4**—, but there's also a need to understand more than just the words. What is the speaker inferring? What does his or her intonation suggest? Whose ideas does the lecturer support or —**5**—?

What is tested in the Listening test?

700	attitude	global	not	spelling

The Listening test wants candidates to: identify speakers; assume what is happening; find —**6**— information; find specific information; understand negative language; or, a speaker's —**7**—.

It also tests their reading ability since each test has around —**8**— words. Vocabulary, grammar, and —**9**— are important as well. All answers must be spelt correctly. This book has 18 pages on spelling for this reason.

Of the four tests, many candidates do best or second-best in Listening. However, around the world, men do —**10**— score as highly as women.

How is the Listening test marked?

What are the missing words below? Write the letters to complete each one.

There are 40 questions in the Listening test. Each one is worth one mark. There are no half marks even when a question asks for two answers as it does occasionally. Candidates should answer every question because if they get one wrong, they don't **lo __ __** a mark.

Typically, a Six thinks the test is quite easy, but **sco __ __ __** around 23 out of 40. This is because the questions are, in fact, not so easy, and spelling counts. A Six makes **sev __ __ __ __** spelling mistakes. A candidate below a Six has serious problems with Section 4, and leaves many answers blank, or **gue __ __ __ __** them. He or she doesn't have time to read all the questions. Only a Seven or above is completely comfortable with the test.

The people who mark the Listening test have strict instructions. Each paper is marked **tw __ __ __**. A candidate can ask for his or her Listening paper to be marked again, but this is expensive, and the **v __ __ __** majority of candidates do <u>not</u> get any more marks. IELTS is so confident about its marking that a candidate who does go up gets his or her re-marking fee **b __ __ __**!

Bands

Here is a table of *approximate* marks for IELTS bands.
Refer to this page when you do your practice tests.

Band	4	4.5	5	5.5	6	6.5	7	7.5	8	8.5
Mark out of 40	9	12	16	19	23	27	30	33	35	37

In a real IELTS test, these bands could be one or two marks higher or lower. For example: a Four might equal 8 or 10; a Seven might be 29 or 31. Each test is slightly different.

How to fill out the Listening and Reading answer sheets

The Listening answer sheet

Let's imagine one candidate wants to move to Canada, another hopes to become an accountant in Australia, and a third would like to work as a registered nurse in the United States. All of these people need a Seven in all four tests, which is difficult. If they get 32/40 or 33/40 in Listening or Reading, their applications will be rejected. Only one or two marks in IELTS can make a huge difference to a person's future.

Sometimes candidates know the answers in the Listening test, but don't fill out the answer sheet properly. Or, their spelling is poor.

Below is a fake answer sheet. You don't need to know what the questions are to understand the problems with the answers.

The incorrect answers are marked according to the following:

G = Grammatical mistake	
Sp = Spelling mistake	**T** = Too many words
U = Unclear answer	**V** = Vocabulary mistake

Suggest a solution for each one as in the examples.

	Candidate's answers	Problem	Solution
Eg	quater	Sp	**quarter / ¼**
Eg	to expensive	V	**too expensive**
Eg	B / D	U	***Which one?***
1	new acommodation	Sp	
2	high buildings	V	
3	studing in groups	Sp	
4	differents nationalities	G	
5	ivi	U	
6	spreaded throughout Asia	G	
7	150,00$	U	
32	Mz Masters	Sp	
33	school principle	V	
35	obey traffic rules & regulations	T	
36	local goverment	Sp	
37	due to late	G	

Here are three more answers. Which one is correct?

38	barbecue ~~barbicue~~ with neighbours	
39		
40	comunity sense of ~~community~~	

The Reading answer sheet

What are the missing words below? Write the letters to complete each one.

The Reading test is similar to the Listening test in its format. If answers are illegible, they're marked **wro** __ __. If there are two many or too **f** __ __ answers, again, they're wrong. If there's a word a candidate provides from his or her head in a **sum** __ __ __ __ question, for example, the spelling must be perfect, but if there's a word given in a box which the candidate **accid** __ __ __ __ __ __ __ copies down wrongly, then he or she still gets a mark.

Unlike the Listening test, there is no **trans** __ __ __ time at the end of the Reading test. Candidates must read, answer, and fill out the sheet **with** __ __ the one hour.

Some candidates answer Passage 3 in the Reading **fir** __ __ because it's the longest and most difficult. If you do this, be **ca** __ __ __ __ __ where you write your answers on your answer sheet.

It's a good idea to make a little **ma** __ __ after questions 14 and 27 on your answer sheet to show where Reading passages end. This way, if you need to go **b** __ __ __ to answer anything in the last few minutes of the test, you can quickly find the place on your sheet.

IF YOU WANT A SEVEN

Here are 12 more incorrect Listening answers. What should they be?

	Candidate's answers	Problem	Solution
1	writting a journal	Sp	
2	six-pages story	G	
3		U	
4	footbreak	Sp	
5	adjust review mirror	V	
6	discover in 1955	G	
7		U	
8	opposing thumbs	V	
9	gorillas, orangutans, chimps, humans	T	
10	made researches	V & G	
11	three millions people	G	
12	endangered specious	V	

Listening strategies
Section 1

In Section 1 of the Listening test, candidates identify speakers and understand simple specific information.

It's a good idea to work out as much as possible about the recording before it's played. In the instruction time and the 30 seconds reading time, ask yourself: Who are these speakers? What are they talking about? Who wants what? Don't forget to read the title to help you.

Remember, there's more information in the recording than you're tested on. It's important to know *exactly* what you want to find out, so you don't get tired concentrating on every single word. Underline key words in the questions – not almost every word. Circle any negative ideas.

Now, let's look at which question types are easy, and which may need more practice.

Read all the questions on the next two pages. They are for the first part of Section 1 of a Listening test.

Which set – I, II, or III – do you think would be the hardest to answer? Why?

 PLAY RECORDING 1 and answer the Set III questions shown.

The first part of Section 1

LOST PROPERTY AND THEATRE TICKETS

Set I

Choose the correct letter: A, B, or C.

1   Emma left her raincoat at the theatre

    A   on Saturday.

    (B)   last night.

    C   two nights ago.

2   The man at the theatre has

    A   one coat and one umbrella.

    B   two coats and one umbrella.

    (C)   two coats and two umbrellas.

Choose two letters from the list below.

3   What features does Emma's coat have?

    (A)   a hood

    B   embroidery

    C   outside pockets

    (D)   inside pockets

    E   a short zipper

*Write **ONE WORD AND/OR A NUMBER** for each answer.*

4   What time does the woman start work?

5   How does the man say he feels about helping Emma?

Shally
95413828

Set II

Complete the sentences below.

*Write **NO MORE THAN THREE WORDS AND/OR NUMBERS** for each answer.*

1   Emma is calling the ....*magestic*.... Theatre.

2   Emma describes her coat as being quite ....*ood record*.....

3   Emma says her two coat pockets are ....*two Umbrella*....

4   The man's colleague is called ....*Shally*..... .

5   Emma shouldn't collect her coat between ....*6 to 6:30*.... .

Set III

1   *Which picture shows Emma's coat?*

A   B   C

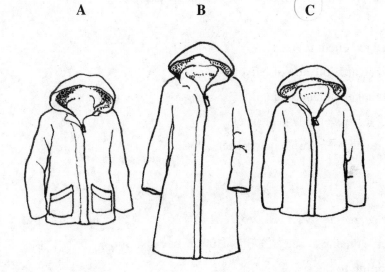

Complete the notes below.

*Write **NO MORE THAN TWO WORDS AND/OR A NUMBER** for each answer.*

LOST PROPERTY REPORT	
Name:	Emma **2** *Gordon*
Item(s) lost:	Green Gore-Tex coat
When this item will be collected:	**3** *Evening*
Phone:	**4** *98413678*
PM duty officer:	**5** *Sally* McPherson

The second part of Section 1

Listening sections are usually divided into two parts with a pause for you to read the second lot of questions.

Which set is harder here: Set IV or Set V?

 PLAY RECORDING 2 and answer either Set IV or Set V.

Set IV

Classify the following statements according to whether they are related to

    A   'A Christmas Carol'

    B   'A Doll's House'

    C   'Romeo and Juliet'

*Write the correct letter, **A**, **B**, or **C**, on your answer sheet.*

This play:

  6   has had excellent reviews.

  7   opens towards the end of November.

  8   might make audiences laugh.

  9   has no seats available next week.

 10   can only be seen with a new ticket.

Set V

*Choose the correct letter: **A**, **B**, or **C**.*

  6   Emma is unable to see 'A Doll's House' because she is

    A   going to the seaside.

    B   making a presentation.

    C   attending a conference.

  7   Letter Z on Emma's ticket means that she can

    A   change it for another one.

    B   get her money back.

    C   do either A or B.

  8   Emma won't see 'A Christmas Carol' because

    A   the critics didn't rate it highly.

    B   it's not the kind of production she likes.

    C   it's booked out.

Complete the sentences below.

*Write **NO MORE THAN TWO WORDS AND/OR A NUMBER** for each answer.*

  9   The final performance date of 'A Doll's House' is ....

 10   Emma's refund will be put into her .... account.

Play Recording 1 again, and answer Sets I and II to see why they're more difficult than Set III and are unlikely to be in a real IELTS test. Then answer the following questions. Write your answers in the blanks.

1   Looking back at Set II on page 21, why would question 4 never be in the IELTS exam? ___

_____

2   Which other question in Set II would *not* be in Section 1? _____

Why not? _____

3   Which section(s) could the question above be in, *Section 2, Section 3, or Section 4?* ____

4   Why might Sets IV and V be equally difficult? _____

_____

Always listen for evidence

There's no recording script given to you in the Listening test, but let's analyse one. Why is some writing below *italics*, and other writing **bold**?

Line #

Woman	Before I forget. I've got a ticket for a play **'A Doll's House' in November, but I won't be able to use it. I have to go to a conference abroad.** I wonder if I could exchange it, or get a refund?	
Man	Do you have the ticket there with you?	
Woman	Yes, I do.	5
Man	In the top right-hand corner of the ticket there's a letter: X, Y, or Z. Which letter do you have?	
Woman	Um ... **I've got Z.**	
Man	**That means your ticket is exchangeable or refundable.** So, which would you like: another date for the same show; another show; or, your money back?	10
Woman	*The critics have been raving about your production of 'A Doll's House'.* I'd love to see it. **What's the last date it's on?**	
Man	**The twenty-first of November.**	
Woman	That's no good. I'll still be at the conference – that might even be the day of my presentation. *What show's next?*	15
Man	*'A Christmas Carol'.* I'm sure you know it. However, it's been updated, and *it's more of a comedy than the original.*	
Woman	**I'm afraid that's not my cup of tea.** What about *next week*? Is there a performance of *'A Doll's House'* then, before I go away?	20
Man	Yes, there is, *but it's completely booked out.*	
Woman	Could I use my ticket for another play next year? Aren't you doing *'Romeo and Juliet'*?	
Man	*That's scheduled for February – opening on Valentine's Day. Unfortunately, we only exchange tickets within the same season, so you'd have to buy another ticket if you wanted to see that.*	25

Woman It looks like a refund is my only option.

Man Would you like me **to put the money into your credit card account directly?** 27

Woman If you can, that'd be lovely.

YOUR TURN *For each sentence below, find words in the script above that provide evidence for the idea expressed. Write the words in the blank provided. Quote line numbers. There is an example.*

Set IV

6 'A Doll's House' has had excellent reviews ➞ *The critics have been raving about…* (line 11)

7 'A Christmas Carol' opens towards the end of November. ➞ ____________________

____

8 'A Christmas Carol' might make audiences laugh. ➞ ____________________

____

9 'A Doll's House' has no seats left next week. ➞ ____________________

____

Set V

7 Emma can either change her ticket for another one, or get her money back. ➞ ____________________

____

8 'A Christmas Carol' is not the kind of production Emma likes. ➞ ____________________

____

Answer the following question.

9 This date 'the twenty-first of November' (line 14) *isn't* hard to hear, but many candidates don't write it correctly on their answer sheet. What does this date look like when written?

____

Timing

What are the missing words below? Write the letters to complete each one.

You have about 2¾ ***m*** _ _ _ _ _ _ of speaking to listen to in each part of a Listening section. That makes 5½ minutes for one whole section. You have at least one minute of ***pau*** _ _ _ for reading questions and checking answers. That's about seven minutes. You have ten questions to answer in that time. Therefore, you have 40 **S** _ _ _ _ _ _ PER QUESTION while the recording is playing.

At the beginning, there is some time for instructions that you can ***ig*** _ _ _ _ and use instead for reading ahead. There are ten minutes after the fourth recording for you to ***tra*** _ _ _ _ _ _ your answers from the booklet to the answer sheet. You need to practise so you can do this neatly in just ***fi*** _ _ minutes, and spend the rest of the time checking or guessing.

Strategies for each question type (i)

The following pages may be some of the most important in this book. The strategies are the same for Reading test questions.

Again, what are the missing words? Write the letters to complete each one.

How do you *an* _ _ _ _ MCQs?

1   In Sections 1 and 2 of the Listening test, try to read the stems (underlined) *and* the three choices (A, B, and C) in the 30 seconds before the recording is played. (A Six can read both stems and choices easily.)

> **1**   <u>Emma left her raincoat at the theatre</u>
>   **A**   on Saturday.
>   **B**   last night.
>   **C**   two nights ago.

In Sections 3 and 4, it's better to **read *only* the stems in the reading time**. In Section 4, there's slightly more reading time at the start (45 seconds), but there's no break in the middle to read as in the other three sections. Therefore, it's essential to work as fast as possible, keeping stems for MCQs in your head while the recording is played. **Read the choices, and answer as you listen.** Use this technique in the tests.

2   MCQs work in different ways. At the very beginning of the test (questions 1-5), you're listening for the same simple words or phrases like 'last night' above. Later, you're listening for synonyms or paraphrases. For question 7 in Set V, we hear that Emma can either 'exchange' or 'refund', which are another way of saying choices A and B, so the answer is choice C.

> **7**   Letter Z on Emma's ticket means that she can
>   **A**   change it for another one.
>   **B**   get her money back.
>   **C**   do either A or B.

3   MCQs are about eliminating wrong answers. Look at question 8 in Set V.

> **8**   Emma won't see 'A Christmas Carol' because
>   **A**   the critics didn't rate it highly.
>   **B**   it's not the kind of production she likes.
>   **C**   it's booked out.

You might not know the idiom used in the recording, 'not my cup of tea' (line 19) (check in your dictionary), but you can still get this question right. We don't know what the critics said about 'A Christmas Carol'; critics are only mentioned in relation to 'A Doll's House'. Therefore, choice A is wrong. 'A Doll's House' is 'booked out'; we don't know about 'A Christmas Carol', so choice C is wrong. That leaves choice B as the correct answer.

4   Another type of MCQ has two close answers, but one of them may be too specific. For question 6 in Set V, Emma does say she's making 'a presentation' (line 16), but she's doing this at 'a conference', so the more general answer, choice C, is better.

> **6**   Emma is unable to see 'A Doll's House' because she is
>   **A**   going to the seaside.
>   **B**   making a presentation.
>   **C**   attending a conference.

5   Section 3 and 4 MCQs can be difficult because both stems and choices are long. Reading the stems *only* in your preparation time is the best thing to do.

One MCQ (often called a global MCQ – usually question 30 or 40) is about a speaker's attitude. You may have to work this out from intonation as much as vocabulary.

6   When you have no idea, or you've run out of time with MCQs, choose choice B.

How do you choose two answers from a *l* __ __ __ (like question 3 in Set I)?

1   Eliminate in the same way as in an MCQ.

Unlike with MCQs, read the stem *and* the choices.

Again, the choices are in order in the recording.

Watch out in question 3 below for similar-sounding options like 'inside/outside pockets'. Choice E is wrong because the coat is 'shortish', but the zipper is 'long'. Emma doesn't mention any embroidery, so choice B is wrong.

> **3**   What features does Emma's coat have?
>
> **A**   a hood
>
> **B**   embroidery
>
> **C**   outside pockets
>
> **D**   inside pockets
>
> **E**   a short zipper

2   Remember, there are no half marks in IELTS: if you write one answer or three answers to this type of question, you do not get a mark.

How do you choose *gra* __ __ __ __ __ (like question 1 in Set III)?

1   The same way you choose MCQs.

If you have time, circle key similarities or differences.

In the drawings of the coats on page 21, notice that one coat (choice A) has pockets, so circle the two other coats. There is one longer coat (choice B), so circle the two shorter ones. Then, listen for 'pockets', and words about length. Emma says her coat is 'shortish', a word you might not know, but which is close to 'short'. This makes coat B less likely. Now, there are often little tricks in IELTS, and here's one. Emma *does* talk about her two pockets, but she says they're 'on the inside', which means you can't see them in the drawings. Therefore, coat A with pockets is wrong; coat B we think is wrong because it's too long, which leaves coat C.

Recently, IELTS hasn't had many graphical questions because they're quite easy.

How do you answer note / table *comp* __ __ __ __ __ __ questions (like questions 2-5 in Set III)?

1   Firstly, remember that your answer must be a word or words you've heard in the recording. You can't answer with other words from your head even if they're logically and grammatically correct. Sorry. This makes these answers easy unless they're three words long.

2   These answers are usually specific facts.

3   The majority of IELTS Listening answers are nouns. Next come gerunds, other kinds of verbs (usually past participles) and adjectives. A three-word answer is likely to be an adverbial phrase like 'on the inside' in question 3 of Set II.

How do you label plans or *m* __ __ __? (See questions 5-8, Academic Practice Test 2.)

1 Notice *where* the questions are. Do they go across or down? This is the most common way candidates make mistakes with this question type.

2 Focus on the words and phrases in the recording (probably prepositions) that describe relationships. Eg: 'The post office is opposite the bank.' 'Opposite' tells us where the buildings are in relation to each other. Or: 'The yoga studio is at the back of the building'. 'At the back of' tells us where the studio is within the building.

How do you give *sh* __ __ __ answers (like questions 4-5 in Set I)?

1 Again, your answer must be a word or words you've heard in the recording. You don't need to include the subject in your answer. In question 4 of Set I, you don't write: 'She starts work at 4 PM', or 'The woman starts work at 4 PM.' '4 PM' is enough. The other answers are six or seven words long, and will be marked wrong.

2 These answers are usually specific facts. Occasionally, they're feelings.

How do you answer *mul* __ __ __ __ __ matching questions (like Set IV)?

1 Don't panic.

2 Remember the statements (the numbers, here questions 6-10) are in the order you hear them in the recording, but the choices (A, B, and C) are in any order.

Read the choices first. Then, read the statements <u>twice</u>.

Classify the following statements according to whether they are related to

    A   *'A Christmas Carol'*

    B   *'A Doll's House'*

    C   *'Romeo and Juliet'*

*Write the correct letter, **A**, **B**, or **C**, on your answer sheet.*

This play:

    6   has had excellent reviews.

    7   opens towards the end of November.

    8   might make audiences laugh.

    9   has no seats available next week.

    10   can only be seen with a new ticket.

---

3 As with EVERY question in the Listening test, mark key words. <u>Underlining</u> is the fastest. Circling negatives is useful (see 'no seats' above).

4 Multiple matching questions usually rely on synonyms or paraphrases. Beware of phrases in the recording that sound exactly the same as or similar to your numbered statements – it's possible they refer to something else.

5 Almost always each of the three choices is mentioned. It's very unlikely (and unlucky) if you have an answer like AAACA.

6 Guess if unsure, and revisit multiple matching questions in your transfer time.

Section 2

Strong candidates read ahead to Section 2 in the checking time at the end of Section 1.

Section 2 question types may be more difficult than Section 1. Although the topic is of general interest, you may not be interested in it. Don't lose concentration just because the topic is a little dull.

Below are two sets of questions for one recording. Do Set VI the first time you listen to the recording. Do Set VII on your second listening.

 PLAY RECORDING 3.

GEOTHERMAL AIR CONDITIONING

Set VI

Complete the summary below.

*Write **NO MORE THAN TWO WORDS AND/OR A NUMBER** for each answer.*

Geothermal air conditioning systems have been available for about **11** .... , and can reduce energy bills by **12** ....

These systems work by piping water deep under ground, where the temperature is about the same all **13** .... and never very hot nor very cold. This water is returned to the building for heating and **14** .... purposes.

Pipes are normally sent down **15** .... beneath a car park that already exists.

Label the diagram below.

*Write **NO MORE THAN TWO WORDS OR A NUMBER** for each answer.*

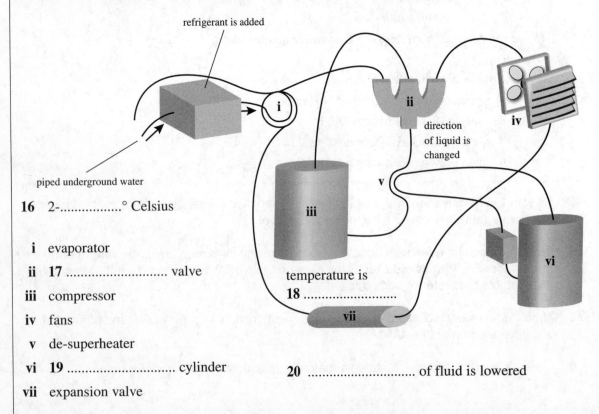

refrigerant is added

piped underground water

direction of liquid is changed

v

temperature is **18** ....

16   2-................° Celsius

  i   evaporator

 ii   **17** .... valve

iii   compressor

iv   fans

 v   de-superheater

vi   **19** .... cylinder

vii   expansion valve

20 .... of fluid is lowered

Set VII

Choose the correct letter: A, B, or C.

11 Heat Smart Solutions sells geothermal air conditioning to

   A   commercial buildings.

   B   individual homes.

   C   commercial buildings and individual homes.

12 The speaker suggests businesses should be interested

   A   mainly in profit.

   B   in both profit and responsibility.

   C   far more in global responsibility.

13 Geothermal A/C can reduce energy bills by

   A   a significant amount.

   B   a moderate amount.

   C   a small amount.

14 A limitation of traditional A/C is that it draws from the air outside which

   A   may be very hot.

   B   may be very cold.

   C   may vary greatly in temperature.

15 A large supermarket might need

   A   15 pipes.

   B   50 pipes.

   C   150 pipes.

Complete the flowchart on the following page.

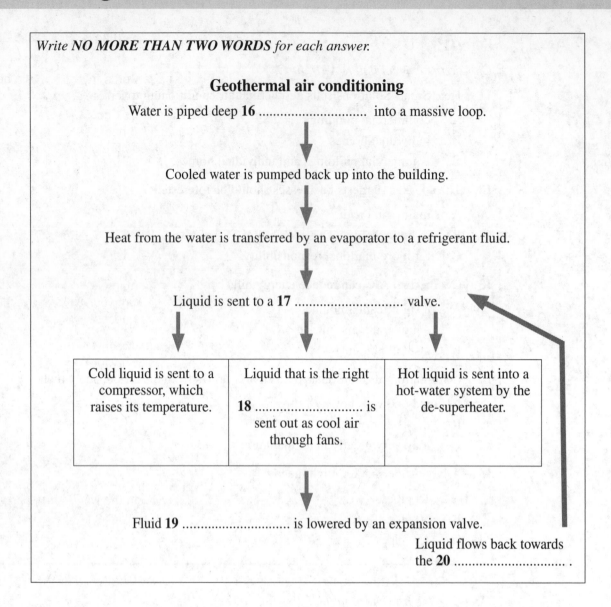

*Write **NO MORE THAN TWO WORDS** for each answer.*

Geothermal air conditioning

Water is piped deep **16** .... into a massive loop.

↓

Cooled water is pumped back up into the building.

↓

Heat from the water is transferred by an evaporator to a refrigerant fluid.

↓

Liquid is sent to a **17** .... valve.

| Cold liquid is sent to a compressor, which raises its temperature. | Liquid that is the right **18** .... is sent out as cool air through fans. | Hot liquid is sent into a hot-water system by the de-superheater. |

↓

Fluid **19** .... is lowered by an expansion valve.

Liquid flows back towards the **20** ....

Strategies for each question type (ii)

What are the missing words? Write the letters to complete each one.

How do you answer *sen __ __ __ __ __* completion questions?

1   Check how many words are needed in your answers. If the answer asks for two, don't write three. If it asks for a number, there has to be a number in one of your answers.

2   As with EVERY question in the Listening test, mark key words. Underlining is the fastest. Circling negatives is useful.

3   The language around your answer is a paraphrase or contains synonyms of what you hear in the recording. Your answer, however, is a word or words that you hear. Beware of phrases in the recording that sound exactly the same as the language around your answer. They probably refer to something else.

4   Take notes during the recording in the margin of your Listening booklet so that if you guess, you have words to choose from. Answers must come from the recording, not your head.

5   Spelling and grammar count, so check these in your transfer time.

How do you answer *sum* __ __ __ __ completion questions (like questions 11-15 in Set VI)?

1 In summary completion questions, candidates may use words from their own heads to fill in the gaps. These must be grammatically accurate, logical, and correctly spelt.

In Set VI, you hear: 'decade', but the answer to question 11 could also be '10 years'. Your vocabulary is being tested here. In the recording you hear: 'to cool', but the answer to question 14 is 'cooling'. Your grammar is being tested here as a gerund follows the preposition 'for'.

2 Always check these questions again in your transfer time!

How do you label *flow* __ __ __ __ __ __?

1 Don't panic.

2 Analyse the grammatical structures used. Is the first word in each line / box in the chart a gerund, or a noun? Are the statements passive? Make sure your grammar is the same as that which is used. (In the flowchart in Set VII, this is not necessary.)

3 Consider that the majority of missing words inside the flowchart sentences are nouns. (This is true in Set VII with 'temperature', 'pressure', and 'evaporator'.)

4 Take notes during the recording in the margin of your Listening booklet so that if you guess, you have words to choose from. Answers must come from the recording, not your head.

How do you label *di* __ __ __ __ __ __?

1 Don't panic.

2 Don't worry if you don't understand the diagram. Focus on the words in the diagram rather than the pictures.

3 Spend three seconds looking at the direction the questions go in. Where is the first question; where is the second? Are they going across the diagram, down the diagram, around it clockwise, or in some other order? (The arrows on the diagram in the answers on page 28 show the zigzag of the questions there. They are very nasty.)

4 Take notes during the recording in the margin of your Listening booklet so that if you guess, you have words to choose from. Answers must come from the recording, not your head.

5 Listen for prompts – phrases that get a listener ready for what's coming next. Things like 'In the diagram, you can see' or 'In the top right-hand corner, you'll notice' are prompts. In Set VI, the man says, 'Oh, I've forgotten the expansion valve at the bottom of the diagram.' 'Oh, I've forgotten' is the prompt.

6 Listen for sequencing language like: 'The first thing that happens is' or 'then', after that', or 'finally'. Be completely familiar with pronouns and what they refer back to.

7 Listen for language in the recording that describes processes (usually the passive) or functions (the passive, or 'used for' + gerund).

8 Nouns, past participles, and numbers are the most likely missing items.

Make sure your grammar is the same as that which is used. (In Set VI, 'raised' is a past participle, part of a passive verb. The short statements describing the functions of the parts are passive here.)

9 Guess intelligently. This may mean the difference between a Six and a 6.5.

The alphabet and numbers in the Listening, Speaking, and Writing tests

Accuracy can be critical in IELTS. In the Listening test, a tiny mistake loses a candidate a mark, and as a result he or she does not get the band needed.

The following pages revise work you've probably done before on the alphabet and numbers. These are particularly important in the Listening test.

YOUR TURN   *A good way to practise numbers is to listen to or watch the news, and write a summary of two stories.*

Look at the examples below, and fill this out tonight.

Who?	What?	Where?	When?	Anything else of interest?
Thunder Bolt	Broke the world record for running 100m	France	23rd July	Ran in 9 mins 47 secs; says he'll go under 9.4 eventually
	Forest fires	Around Moscow	For a week	Highest temperature recorded in summer 42°C; thousands of hectares burnt; 15 deaths
Two news stories from ___ / ___ / ___:				

The alphabet

In Sections 1 and 2 of the Listening test, there are sometimes answers which speakers spell out. Therefore, candidates need to know the alphabet in English perfectly.

YOUR TURN   *Listen to the alphabet. Put the letters into their columns according to how they sound. There are examples. (Go to page 214 for the International Phonetic Alphabet if you don't already know the symbols.)*

Play
Audio **PLAY RECORDING 4.**

/iː/	/uː/	/e/	/aː/	/eɪ/	/aɪ/	/əʊ/
B		F		A		

Zed or zee?

In America, people say 'zee' for 'z'. In Canada, most people say 'zed,' but 'zee' is also acceptable. In other English-speaking countries and IELTS it's 'zed'.

Commonly confused letters

Here are letters IELTS candidates mix up.

YOUR TURN

1 In the first group, the letters sound similar.

Choose the missing letters from below. Write your answers in the blanks.

N P T

i Did the speaker say: B or ___?   **ii** Did the speaker say: D or ___?

iii Did the speaker say: M or ___?

In questions i and ii, the initial sounds of 'B' and 'D' are unvoiced – the speaker doesn't use as much air to send the sound out of his or her mouth. 'P' and 'T', by contrast, are voiced. (See page 214.)

The sound /em/ is slightly longer than /en/. 'N' is also a more common letter than 'M'.

2 In the second group, the candidate has a letter in his or her own language that causes confusion. For example, in French the letter 'I' is called /iː/, like 'E' in English.

Choose the missing letters from below. Write your answers in the blanks.

E G S U V W

i Did the candidate write: C or ____?   **ii** Did the candidate write: ____ or I?

iii Did the candidate write: F or ____?   **iv** Did the candidate write: ____ or J?

v Did the candidate write: ____ or V or ____?

Try this at home. To improve your speed with the alphabet, find five maps of five countries you know little about. Write down the capital cities and the countries. Then, spell them aloud, or get another person to spell them to you.

Eg: You write: *Ouagadougou is the capital of Burkina Faso*.

You say: 'It's spelt: oh, you, a, gee, a, dee, oh, you, gee, oh, you. And Burkina Faso is: bee you are kay I en a, eff a ess oh.'

Or: look at an article where the journalist's name is written, and do the same.

Eg: You write: *This article on diplomatic leaks is written by Toby Leigh*.

You say: 'That's tee oh bee why, ell ee I gee aitch.'

Addresses

There are a lot of different places where people live, but IELTS almost always uses *Street* or *Road*. *Avenue* or *Lane* might occur. Their abbreviations are: *St*, *Rd*, *Av* or *Ave*, and *Ln*.

In the Listening test, you may hear: 'I live at flat three number nineteen Brook Street.' If a person spells out Brook, it is: 'Bee are double oh kay'. The address is written: 3/19 Brook St. A speaker may say 'unit' instead of 'flat', which is written: Unit 3, 19 Brook St. Sometimes, the word 'apartment' is used. A unit, flat, and apartment are the same kind of accommodation.

A person may live at an *A* or a *B*, as in *32A Oldham Rd* or *161B Elizabeth St*.

An email address may be a Listening test answer. Remember: 'at' is written @.

Dates

We say dates one way, but write them another.

We say:	We write:
'Independence Day's on **the** seventeen**th** of August.'	*Independence Day is on 17ᵗʰ August.* or *Independence Day is on August 17.*
But: 'Father's Day's on the first Sunday in September.'	*Father's Day is on the first Sunday in September.*

IELTS prefers this system for dates: *day/month/year*. For example: My date of birth, the twenty-sixth of July nineteen seventy-four, is written *26 July 1974* or *26/07/74*.

With years, we say 'eighteen forty'. We write *1840*.

'Nineteen ninety-five' = *1995*

'Two thousand and twelve' **or** 'twenty twelve' = *2012*

Americans don't say 'and' above. Speakers in the Listening test use British numbers.

Phone and card numbers

A phone number is written like this: *996 4202*. Usually, numbers in the Listening test have seven digits.

The number *996 4202* is said: 'Double nine six (*pause*) four two zero two.'

Sometimes a credit card or an ID card number may be needed.

YOUR TURN *Fill in the forms. Write* **NO MORE THAN TWO WORDS AND/OR A NUMBER**.

Play Audio **PLAY RECORDING 5.**

1

Name:	Simon _____
Address:	Unit 4, _____ St
Phone #:	_____
Email:	_____@hotmail.com

2

Name:	Kirsten _____
Nationality:	_____
Passport #:	_____
Date of Birth:	06 May 1991
Place of Birth:	_____

The time

In Listening Section 1 or Speaking Part 1, a candidate may need to understand the time.

YOUR TURN *Listen to the dialogues. Write your answers as numerals with AM or PM, eg: 7:20 AM.*

Play Audio **PLAY RECORDING 6.**

1   What time is the woman's flight?   _____

2   When does the second film start?   _____

3   Who is correct: A or B?   _____

4   What should the other candidate have said?   _____

Money

Like dates, money is said and written differently.

In speaking, the currency goes second. In writing, the symbol for the currency goes first. The exception is cents, or *c*, which follows the amount.

YOUR TURN   *Listen, and write down the money answers. Three currency symbols have been written for you. IELTS does not expect you to know these.*

 PLAY RECORDING 7.

1   How much money has the man won?   _____

2   How much money has the woman lost?   €_____

3   How much was the man earning in the past?   ¥_____

4   How much does a pub meal cost?   £_____

5   How much is a NZ dollar worth in relation to a US dollar?   _____

IF YOU WANT A SEVEN

PLAY RECORDING 8.

AMAZING FACTS

Listen to some amazing facts.

Write **NO MORE THAN TWO WORDS AND/OR A NUMBER** in the gaps. There are examples.

	What/Who?	Where?	When?	What?	How tall/high/ far/heavy/long?
Eg	The _Khalifa Tower_	In Dubai	2010	The world's tallest building	_828_ metres
1	_____	In Hawaii		The world's highest mountain when measured from the sea floor	_____ metres
2	The planet HD _____	Outside our solar system		Too hot to inhabit, but not too far away	_____ light years away from Earth
3	Japanese royal family		Since _____ BC	Been ruling continuously	
4	A camel			Its brain weighs just over _____ that of a human	_____
5	Darko Novovic	From _____	2010	Swam the Amazon River – _____ kilometres	In _____

Numbers

Spend a few minutes reading the tables below.

Numeral	Cardinal	Ordinal	Anything else? (Words in *italics* below are written. Spoken sentences, from the Listening or the Speaking test, have quotation marks '…'.)
1	one	1st = first	In IELTS Writing, sometimes candidates write: *Firstable* instead of *First of all*. 'This is **the** first time I've taken the exam.'
2	two	2nd = second	Look up the verb *tow* in your dictionary. Remember the letter *w* is silent in 'two', but is pronounced in 'twelve', 'twenty', 'twice', 'twin', and 'between'. 'It's **the** second-largest city.'
3	three	3rd = third	*third* not *therd* 'I'm **the** third child.'
4	four	4th = fourth	*fourth* not *forth* Check what *forth* means.
5	five	5th = fifth	The /θ/ ending of 'fifth' is hard to say for some candidates.
6	six	6th = sixth	Hard to say for some candidates
7	seven	7th = seventh	Hard to say for some candidates
8	eight	8th = eighth	Don't spell this *eightth*.
9	nine	9th = ninth	Don't spell this *nineth*. Remember: *nine, nineteen, **ninth**, ninety, ninetieth*.
10	ten	10th = tenth	Some speakers confuse 'tenth', and 'tense'.
11	eleven	11th	'e-LE-ven' has second-syllable stress.
12	twelve	12th	*twelfth* not *twelvth* Hard to say for some candidates
13-19	thirteen… nineteen	13th-19th	'thirteenth'…'nineteenth' Remember the stress patterns: thir-TEEN and thir-TEENTH, but THIR-ty and THIR-ti-eth.
20	twenty	20th	*twentieth* The *y* becomes an *i*.
21	twenty-one	21st	Notice the hyphen (-) in *twenty-one*. *21st* not *21th*, and *31st* not *31th* Chinese candidates sometimes write *-th* for *-st*, *-nd*, or *-rd* in the Listening test. Their answers are wrong.
22	twenty-two	22nd	*22nd* not *22th*
23	twenty-three	23rd	*23rd* not *23th* 'There are twenty-three students in my class.'
24	twenty-four	24th	'Classes start on **the** twenty-four**th of** January', or 'Classes start on January twenty-fourth'.
40	forty	40th	***forty*** not *fourty*. Remember the *i* in *fortieth*.

Larger numbers, fractions, and zero

100	hundred	'More than **a / one** hundred schools took part in the competition.'
1,000	thousand	Pronunciation of /θ/ is hard for some candidates.
		'More than **a / one** thousand people ran the marathon.'
10,000	ten thousand	'My car cost ten thousand dollars.' Not 'ten thousand<u>s</u> dollars' – it's a singular adjective.
100,000	hundred thousand	'The floods caused over **a / one** hundred thousand people to flee their homes.'
		'Lakh' is common in Indian English, but no one else speaking English understands it. If you're an Indian speaker taking IELTS *outside* India, don't use words the examiner won't know. You will go down in Vocabulary.
1,000,000	million	'My city reached **a / one** million people when I was a teenager. It's now got about one point three million.'
1bn	billion	'Africa now has more than **a / one** billion people.'
½	half	Pronunciation: /haːf/
		The verb is *halve*. 'The bird population <u>has halved</u> since cats were introduced.' Pron: /haːvd/
⅓	third	*About **a** third of TV viewers said they often watched documentaries.*
		'My brother came third in a talent quest.'
¼	quarter	*About **a** quarter of teenage girls smoke.*
		Don't write *quater*.
		'It's a quarter to nine.' Or 'It's quarter to nine.'
¾	three-quarters (This is plural.)	*Three-quarters receive money from their parents while studying at university.*
1½	one-**and-a**-half (This is plural.)	'I think one-and-a-half-days **aren't** long enough for my weekend.'
1.66	one point six six	This is said: 'one point six six', not 'one point sixty-six'. Note: a point, not a comma, is used in written English. *Wages rose 1.6% in 2010 while house prices rose 8.2%.*
0.375	zero point three seven five	This is said: 'zero point three seven five.' You may occasionally hear this in the Listening test, but it's unlikely you'll have to write it. You may have to choose it in an MCQ.
0	zero	Although there are several ways to say 0 in English, IELTS uses 'zero'. You might need to write out a phone number in the Listening test.

YOUR TURN *Find one correct sentence below, and three with mistakes. Fix the mistakes.*

Eg		*two* *There are ~~tow~~ main reasons why teenagers smoke.*
Eg	✓	'Ten thousand people auditioned for the TV show.'
1		*Approximately a therd of the countries have coal-fired power stations.*
2		*Over quarter of international students have scholarships.*
3		'My grandparents have just had their fifty wedding anniversary.'
4		'There are two point six million people in my city.'

Percent or percentage?

Candidates often confuse these words.

Percent or *per cent* is an adverb. It has a number just before it and can be shown by the symbol: %. *Percentage* is a noun or part of a quantifier. The phrase *the percentage of = the number of*.

These sentences show the differences above. *Eighty percent own cars.* Or: **The** percentage **of** *car owners is high.*

YOUR TURN *Fix the mistakes below.*

1   Only two percentage walk to work.

2   Percentage of walkers is low.

Numbers that are quantifiers

In this sentence: 'I've got a lot of friends', 'a lot of' is a quantifier, telling me how many. I can also say (though not write), 'I've got lots of friends'. 'Lots of' is a less formal quantifier.

Hundreds of, *thousands of*, and *millions of* function the same way as *a lot of*. They are all followed by plural nouns.

Two common IELTS mistakes are: a candidate doesn't make the quantifier plural, or doesn't make the following noun plural.

YOUR TURN *Find one correct sentence below, and three with mistakes. Fix the mistakes.*

1		Hundreds of students took part in the protests.
2		People have been living in caves on the Tigris for thousands years.
3		Million of dollars were spent on security when Oprah Winfrey visited.
4		An inexpensive vaccine would save millions of life.

Writing numbers in the Writing test

In Task 1 of the Academic Writing test, there are often numbers to write. There are two basic rules about writing numbers in English.

YOUR TURN *Put the words in the box into the summary below. Write the words in the spaces provided.*

inside	larger	numeral	start	twelve

Firstly, a number from one to _____ is written as a word: eg: *Ten percent of people interviewed had visited Bali more than twice.* A number above twelve is written as a _____: eg: *Around 25% had visited both Bali and Jakarta.*

    Secondly, sentences can't _____ with numerals, only words, so _____ numbers are put _____ the sentence as above.

YOUR TURN *Find two correct sentences, below, and two with mistakes. Fix the mistakes.*

1		Five percent had visited Lombok or other small islands.
2		70% had stayed for two weeks.
3		One sixth had stayed for more than a fortnight.
4		Of the 300 people surveyed, only 3 had not enjoyed their holiday at all.

Compound adjectives with numbers

IF YOU WANT A SEVEN

Compound adjectives cause problems for all IELTS candidates except Nines. There are **no** plural adjectives in English, so a compound adjective can't end with an s or es.

We say and write:	
1	the one-child policy; a one-legged or one-eyed dog; a one-time movie star
2	a two-person tent; a two-bedroom apartment; a two-year contract (A plural is: **two** two-bedroom apartment**s**)
3	a three-hour exam; a three-day workshop; a three-course meal
4 and 5	a four-star hotel; a five-year plan
6 and 7	a six-month course; a seven-year drought; a seven-hour flight
8	an eight-hour day (A plural is: **five** eight-hour day**s**)
9	a nine-month-old baby (not *months*)

We say:		We write:
12	'a twelve-month contract'	*a twelve-page report*
18	'an eighteen-month-old son / daughter'	*an 18-month-old child*
20	'a twenty-year-old man' (*not* years)	*a 20-year-old man*
50	'a fifty-year-old bottle of wine'	*a 50-year-old bottle*
120	'a one-hundred-and-twenty storey building' (*not* storeys)	*a 120-storey building* (*not* an)
2000	'a two-thousand-year-old body'	*a 2000-year-old body*

YOUR TURN *Find two correct sentences, below, and three with mistakes. Fix the three with mistakes.*

1	My husband has just signed three-year contract to teach in Abu Dhabi.
2	I read a 950-page report on the forest fires around Moscow for work.
3	I believe there are too many four-wheel drives in the city.
4	Taipei has lots of hundred-storey building.
5	A 50-cents vaccine could end meningitis in Africa.

If you are from China or India

What are the missing words? Write the letters to complete each one.

Speakers of Chinese and Indian **l** __ __ __ __ __ __ __ __ have problems with larger numbers in English. It's common for an IELTS Four or **F** __ __ __ to say, 'My village has one million people', when the candidate means, 'My village has **t** __ __ **t** __ __ __ __ __ __ __ people'. Or: 'The company I work for has ten million workers', whereas perhaps 'one hundred thousand' may be more **lik** __ __ __.

Listening Taster Test

A 'taster' is a small sample.

This Taster Test has model IELTS Listening test questions, followed by their answers and tape scripts.

Copy the answer sheet on page 456, or make your own with 40 questions. Do each section as though it were a real test. Then, read through the scripts carefully to see why any of your answers were incorrect.

Write new vocabulary on flash cards or in your vocabulary notebook.

Section 1

 PLAY RECORDING 9.

You hear:

Narrator	Section 1. Community College Courses. You will hear a woman calling a community college about courses. Read the example.

You read:

COMMUNITY COLLEGE COURSES

Complete the notes below.

*Write **NO MORE THAN TWO WORDS** for your answer.*

Example: Sonya would like some ***information*** and help to choose a course.

You hear:

Receptionist	Good afternoon, East Coast Community College. How may I help you?
Sonya	Good afternoon. My name's Sonya Stamp. I wonder if you could give me some information about your courses.
Receptionist	Certainly.
Sonya	And perhaps help me make a choice.
Narrator	The answer is 'information'. On this occasion only, the first part of the conversation is played twice.

Let's do the rest of Section 1.

Play Audio **PLAY RECORDING 10.**

SECTION 1 Questions 1-10

Questions 1-6

Complete the sentences below.

*Write **NO MORE THAN TWO WORDS** for each answer.*

COMMUNITY COLLEGE COURSES

1   Sonya is good at .... , which may be useful for Graphic Design or Desktop Publishing courses.

2   The receptionist tells Sonya desktop publishers create leaflets or brochures, or even whole ....

3   Sonya would prefer to study at Randwick because it is close to her ....

4   The community courses are either two-hour classes during the week, or all-day ....

5   Sonya thinks her .... might take a course with her.

6   Since the Web Design courses are very .... , the receptionist suggests Sonya pay immediately.

Questions 7-10

Complete the notes below.

*Write **NO MORE THAN TWO WORDS AND/OR A NUMBER** for each answer.*

Name of course:	Web Design for Beginners
Course pre-requisites:	Good 7 .... and familiarity with Windows
Course day(s) & times:	Fridays 12:00-2:00
Length of course:	8 ....
Course location:	9 ....
Discounts available:	For students or 10 ....

Here is the script.

Answer to question #

Receptionist	Good afternoon, East Coast Community College. How may I help you?	
Sonya	Good afternoon. My name's Sonya Stamp. I wonder if <u>you could give me some **information** about your courses</u>.	**eg**
Receptionist	Certainly.	
Sonya	And perhaps help me make a choice.	
Receptionist	I'll see what I can do. What were you thinking of studying, Sonya?	
Sonya	Well, a while ago, I started a Bachelor's degree in Accounting, but I only completed the first year. I'd like to study again, only this time something a bit more creative.	
Receptionist	Then, you've come to the right place. We've got courses in drawing, painting, photography, music, dance, and drama.	
Sonya	I'm not sure I could make a career out of those although <u>I'm not bad at **drawing**</u>.	**1**
Receptionist	Yes, it's not easy to earn a living as an artist. Still if you like **drawing**, why not consider Graphic Design or Desktop Publishing?	**1**
Sonya	To tell the truth, <u>I'm not sure what Desktop Publishing is</u>!	
Receptionist	<u>It's creating leaflets or brochures for advertising, or even entire **books**</u>. You manipulate the text and images on your computer. We've got some really good tutors on that course, and lots of our students get work afterwards.	**2**
Sonya	That sounds interesting. Where could I study Desktop Publishing?	
Receptionist	There's a Beginner's course at East Lakes, and we've just started one at the Randwick Community Centre.	
Sonya	Really? <u>That's close by. I could walk from **home**</u>.	**3**
Receptionist	Wait a minute…<u>The Randwick course is a series of **weekend workshops**</u>. You'd have to give up Saturdays and Sundays.	**4**
Sonya	Oh that's no good. I waitress on Saturday, and I need that income. Tell me about the course at East Lakes.	
Receptionist	East Lakes? Oh, sorry, that course has been filled, and there are already two people on the waiting list.	
Sonya	No problem.	
Receptionist	Have you thought about Web Design?	
Sonya	Yes, I have. My **cousin**, who makes jewellery, wants to set up an online business. We've been talking about making our own website for ages.	**5**
Receptionist	<u>Because these courses are so **popular**</u>, you'd have to pay straight away.	**6**
Narrator	Before you listen to the rest of the conversation, you have 30 seconds to read questions 7 to 10. (*30-second pause*)	
Receptionist	So, Sonya, you've chosen Web Design.	
Sonya	Yes. Just one more thing. How familiar would I need to be with computers before I start?	
Receptionist	According to the information here, <u>you need good **keyboarding skills**, and a working knowledge of the Windows environment</u>.	**7**
Sonya	I've got both of those, but I'm not sure about my **cousin**. I'd like to study Web Design at your Randwick centre. Is that possible?	**5**
Receptionist	I'm afraid our courses there are full. Another option is a daytime class. Do you have any commitments on weekdays?	

Sonya	I'm busy on Mondays and Tuesdays.	
Receptionist	OK. There's a course at Daceyville on Fridays at noon for two hours. It runs from August to November – for **thirteen weeks**.	8
Sonya	That's a fairly long time – **thirteen weeks**. I mean, long enough to really learn something.	8
Receptionist	Yes, I agree. So, shall I put you down for Web Design at **Daceyville**?	9
Sonya	Ah…I'm new to this area, and I'm not sure where Daceyville is. Could you spell it for me, and I'll look it up?	9
Receptionist	It's Daceyville – D-A-C-E-Y-V-I-double L-E.	
Sonya	Thanks. Is it easy to get to by bus from Randwick?	
Receptionist	The 400 bus stops right outside the school where the course is held, and the service runs until midnight.	
Sonya	Great. One last question. My cousin's a pensioner. Would she get a discount?	10
Receptionist	Yes. There's 20% off for fulltime students or **pensioners**. She'll just have to bring her pension card to the first class.	10
Sonya	No problem. Speaking of cards, I've got my credit card here. I'd like to pay.	
Narrator	You now have 30 seconds to check your answers. (*30-second pause*) That is the end of Section 1.	

Here are the answers. How did you do?

Section 1: 1. drawing; 2. books; 3. home; 4. weekend workshops; 5. cousin; 6. popular; 7. keyboarding skills; 8. 13/thirteen weeks; 9. Daceyville (*capital optional*); 10. pensioners.

KEY POINTS

- Although the Listening is only played once, there's lots of time for reading questions and checking answers. (How many 30-second pauses were there?)
- The most common question type in Section 1 is a gapfill (#1-10).
- The number of words and/or numbers in gapfills changes. 'No more than two words and/or a number' means: one word, eg: 'drawing'; or, a word + a number, eg: '13 weeks'; or, two words, eg: 'weekend workshops'; or, an answer like: 'three working days'. Sometimes the instruction does <u>not</u> ask for a number. Sometimes it asks for one word only. Occasionally, it asks for 'no more than *three* words'. **No IELTS answer is longer than three words**. Usually, there is only one set of questions in a Listening test asking for 'no more than three words'.
- Some of the answers are given more than once, eg: questions 1, 5, 8, 9, and 10 above.
- Notice that most of the answers are nouns or gerunds. Sometimes there's an adjective, eg: 'popular'. In fact, **the majority of IELTS answers in the Listening and Reading tests are nouns.** Be careful with uncountable, singular, or plural nouns. There are five plurals above which need 's'.
- IELTS cares about spelling, but there are no marks lost for incorrect punctuation. 'Daceyville' is the name of a place, so it has a capital, but if you forget this in IELTS, it doesn't matter. You'll still get the mark if your spelling is correct.

> **WATCH OUT!**
> Of course, this is Section 1 of the Listening, and your first experience of the whole IELTS exam. To settle you down, Section 1 is easy. However, I hope you didn't forget the plurals in questions 2, 4, 7, 8, and 10. Did you spell 'drawing' and 'pensioners' right?

Going on to Section 2

Let's go on to Section 2. In Section 2, you will hear just one main speaker.

Play
Audio **PLAY RECORDING 11.**

SECTION 2 Questions 11-20

Questions 11-15

Complete the sentences below.

Write **ONE WORD OR A NUMBER** *for each answer.*

28-DAY TOURS

11   The Go-16 company takes students aged 16 to .... on tours.

12   Last year, Go-16 groups visited China, ... , Vietnam, and Peru.

13   Go-16 is equally interested in .... responsibility and travelling.

14   All Go-16 trips include: .... learning, volunteering, and trekking.

15   Go-16 students volunteer for a local organisation for .... weeks.

Questions 16-17

*Choose the correct letter: **A**, **B**, or **C**.*

16   In western China, Go-16 students worked on a project
    A   to plant trees.
    B   to help people with AIDS.
    C   to stop the desert spreading.

17   The speaker suggests students are safe when travelling with Go-16 because
    A   it has very good insurance.
    B   the students are bilingual.
    C   the tours are expensive.

Questions 18-20

*Choose **THREE** letters: **A-F**.*

*Which **THREE** reasons does the speaker give for Ukraine becoming a destination?*
    A   Trekking in the mountains is fantastic.
    B   Its history is now being studied at high school in America.
    C   Go-16 students will enjoy volunteering there.
    D   Americans and Ukrainians want better relations between their countries.
    E   Many Americans have relatives who emigrated from Ukraine.
    F   He is Ukrainian himself.

Here is the script.

Answer to question #

Narrator	Section 2. Twenty-eight-day Tours. You will hear a man talking about 28-day tours that his company organises for students. Before you listen, you have 30 seconds to read questions 11 to 15. (*30-second pause*)	
Stan Manko (an American man)	Welcome to Go-16, the adventure tour company for high school students. I've met some of you young people before at our last meeting, and I'm glad your parents could make it tonight.	
	Let's get started. You probably know that <u>our company takes students, aged 16 to **18**, to around 40 destinations worldwide</u>. Our maximum group size is 14, and we're away for 28 days. We usually go in the long summer vacation, but a couple of groups go in winter. Last year, <u>Go-16 groups visited China, Indonesia, Vietnam, and Peru. Sorry, **not Indonesia, Malaysia**</u>. And this year, we're adding Ukraine. That'll be a winter trip because Kyiv is gorgeous in the snow, but the climate brings additional challenges.	**11** **12**
	But what you may not know is that Go-16 is no ordinary business. <u>We're as concerned about **social** responsibility as travelling.</u> Of course we go to beaches and restaurants, like ordinary tourists, but <u>every Go-16 tour must include three things. Firstly, students learn some of the local **language** through a ten-day stay with a family. Then, they go on a trek.</u> In Peru, we climb for three days in the mountains up to Machu Pichu. It's fantastic. <u>Lastly, Go-16 students volunteer for **two** weeks for a community organisation.</u>	**13** **14** **15**
Narrator	Before the talk continues, you have 30 seconds to read questions 16 to 20. (*30-second pause*)	
Stan Manko	While I'm on this topic of volunteering, <u>our Go-16 group in China, in 2009, took part in an environmental project to prevent the desert spreading.</u> Our students saw the Great Wall and the Forbidden City in Beijing first, then they flew 3000 kilometres west to Kashgar. They assisted scientists from a well-known research institute with laying plastic netting in the Taklimakan Desert. Over time, seeds are caught in this netting, and eventually plants grow to create a barrier against sand. In 2012, another Go-16 group went to see the progress, and they were amazed – grasses, bushes, and even trees had grown that <u>stopped the desert spreading</u>.	**16** **16**
	I can hear you mothers thinking: Laying plastic netting in the Chinese desert – that doesn't sound safe, or educational. Why would my child be doing that? As to the safety, <u>Go-16 has very good **insurance**</u>; all our staff is bilingual and familiar with local conditions. Furthermore, we follow New York State Health and Safety regulations in every country we're in. Concerning the educational value of the desert project. I think all of those Go-16 students got straight As in Biology and Geography back home.	**17**
	Perhaps you're wondering: What does this all cost? Go-16 has two packages which you can read about in the brochure I'll pass round. Since the kids raise some of the money themselves, it's less expensive than you might think.	
	As I said before, we've added Ukraine this year. We chose this country because the history of **Eastern Europe is now part of the school curriculum**. Some of you here tonight might be studying the communist period and the break-up of the former Soviet Union. Many **Americans also have family members from there**. Lastly, **I was born in Kyiv,** the capital, **so I'm a Ukrainian-American**. I can give a special insight into the country and culture.	**18** **19** **20**

Stan Manko (continued)	Now, I said earlier that Ukraine is lovely in winter. However, some of the community projects Go-16 will be involved with are connected to AIDS and drug use. These may be challenging for teenagers. In my opinion, the world is a complex place, and understanding complexity is an important part of education.
	Of course, Go-16's tours are fun – trekking is fantastic fun – but they're also about personal development and understanding our ever-changing world.
	Now, it's your turn. Any questions?
Narrator	You now have 30 seconds to check your answers. (*30-second pause*). That is the end of Section 2.

Here are the answers. How did you do?

Section 2: 11. 18/eighteen; 12. Malaysia; 13. social; 14. language; 15. 2/two; 16. C; 17. A; 18-20. *in any order*: B,E,F.

KEY POINTS

- Section 2 is harder than Section 1 because there's only one main speaker. He or she still uses informal language as in Section 1. However, there is more specific vocabulary related to one topic.

- Fewer answers are given more than once.

- There are gapfills again, and multi-choice questions (MCQs). One benefit of MCQs is you've got a 33% chance of being right by guessing. A drawback is there may be a lot to read in each question.

- Multiple matching (questions 18-20), also called matching lists or classification in other text-books, can be tricky. You need to decide which choices are not possible until you're left with the correct answers.

> **WATCH OUT!**
> Section 2 is still easy, but I'm sure not all of you got the spelling of 'Malaysia' right.
> By the way, it's always safer to write numerals rather than words for numbers, I mean '2' instead of 'two', or '40' for 'forty' because there are lots of numbers people don't spell correctly.
> Did you notice how the speaker corrected himself in question 12? This is common in IELTS. Almost always, the second answer is what the speaker intends and what you write.
> In the multiple matching: choice A is more likely to relate to Peru. Choice C may not be true since Stan Manko says volunteers work with 'AIDS and drugs', which could be 'challenging for teenagers'. This is a negative idea. Choice D is not mentioned. Therefore choices B, E, and F are correct. Double-check multiple matching questions in your transfer time.

Going on to Section 3

Let's go on to Section 3. Listening Sections 1 and 2 are on everyday topics, but Sections 3 and 4 are more academic. Section 3 is a discussion about situations at college or university. Section 4 is a short lecture. Maybe you're familiar with the topics, maybe not.

Play Audio **PLAY RECORDING 12.**

SECTION 3   Questions 21-30

Questions 21-25

Complete the notes below.

*Write **NO MORE THAN TWO WORDS AND/OR A NUMBER** for each answer.*

SPACE FOOD ASSIGNMENT

Class:	**21** .... Methods
Presentation topic:	Food issues related to living in space
Date due:	**22** .... time
Research sources:	• Internet • library books • ESA **23** ....
Ideas students have considered so far:	• nutritional value of food • **24** .... of food • astronauts' food preferences
Location students are focusing on:	The **25** .... Station (ISS)

Questions 26-28

*Write **ONE WORD** for each answer.*

According to the lecturer, the students should also look into:

26   experiments in creating artificial environments on ....

27   the Vietnam War because there is already research into food ....

28   how planets that could sustain life might be ....

Questions 29-30

*Choose the correct letter: **A**, **B**, or **C**.*

29   The lecturer wants to see the students the following day with

    A   a clearer research topic.

    B   another research topic.

    C   research from other experts.

30   Overall, the lecturer

    A   thinks the students have done good work.

    B   does not show how she feels about the students' work.

    C   is disappointed with the students' work.

Here is the script.

Answers to question #

Narrator	Section 3. Space Food Assignment. You will hear a university lecturer and two students discussing an assignment. Before you listen, you have 30 seconds to read questions 21 to 25. (*30-second pause*)	
Gabrielle Anderson (a woman)	Come in, gentlemen. How can I help you?	
Ravi Kaur (a man)	Good afternoon, Dr Anderson. Chen and I are students in your <u>**Research** Methods class</u>, and we're having some problems with our assignment.	**21**
GA	Yes, you told me that on the phone. What was your topic again?	
Ma Chen (a man)	Food issues related to living in space.	
GA	What exactly are you finding difficult?	
RK	We can't find much information, and our presentation's in **two weeks'** time. We've done all the usual things: look online...	**22**
GA	Go to the library.	
RK	We've even contacted <u>the ESA</u>.	
GA	<u>The European Space Agency</u>?	
RK	<u>Yes. For its 2012 **report**</u>.	**23**
GA	Well done. What have you learnt so far?	
MC	Not much, I'm afraid.	
RK	It's going to take three weeks for the **report** to get to us – too late for our presentation.	**23**
GA	You can still use the data in your essays. By the way, how have you defined your topic? It needs to be clearer and more specific. I mean, food issues in space is a pretty big area!	
MC	We've decided on: the nutritional value of food, and <u>the **cost** of food</u>.	**24**
RK	And food preferences: whether astronauts like chocolate or strawberry ice cream for example.	
GA	What about the social aspects? Can you sit down to a meal together in a rocket?	
RK	Apparently astronauts did in Skylab in 1973. And they do at <u>the ISS – the **International Space** Station</u>. We're focusing on the **International Space** Station rather than rockets.	**25**
Narrator	Before you listen to the rest of the discussion, you have 30 seconds to read questions 26 to 30. (*30-second pause*)	
GA	All right. **Now, you may not like this, but I find your considerations minor; your research areas aren't that interesting or academic**. How about looking into the future? How could agriculture, for example, be developed in space?	**30**
RK	Well as far as we know, there's no planet in our solar system with an atmosphere suitable to sustaining life – that's any kind of life: human or plant.	
GA	What about <u>setting up an artificial environment</u>? You might remember the experiments in greenhouse production <u>here on **Earth**</u>: there was a major one in Texas in 2006, and there's another underway in the south of England. The ESA should mention that.	**26**
RK	That's an idea.	
GA	Of course an alternative is importing food until a colony can produce its own.	

MC	That's what I meant about the cost. Flying food into space is very expensive. Not to mention all the waste produced. Around 25% of the weight of food products for astronauts at the ISS is their packaging.	
GA	OK. Why don't you examine the logistics of sending food into space and bringing back the waste? Do all the maths on it, since you're Engineering students. This could be interesting.	
MC	I've seen a couple of articles already on feeding groups of people who are far from home.	
RK	Like soldiers?	
GA	Exactly. <u>There've been lots of PhDs on the Vietnam War and food **logistics**</u>. The use of container ships began then as a response to supplying so many men.	**27**
	Anyway, isn't it likely that <u>moons or planets outside our solar system will be better for growing food? I think around 400 exo-planets are in the habitable zone – not too far for us to travel to. When might these be **explored**</u>?	**28**
RK	We're still waiting for <u>the ESA **report**</u>.	**23**
GA	**I'd like you to spend tonight refining your research topic. Come back to me tomorrow. You've done some good work, but you need to focus.** At this level of your studies, you should try to become experts.	**29** **30**
MC & RK	Thank you, Dr Anderson. We'll see you tomorrow.	
Narrator	You now have 30 seconds to check your answers. (*30-second pause*) That is the end of Section 3.	

Here are the answers. How did you do?

Section 3: 21. Research (*capital optional*); 22. 2/two weeks' (*apostrophe optional*); 23. (a) report; 24. (the) cost; 25. International Space (*capitals optional*); 26. Earth (*capital optional*); 27. logistics; 28. explored; 29. A; 30. C.

KEY POINTS

- You have three sets of questions here. Don't panic. This only happens in one section in an IELTS test if at all.

- In Section 3, question types are again gapfill or MCQs. Short answers, matching lists, flow-charts, or diagrams to label are also possible.

> **WATCH OUT!**
> Notice how the MCQ in question 30 asks for a feeling. The speaker's intonation is as important as her language. Usually if an MCQ question is at the end of a section, it's looking for an overall idea or an emotion.
> 'Logistics' is always plural.

Going on to Section 4

Let's go on to Section 4. As mentioned earlier, Section 4 is a lecture. Most Section 4s are on less familiar topics. In this taster test, the lecture is descriptive, dealing with facts. However, often the lectures are argumentative – they contain the speaker's opinions or theories, and those of other people he or she is discussing.

The format of Section 4 is slightly different from the other three sections. There is no 30-second break in the middle for candidates to read the last set of questions. Instead, at the start, there is 45 seconds' reading time.

Since Section 4 is difficult, a candidate below a Six will guess a lot of the answers. There will usually be one or two questions that are hard even for an Eight.

 PLAY RECORDING 13.

SECTION 4   Questions 31-40

MACQUARIE ISLAND

Question 31

Which map describes Macquarie Island?

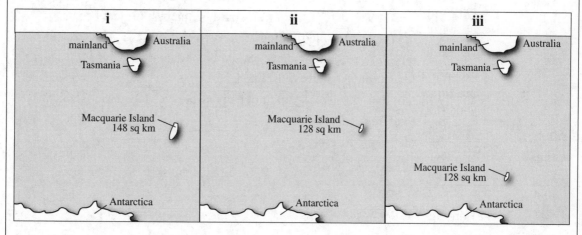

Questions 32-36

Complete the table below.

*Write **ONE WORD OR A NUMBER** for each answer.*

Time or period	Important event(s)
Millions of years ago	Creation of Macquarie Island It is between two tectonic plates: the Indo-Australian and the **32** ....
33 ....-1919	Discovery of Macquarie Island by Hasselborough Killing of seals and penguins for their skins and blubber. Animals almost become **34** ....
1948 onwards	Antarctic **35** .... is set up, which is still in use.
1997	World Heritage Site is declared.
1985-2000	Over 2,500 cats are destroyed.
2004	Massive earthquake occurs.
2007-2014	Plan to get rid of **36** .... is put into action.

Questions 37-40

*Choose the correct letter: **A**, **B**, or **C**.*

37   Macquarie Island is well known for its research into

    A   fish species.

    B   climate change.

    C   Emperor Penguins.

38   .... seabirds are thought to breed there annually.

    A   80,000

    B   one million

    C   3.5 million

39   The speaker suggests pest control would be the best project because

    A   it has considerable funding.

    B   rats, cats, and rabbits have caused great damage.

    C   Macquarie Island is so isolated.

40   Which of these projects would <u>not</u> be possible on Macquarie Island?

    A   Studying seals

    B   Surveying forests

    C   Analysing rocks

Here is the script.

Narrator	Section 4. Macquarie Island. You will hear a lecture about an island near Antarctica called Macquarie Island. Before you listen, you have 45 seconds to read questions 31 to 40. *(45-second pause)*
Lecturer (a man)	Good morning. Today's lecture is on Macquarie Island. We'll be using this island for our next assignment in which I'd like you to write a practice proposal for a research grant there.

Macquarie Island is halfway between the Australian mainland and Antarctica. **To be precise, it's fifteen hundred kilometres south-southeast of Tasmania. It's quite a small island, only 128 square kilometres,** but its geological value is immense. In 1997, it was made a UNESCO World Heritage Site for this reason.   **31**

Macquarie Island is the only place on Earth where rocks from the mantle are exposed at sea level. Macquarie Ridge, which the island is part of, <u>is right between two tectonic plates – the Indo-Australian and the **Pacific**</u>. As you may imagine, earthquakes are common. One, in 2004, registered 8.1 on the Richter scale! Luckily, there was no loss of human life.   **32**

<u>Discovered by Frederick Hasselborough in **1810**</u>, Macquarie Island was named after the governor of New South Wales, a British colony which is now an Australian state. Hasselborough was looking for seals to kill. In those days, sealskin and blubber, or fat, were in great demand. They were used around the world for clothing and heating. It was Hasselborough's lucky day when he found Macquarie Island since there were possibly a million animals there. Hasselborough and his men slaughtered as many seals as possible, boiled down their blubber, and shipped it back to Australia. This industry continued for over a century. <u>Both the seals and penguins were very nearly made **extinct**</u>.   **33**   **34**

After sealing ended, Macquarie Island became a nature reserve and a giant science lab. At present, there are no permanent inhabitants, and only 40 people, nearly all scientists, stay there temporarily. <u>There's been an Antarctic **base** there since 1948</u>. I think it's now called the Australian Antarctic Division.   **35**

But back to some unfortunate events. In **1810**, by accident, Hasselborough carried rats on his ships. Deliberately, he brought rabbits to feed his workers. Later, cats were intro-duced to kill the rats, but the cats bred like rabbits. By the 1950s, there were huge rat, cat, and rabbit populations. It is believed the cats killed 60,000 seabirds each year. From 1985 to 2000, more than twenty-five hundred cats were destroyed by park staff. Rabbits don't eat birds, but they do cause erosion. Landslides, caused by rabbits, have reduced the area where birds make their nests. In 2007, a seven-year plan to rid the island of **rabbits** was put into action. **33**

36

...So, what areas might your research proposals cover? Well, the geology of Macquarie Island is unique. Seismology is another possibility. There are also meteorological and magnetic stations for weather reporting. **There's been a long-term study on rising temperatures collected by these stations**, which has been fundamental in our under-standing of global warming. **37**

Animal life is abundant. More than 80,000 elephant seals call this place home. There are flocks of rare birds, including six penguin and four albatross species. In fact, it's estimated that **3.5 million** seabirds breed on Macquarie Island each year. Studying animal populations might be worthwhile. **38**

But the big money these days is in pest control. Twenty-four million Australian dollars to be precise are going towards this, so you'd have to be crazy not to get in on the act. 39

What about the island's flora? Plants share an affinity with those of southern New Zealand, rather than mainland Australia. Yet, due to the bitter wind, **none grows more than a metre high, and woody plants are absent**. If you're curious about mosses or bushes, then this could be the place for you. **40**

Anyway, whether you're into weather patterns, earthquakes, seals, birds, or strange plants, scientific research on Macquarie Island certainly sounds exciting.

Research one specific area this week, and in tutorials next week, we'll look at how to write up a research proposal, and what its budget might be.

Narrator   You have 30 seconds to check your answers. (*30-second pause*) That is the end of Section 4.

In a real test, the Narrator adds: 'You now have ten minutes to transfer your answers onto your answer sheet.' (*10 minutes of silence*) 'That is the end of the Listening test.'

Here are the answers. How did you do?

Section 4: 31. ii; 32. Pacific (*capital optional*); 33. 1810; 34. extinct; 35. base; 36. rabbits; 37. B; 38. C; 39. A; 40. B.

KEY POINTS

- Vocabulary and grammar are now closer to native-speaker level, and not rewritten more simply for IELTS candidates as in the previous sections.

- There is more idiomatic language. (See page 199.) In question 39, 'the big money' and 'get in on the act' are idioms.

- The speaker's tone of voice may be important to show if he or she approves or disapproves of something.

- MCQs in Section 4 may be negative as in question 40.

- Answers to questions are usually spaced out in IELTS – say one per paragraph. However, sometimes they're close together.

- Only a few answers are repeated, and one of the numbers, '3.5 million', you only hear once.

- You can write anything you like on your answer booklet. It's EXTREMELY USEFUL to take notes during Section 4. I'd strongly advise writing down dates and numbers and any clues about the speaker's feelings.

WATCH OUT!

In question 35, the speaker mentions the Antarctic base and the Australian Antarctic Division, but only the former is connected to 1948. Now, the spelling of 'base' is like 'case' and 'vase', but there's another word in English which sounds the same, but is written 'bass', as in 'bass guitar'. Words which sound the same but mean different things and are spelt differently are called homophones, and sometimes IELTS answers are homophones. Nasty!

Your vocabulary is tested in question 40 with 'considerable funding'. If you don't know either of these words, you can't answer the question. MCQs are often about vocabulary, either paraphrases or synonyms.

CHAPTER **3** IELTS Reading

What happens in the Reading test?

YOUR TURN *Match each item in the box with a number in the text below. Write the number in the space provided. There is an example.*

					eg		
60	2700	answers	as	dictionaries	follows	no	wrong

The Reading test —**eg**— the Listening test in the IELTS exam. It is a different test for Academic and General Training candidates.

Both Reading tests have 40 questions to be answered in —**1**— minutes. The question types are the same, but the text types and lengths differ slightly. Journal, magazine, and newspaper articles form the basis of the Academic test, which has around —**2**— words. —**3**— are common words in English as well as words from the Academic Word List. For more information about GT, see page 81.

Each candidate is given a question booklet and an answer sheet, which are collected at the end of the test. The booklet contains the instructions, questions, and reading texts. Candidates can write on it.

Unlike the Listening test, there is —**4**— time to transfer answers at the end of the Reading test. Candidates write their answers on the answer sheet —**5**— they read. People who supervise the Reading test remind candidates to do this. Any answer that can't be read easily is marked —**6**—.

Candidates are not allowed to use —**7**— in either test, nor ask anyone for help. Candidates who copy from others are warned to stop, and are asked to leave the exam if they continue.

Reading question types

There are two or three question types for each text. The following are the —**eg**— as those in the Listening test:

			eg	
missing	once	questions	same	title

- **gapfill** – Fill in a gap with the —**8**— word or words. Answers are one, two, or three words long. Answers must be grammatically correct.

- **short-answer** – Provide answers, usually to 'Wh-' —**9**—. These may be words chosen from the text, or words that are a little different from the text. These occur more often in GT tests.

- **multi-choice (MCQs)** – Choose answers from A, B, C, or D. These could be single-word answers, whole-sentence answers, the ends of sentences, or a graphic. In questions that ask for a suitable —**10**— for a passage, there may be five choices: A, B, C, D, or E.

- **multiple matching** – Choose two or more answers from a list. There are never more than seven items: A, B, C, D, E, F, or G. If instructed, candidates may use any letter more than —**11**—. In an entire Reading test, there is only likely to be one multiple matching question.

- **labelling** of plans, diagrams, or flowcharts with one-, two-, or three-word answers from the passage.

Read the text below. Then answer the questions on page 57.

Strategies for answering the question types already mentioned are the same for both Reading and Listening.

The following question types do **not** exist in Listening; they are only in Reading. (eg)

- **Matching headings**: Paragraphs in the Reading are given letters: A-J. Candidates choose suitable headings from a list numbered with Roman numerals: i-x.* Unlike other question types, heading questions go before a reading passage.

- **True/False/Not Given**: A statement is given which the candidate decides is *True* if it matches what is written in the Reading passage, not what the candidate knows from real life. Or, a statement is given that is *False* – the opposite of what is written in the Reading, or only partly what is written. If there is no information about the statement, the answer is *Not Given*. These questions are about facts described by the writer.

- **Yes/No/Not Given**: A statement that agrees with the views of the writer of the text gets a *Yes* answer. A statement that disagrees with the views of the writer gets a *No*. If there is no information about what the writer thinks, then *Not Given* is the answer. These questions are about the opinions, views, or beliefs of the writer, or other experts mentioned.

- **Matching sentence endings**: Seven sentences that restate what is in a Reading passage do not have endings. Candidates choose endings from a list of ten: A-J.

- **Summary with a list of answers**: A summary of part of the text is given with some missing words. A list of up to 15 words, A-O, is provided. Candidates choose the correct ones. Here, not only is reading comprehension being tested, but also knowledge of grammar.

No answer in the IELTS Reading test is more than three words. There are usually only two or three three-word answers in an entire test. Listening tests have a lot more written words as answers than Reading. Reading is more likely to have letters, numerals, or T/F/NG etc. Look at the proportion of answer types in the Practice tests.

Reading questions are almost always in order. That is, the information related to question 1 appears in the text before 2. However, where there are headings to choose, these are mixed up in the question box as otherwise there'd be no point in the activity. Also, as in Listening, MCQ stems are in passage order, but the options are not.

Questions become more difficult as the test progresses. More complex vocabulary is used, and questions become longer.

Go to page 381 for the answers.

---

* i = 1; ii = 2; iii = 3; iv = 4; v = 5; vi = 6; vii = 7; viii = 8; ix = 9; x = 10

YOUR TURN   *The following statements refer to the text that you have just read. For each statement, write T (True), F (False), or NG (Not Given) in the space provided. Underline your evidence in the text. There is an example.*

Eg Question types in the Listening and Reading tests are the same. _F_

12 All Reading questions precede the passages. ___

13 Candidates find Yes/No/Not Given questions difficult. ___

14 Candidates should answer according to what is written in the text, not what they believe is true from their own knowledge. ___

15 Yes/No/Not Given questions are about facts. ___

16 Summary questions test understanding of the reading and grammatical awareness. ___

17 A Reading-test answer can be any number of words. ___

18 An answer may be two letters. ___

19 Generally, question 5 comes in the text after question 4. ___

20 Many IELTS candidates do not finish the Reading test. ___

What are the missing words below? Write the letters to complete each one.

What are the three different passages of the Academic Reading test?

In the Academic test, there are **thr** __ __ passages. The lengths of the passages vary from test to test. Generally, the first passage has between 600-700 words; the second passage has 700-850 words; and, the last passage contains more than **1** __ __ __ words.

There is no connection **be** __ __ __ __ __ the topics of any of the passages.

Two of the passages are descriptive; one contains a logical argument, or opinions expressed against another writer. The topics themselves are of **gen** __ __ __ __ interest.

What is tested in the Reading test?

The Reading test wants candidates to: find **spec** __ __ __ __ information; find global information; understand negative language, inference, and a writer's **vie** __ __. Scanning, **sk** __ __ __ __ __ __, and reading carefully are all tested.

Some nationalities do well at Reading; others do poorly. Check out ielts.org for the **da** __ __ on how people from your country or language background perform. Like the Listening test, unfortunately, men generally score **lo** __ __ __ than women.

How is the Reading test marked?

The 40 questions in the Reading test are worth one mark each. There are no half marks even when a question asks for two answers. Candidates should answer every question because if they get one wrong, they don't **l __ __ __** a mark.

Typically, a Six thinks the test is quite easy, but **sco __ __ __** around 23 out of 40. The Academic Reading test is **desig __ __ __** so that a Six finishes with a few minutes left. A Five is unable to finish with any time left. A Four has serious problems with Passage 3, and leaves many answers blank, or **gu __ __ __ __ __** them. Only a Seven or above is completely comfortable with the test.

The people who mark the Reading test have strict instructions. Each paper is marked **tw __ __ __**. A candidate can ask for his or her Reading paper to be marked again, but this is expensive, and most candidates do **n __ __** get any more marks.

See page 7 for the differences between Academic and GT marks for each band.

Statistical information about IELTS Reading tests

YOUR TURN   *Put the words and numbers from the box into the text below. There is an example.*

16	20	1000	another	~~designed~~	infer	sentence	syllables	underestimated	undergraduate

IELTS Reading tests are carefully (eg) <u>designed</u> and tested with special computer programs. (If you're interested in this, check online for 'Readability'.) Three main elements the programs analyse are:

- passage length
- _____ length
- word length and complexity

The levels set by IELTS mean that Academic reading tests should be easily understood by first-year _____ students. (GT tests are slightly easier.)

Total test length varies from 2500-2700 words with Passages 1 and 2 having up to 850 words, and Passage 3 up to _____. Therefore, it is always better to spend more time on the last passage.

Sentences are mostly compound-complex (see pages 299-300) and contain around _____ words each. (Think about this: most newspaper and magazine articles have sentences that are fewer than ten words long.) The percentage of complex words in one IELTS passage will range from 11-17%. Usually, Passage 1 has 11%; Passage 2 has 13%; and, Passage 3 has _____% or more. Most complex words are originally from the Latin language, containing three _____ or more. (Look through this text, and see how many words fit that description.) Many IELTS words can be found on the Academic Word List (see page 257). The importance of understanding vocabulary to reading success should not be _____.

Computer programs cannot judge how difficult reading questions are in relation to what readers must _____ from a passage, but, once again, they can test the lexical level of questions.

Overall readability programs ensure one IELTS test is the same level as

_____.

Academic Reading Taster Test

To prepare you for IELTS, here is a slightly easier reading test than in a real exam.
Copy the reading answer sheet on page 456, or make your own.

When you do the test below, use a stopwatch. Time yourself, noting how long each question type takes. Write your time – minutes and seconds – where you see this symbol: 00:00.

In Passage 1, candidates find specific information, usually facts, by scanning then skimming. Only one or two questions require careful reading.

PASSAGE 1   Questions 1-14

Questions 1-6

Reading Passage 1 below has seven sections: A-G.

Choose the correct heading for sections B-G from the list of headings.

Write the correct number, i-ix, in boxes 1-6 on your answer sheet.

List of Headings

i	Buy it at the co-op
ii	A composite word
iii	A different kind of farming
iv	The dream of Warren Oakes
v	Media v Freegans
vi	Origins and activities
vii	What is freeganism?
viii	Use less; waste less
ix	The UK is OK for freegans

FREEGANISM

A Freeganism is a lifestyle in which people try to use less. Freegans find free food, or grow their own in community gardens. They recycle and help each other fix things instead of throwing them away. They might live in houses which are empty so as not to pay rent. Often, they ride bicycles or rely on public transport. As a result, they are able to work fewer hours because they do not need so much money. A few freegans even try to avoid money.

B Freegan is a new word, made up of the two words: 'free' and 'vegan'. A vegan is someone who does not eat or use any animal products. However, not all freegans are vegans. Some are vegetarians; others enjoy meat.

C Freeganism started in the 1960s in the US. It arose from environmental and anti-globalisation movements. It did not grow much until the mid-90s. A famous booklet called 'Why Freegan', written in 1999, by Warren Oakes, a musician, describes common things freegans do or believe. For example: to get food, freegans may go 'dumpster diving', 'plate scraping', wild foraging, or they may garden, or barter. A dumpster is an American word for a very large rubbish bin like the one in the illustration. 'Plate scraping' is taking leftover food from restaurants. Wild foraging is looking for food that is not grown on farms, but in parks or wild places. Of course, gardening is growing one's own food. Bartering is the process whereby people swap things that they both want without using money.

D People become freegans for different reasons. Perhaps they think it is better for the world environment to consume less; or they think people should spend more time with their friends and families, and less time working for money. Certainly, they do not like useful items being put into rubbish or landfill. A large area outside the city where large amounts of rubbish are buried is called landfill. Due to all the rubbish in landfills, the sites remain unusable for farming or housing for many years, which upsets freegans.

E Reports on television and in magazines have shown how weird dumpster-diving freegans are: how desperate and antisocial – pulling food out of the rubbish like homeless or very poor people. After all, this practice is dirty, smelly, and illegal. What journalists do not say is that the UK and Australia currently consume and discard equal amounts of good food. In the US, even more good food is destroyed. Meantime, one billion people worldwide are unable to eat the World Health Organisation's recommended daily intake of nutrients, and these people exist in both rich and poor countries. Freegans hope to change this. Despite bad press, the number of freegans worldwide is growing: a recent estimate by a Swedish organisation suggested more than 500,000 in 50 countries.

F Not all freegan dumpster divers search for food; not all freegans are dumpster divers. Many dumpster divers search for anything that can be recycled or reused, from clothes, to furniture, to tools in need of small repairs. An alternative source of inexpensive food exists in the form of co-operatives. These are shops which are owned by groups of local people. They do not aim to make a large profit, but to sell food at reasonable prices, and to provide what is in season and grown locally. Imported food may be forbidden as it is costly to the environment to transport it great distances.

G Some freegans plant their own crops at home or in community gardens. They may also take small amounts of food from the wild, particularly things which are not sold commercially. They feel they are fighting against a huge army of farmers and consumers because freegans believe large-scale farming, as currently practised, is bad for the environment. They also do not support the giant multinational companies that control large amounts of land worldwide. Methods such as factory farming, where animals are kept in very small areas inside, freegans hate. Many crops are sprayed with chemicals, or have things added to them like colour or wax, which freegans think are dangerous and wasteful. They support organic farming if they buy from farms at all.

Freeganism may not be a movement that ever becomes mainstream, but its central concerns may encourage people to modify their wasteful behaviour.

Questions 7-10

Do the following statements agree with the information in the text on the previous pages?

In boxes 7-10 on your answer sheet, write:

TRUE	*if the statement agrees with the information*
FALSE	*if the statement contradicts the information*
NOT GIVEN	*if there is no information on this*

7   Although freeganism began more than 40 years ago, it did not take off until the late 1990s.

8   Rubbish dumps or landfill sites are quite disturbing to freegans.

9   In developed countries, barely any food is thrown away.

10   It is predicted that freeganism will grow significantly in the next decade.

```
00:00 =
____:____
```

Questions 11-14

*Complete each sentence with the correct ending: **A-H** below.*

*Write the correct letter, **A-H**, in boxes 11-14 on your answer sheet.*

11   Freegans always

12   Freegans generally do not buy imported food because

13   Freegans have a special interest in

14   As a way of living, freeganism

A	dumpster dive.
B	transporting it long distance is another environmental cost.
C	the media.
D	agriculture.
E	challenges patterns of consumption and employment.
F	is probably hard to follow.
G	recycle.
H	grown locally is less expensive.

```
00:00 =
____:____
```

Passage 2

The second passage in the Reading test is more complex.

All different question types are used here: MCQ, gapfill (one, two, or three missing words), short answer, labelling diagrams etc. You'll find these again in the Practice tests; you know them already from the Listening.

Two question types that only appear in the Reading test are: a summary question (questions 15-22 below); and, choosing proper-noun answers from a list (questions 23-27).

Continue the Reading test under exam conditions. A Seven should read the passage and answer the questions in 17 minutes. Do you have your stopwatch ready?

PASSAGE 2   Questions 15-27

- - - - - - - - - - - - - - - - - - - -

THE GIANT RED BOX

Any day of the week, it's highly likely you'll see a giant long red metal box, otherwise known as a container, being hauled by a truck. Even if you don't live near a port or railway station, containers are transported long distances in order to meet our insatiable demand for goods. According to a World Bank report, in 2007 alone more than 18 million containers made more than 200 million trips. Now, over a quarter of global container traffic originates in China, and the world's largest port is in Shanghai.

Invention

But what are the origins of containerisation? In 1956, Malcolm McLean, who owned a trucking firm on the east coast of America, set this freight revolution in motion by using a converted tanker ship – the *Ideal-X* – to convey 58 aluminium truck bodies in a single shipment. McClean reasoned that loading and unloading goods are extremely costly, so he found the biggest ship, and designed the largest packaging to simplify and economise on this process. Aluminium containers are convenient due to their lightness, size, and stackability – that is, being uniform, like bricks, they're easily stacked alongside each other and on top of one another, which means little space is wasted when carrying them. Initially, McLean's company, Sea-Land Services, operated domestically, but in 1969 it won a contract to build a container port at Cam Ranh Bay in Vietnam. Its core business was shipping food, housing equipment, and medical supplies to the US military.

Three players

Aware of McLean's logistical success, the Japanese government developed its own container capacity to assist in its export drive, and special terminals with massive cranes – the first of their kind – were built in the Tokyo-Yokohama and Osaka-Kobe areas. However, at the time, the Japanese national rail carrier was not equipped to transport anything as long as 6 metres (20 feet) – the length of the first containers – and it was several months before this was possible.

Meantime, another American company, Matson Navigation, commenced a mostly commercial container service between the US west coast and Hawaii, with plans for expansion to East Asia. As the Japanese forbade a wholly-owned foreign firm from operating in its facilities, Matson Navigation was obliged to find a local partner – the Nippon Yusen Kaisha Line – before it could infiltrate the Japanese market. Their maiden container voyage took place in 1968. Only six weeks later, McLean's Sea-Land company competed with them for a service between Yokohama and California.

Rapid expansion

By the end of that same year, there were seven different companies on the US-Japan route, and 7000 tons of eastbound freight were being transported each month. Once again, only outdated infrastructure hampered growth, especially the American rail networks, but after their redevelopment, rail transport of containers in the US went from 3.1 million in 1980 to 25 million in 2015. No one is certain how many containers were taken by road, but heavy 18-wheeler trucks were manufactured to accommodate them, and these soon became common sights.

Size matters

Early containers were 6 metres (20 feet) long and mostly red. They had a gross mass of 24 metric tons (26.5 tons), and were measured in Twenty-foot-Equivalent Units or TEUs. Within two decades, 40-, 48-, and 53-foot (12-, 14-, and 16-metre) container models had been developed. Ports, cranes, trucks, and trains were all scaled up; the Panama Canal was expanded, but the Suez Canal remains too narrow for most modern vessels. These superships, carrying thousands of containers at one time, make the 1956 *Ideal-X* look like a child's paper boat. For example, the *MSC Oscar*, owned by a Swiss company, is nearly 400 metres (1311 feet) long, with a capacity of 19,224 TEUs. Ships owned by the highly successful Danish company Maersk hold around 15,000 TEUs.

Engineers believe that even larger container vessels can be built, but nature may prevent their sailing the seas. For instance, the link between the Indian and Pacific Oceans – the Malacca Straits between Malaysia and Indonesia – is narrow and relatively shallow, and therefore has limited shipping capacity. Thus, a ship with a length of 470 metres (1,541 feet) and a width of 60 metres (197 feet) is described as being 'the Malacca-max'.

Are there any downsides to the container revolution? Marine biologists cite high levels of pollution, particularly from the bilgewater of container vessels. This is waste matter originally taken on to stabilise a light or empty vessel, then subsequently tipped into the sea when the ship is weighted by its full load of freight. Other social scientists believe that the ever-increasing volumes of goods travelling internationally mean an easier time for organised crime. Guns, drugs, and other illegal items are imported in large amounts, and due to ports' wishing to seem efficient, moved out so rapidly that Customs checks may not be thorough. These days, sophisticated scanners are used to view the contents of containers, but it might be one in a thousand that is put under extreme scrutiny. Even more deplorably, there have been numerous cases, particularly of containers travelling by road in Europe, where people smuggled into them – illegal immigrants, mostly headed for the UK – have suffocated to death. What is the alternative? A return to smaller oddly-shaped crates, chests, and parcels that remind people of the back of a suburban post office or the over-sized baggage section of an airport? It's doubtful.

Ecological and social concerns aside, economic crises, like the sharp decline experienced in 2008, may be mechanisms for the reduction of freight. However, to date, the world's largest container company – Maersk – is doing fine, as it moves more than three million giant, still mostly red, metal boxes each year. And there's probably one passing by on your street right now.

Questions 15-22

*Complete the summary using the list of words, **A-O**, below:*

*Write the correct letter, **A-O**, on your answer sheet.*

Containers are everywhere! However they are a relatively **15** .... phenomenon. The first ones came out only in **16** .... While they were invented by an American, they were **17** .... by the Japanese in a period of rapid economic growth. Now, the Chinese use the most. The success of containers is due to lower labour **18** .... in their loading and unloading as they are far larger than previous packaging, and their **19** .... makes them easy to stack and transport.

Almost unbelievable numbers of containers **20** .... the world's oceans daily. Unfortunately, **21** .... dictated by ports and markets has meant insufficient checks on illegal goods also entering countries in vast quantities.

All in all, international trade has been changed **22** .... by the giant red aluminium box. Most of us would agree: it's for the best.

A	efficiency	**B**	travelling	**C**	uniformity
D	produced	**E**	recent	**F**	numbers
G	dramatically	**H**	1968	**I**	cross
J	costs	**K**	popularised	**L**	increasingly
M	1956	**N**	current	**O**	effectiveness

```
00:00 =
_____:_____
```

Questions 23-27

*Complete each sentence with the correct country, using the letters, **A-H**, below:*

23   More than 25% of the world's container freight starts in ....

24   Early public sector involvement in infrastructure was critical in ....

25   Geographical limitations in .... will determine the size of container ships.

26   Fatalities inside containers are associated with ....

27   The most successful container company is currently from ....

A	China	**B**	Denmark
C	Japan	**D**	Malaysia & Indonesia
E	Panama	**F**	United Kingdom
G	Switzerland	**H**	Vietnam

Passage 3

This is the hardest passage with the most difficult questions. Only a Seven or above can complete it in 20 minutes. Therefore, it's safer to give yourself 25 minutes for it.

The views of the writer are expressed, and not just a description of facts or events. Sentences are longer at an average of 23 words; vocabulary is more complex. Careful reading is essential.

Make yourself a nice drink, have a stretch, settle down with your favourite pen and a stop-watch for 25 minutes.

PASSAGE 3   Questions 28-40

Anyone who owns a pet is familiar with the range of communication possible between animals and humans. A cat, for example, makes noises to indicate it's hungry, injured, scared, contented, or playful, and if the owner calls its name, it usually comes, even from a distance. Cats signal each other vocally – they hiss to threaten intruders; they wail when seeking a mate. But to what extent is their communication a form of language similar to our own?

Myths and legends in all cultures contain stories with speaking animals, so presumably people once believed animals possessed language. The power and wisdom of animals were also a significant component, and in English today, we still describe someone as 'a wise old owl'. But were these tales merely indirect ways of teaching moral concepts? Were the 'wise' animals considered more effective messengers than human characters? Perhaps once it was considered easier to learn from a bear stung by bees while stealing honey that theft is antisocial, or from a tortoise who says: 'I shall win this race with the hare!' that being slow but determined results in success. However, because human relationships with animals have diminished due to today's highly urbanised culture, our overall interest in them has dwindled.

For thousands of years, people have recognised that parrots can speak, or more precisely, that they reproduce words and phrases taught to them. Likewise, mynah birds are mimics and can produce around 200 different sounds, ranging from the songs of other birds to the ring tones of mobile phones. Yet none of this confirms that birds understand the sounds they make since vocalisation does not define language. Moreover, deaf people communicate effectively without vocalisation through signing, and all humans react to body language.

An important feature of human language is that it employs a finite set of sounds or gestures, which, when combined, generate infinite meanings, whereas animals may learn discrete sounds or sentences, but lack the ability to create new meaning from individual elements. A parrot can announce: 'Polly wants a cracker' when seeking food, and: 'Oh, what a lovely morning', but it cannot spontaneously compose: 'Polly doesn't want a cracker' or: 'Oh, what a lovely after-noon' although it's heard the words 'doesn't' and 'afternoon' a thousand times.

In the 1970s, ornithologists thoroughly researched the sounds birds make to each other. Bird-calls (one or more short notes) provide information to other birds of the same species concerning the immediate environment: whether danger is present; whether it's time to return to the nest for food; or, whether it's time to depart together in a flock. Birdsong (longer, more complex note patterns) claims territory and attracts mates, but research into many bird species has demonstrated that a bird may sing the notes of its song in any order, suggesting that the individual notes lack particular meaning. By contrast, consider the sentences: 'The boy killed the dog.' and 'The dog killed the boy.' – clearly different, and clearly proof of an underlying grammatical system. Secondly, the pitch of the notes in birdsong is the only indicator of what a bird feels about its territory. A higher-pitched song indicates: 'I'll defend this place or die.' In English, prosodic features like pitch, stress, and intonation convey some, but not the entire meaning, for as we know from automated voices on the telephone, even with slightly strange prosody, we understand the message.

But what about animals with larger brains than birds? A dog can distinguish between the words 'sit' and 'fetch', and phrases like 'go around the back', and act accordingly. Show dogs, guide dogs, and farm working dogs have learnt more commands than others, yet the total is still not high, and estimated to be around 30. Just as the parrot speaks because it knows it'll be fed, dogs respond to stimuli rather than actually understanding language.

What about primates – chimpanzees, gorillas, monkeys, and others – who are more closely related to humans? They certainly make numerous sounds in the wild, yet once again, their vocalisations and gestures relate solely to their immediate environment. Unlike humans, they are unable to hypothesise, ponder the future, or discuss the past.

There have been numerous attempts to teach primates language as we know it, yet all have proven useless. The primary reason for this failure is that the animals do not spontaneously apply the target language as human children do. When with a trainer, they will answer a question, but they won't then ask the trainer a question, and in the company of other animals of their species, they don't use or teach the language as human parents do with their children. People who find themselves in any environment where they can't speak the language, however, will attempt to use the new language. Secondly, primates never learn grammar. Kanzi, a male bonobo chimp, considered one of the best non-human language users, was taught a special sign language since chimp mouths cannot form most human sounds. Although evidently clever, Kanzi never passed the grammatical level of a three-year-old – his language remained simple (two to three words combined) and inflexible. Lastly, primates imitate sign language, but rarely create anything new with it themselves. Conversely, human children, as early as 18 months old, are creative, copying language only 40% of the time, while also generating completely new sentences from the elements they have learnt. Even if not totally accurate, all these new sentences follow the grammatical structure of their particular language.

Studies into the linguistic abilities of animals are far less popular now than 50 years ago, due largely to the widely accepted theory proposed by Noam Chomsky in the 1980s. It declares that language is innate to humans – we are all born with the capacity for it – and despite needing to be exposed to language at a critical period in early childhood to learn it perfectly, almost all humans everywhere have language.

Mickey Mouse may talk in cartoons; Aslan the lion may save Narnia; clever chimps may live at the zoo, but flexible, creative, heritable language remains a uniquely human preserve.

Questions 28-33

Do the following statements agree with the claims of the writer in Reading Passage 3?

In boxes 28-33 on your answer sheet, write:

YES	*if the statement agrees with the claims of the writer*
NO	*if the statement contradicts the claims of the writer*
NOT GIVEN	*if it is impossible to say what the writer thinks about this*

28   A cat appears to understand when a human calls its name.

29   The speeches of animals in myths and legends were mainly for entertainment.

30   Mynahs make an amazing number of different sounds.

31   Parrots lack the ability to combine language elements creatively.

32   For some birds, the order of the notes in their songs alerts other birds.

33   It is more likely that a dog responds to the stimulus attached to language than the language itself.

```
00:00 =
____:____
```

Questions 34-39

Complete the summary below.

*Choose **ONE WORD** from the passage for each answer.*

Write your answers in boxes 34-39 on your answer sheet.

Like birds and small mammals, **34** .... only produce sounds connected to their environment. One reason they do not learn language is they fail to use the language they have been taught **35** .... Secondly, they do not master **36** .... ; their language stays **37** .... and fixed.

The number of scientific **38** .... into the linguistic ability of animals has probably decreased because Chomsky's theory of the innateness of language is **39** .... universally.

Question 40

*Choose the correct letter: **A**, **B**, **C**, **D**, or **E**.*

Write the correct letter in box 40 on your answer sheet.

Which of the following is the most suitable title for Reading Passage 3?

A   Fascinating animal language

B   Effective animal communication

C   Animals make good companions.

D   Animal language – fact or fiction?

E   Language is a purely human creation.

```
 00:00 =
____:____
```

Here are the answers. How did you do?

1. ii; 2. vi; 3. viii; 4. v; 5. i; 6. iii; 7. F; 8. T; 9. F; 10. NG; 11. G; 12. B; 13. D; 14. E;
15. E; 16. M; 17. K; 18. J; 19. C; 20. I; 21. A; 22. G; 23. A; 24. C; 25. D; 26. F; 27. B.

28. Y/Yes; 29. NG/Not Given; 30. NG/Not Given; 31. Y/Yes; 32. N/No; 33. Y/Yes;
34. primates; 35. spontaneously; 36. grammar; 37. simple; 38. studies; 39. accepted;
40. D.

For explanation of the answers, see pages 70-74.

Reading strategies

YOUR TURN   *Choose the correct item in each pair below. There is an example.*

Reading is (eg) *a transferable skill/innate*. Research has shown that if people read a lot in their first language, their English reading will (1) *also be good/not be so good*. Look around next time you're on a bus or train to see how many people are reading. If you come from a culture that doesn't read much, you need to read for at least 20 minutes in English (2) *every day/once a week*. Keeping a log of your reading with recorded times is essential. See page 444.

Both speed and comprehension are important in the IELTS Reading test. A reasonable aim is to read (3) *70/90* words per minute. If you leave five minutes' checking time, that means about (4) *60/80* seconds for each of the 40 test questions.

To improve speed:

- Make sure you know exactly what you're answering, so you don't waste time reading every single word. (There's more information than you're tested on.) Always read the questions (5) *after/before* you read the passage. Underline key words in the questions; circle any negative ideas.

- Work out as much as you can about the passage by quickly looking at the title, headings, or graphics. If you've been reading widely, you might already know something about the topic.

- Most Reading question types are (6) *different from/the same as* those in the Listening test.

- Skills used to read faster include: scanning and skimming. Scanning is moving your eye over a whole text, or one section, until you find one word or phrase you're looking for. (7) *You do not read any complete sentence until you've found what you want./You may read any sentences at any time you like*. Capital letters help when scanning for names. Finding nouns on the same topic will also lead you to your answer. Skimming means reading everything (8) *quickly/slowly*.

- In each Reading Practice test that you do, notice how one passage is divided into two, three, or four question types. If there are three question types in a passage, you've got (9) *five/three* minutes for each one. If there are two, you've got about eight. Work as fast as you can, and move on if you can't do one question; answer it at the end. You should (10) *guess/leave the answer* if you have to.

To improve comprehension:

- Most IELTS Reading questions rely on understanding (11) *grammar/vocabulary*. Where there are words that you don't know, use the language around them to work them out. Other nouns in the same sentence are likely to be on the same topic. Develop your vocabulary by reading as much as you can. Linguists estimate it takes (12) *seven/three* times reading one word in different contexts to learn it.

- Candidates need to know the connotations of words: whether they are positive, negative, or neutral.

- Qualifying words change the meaning of nouns. Often (13) *adjectives/verbs* indicate a writer's opinion. Watch out for adverbs in the questions which might have a different meaning from similar words in the text.

- Reference – identifying which (14) _noun/pronoun_ refers backwards or forwards to the original idea – is common in IELTS Reading. (See pages 267 and 272.)

- Another skill is understanding inference. This is making a judgment about information that is given but not stated directly. Inference is tested in Passages 2 and 3. (15) _A Five/A Six_ generally can't infer, and guesses these questions. Reading reputable magazines (_The Economist_ not _Grazia_), academic journals, or literature in English exposes you to inference.

- Careful reading, word by word, more than once, is necessary for around (16) _25%/50%_ of IELTS questions.

- Exam technique is useful, (17) _and it is underestimated/but it is overestimated_ by most candidates: either you understand the meaning of the words, or you don't.

Additional strategies if you scored a Six in your last test

- Very fast readers say they read down the middle of a page, rarely looking to the left or the right. They take in a whole paragraph, rather than individual words or sentences. This is particularly useful for (18) _gapfilling/heading and labelling_ questions.

- Try to answer (19) _each question separately/a group of questions together_. Understand the relationship between or among questions.

- Don't think (20) _too little/too long_ about a question; you're likely to run out of time, and sometimes you might come up with a convoluted argument that is wrong. IELTS Reading answers are never very complicated.

- (21) _Make sure you have time for a slow, careful transfer; checking answers is less important./Never sacrifice checking time. Practise a speedy, accurate transfer in your exam preparation_.

Very important information about timing

In the IELTS exam, there is advice given about spending 20 minutes on each passage (as written in the Practice tests). However, Passage 3 is more difficult than the other two, so you may want to save time in the first two passages to add to the last one. Also, checking time is extremely important. A better way to divide your time is:

Passage 1	**15 minutes**
Passage 2	**16 minutes**
Passage 3	**25 minutes**
Transferring and Checking	**04 minutes**
Total	**60 minutes**

Strategies for question types that are _only_ in the Reading test

The examples on the following pages refer to the questions and answers in the Academic Reading Taster Test on pages 59-67.

1B = ii	**List of Headings**
	i Buy it at the co-op
2C = vi	~~ii A composite word~~
	iii A different kind of farming
3D =	iv The dream of Warren Oakes
	v Media v Freegans
4E =	~~vi Origins and activities~~
5F =	~~vii What is freeganism?~~
	viii Use less; waste less
6G =	ix The UK is OK for freegans

Example *Answer*

Paragraph A **vii**

YOUR TURN *What are the missing words below? Write the letters to complete each one.*

How do you match hea __ __ __ __ __ (like questions 1-6 in the Taster Test)?

1 Firstly, write the question numbers down the page next to the heading box with the letters (here B-G) as above, so you won't make a mistake in the transfer. Your answers are Roman numerals, not letters from the alphabet. A common mistake with this question type is accidentally writing letters instead of numerals, or writing *ivi* or *viiii*, which do not exist.

   Cross out the example answer, so you won't choose it. Cross out the headings as you find them as well.

2 Don't **bo __ __ __ __** reading the example paragraph (usually A) because you know what it's about from the heading.

3 Choose a heading which gives the **m __ __ __** idea of a paragraph.

   In the example above, Paragraph D talks about 'rubbish' and 'landfill', so heading **viii** is suitable. It also says wasting land 'upsets' freegans, from which we may infer that freegans believe everyone should use less.

   If necessary, measure with your finger how much text is about one idea if you think there are two ideas in a paragraph.

4 Avoid an answer that is too specific.

   In question 2, Warren Oakes is mentioned (heading **iv**), but there is more information about the 'origins' (when freeganism started) and 'activities' (what freegans do), so heading **vi** is co __ __ __ __ __.

5 Look for parallel phrases or **syn __ __ __ __ __**.

   'Composite' means 'made up of two or more things', so heading **ii** goes with Paragraph B, which says: 'Freegan is a new word, made up of the two words: "free" and "vegan".'

6 Look for **exa __ __ __ __ __** that illustrate a more general concept.

   'Television', 'magazines', and 'journalists' in Paragraph E = 'media' from heading **v**.

7 Remember: some headings or titles in English are like jokes.

   'The UK is OK for freegans' is an example. Some titles use abbreviations or **sym __ __ __ __** to save space: 'co-op' is a short form of 'co-operative'. Scan for the hyphen (-) to find the word. The letter 'v' in 'Media v Freegans' is used in sporting competitions or legal battles. It stands for 'versus', and means 'against'.

8 Choose each heading quickly. Once you have chosen, **st __ __** reading the paragraph.

How do you match sentence en __ __ __ __ __ (like questions 11-14)?

1 Remember: there are usually two or more possible endings for each question.
Elim __ __ __ __ __ the wrong ones. To do this, ask yourself: Is the complete sentence:

      (a) a true, given statement?
      (b) general enough (not too specific)?
      (c) correct according to grammar or vocabulary?

    For (a): In question 13, the choices are 'agriculture' or 'the media'. We don't know if freegans have a special interest in the media, so 'agriculture' is the answer.

    For (b): In question 11, the choices are 'dumpster dive' or 'recycle'. 'Recycle' is correct because not all freegans dumpster dive.

    For (c): In question 12, 'Freegans generally do not buy imported food because...' has to be followed by a clause (underline{subject} + boxed{complete verb}) as in: 'underline{transporting it long distance boxed{is} another environmental cost}'. The answer 'H' is true, but 'grown locally is less expensive' does not make grammatical sense as there is no subject, and the verb is a participle.

2 Do not think about your *o __ __* beliefs; only look at what's written in the text. I'm sure most people think freeganism is 'hard to follow', but a better answer for question 14 is that it 'challenges patterns of consumption and employment'.

How do you choose the correct proper noun from a list of answers (like questions 23-27)?

1 *Sc __ __* for names of people, companies, cities, or countries, by looking for capital letters. Circle them once you find them.

2 Remember: questions are often parallel expressions for what is in the text.
    For example, in question 23: 'underline{More than 25%} of underline{the world's container freight starts in}...' *me __ __ __* 'underline{over a quarter} of underline{global container traffic originates in}...'.

3 *Inf __ __* as much as possible. It is likely in question 27 that 'underline{the world's largest container company}' is also 'the most successful logistics company'.

How do you answer True / False / Not G __ __ __ __ questions (like questions 7-10)?

1 Find and *underl __ __ __* the evidence in the text that supports your choice. Remember, *True* means it's stated there as a fact; *False* means the opposite is stated, or something only partly true. If you can't find evidence, *Not Given* is the answer.
    True answers mostly rely on vocabulary that means the same thing being used in both the *te __ __* and the question. In question 8, we're told freegans find landfill 'quite disturbing'; in the text, they are 'upset'.
    In question 7, the question says: 'the late 1990s', but in the text, it is written: 'the mid-90s', so the answer is False.
    With NG, don't be fooled by something similar. It is stated in the text: 'the number of freegans worldwide is growing', but that is *n __ __* the same as question 10: freeganism is 'predicted to grow significantly'. Adverbs, like 'significantly', 'never', or 'always' *always* need to be checked.

2 Watch out for *neg __ __ __ __ __* language.
    In question 9, 'barely any' means 'almost none'. In the text, it is written: 'the UK and Australia currently consume and discard equal amounts of good food.' which means they throw away huge not small amounts.

How do you answer Yes / No / Not Given questions (like questions 28-33)?

1 Yes/No/Not Given questions are about the writer's **op __ __ __ __ __ __**, views, or beliefs.

A statement that **ag __ __ __ __** with the views of the writer of the text gets a *Yes* answer. A statement that disagrees with the views of the writer gets a *No*. If there is no information about what the writer thinks, then *Not Given* is the answer.

Many candidates find these the most difficult Reading questions.

2 Always underline the **evi __ __ __ __ __** in the passage.

Question 28 = Y. The question is: 'A cat appears to understand when a human calls its name'. In the text, it is written: 'If the owner calls the cat by its name, it usually comes'.

Question 29 = N. The question is: 'The speeches of animals in myths and legends were mainly for entertainment.' In the text, it is written: 'Were these tales [about speaking animals] just indirect ways of teaching moral concepts?'

Question 30 = NG. The question is: 'Mynahs make an amazing number of different sounds.' In the text, it is written: 'They [mynahs] produce more than 200 different sounds.' But the writer doesn't say that's 'amazing'. Beware of emotive adjectives.

3 Scan to find one or two **k __ __** words; **sk __ __** over all the lines needed for each answer. Sometimes there's not much to read; other times, there are several lines containing the information.

To answer question 32, you have to read seven lines, while for question 33, the answer is in one line. Expect one or two questions like question 32 in each IELTS test.

How do you choose the correct word from a list of answers for summary questions (like questions 15-22)?

1 You can usually answer most of these questions **with __ __ __** reading the text. Strong candidates do this, and then go to the text for the remaining answers that are facts, like the date '1956' or '1968' in question 16; or, whether Japan 'mass produced' or 'popularised' containers (both these past participles are grammatically possible).

2 As with matching sentence endings, look for grammatical **connec __ __ __ __ __**.

In question 15, the missing word is an adjective to qualify the noun 'phenomenon'. 'Recent' (E) is the only possibility. 'Current' (N) is an adjective, but we can't say 'a current phenomenon' because 'current' means 'happening now, and not related to the past'; but 'recent' means 'happening just a short time ago, and probably now as well'.

In question 20, a complete verb is missing; it follows 'containers', the subject. 'Cross' (L) is that verb. 'Travelling' (B), a present participle, is only part of a verb, so it is wrong.

In question 21, the subject, which is missing, needs to be singular because the main verb is 'has' in: 'Unfortunately, _____ dictated by ports and markets **has** meant...' (This sentence also contains a reduced relative clause because 'which is' – before 'dictated' – has been removed.) 'Numbers' (F) is not possible because it's plural. 'Efficiency' (A) is correct, as an uncountable noun takes a singular verb.

3 Find vocabulary that **collo __ __ __ __ __**.

In question 18, 'lower labour' can only go before 'costs' (J).

4 When in doubt, choose **n __ __ __ __**. Most IELTS Reading answers that are single words are nouns. Half of the answers in this Taster passage are nouns.

How do you choose the correct word from the text for summary questions (like questions 34-39)?

1 Firstly, **sc** __ __ to find the paragraphs the summary is about. **Ma** __ __ them.
   In the Taster passage, these are paragraphs 8-10.

2 Read for main ideas; skim over examples. Read carefully to find each word you need. Check the words make **sen** __ __ for meaning and grammar when put into the summary.

Here is a comparison of the text and the summary:

Text:

'…their [**primates**] vocalisations and gestures relate solely to their immediate environment….The primary reason for this failure is that the animals do not **spontaneously** apply the target language as human children do…Secondly, primates never learn **grammar**….
His [a chimp's] language remained **simple**…and inflexible.

  Studies into the linguistic abilities of animals are far less popular now…due largely to the widely **accepted** theory proposed by Noam Chomsky in the 1980s.'

Summary:

'Like birds and small mammals, **34** only produce sounds connected to their environment. One reason they do not learn language is they fail to use the language they have been taught **35**. Secondly, they do not master **36**; their language stays **37** and fixed.

  The number of scientific **38** into the linguistic ability of animals has probably decreased because Chomsky's theory of the innateness of language is **39** universally.'

3 Understand referents **thor** __ __ __ __ __ __. (A referent is a word like 'their' or 'his', which refers back or forward to a subject or object.)
   In question 35 and question 37, what does 'their' refer to? What does 'his' refer to?

4 Word **or** __ __ __ may be different between the text and the summary.
   In question 35, 'spontaneously' comes before the verb 'apply' in the text, but after 'taught' in the summary; the same is true of 'accepted'.

5 Recognise synonyms **aro** __ __ __ the words you're choosing.

6 Always read the questions before the passage. In this case, unlike a summary question with a list of answers supplied, only work out which part of **spe** __ __ __ is needed; don't guess the exact word. Your guess may be correct, grammatically and logically, but will be marked wrong if the word isn't in the text because the instructions ask for: 'one word from the passage'.
   In question 39, the answer is 'accepted', but other words like 'acknowledged' or 'recognised' do fit there.

7 Make sure you write the **nu** __ __ __ __ of words asked for.
   In the Taster it's: 'one word only', so don't write two.

8 **Co** __ __ the words correctly.
   You may think 'grammer' is spelt with an 'e', but it's not. You might know that 'excepted' and 'accepted' sound the same, and by accident write the former. You might write 'privates' instead of 'primates'. Perhaps you're tired, and you write a word from your own language by mistake.

How do you choose the correct title (like question 40)?

As with many other question types, choose a **gen** _ _ _ _ title – though not too general.

Eliminate those that are unlikely one by one. Usually, two **sim** _ _ _ _ titles are left.

In the Taster passage, the writer believes animals don't have language, so choice A ('Fascinating animal language') can't be the title. Choice B is also wrong: the writer does discuss 'Effective animal communication', but it's not the main idea. Choice C is off topic. Choice D ('Animal language – fact or fiction?') is possible. Choice E ('Language is a purely human creation') is also possible. Choice D is better than choice E because the focus of the passage is on animals rather than humans.

Extra practice filling in a flowchart

Many IELTS candidates panic when they see flowchart questions, but these are not so difficult because the passages they accompany may have a lower reading level than other IELTS passages. That is: they do not have as many long sentences, nor as much complex vocabulary.

Furthermore, flowchart questions are logical. The process described has a beginning and an end, and certain vocabulary alerts a reader to the different stages. Look for 'first of all', 'during', 'then', and 'finally'. There are also nouns such as 'stage', 'part', or 'phase'. Do watch out for stages that may be written slightly out of sequence order. (There's one in the passage below.)

Sometimes a reader has to identify two possible options – shown by the flowchart splitting in two. Finding sentences that contain 'if' or 'whether' will help here. 'If' may also signal some kind of failure in the process, meaning a part of it should be repeated. Arrows going back up to boxes show this repetition.

Remember: with missing verbs in a flowchart, the passive may be needed.

Treat the following passage as though it were a real IELTS exam.
Record your time at the end. It should be around 18 minutes.

PASSAGE 2 Questions 14-27

HOW MEDICINES ARE DEVELOPED

Strolling into a pharmacy for a prescribed medication or an over-the-counter remedy, few people are aware of the long developmental process of the product they are purchasing.

In fact, any medicine dispensed by a pharmacy or hospital is the sole successful compound out of hundreds of similar ones that underwent rigorous testing, and it has taken around 15 years' research and considerable expenditure before it has reached the shelves.

First, a pharmaceutical company selects an illness, preferably one for which there are quantities of sufferers. Then, research and development commence. Research is conducted in a laboratory whereas most testing occurs in hospitals and clinics ideally across several countries.

In laboratory tests, over a two-year period, a particular drug molecule is identified. Studies are performed on its toxicity before the molecule is clinically trialled on humans.

Clinical testing can take up to ten years. Throughout, patients are monitored continually. As soon as any serious problem is encountered, the medicine is withdrawn.

In Phase I, healthy volunteers take the drug to see what a safe dosage is, and what constitutes its side effects – those annoying reactions like nausea, drowsiness, tingling, tremors, or weight gain. The medicine may be returned to the lab if it seems too toxic, or its side effects are too distressing.

Small groups of patients are used to determine the effectiveness of treating their particular disease or condition in Phase II. Dosage levels may be adjusted as a result of this phase.

Phase III is a comparative trial in which thousands of patients compare the new medicine with one already widely in use, or with a placebo (a sugar pill which patients believe is the drug).

If all proceeds smoothly, medical journals review the results, indicating whether the benefits of the medicine to a large number of patients outweigh any deleterious effects.

National regulatory bodies grant final permission for sale. Sometimes, where there are existing treatments which are cheaper and equally effective, the body may refuse a licence to the pharmaceutical company. The regulator also decides whether the cost of the final product will be borne entirely by patients, or subsidised in part by the state.

Just before the regulator has its say, a name is chosen for the medicine – a process involving three months' work by an advertising agency. There are so many pharmaceutical products available today that it is no longer easy to distinguish one from another. Three-syllable product names are considered memorable for medicines, and ones with a whiff of Greek about them too since many scientific words in English are derived from this language.

After the newly-named medicine has been approved for sale by the national authority, it is launched onto the market. Further monitoring takes place post release, and if problems are reported, a decision is made by the national body as to whether the product should be withdrawn, or sold to the public accompanied by a warning label.

Pharmaceutical companies usually patent their new medicines for a decade or more to prevent other companies from copying them, and to profit from sales since their investment has been onerous. However, on expiration of the patent, other companies can manufacture their own versions, dubbed generic medicines. In spite of their having lower profit margins, generics may steal the market from pharmaceutical majors, being far less costly to consumers.

With this lengthy process of checks and balances, it may seem unlikely that any medicine could reach the public that was still unsafe. However, there have been examples of this – some disastrous. In the early 1960s, a drug to relieve pregnant women of the symptoms of morning sickness, called Thalidomide, was prescribed in the UK and elsewhere. A small proportion of children born to these women had serious physical defects including too few fingers, or limbs that were severely stunted.

Conversely, there is the Aspirin phenomenon. The active ingredient in this drug comes from the bark of the willow tree, meaning its manufacturing costs are negligible. There is a growing body of scientific evidence that shows this inexpensive painkiller is effective against a wide range of other ailments from heart disease to cancer. For patients, Aspirin wins out over far more expensive and extensively-tested compounds. It may even become the out-of-patent wonder drug.

Next time you dash in to your pharmacy for Xenyphol or Zilovin, or some other improbably-named concoction, ponder for a moment on the arduous process of producing that pill.

Questions 14-22

Choose **NO MORE THAN TWO WORDS OR A NUMBER** *from the passage for each answer.*

Time period	Process	Constraints
1 year	**SELECTION** An illness is chosen.	
2 years 7-10 years	**RESEARCH & DEVELOPMENT** In the lab: A drug molecule is identified. Toxicity studies are **14** .... In hospitals & clinics: The molecule is trialled on humans. Phase I: The drug is taken by healthy **16** .... to determine safe dosage levels and side effects. Phase II: Small groups of patients are given the drug to test how effective it is for their particular disease or condition. Phase III: The drug is tested against another medication already on the market and a sugar pill or **18**	If, at any time, **15** .... are encountered, the drug is withdrawn. If the drug is too toxic or its **17** .... are too great, it is returned to the lab. If the dosage level is too low or too high, the drug is returned to the lab.
6 months	**REVIEW** The drug is appraised in medical journals.	
19 .... months	**NAMING** The drug is given a trade name.	
1 year	**REGULATION** A national regulatory body gives permission for sale of the drug, or refuses permission because other similar but **20** .... medications already exist. The body decides who will bear the cost of the drug: the patient alone, or the patient in conjunction with the **21**	
3 months	**LAUNCH** The drug becomes available to the general public.	If minor problems occur after launching, the regulator decides whether to withdraw the drug, or to sell it with a(n) **22** ....

Questions 23-26

*Choose the correct letter: **A**, **B**, **C**, or **D**.*

23 An out-of-patent medicine made by any pharmaceutical company is called

    A   a copy.

    B   generic.

    C   onerous.

    D   a version.

24 Thalidomide was given to women who were

    A   suffering the ill effects of pregnancy.

    B   trying to get pregnant.

    C   suffering from physical deformities.

    D   very stunted.

25 Since the active ingredients in Aspirin come from a tree, its production costs are

    A   quite high.

    B   very high.

    C   quite low.

    D   very low.

26 The writer suggests patients will buy Aspirin because

    A   it is cheap and particularly effective against heart disease.

    B   it is a highly effective painkiller.

    C   it is inexpensive and suitable for multiple conditions.

    D   it has been extensively tested.

Question 27

*Choose **TWO** letters: **A-E**.*

*Which **TWO** of the following are the writer's views of some names of medicines?*

    A   They are more readily accepted if they have three syllables.

    B   They should come from Greek.

    C   They are sometimes hard to pronounce.

    D   They are made up too quickly.

    E   They do not sound believable.

```
00:00 =
____:____
```

Extra practice labelling a diagram

Some candidates find labelling diagrams difficult.

In the months before your IELTS exam, try to find short texts on scientific topics that interest you. There are countless online materials. Google 'How X works', for instance, to find out all about X. There's bound to be a diagram. This may also help you in answering Writing Task 1.

Below is some extra practice in labelling diagrams.

Remember:

1 Always read the questions before you read the passage.

2 Study each diagram quickly but carefully.

3 Note the direction of the questions you must label: clockwise, anticlockwise, in a spiral, across, or down.

4 While reading, use headings to find the section that the diagram refers to. It won't be about the whole text.

When you do the passage below and on the following page, time yourself (minutes and seconds). A Seven should finish in just under 20 minutes.

PASSAGE 2 Questions 15-27

FLUORESCENT MICROSCOPY

In 2008, the Nobel Prize for Chemistry was awarded for work on dyes used in fluorescent microscopy. This refinement has improved a technology already at the forefront of molecular biology, and an invaluable aid to disease and pollution detection.

Differences between conventional and fluorescent microscopes

All of us are familiar with microscopes. The ones that we peered into in school biology classes work with magnifying lenses and visible light, produced by a 100-watt bulb beneath the specimen. The enlarged image, called the Objective, is viewed through an eyepiece.

A fluorescent microscope, however, uses a far stronger light source, so it is capable of revealing much greater detail. These days, this light is an argon-ion laser of around 50 megawatts.

The laser excites a fluorescent species in the specimen, which, in turn, produces the Objective, made highly visible due to the contrast between glowing dyed material and the rest. The Objective is not only studied through an eyepiece, but is also linked to a camera, computer, and monitor.

How a fluorescent microscope works

The laser in a fluorescent microscope focuses repeatedly on one infinitesimal point after another in the specimen. Prior to imaging, the sample is prepared with a fluorochrome, or fluorescent dye, and the microscope is fitted with special filters.

The radiation from the laser is absorbed by the fluorochrome, which collides with atoms in the specimen. Electrons within the atoms are excited to a higher energy level – hence the name Laser Excitation Source. As the atoms relax to a lower energy level, they emit photons, or small packets of light. These photons have a longer wavelength than that of the laser. To be visible to the human eye, and captured on camera, these waves are separated from the brighter laser light, firstly by a Dichromatic or Beam-splitting Mirror at 45 degrees, and then by an Emission Filter. A computer program pieces together the points of data into a 3-D reconstruction of the target.

The majority of today's fluorescent microscopes are epi-fluorescent, meaning both the excitation and the observation of the fluorescence occur above the specimen as in the diagram.

Applications of fluorescent microscopy

Environmental monitoring, public health, and biological research all rely on fluorescent microscopy. Microbial contamination of air, water, dairy products, and other consumables can easily be identified. Fluorescent microscopy is used to image the structural components of cells, for example their DNA or RNA, to reveal abnormalities, or indicate whether a cell is dead or alive. Extremely small features, like organelles, can be visually enhanced, and fluorescent tags may even be attached to antibodies which in turn attach themselves to the target. The most common use of fluorescent microscopy is as a diagnostic tool in medical laboratories.

As mentioned previously, specimens are stained with fluorochromes: for example, acridine orange (AO) or fluorescent antibody (FA). AO is favoured in the diagnosis of Tuberculosis (TB), in parasitology (for malaria or menigitis), exfoliative cytology (for cancer), and biological research (to study tissue and cellular structures). FA is used for diarrhoea, hepatitis, HIV, and a number of other infectious diseases.

Fluorochrome dyes work even when diluted to concentrations of 1:10,000, and the time between slide preparation and analysis is minimal. A TB sputum slide which uses a standard Ziehl-Nielsen stain may require 15-20 minutes before it can be read, whereas an AO-stained sample takes only two to three minutes.

The obvious benefits of fluorescent microscopy have meant it has been adopted worldwide. Doubtless, it will be a laboratory fixture for some time to come.

• •

Questions 15-21

*Choose **ONE WORD** from the passage for each answer.*

15 The 2008 Nobel Prize for .... was awarded for work on dyes used in fluorescent microscopy.

16 A conventional microscope relies on visible ....

17 A fluorescent microscope shows specimens in far more .... than a conventional microscope.

18 In fluorescent microscopy, a dyed specimen produces its own ....

19 For a microscope to work as a fluorescent microscope, it needs two special

....

20 A laser lights up millions of tiny spots on a specimen. These are combined into an image by a computer .... program.

21 AO and FA are .... with which samples are prepared.

Questions 22-26

Label the diagram below.

*Choose **ONE WORD** from the passage for each answer.*

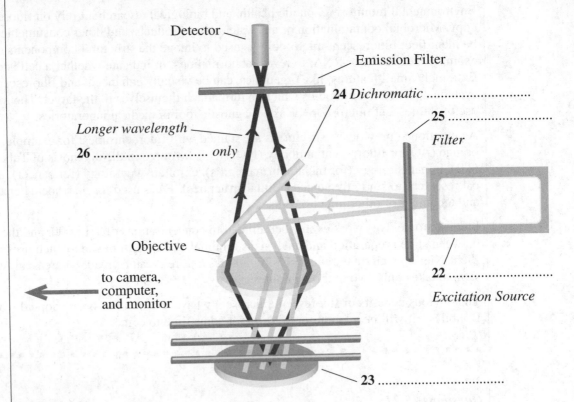

Question 27

*Choose **TWO** letters: **A-E**.*

*Which **TWO** of the following are likely about fluorescent microscopy?*

A   It is slow and difficult to perform.

B   Other imaging technology is challenging it.

C   It is only available for use in developed countries.

D   It is relatively cheap and effective.

E   Genetic research benefits from it.

```
  00:00 =
  ____:____
```

Go to page 385 for the answers.

Special information about the General Training Reading test

Read the text below, then answer the questions that follow.

Like the Academic test, the General Training (GT) has 40 questions to be answered in 60 minutes. Question types are the same, but some text types differ. In a GT test, there are up to 2500 words – 200 fewer than possible in an Academic test.

Most GT tests contain at least five texts in three sections. Sections 1 and 2 have a variety of short texts. They use material from daily life – advertisements, flyers, notices, timetables, instructions etc. Section 1 is focused on facts like dates, times, numbers, prices, categories etc. Scanning is the main reading skill being tested.

Section 2 is again connected to daily life – usually the work or training context. Skimming is useful here.

Section 3 is similar to an Academic Passage 3 with at least 1000 words. It tests a deeper understanding of a text. It is usually a description whereas Academic passages may include different opinions of scholars.

In GT, there are only 5-10 answers out of 40 that are words; all other answers are letters or numerals. Due to this, GT candidates need to get higher scores for each band because guessing is more likely to be correct.

Many people find a GT test easier than an Academic one, but since the scoring is different, in reality it is similar. In one way, GT may be more difficult: with several texts, candidates must manage their time better.

See page 7 for how the scoring works.

YOUR TURN　*The following questions are based on the text you have just read. Choose* **NO MORE THAN THREE WORDS OR A NUMBER** *from the text for each answer.*

1 How many questions are there in a GT Reading test?　......................

2 How many words are there in a typical test?　......................

3 How many texts are there in a test?　......................

4 Which reading skill is tested in Section 1?　......................

5 Which two contexts does Section 2 generally focus on?　......................

6 What does Section 3 test?　......................

7 For each band, what do GT candidates need to get in relation to Academic candidates?　......................

8 Because it has so many texts, what should candidates do carefully in the GT Reading test?　......................

9 What score is a Seven in Academic Reading?　......................

10 What score is a Six in GT Reading?　......................

GT Reading Taster Test

Copy the answer sheet on page 456, or make your own.

Do the Taster Test in a quiet place. Do it as though it were an exam. That is, take 60 minutes for the whole test, including writing your answers on the answer sheet.

There are three sections in a GT Reading test, but there are at least five different texts: two or more for Section 1; two for Section 2; and, one for Section 3.

In the IELTS exam, there is advice given about spending 20 minutes on each section. However, Section 3 is more difficult than the other two, so you may want to save time in the first two sections to add to the last one. Also, checking time is very important. A better way to divide your time is this:

Section 1A	**07 minutes**
Section 1B	**07 minutes**
Section 2A	**08 minutes**
Section 2B	**09 minutes**
Section 3	**25 minutes**
Transferring and Checking	**04 minutes**
Total	**60 minutes**

Find a stopwatch, and time yourself. Write your time – minutes and seconds – where you see this symbol: 00:00.

While doing the Taster Test, you might like a break after each section to review the answers, which follow.

There are two complete GT Practice Tests on pages 367. You should also do the remaining four Academic Practice Test Passage 3s.

SECTION 1   Questions 1-14

Read the text below and on the next page, and answer questions 1-7.

FINDERS KEEPERS – Australia's newest employment website	
Name	Cathy Ng
Password	Ng93Blue
Location	Perth
Phone	0413 223 604
Preferred jobs	Accountant; accounts assistant; payroll clerk

Services for job seekers	This week's jobs	Services for employers
Advice on pension funds & savings	Banking & Finance	Contributing to pension funds
Continuing education	Hospital & Medical	Locating technicians abroad
Finding industry mentors	Human Resources	Providing staff development
Negotiating a salary & benefits package	IT	Safety at work
Writing résumés & cover letters	Restaurants & Catering	Understanding state and federal employment laws

Today's job tip	It may seem time-consuming, but it pays to write a different résumé for each job you apply for. Tailor your information to a specific employer and a specific position.
Messages waiting for you	12

Questions 1-7

Answer the questions below.

Choose **NO MORE THAN THREE WORDS** *from the text for each answer.*

1   Where is Cathy Ng based? ....

2   In which of this week's job categories is Cathy most likely to find work as an accountant? ....

3   If Cathy would like to find a respected person already working in the accountancy field who might advise her, where would she search? ....

4   If an employer is having trouble finding an IT expert in Australia, which category might he or she consider? ....

5   If an employer wants to improve the skills of his or her employees, which category offers advice? ....

6   If an employer is concerned about work-related injuries, where could he or she search? ....

7   What should a job seeker write for each job application? ....

```
00:00 =
____:____
```

JOB ADVERTISEMENTS

Questions 8-14

Read the advertisements below, and answer questions 8-14.

A

Stiletto imports shoes for major retail outlets. We are looking for an accountant who is a hardworking self-starter.

The main duties are:
- Accounts Payable
- Accounts Receivable
- Payroll

An excellent knowledge of MYOB is needed.

Other duties include:
- Debtor control
- General ledger
- Stock overview
- Customer supply
- Generating invoices
- Preparation of financial statements and tax returns
- Preparation of activity statements
- Development & management of customer database
- Freight bookings

An Intermediate knowledge of Word and Excel is needed.

Hours are 9 to 5. There is a local bus, but own transport is preferable due to frequent overtime.

Email your résumé to Tanya@Stiletto.com.au.

B

Randall's Recruitment
Location: Sydney CBD

Type: Permanent; Temporary hourly-paid

Title: Payroll officer

Salary range: Permanent: $50-60k + superannuation; Hourly-paid: $26-33 per hour dependent on experience.

Randall's is recruiting several payroll officers for positions in the city. Opportunities exist for experienced and less experienced officers. We supply staff to government departments as well as leading private companies.

We are looking for people with high-volume experience, able to process timesheets for more than 200 employees.

Email your résumé to daniel.randall@Randalls.com.au, or click on the appropriate link.

C

Family-run business is seeking a part-time accounts assistant (April-July)

This would be ideal for a person with school-age children returning to the workforce. Hours are flexible between 10-3.

The owner is a chartered accountant who requires assistance at the end of the tax year.

If the candidate is suitable, there is an opportunity that this would become a long-term position.

Email your CV to BJPark@gmail.com.

D

WorkPower Agency

Job reference #: D: 2013-446 Payroll5

Payroll Clerk (using PeopleSoft)

- North Sydney
- Immediate start
- 2-month assignment

Located just over the Harbour Bridge, this not-for-profit organisation touches the lives of millions of people. Our agency needs an experienced payroll clerk to assist a small, friendly team in its transition from PeopleSoft 9.3 to 10.1.

This 7-week assignment requires an immediate start. You will conduct payroll systems testing.

It is essential you are proficient in PeopleSoft 10.1.

It is desirable that you have:

- Good numerical skills
- The ability to maintain accuracy while completing repetitive tasks
- Good communication skills
- The ability to work within a team

Overtime is expected.

To apply for this position, submit your résumé by clicking on the Apply Now icon.

---

*Look at the seven descriptions of the advertisements: **A-D** above.*

For which descriptions are the following statements true?

*Write the correct letter, **A-D**, in boxes 8-14 on your answer sheet.*
NB: You may use any letter more than once.

8 This job would suit a payroll clerk with little experience.

9 Although this job is for a short period, it may continue.

10 An employee is needed for this position straight away.

11 The duties in this advertisement are quite specific.

12 A car would be particularly useful to reach this job.

13 For this position, applicants can only submit their details directly to the website.

14 The agency that published this advertisement finds employees for both the public and private sectors.

```
00:00 =
____:____
```

Here are the answers. How did you do?

Section 1: 1. Perth (*capital optional*); 2. Banking and Finance (*capitals optional*); 3. Finding industry mentors (*capital optional*); 4. Locating technicians abroad (*capital optional*); 5. Providing staff development (*capital optional*); 6. Safety at work (*capital optional*); 7. a different résumé (*symbol above the 'e' optional; the article 'a' is necessary*); 8. B; 9. C; 10. D; 11. A; 12. A; 13. D; 14. B.

KEY POINTS

- Short-answer questions (questions 1-7 above) are common in Section 1. The instructions will tell you to choose words from the text. If this is *not* said, then answers can come from your head as well as long as they're logical and grammatically correct.

- Remember: **No IELTS answer is longer than three words**. Usually, there is only one set of questions in a GT Reading test asking for 'no more than three words'.

- Remember: *Always read the questions before you read the text.* For questions 8-14, underline your evidence in the text. Many parallel expressions are used, for instance: '... short period, it may continue' in the question = '... would become a long-term position' in the text. 'Straight away' in question 10 = 'immediate' in Text D.

- Notice the distribution of answers. In a whole IELTS Reading test, letter answers will be fairly evenly distributed. That is: there won't be one letter, say 'B', that appears much more often than others.

WATCH OUT!

The most common mistake in Sections 1 and 2 is a careless one: copying words from the text wrongly (forgetting to write the article 'a' in question 7), or writing a wrong letter (*F* instead of *E*).

SECTION 2   Questions 15-27

Not only has the method of job application changed recently, with over 75% of vacancies in developed countries advertised online, but the style of application has undergone metamorphosis as well. Many companies and organisations now use a rigorous selection process which is criterion-based. Carla Mhando explores this phenomenon.

My first job was waitressing at weekends in an Italian restaurant. I'd seen an advert stuck on the window, walked in – in my school uniform – and got the job on the spot. Three years later, I became a cadet journalist for a regional newspaper. The traineeship was arranged by my uncle, who knew the editor. I stayed with the paper for twelve years. In the late 90s, when journalism was in decline, I decided on a career change – working in administration. To my dismay, the application process seemed like a job in itself. Not only was I asked for a detailed CV, but I was also required 'to address selection criteria'. These were a set of behavioural competencies which were meant to prove that I could do the job.

I was unfamiliar with the word 'competency', but I read through all the material my prospective employer had supplied. This came in the form of a 'competency dictionary' – a lengthy document outlining what is expected of employees at each level since competencies exist at entry, post-entry, supervisory, and senior managerial levels.

In alphabetical order, these were the following competencies: Achievement; Analytical Thinking; Customer Service Orientation; Entrepreneurship; Flexibility; Holding People Accountable; Intercultural Competence; Leading and Developing Others; Self-awareness; Team Working; and, Working Strategically. I felt dizzy just reading the contents page.

Typically, three or four competencies or criteria had to be addressed in any application. As a new employee for an entry-level position, mine were: Customer Service Orientation, Flexibility, and Team Working. For Customer Service Orientation, this meant I needed to demonstrate the 'ability to deliver a service'. For Flexibility, I had to display an 'ability to change ideas or perceptions based on new information or contrary evidence', and show 'willingness to listen to other people's points of view'. While for Team Working, I needed to be 'co-operative; unafraid to seek advice; and keen to put in extra effort to assist others'. Once again, the amount of stuff to absorb made me worry I could ever do the job, which was a humble receptionist.

For my application I had to write 600 words on the competencies. To my way of thinking, a receptionist needs a tidy appearance, a welcoming smile, a pleasant phone manner, and a degree of skill with a switchboard – all of which I had. Six hundred words about abstractions hardly seemed necessary. Needless to say, although I wrote what I considered to be excellent and pertinent prose, I wasn't even interviewed for the job.

A week later, I tried my luck with a Level Two position – a job as a Press Officer. For Customer Service Orientation, I now needed to show I could 'add value; make decisions with the customer in mind; take pride in delivering a high-quality service; investigate service delivery problems, and provide solutions for them.' I couldn't see how this related to what a Press Officer actually does on a day-to-day basis. Desperate for demystification, I rang an acquaintance who worked in HR*.

The first thing Taylor Lexington asked me was, 'Are you using star, Carla?' 'Star?' I queried. 'Yes, STAR,' she said. ' "S" for your "specific situation"; "T" for your "target"; "A" for the "action" you took; and, "R" for the "result"? If you don't use STAR,' Taylor admonished, 'you can't address a criterion effectively.' 'Thanks,' I said, adding under my breath, 'Beam me up.'

Through word of mouth, I found a job as a registrar in a language school. In 2010, I decided to apply for a managerial position at the school next door. When I discovered that the application included addressing four criteria at Level Three, I went into panic mode. Flexibility now meant I had to 'identify a pragmatic approach in order to get a job done quickly and effectively'; 'be aware of the bigger picture when interpreting and implementing policy'; and, 'be comfortable with ambiguity'. Although I'd just spent three months as a manager, covering for someone on leave, and I'd successfully introduced a new database and registration process, I was completely at a loss as to how I should reframe all this as Flexibility. Once again, I did not get the job.

Questions 15-21

Complete the summary using the list of words, A-O, below:

Write the correct letter, A-O, in boxes 15-21 on your answer sheet.

Carla Mhando decided to write about criterion-based selection when she was looking to change 15 .... herself. Prior to the late 1990s, she had found jobs easily, and the application process had been uncomplicated. In the new job-seeking environment, she was forced to submit lengthy applications that address criteria or 16 .... These exist at different levels, according to how much 17 .... an employee has. For Customer Service Orientation, Level One, Carla had to prove she could deliver a service, change ideas based on new data, and willingly listen to other perspectives. At Level Two, it was necessary to add value and 18 .... to service delivery problems. Taylor Lexington advised Carla to use the STAR system in her applications. The 'R' in STAR stands for 19 .... When Carla applied to be a manager of a language school, she knew she could do the job well because she had sufficient 20 .... However, she was unsuccessful with her application probably because she did not 21 .... her achievements under the criterion of Flexibility.

A experience	B jobs	C reason
D careers	E Starland	F receptionist
G competencies	H result	I attention
J qualifications	K describing	L responsibility
M countries	N attend	O spell out

---

* Human Resources

Carla Mhando continues her exploration of criterion-based applications.

When I ran into Taylor Lexington a week later, she was with two friends: Adrienne Fuamana, who hires and fires for the civil service; and, James Godden, who screens volunteers for an aid agency.

Over lunch, I quizzed the experts on the value of this new application process. They all agreed competencies and levels are favoured by employers as generic questions make it easy to mix and match to suit any job. Taylor Lexington added that the process of writing a competency dictionary helps a company or organisation focus on its core business. Adrienne Fuamana noted that since the writing process takes time and effort, it weeds out people who are not committed to hard work or to the principles of the employer.

James Godden, however, was more circumspect. 'I've been in this business since 1987 and have seen it all. There was a time when personality tests were touted as the surest way to find ideal employees, and there was a fashion for left-of-field interview questions to see who reacted best to stress.' He continued, 'I think writing 200 words for a competency encourages people to embellish their work history in order to meet the criterion. Or, even worse, to fabricate events altogether. In an aid organisation where it's imperative to have moral boundaries, that's a grave concern.'

Adrienne Fuamana took up his argument, 'There are also people who don't like to blow their own trumpet – they're reluctant to recount their actions explicitly. Or, they interpret the competencies in a way a recruiter with a rigid mind-set can't fathom. These applicants write answers which are considered off-topic. A company or organisation therefore rejects people who may be extremely capable.'

Taylor Lexington interrupted, 'But at interview, it's a much fairer process – sticking to a set of questions for each competency.' She went on, 'In the old days, an employer could ask about anything – if you were married, which church you went to. Criterion-based interviews have narrowed questions down to what's relevant to the job.'

Here's Godden again: 'I have qualms about the restricted nature of questions. With competencies like Intercultural Competence, Self-awareness, or Analytical Thinking, these concepts are about a sensibility rather than specific actions people took to meet targets and get results. In my experience, people who are really self-aware are beyond the stage of self-reflection. Furthermore, genuine analytical thinkers are so rare that almost nobody meets that criterion!'

Paying for my bill, and observing how well the schoolgirl waitress performed her Customer Service Orientation (Level One), I hoped, like James Godden, that criterion-based job applications were a passing fancy. After all, why is there never a criterion called 'Loving one's job' or 'Just getting through each day'?

Questions 22-27

Look at the following statements and the list of people below.

*Match each statement with the correct person: **A**, **B**, **C**, or **D**.*

*Write the correct letter, **A**, **B**, **C**, or **D**, in boxes 22-27 on your answer sheet.*

This person:

22   recruits people to work for the government.

23   thinks a long written application discourages those who are less serious applicants.

24   has reservations about the lies people may tell when forced to write at length about their work experiences.

25   notes that companies or organisations using criterion-based selection may miss out on excellent candidates whose answers are modest or just a little different.

26   believes personal questions at interview are more discriminatory than criterion-based ones.

27   wonders why there is no criterion about whether a person is passionate about his or her work.

List of people	
A	Carla Mhando
B	Taylor Lexington
C	Adrienne Fuamana
D	James Godden

```
    00:00  =
   ____ : ____
```

KEY POINTS

- Read Section 2 more carefully than Section 1, but still skim – that is, read quite fast, moving your eye down the middle of the page.

- Answers to summary questions (questions 15-21) must be grammatically correct. Most answers are nouns. Where answers are verbs, do you need an infinitive, a bare infinitive, a present or past participle?

- Where there is a list of proper nouns (questions 22-27 – here, people's names), circle these in the text – they're easy to find as they start with capital letters.

Here are the answers. How did you do?

Section 2: 15. D; 16. G; 17. L; 18. N; 19. H; 20. A; 21. O; 22. C; 23. C; 24. D; 25. C; 26. B; 27. A.

SECTION 3

Go to page 65 for Passage 3 of the Academic Reading Taster Test.

What happens in the Academic Writing test?

YOUR TURN *Unscramble the words in parentheses below. Write the words in the spaces provided. There is an example.*

Candidates answer two questions in (eg) (*eno*) <u>one</u> hour. The first question, called Task 1, is a 150-word report. The second, Task 2, is a 250-word essay.

As there is one hour, most candidates write over these word limits; they are not penalised. Writing fewer, however, leads to a penalty, and a maximum of Five is awarded for Task Fulfilment, which represents 25% of a candidate's score.

Some candidates, like Indians, seem used to writing a lot in exams and may believe that more writing equates with a (*herghi*) _____ score. However, the score has to be earned according to the marking criteria. If a candidate's script is full of errors, its length won't help.

For Task 2, IELTS research has shown that a Four usually writes between 110-370 words; a Six, up to 485 words; and an Eight, up to 455 words. Higher-level candidates write fewer words than mid-level ones because their writing is well-organised, and their vocabulary is (*ciprees*) _____.

What is Task 1?

Task 1 is a short report. The writing style is (*marfol*) _____. Candidates use complete sentences in clear paragraphs. Bullet points or notes are not accepted.

Task 1 inputs are non-verbal devices (NVDs) with titles and keys. These may be graphs, tables, charts, maps, plans, or diagrams. Candidates transfer the non-verbal information into at least 150 words. If the NVD is a (*gradima*) _____, there is only one to describe. It is usually a process like the life cycle of an animal, or how something works or is made. Otherwise, there are NVDs to compare and contrast. These could be: two bar charts; a graph and a table; or, two plans. Often different (*mites*) _____ are mentioned, for example: a plan of a community centre in 2005, and a second plan in 2015; or, literacy rates in three countries from 1800 to 2000. Occasionally there are three NVDs to compare.

The instructions for Task 1 are something like: *Write a summary of the information below by selecting and reporting the main features.*

What is Task 2?

Task 2 is a formal essay. Again, candidates use complete sentences with suitable academic vocabulary. (ra**ce**l) _____ paragraphing is essential.

Candidates are given a proposition with a question. There are three basic types:

A   <u>Argument</u>: The proposition is a social issue. The question asks candidates to write about both sides of the issue, favouring one.

Or: There are two similar ideas in the proposition. Candidates discuss both, saying which one they think is better.

O   <u>Opinion</u>: The proposition is a social issue. Candidates give (e**r**anoss) _____ for this development, and say whether it is positive or negative. They do not discuss both sides.

P-S   <u>Problem-solution</u>: In the proposition, a social problem is posed. Candidates describe the problem and provide a solution.

Match the Task 2 inputs with the question types above. Write the letter symbols in the spaces provided. There are examples.

Eg = **<u>A</u>**   *In some countries, the government gives money or other help to people who are unemployed. (Proposition)*
What are the benefits and drawbacks of this? (Question)

Eg = **<u>O</u>**   *These days more and more people are retraining for different careers in their thirties or forties.*
Why is this happening? Do you think it is advantageous for individuals?

i = ___   *Many people around the world dream of buying their own home even though this may cost a lot of money.*
Consider opposing views on this, and present your own.

ii = ___   *Schools these days teach subjects like Art and Music to students aged 7-14. Explain why schools do this. Some parents and students believe this is a waste of time. Do you agree or disagree?*

iii = ___   *People worldwide are leaving the countryside to live in the city. This causes disruption to both the city and the countryside.*
Describe these disruptions, and suggest how they might be reduced.

iv = ___   *Cities worldwide are trying to make people use private cars less. However, private car use continues to increase.*
If cities cannot make people forego their cars, what other ways are there to reduce the negative effects of so much car traffic?

v = ___   *Some universities assess students only on examinations; others have a mix of assignments throughout the course and examinations.*
Discuss both systems. Which one do you think is better?

After the proposition and question, there is some advice: *Provide reasons for your answer, including relevant examples from your own knowledge or experience.*

What happens in the GT Writing test?

YOUR TURN *Unscramble the words in parentheses below. Write the words in the spaces provided. There is an example.*

Candidates (eg) (*swaner*) <u>answer</u> two questions in one hour. Task 1 is a 150-word letter.

Some short information in (*tebull*) _____ points is given. Candidates must use all of this as the basis of their letter.

The letter may be:

- a (*queters*) _____ for information
- an offer of information
- some advice, usually to a friend
- a (*lontmapic*) _____
- an apology
- an invitation
- a personal view (eg: writing to a local newspaper)
- some other expression (eg: congratulating another person).

The letter may be formal, semi-formal, or informal, depending on who will receive it.

GT Task 2 is virtually the same as Academic Task 2, although problem-solution essays are (*remo*) _____ frequent.

How is the Writing test marked?

The Academic and GT modules of the Writing test are marked the same way.

Task 2 is worth twice as much as Task 1.

Both tasks are marked according to four criteria: Task Fulfilment, Coherence and Cohesion, Vocabulary, and Grammar.

Only the band (on the right) appears on a candidate's report. He or she doesn't know about the individual criteria.

MARKING CRITERIA AND WRITING BANDS

TF	C&C	V	G	Band
7	7	7	6	6.5
7	6	6	6	6
5	6	6	6	5.5
5	5	5	6	5

TF	C&C	V	G	Band
7	7	6	6	6.5
6	6	6	6	6
5	5	6	6	5.5
5	5	5	5	5

YOUR TURN *Before you read about the four marking criteria, which statement on the left refers to which criterion? Place a tick (✓) in the appropriate box. There are examples.*

For this criterion, a candidate:		Task Fulfilment	Coherence & Cohesion	Vocabulary	Grammar
Eg	Gives an overall impression of the visual inputs. / Covers all the material in the bullet points.	✓			
Eg	Uses words specifically related to the topic.			✓	
Eg	Includes topic and supporting sentences in each paragraph.		✓		
Eg	Punctuates clearly.				✓
1	Orders ideas in a logical way.				
2	Provides examples closely connected to arguments.				
3	Varies sentence types.				
4	Understands collocation.				

Task Fulfilment

The first criterion for Writing is Task Fulfilment. Here is a checklist of what an examiner is looking for.

For Task 1 Academic, does the candidate:

- provide an overview of what is happening in the visual input?

[handwritten: 1 - Introduction]

- identify the main features (trends and counter-trends)?

[handwritten: 2 - overview: - General de]

- note any startling features?

[handwritten: 3 - detailed description.]

- make clear and relevant comparisons without mechanically reporting data (eg: starting on the left of a graph, and describing all the data on the horizontal axis by moving along to the right)?

- give enough detail, which means deciding what *not* to report since the word limit is low?

- describe the data or stages accurately? *[handwritten: ∧ graph   process]*

- describe only what is shown in the visual input, and not something else from his/her own knowledge?

- write enough words? A candidate cannot score more than a Five if fewer than 150 words are written.

- format the report appropriately (no notes or bullet points)?

For Task 1 GT, does the candidate:

* clearly explain the purpose of the letter?

* address all the information in the bullet points?

* include suitable examples?

* lay the letter out correctly?

* use a tone appropriate to the task: formal, semi-formal, or informal according to who the recipient is, and not a mix of these?

* offer a reasonable solution where necessary, and not a threat?

For Task 2 Academic and GT, does the candidate:

* answer the specific question (not another similar one)?

* introduce the topic (preferably without a rhetorical question)?

* establish a position with a logical argument?

* include relevant examples?

* write with an even tone (not too personal, not too dogmatic)?

* draw a conclusion, which includes a summary, recommendation, or speculation?

Note: Both Task 1 and Task 2 need introductions. In the introduction to Academic Task 1, the title and keys are turned into sentences; an overall statement is given. In Task 2, a candidate paraphrases the question, stating clearly what he or she supports.

Task 2 needs a conclusion, but Task 1 does not – there are too few words.

In both tasks, candidates who do not write the required number of words (150 or 250), go down one band in Task Fulfilment.

Coherence and Cohesion

The second criterion is Coherence and Cohesion (C&C). It is essentially the same for Academic and GT for Tasks 1 and 2.

Here's the examiner's checklist.

Does the candidate:

* organise material logically with the most important idea first?   *= i.e overview*

* in Task 1: have at least three paragraphs (introduction; overall statement; detailed description)?   *↗ 2 paragraphs*
A Four or a Five is given if there are no paragraphs, or if the paragraphing is faulty.

* in Task 2: have at least five paragraphs, each containing topic and supporting sentences?
A Four or a Five is given if there are no paragraphs, or if the paragraphing is faulty.

* link information well within and between sentences, and not overuse any linkers?

* write neatly?

In both tasks, candidates who do not use paragraphs go down one band in Coherence and Cohesion.

Grammar

Does the candidate:

* use a wide range of grammatical structures? (These include: complex verb phrases with modal/passive verbs/adverbial modifiers, and complex noun phrases.)

* include a mix of simple, compound, and complex sentences?

- show grammatical accuracy?
- punctuate correctly?

Vocabulary

Does the candidate:

- use a wide range of vocabulary?
- use precise vocabulary, including academic language, topic-specific items, and less common phrasal verbs or other idioms?
- collocate naturally?
- form the correct parts of speech?
- spell well?
- have a sense of style?

Model answers to Academic Writing Task 1 questions

[handwritten: → charts → MAPS → PROcesses]

The following three answers to Academic Writing Task 1 questions would each receive an IELTS Nine. They involve a table, a graph, and a diagram.

[handwritten: 20 min duration/task]

Summarising information in a table

Here is a Task 1 question.

The following table shows the main hobby for people in New Zealand.
Write a summary of the information. Select and report the main features, and make comparisons where relevant.

YOUR TURN   *Read through the model answer to reconstruct the table on the following page.*

[handwritten: illustrates]

[handwritten: introduct] = This table shows which main hobby male and female New Zealanders pursue. These hobbies are art and craft, cooking, DIY, gaming, gardening, and reading.

[handwritten: overview providing big picture w/out given %, n°.] = Overall, there is no single hobby both genders mostly enjoy, and there is only one, gardening, they like equally at a low twelve percent. Typically the principal hobby for men is evenly spread among the six categories, whereas women are concentrated largely on reading (38%) and cooking (24%).

[handwritten: Detailed description] = Cooking and gaming share the top spot for men at 21% each, followed by reading at 20%, and DIY at 16%. After reading and cooking, for women, comes art and craft at 13%. The least likely main hobby for men is art and craft (10%), while for women, it is gaming (5%). Significant differences between the genders can be seen in gaming, where male hobbyists enjoy it four times more than female; and in reading, where women favour it almost twice as much as men.

(157 words)

Use the model on the previous page to reconstruct the data.

What are the missing words and numbers in the table?

MAIN HOBBY FOR PEOPLE IN NEW ZEALAND

	Men (%)	Women (%)
_____	___	13
Cooking	21	24
DIY*	___	8
Gaming	21	___
_____	12	___
_____	20	38

What are the missing words below? Write the letters to complete each one.

Sometimes there is only **o** __ __ simple visual input in Task 1 as above. This does
n __ __ mean the task is **ea** __ __ __ __ than others, or that candidates write
less **soph** __ __ __ __ __ __ __ __ __ answers. In fact, it may be harder to reach the
word **l** __ __ __ __ in this case. Using a **var** __ __ __ __ of vocabulary and grammar
can also present a challenge.

---

*DIY = Do It Yourself – Building or fixing things in your home or garden yourself.

Summarising information in a graph

Here is another Task 1 question.

The graph, below, shows people with PhDs in three countries.
Write a summary of the information. Select and report the main features, and make comparisons where relevant.

YOUR TURN   *Read the model answer to reconstruct the graph below.*

This graph shows the number of people with doctoral degrees per 10,000 in three countries: America, Australia, and South Korea from 1980 to 2020.

Overall, the total number of PhD-holders has risen, and most dramatically in South Korea.

While South Korea had the fewest PhDs in 1980 (0.1% of its population), this had doubled by 1990, and quadrupled a decade later. By 2020, it may even be five times the 1980 figure. Australia, in contrast, began the 1980s with the highest number (0.3%), maintained this until the mid-1990s when it was overtaken by South Korea, but afterwards suffered a marked decline: it will probably have the fewest PhD-holders by 2020, with only 0.15%, half as many as forty years earlier. In 1980, the United States was in second place, (0.2%), and by 2020 was still second. However, although its percentage remained stable until 2000, it is predicted to rise to 0.25% by 2020.

In conclusion, there have been significant changes in the three countries surveyed with regard to how many of their people have gained PhDs, and a country that was once less well-off, South Korea, will far out-do two developed nations within the next few years.

(197 words)

People with PhDs per _____

10

0

1980   2000   2020

Key:
(1) _____   _____
(2) ....   _____
(3) - - - - -   South Korea

Describing a procedural diagram

Comparing tables or graphs is a more common IELTS Task 1 question, but you do need to be able to describe processes.

Take your time to work out what is happening in the diagram. If there is a key, refer to it. There's usually more information than you can describe, so decide what is less important and may be left out.

Use the present tense (easy), and the passive (not so easy because you need correct past participles of irregular verbs + singular/plural of 'to be').

No conclusion is necessary.

Here is a third Task 1 question.

This diagram shows how water is recycled within a house.
Write a summary of the information by selecting and reporting the main features.
Write at least 150 words.

YOUR TURN *Here is an IELTS Nine answer. Read it, then follow the directions.*

This diagram shows the process of recycling water within a private home. Instead of sending all used water into a municipal sewerage system, some water is treated on site to be used outdoors (grey water); other water is treated more thoroughly, so it can be drunk again (white water); and, only a small amount of water (black water) goes back into the municipal sewerage system, or into an on-site treatment system.

Firstly, water is supplied to this home by either a municipal supplier or a well.

The water from the municipal supply is called white water because it can be drunk immediately. The well water, which may be impure, is filtered through an upflow filter until it becomes drinkable (ie: white water), and is pumped into the house.

Inside the house, used water (grey water) from sinks, showers, washing machines, etc either goes into a filtering system which purifies it to a certain extent for use on the garden or in the yard, or it goes back into the upflow filter for complete repurification. Roof water may be used likewise.

Water from the toilet, however, does not go into the same purification system as grey water. This black water either returns to the municipal sewerage system, or goes into a septic system or other waste water system for treatment. (218 words)

Use the model to label the diagram.

Where do these labels go? Write them in the Key at the right of the diagram.

black water	grey water	white water
on-site treatment system	upflow filter	well

A GREY-WATER SYSTEM IN A PRIVATE HOME

KEY

Water sources

(1) _____

(2) Municipal supplier

(3) Roof

(4) _____

(5) _____

(6) _____

Equipment

■	Valve
✳	Pump
∧	_____
▭	Tank
♣	Optional _____

Go to page 382 for the answers.

A single table in Task 1

Often candidates find it difficult to describe a single table. However, research has shown that IELTS writing scores are higher when there is less visual input as candidates attempt more complex sentences, and use more varied vocabulary. Therefore, there is no need to panic when only one device appears in Task 1.

What are the missing words below? Write the letters to complete each one. There is an example.

The task below is **not** easy for two reasons:

- What is the most **log** _ _ _ _ way to organise the information? (Describe similarities then **dif** _ _ _ _ _ _ _ _.)

- How can a candidate include the relevant information without **cop** _ _ _ _ a lot from the table? (Use synonyms, different parts of **sp** _ _ _ _, and **pron** _ _ _ reference.)

How would you answer the following question?

The table, below, gives data about two countries.
Write a summary of the information. Select and report the main features, and make comparisons where relevant.

	Comoros	Luxembourg
Date of formation	1975	1867
Population	800,000	470,000
Total area	2170 sq km (838 sq miles)	2586 sq km (998 sq miles)
Languages	Arabic, Comoran, and French	Luxembourgish, German, and French
Location	Off East Africa (between Mozambique and Madagascar) 3 main islands + a number of very small islands	Plateau – western Europe (between Germany, Belgium, and France)
Economy	Very small. Vanilla + cloves = main exports. Receives international aid.	Strong. Banking + services = main industries. Many European Union institutions based there.

There is a model answer on page 382.

Assessing candidates for Academic Writing Task 1

Task 1

Here is an Academic Writing Task 1.
Spend about 20 minutes on this task.

The plans below show Randwick Road in 2000 and 2010.
Write a summary of the information. Select and report the main features, and make comparisons where relevant.

Write at least 150 words.

Randwick Road 2000

Bakery	Newsagent	Real estate agent	Thai restaurant	Video shop

All-day Parking

All-day Parking

Charity shop	Vacant	Shoe shop	Pet shop

Randwick Road 2010

Bakery	Newsagent	Charity shop	Real estate agent	North Indian restaurant	Organic grocery

Parking 10-3 only

No Parking _____ Bus Stop _____

Childcare centre	Pharmacy	Brazilian restaurant	Pet shop

_____

_____

_____

_____

_____

_____

_____

_____

_____

_____

_____

_____

Model answer

YOUR TURN   *Below is an IELTS Nine answer. The paragraphs are out of order.*
Number the paragraphs in the correct order from 1 to 3. How similar is the answer to yours?

_____ In 2000, there were eight operating businesses, the largest of which was a charity shop. In 2010, there were ten businesses, and the charity shop had relocated into a smaller space. The newsagent, the second-largest shop in 2000, had reduced its size by fifty percent by 2010. A childcare centre had occupied the premises of the old charity shop, and a pharmacy opened in the one site vacant in 2000.

_____ Around half of the shops on Randwick Road in 2000 were the same ten years later. However, some shops contracted, and two closed down altogether. A new childcare centre and pharmacy appeared; the number of food outlets doubled. Significantly, in 2000, parking was permitted on both sides of the road, but by 2010 was restricted to one side from 10 AM until 3 PM, and forbidden on the other, where a bus stop was added.

_____ The bakery was exactly the same in 2010 as a decade earlier. The Thai restaurant had changed its cuisine to North Indian, and a Brazilian restaurant had taken over the shoe shop. An organic grocery had replaced the video shop. **(185 words)**

Analysis of the model

Analyse the model by circling the correct answer to each question below.

Does the candidate:

1 Mention every shop? <u>Yes / No</u>

2 Give an overview of changes? <u>Yes / No</u>

3 Describe where the shops are located? <u>Yes / No</u>

4 Detail changes from left to right along the road? <u>Yes / No</u>

5 Say which shops changed their size? <u>Yes / No</u>

6 Group together similar kinds of shops? <u>Yes / No</u>

7 Provide reasons for the changes? <u>Yes / No</u>

8 Say which shops he or she likes the best? <u>Yes / No</u>

9 Mention the transport changes? <u>Yes / No</u>

10 Have a conclusion? <u>Yes / No</u>

Candidates' scripts

Below are answer scripts to the same question by four other candidates labelled A though D.

Rank the scripts from the best (1st) to the worst (4th). One has been done for you.

A = ____

> As can be seen in this digram RANDWICK ROAD in 2000 and 2001. This digram illustrate RANDWICK ROAD in 2000 and 2001. Shopping popular in dubai. the city of RANDWICK ROAD in LONDAN. difrent the PARKING in 2000 and 2010. Biggest shop CHILD CARE CENTRE. smallest shop BAKERY. Didn't had VIDEO SHOP in 2010 because MP3.
>
> In concolusion few changes 2010. Mainly CHILD CARE. **(64 words)**

B = 3rd

> Re: Alterred commercial arrangements on Randwick Road 2000 and 2010
>
> In general, slightly more than half (5 out of 9) of the shops on Randwick Road in 2000 were existing the same ten years later. However, some shops were reduce in size, and two close completely. A new childcare centre and pharmacy appeared, doubtless because the demography was changed. The number of food stores was increasing substantively, in fact by 100 per cent. Significantly, in 2000, parking was permitted on both sides of Randwick Road, but by 2010 was being restricted to one side from 10 AM until 3 PM, and forbiden on the other, where a bus stop added. The era of public transportation has surely arrived in this municipality.
>
> In 2000, there were eight business, the largest was charity shop. In 2010, there were ten business, and the charity shop had relocated to a smaller space, commensurate with it's reduced status. The newsagent, the second largest shop in 2000, had fined down it's dimensions by fifty per cent by 2010. A childcare centre had occupied the premise of the old charity shop, and a pharmacy thrown open it's doors in the one sight that was being empty in 2000.
>
> The bakery was remaning exactly same in 2010 as a decade prior. The Thai restaurant had convert its culinary style to North Indian, since food from Srinagar is notoriously tasty, and a Brazilian restaurant had superseeded the shoe shop. An organic grocery had replaced the video shop. **(248 words)**

C = ___

Around half of shops on Randwick Road in 2000 were the same ten years later. However, some were smaller, and two had close down all together. A new childcare centre and pharmacy had opened; the number of food outlets doubled. Significantly, in 2000, parking was permitted on both sides of road, but by 2010 was restricted to one side, and forbidden on another due to erection of bus stop.

In 2000, there were eight small businesses, the largest of which was charity shop. In 2010, there were ten and charity shop had relocated into smaller space. The newsagent, the second-largest shop in 2000, had reduced its size by fifty per cent by 2010. Childcare centre had remont the old charity shop, and pharmacy began operation in one site vacant in 2000. Bakery was exactly the same in 2010 as the decade earlier. The thai restaurant had changed its cuisine to North Indian, and Brazilian restaurant had overtaken shoe shop. Organic grocery had replaced the video shop. (**166 words**)

D = ___

These plans show Randwick Road in 2000 and 2010.

In a nutshell, half of shops on Randwick Road in 2000 were same after ten years. However, some shops were smaller, and some closed. A new Childcare Centre and pharmacy open. Numbers of food shop dubbled. Amazingly, in 2000, parking was permited on both sides of Randwick road, but by 2010 was limit to one side from 10 AM til 3 PM, and No Parking on the other. Randwick road must of been very busy road.

In 2000, there were eight shops, the most large was charity shop. While in 2010, ten shops, and the charity shop moved into smaller shop. A Childcare Centre take over the old charity shop. While a pharmacy opening in vacant shop.

The bakery and the pet shop was exactly the same in 2010 as ten year a go. Further more, Thai restaurant changed its cooking style to North Indian, while, intrestingly, a shoe shop become brazilian restrant. Last but not least, organic grocery replaced the video shop. (**172 words**)

Examiner's reports

Read the examiner's reports below. Which two scripts on pages 104-105 are being described?

1 = ___

TASK FULFILMENT: This script is long enough. It has an overall statement at the beginning. All the key information is included. It is generally easy and pleasurable for the reader. This criterion gets a Seven.

COHERENCE & COHESION: Paragraphing is clear. However, there is overuse of the linking word 'while' (three times); and, there are some unnecessary adverbs: 'amazingly' and 'intrestingly'. Along with 'must [of] been', these words contain the candidate's opinion, and Task 1 does not ask for this – it is purely descriptive. 'Til' (misspelt) is for speaking or informal writing; here, it should be 'until'. The idiom 'in a nutshell' is completely inappropriate for academic writing. Avoid idioms or proverbs – they are used occasionally in spoken English. There are some problems with capitalisation: it should be 'Randwick Road' but 'road' when its name is not given. 'Childcare Centre' is not the name of a company, so it should not be capitalised. The adjective 'Brazilian' needs a capital. This script gets a Six for C&C.

VOCABULARY: There is a range of vocabulary: simple and more complex, but it lacks sophistication. Some of the more complex language is not always accurate: 'dubbled' and 'permited' are misspelt. 'Furthermore' and 'ago' are not two words as the candidate has made them. There is one phrasal verb: 'take over' although its grammar is incorrect. The phrases 'exactly the same' and 'changed its cooking style' are good. Vocabulary gets a Six.

GRAMMAR: Again, there is a mix of simple and complex structures, but there is not one correct sentence in the script. The passive is used with varying success: 'closed' is correct; 'open' should be 'opened'. Likewise: 'was permited' is correct; 'was limit' is not: it needs to be 'limited'. Tenses are fairly well handled, and the past is mostly consistent, although the second paragraph needs attention. Expressions of quantity are uneven: 'on both sides of Randwick road' is correct; 'half of shops' should be 'half of the shops'. Subject-verb agreement is variable. Grammar gets a Six.

TF	C&C	VOC	GRA
7	6	6	6

2 = ___

TASK FULFILMENT: This answer provides both an overview and details. Comparison and contrast are well balanced. As it would benefit from an introductory paragraph, it has been awarded an Eight.

COHERENCE & COHESION: Paragraphing is a minor problem here. It might be better to start a third paragraph with 'Bakery was exactly...'. There are two punctuation errors: 'Thai' should have a capital; a comma is needed in the second paragraph after 'there were ten'. Otherwise C&C are expertly managed: Eight.

VOCABULARY: There is a range of vocabulary: simple and complex. Excellent examples are: 'food outlets', 'second-largest', 'operation in the one site vacant', and 'changed its cuisine'. There are a number of errors: 'all together', which should be 'altogether'; 'on another' should be 'on the other'; 'erection' is too formal; 'remont' is not English; and, 'overtaken' does not mean the same as 'taken over'. The error density means it can only get a Seven.

GRAMMAR: There is a nice mix of simple and complex structures. The past perfect is used accurately except for 'close' and 'began', which should be past participles. However, most sentences contain errors with the use of articles. There are numerous omissions of articles, and some use of the definite when the indefinite is needed. A Six is the highest the candidate can score here.

TF	C&C	VOC	GRA
8	8	7	6

Why script C gets a Seven

Although C is the best script, it is only likely to be awarded a Seven. It's easier to understand why visually.

Why is the text highlighted in grey? Why are two words **underlined**?

Why is some language written like this?

Around half of shops on Randwick Road in 2000 were the same ten years later. However, some were smaller, and two had close down all together. The new childcare centre and pharmacy had opened; the number of food outlets doubled. Significantly, in 2000, parking was permited on both sides of road, but by 2010 was restricted to one side, and forbidden on another due to erection of bus stop.

In 2000, there were eight small businesses, the largest of which was the charity shop. In 2010, there were ten and charity shop had relocated into smaller space. The newsagent, the second-largest shop in 2000, had reduced its size by fifty per cent by 2010. Childcare centre had remont the old charity shop, and pharmacy began operation in one site vacant in 2000. Bakery was exactly the same in 2010 as the decade earlier. The thai restaurant had changed its cuisine to North Indian, and Brazilian restaurant had overtaken shoe shop. Organic grocery had replaced the video shop.

Go to pages 382-383 for the answers.

Assessing candidates for GT Writing Task 1

Task 1

Here is a GT Writing Task 1.

Spend about 20 minutes on this task.

You are looking for a job, and you need a referee.*

Write a letter to your previous boss. In your letter:
• **Introduce yourself and the job(s) you are applying for.**
• **Ask your boss to be your referee or suggest another referee.**
• **Describe the work you did together in the past.**

Write at least 150 words.

You do NOT need to write any addresses.

Start your letter with

Dear .... ,

_____

_____

_____

_____

_____

_____

_____

_____

_____

_____

_____

_____

_____

_____

_____

_____

_____

_____

_____

* Here, a 'referee' is a person who will write or speak positively about you and your work.

_____

_____

_____

_____

_____

_____

_____

_____

_____

_____

_____

_____

_____

_____

_____

_____

Candidates' scripts

YOUR TURN _Read the following three letters. Which one is the best?_

A

Dear Mrs Anne,

How are you? I'm Mahesh. I was having the great pleasure of working for you from 2008 until 2011 when I moved interstate because my wife was offer better job.

I'm writing to you to ask for your help. I'm looking for work as part-time Hindi teacher in the tertiary sector while continue work as salesman. I'm wondering if you can provide to me a reference as considering you were my maneger for 3 years. And we always had good relations.

BTW I was teaching all levels from beginer to advanced and performing the co-ordination duties for the Translators Course. I was also ET as well as OHS&S specialist including FW.

It is my understanding you will contact by phone persons from the Eastern Suburbs Community College or the University of New South Whales.

If you cannot to do this for me, might you ask other colleage whom can I contact?

Best wishes,

Mahesh Kumar (**154 words without counting 'Dear' or the writer's name**)

B

Dear Mrs Hansen,

My name is Fumiko Sato-Anderson, and I was an employee at your centre 18 months ago. How are you? How's the language centre these days?

I am writing to you to ask a small favour. As you may recall, my husband and I moved inter-state to build our own home. As this project is now complete, I've decided to return to work – either full or part-time – teaching Japanese. I wonder if you would be one of my referees as you were my manager for nearly three years, and we always had a good working relationship.

Just to jog your memory: I started at your centre in April 2011, and taught all levels from Beginner to Advanced. I also co-ordinated a special Translator's Course. Quite possibly, you will be contacted by phone or email by someone from the Eastern Suburbs Community College or the University of New South Wales.

If you are unable to do this for any reason, could you suggest another colleague I could contact?

I look forward to hearing from you.

Yours sincerely,

Fumiko Sato-Anderson **(175 words)**

C

Dear Mrs Hansen,

How are you? How's the language center at the moment? I am writing to you to ask you a favor. As you know, nine months ago when my husband was promoted, our family moved to Sydney. we are really living life to the full here and go to the beach almost every weekend! Since my son Aziz is now at pre-school, I am looking for work either full time or part-time. Could you be one of my referees as you were my manager for three years. We always had an exellent work-ing relationship. Just to remaind you, I started at your centre in April 2011 and tought all levels. Probably someone from the Eastern Suburbs Community College or University of New South Wales will contact you in regard to my application.

I look forward to hearing from you.

Yours sincerly,

Pinar Sinan **(140 words)**

Analysis of the best letter

Analyse the letter by circling the correct answer to each question below.

Does the candidate:

1 Address all the bullet points? *Yes / No*

2 Reach 150 words? *Yes / No*

3 Have a consistent tone? *Yes / No*

4 Include irrelevant detail? *Yes / No*

5 Repeat him/herself too much? *Yes / No*

6 Have clear paragraphs? *Yes / No*

7 Use appropriate linkers? *Yes / No*

8 Use a range of vocabulary? *Yes / No*

9 Use vocabulary accurately? *Yes / No*

10 Have occasional spelling mistakes? *Yes / No*

11 Use a range of grammatical structures? *Yes / No*

12 Use grammar accurately? *Yes / No*

13 Punctuate correctly? *Yes / No*

The other two letters

IF YOU WANT A SEVEN

Choose one criterion below (TF, C&C, Voc, or Gra) to go with each of the examiner's comments. Then, decide which comments relate to Letter A or Letter C. There are examples.

Task Fulfilment (TF – 1 more to find); Coherence & Cohesion (C&C – 2 to find); Vocabulary (Voc – 1 more to find); Grammar (Gra – 2 to find).

	Criterion	A or C	Examiner's report
1	Eg: *TF*	C	The semi-formal tone of the letter is appropriate. However, the candidate does not include all the information in the bullet points. It is unclear what was or will be taught. An alternative referee is not requested. Despite some irrelevant information, the letter is still under length. (Not so good)
2			Simple grammatical structures are accurate, but more complex language contains errors. The continuous is used inaccurately. The passive is also imperfectly formed, or absent when needed. (Good)
3	Eg: *Voc*	A	This is generally appropriate, and there are some very good examples like 'tertiary sector' and 'performing the co-ordination duties'. Unfortunately, 'good relations' does not mean the same as 'good relationship' – the former is a sexual expression. The name of the university is not connected to animals. BTW, ET, OHS&S, and FW are hard for a reader to understand, and should be avoided. There are several spelling mistakes. (Good)

4			All of the bullet points are mentioned, and information is detailed. However, the tone of the letter is variable – sometimes strangely formal, at other times informal. This would confuse or annoy the reader. (Good)
5			This is suitable throughout and includes the high-level idiom 'living life to the full'. There are still a few spelling mistakes. (Very good)
6			There is a range of structures, and they are nearly all accurate. There are long, complex sentences that are a pleasure to read. (Excellent)
7			Paragraphing is clear, but many sentences start the same way with 'I'. Linkers are a bit too basic. (Good)
8			This is well managed within sentences except that some punctuation is missing. Paragraphing is poor, which causes strain on the reader, and is penalised in IELTS. (Good)

Complete the missing words.

Although the two **let** __ __ __ __ above have different **str** __ __ __ __ __ __ and

weaknesses, they will probably **sc** __ __ __ about the **s** __ __ __: Six.

Assessing candidates for Academic and GT Writing Task 2

Here is a Writing Task 2 question.

Many countries these days have high immigration.
In your opinion, what are the disadvantages of this for the receiving country? How could these disadvantages be reduced?

How might you answer it?

YOUR TURN *Read the essay below.*		
Paragraph 1	At present, large number of people are moving from the developing into the developed world in order to flea poverty. Within the developed world, there is also movement as people seek to improve their lives. In this essay, I shall discuss drawbacks of high immigration on the receiving country, and how these could be reduced.	**Line 1** 5
Paragraph 2	Firstly, what is high immigration? I belive this is when many thousands of people arrive in a country in one year. I heard last year, the city of Melbourne have 40,000 immigrants, which I think is high number for city of around four millions. It is not flood like when there are millions of refugees in camps. But it's kind of complicated. Anyway, migrants and refugees are different.	 10
Paragraph 3	A sudden influx of newcomers who may not speak the language of the country well nor understand its culture may cause disruption. This is one problem with high immigration. Furthermore, these people choose to live altogether in one area, which might become kind of slump. This means the government need to encourage spread out of monoculture, as well as introduce mechanism to integrate newcomers such like language classes or more TV program about the culture. People who are indigenes of that country may also feel there culture is deterating day by day.	 15 20

Paragraph 4	Secondly, local people, who have low skill, may consider immigrants are stealing their jobs since many immigrants work as manual labours. This means there is tension with migrants and locals that could lead to violence. In Melbourne, some Indian students who drive taxis were attacked and even merdered a few years back for this reason. I reckon this is major problem.	25
Paragraph 5	Unfortunately, immigrants may also bring their own conflicts. For instance, the Sudanese in Melbourne from North and South Sudan had a long war in Africa. Now they find themself as nieghbours and continue their dispute. This mean Australian police and social worker need involvement in reparation of this situation rather than other works. Therefore, higher taxes become necesary. More seriously, international criminal networks like the Mafia might also come with immigrants, meaning further stain on police and legal system.	30
Paragraph 6	To conclude, immigration is essential for prosperite. But high immigration may only be necessity when there is rapid development with lots of employment oportunities. Social problems in receiving country as a result of immigration can be less if governments introduce certain social or policing measures, or immigrants are restricted to people who have passed IELTS exam and posess jobs on skilled migrant list.	35
		40

Examiner's summary

Overall, this is a mid-level essay. The writer has a point of view – that immigration is problematic, exemplified by the situation in Melbourne. Solutions are provided in terms of education, policing, and limiting applicants.

The candidate has good control of English. The errors in grammar do not affect communication greatly. Coherence and cohesion are mostly well managed. However, vocabulary is variable.

Task Fulfilment
(What convincing arguments and supporting examples does the candidate have?)

This essay has 418 words. All of the question is addressed. 'High immigration' is defined as 40,000 immigrants out of four million inhabitants and, the writer makes a distinction between migrants and refugees. Arguments are mostly clear and well supported. The conclusion, however, does contain an example – 'pass the IELTS exam and posess jobs on the skilled-migrant list' – when it would be better to generalise with a statement like: 'possess desirable language and employment skills'.

Coherence and Cohesion
(How does the essay flow? What logic and linking words does the writer use? Are linkers subtle, or overused or simplistic?)

The essay is mostly logical. Paragraphing exists. Referencing is effective. Punctuation is excellent. The second, stronger, argument about perceived stealing of local jobs, however, should open the essay. There is a slightly annoying habit (three times) of starting sentences with 'but', which should be used in the middle of a sentence to join clauses.

Vocabulary
(How much vocabulary is there related to the topic? Are there less common idiomatic words and phrases? Is the vocabulary formal enough?)

In general, there is considerable topic-related vocabulary. Less common phrases include: 'a sudden influx', 'introduce mechanism to integrate', and 'international criminal network'.

The writer is a risk-taker, so some words are not quite correct: 'deterating' should be 'deteriorating', 'labours' should be 'labourers', and 'altogether' should be 'all together'.

'Resolve' makes more sense than 'reparation'. 'Monoculture' in line 16 is inappropriate; 'a single ethnic group' would be better. 'Citizen' is preferable to 'indigene' in line 19.

There are quite a few spelling mistakes: 'flea' instead of 'flee' in line 2. (The former is an insect; the latter is the verb meaning 'to run away'.) 'Slump', in line 15, should be 'slum'; 'stain', in line 34, should be 'strain'. (Check the meaning of 'slump' and 'stain'.) 'Belive', 'merdered', 'oportunities', 'necesary', 'nieghbours', 'posess', and 'prosperite' are all misspelt, reducing the level of vocabulary.

The writer uses the modal verb 'may' successfully, and is never dogmatic. However, there are some minor inconsistencies in tone: 'Kind of', Anyway' and 'reckon' are used in informal speaking.

Grammar
(Is there a pleasing mix of simple and complex sentences? How dense are the errors? Is the message prevented from coming through by the grammar?)

Along with Task Fulfilment, grammar is the best part of the essay. There is a satisfying mix of sentence types, with longer complex sentences predominating. Many complex sentences are error free.

The commonest grammatical mistakes involve article and preposition use. The clause 'which I think is high number for city of around four millions' is missing two articles. It should be: 'tension between' not 'tension with'. Some words should be plural, like: 'large numbers', 'social workers', 'skills', and 'TV programmes'. There are minor problems with tense as in line 8.

Understanding Task Fulfilment in Writing Task 2

Read the definitions of Task Fulfilment for Writing below.

An IELTS Seven = The candidate addresses all parts of the question appropriately. He/She has a position, but there is some over-generalisation, or examples that are a little less relevant.

An IELTS Six = The candidate addresses the question, but some parts of it are more fully covered than others. He/She presents a position, but the conclusion is unclear, unjustified, or repetitive. There are some clear main ideas, but others are less clear, and examples are less relevant.

An IELTS Five = The candidate only addresses the question partially. The format may be inappropriate. He/She expresses a position, but it is not always clear, and there may be no conclusion. There are not enough main ideas, and some of these may be limited. Some examples are irrelevant, or they do not exist. There is some repetition.

YOUR TURN *Here is a Writing Task 2 question:*

> *In some countries, many old people live in retirement homes.*
>
> *Why does this happen? What are the benefits and drawbacks?*

*Circle **five** key words or phrases in the question above.*

To score well in IELTS, you need to write about each of these, some in more detail than others.

I'm sure you found:

some countries... retirement homes... Why... benefits... drawbacks...

You'll probably define 'some countries' briefly in the introduction. Most of your essay will be about the reasons for living in retirement homes, and the benefits and drawbacks.

You'll also need to conclude that there are more benefits *or* there are more drawbacks.

Use a stopwatch to set yourself exactly 60 seconds to brainstorm ideas. Fill in the boxes below.

Retirement homes
Reasons

Benefits	**Drawbacks**

Conclusion

Read two body paragraphs for a Task 2 essay. Which one is a Nine for Task Fulfilment? Which is a Six?

A (i) With a more and more competitive society, young people are too busy working to care for the elderly. **(ii)** Therefore they put family members into retirement homes. **(iii)** These places have good medical care. **(iv)** In addition, old people do not want to shop, cook, or clean. **(v)** Luckily, there is delicious food in old people's homes. **(vi)** It is well known that the elderly really enjoy being with people their own age to play games, sing songs, and talk about the past. **(vii)** Furthermore, they no longer have to worry about money, although some old people's homes are expensive. **(94 words)**

B (i) Some people choose to live in retirement homes since they feel, as they age, they need a higher level of assistance than independent living allows. **(ii)** This could take the form of around-the-clock medical care as well as considerable help with household chores or budgeting. **(iii)** It might also mean the organisation of social activities, particularly with others their own age. **(iv)** Some older people do not want to burden their families with these responsibilities; others may not have family, and so opt for assisted living. **(83 words)**

Here are the functions of each sentence in paragraph B, related to Task Fulfilment.

(i) This topic sentence says people choose retirement homes because they need assistance. This is convincing.

(ii) This example of 'assistance' is connected to health and living conditions.

(iii) This one is about entertainment.

(iv) These reasons relate to the families of the elderly. Often, in English, ideas in the final position are powerful.

Circle the correct answer about A.

1	Does the topic sentence focus on the young or the elderly?	*Young / Elderly*
2	What is the focus of the paragraph?	*Young / Elderly*
3	Are there any examples that are too general, and could relate to life outside retirement homes?	*Yes / No*
4	Is any information too specific?	*Yes / No*
5	Are all examples entirely relevant?	*Yes / No*
6	Is there a sentence that contains a contradiction?	*Yes / No*

Read A and B again. What other differences can you find?

Write a second body paragraph about benefits and drawbacks related to the material in paragraph B, or use your ideas from your brainstorming to write the whole essay another way, as there are many ways to write IELTS essays. Make sure you avoid the mistakes in paragraph A.

Writing penalties

Examiners count words in IELTS tasks, so losing bands is a real danger, especially for a candidate who doesn't have enough main ideas or examples.

Here are the rules:

For Task 1:   A candidate who writes 50 words or fewer loses three bands in TF.
A candidate who writes 51-100 words loses two bands in TF.
A candidate who writes 101-140 words loses one band in TF.

For Task 2:   A candidate who writes 100 words or fewer loses three bands in TF.
A candidate who writes 101-175 words loses two bands in TF.
A candidate who writes 176-240 words loses one band in TF.

Tone in Academic Writing Task 2 and GT Writing Task 1

In any communication, it is necessary to establish both the level of formality and a suitable tone.

In the Speaking test, language is informal and the tone may be personal. However, in the Writing test, language is formal and academic. This means it should be balanced and impersonal.

Unfortunately, many IELTS candidates, in essays and in GT letters, mix formal and informal language. They also write with an uneven tone that annoys the reader. This tone may be partly academic, then suddenly personal, while at other times even dogmatic (being absolutely sure what you believe is right even though you give little or no evidence). To score a Seven in Task Fulfilment, there can be no lapses in tone.

As we have already seen, the language of writing differs from speaking. Writing follows certain conventions: complete sentences, nominalisation, different vocabulary, and no contractions.

In Task 2, in particular, candidates need to observe the conventions of writing, and include structures that create an even tone while persuading the reader of his or her viewpoint.

Persuasive techniques

YOUR TURN *What are the missing words below? Write the letters to complete each one.*

Here are some techniques to gently **per __ __ __ __ __** the reader.

A candidate should:

1 Draw on the ideas of **ot __ __ __ __** to support his/her arguments by using phrases like: 'X, a well-known _____, has suggested...', or 'Research has shown...', or 'It has been reported in the media that...'.

2 **Rest __ __ __ __** the use of 'I' to examples from experience that support arguments, and occasional phrases like: 'I think' or 'I believe'.

3 Use mild language including:

   • the verb 'seem' as in: 'It seems...' or 'It might seem...'.

   • the adverbs: 'rather' or 'quite', or 'very' instead of 'completely' or 'extremely'.

   • the modals + adverbs: 'might possibly', 'may conceivably', 'could potentially', or 'would **prob __ __ __ __**' rather than 'will absolutely/certainly/definitely/totally'.

4 Avoid **ext __ __ __ __** adjectives like: 'amazing', fantastic', 'wonderful', 'appalling', 'disgusting', or 'terrible'.

5 **N __ __ __ __** use 'always' or 'never' except in inversion (see below).

6 Avoid **vag __ __** language like: 'stuff' or 'thing'.

7 Never use idioms or proverbs translated from his/her first **l __ __ __ __ __ __ __**.

8 Not start sentences with 'And' or '**B __ __**'.

Note: Despite what you've read elsewhere, avoid a rhetorical question or a hook at the start of your essay. Most of these backfire because they seem **chil __ __ __ __** to an examiner. (Check 'backfire' in a dictionary.)

IF YOU WANT A SEVEN

A candidate should:

1 Avoid clichés. (See below.)

2 Express doubt with sophisticated adjectives such as: 'dubious', 'illusory', or 'questionable'.

3 Start some sentences with adverbials like: '<u>Without a concerted effort by individuals and the state</u>, pollution will not be reduced.' Or '<u>With the greatest of ease</u>, people have adopted a consumerist lifestyle that has led to environmental degradation.' These manner adverbials (telling us 'how') often begin with 'with', 'without', or 'by', as in: '<u>By doing this</u>, the negative information in the main clause seems less painful.'

4 Use inversion or an It-clause for emphasis. (See below.)

5 Disagree with the proposition in the question cautiously, perhaps using concession. (See below.)

What are clichés?

Clichés are expressions that are very frequently used. Many people think they are overused.

What are the missing letters below? What do the clichés mean?

1   'It's raining cats and *d* __ __ __.'

2   'Penicillin was a quantum *l* __ __ __.'

3   'There should be a level *pl* __ __ __ __ __ field in international trade.'

4   'We're not out of the *w* __ __ __ __ yet.'

In the Speaking test, a candidate may be rewarded for using an occasional cliché because it takes some skill to do so correctly. However, in writing, clichés should be avoided because they reduce the persuasive power of arguments. Writing for Task 2 is serious, but clichés are so familiar they are like bad jokes.

What is inversion?

This is a sentence in which the word order is slightly different from normal. It presents a strong idea, like 'never' or 'rarely', in a gentle but emphatic way.

A man who became a father late in life wrote inside a precious book he gave to his baby: '<u>Never</u> *have I* felt so much happiness as at your birth.' This is inversion. The same sentence could also be expressed as: '*I have* <u>never</u> felt so much happiness as at your birth.'

Here is another example:

'*Doctors are* <u>seldom</u> sympathetic to men who use drugs or alcohol to mask depression.'

'<u>Seldom</u> *are doctors* sympathetic to men who use drugs or alcohol to mask depression.'

Here is a third example: '<u>Rarely</u> **do** *the victims of rape* **have** the opportunity to bring the criminals to court.' The auxiliary 'do' is used with the bare infinitive, here 'have', because there is no auxiliary verb in the sentence as in the example above with the present perfect; nor is the verb 'to be' present.

Here is a final example: '<u>Never once</u> **did I say** I was bored when I was a child.'

Can you invert these four sentences?

1   The time has never been more opportune to consider alternative energy sources.

_____

_____

2   There are seldom occasions when volunteers are recognised publically.

_____

_____

3   We rarely see such convincing acting in Bollywood films. *(Use 'do' + the bare infinitive.)*

_____

_____

4   People never even ventured beyond their village. *(Use 'did' + the bare infinitive.)*

_____

_____

What is an It-clause?

A writer may give emphasis to a negative idea by using the construction: 'It is the X who/which + verb' instead of 'X + verb'. This construction is called an It-clause.

Consider the following: 'Only children suffer from loneliness' and 'It is only children who suffer from loneliness.' Or: 'Wetlands are being destroyed for hotel development' and 'It is the wetlands which are being destroyed for hotel development.'

What is concession?

In concession, the main clause is preceded by a clause that starts with something like: 'While', 'Despite', or 'Although'. As with adverbials, it leads the reader slowly into the trap of the argument. However, the first part of the sentence includes a restatement of the opposing viewpoint. Consider the following with the concessive clauses underlined:

1   <u>**While** large numbers of people use cars for every journey in a day</u>, I believe reducing the number of trips by walking or using public transport is preferable.

2   <u>**Although** the European Union seemed keen to accept Turkey's application some years ago</u>, accession appears to be less likely now.

3   <u>Naturally, parents are concerned about their children</u>, **but** refusing to let them play in public parks may be overprotective and even counterproductive to overall public safety.

4   <u>Admittedly, private school education provides less able students with a strong academic environment and a network of rich friends</u>, **but** its overall effect on the social fabric is detrimental.

Unscramble the following clauses to make a sentence.

<u>Concessive clause</u>: ~~the~~ and health ~~expense~~ problems ~~Despite~~ well documented ,

Despite the expense _____ ,

<u>Main clause</u>: cigarettes continue to ~~people~~ smoke.

people _____ .

Creating an even tone

YOUR TURN *Which good feature or features, from i-ix below, do sentences 1-6 on the following page contain? There are examples.*

   i   conceding

   ii   drawing on others' ideas

   iii   expressing doubt with a sophisticated adjective

   iv   inverting for emphasis

   v   using an It-clause for emphasis

   vi   starting with a manner adverbial

   vii   using a modal + an adverb

   viii   using the passive

   ix   using 'seem'

		An even tone is created by:	
Eg	It is questionable whether more people can be persuaded to use public transport when it is so expensive.	*iii*	*viii*
1	With the competition among channels for viewers, there has been an increase in the number of reality TV shows since these are popular.		
2	Despite some regulation of the industry, I think there is still too much television advertising.		
3	The European Space Agency has indicated that the colonisation of planets outside our solar system could conceivably occur before the end of the century.	*ii*	
4	Rarely have children been subjected to such a barrage of advertisements.	*iv*	
5	It seems likely that the infrequency of buses and trains in Sydney means that few people use them.		
6	As tourism encroaches on the Amazon, I believe it is the local indigenous people who benefit the least.		

Identifying strange tone

YOUR TURN *Two passages from 1-7 on the following page are perfect. Which strange feature or features, from i-ix, do the remaining five contain? There are examples.*

i	appears to concede, but does not.
ii	contracts.
iii	includes clichés.
iv	is dogmatic.
v	is overly personal.
vi	starts with 'And'.
vii	uses extreme punctuation.
viii	uses extreme adjectives or adverbs.
ix	uses informal vocabulary.

		The tone is strange because the writer... /	The tone is perfect.
Eg	Although I am against wider roads, many people support them.	*i*	*ix*
Eg	With the rising popularity of video games, large numbers of teenage boys spend long periods of time at a computer.		✓
1	Overpopulation is an accident waiting to happen! We should all do our best to reduce the numbers of humans.	*iii*	
2	While higher income is assured, I couldn't get used to sticking my hand into someone's mouth.	*ii* *v*	
3	The fact that soon there will be eight billion people on Earth disgusts me. The only thing that will prevent massive wars and famines is if international laws are passed to limit family size, especially in the Gulf, where I know women still have more than ten children.		*viii*
4	Agricultural land is already threatened by the growth of cities. Road-widening within cities only increases that pressure on farmers.		
5	And there is the possibility that students consider Dentistry takes longer to study than Accountancy or Marketing.		
6	Despite opposition to video games, they never hurt anyone. In fact, they are amazing entertainment.	*iv*	
7	Colonising other planets is not feasible within the next two to three generations.		

See the improved sentences, above, in the answers on page 383.

Special information about tone in GT Writing Task 1

GT Task 1 has three letter types: formal, semi-formal, or informal. Vocabulary and grammar need to match the level of formality. Balance is created as shown above.

In particular, there should be no formulaic expressions used in the wrong situation. For example: 'Please accept my sincere apologies' is unsuitable when writing to a friend. It should be: 'I hope you will forgive me.' Likewise: 'The matter has recently been brought to my attention.' may be used to write to your manager, but not to your cousin, who expects: 'I've just found out...' For a letter of formal request, a candidate who writes the following is in trouble: 'Hope you can get onto this right away for me.' It would be better to write: 'As this matter is rather urgent, I wonder if you could answer as soon as possible.'

In reality, many candidates mix up expressions, creating bizarre sentences like: 'Hope you can get onto this as the matter is rather urgent.'

There are some nationalities who do quite a lot of business in English with other people whose first language is also not English. It seems everyone has developed some bad habits of which the previous example is one. Remember: wherever tone is variable, a candidate won't get more than a Five for Task Fulfilment.

Threats are completely inappropriate: after all, IELTS isn't asking you to write a final letter recovering debt, or forcing a troublesome employee to resign.

YOUR TURN   *The following letter has a lot of mistakes in the three other Writing criteria. However, concentrate only on Task Fulfilment and the variable tone.*

Can you find some words and sentences that need deleting or changing?

Dear My Neighbour,

Hello! My name is maha sabagh, and i am live below you in the number 7.

I am very happy here, and your family is very nice.

However, I'm writting to you about a problem in our block of flats. Recently, I notice too much rubbish left on the stairs. It seem to come from your renovations. I know that you and your family is not living in your flat while the renovation happening, and probably your not aware that the workers are leave their stuff on the stairs for many days before take it out of building. I spoke to the man who is boss of the renovation, and he said that i am a liar, and the rubbish not come from your flat! However, I have seen him puting out it, and two time, i have tripped over bricks left there. As you know, the lighting is not so good at night, and I or my old mother may have accident.

I hope this letter can resolve matters, and you can ask to foreman to remove the litter daily. Otherwise I will go to police. I'm available for chatting concerning this matter on my mobile: 0416 964 088 anytime.

Yours sincerly, Maha

Here is the letter again. The information in parentheses shows changes. Some writing has been crossed out altogether. Spelling and grammar, however, have not been corrected.

Dear My Neighbour **(Dear Neighbour,/Dear Mrs Shibani,)**

~~Hello!~~ My name is maha sabagh, and i am live below you in the number 7. I am very happy here, and your family is very nice **(seems rather nice)**.

However, I'm **(I am)** writting to you about a problem in our block of flats. Recently, I notice too much **(a lot of)** rubbish left on the stairs. It seem to come from your renovations. I know that you and your family is not living in your flat while the renovation happening, and probably your not aware that the workers are leave their stuff on the stairs for many days before take it out of building. I spoke to the man who is boss of the renovation, and he said that ~~i am a liar, and~~ the rubbish not come from your flat! *(Your neighbour is likely to throw away this letter as soon as she sees the word 'liar'. Something like:* **'We had a slight disagreement over the origin of the rubbish'** *may work better. Avoid exclamation marks.)* However, I have seen him puting out it, and two time, i have tripped over bricks left there. As you know, the lighting is not so good at night, and I or my old mother may have accident.

I hope this letter can resolve matters, and you can ask to foreman to remove the litter daily. ~~Otherwise I will go to police.~~ I'm available for chatting concerning this matter on my mobile: 0416 964 088 anytime. *(Threats – going to the police – don't work, especially when followed by a friendly suggestion about 'chatting'. The reader may be confused.)*

Yours sincerly,
Maha Sabagh

The introduction in Writing Task 2

For a university assignment or a work report, a person is likely to write more words than in an IELTS essay. Therefore, a Task 2 introduction should be short and to the point.

Read the 100 words below. There are no problems with coherence, cohesion, grammar, or vocabulary. What is unclear, and will give the candidate a low score in Task Fulfilment?

> Communication is a blessing to humanity! Nowadays, with the rapid development of technology, more and more people, including my friends and relatives, have become connected to the Internet: a digital system in which computers communicate with each other via satellites. Currently, many work places, schools, universities, and libraries have the Internet. In addition, significant numbers of people access it in their houses, apartments, and holiday homes. Many mobile phones also have Internet applications. Surely, since so many individuals use this invention, it must be advantageous. However, every coin has two sides, especially the hot-button issue of the Internet at home.

The revised introduction has 20 words. What are the missing words?

> In this **e**__ __ __ __, I shall **di**__ __ __ __ __ having the Internet at home. In my
> **o**__ __ __ __ __ __ __, its **be**__ __ __ __ __ __ __ far **outw**__ __ __ __ its drawbacks.

Here is a longer introduction.

> Education is a life-long process. The foundations begin with primary school, at the age of five, and continue at secondary, which ends at 18. During this time, students mainly learn academic and social skills, but they also play sport, enjoy extra-curricular activities, and develop a knowledge of their own and other people's cultures. I believe that art, craft, and music play a small but important role in school education.

Circle the correct answer.

1   Is the writer's view clear?   Yes / No

2   Is the topic defined?   Yes / No

3   Are there any clichés (words or phrases that are overused

    and so meaningless, and not academic)?   Yes / No

4   Are there any examples which should be in the body of the essay?   Yes / No

Assessing introductions

IF YOU WANT A SEVEN

Here is another Task 2 question:

Many parents these days are sending their teenage children to another country to continue their education.
What are the advantages and disadvantages for the child's family of doing this?

Read what five IELTS candidates wrote to introduce their essays. Rank the paragraphs from the most (1st) to the least successful (5th). There are examples.

A = 3rd   Now a day more and more people are sending their adolesent children to foreign countries to continue their education. I think there are some positives, but mainly it can result in financial difficulties for the child's family because it's too expensive to live in Britain or USA. Also, children won't have so good relationship with other borthers and sisters and may feel supeerer living in other culture.

B = __   To send one's teenage child abroad for further study currently appealing to more and more people, specialy the middle classes in developing countries. In this essay, I shall discuss benefits and disadvantages of this phenomenon with relation to the child's family. In my view, the family makes short-term sacrifises, but long term benefits from their child's higher level of education and better job chances.

C = __   There is broverb in my country, if will take camel baby it's mother young it will never win the race. so I not think good idea for teenager go abroad to study Teenager, childs 13-19 inclusive is not ready enough leaving family, and may get troubles like drink alcohol or gumble if very like horseracing.

D = <u>2nd</u>   Sending a teenager aboard for education is getting increasingly popular in some countries. In this essay I shall talk about 'the prose and cons' of this with regard to the affect's on the childs family. Overall I consider education aboard is benificial.

E = __   In this highly competitive society, is very important have best education, particully the University. In this essay, I shall discuss if teenager should studing oversea or in own country. And university in indonesia not so high so if rich why not to australia or an other place?

Match an examiner's comments with the introductions you have just read. Write the letters in the spaces provided. There are examples.

i = ___ This introduction is relevant to the question, and clearly states the writer's viewpoint. Errors in grammar, spelling, and punctuation make it hard to read, and some vocabulary is better suited to speaking.

ii = ___ This introduction is relevant to the question, and clearly states the writer's viewpoint. However, it includes arguments and examples that should be in the body of the essay. There are some errors in grammar, spelling, and punctuation. Contractions are too informal for an essay. 'Nowadays' (even correctly written) is overused and not really academic. Despite these things, this is quite a good start.

iii = C It is not appropriate to start an academic essay with a proverb. Furthermore, the candidate has answered another question: Do you think teenagers should study abroad or not? Using camel racing and horseracing adds to the confusion. Grammar, vocabulary, spelling, and punctuation are all low-level.

iv = ___ This introduction is relevant to the question, and clearly states the writer's viewpoint. There are only a few errors in grammar and spelling. Vocabulary could be improved. What is the opposite of the noun 'benefits'? How can the candidate avoid using the word twice? Which preposition should replace 'with' in the phrase 'with relation to'? Which noun(s) should replace 'chances' in the phrase 'job chances'? Overall, this introduction is good.

v = E This introduction is not relevant to the question as teenagers study both at secondary school and at university. It does not refer to the advantages and disadvantages of study abroad on the teenager's family, and its example should be in the body of the essay. Errors in grammar and spelling are quite intrusive. The conjunction 'and' does not logically join the last two sentences. The phrase: 'In this highly competitive society' is inappropriate at the beginning of an academic essay. 'In this essay, I shall discuss if...' is preferable.

Writing the essay

Choose one 'for' introduction from the previous pages, and improve it by taking the examiner's advice.

_____

_____

_____

_____

_____

_____

Choose one 'against' introduction, and improve it by taking the examiner's advice.

_____

_____

_____

_____

_____

Continue writing the rest of the essay, in 30 minutes, using one of the introductions above.

_____
_____
_____
_____
_____
_____
_____
_____
_____
_____
_____
_____
_____
_____
_____
_____
_____
_____
_____
_____
_____
_____
_____
_____
_____
_____
_____
_____
_____
_____
_____
_____
_____
_____
_____
_____
_____

Topic and supporting sentences in Writing Task 2

YOUR TURN *Put the words in the box into the text below. There is an example.*

developed	examples	main	opens	relevant	~~Six~~

To achieve a (eg) <u>Six</u> or more in Task Fulfilment for Task 2, a candidate needs to present a logical argument with _____ support.

In academic writing, a topic sentence gives a reader the _____ idea, or topic, of a paragraph. It _____ or closes the paragraph. Sometimes, there may be two topic sentences when there are two parts to an essay question.

The topic sentence is _____, or supported, by sentences that give reasons, results, or _____.

Read the Task 2 essay below. Why is some writing shaded, and some in italics?

Doing voluntary work is far better for the volunteer than the community. To what extent do you agree?

In this essay, I shall discuss voluntary work, and whether it is more beneficial for the volunteer or the community. In my opinion, both gain from it.

First of all, the worker acquires new skills and experience. *Examples of this are when a person who works mainly with figures, like an accountant or IT specialist, does voluntary work with children, which focuses more on people skills; or, when someone who works predominantly indoors – a doctor or a lawyer – does voluntary work outdoors, in a park or national park.* Meanwhile, the community benefits because the volunteer offers his or her labour and know-how for free.

Secondly, volunteers become more tolerant of those less fortunate than they, or they may mix with other ethnic groups with whom they have previously had little contact. For the community, this leads to greater social cohesion between classes and cultures. *My aunt, for instance, while she was a housewife, spent two hours a week helping adults with literacy difficulties. Some of these people were from migrant families or the countryside. Before tutoring them, she had rather fixed ideas about their abilities, but during the process, she learnt that their lack of access to primary education or their moving around had been a major factor in their never having learnt to read properly. She became friendly with some of her students, and was invited to a farm where one of them lived in a remote area.*

To conclude, it is up to the individual how much he or she makes of any work experience, and volunteering is the same. Communities are fortunate if anyone gives time, energy, and expertise freely, and there are almost never negative outcomes: both the individual and society benefit equally.

Here is another Task 2 question:

In some countries, art, craft, and music are taught at both primary and secondary school to all students.
Why might this be a good idea?

The following essay *does not* have an introduction or a conclusion. They are on pages 123 and 129.

Seven phrases or sentences, below, are missing from the essay that follows. Match each one with a numbered blank. Write the numbers in the spaces provided. There is an example.

they develop lateral thinking = ____

are part of a universal cultural heritage = *eg*

exposure to different aesthetics at school = ____

develop discipline and teamwork = ____

Through art, craft and music, students learn to relax = ____

national identity is formed not only through momentous events, but also through music
    and art = ____

A talented few might even pursue careers as artists or musicians as a result of studies
    at school = ____

Drawing, painting, film, design, woodwork, metalwork, and all kinds of music from classical to hip hop __**eg**__. Learning a song from another country, possibly in another language, introduces children to something beautiful and mysterious. It reminds us that we are all part of one human family.

Indeed, __**1**__. How often have you heard a tune on the radio and nearly cried because it has reminded you of your country?

However, in my opinion, the greatest value of teaching these subjects is that __**2**__, which is extremely useful for a tertiary student, a researcher, or even an employee. Lateral thinking is when a person solves a problem by looking at it from different angles. Significantly, art and music activate different parts of the brain from language or chemistry, so they encourage problem-solving.

Activities like building a theatre set or playing in an orchestra __**3**__, also useful in later life. These more complex skills are more easily learnt at secondary school.

__**4**__, which will improve their capacity for study.

Today the world is full of products; it is nice to be able to appreciate good design, or to decorate one's own home tastefully after __**5**__.

__**6**__. Since these continued to secondary level, students received a solid foundation.

Answer this opposing question:

In some countries, art, craft, and music are taught at both primary and secondary school to all students.
Why do some people think this is a waste of time?

The conclusion in Writing Task 2

It is not necessary to write a conclusion in Task 1 although candidates are not penalised for doing so.

Task 2 requires a conclusion, but it does not need to be long. There are three kinds of conclusion. A candidate may:

- restate his or her opinion, which was indicated in the introduction;
- give his or her opinion if it was not mentioned in the introduction;
- or, for a problem-solution essay, say which solution he or she thinks is the most effective.

YOUR TURN *The lettered sentences below are possible conclusions to the three essays listed below. Match the conclusions to the essays. Write the letters in the spaces provided.*

Essay 1 (shopping malls) = ____, ____ and ____

Essay 2 (car accidents) = ____, ____ and ____

Essay 3 (art at school) = ____, ____ and ____

a. People everywhere flock to shopping malls.

b. Sadly, the days of many small businesses are over.

c. To conclude, driving is a social contract as well as a means of transport.

d. Music, art, and craft stretch, nourish, and unite people.

e. The convenience and value to individuals that malls offer outweigh the social dysfunction they cause, or their banality.

f. Modifying human behaviour through education is the key.

g. They help them become well-rounded individuals, and not just automatons who provide standard answers to standard questions.

h. Therefore, teaching music, art, and craft throughout primary and secondary school is essential.

i. Drivers, the police, and governments all play their part in averting the daily tragedy of death on the road.

Understanding Coherence and Cohesion in Writing

Read the definitions of Coherence and Cohesion for Writing below.

An IELTS Seven = The candidate mostly presents ideas logically. Each paragraph contains a main idea with supporting sentences. Various cohesive devices are well used, but there are occasional mistakes with pronouns and what they refer to.

An IELTS Six = The candidate presents ideas in a generally logical manner although a main idea may not be so clear. Many cohesive devices are correctly used, but some are misused, overused, or omitted. Reference is sometimes faulty.

An IELTS Five = The candidate presents information in such a way that the reader has to work out what the logical order is – it is not immediately clear from the writing. Clauses, sentences, and paragraphs may not be joined together naturally. There is a lot of repetition due to inadequate referencing. There may be no paragraphs, or an appearance of paragraphs, but their contents do not match their divisions.

YOUR TURN   Here is a candidate's writing about road accidents.

There are very few mistakes in grammar, and vocabulary is largely correct. While the response is logical and examples are excellent, there are still some problems, making this a Six for Coherence and Cohesion.

The behaviour of drivers is to blame for accidents as well as the condition of the roads. First of all, some drivers are inexperienced, and unsure how to handle problems. But a large number of drivers drive in an unfit state. It is drunk, drugged, or exhausted. Secondly, drivers speed and disobey rules. Changing driver mentality is difficult. Nationwide drink-driving and awareness-raising campaigns like 'Click clack, front and back' for seatbelts, or 'Drive Rest Survive' for exhaustion, which are effective. So is fixing roads. In addition, disturbing TV advertisements work. Moreover, a proven shock tactic is to show schoolchildren destroyed cars and graphic photos of the dead. Some defensive driving taught in the senior school is probably useful. **(118 words)**

Below is an explanation of the problems that the Six above has with Coherence and Cohesion.

Put the words from the box into the text. Write them in the spaces provided.

avoid	but	instead	last	refer	slow down	topic

1   Two ideas are mentioned in the _____ sentence, but only one is developed in the paragraph.

2   '_____' and 'so' join clauses, not sentences. Don't start with these in academic writing. 'However' and 'Therefore' can start sentences.

3   The linkers 'First of all', 'Secondly', and 'In addition' _____ the text, and are unnecessary. One adverb, 'moreover' is misused. ('Moreover' signals the greatest problem/solution that is written _____: here, 'defensive driving' follows. It is better to _____ 'moreover' in IELTS.)

4   Words related to 'drive' appear seven times when they could be omitted, or pronouns used _____. See the two underlined words in the IELTS Nine writing on the following page. (The Nine uses only four words derived from 'drive'.)

5   Two pronouns are misused. One, 'it', in line 3, does not _____ back to a noun correctly; the other, 'which', in line 6, needs a clause with subject + verb to follow.

Note: The Six's writing could be divided into two paragraphs, but it is not essential.
Note: Vocabulary which creates an even tone in the Nine's writing is largely absent from the Six's. (There are only two examples in the Six's: 'some' in line 2, and 'probably' in the last line.)

Here is a Nine's response.

In my view, the behaviour of drivers is mostly to blame for accidents. Admittedly, some may be inexperienced, and unsure how to handle problems, but a large number go on the road in a state unfit to drive: drunk, drugged, or exhausted. They speed, disobey other rules, and appear not to notice any other road-user.

Changing driver mentality is difficult, but possible. Nationwide drink-driving and awareness-raising campaigns – like 'Click clack, front and back' for seatbelts, or 'Drive Rest Survive' for exhaustion – are generally effective. I understand that disturbing TV advertisements also work. Showing destroyed cars and graphic photos of the dead to schoolchildren is another proven shock tactic. Introducing defensive driving to the senior-school curriculum could be useful. (118 words)

Paragraphs

All IELTS writing needs paragraphs. Without them, or with strange paragraphing, a candidate can only score a Five in Coherence & Cohesion.

In general, each academic paragraph contains a major new idea.

YOUR TURN *Read the following IELTS Nine essay.*
Separate the four paragraphs by inserting two slashes (/ /).

Around the world, children learn English as a second language at school. However, in some places, they also learn at kindergarten (pre-school care, when children are aged two to five).
Discuss the advantages and disadvantages of learning English at kindergarten.

As English has become the dominant language worldwide, vast numbers of people are learning it. The age of English-language acquisition is also lowering at the same time. Personally, I believe it is essential for a person from a non-English speaking community to learn English, but I think it is not necessary to do so until a child is around seven or eight. Supporters of teaching English at kindergarten – that is, when a child is aged between two to five – believe that early exposure will produce more competent speakers. Parents who are keen to give their child a head start in an ever more competitive world are persuaded by this idea. They think that if English is combined with play, it will be easily absorbed, and not seem like study at all. However, there are strong arguments against teaching English at kindergarten. Firstly, linguists claim that a child needs to be literate in his or her own language before another is begun unless that child is already living in a completely bilingual environment – that is: his or her parents are native speakers of both languages, and both languages are used around the child. Secondly, kindergarten teachers are less likely to be native English speakers themselves, or to be competent language teachers, which means that what children learn at kindergarten could be no more than a smattering of words – 'Hello' 'Goodbye', numbers, colours, and the names of animals. All of these could be learnt very quickly in a school classroom at the age of seven in addition to proper grammar and good pronunciation. Then there is the issue that kindergartens provide 'English' more as a marketing tool than an educational one, cashing in on concerned parents. It could also be a status symbol that a child is learning English at the age of three among the friends of his or her parents, meaning that the child's learning experience is subordinated to the parents' prestige. In my view, kindergarten is a time to acquire social skills, motor skills, and a deeper understanding of a child's own language. English can come later when a child is more capable of focused learning, and when the teaching is likely to be better. In an age where the endless pursuit of qualifications and accomplishments seems the norm, why not let a child be a child at kindergarten? (390 words)

Coherence and Cohesion in a Task 2 model

The essay on the following page is a model answer for the GT Practice Writing Test. Let us consider it in relation to coherence and cohesion.

YOUR TURN   *Unscramble the ends of the following sentences. Write the words in the spaces provided. There is an example.*

Eg   This essay is coherent because there is a logical order <u>and each paragraph contains a clear idea.</u>

~~a~~   ~~and~~   ~~clear~~   ~~contains~~   ~~each~~   ~~idea~~   ~~paragraph~~

1   If the essay were cut up into sentences, _____ .

again   back   be   easy   it   put   to   together   would

2   It is also cohesive. For linking, the writer uses conjunctions, reference, clear punctuation, and _____ .

essay   knit   sentence   sophisticated   structure   the   to   together

3   Note: there are no words or phrases like 'firstly', _____ .

in   in   addition   conclusion   or   to   sentences   start

4   A writer who is a Seven or _____ .

above   avoid   can   items   mechanical   such

IF YOU WANT A SEVEN

Read the following IELTS Nine essay.

Twelve words are missing from it. What are they? Write the missing letters in the spaces provided.

In some countries, fathers are playing a greater role in raising their children. Why is this happening? What are the benefits of it?

S__ __ __ __ women have entered the workforce in large numbers in many societies, they have also chosen to have fewer children. Their husbands, **mean** __ __ __ __, are expected to play more of a role in raising children not only because their wives are working but **a** __ __ __ because fatherhood has been redefined by men and women alike. A generation ago, fathers were more clearly financial providers; now they are also emotional anchors **w** __ __ spend more time with their children.

The benefits of fathers' assuming a greater role in childrearing are **m** __ __ __. From the perspective of the child or children, they have a more accessible male figure they can both look up to and rely on. **T** __ __ __ leads to their being more rounded individuals better able to cope with today's complex world. Research has shown that children who lack confidence or have some other problem develop faster with paternal as **w** __ __ __ as maternal love and attention.

F __ __ __ the father's point of view, he enjoys a period of time with his children that passes all too quickly, and is nourished by their daily accomplishments, by their intellectual and emotional growth. A man may count it a great achievement if his children are stable and able; his employment or earning capacity does not only confer status upon him.

For the mother, she feels as though her partner is assisting **h** __ __ physically and emotionally, and not just financially. While her partner is caring for their children, she may have more space and time for her own pursuits be **t** __ __ __ connected to her career or to other creative endeavours.

The notion of manhood has changed in recent times to include more active fatherhood, **a** __ __ I believe **t** __ __ __ is a positive development for all concerned. **(285 words)**

Go to pages 383-384 for the answers.

Paragraph organisation in Writing Task 2

By now, you probably have a good idea about what coherence and cohesion are.

YOUR TURN   In the following Task 2 answer, the grammar is perfect, but the paragraph is poorly organised.

1   Reorder the paragraph, so that the strongest arguments, related to society, go first.

2   Add *A wide variety of shops also exist in major cities* and *restaurants, clubs, cinemas.*

3   Delete one example sentence, which is not academic.

4   Delete two linkers – one word, and a two-word phrase – to make the writing faster.

Here is a GT Task 2 question:

More and more people are living in big cities these days.
Why is this happening? What are the advantages and disadvantages of this for society and the individual?

> People like to live in big cities because life is easier there. For example, there are more shops, parks, and museums. Moreover, there are more facilities like hospitals and universities. Very often, the best university is located in the capital. More entertainment can be found there. My favourite cinema is the Encore. In addition, cities offer better infrastructure with newer roads and more reliable utilities.

Rewrite the improved paragraph below.

_____
_____
_____
_____
_____
_____
_____
_____
_____
_____

The new paragraph, Version 2, is better:

> (1) People like to live in big cities because life is easier there. (6) ~~In addition,~~ Cities offer better infrastructure with newer roads and more reliable utilities. (3) ~~Moreover,~~ There are more facilities like hospitals and universities. (4) Very often, the best university is located in the capital. **A wide variety of shops also exist in major cities.** (5) More entertainment can be found there. (2) For example, there are more ~~shops,~~ **restaurants, clubs, cinemas,** parks, and museums. ~~My favourite cinema is the Encore.~~

There is one word, 'more', that occurs four times, above.

Go back to your writing on the previous page, and make sure 'more' is used only twice. (This improves Vocabulary because it avoids repetition.)

Version 2 contains around 70 words. Add sentences about employment and culture, and give more examples to reach at least 120 words. (This improves Task Fulfilment.)

_____

_____

_____

_____

_____

_____

_____

_____

_____

_____

_____

_____

_____

_____

_____

_____

_____

_____

_____

_____

_____

_____

_____

Here is a model of the expanded paragraph. The words in **bold italics** have been added. The word 'more' appears only three times now; it has been replaced in some instances by 'greater access', 'numerous', and 'better'.

People like to live in big cities, *especially capitals*, because life is easier there. Cities offer better infrastructure with newer *faster* roads and more reliable utilities *in particular water and electricity*. There is *greater access* to facilities like hospitals and *educational institutions*. Very often, the best *schools and* universities are located in the capital. *Employment opportunities attract people to the city: there are both more jobs, and more interesting IELTS highly-paid jobs. A range of employment prospects means a range of people as well. Cities are made up of many different cultural groups.* A wide variety of shops also exist in major **urban areas. These range from open-air markets for fruit and vegetables to glitzy shopping malls.** Better entertainment can be found there. For example, restaurants, clubs, cinemas, parks, and museums are **numerous.**

(133 words)

Now, write a paragraph on the disadvantages below.

_____
_____
_____
_____
_____
_____
_____
_____
_____
_____
_____
_____
_____
_____
_____
_____
_____
_____
_____
_____

Linkers

Linkers are words or phrases that link clauses, sentences, or paragraphs. They are usually conjunctions, adverbs, or adverbials.

Linkers perform different functions:

- Addition – 'also', 'and', 'furthermore', 'in addition', 'moreover'
- Contrast – 'but', 'however', 'on the other hand'
- Reason – 'as', 'because', 'since'
- Result – 'as a result', 'so', 'therefore'
- Sequence – 'first of all', 'secondly', 'next'
- Conclusion – 'in conclusion', 'to sum up'
- Exemplification – 'except for', 'for example', 'for instance'

- Opinion – 'in my view', 'the way I look at it'
- Condition – 'if', 'whether'
- Concession – 'although', 'in spite of', 'while'
- Emphasis – 'certainly', 'without a doubt' etc.

In speaking, one-word linkers like: 'and', 'but', 'because', and 'so' are favoured. In the Speaking test, it is strange to use 'in addition' or 'as a result', which are more appropriate in writing. However, a phrase like: 'the way I look at it' is a natural spoken alternative to 'in my opinion', which is used too much.

Writing for Task 2 requires the most careful use of linkers. Misuse is the mark of a Five; mechanical use – usually at the beginning of a sentence – and overuse define a Six; only a Seven manages to write so skillfully that linkers are barely noticed or needed. (Consider this paragraph in which punctuation, parallel structure, and logic have been used instead of linkers.)

Many IELTS books and websites mislead candidates by indicating that linkers must be used frequently. This is not so.

Using correct linkers

YOUR TURN   *Choose linkers from the box below to go into the text. Write them in the spaces provided. There is an example.*

although	and	~~as~~	certainly	except for	however
moreover	since	view	whether	while	

1   I believe a system whereby workers are obliged to contribute a small proportion of their earnings to health insurance is a good one (eg **as** it is fair, _____ it raises a significant amount of money. _____, once the tax is in place, it can easily be raised should this be required.

2   _____ nurses are well-paid in Britain, there is still a shortage of them. In my _____, more should be recruited from Eastern Europe.

3   With an ageing population, there are _____ more calls upon health care.

4   It is the aim of each administration to have healthy citizens. Even rich countries, _____, may not be able to afford free universal health care.

5   _____ it is a very large industry in many countries, alternative medicine has been found to be generally ineffective _____ the fact that the personal attention of a therapist makes patients feel better.

6   It is debatable _____ running is a safe form of exercise _____ it can damage the knees, but swimming appears to have no drawbacks at all.

A question of style

YOUR TURN

In speaking, it is acceptable to begin sentences with 'and', 'but', or 'so', but in writing, this is poor style. To avoid this:

a. join the two clauses with a comma;
b. begin a new sentence with another longer linker;
c. restructure slightly; or,
d. use more sophisticated punctuation (semicolons and colons).

Change each of the following sentences below according to one of the four lettered choices above. Write the new version. There are examples.

The United States and Qatar pumped comparable amounts of oil in 2010. But Qatar has four times the reserves of the United States.

Eg a. The United States and Qatar pumped comparable amounts of oil in 2010, but Qatar has four times the reserves of the United States.

Eg b. The United States and Qatar pumped comparable amounts of oil in 2010. However, Qatar has four times the reserves of the United States.

Eg c. While the United States and Qatar pumped comparable amounts of oil in 2010, Qatar has four times the reserves of the United States.

Eg d. The United States pumped 30 billion barrels of oil in 2010; Qatar pumped 25. Nevertheless, Qatar's reserves are four times those of the United States: 45.2 as opposed to 11.3 years.

1   Known reserves of oil rose by 6.6 billion barrels in 2010. Because major discoveries were made in Brazil, India, and Russia. (a)

_____

_____

2   More than 50% of the world's oil reserves are in the Middle East. So this region has become important politically. (b)

_____

_____

3   Currently, China does not have much oil. China's reserves will be exhausted within ten years. (c – Make this sentence conditional using 'pump out' and 'current rate', or use 'Since'/'As'.)

_____

_____

4   [*Production 2010: Saudi Arabia: 260 billion barrels; Reserves: 72.4 years. Production 2010: Venezuela: 210 billion barrels; Reserves: 234.1 years.*]
     Although Saudi Arabia pumped more oil in 2010 than Venezuela. It has three times the reserves of Saudi Arabia. (a + change 'three times' because logic is wrong)

_____

_____

5   Nigeria and Canada each pumped out about 40 billion barrels in 2010. Nigeria has 42.4 years' worth of reserves. Canada has 26.3 years' worth of reserves. (b and d)

_____

_____

IF YOU WANT A SEVEN

There are no mistakes in the following paragraphs. Which two are better because they use fewer linkers?

A *In some countries, for example Italy, the participation rate for women in the workforce is low by international standards. Although I cannot give a figure, I know that even university graduates often become housewives on marriage. They stay home even when there is no child to look after. There are two main reasons for this. Firstly, there is a culture of machismo. In addition, the economy appears unable to support more workers.*

B *In some countries, like Italy, the participation rate for women in the workforce is low by international standards. I cannot give a figure, but, from my experience, I know that even university graduates often become housewives on marriage even when there is no child to look after. This is due to a culture of machismo, and an economy which appears unable to support more workers.*

C *First of all, many people who choose euthanasia have terminal illnesses with undignified and very painful ends. They think it would be better to die while they still feel relatively fine and look good, meaning their friends and family have a pleasant memory of them. People may opt for euthanasia instead of burdening their families financially as they die. One surprising statistic suggests that in the last year of life, a person with a terminal illness spends half as much money as in the rest of his or her life on medical treatment. Finally, from a moral perspective, fewer people object to taking their own life as they did in the past.*

D *First of all, many people who choose euthanasia have terminal illnesses with undignified and very painful ends. As a result, they think it would be better to die while they still feel relatively fine and look good, so that their friends and family have a pleasant memory of them. Furthermore, I have seen one surprising statistic: in the last year of life, a person with a terminal illness spends half as much money as in the rest of his or her life on medical treatment. Therefore, such people may opt for euthanasia instead of burdening their families financially as they die. Moreover, many people are not religious, which means they do not have any moral objection to taking their own life as they did in the past.*

Punctuation

Without good punctuation, a text does not flow smoothly, making it hard for someone to read. Poor punctuation can sometimes change meaning.

All punctuation marks (capital letters, full stops, commas, apostrophes, question marks etc) are part of the IELTS Grammar criterion; paragraphing is part of Coherence & Cohesion.

YOUR TURN   Here is a GT Task 1 question:

You are studying a short course in another country. Your accommodation was arranged by the course provider. There is a major problem with the accommodation.

Write a letter to the course provider. In your letter:

- *Say what the problem is.*
- *Describe the accommodation you thought you were getting.*
- *Ask the provider to solve the problem.*

Read the letter below. It is an IELTS Nine answer except for its punctuation. There are 15 mistakes, shown in the column on the right. Fix the mistakes.

	# of punctuation mistakes
Dear Mr Brown,	
My name is Joseph Denka, and I am taking a six week intensive course at the school of	2
commerce. My company is paying for my tuition and I am using my Summer vacation	3
to study It is expected I will pass an international actuarial exam as a result, and be	1
transferred abroad. Therefore, it is rather important to me that i am able to study in	1
the best environment.	0
I am staying in West Hostel on campus. While my room is pleasant and the facilities are	0
very good the hostel is extremely noisy. When I organised my accommodation,	1
I was assured I would be staying only with post-graduate or intensive-course student's.	1
However, most of the people in this hostel are doing summer-school courses due to	0
academic failure, and they are all under 25. It seems to me they are enjoying 1 long	1
party certainly no-one observes lights out, or turns down music despite being asked to.	2
I wonder if I may be moved to a hostel, which is more conducive to serious study, or	1
I may use the remainder of my accommodation fee to go towards payment for a Hotel.	1
I look forward to hearing from you.	0
Your's sincerely,	1
Joseph Denka (197 words)	0

IF YOU WANT A SEVEN

Fill in the missing words below. Write the letters in the spaces provided.

Example	Problem	Reason for the correct punctuation
✗ ...a six week intensive course... ✓ ...a six-week intensive course...	A punctuation mark is missing.	A hyphen is needed for a compound *adj* __ __ __ __ __ __.
✗ school of commerce ✓ School of Commerce	Capitalisation	The School of Commerce is a *pro* __ __ __ noun, so it needs capitals.
✗ My company is paying for my tuition and I am using my summer vacation to study. ✓ My company is paying for my tuition, and I am using my summer vacation to study.	A punctuation mark is missing.	There are two clauses here: 'My...tuition', + 'and...study'. Two separate clauses are *j* __ __ __ __ __ with a comma before 'and', 'but', and 'so'.
✗ ...and I am using my Summer vacation to study. ✓ ...and I am using my summer vacation to study.	Capitalisation	English days of the week and months are capitalised. However, the *sea* __ __ __ __ are not.
✗ ...I am using my summer vacation to study ✓ ...I am using my summer vacation to study.	A punctuation mark is missing.	A full stop* is needed at the *e* __ __ of a sentence.
✗ ...that i am able to study ... ✓ ...that I am able to study ...	Capitalisation	The pronoun 'I' is *al* __ __ __ __ capitalised in English.
✗ While my room is pleasant and the facilities are very good the hostel is extremely noisy. ✓ While my room is pleasant and the facilities are very good, the hostel is extremely noisy.	A punctuation mark is missing.	There are two clauses here: 'While...good' + 'the...noisy'. The first clause is dependent, it can't *st* __ __ __ alone. When a word like 'while', 'when', 'if', 'although', or 'despite' starts the first (dependent) clause, there is a *c* __ __ __ __ at the end of this clause. If 'while' etc starts the second clause, there is no comma.
✗ ...post-graduate or intensive-course student's. ✓ ...post-graduate or intensive-course students.	*Un* __ __ __ __ __ __ __ __ punctuation has been added.	In this letter, 'students' is a plural noun and it does not show possession. Be careful with *ap* __ __ __ __ __ __ __ __ __. Put in the wrong place, an apostrophe is the mark of an uneducated or careless person.

*A 'period' in US English.

✗ they are enjoying 1 long party ✓ they are enjoying one long party	Numeral or word?	The rule is: numbers one to ***tw*** __ __ __ __ are written as words; 13+ are numerals, except at the start of a sentence, where all numbers become words.
✗ It seems to me they are enjoying one long party certainly no one observes lights-out or… ✓ It seems to me they are enjoying one long party – /: certainly no one observes lights-out or…	A punctuation mark is missing.	The writer is giving an ***e*** __ __ __ __ __ __ after 'party'. Therefore, either a long dash (–) or a colon (:) should be used.
✗ …no-one observes lights out … ✓ …no one observes lights out …	Unnecessary punctuation has been added.	These are two ***sep*** __ __ __ __ __ words although 'anyone', 'everyone', and 'someone' are not.
✗ …to go towards payment for a Hotel. ✓ …to go towards payment for a hotel.	Capitalisation	This is a common noun, so no capital is needed.
✗ I wonder if I may be moved to a hostel, which is more conducive to serious study… ✓ I wonder if I may be moved to a hostel which is more conducive to serious study …	Unnecessary punctuation has been added.	Here, 'which' begins a defining relative ***cl*** __ __ __ __. There is no comma before it, which would show a non-defining clause. Basically, if you think about the first clause: 'I wonder if I may be moved to a hostel', it doesn't make sense standing alone because the writer is already *in* a hostel (not a house or a tent or a hotel). Therefore, to define, or make clearer, his situation, the writer has added the 'which …' clause. (Check *defining* and *non-defining relative clauses* in a grammar book if you think you are a Seven.)
✗ Your's sincerely, ✓ Yours sincerely,	Unnecessary punctuation has been added.	'Yours sincerely' is an abbreviation of the ***phr*** __ __ __: 'I am yours, sincerely.'. 'Yours' is an adjective like 'mine', 'hers', or 'theirs'.

Handwriting

Which would you prefer: a neatly handwritten thank-you card, or one scrawled in a hurry?

YOUR TURN *Read the text below about handwriting in IELTS. Then answer the questions that follow.*

The IELTS exam is handwritten, and good handwriting counts (**eg**). In the Writing criterion of Coherence and Cohesion, a candidate only gets a Five if any of his or her handwriting is too hard to read. Illegibility affects the flow of meaning, or the coherence.

Examiners read from six to twelve Writing scripts at a time. In some countries, like China, they have a lot more. This means they process between 3,000-12,000 words per exam.

As you can imagine, examiners enjoy scripts that are easy to read, both in terms of level and appearance. There is almost always a correlation between the neatness of a script and a candidate's band score: the neater the writing, the higher the score. This does not mean that candidates should avoid correction – crossing-out or erasing. A candidate may even add a whole sentence or paragraph, indicating its position in the text with an arrow. Scripts which show evidence of editing are always better than those where nothing has been changed.

In general, IELTS handwriting is fine. However, some is hard to decipher, and annoying to do so. Sometimes words are too small; other times they are too large, which could lead to too few words written. A person who is trying to disguise the fact of giving a short answer may write large, or on alternate lines. A candidate automatically loses marks for Task Fulfillment if the word limits are not reached.

If a candidate's first language is Arabic, for example, the Roman letters of English may be ill-formed. There are often problems with capitals, either unused, or used in an apparently random fashion. Vowels may be missing; letters may be in the wrong order. Naturally, the candidate goes down in Vocabulary with these problems. French or German writers may be messy because their own education systems place less emphasis on handwriting. A few candidates write crudely, like children, and this may affect how the examiner views their content: is it juvenile as well?

Recently, a handful of candidates have been including texting abbreviations or symbols, like 'R U up 4 it?' or :), which are not suitable, particularly in academic writing.

Remember, IELTS is an exam for tertiary study, immigration, or registration with professional bodies. It is serious and life-changing. Examiners want to assess fairly what candidates have to say, and not be distracted by poor handwriting, childishness, or inappropriate language.

Currently, there is talk of all IELTS exams being done on computers, so there would be no issue of handwriting. But, for now, handwriting counts.

The following statements refer to the text you have just read. Mark each one as True (T), False (F), or Not Given (NG). Underline your evidence in the text. There is an example.

Eg Good handwriting is not so important in the IELTS exam. _F_

  1 Examiners have quite a lot to read. ___

  2 Chinese candidates get higher marks than Arabs. ___

  3 Examiners prefer scripts from women, whose handwriting is usually better than men's. ___

  4 Generally, neat scripts get higher marks than others. ___

  5 There is no benefit in deleting or adding words. ___

  6 Examiners are never irritated by poor handwriting. ___

  7 There is not really any danger in having large handwriting. ___

  8 Texting is acceptable in the IELTS exam. ___

9 Illegible writing may take an examiner's mind away from a candidate's content. ___

10 IELTS exams will be computer-based in future. ___

Understanding Vocabulary for Writing

Read the definitions of Vocabulary for Writing below.

An IELTS Seven = The candidate uses a variety of words, and shows some precision. There are some less common items, including idiomatic ones. He or she collocates correctly nearly all of the time, and has a certain style. There are some errors in word choice or collocation. There are occasional spelling mistakes, but they do not affect communication.

An IELTS Six = The candidate has a mostly adequate and appropriate resource, and meaning is generally clear. There is a restricted range of words, and wrong word choice does mean some lack of precision. Some writers who take risks with vocabulary at this level use a wider range, but there is a higher degree of inaccuracy. There are some spelling mistakes, but they do not affect communication.

An IELTS Five = The candidate can use simple vocabulary connected to the task, but there is quite a lot of repetition. Other more complex language is frequently wrong. Errors in word choice and spelling are noticeable; a reader may have to work out what the writer means.

YOUR TURN *Read two body paragraphs for a Task 2 essay. Which one is a Five for Vocabulary? Which is a Six?*

A People enjoy shoping molls becouse the very big supermarkets have all the things people need, and sometimes they have cheeper prizes. Molls are clean and air-conditioning. When I lived in Krakow, Poland, I prefered shoping at the moll instade walking on the cold streets in the snow.

B People enjoy shopping malls because the grand supermarkets provaid all the necessary, and discouns are offerred. Malls are clean and air-conditioned. When I lived in Krakow, Poland, I preferred shopping at the mall to trumming thru the cold, snowy streets.

Choose the correct item in each pair. There is an example.

In my (eg) ~~opion~~ / view, the behaviour of drivers is mostly (1) responsibility / to blame for (2) accidents / acidents. Certainly, some may be inexperienced, and unsure how to (3) deal / handle problems, but a large number (4) drive / go on the road in (5) a badly state / a state unfit to drive – drunk, drugged, or exhausted. They (6) sped / speed, disobey other road (7) laws / rules, and appear not to notice any other (8) road-user / user of the road. Imposing (9) big / high fines and (10) take / taking licences away from repeat (11) fencers / offenders do influence behaviour to some (12) extend / extent.

Describing graphs and charts in Academic Writing Task 1

In Task 1, there are many different NVDs, but graphs are common.

If you look online at various organisations that collect data like national bureaus of statistics, or the UN, or at a magazine such as *The Economist*, you'll find plenty of real NVDs already described for you. Some of them, like the graph below, don't include dramatic information. However, reading will expose you to suitable language, and broaden your general knowledge, helpful in the Reading and Listening tests.

YOUR TURN   *Study the graph below.*

VALUE OF THE AUSTRALIAN AND NEW ZEALAND DOLLARS AGAINST THE US DOLLAR

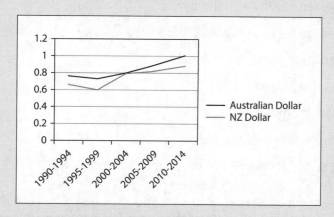

Which statements about the dollars are true?

1   Over time, both currencies rose against the US dollar.
2   At one point, they were on par with the greenback*.
3   In 2002, they were worth the same.
4   The Australian dollar has almost always been more valuable than the New Zealand dollar.
5   The New Zealand dollar is slightly less volatile than the Australian dollar.

Here are some mythical countries and their more volatile currencies.

VALUE OF FOUR CURRENCIES AGAINST THE EURO

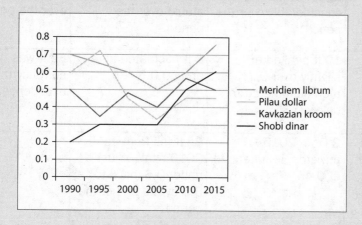

* A common way of describing the US dollar.

Match the statements with the currencies. There are examples.

Eg <u>ML</u>   It was the most valuable currency almost the entire time.

Eg <u>PD</u>   It declined considerably over the period.

Eg <u>SD</u>   It was the only currency that never experienced a fall.

Eg <u>KK</u>   It fell from its 2010 peak of just under 0.6, back to 0.5 by the end of the period.

1 ____   It was moderately valuable throughout.

2 ____   From 2010 onwards, it plateaued at 0.45.

3 ____   It began as the second-strongest currency, but ended as the weakest.

4 ____   It strengthened slightly over the period.

5 ____   It began as the weakest currency, but tripled in value.

6 ____   It remained fairly stable over the period.

7 ____   Its lowest point was at 0.5.

8 ____   It fluctuated at around 0.5.

9 ____   It rose dramatically over the period.

10 ____   It peaked at slightly over 0.7; then plummeted to below 0.35.

Here are the answers. Use the material below to write your own Task 1 answer. To make sure you have 150 words, add an overall statement as your first paragraph, and don't forget to mention the year 2005.

Meridiem librum	Pilau dollar	Kavkazian kroom	Shobi dinar
Eg It was the most valuable currency almost the entire time.	**3** It began as the second-strongest currency, but ended as the weakest.	**1** It was moderately valuable throughout.	**5** It began as the weakest currency, but tripled in value.
4 It strengthened slightly over the period.	**Eg** It declined considerably over the period.	**6** It remained fairly stable over the period.	**9** It rose dramatically over the period.
7 Its lowest point was at 0.5.	**10** It peaked at slightly over 0.7; then plummeted to below 0.35.	**8** It fluctuated at around 0.5.	**Eg** It was the only currency that never experienced a fall.
	2 From 2010 onwards, it plateaued at 0.45.	**Eg** It fell from its 2010 peak of just under 0.6, back to 0.5 by the end of the period.	

Collocation

A number of common collocations are used to describe NVDs.

What are the missing words below? Write the letters to complete each one. There is an example.

Adverb + adjective: (eg.) *moderately* valuable

Adjective + noun: the **stro** _ _ _ _ _ currency // the **wea** _ _ _ _ currency

Adverbials about equality: They were **on p** _ _ **with** the dollar. / They were **wo** _ _ _ **the same**.

Time expressions: the **ent** _ _ _ time // over the **per** _ _ _

It declined **consi** _ _ _ _ _ _ _. / It experienced a **f** _ _ _. / It fell from its **pe** _ _. / It **plum** _ _ _ _ _ to ... / Its lowest **p** _ _ _ _ was...

It **plat** _ _ _ _ _ at... / It remained fairly **sta** _ _ _. / It **fluc** _ _ _ _ _ _ at around...

It **stren** _ _ _ _ _ _ _ slightly. / It **trip** _ _ _ in **va** _ _ _. / It rose **dramat** _ _ _ _ _ _. / It **pe** _ _ _ _ at...

Here is some more vocabulary for Task 1. The words are NOT synonyms. That is, you can't just exchange one word for another in your writing. They are related closely to a context and to a level of formality – some are more academic than others. Furthermore, you need to learn which words they collocate with.

Up	Down	The same
Nouns		
expansion	collapse	reach a plateau
growth	contraction	
improvement	decline	
increase	decrease	
recovery	downward trend	
rise	drop	
upward trend	fall	
Verbs		
climb	collapse	plateau
expand	contract	level off
go up (irreg)	decline	maintain (its level)
grow (irreg)	decrease	remain stable
improve	deteriorate	remain steady
increase	drop	stay the same
recover	fall (irreg)	
rise (irreg)	go down (irreg)	
soar	nosedive	
strengthen	plummet plunge weaken	
A quantifier + a noun:		no change

YOUR TURN   *Put the phrases below about the degree of change into order from least to greatest. There is an example.*

a complete change	a dramatic change	~~an extremely slight change~~	
an insignificant change	a major change	a marked change	a minor change

no change → almost no change / (eg) <u>an extremely slight change</u> / (1) _____

_____ → (2) _____ / a slight change → a moderate change →

(3) _____ / (4) _____ / a noticeable change/a significant

change → (5) _____ / a very great change → (6) _____

Other useful language

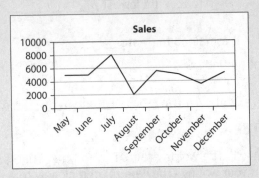

Cross out the phrase that **cannot** *be used in the sentences below.*

1   Overall, sales <u>fell / fluctuated</u>.

2   They reached a peak in <u>July / August</u>.

3   In August, sales fell to the lowest point of <u>1000 / 2000</u>.

4   Between September and October there was a <u>modest / rapid</u> decline.

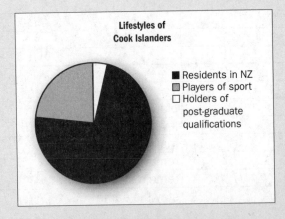

Cross out the phrases which are not true.

5   <u>A small minority/A reasonable number/The vast majority of Cook Islanders</u> play sport.

6   <u>A small minority/A reasonable number/The vast majority of Cook Islanders</u> hold post-graduate qualifications.

7   <u>A small minority/A reasonable number/The vast majority of Cook Islanders</u> live in New Zealand.

IF YOU WANT A SEVEN

Read the following Task 1 report.
   Choose the correct collocation each time. There is an example.

BIRD NUMBERS IN WOLLAI PARK 1990-2010

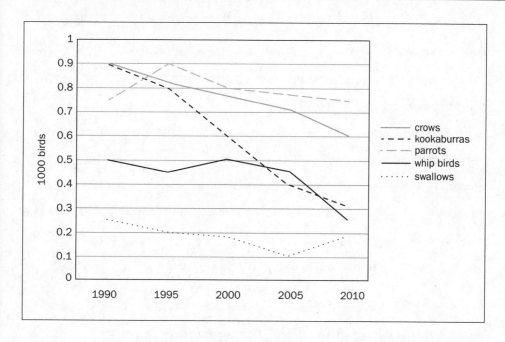

In the twenty-year (eg) *period / ~~time~~* from 1990 to 2010, there was an overall *decline / drop* in the number of birds in Wollai Park. There were around 3,300 birds in 1990, but only 2,000 by 2010. For three species, this decline was *marked / noticed*. Only parrots *kept / maintained* their 1990 numbers, which were 750 birds.

Kookaburras, along with crows the most numerous birds in 1990, *enjoyed / experienced* the most dramatic fall, losing two thirds of their numbers, ending with only 300 birds. The number of crows decreased steadily from 900 in 1990 to 600 two decades later. Whip bird numbers fluctuated at *about / around* 500 birds between 1990 and 2005, but *fell / plunged* after that, ending at just 250 birds. Swallow numbers were *little / low* to start with at around 250 birds. They also fell gradually until their lowest point of 100 in 2005. After that, they *had / made* a modest recovery to just under 200 birds. Parrots seemed to *live / survive* the best. When first surveyed there were 750 of them; they peaked *at / on* 900 in 1995, but had returned to their 1990 numbers by 2010. (**177 words**)

Using approximate language in Task 1

YOUR TURN *Put the words from the box into the following text. There is an example.*

150	add	approximate	data	~~hardest~~	in	kinds	subcategories

One of the (eg) *hardest* tasks in Writing is a single visual input in Task 1. This is because candidates need to make sure they write the required _____ words. Also, identifying trends is more difficult with less _____.

   In the chart below, many candidates fail to see what the major change *in* _____ *of products sold* is (*used* to *new*). They do not _____ up the _____ (two kinds of clothes; three kinds of food etc) to see if these totals are significant. They may also get caught up _____ the percentages, ruling lines to work out exactly what they are when this is mostly unnecessary. IELTS is testing _____ language here. (You can see this as only a few products are on a zero or five line on the percentage axis.)

Read the IELTS Nine answer below. What are the missing words?

PERCENTAGE OF PRODUCTS SOLD AT WETHERBY MARKET

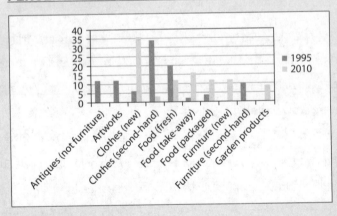

   In the fifteen-year period from 1995 to 2010, there were significant changes in the types of products sold at Wetherby Market. There were **roug** __ __ __ the same number of product categories, but, in 1995, the market specialised in used goods, art works, and food, while by 2010, it had converted to selling **mai** __ __ __ new products. Some things, like antiques, art works and second-hand furniture, were no longer available in 2010. Garden products and new furniture had replaced them in **sim** __ __ __ __ amounts. Further-more, clothing – new and used – represented **ab** __ __ __ 40% of goods sold in both 1995 and 2010. However, by 2010, food – fresh, take-away, and packaged – also took up 40% of sales, while it had only been 25% in the past.

The least noticeable change was in fresh food sales even though these *al*_ _ _ _ halved in the period surveyed. The most noticeable change was in clothing. In 1995, *j*_ _ _ *o*_ _ _ five percent of clothes sold were new, but this figure had increased six times by 2010. In that year, *a frac*_ _ _ _ _ *of* clothing was second-hand – *per*_ _ _ _ only two percent – whereas fifteen years earlier, it had been *ap*_ _ _ _ _ _ _ _ _ _ _ one third of all sales. (191 words)

IF YOU WANT A SEVEN

Look at the following chart. Spend a minute working out the main trends before you write. Add up the subcategories to help you. Find which activities dominate in 2010, and write about them first, because visually this is the most remarkable feature (the two long light grey lines). Then, describe which activities are most popular in 1995. Find which activities change the most over time, and write about them next. Finally, mention the activities that change the least.

Do NOT write about 'Art' and end with 'Swimming'. This is what a Four or a Five does. You also do not need to give details about every activity.

Use as much approximate language (the words and phrases you filled in above) as possible.

Task 1

The graph, below, shows children's leisure-time activities in California, USA.
Write a summary of the information. Select and report the main features, and make comparisons where relevant.

PERCENTAGE OF CHILDREN'S LEISURE-TIME ACTIVITIES IN CALIFORNIA, USA

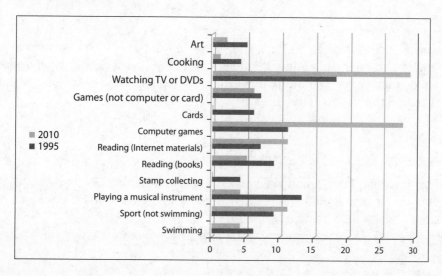

Nominalisation

YOUR TURN *The headings have been removed from the text below. Put them back in.*

- **i** Capabilities of different IELTS bands
- **ii** Nominalisation in IELTS
- **iii** Spoken v written structures
- **iv** Striking a balance
- **v** What is nominalisation?

1 _____

Nominalisation means that the main information in a clause is a noun phrase, often including an **abstract** noun.

It occurs mostly in academic essays, where writers convince readers by using abstract ideas, which may seem more powerful than others.

2 _____

In speaking, to express the same idea, structures like common noun subject + verb and common noun subject + 'to be' + adjective are more likely. Consider the written, nominalised, statement: *The **popularity** of the motor vehicle has resulted in urban sprawl.* Here is a spoken version: 'People like to own cars, so cities have just kept on growing.' Or: 'Cars are very popular, which has led to urban sprawl.'

3 _____

Naturally, it is easier to learn the vocabulary used in the spoken versions than in the nominalised one.

A Five almost never nominalises. A Six may do so occasionally. Only a Seven or an Eight has an extensive enough vocabulary, and an understanding of academic style, to nominalise appropriately.

4 _____

While a native speaker, or an IELTS 9, knows the convention of nominalisation, he or she is also aware that nouns are heavy in a text – that they slow it down – as they are usually longer words than verbs. Therefore, this extremely sophisticated writer uses a subtle mix of nominalised and verbalised structures.

5 _____

As well as in Writing Task 2, nominalisation occurs in Listening Sections 3 and 4 and throughout the Academic Reading test. GT Reading Sections 1 and 2 have less nominalisation, but Section 3 contains it.

YOUR TURN   *Mark each of the following sentences referring to either Home schooling (HS), or Learning English at kindergarten (LE). There is an example.*

Eg   <u>HS</u> The phenomenon of home schooling, or educating school-age children at home, is not new.

1   _____   However, it has gained momentum recently with the rise of the Internet.

2   _____   In many countries, English-language education begins at the age of seven or eight within the school system.

3   _____   Research has shown that literacy in a child's first language should be established before exposure to a foreign language begins.

4   _____   In the past, there was limited availability of teaching material through the post or at libraries, but information is limitless with the Internet. The idea of interaction with a virtual or distant teacher was also unknown.

5   _____   Nevertheless, there is a movement by concerned parents to introduce their children to English earlier, even at kindergarten.

Here is one whole paragraph from three of the items above. The highlighted language is nominalised.

In many countries, English-language education begins at the age of seven or eight within the school system. Research has shown that literacy in a child's first language should be established before exposure to a foreign language begins. Nevertheless, there is a movement by concerned parents to introduce their children to English earlier, even at kindergarten.

Speaking versus writing

Here is part of a Speaking Part 3 interview from Japan. The candidate is a Nine.

Examiner	What do you think is the value of children learning English at kindergarten?
Candidate	I think it's a great idea. I mean, if <u>parents want</u> their children to get a head start in life, <u>why not expose</u> them to some basic English, like numbers and colours, in some fun activities?
Examiner	Why might some people think it's a waste of time at kindergarten, and better left until school?
Candidate	Well, I suppose there are already lots of things to learn at kindergarten, like getting on with other kids, and the child's own language. Maybe it's better that <u>children can read</u> in their own language before <u>they move on</u> to English. Also, <u>kindergarten teachers mightn't have</u> such good English themselves.

Most constructions are <u>subject + verb</u>.

IF YOU WANT A SEVEN

Read the following IELTS Nine Task 2 essay about extended families.
Choose the nominalised item in each pair.

In this essay, I shall discuss the benefits and drawbacks of extended families, and provide reasons for (1) *their diminishing popularity. / why they are less popular*. I believe the drawbacks outweigh the benefits, which mainly explains their decline.

In the 19th and early 20th centuries, almost all families were extended; in the last seventy years, however, this has changed. In my country, Sweden, (2) *extended families only exist within / the existence of extended families is limited to* immigrant communities and farming families.

In Stockholm, there is a small number of extended families. These are typically immigrants from Iran or the Middle East who live together (3) *for financial reasons / to save money*, or because the older members cannot speak Swedish. (4) *Living alone may be difficult for these people. / These people do not want to live alone because it may be difficult*. Some people are satisfied with this arrangement, but as far as I know, second-generation Iraqis who have more money and better jobs than their parents move out to live as nuclear families, in shared houses, or alone. They value (5) *being independent and private / their independence and privacy* over the larger family unit.

Admittedly, there are some positives about life in an extended family. Relatives can provide 24-hour childcare, and the older generation can give on-the-spot advice. Nevertheless, grandparents (6) *may feel exploited / may have a feeling of exploitation*, at babysitting or housekeeping for free; the younger generation may want neither instant advice nor the constant examination of their lives.

On farms, (7) *some extended families have survived / the survival of some extended families has continued*, since having as many related people as possible to provide labour may be cost-effective. However, (8) *more farmers these days use machines, and / with the steady mechanisation of agriculture*, (9) *fewer people work / there is less employment* in the countryside, so there are fewer extended families.

To sum up: cultural and economic imperatives have made extended families a thing of the past about which (10) *nostalgia is unnecessary. / we need not be nostalgic*.

Note: In reality, there are no right answers for this activity. The important thing is that there are at least ten nominalised phrases in an IELTS Task 2 essay. More than 15 make the essay too heavy; fewer than five make it too chatty.

Here are the answers: 1. a (the item on the left of the pair); 2. b (the item on the right); 3. a; 4. a; 5. b; 6. b; 7. b; 8. b; 9. b; 10. a.

Understanding Grammar for Writing

Read the definitions of Grammar below.

An IELTS Seven = The candidate uses a variety of complex structures flexibly and accurately. Error-free sentences are frequent. There are a few grammatical and punctuation mistakes, but these do not affect communication.

An IELTS Six = The candidate uses both simple and complex sentences, but complex structures are less likely to be accurate. He or she makes quite a few grammatical mistakes, although these do not generally affect communication. There are occasional problems with punctuation.

An IELTS Five = The candidate uses a limited range of structures. Occasionally, he or she tries to use complex sentences, but these are nearly always wrong. Simple sentences may be correct, but there are so many errors throughout that the reader has some difficulty understanding. There are some problems with punctuation.

YOUR TURN *Read two introductions for Task 1 Academic. Which one is a Four for Grammar? Which is a Five?*

A This table and map show 17 countries, which they are involve in Antarctica. Most of country have scientific bases in Antarctica. Seven countries have territorial claim. 13 signed the Antarctic treaty in either 1960 or 1961 but four countries sign in 1980s.

B This table and map showing 10 country in the Antarctica have scientific base and 7 country having territorial claims. four countries signed 1980s Antarctic Treaty 13 sign 1960 or 1961.

IF YOU WANT A SEVEN

Here is a Task 2 question:

More and more information about the lives of celebrities is now found in newspapers, magazines, and online.
Why is this happening? What are the drawbacks for the reading public?

The following text is very simple. It needs more complex sentences (and vocabulary) and less repetition of structures or individual words.

   It also needs 'you' and 'we' removed, and more general statements made.

Fill in the missing words. There is an example.

Eg Life is stressful now. People need to relax because of too much stress. → *Life is more stressful now, **which** means people need more **re**laxation.*

   You can relax if you read about celebrities. → *It is **po** __ __ __ __ __ __ to relax by* **re** __ __ __ __ __ *about celebrities.*

   It is interesting to find out about their lives. Their lives are very different from our lives.

→ *It is interesting to find out about their lives,* **wh** __ __ __ *are very different from* **o** __ __ __.

When we read about celebrities, we can dream about nice lives with lots of money and lots of lovers. → *This* **allo** __ __ *people to dream about* **hav** __ __ __ *lots of money and lots of lovers.*

Usually news is about terrible things like wars or earthquakes. It is better if you read about nice things like celebrities. → *Usually news describes terrible* **eve** __ __ __ *like wars or earthquakes; it is better to* **r** __ __ __ *about more* **plea** __ __ __ __ *things like celebrities.*

Furthermore, in articles about celebrities, sometimes we learn that celebrities may be famous, but they are not perfect. They have problems. → *Furthermore, in reading about* **th** __ __, *people learn that* **alth** __ __ __ __ *celebrities may be famous, they are not perfect: they* **a** __ __ __ *have problems.*

When we read about the problems of celebrities, we get ideas about how to solve our problems. I think reading about celebrities is more than just relaxing. → *When* **p** __ __ __ __ __ __ *read about the* **cele** __ __ __ __ __ __ __ *problems,* **t** __ __ __ *may learn how to solve* **t** __ __ __ __ *own.* **Ther** __ __ __ __ __ __, *I believe, reading about celebrities is more than just relaxing.*

Here are the completed paragraphs. They are still rather simple, and you might like to improve them. How would you continue the essay?

Life is more stressful now, which means people need more relaxation. It is possible to relax by reading about celebrities. This allows people to dream about having lots of money and lots of lovers.

Usually news describes terrible events like wars or earthquakes; it is better to read about more pleasant things like celebrities. Furthermore, in reading about them, people learn that although celebrities may be famous, they are not perfect: they also have problems. When people read about the celebrities' problems, they may learn how to solve their own. Therefore, I believe, reading about celebrities is more than just relaxing.

The following text gives an opposing view of the same topic.
Choose the correct item in each pair. There is an example.

'Brangelina split!' 'Lady Gaga's ex in rehab.' 'Russian tennis ladies start fashion empire.' (eg) ~~This~~ / These are the kinds of headlines in (1) <u>todays newspaper's and magazine's /</u> <u>today's newspapers and magazines</u>. Increasingly, news space (2) <u>are / is</u> being taken up by stories (3) <u>about / of</u> celebrities, some of whom – like a pop singer's former partner – it is questionable whether they are well known at all. (4) <u>For older readers who are interested in</u> <u>real news / For older readers, who are interested in real news</u>, this (5) <u>represent / represents</u> a serious deterioration of journalism, meaning it is harder to find out what other (more impor- tant) things (6) <u>are happening / happen</u>. For younger readers, it (7) <u>threaten / threatens</u> their ability to judge what is important. Doubtless, the media magnates who popularised this genre aimed (8) <u>only to sell / to only sell</u> products. However, I consider that a lack of hard news, (9) <u>combined / combining</u> with a frivolous, amoral interest (10) <u>in / of</u> the lives of the rich and famous may lead to the erosion of a cohesive, moral society.

Grammar and Vocabulary Test 1

Here is a model answer to the Academic Practice Writing Test 3.

Which item is correct in each pair? There is an example.

(eg) <u>These / ~~This~~</u> plans show a community centre that has been remodelled. While the total size of the property and the building <u>remain / remains</u> the same, the configuration and use of space, both internal and external, are substantially different.

With regard to the outdoors, after remodelling, the yard is still a rectangle, but its length is longer than its <u>wide / width</u>. There is no parking allowed, and since there is now an indoor café, there are tables and chairs outside. There are also plants, and the possibility of exhibitions <u>being held / held</u> in the yard.

Inside, after remodelling, the centre is a large rectangle rather <u>than / then</u> L-shaped. There are six spaces instead of five, the largest of which – Gallery 2 and the Art Studio – have maintained their original size and location. Gallery 2 is <u>approximately / roughly</u> the middle third of the building, with the Art Studio, now for rent, <u>occuping / occupying</u> one corner.

Gallery 1 and the toilets still <u>exist / same</u>, in slightly smaller form and different locations. The kitchen has disappeared <u>altogether / all together</u>; there is now a café between Gallery 1 and the toilets.

The <u>function / purpose</u> of one space has altered considerably: what was once Gallery 1 is now a recording studio, also for rent, <u>meaning / meant</u> the name of the centre has been changed accordingly.

(205 words)

Grammar and Vocabulary Test 2

Here is a model answer to the GT Practice Writing Test 2.

Which item is correct in each pair? There is an example.

Dear Khuloud and Abdulwahid,

I'm (eg) <u>writing / ~~writting~~</u> to thank you for the lovely time I had <u>stayed / staying</u> in your gorgeous house in Bab Touma while I was <u>studing / studying</u> Arabic <u>last / the last</u> summer.

As you know, I'd <u>been never / never been</u> to the Middle East when I arrived <u>in / to</u> Damascus, and I was thrilled to <u>find / finding</u> so many wonderful <u>people / persons</u> and amazing archaeological sites. I really had no idea about Syria's _heritage rich / rich heritage._ Almost all the stereotypes we _had / have_ in Norway of Syria _was / were_ soon proven wrong. I met many people _who's / whose_ worldview is pretty much the same as my own. I've _certainly told / told certainly_ everyone back home about the _fascinated / fascinating_ and generous community of Bab Touma.

My most memorable experience was _celebrate / celebrating_ Easter with you – that incredible Palm Sunday _parade / perade_ and those bonfires, as well as the Easter Mass in four _language / languages_. I'm so _grateful / greatful_ you shared those things with me.

Please _accept / except_ a small token of my gratitude, enclosed, and _remember / remind_, if you're ever in Oslo, I'd be delighted _to put you up / to put up you_, and show you around.

Your friend,

Hege

Grammar and Vocabulary Test 3

Here is a model answer to the GT Writing Taster Test.

Which item is correct in each pair? There is an example.

To the Editor,

My name is Warawan Chattaporn – a resident of Burtonville (eg) _for / since_ two years. My family moved here due to _it's / its_ affordability and _approximation / proximity_ to the city. We also enjoy several small parks in which our sons and their friends play. One of _these / this_ parks is Davis Park, _on / on the_ Bellingham Street. It is not large, but it is well-used, clean, and _safe / safety_.

Recently, I learnt that Burtonville Council _has / have_ decided to sell this _pubic / public_ amenity for development. The land has already been _reasoned / rezoned_ residential, so I assume as many dwellings as possible – perhaps even fifty apartments – could be _building / built_ here.

While I am not a _lawer / lawyer_, and do not know by which legal process this land could be _selled / sold_, as a resident, I was neither informed nor _consultation / consulted_ about it. All my neighbours say the same thing. We have _asked / petitioned_ the council, and I hope this letter _reach / reaches_ a wider public.

Our / Us website, SaveDavisPark.com, lists a number of protest activities in which we _hop / hope_ your readers may join us.

To / Too few green and tranquil public spaces remain in this over-developed city. Save Davis Park before _it is / it will be_ too late.

Warawan Chattaporn

GT Task 1 formal letters – a request

In GT Task 1, a candidate is expected to be able to write both formal and informal letters.

YOUR TURN *Put the formal or informal items in the box into the table below. There is an example.*

> I can hardly believe that Michael is getting married.
>
> I expect you will be tired on arrival.
>
> I need not describe all the details now.
>
> I would like some information on spring semester courses.
>
> My sister has invited quite a few guests to her party.
>
> The changes won't affect many people.
>
> Yours sincerely,
> Abdulwahab Alkurdi

Formal	Informal
Correct grammar is used throughout. Eg: I look forward to seeing you in March.	**Occasional sentence fragments are possible.** Eg: *See you in March.*
There are no contractions or abbreviations.	**Contractions and some abbreviations are acceptable.**
1.	I can't believe that Mick's tying the knot.
More formal vocabulary is used.	**Less formal vocabulary is used.**
2.	My sister's asked heaps of people to her party. I need some information on spring semester courses.
Nouns phrases are common.	**Verbs are used more often.**
3.	I'm sure you'll be worn out by the time you arrive.
Long verbs from Latin are preferred. There may be more passives.	**Phrasal verbs and the active are preferred.**
4. Few people will be affected by the changes.	I won't go into all the details now. 5.
The opening and close are different.	
Dear Mr Koussa, 6. Dear Sir or Madam, Yours faithfully, Mr Abdulwahab Alkurdi	Hi Idris, Your friend, Abdul Dear Idris, Best wishes, Abdul

YOUR TURN   Here is a Task 1 question:

You live in a complex of 50 flats. You want to make your flat bigger. Before you do this, you need the body corporate (the organisation that controls your flats) to agree to this change.

Write a letter to the body corporate. In your letter:

- *Introduce yourself and your flat.*
- *Say what change(s) you want to make, why, and when.*
- *Ask the body corporate to let you do this.*

The letter below is a little too informal.

Replace crossed-out items with more suitable language, referring to the table on the previous page. There is an example.

Dear Mr Mukherjee,

(eg.) *My name is Ashoke Gupta.*

~~I am Ashoke Gupta.~~ My family and I own flat 26B in the Forest Lake Complex. ~~We've~~ been living here for ~~ages~~.

~~I'm~~ writing to you ~~about~~ extending my flat now that ~~we've got~~ three children. I ~~wanna~~ add three square metres to the western side of my ground floor, and ~~make~~ a terrace on the roof of this addition. ~~Now, there's~~ a service lane on the western side, which ~~no one ever uses~~. My addition would not ~~block off~~ this lane, ~~and it wouldn't make~~ my neighbours lose any light ~~cos there's~~ already a high wall around our complex which ~~makes everything dark~~.

I ~~want~~ to begin work on this addition ~~right away~~. I ~~pray to God~~ the body corporate will ~~say yes~~ to my plan.

~~Looking forward to your reply.~~

~~Best wishes,~~

Mr Ashoke Gupta

GT Task 1 formal letters – a complaint

A common problem in GT Task 1 is that candidates use a strange mix of formal and informal language. In formal letters, they may include inappropriate informalities; in informal letters they may suddenly be too formal, usually including a memorised chunk. This mix confuses the reader and affects the candidate's score in Task Fulfilment.

YOUR TURN   Here is a Task 1 question:

You live in an area where the local council has made some changes to regulations. You believe these changes are not good for residents.

Write a letter to a councillor. In your letter:

- **Introduce yourself.**
- **Describe the problem.**
- **Say what you think the council should do about the situation.**

In the letter below, choose the more formal item in each pair. There is an example.

Dear Sir,

My name is Mrs Penny Wu. (eg) *I have been a resident of / I've been living in* Smithfield Avenue, Coogee, for several years.

I am writing to you *about / in reference to* the changed parking conditions in Coogee that *came into effect from / started on* the first of October last year. *I believe these are an inconvenience to residents, and should be reconsidered. / I believe these inconvenience residents, and you should think about them again.*

In the past, I was always able to park my car on the street outside my house without any *difficulty / problems*. When metered parking *began in / was introduced to* my suburb, particularly near the beach, some visitors started parking their vehicles further away from the beach *in order to avoid payment / so they didn't have to pay*. My street *appears to be / is* the perfect place for these people: it is not too far from Coogee Beach, and the parking is still free. Between October and December, I occasionally found it hard to park, but when summer finally *arrived / hit*, there were two days a week when I *had to / was forced to* park hundreds of metres away from my home. On public holidays, I *ended up using / resorted to* metered parking myself.

I understand the local council *hopes to benefit financially / wants to make some money* from metered parking, or perhaps to encourage people to use public transport. Nevertheless, residents like myself are inconvenienced by this system. I suggest either residents be allowed to park free in metered zones which *are bigger / extend a greater distance* or metering cover a smaller area, and ticket prices be raised. *Additional / More* bus services would also reduce congestion.

I look forward to hearing from you.

Yours faithfully, / Yours truly,

Mrs Penny Wu

GT Task 1 formal letters – an offer

YOUR TURN Here is a Task 1 question:

You have seen an advertisement for a community college that needs teachers for night classes.

Write a letter to the community college. In your letter:

- **Say which advertisement you are answering.**
- **Describe which course(s) you want to teach, and what it/they would be about.**
- **Explain why you would be a suitable teacher.**

The IELTS Nine letter below is missing 20 prepositions. Put them back in, using the choices in the box.

> at **x** 2; for **x** 3; from **x** 1; in **x** 4; of **x** 4; on **x** 3; to **x** 3

Dear Sir,

I am writing to City Evening College _____ reference _____ an advertisement I saw in *The Echo* _____ July 12th _____ language teachers _____ your college.

I am interested _____ teaching Korean and Korean Cookery. I have seen that your guide _____ last term does not include these courses, but I understand there are now large numbers _____ second- and third-generation Koreans living in this part _____ the city who may be keen to learn more about their language and culture.

I have a Bachelor of Science degree and a teaching diploma. I hold special qualifications _____ language teaching and cookery. I was a science teacher in Korea, but moved _____ Los Angeles _____ 2002. There, I taught Korean _____ Beginners and Korean Cookery _____ two community colleges. The language course assumed students had no prior knowledge _____ Korean. It gave them simple everyday language, as well as recognition of the alphabet. The cookery course focused _____ easy meal preparation and the art _____ pickling or kim chi.

In Vancouver, I could teach the same courses as previously, or we could devise new ones, depending _____ what the college considered its market to be.

I look forward _____ hearing _____ you.

Yours faithfully,

Mrs Won-Kyong Stevenson

Go to page 386 for the answers.

GT Task 1 semi-formal letters – a view

A letter to a newspaper may be in a semi-formal style. This means the grammar is formal, but some language is more colloquial to draw the reader's attention to the issue.

YOUR TURN   Here is a Task 1 question:

You live in an area where a motorway is being made wider. You believe this is unnecessary. Write a letter to a local newspaper. In your letter:

- *Introduce yourself.*
- *Describe the problem.*
- *Say what you think a better solution would be.*

The letter below is excellent. Some lines are completely correct, as shown by *OK*. In other lines, there is one word that is not needed (*NN*), or one word that is missing (*M*).

Cross out the extra words, and add others where necessary. There are examples.

Line		Problem
	To the editor,	
1 Eg	My name is Graziella Mara, and I've been living in ~~the~~ Peterton for	**NN**
2 Eg	the past six years. When I heard that the Southern Motorway	**OK**
3 Eg	was ^being widened, I was livid. Frankly, this roadway has all but ruined my	**M**
4	suburb by dividing in two and creating pollution. Many residents sold	**M**
5	at a loss when the first extension was made in 2009 since the	**OK**
6	concrete sound barriers little to prevent noise, and the air pollution	**M**
7	has worsened with more traffic. Adding two more city-bound lanes a	**M**
8	Band-Aid solution. I bet they'll be gridlocked within 12 months, and we'll	**OK**
9	be returned back to square one.	**NN**
10	In an era when the people are seriously questioning the reliance on	**NN**
11	private cars, the government should developing public transport, or	**M**
12	discouraging people from living so far distance from the city for them	**NN**
13	to need a motorway. I would very support a dedicated bus lane or a	**NN**
14	tramway any extension were to be made, but I understand it's just	**M**
15	going to be ordinary vehicular lanes. Furthermore, the green space will	**M**
16	be requisitioned is used by joggers and people walking dogs. You may	**OK**
17	not imagine, but there are a number of native birds that make their	**M**
18	home in that strip.	**OK**
19	As a local paper, I hope you can to promote sustainable development	**NN**
20	and publicise campaign to stop this motorway widening.	**M**
	Yours faithfully,	
	Graziella Mara	

Academic Writing Taster Test

Do this Taster Test in a quiet place, under exam conditions.
You have one hour for this test.

Task 1

The graph shows student enrolments at the University of Westchester.

Spend about 20 minutes on this task.

Write a summary of the information.
Select and report the main features, and make comparisons where relevant.

Write at least 150 words.

Student enrolments at the University of Westchester

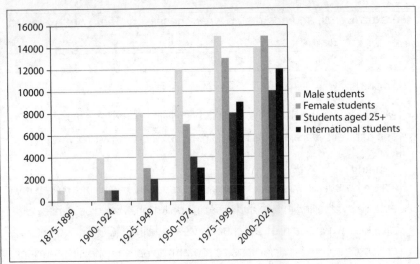

Academic and GT Task 2

Spend about 40 minutes on this task.
Write about the following topic:

There are many stages to life, for example: childhood, adolescence, young adulthood, and middle age.

Choose one that you consider is the most difficult for men, and one for women. It may be the same one.

Provide reasons for these difficulties, and say how they may be overcome. Include relevant examples from your own knowledge or experience.

Write at least 250 words.

GT Writing Taster Test

Do this Taster Test in a quiet place, under exam conditions.
You have one hour for this test.

Task 1

Spend about 20 minutes on this task.

There is a public park near where you live. You have heard that the local council wants to sell this park.

Write a letter to a local newspaper. In your letter:

- ***Introduce yourself.***
- ***Describe the importance of the park.***
- ***Say what action you will take if the council continues with its plan.***

Write at least 150 words.

You do NOT need to write any addresses.

Start your letter with:

To the Editor,

_____

_____

_____

_____

_____

_____

_____

_____

_____

_____

_____

_____

_____

_____

_____

_____

_____

_____

_____

_____

_____

_____

_____

For Task 2, see page 166.

(Page 387 has model answers for Tasks 1 and 2.)

Writing – Putting it all together

We've looked at the four marking criteria for Writing: Task Fulfilment, Coherence and Cohesion, Grammar, and Vocabulary. They are equally important. Each candidate, however, will have strengths and weaknesses.

If candidates do not write enough or they have no paragraphs, IELTS awards a Five as the maximum for TF or C&C.

Although most candidates work on improving their grammar, in fact, they need to devote much more time to vocabulary. Furthermore, written academic language differs from informal spoken language.

IELTS writing is a skill learnt through practice. A person cannot show up for the test with only ever having written one or two IELTS-style essays and expect to get a high score. There are also thousands of candidates who have received post-graduate degrees from English-speaking countries yet who have never demonstrated that their written English is good. These people do not automatically get high IELTS scores.

There are 83 pages in this book on writing because it is complex, and because most language learners get little feedback on their efforts.

Assessing candidates

YOUR TURN *The plans, below, show Randwick Road over time.*

Write a summary of the information. Select and report the main features, and make comparisons where relevant.

Randwick Road 2000

Bakery	Newsagent	Real estate agent	Thai restaurant	Video shop

All-day Parking

All-day Parking

Charity shop	Vacant	Shoe shop	Pet shop

Randwick Road 2010

Bakery	Newsagent	Charity shop	Real estate agent	North Indian restaurant	Organic grocery

Parking 10-3 only

No Parking _____ Bus Stop _____

Childcare centre	Pharmacy	Brazilian restaurant	Pet shop

Read the scripts on the following page. What can these candidates do to improve?

A Fristly, in 2000 have the bakery, the news agent, the real estate agent, the thailand restarant, the vidio shop. Oposit have the charity shop, the vacant shop, the shoe shop, the pest shop.

In the other hand, in 2010 have the bakery, the newsagent the smoller, the charity shop move and smoller, the real estate agent same, the north india restaurant, the organic grocery. Cross the street have the child care centre, the pharmacy, the Brasilia restaurant, the pet shop.

Moreover have the parking diffrent rule and regration.

In addition, the child care center in 2010 was biggest place, but the charity shop smaller because people in this aria the richer. The news agent in 2010 was second shop, but same size as other's shops in 2000.

In summery, I think the Randwick Road for shopping nice place. Many facilities. Too much place for eating. But you have to cought bus becouse privat cars No Parking in 2010. (**158 words**)

B These planes show Randwick Road in 2000 and 2010.

Most of shops on Randwick Road in 2000 were the same ten years later. But some shops were smaller, and two shop had closed. In staid childcare centre and pharmacy opened. Food shops in 2010 were twice than 2000.

In 2000, there were eight shops. The largest shop was the charity shop. In 2010, there were ten shops, and the charity shop moved across the road into a shop which was half-size. The newsagent, in 2000 was quite large, but had down size in 2010 maybe because everyone have Internet and read newspapers online. A childcare centre and pharmacy opened in 2010 that didn't exit before.

The pets shop and the bakery were exactly the same in 2010 as 2000. The Thai restaurant was different, now North Indian, and Brazilian restaurant had overtaken shoe shop. There was organic grocery shop in stade of video shop.

In conclusion, there were many changes on Randwick Road between 2000 and 2010 especialy the parking. (**172 words**)

C Re: Alterred commercial arrangements on Randwick Road 2000 and 2010

In general, slightly more than half (5 out of 9) of the shops on Randwick Road in 2000 were existing the same ten years later. However, some shops were reduce in size, and two close completely. A new childcare centre and pharmacy appeared, doubtless because the demography was changed. The number of food stores was increasing substantively, in fact by 100 per cent. Significantly, in 2000, parking was permitted on both sides of Randwick Road, but by 2010 was being restricted to one side from 10 AM until 3 PM, and forbiden on the other, where a bus stop added. The era of public transportation has surely arrived in this municipality.

In 2000, there were eight business, the largest was charity shop. In 2010, there were ten business, and the charity shop had relocated to a smaller space, commensurate with it's reduced status. The newsagent, the second largest shop in 2000, had fined down it's dimensions by fifty per cent by 2010. A childcare centre had occupied the premise of the old charity shop, and a pharmacy thrown open it's doors in the one sight that was being empty in 2000.

The bakery was remaning in stasis same in 2010 as a decade prior. The Thai restaurant had convert its culinary style to North Indian, since food from Srinagar is notoriously yummy, and a Brazilian restaurant had superseeded the shoe shop. An organic grocery had replaced the video shop. **(249 words)**

Strategies for improvement

Match the strategies below with the candidates above.

1 = ___: It seems you've been working in an English-speaking environment for some time to have picked up some useful language. However, your vocabulary is a strange mix of overly formal ('commensurate with', 'prior' & 'in stasis') and informal ('fined down', 'thrown open its doors' & 'yummy'), which alienates a reader. Your spelling needs attention. (See the highlighted words.) Your overdependence on the present continuous is a significant problem. Consult a good grammar book for when the simple is needed – it is far more frequent than the continuous. It is inappropriate to start this task with a subject line, 'Re:...'. You've also written more than is necessary; writing a longer IELTS task does not guarantee a higher score! It might be an idea to find a private tutor who could draw your attention to these problems, which prevent you from getting a Seven.

2 = ___: You have a lot of work to do before your English is good enough for post-graduate study or immigration. There is not one correct sentence in your writing, so you need to focus on grammar. Your spelling and punctuation are poor, which makes reading difficult. You need to improve all aspects of General English before you think about taking the IELTS exam again.

3 = ___: Your writing is mid-level, but it will be some time before you reach a Seven unless you work intensively. Your grammatical accuracy is variable, and your vocabulary is a little basic ('large', 'small', 'open', and 'close') or repetitive ('shop' and 'same'). More sophisticated language is not quite correct ('down size' should be 'downsized'; 'overtaken' should be 'taken over'). Extensive reading will expose you to vocabulary, and working through grammar exercises related to verbs will help.

What happens in the Speaking test?

YOUR TURN *Match the items in the boxes with the numbered blanks in the text below. Write the numbers in the spaces provided. There are examples.*

eg					
14	25	abstract	change	followed	functions

				eg	
judge	personal	two	unfriendly	up	will

The Speaking test is the last part of IELTS. It takes between 11 to –eg– minutes. During this time, an examiner asks a candidate about –1– questions. The examiner may seem a little –2– because he or she does not give any opinions or encouragement.

There are three parts to Speaking. Part 1 deals with –3– questions – where you live, what you do – plus two short familiar topics. In Part 2, the candidate speaks on one topic that the examiner chooses for –4– minutes. That's around 350 words. In the last part, the examiner asks questions related to the Part 2 topic. These are no longer about the candidate but about the world beyond. Since these questions are more –5–, they are more difficult.

The examiner asks questions from a script for Parts 1 and 2, but makes –eg– the questions based on general ideas in Part 3. For example, a Part 1 question written in the script for the examiner might be: 'Where is your home town?', or: 'Do you like sport?' In Part 3, the examiner is interested in language –6–, or the ideas behind words. One function might be: suggestion. The examiner's information is: (*Suggest*) *how urban sprawl could be controlled*. The examiner will –7– this into a question like: 'What are some ways land in cities might be used so that cities don't keep growing?' Or, for: (*Speculate*) *on the development of mega-cities*, the examiner might ask: 'What do you think might happen in future: will there be more medium-sized cities, or more very, very big cities, like Shanghai?' This could be –8– up with: 'What are the advantages of extremely large cities?' or: 'What challenges do extremely large cities present for governments?'

Examiners do special training for the IELTS Speaking test. During this they learn how to ask easy questions in Part 3 for IELTS Fours and Fives, and harder ones for higher-level candidates. Because the examiner works at the candidate's level, it's quite hard for someone to –9– how well he or she did in the test.

If a candidate doesn't understand anything, he or she can ask the examiner to say the question in another way, or to explain an item of vocabulary. Naturally, candidates are nervous, and sometimes forget things. However, asking for these more than once in a test –10– affect a person's score.

How is the Speaking test marked?

There are three parts to the Speaking test, which are marked all together – not separately as the tasks are in Writing.

There are four criteria: Fluency and Coherence; Vocabulary; Grammar; and, Pronunciation.

Only the band (on the right) appears on a candidate's report. He or she doesn't know about the individual criteria.

MARKING CRITERIA AND SPEAKING BANDS

F&C	V	G	Pron	Band
7	7	7	6	6.5

F&C	V	G	Pron	Band
7	7	6	6	6.5

F&C	V	G	Pron	Band
7	6	6	6	6

F&C	V	G	Pron	Band
6	6	6	6	6

F&C	V	G	Pron	Band
5	6	6	6	5.5

F&C	V	G	Pron	Band
5	5	6	6	5.5

F&C	V	G	Pron	Band
5	5	5	6	5

F&C	V	G	Pron	Band
5	5	5	5	5

YOUR TURN   *Before you read about the four marking criteria, which statement on the left refers to which criterion? There is an example.*

	For this criterion, a candidate:	Fluency and Coherence	Vocabulary	Grammar	Pronunciation
Eg	Produces sounds the English way rather than the way of his or her first language				✓
1	Uses phrasal verbs				
2	Does not pause while looking for language				
3	Chunks words together				
4	Uses a range of tenses when telling a story				
5	Stresses syllables and words correctly				
6	Is confident with little words like articles, auxiliaries, and prepositions				
7	Does not translate idioms or proverbs from his or her own language				

Detailed information about the criteria

YOUR TURN *There are two words missing from the description of each criterion. Find them in the box below, and put them back into the text. Write them on the lines provided.*

> chunking complex hesitation modal overuse own precise style

Fluency and Coherence

The first criterion for Speaking is Fluency and Coherence. Here is a checklist of what an examiner is looking for.

Does the candidate:

- keep going without too much self-correction, _____, or slow speech?
- produce long answers which include complex sentences?
- use and not _____ linkers appropriate to speaking?
- give relevant and logical answers?

Grammar

Does the candidate:

- use a wide range of grammatical structures? (These include: complex verb phrases with _____ / passive verbs / adverbial modifiers, and complex noun phrases with suitable adjectives and determiners.)
- include a mix of simple, compound, and _____ sentences?
- show grammatical accuracy?

Vocabulary

Does the candidate:

- use a wide range of vocabulary?
- use _____ vocabulary, including topic-specific items, and less common phrasal verbs or other idioms?
- collocate naturally?
- form the correct parts of speech?
- have a sense of _____?

Pronunciation

Does the candidate:

- speak so that he / she can always be understood?
- have minimal interference from his / her _____ language?
- use appropriate pitch, intonation, word and sentence stress?
- separate grammatical words from content words by using weak forms and _____?

Comparing speakers

YOUR TURN   Jamila (a woman) and Michel (a man) have both taken an exam preparation course in London. Now, they're chatting after their real IELTS test.

> Play
> Audio **PLAY RECORDING 14.**

1   Who do you think is likely to score more in IELTS: Jamila or Michel? Why?

_____

> Play
> Audio **PLAY RECORDING 14 again** and answer the questions below.

Fluency and Coherence

2   Michel says he's a fluent speaker. Is this <u>true / not true</u>? Why?

_____

3   Michel's Speaking Part 2 topic was: 'A national celebration'. He talked about: 'A football match in his village'. How will this affect his score?

_____

4   Should a candidate ask an examiner to 'repeat' a question?

_____

Write the letters to complete the missing words.

5   Jamila is fairly fluent. She doesn't **hes** __ __ __ __ __. Rather than stopping when she doesn't know a word for a woman's job, Jamila describes the job. She keeps going.

6   Jamila uses chunking (words said together in groups). These include contractions. Examples of these are:

i _____   ii _____   iii _____

7   However, Jamila <u>doesn't</u> have many **w** __ __ __ forms of prepositions.

Vocabulary

8   Michel has *no* high-level vocabulary. What are four examples of Jamila's vocabulary that are quite good?

i _____   ii _____

iii _____   iv _____

9   Jamila makes a mistake with 'angry'. She should say: **ner** __ __ __ __.

Grammar

10 Both Michel and Jamila have numerous grammatical errors. Correct part of Michel's speech. There are at least <u>eight</u> mistakes.

Best part for me Speaking. I am very fluent. And good pronunciation.

English and French almost the same. My teacher has given me last

semester 90% for Speaking, so IELTS gonna be the same.

Pronunciation

11 Michel's main pronunciation problem is he speaks English as though it were French. He doesn't have consistent word stress, where one **syl __ __ __ __ __** in a word is stronger than the others.

12 Which consonant sounds, or phonemes, does Jamila have problems with throughout?

i _____   ii _____

When her cousin got married, Jamila went to the wedding. Jamila doesn't say 'wedding' but '**w __ __ ding**'. (Check this word in a dictionary.) Jamila is unsure about the vowel sound /___/.

What other problems with phonemes does Jamila have? _____

_____

13 Jamila gives stress to the second syllable of 'Le**ba**nese'. What should she do? _____

_____

14 Jamila also has some problems with **sent __ __ __ __** stress.

Other questions about the IELTS exam

15 Michel suggests note-taking during the Listening test. Is this good advice?

16 What do you think it means if a candidate finds there is not enough time to answer everything in the Reading test?

_____

17 How useful is Michel's cousin's strategy? _____

_____

18 To what extent is Jamila right about the Writing test that quality is more important than quantity?

_____

Here is the recording script:

Jamila	Hi Michel. How are you?	Line 1
Michel	Fine thanks, Jamila. Are you wait for the bus?	
Jamila	No. My brother's coming to pick up me, but he's late.	
Michel	What do you think about IELTS?	
Jamila	It was difficult.	5
Michel	What score you need?	
Jamila	Six. And you?	
Michel	Six and half.	
Jamila	That's hard to get, I hear.	
Michel	I think Speaking and Reading very easy,…but for Reading I just not have enough time.	10
Jamila	Oh? I finished; then I heard the lady – I forgot her job, the lady who controlled the test – say, 'You have five minutes left'.	
Michel	When she say that I just write B B B C in all space. My cousin tell to me this best strategy.	
Jamila	Have your cousin take IELTS?	15
Michel	Yes, in Madagascar, but he get five and half three time. Now he will try in India because he think exam more easy in India. What do you think?	
Jamila	I dunno. I understand it's the same exam everywhere. *(Jamila's phone rings, and she answers.)*	
Michel	…What language do you speak with your brother?	20
Jamila	Arabic. What's your first language?	
Michel	French. How about the Writing? How do you find the Writing?	
Jamila	That was very tough for me. I couldn't describe the process for make chocolate in Task 1. All I can think about is: I love chocolate. Next week the Valentine's Day.	
Michel	Well, Task 1 was…fine for me; I am study Engineer, but Task 2 – Oh my God! I have no idea – *absolument* – about 'the generation gap'. My grandfather, he live in Tanzania, and my…my grandmother in Espana. I am not care about any of old persons. I haven't time for counting all the words of my essay. It is really important to write 250?	25
Jamila	I'm not sure, Michel. Maybe it's quality; not quantity. You will have to ask our teacher in Wednesday. For me Listening was most hardly. I am very bad in spelling. 'C.O.L.L.E.G.E' or 'A.G.E' for 'college'. I don't know how many Cs or Ms are there in 'accommodation'. I have to guess most of last part with lecture.	30
Michel	Do you…Did you made notes on your test paper for Section Four?	
Jamila	No. Perhaps I should of did that.	35
Michel	Best part for me Speaking. I am very fluent. And good pronunciation. English and French almost the same. My teacher has given me last semester 90% for Speaking, so IELTS gonna be the same.	
Jamila	Some of question were challenging for me. The test seemed rather fast – just 12 minutes.	
Michel	Many of question was Yes or No. Too easy. And topic a little bit stupid: 'A national cele-bration you have gone to'. Do you think it is OK to ask examiner to repeat the question?	40

Jamila	Why not? Maybe you're angry; maybe you don't hear well.	
Michel	Maybe. What was your topic?	
Jamila	A wedding you have been to. That was lucky since my sister married with Lebanese man before two weeks.	45
Michel	I talk about . . . about football match in my village.	
Jamila	(*Her phone rings again.*) That's Nasser. I'm afraid I have to go now. See you on Wednesday.	
Michel	I am not come to class now I have done test. I will make application to university in Australia.	50
Jamila	Well, goodbye, then. All the best.	

Here are the answers to the questions about the conversation between Jamila and Michel.

1 Overall, Jamila is better than Michel at Speaking in three criteria: Fluency and Coherence, Vocabulary, and Grammar. Their Pronunciation is about the same. In terms of the rest of the test, it's hard to tell. However, Michel didn't finish the Reading, so he's <u>unlikely</u> to get a Six. He also may not have written enough words in the Writing. Jamila had difficulty with Section 4 of the Listening, so a Six will be her maximum. She was unsure how to describe the process in Task 1 of the Writing.

2 Not true. He hesitates and self-corrects quite a lot in lines 10, 27, 34, and 46.

3 Michel's Part 2 answer is off the topic in lines 40 and 41. He will go down in Coherence, part of the criterion: Fluency and Coherence.

4 It's fine to ask for clarification in the Speaking, especially when nervous. However, if a candidate does this more than once in a test, he or she loses marks for Fluency or Vocabulary.

　If a candidate asks an examiner to 'repeat' a question, the examiner will do just that: say exactly what was said before again. A better idea is to ask: 'Could you say that in another way?' or 'What does x mean?'

5 In general, Jamila doesn't **hesitate**. In lines 11-12, rather than stopping when she doesn't know the word for a woman's job, Jamila describes the job. She keeps going.

6 Jamila's speech is fluent where she uses chunking and contractions in lines 3, 9, 18, 21, 23, and 29.

7 However, Jamila doesn't have any **weak** forms of prepositions. 'To' in line 3, should be /tə/, not /tu:/ etc.

8 Examples of Jamila's vocabulary that is quite good are in: (i) line 3: 'pick up me' although it should be 'pick me up' (ii) line 23: 'tough' (iii) line 29: 'maybe it's quality, not quantity' (iv) line 39: 'challenging'

9 Jamila should say **nervous** instead of 'angry' in line 42.

10 *The* best part for me **was the** Speaking. *I'm* very fluent, **and have** good pronunciation. English and French **are** almost the same. My teacher **gave** me **90% last semester** for Speaking, so *IELTS'll be / IELTS* **should be** the same. ('Gonna' or 'going to' is for a plan, whereas this is a prediction.)

11 Michel's main pronunciation problem is he speaks English as though it were French. He doesn't have consistent word stress, where one **syllable** in a word is stronger than the others.

12 Jamila has problems with the consonant sounds /p/ and /tʃ/. (i) She says 'brocess' for 'process' in line 23, and 'bart' for 'part' in line 33. (ii) She says 'teasher' for 'teacher' in line 29; 'shallenging' for 'challenging' in line 39. She says 'shock-o-late' for 'chocolate' in line 23. (iii) She says '**weeding**' for 'wedding' in line 44. She is unsure of the vowel sound /e/. (iv) She over-emphasises the '-ing' suffix of present participles. The sound at the end of 'coming' is /ŋ/. (Michel also does this.) (v) Jamila rarely has a schwa /ə/ in unstressed syllables. In the word 'controlled' in line 11, she says /kɒn/ when she should say /kən/.

13 Jamila says 'Lebanese' with second-syllable stress (le-BA-nese), instead of final-syllable (le-ba-NESE).

14 She sometimes has strange **sentence** stress. When she says, 'A wedding you have been to', Jamila puts stress on 'to', when it should be on 'wedding'. When she says, 'That was lucky since my sister married with Lebanese man', she puts stress on 'since' when it should be on 'lucky'.

15 Michel's note-taking suggestion is excellent.

16 He or she is unlikely to get a Six in Reading. The test is designed for a Six to finish in time.

17 Michel's cousin's strategy is useful for low-level candidates. Never leave an IELTS question without an answer! However, IELTS is designed so that multi-choice answers in both the Listening and the Reading are *not* random. If there are 10 (the maximum number) MCQs in Listening, they are likely to be A x 4, B x 3, and C x 3; or, A x 3, B x 4, and C x 3; or, A x 3, B x 3, and C x 4. There won't be five Bs, for example. Check MCQ answers to the practice tests for this.

18 Jamila is mostly right that quality is more important than quantity in the Writing test. However, if a candidate writes fewer than 150 words, no matter how good, in Task 1, or fewer than 250 in Task 2, he or she will be penalised.

Speaking Taster (Buzzer) Test

Listen to a model IELTS Speaking test. It is complete, and rather typical.

After each question, there's a buzzer. When you hear this, pause the recording, and answer the question as you would in a real Speaking test. Continue with the next question. Don't stop to prepare for anything except for the Part 2 topic.

When the examiner says: 'You can make some notes if you wish', turn to page 401.

 PLAY RECORDING 15.

Fluency and Coherence

The first criterion for Speaking is Fluency and Coherence.

The main features of Fluency

These are:
1. speech rate
2. continuity

YOUR TURN *Fill in the missing words about Fluency. There is an example.*

1 *Speech rate* is how (eg) **_fast_** someone speaks. Generally, a Five speaks too slowly. A Six is better, but still unnatural. A Seven is closer to a native speaker although he or she may sometimes slow *d __ __ __*.

   If you think of this as the number of spoken words per minute (wpm), then aim for 150 words. On English-speaking *r __ __ __ __* and TV, newsreaders speak at 180 wpm.

   Speech rate means how quickly the speaker can form individual sounds, as well as how he or she uses **conn** __ __ __ __ __ speech. The individual sounds are called phonemes, which we'll look at in Pronunciation.

   Connected speech is many things. Here, our focus is on chunking and **rhy** __ __ __. (In Pronunciation, we'll examine word stress, sentence stress, and intonation.)

   Chunking is:

   - dividing speech into meaningful **gr** __ __ __ __ of words or chunks
   - pausing to add meaning, not because the speaker is searching for words.

   Rhythm is:

   - using stress timing (don't worry about this now)
   - producing weak forms (with /ə/ or /ɪ/ in the IPA)
   - **lin** __ __ __ __ words together. (Contractions, like 'I'm', 'it's', or 'doesn't', are important.)

2 *Continuity* is the ability to keep **g** __ __ __ __. Is the speech smooth and continuous, or are there too many **pau** __ __ __, hesitations, or self-corrections?

The main features of Coherence

YOUR TURN *The following headings have been removed from the text below. Put them back in.*

i *Logical order of sentences* ii *Cohesive devices* iii *Relevance of answers*
iv *Fillers* v *Discourse markers*

1 _____: Does the candidate understand the question, and give an answer related to it? Does the candidate give a memorised answer, which will lower his or her speaking band?

2 _____: Does the candidate present information in a way that is easy to follow and sensible?

3 _____ are little words and phrases that people use when they're thinking of an answer. For example: 'well,' at the beginning of a sentence, or 'sort of', or 'if you know what I mean'. They're correct, and natural, but a candidate <u>cannot</u> get a Seven when there are too many of these.

4 _____ show the stages of a discussion. There are many kinds of these like: 'first of all', or 'generally speaking', or 'I'm afraid'. A candidate needs to know which of these to use in speaking, and which in writing. Many Fives overuse discourse

markers, possibly starting each sentence with one. The difference between a Six and a Seven is that a Seven uses markers that are more interesting.

5 _____, like pronouns and conjunctions, join phrases or sentences, for instance: 'which', 'this', 'it', 'because', and 'and'. Having too few or being repetitive limits a candidate to a Five.

Identifying Coherence

Now we're going to analyse some answers for Coherence from Part 1 of the Speaking test. For this exercise, the candidates don't have mistakes with grammar or vocabulary. We don't know how fluent they are or what their pronunciation is like because there's no recording. Our interest is *only* in understanding Coherence.

Examiner   First of all, I'd like to ask you some questions about yourself.
                  Let's talk about your home town. Where is your home town?

Candidate A   My home town is Pusan in the south of Korea.

Examiner   What do you like most about your home town?

Candidate A   Firstly, my home town is very beautiful. Secondly, the people are friendly in my home town. However, my home town has lots of factories and pollution.

Here are the problems that Candidate A has. Can you see why?

	Relevance	Logic	Fillers	Discourse markers	Cohesive devices
Candidate A		X		X	X

Examiner   First of all, I'd like to ask you some questions about yourself.
                  Let's talk about your home. Do you live in a house or an apartment?

Candidate B   An apartment.

Examiner   Which is your favourite room in your apartment?

Candidate B   Well, I think the kitchen is kind of my favourite room although my family has dinner there every night. Actually, it's a big room. My family is very rich because my father is a businessman.

Here are the problems that Candidate B has. Can you see why?

	Relevance	Logic	Fillers	Discourse markers	Cohesive devices
Candidate B	X		X		X

Here is candidate A after improvement. The order has been changed to make it more logical. 'Firstly' and 'secondly', which are better in writing, have been removed. Other cohesive words like 'there' and 'it' now refer to 'home town'. 'Unfortunately' has been added for emphasis.

Candidate A

Examiner   First of all, I'd like to ask you some questions about yourself.
                  Let's talk about your home town. Where is your home town?

Candidate A   It's Pusan, in the south of Korea.

Examiner   What do you like most about your home town?

Candidate A	The people are friendly there, and it's a beautiful place. However, unfortunately, there's a lot of pollution from factories.

Here is Candidate B. It's not relevant to tell the examiner about your father's job here. It's better to say 'quite well off' than 'rich'. 'I think', 'kind of', and 'actually' have been removed; there shouldn't be fillers in a short answer.

Candidate B

Examiner	First of all, I'd like to ask you some questions about yourself. Let's talk about your home. Do you live in a house or an apartment?
Candidate B	An apartment.
Examiner	Which is your favourite room in your apartment?
Candidate B	Well, the kitchen's my favourite room because we have dinner there every night together. It's a big room since my family's quite well off.

YOUR TURN	*For candidates C and D, study the table of Coherence problems, and reduce the candidates' answers. Use as many contractions as possible.*

	Relevance	Logic	Fillers	Discourse markers
Candidate C		X	X	X
D	X			X

Candidate C

Examiner	First of all, I'd like to ask you some questions about yourself. At the moment, are you working or studying?
Candidate C	I'm a student.
Examiner	What subject are you studying?
Candidate C	Mechanical Engineering.
Examiner	What do you find difficult about this subject?
Candidate C	That is an interesting question. Well, firstly, I did not study a lot of maths in my country. Secondly, I have a part-time job.
Examiner	What do you find difficult about this subject? (Rewrite the candidate's answer above.)
Candidate C	

Candidate D

Examiner	First of all, I'd like to ask you some questions about yourself. At the moment, are you working or studying?
Candidate D	I'm working.

Examiner	What sort of job do you do?
Candidate D	I'm an assistant nurse.
Examiner	What do you find difficult about your job?
Candidate D	The hospital is close to my home, and the doctors are really nice. In addition, I like to make people happy and healthy.
Examiner	What do you find difficult about your job? (Rewrite the candidate's answer above.)
Candidate D	

IF YOU WANT A SEVEN

Here is a Speaking Part 3 answer with Coherence problems underlined. We aren't listening to this speaker, so we don't know how fast he speaks, or what his connected speech is like. We can't hear his pronunciation either. His grammar and vocabulary are perfect just for this exercise, but in reality they would contain errors.

Examiner	We've been talking about a toy you remember from childhood. Now, I'd like to discuss some more general questions related to this. First of all, in your country what are some different toys for boys and girls?
Candidate	Umm. I think boys are more active than girls. Boys-boys like to play sport especially football although football-basketball. Now they play basketball. They also play computer games.
Examiner	What about girls?
Candidate	Girls? Let me see. Girls like chatting and cooking.
Examiner	Do you think children these days have too many toys?
Candidate	No.
Examiner	What toys from the past are still played with today, and which ones do you think might be popular in future?
Candidate	Actually, I have never thought about that question before. Well, I think my father played football, and um maybe my son will play football. Computers will be popular, but the games will be more advanced. But computer games are bad for children's eyes.
Examiner	Now let's consider the toy industry, and advertising in particular. How much advertising is there for toys on TV in your country?
Candidate	I do not know because I do not watch TV for children.
Examiner	What do you think about advertising that's targeted towards children?
Candidate	Actually, the biggest problem is fast food. As we all know fast food contains a lot of fat and sugar. In addition, sugar and fat can make you fat. Nowadays, too many children eat McDonald's because it is delicious. Moreover they want to eat it, but it is bad for their health.
Examiner	What about the advertising of fast food that's directed specifically at children?

Candidate	Well, I'm not sure about that. The companies that produce fast food want to make-make…what do you say?… profits. Furthermore, they need to advertise. It is part of their marketing plan. I studied Marketing at university. You must have P, P, P: Price, Product, and Posit–
Examiner	Let's go back to advertising directed towards children. How might their parents feel about it?
Candidate	I do not have children, so I am not sure.

Put the words and phrases below into the numbered blanks in the examiner's report. There is an example.

> Barbie   chatting   contractions   contradicts   discourse markers   fillers
> Five   ~~games and sport~~   irrelevant   memorised   targeted advertising

This candidate has poor Fluency because he talks about (eg) *games and sport* not toys. He says nothing about girls except that they like (1) _____ and cooking. Cooking is an activity, not a game or a toy. If he wants to talk about cooking as part of play, he needs to mention 'toy tea sets', or 'toy pots and pans', or 'toy stoves' etc. I'm sure he's heard of (2) _____ and some other dolls girls like to play with! His answer about whether children have too many toys is just 'No'. He has no idea about TV advertising for toys, which is unlikely, and then he gives a long, possibly (3) _____, speech about fast food. He (4) _____ himself by suggesting that children are affected by fast food ads, but it's OK for the producers to screen them. If he's studied Marketing, then he should have more to say on the subject of (5) _____. When the examiner interrupts him because his answer is (6) _____, and asks the question a second time, the candidate can only think about himself. This shows he doesn't have the English language for abstract ideas.

The candidate wrongly uses some (7) _____, like 'moreover' and 'furthermore'. He has too many (8) _____, and too much hesitation and self-correction. He doesn't use many (9) _____, so he sounds a bit angry.

All of this is like a (10) _____.

Identifying Fluency

Chunking

Read the text about Chunking and Rhythm below. Then answer the questions that follow.

A speaker puts words into chunks, or small groups, to make it easier for the listener to understand. In fact, when words are said <u>separately</u>, it shows that a speaker is angry.

Some students don't believe a teacher who says it's more important to chunk than to say each word clearly. In fact, it's WRONG to say each word clearly.

Let's look at the first sentence above, and see where the chunks are.

'A-speaker / puts-words / into-chunks / to-make-it-easier / for-the-listener / to-w-understand.' (For linking, we need to add /w/ between the vowel sounds of /u:/ and /ʌ/.)

There are six chunks here. One word in each chunk will have more stress or force or loudness than the others. Basically: 'speaker-words-chunks-easier-listener-understand'. You'll notice that these are lexical or content words, not grammatical words. With this information alone, we know what the speaker means.

Sentence stress

In the whole sentence, there might be a few more strongly stressed words, perhaps: 'chunks-easier-understand'. After each of these, there's a short pause so the listener can process the most important words. These deliberate pauses also improve understanding; they're not there because the speaker is having trouble finding the right vocabulary.

Rhythm

Stress timing

If English is compared to French, English is said to be a stress-timed language because at least one syllable is stressed, being louder, longer, or higher pitched than the others in each word. In French, for example, the syllables are given equal stress, and it's called a syllable-timed language. If a speaker has French as a first language, he or she needs to pay particular attention to this feature in English.

Weak forms

These are words, in the table on page 187, that contain the schwa, or /ə/, or /ɪ/ as their vowel sound. They are all grammatical words. The words exist in strong forms as well, mostly used at the end of sentences or before vowel sounds.

Let's take the preposition 'for'. It is mostly weak, and pronounced /fə/, not /fɔ:/, like the number four. Only at the end of a sentence does it sound like the number. Often 'for' almost disappears, as in 'My city's famous fritz beaches'. Remember: 'Famous Fritz'.

Linking is when sounds disappear (*elision* is the technical term for this). In the phrase: 'her afternoon tea', we hear the /r/ in 'her'; but, in the phrase 'her morning tea', we don't. In the sentence, 'I can't do it', we lose the /t/ at the end of 'can't'. Sometimes, sounds are added, as in: 'I agree'. There's a /j/ between the words, so the two words sound like the single word 'Iyagree'. With 'to understand', there's a /w/ between the vowels. (*Intrusion* is the technical term.) Some final sounds also change: the 't' at the end of 'that' in 'that cat', becomes a /k/ sound. (*Assimilation* is the term for this.)

Contractions are part of linking. They are two words said (or written) as one.

On page 188, there is a list of nearly all the contractions you'll need for IELTS Speaking. (None in your writing, please.) Learn the correct pronunciation of each one. If a candidate does not use contractions, he or she sounds too formal or rude. Without contractions, a candidate stays at a Five.

Continuity is how much extra pausing, hesitation, or self-correction there is. It's also how willing a candidate is to give a longer answer. Sometimes short answers are fine, especially in Part 1. In fact, longer answers may be inappropriate.

YOUR TURN   *The following statements refer to the text that you have just read. Mark each one as True (T), False (F), or Not Given (NG). Underline your evidence in the text. There is an example.*

Eg   Saying each word separately and clearly shows good fluency. *F*

1   Pausing means a person is not fluent. ____

2   French pronunciation is more difficult than English. ____

3   Content words can be both strong and weak. ____

4   Sometimes, in linking, sounds are added between words. ____

5   Without contractions, a person may sound impolite. ____

6   A candidate who can keep on talking when appropriate has good fluency. ____

Weak forms and Contractions

Study the tables that follow. To get a Seven, you need to use all these forms.

WEAK FORMS

Verbs – mostly auxiliary	Prepositions or particles	Articles	Other
be /bɪ/ is /z/ are /ə/ was /wz/ were /wə/ been /bɪn/ has /z/ have /v/ had /d/ do /d/ does /dz/ can /kn/ could /kd/ should /ʃd/ would /wd/ going to /gənə/	to (always weak before a consonant sound) /tə/ at for from in of with	a /ə/ an /n/ the (always weak before a consonant) /ðə/ some ('some time', 'some people' = weak /sm/. 'some do' = strong /sʌm/)	and /n/ (eg: in a list, 'milk and honey') but /bt/ (not 'butt' as in 'cigarette butt' /bʌt/) me /mɪ/, you /jɪ/, he, she, we, us, them, my his her their that which than /ðn/ (this doesn't sound like 'man') as ('as big as' = weak /z/. 'As I said before' = strong /æz/)

YOUR TURN   *There are 10 missing contractions. What are they? Write them in the spaces provided. There is an example.*

CONTRACTIONS

		I	you	he	she	it	we	they	Other
Positive									
To be		I'm (a student) (sure) (trying)	**(eg)** *you're*	he's	**(1)** _____	it's	we're	they're	(t)here's mine's
The auxiliary 'have'		**(2)** _____ (been)	you've	he's	she's	it's	we've	**(3)** _____	someone's no one's anyone's everyone's
The auxiliary 'will'		I'll (see)	you'll	**(4)** _____	she'll	it'll	we'll	they'll	this'll
The auxiliary 'would'		**(5)** _____ (like)	you'd	he'd	she'd	**(6)** _____	we'd	they'd	that'd
'Have' as a second auxiliary verb		I may've (heard)	you might've (visited)	she would've (gone) / she wouldn't've (gone) (*only spoken, not written*) it could've (been) / it couldn't've (been) it should've (happened) / it shouldn't've (happened) they ought to've (taken) / he will've (been)					
Negative									
To be		I'm not (going) you're not/you aren't	he/she/it isn't (happy) there isn't (time)				we/they aren't (feeling)		
The auxiliary 'have'		I/you haven't (got)	he/she/it hasn't (been)				we/they **(7)** _____ (done)		
The auxiliary 'do'		I **(8)** _____ (believe) you **(8)** _____ (want)	he/she/it doesn't (seem)				we/they don't (imagine)		
The auxiliary 'can'		I/you/he/she/it/we/they/there can't (be)							
The auxiliary 'could'		I/you/he/she/it/we/they/there couldn't (be)							
The auxiliary 'will'		I/you/he/she/it/we/they/there **(9)** _____ (be)							
The auxiliary 'would'		I/you/he/she/it/we/they/there **(10)** _____ (be)							
The auxiliary 'should'		I/you/he/she/it/we/they/there shouldn't (be)							

When are short answers appropriate in the IELTS Speaking test?

Read the dialogue at the very beginning of the IELTS Speaking test. Look at the long and short answers.

This short answer is fine ✓
This answer is <u>too</u> long x

Examiner	Could you tell me your full name, please?	
Candidate	Pang Xiao Shun, but you can call me Teresa. This is the name my boyfriend —	x
Examiner	And where are you from?	
Candidate	I am from the south of China, from Fujian Province, an ancient coastal city called Zhenzhou, which is famous for its tea and —	x
Examiner	Could I have a look at your passport, please?	
Candidate	Certainly.	✓

It's not necessary to give extra information at the start of the test, and if it's memorised the examiner will probably interrupt.

By the way: if the candidate is taking the exam in China, a natural answer here is 'Zhenzhou' only. If the candidate is taking the exam in another country, a suitable answer is 'Zhenzhou, a city in the south of China'. That's enough.

YOUR TURN   *Read a Part 1 dialogue that could follow the one above. Which <u>two</u> short answers are fine?*

This short answer is fine ✓
This answer is <u>too</u> long x

Examiner	First of all, I'd like to ask you a few questions about yourself. At the moment, are you working or studying?
Candidate	I'm a student.
Examiner	Where are you studying?
Candidate	At a college.
Examiner	Why did you choose this college?
Candidate	I didn't.
Examiner	What do you like about your college?
Candidate	I have some new friends.
Examiner	Do many people from your country choose the same subject that you're studying?
Candidate	Yes.
Examiner	Why?
Candidate	I have no idea.

Remember, if you give an answer that's too long, the examiner will stop you. If it's too short, then you won't score well in Fluency, Vocabulary, or Grammar.

Here is another Part 1 dialogue. Extend the answers (x) that are too short.

Examiner	Now, I'd like to talk about music. Do you like music?	
Candidate	Yes, I do.	✓
Examiner	Why?	
Candidate	It is relaxing.	x
Examiner	Did you study music at school?	
Candidate	No.	x
Examiner	Do you think every child should learn to play a musical instrument?	
Candidate	No, I don't.	✓
Examiner	Why not?	
Candidate	Because not everyone is interested.	x

Go to page 388 for a possible answer.

Long and short sentence types

We've seen that to keep going, answers should be long where necessary. The best way to do this is to include more compound and complex sentences. (See pages 285-286.)

The IPA

Have you ever studied the International Phonetic Alphabet or IPA? There's an example of this on page 214. Refer to the IPA when you do the following exercises.

Unscramble this very important sentence.

need to ~~get~~ you the Seven know ~~to~~ a IPA

To get _____.

YOUR TURN   *Let's listen to an IELTS Nine candidate in Speaking Part 1. The first time you listen, just enjoy the dialogue.*

 PLAY RECORDING 16.

Now write down exactly what the examiner says at the start. Each line on the following page is for one word. A contraction = one word. You may need to play this recording three or four times.

 PLAY RECORDING 17.

Examiner _____ _____ _____ _____

_____ _____ _____ _____.

_____ _____ _____ _____

_____ _____ _____ _____

_____ _____ _____ _____.

This time, write down exactly what the candidate says. You may need to play this recording three or four times.

 PLAY RECORDING 18.

Candidate _____ _____ _____ _____

_____, _____ _____ _____

_____ _____ _____ _____.

_____ _____ _____, _____

_____ _____ _____ _____

_____ _____ _____.

Can you hear the chunking and rhythm? Words that are written as two are often joined together and spoken as one, eg: 'There are' sounds like 'thera'; 'made a lion' sounds like 'maidalion'. This exercise shows a major difference between writing and speaking. Although we write each word separately, we say them in chunks.

Now, let's listen to some more of the candidate's answer. The weak forms are highlighted in grey. Slashes (/ and //) show chunks. **Bold** words are stressed.

 PLAY RECORDING 19.

Candidate . . . Then, / in **sixth** class / I was part of a group / that made a **model** / of an **ancient city**. // It was **pretty good**. // My **father** / took us to the **site** / where the **archaeologists** were **working**, / so we could **imagine** / what our **model'd** be like.

The grey words, above, are all grammatical words, and many of them are in the table on page 187.

Play Recording 19 several times, saying the chunks after the speaker.

Listen for the stressed words and the chunks once more in Recording 20.

PLAY RECORDING 20.

Weak forms

YOUR TURN   *Let's see now if you can guess when the word 'the' will be weak or strong. Mark (W) when it's weak / θə /, or (S) when it's strong /θiː/.*

 PLAY RECORDING 21.

Eg   'My father took us to <u>the</u> site where <u>the</u> archaeologists were working.'
                                    W   S

1   'I listen to my iPod on <u>the</u> way to work, which makes <u>the</u> journey go faster.'

2   '<u>The</u> only thing I like about my college is <u>the</u> friends I've made.'

What is the pattern?
Can you hear how /j/ is added to link 'my-j-iPod', and when 'the' is strong in sentence 2? Play Recording 21 again, and practise saying these sentences yourself after each speaker. Another way of thinking about this is: which content words are stressed?

'My **father** took us to the **site** where the **archaeologists** were **working**.'

'I listen to my **iPod** on the **way** to **work**, which makes the **journey** go **faster**.'

'The **only** thing I like about my **college** is the **friends** I've made.'

Now, let's listen to some prepositions. Mark each one as weak (W) or strong (S).

PLAY RECORDING 22.

Eg   'Who do you work <u>for</u>?'
                              S

   'I work <u>for</u> myself.'
              W

1   'Where do you come <u>from</u>?'

   'I come <u>from</u> the south of China.'

2   'Zhenzhou is famous <u>for</u> its tea.'

3   'I made a lion mask <u>for</u> a play that we put on.'

4   'What are you looking <u>at</u>?'

5   'I'm studying <u>at</u> a college in the city.'

6   'I listen <u>to</u> my iPod on the way <u>to</u> work.'

7   'I'd like <u>to</u> apply <u>for</u> another job.'

What is the pattern?

Can you hear the /w/ for linking in sentence 7? Did you hear 'fra-nother'?

The verbs 'are', 'was', and 'were' are weak. Other forms of 'to be' are usually contracted.

Mark (W), when the forms of 'to be' are weak, or (S) when they're strong.

 PLAY RECORDING 23.

1 'Do you think children these days <u>are</u> better educated than 20 years ago?'

'Yes, I think they <u>are</u>.'

2 'I didn't make many things, but there <u>are</u> two I remember well.'

3 'I <u>was</u> part of a group that made a model of an ancient city.'

4 'My father took us to the site where the archaeologists <u>were</u> working.'

Unless it's at the end of a sentence, 'are' is <u>not</u> said like the letter 'R', but like the article 'a'. It's a schwa. 'Were' does not sound like 'word' because it's also a schwa. It's pronounced /wə/.

The verb 'going to' is almost always weak. It can be said 'gonna' or 'going ta'. If there is the verb 'going' and the preposition 'to', then it can't be 'gonna', but 'going ta' is possible unless a vowel sound follows. There is only one strong form of 'going to' here. Can you find it before you listen?

Practise saying the sentences after the speakers.

PLAY RECORDING 24.

1 'I'm <u>going</u> to be a radiographer. I've done my first two years of study.'

2 'My brother's <u>going</u> to organise my graduation party.'

3 'My sister's <u>going</u> to have a baby in two weeks' time. I'm really excited.'

4 'My parents are <u>going</u> to Europe for a holiday.'

5 'My uncle who's a banker says there's <u>going</u> to be another financial crash.'

Chunking

YOUR TURN   *Listen to two speakers saying the same sentences. Whose chunking is better? The examiner has asked the question: 'Tell me about a wedding you've been to.'*

PLAY RECORDING 25.

1 A / B   **2** A / B   **3** A / B   **4** A / B

Natural or unnatural? Listen to eight more speakers, and decide who is natural (N) with good fluency, or unnatural (U).

PLAY RECORDING 26.

	N	U	Why is the speaker unnatural or not fluent? Possible reasons are: *hesitation, self-correction, slow speech, strange chunking, no weak forms, and/or no contractions.*
1			
2			
3			
4			
5			
6			
7			
8			

Now, say the natural ones after each speaker.

PLAY RECORDING 27.

The unnatural ones are now natural. Say them after each speaker.

PLAY RECORDING 28.

Longer Part 1 answers

Listen to this Part 1 dialogue. Write down exactly what the examiner says.

PLAY RECORDING 29.

Examiner _____

_____

Candidate _____

_____

_____

_____

Examiner Have you ever played sport?

Candidate _____

_____

_____

_____

How might you answer these questions?

PLAY RECORDING 29 again.

Write down exactly what the candidate says.

The candidate makes five contractions. Did you find them? Can you also hear the rhythm and chunking?

PLAY RECORDING 29 once more, and practise by saying the sentences.

IF YOU WANT A SEVEN

Write down exactly what the examiner says.

PLAY RECORDING 30.

Examiner _____

_____

Candidate _____

_____

_____

Examiner   What do people like about the sea?

Candidate   _____

_____

_____

_____

How might you answer the questions above?

 PLAY RECORDING 30 again.

Write down exactly what the candidate says.

In the speech of both the examiner and the candidate, find six contractions, and underline all the weak forms.

Fluency in Part 2

In Part 2 of the Speaking test, the examiner chooses a topic for the candidate to speak on for two minutes. (Remember, that's around 350 words!) The candidate has one minute to think about the topic before speaking.

YOUR TURN	_Below, there are no mistakes in vocabulary, so don't change this. However, you'll need to make some longer, compound or complex, sentences. (The ones to improve are in **bold**.) Then, you'll need to make 10 contractions._

Examiner   Remember, you've only got two minutes for this, so don't worry if I stop you, I'll tell you when your time's up.

Candidate   I am going to tell you about something I had to save money to buy. It is a car. **This car is an old VW. I bought it from a classmate**. It is about **fifty years old. I love it**. It is quite reliable, and it does not use too much gas. Plus I think the design is nice. It is turquoise, and **it has got a soft top. You can roll down this top when it is a fine day.**

I went for a trip with my classmate in this car, and I loved it. A few months later, he had to go back **to Egypt. He comes from Egypt.** He desperately needed some money. I could not afford to buy the car, so he left it with **his uncle. I paid his uncle** each week until it was enough. At one point, the uncle got mad, and asked for all the rest of the **money. I** had to work overtime at my job as well as study full time to find the money. That is not easy. Anyway, it was worth it in the end. My girlfriend loves the car. In fact, I think all girls do.

The answer above is 190 words, just over a minute long. To make sure the candidate reaches two minutes, the examiner will ask: 'Can you tell me anything more about that?'

 PLAY RECORDING 31 for one possible answer.

You might like to practise saying this speech.

Assessing candidates

YOUR TURN   *Listen to a candidate. Mark the letter below that you think describes her Fluency and Coherence.*

 PLAY RECORDING 32.

A = _____
This speaker is usually able to keep going but often repeats or corrects himself or herself. He or she speaks quite slowly. Hesitations in the middle of sentences are to remember basic vocabulary. There is overuse of a few discourse markers. Producing complex grammar take several attempts, which may never be successful.
B = _____
This speaker talks for a long time on every question without any effort that the examiner notices. There are only occasional moments of hesitation and self-correction, which do not affect coherence.
C = _____
This candidate talks for a long time on almost every question although coherence is sometimes lost. Discourse markers are used, but may be repetitive or wrong.

If the woman you have just listened to is a Six for Fluency and Coherence, which letter above is a Seven, and, which is a Five?

Strategies for improvement

Copy the IELTS Speaking Log on page 445, and fill it in.

When you listen to people who are better than you speaking English, especially on the radio or TV, be aware of their fluency and coherence.

Make a conscious effort when speaking to chunk, contract, speed up, and keep going.

The best thing to do to prepare for the IELTS test is to record yourself speaking on any topic. The first time, do this for 30 seconds, then one minute, and finally two minutes. Listen to your speech as though you were an examiner.

There are lots of good books and websites on pronunciation. They discuss fluency and coherence as 'suprasegmental features'. Remember, any research you do in English will also improve your IELTS Reading score.

Summary of Fluency and Coherence

Listen to the recording, and complete the missing words. There is an example.

 PLAY RECORDING 33.

In this section, we've learnt that Fluency is how (eg) *fast* a candidate speaks, and how easily

he or she can keep **g** _____. Also, are the answers **l** _____ enough? A candi-

date's speed is determined by rhythm and **c** _____, or saying words in **g** _____.

Rhythm is separating **c** _____ from grammar words by using stress and **w** _____ forms. **C** _____ are also necessary.

Coherence is the **k** _____ of answer a candidate gives. Is it relevant and **l** _____? Does it have suitable discourse **m** _____ and connectors?

Spoken vocabulary and grammar

We have looked at Fluency and Coherence and Pronunciation. The two remaining Speaking criteria are Vocabulary and Grammar.

In many ways, vocabulary and grammar are similar in IELTS Speaking and Writing tests. Candidates need to produce varied, precise, and accurate language.

However, *informal* English is used in the Speaking test, while relatively *formal* language is needed in the Writing. (Only General Training Task 1 letters may sometimes be informal.)

IELTS candidates who have a strange mix of formal and informal language do *not* get above a Six in Speaking.

Other books or websites deal with this topic under the headings of *tone* or *register*.

Vocabulary in spoken and written English

YOUR TURN   *Read the statements below. Mark each one as True (T) or False (F).*

1 Contractions like 'I've' and 'it's' should be avoided in IELTS Speaking. _____

2 The verb 'get' is generally a spoken verb. _____

3 Phrasal verbs are equally common in speaking and writing. _____

4 In English essays or formal lectures (Listening Section 4), a person uses more nouns, especially abstract nouns, than in conversation. _____

5 Words are generally shorter in speaking than in writing. _____

6 This vocabulary may be used in IELTS Speaking: 'lots of', 'lovely', 'cool', 'kids', and 'uni'. _____

Grammar in spoken and written English

7 Short answers, like: 'Not really.', or 'Swimming at the weekend.', which do not contain a subject or complete verb, are unacceptable in IELTS Speaking. _____

8 Written English tends to have more compound and complex sentences. These are longer than the simple sentences that are used in speaking. _____

9 The passive is preferred in academic writing; active structures are more frequent in speaking. _____

10 A person may often use simple linkers like 'and' or 'but' in spoken English. _____

11 Sentences may end with prepositions in both spoken and written English. _____

12 In general, an examiner is less likely to notice lexical or grammatical errors in the Speaking test because it goes so fast. _____

Collocation and idiom

Before we go on, we need to consider two extremely important aspects of vocabulary: collocation and idiom. While collocation exists as much in writing as speaking, idiom is more common and colourful in speaking.

In the IELTS marking scheme (the Vocabulary criterion for Speaking), the collocation of a Seven is almost always correct. Also, he or she comfortably uses idiomatic language.

What is collocation?

English is heavily dependent on collocation. In the previous sentence, the adverb *heavily* goes together with *dependent*. We can't say *greatly dependent* although *very dependent* is possible. *Dependent* is followed by the preposition *on*, not *in*, or *at*, or anything else. Therefore, *dependent* collocates with *heavily* and *on*. They're married, if you like.

Since these collocations aren't really logical, they're not so easy to learn.

See page 261 in Vocabulary for more on this.

YOUR TURN   *Choose the correct collocations below. Circle the letter of your choice.*

1   'I _____ a mistake living so far away from my job.'

    a. did   **b.** made

2&3   'I think the number of children a family (2) _____ should be (3) _____.'

    2 a. has   **b.** produces

    3 a. controlled   **b.** limited

4&5   'I often (4) _____ with friends (5) _____ Friday night.'

    4 a. connect   **b.** get together

    5 a. in   **b.** on

6   'My cousin's married _____ a Nigerian.'

    a. to   **b.** with

7   'The furniture I've chosen is _____.'

    a. contemporary   **b.** modern

8   'There are _____ resources in this region.'

    a. dwindling   **b.** reduced

9   'I'm a(n) _____ child.'

    a. only   **b.** single

10   'It's pretty hard being a _____ parent.'

    a. solo   **b.** solitary

What is idiomatic language?

It is words and phrases whose meaning is somehow unpredictable.

Literal language, the opposite of idiomatic, is clear, predictable. If I say, 'I picked up some money from the road.', a language learner can look up the single verb *pick* in a dictionary and the single adverb *up*, and understand what I did with the money.

An idiom, however, is where the separate meanings of the words do <u>not</u> combine to make up the complete meaning, so they're unpredictable. Here's an idiomatic use of the verb *pick up*. If I say, 'I picked up some Russian while I was living in Moscow.' this means: I learnt some

Russian language without studying. However, a second idiomatic meaning of *pick up* is: to meet a person with the aim of having a sexual relationship, so 'I picked up **a** Russian.' could mean: I went to a bar, met a Russian, and brought him back to my place....Phrasal verbs usually have one literal meaning and multiple idiomatic meanings.

Idioms can be just a single word, like the colour *blue*. If I say, 'Cloudy weather makes me feel blue.' it means: 'Cloudy weather makes me a little depressed.'

Here's another common idiom: 'My sister and I just don't see eye to eye.' It means: we seldom agree.

Idiom is a fascinating part of English vocabulary, and any research you do will increase your IELTS score.

YOUR TURN   *What is the meaning of the underlined words and phrases?*

1&2   'I love my dog, but (1) I'm afraid he's a bit (2) thick.'

1 a. I'm scared   **b.** I'm going to say something negative

2 a. stupid   **b.** overweight

3   'Thank you from the bottom of my heart.'

a. very much   **b.** although I'm a bit nervous

4   'My sister's a cool customer.'

a. emotionally distant and focused on her own success

b. quite careful when she goes shopping

5   'My chemistry teacher was a scream.'

a. dominated other people by shouting a lot

b. was very entertaining although a little unconventional

6   'The club I went to last weekend was hopping.'

a. over-crowded and unpleasant

b. full of people and energy

7   'My best friend takes off the Prime Minister very well.'

a. imitates the PM and makes him/her look foolish

b. talks about the PM admiringly

8   'The plane took off late due to bad weather.'

a. left the ground and flew

b. came down to the ground and stopped

9   'I've put up with my boyfriend's daughter for a month.'

a. lived with and enjoyed the company of

b. lived with and accepted although I don't really like

10   'I'm snowed under at the moment.'

a. living in a place like Canada where there's lots of snow

b. extremely busy

Common vocabulary problems in speaking

Low-level mistakes (i)

IELTS candidates below a Six generally rely on simple, repetitive vocabulary. They may translate directly from their own language, or include words from it in the test. Collocation is inaccurate; idiom is rare.

All of the sentences in the following exercises come from real IELTS Speaking tests.

YOUR TURN   *Substitute the incorrect* crossed-out *words and phrases in the sentences with those in the boxes. There is an example.*

cook	the education system	embarrassed/upset	get along	
go	had	improved	tall	thrilled	~~tore~~	turns off

1 'I (eg) ~~broke~~ (*tore*) my coat coming to the exam. I was sad (_____) because people on the train could see it.'

2 'Last month, my sister ~~got~~ (_____) a baby. We're all ~~very happy~~ (_____).'

3 'Sometimes, the city ~~closes~~ (_____) the central heating to save money.'

4 'My father's a ~~long~~ (_____), kind man, and he's a great ~~cooker~~ (_____).'

5 'I'd like to ~~return~~ (_____) back to Tokyo soon.'

6 'I think ~~schools and colleges~~ (_____) in my country could be ~~better~~ (_____).'

7 'Since I've lived abroad for so long, I don't ~~connect~~ (_____) with my school friends any more.'

In sentence 1 above, the speaker lacks the precise verb *to tear* (*to rip* is also possible). He or she uses basic vocabulary like *sad*.

In sentences 2, 3, and 7, the speaker is translating from his or her first language.

In sentence 4, the speaker probably knows some jobs like *farmer*, *singer*, and *teacher*, and thinks a *cooker* is similar. A *cooker*, however, is the large white appliance in your kitchen on which you cook. It's also called a *stove* or an *oven*. Also in sentence 4, *tall* collocates with *man*, not *long*.

In sentence 5, the speaker has confused two verbs: *return*, and the phrasal verb *go back*. *Return back* is impossible in English. *Return* is a written verb; *go back* is spoken.

In sentence 6, the abstract idea of *the education system* is more precise; *improved* is a better word than *better*. This sentence is from Part 3 of the Speaking test, where more sophisticated language is required.

Low-level mistakes (ii)

50,000	a little overweight	also	below	courtyard	memorable
poverty	recall/remember	's got	a state called Uttar Pradesh		undercover

8 'In the west of China, lots of people still live ~~under~~ (_____) the ~~poetry~~ (_____) line.'

9 'Our flat ~~has~~ (_____) six rooms and a small ~~court~~ (_____). ~~In addition~~, there's (_____) ~~coverunder~~ (_____) parking.'

10 'I had such a ~~vivid~~ (_____) holiday in Paris. I can ~~memorise~~ (_____) every-thing I did.'

11 'I'm friendly with my neighbour even though he's ~~fat~~ (_____).'

12 'About ~~five lakh~~ (_____) were badly affected by the flooding in ~~UP~~ (_____).'

In sentence 9, the single verb *have* would be used in writing; *has got* (contracted correctly to "'s got") is used in speaking. *In addition* is a phrase that a Five loves! It is formal, so restricted to writing (although avoided in high-level writing); *also* is far more natural in speaking.

In sentence 11, *fat* is impolite; *a little overweight* is much better. Words like *fat*, *poor*, *short*, and *ugly* are negative in English, so are not used to talk about people we like.

In sentence 12, the candidate has used *lakh*, which means 100,000 in India. It is not, however, used in <u>any other</u> English-speaking country, and for IELTS is considered a non-English word. The acronym UP is also unknown outside India. It is a good idea to avoid such things, or explain them in the Speaking test.

6+ mistakes (i)

Higher-level candidates have some of the mistakes above, but they produce less common items of vocabulary, and are aware of style.

YOUR TURN   *Substitute the incorrect ~~crossed-out~~ words and phrases in the sentences with those in the boxes. There is an example.*

broke/split up	chance/opportunity	different	hazardous	live
put down	run over	tacky	touris**t**y	young

1 'When I was a child, I didn't have the ~~possibility~~ (_____) to learn a musical instrument.'

2 'Unfortunately, ~~dangerous~~ (_____) waste from the chemical industry is polluting our rivers.'

3 'We had our cat ~~put out~~ (_____) because she'd been ~~hit on~~ (_____).'

4 'Actually, I didn't enjoy Bali. It's too ~~touristic~~ (_____) now.'

5 'I thought the acrobatic performance was ~~bad~~ (_____) especially the part where the women writhed on the floor with swords in their stomachs and trays of champagne glasses on top of them.'

6 'My parents ~~separated~~ (_____) when I was ~~a tiny tot~~ (_____), and now they ~~reside~~ (_____) in ~~dissimilar~~ (_____) cities.'

In sentence 3, it is possible to say the cat had been *hit by a car*. Look up the verbs *put out* and *hit on*.

Sentence 6 appears to be sophisticated, but is in fact quite crazy! The verb *separated* is better in writing. *Tot* is a rare, intimate word. *Reside* is formal, and favoured by the police. *Dissimilar* is a synonym for *different*, but needs a detailed description to follow, and is preferred in writing.

6+ mistakes (ii)

> (auto)biographies   bottom   extinction   handwriting   illegible   insidious   inspiring
> large male breasts   pester/pressure/hassle   tight swimming costumes

7 'My grandmother bought me a flat in Sofia. When I found out, I thanked her from the ~~button~~ (_____) of my heart.'

8 'We're trying hard in Chengdu to save the panda from ~~distinction~~ (_____).'

9 'I don't have very nice ~~calligraphy~~ (_____). In fact, it's probably ~~illegitimate~~ (_____).'

10 'I often borrow ~~bibliographies~~ (_____) from the library. I think it's ~~aspiring~~ (_____) to read about famous people.'

11 'Some TV advertising is ~~insiduous~~ (_____) the way it encourages children to ~~hester~~ (_____) their parents.'

12 'I think ~~moobs~~ (_____) and ~~budgie smugglers~~ (_____) are disgusting.'

Check any new vocabulary, above, in a dictionary.

In sentences 7-10, speakers have confused existing English words with comical results.

In sentence 11, the person has made up two new words – one of which, a very sophisticated item of vocabulary, is nearly correct.

In sentence 12, the candidate lived in Australia for a long time, and learnt some local slang. Unfortunately, he took the IELTS exam in the UK, and his female examiner had no idea what he was talking about. Perhaps if she had, she might have been offended.

Grammar in speaking

Sentence types

In the IELTS Speaking test, grammar needs to be accurate. Candidates should use a variety of structures. However, in Part 1 of the test, it's not unnatural to use quite a lot of simple sentences and even short answers. In Parts 2 and 3, however, a candidate is expected to produce compound and complex sentences.

Go to pages 285-286 for more on sentences types.

Trouble with verbs

Verb forms and the little words (articles, prepositions, quantifiers etc) cause the most difficulty in speaking.

Tense and Aspect. Past, present, and future are different tenses. Simple or continuous, and simple or perfect are different aspects.

In general:

- A Five speaks mainly in the present tense, and mainly in the simple.

- A Six uses a variety of tenses and has a grasp of aspect, but makes quite a few mistakes.

- Only a Seven understands the system, and is nearly always correct.

YOUR TURN   *Choose the correct answer, a, b, or c. A Seven should get all of these right.*

1 'I ___ here since last August.'

   a. 'm living   **b.** 've been living   **c.** 've lived

2 'I wish I ___ a brother or a sister.'

   a. 'd had   **b.** have   **c.** would have

3 'I ___ a property for some time.'

   a. don't planning to buy   **b.** 'm not planning on buying   **c.** won't buying

4 'My neighbour ___ in my spot. It drives me nuts.'

   a. 's always parking   **b.** always park   **c.** always parks

5 'I ___ up to be aware of events in other countries.'

   a. brought   **b.** was bringed   **c.** was brought

6 'On my first day at work, my manager ___ me as being quite strict, but now I know him better, that's not the case.'

   a. strike   **b.** stroke   **c.** struck

7 'My girlfriend ___ me to speak English.'

   a. encourage   **b.** encourages   **c.** encouraging

8 'Yes, I would like ___ a musical instrument when I was a child, but my parents couldn't afford it.'

   a. to have learnt   **b.** to learn   **c.** to learning

9 'My husband and I ___ within a few months. We've remained very close.'

   a. did meet and get married   **b.** had met and got married   **c.** met and got married

10 'By the time I get home, the match ___. I hope there's a replay.'

   a. has been finished   **b.** will finishing   **c.** will've finished

Consult a good grammar book or website for more on tense and aspect, and on all the little words.

Functions

Here are some functions that may be tested:

i	Agreement or disagreement	**ii**	Expression of preference
iii	Analysis	**iv**	Justification of an opinion
v	Comparison	**vi**	Narration
vii	Description	**viii**	Prediction or speculation
ix	Expression of possibility	**x**	Suggestion

IF YOU WANT A SEVEN

Match an examiner's questions, below, with the function, on the previous page, that he or she is trying to get the candidate to produce. (Remember: there are numerous grammatical structures to express each function.) There are examples.

Eg i   'Why would you charge people for plastic bags at supermarkets?' *__iv__*

Eg ii   'What would you do if you were in government to reduce the death toll on the roads?' *__x__*

A   'Tell me about a place you visited that made a great impression on you.' ____ and ____

B   'What are some of the reasons for the rise in drug addiction?' ____

C   'Do you think smoke-free restaurants are a good idea?' ____

D   'Which do you think is better: living in a big city, or in a small town in the countryside?'

____

E   'What are some different ways of dealing with criminals?' ____

Match the answers below with the questions above as in the examples.

Eg   'I'd legislate for compulsory seatbelt wearing immediately.' *__Eg ii__*

Eg   'Because the pollution is horrendous – even in the remotest parts of the Libyan desert you see them floating around.' *__Eg i__*

1   'There are several options, but I think community service is a far better one than putting people in jail.' ____

2   'Right now, I'm a fan of the city, but there's a counter-trend in my country of those who can afford it moving into the countryside. I might do that when I've got a family. There's more land and peace and quiet there.' ____

3   'Yes, I'm all for it.' ____

4   'We took a ferry across the lake to a place called Kizhi. Then, we walked around the old village, which is a probably mostly a replica, and went into an amazing cathedral. This was built several hundred years ago from wood but without a single nail.' ____

5   'This is a more complex issue than is generally thought. It's a combination of availability of products, social acceptability, and self-medication in the face of depression.' ____

Here are some functions candidates may need to perform better in the Speaking test:

- asking for clarification
- using circumlocution
- paraphrasing
- self-correcting

Asking for clarification

Most candidates are nervous during their Speaking test. They sometimes lose track of what the examiner has said.

- If a candidate does not **hear a question**, he or she should ask: 'Could you say that again, please?'

- If a candidate does not **understand a question**, he or she should ask: 'Could you say that in another way?'

- If a candidate does not **understand a particular word**, he or she should ask: 'Could you tell me what X means?'

While examiners are happy to help candidates, there are some restrictions upon this. There is no problem with repeating a question, but definitions may not be given in Part 1 of the Speaking test. If a candidate asks for help with vocabulary *more than once* in Parts 2 or 3, he or she is unlikely to score highly.

See pages 250-251 for more on paraphrasing and circumlocution.

Self-correction is a useful skill. Examiners take into consideration that candidates who use it really do know what language is correct.

A candidate may self-correct by saying the right word immediately after the wrong one, or he or she might add: 'What I mean is…' if a phrase or sentence needs reformulation.

Delaying tactics

YOUR TURN   *Unscramble the words below. Write them in the spaces provided. There is an example.*

Many IELTS books and websites (eg) (ge**s**tugs) <u>suggest</u> that if a candidate needs extra

thinking time before answering a Speaking Part 1 or Part 3 question, he or she should use a

delaying tactic, like saying: 'That's an interesting question.' This is very (gerus**d**ano)

_____ because almost no IELTS question *is* interesting. It merely shows a

candidate lacks (nucley**f**) _____, and so is a Six or below.

The one-minute preparation time before Part 2

Candidates are given one minute to prepare for their Speaking Part 2 answer. They read

bullet-pointed information about their (**t**ocip)_____ to help them with their answer,

and they write (ton**e**s)_____ on a little piece of paper.

The examiner is either sitting quietly watching the clock during this, or filling in a mark

sheet. However, he or she does notice what is written on that paper, and makes a judgement

about a candidate's (ve**l**le) _____. Therefore, it is not a good idea to write in one's

first language; and spelling mistakes do count. It is also foolish not to write (thaningy)

_____, unless one is a native speaker.

Comparing the vocabulary and grammar of six Speaking candidates

YOUR TURN   All the candidates below were asked the same question in Part 1 of the Speaking test: 'What do you do most days at work?'
Rank their answers, on the left, from the best (1) to the worst (6). Two have been done for you.

_____ **A** 'I'd have to say that's not such an easy question because as a pediatrician my work's quite varied. I suppose a simple answer is: I see patients, do some admin, and keep up with research.' _____

_____ **B** 'I think oceanographer good luck. Every day different day. Now disaster chemical. Service harbour. Analisation samples, and write report.' _____

5 **C** 'As I tell to you, I am Marketing manager. Factory number three in world make EV. We will be number one. In these days, I am organise advertisement newspaper and internet, and very very lot of TV for small EV.' ___*i*___

_____ **D** 'I've been run my own business for four years, which is exciting. Mostly, I'm at home in office although rarely I go on road with buses to check guides and some of places they visit. Maybe half of each day I deal with money – how is it infested? And planning forward.' _____

2 **E** 'Our shop's at the airport, so I work shifts. Generally speaking, the morning shift is the most busy. I open the shop, make all the equipments work, serve the customers, and clean up after them. I don't deal much with the till – the manager do that. Now and then, I'm requested by an airline to translate into Portuguese.' ___*ii*___

_____ **F** 'I start in 5:30 AM, make centre ready for first kids. They come at 6 AM. I'm responsibility for seven kids each day. I think mostly same kids yesterday and today, but not always. I play with childrens, lunch and dinner childrens, little bit teach to them. Make sure all of persons calm and co-operation.'

Now, match the following examiner's reports on grammar to the candidates' answers above. Two have been done for you on the right of the table.

i Some basic structures are correct, but attempts at more complex language contain numerous errors.

ii Complex, compound, and simple sentences are used effectively. Nearly every sentence is error-free.

iii No sentence is without mistakes. Almost every sentence is short and simple. There are very few verbs. Word order is a problem.

iv A variety of grammatical structures are used with complete accuracy.

v Simple sentence structures are correct, but no attempt is made at more complex ones. This speaker starts almost every sentence with 'I'.

vi Compound and complex sentences are used almost always correctly. Word order is a problem.

The candidates' speaking has been corrected. The highlighted language shows their vocabulary problems.

'I'd have to say that's not such an easy question because as a pediatrician my work's quite varied. I suppose a simple answer is: I see patients, do some admin, and keep up with research.' *(There are no mistakes in vocabulary or grammar.)*

'Our shop's at the airport, so I work shifts. Generally speaking, the morning shift is the busiest. I open up the shop, get all the equipment working, serve customers, and clean up after them. I don't deal much with the till – the manager does that. Now and then, I'm called on by an airline to translate into Portuguese.'

'I've been running my own business for four years, which is exciting. Mostly, I'm at home in my office although occasionally I go out on the road with the buses to check on the guides and some of the places they visit. Maybe half of each day I spend dealing with the money – how it is invested – and forward planning.'

'I start work at 5:45 AM, getting the centre ready for the first kids who come at 6. I'm responsible for seven children each day. I think they're mostly the same kids, but not always. I play with them, feed them, teach them a bit, and make sure everyone is calm and co-operative.'

'As I mentioned earlier, I'm a Marketing manager. Our company is the third-largest producer of electric vehicles in the world, and we're trying to become number one. Right now, I'm organizing print and internet ads, and a massive TV campaign for a small car.'

'I guess, being an oceanographer, I'm privileged that every day's different. Recently, I've been surveying the harbour for traces of chemical pollution after a major spill. I'll be analysing the samples in the lab later, and writing a report.' *(The original answer has so many mistakes in vocabulary and grammar that this is rewritten.)*

More differences between spoken and written English

Listen to a conversation between two people.

 PLAY RECORDING 34.

What are they talking about? _____

Who supports the idea: the man or the woman?
Here are the woman's ideas as part of a Task 2 response. There are no mistakes; it is an IELTS Nine essay.
The <u>underlined</u> vocabulary is different from what the woman said although the meaning is the same.

Essay

Essentially, I <u>do not believe</u> driving should be taught at school. While driving is rather a useful skill, <u>school children have a considerable number of</u> other things to concentrate on.

In the <u>final</u> two years of secondary, study becomes <u>particularly intense</u>. Some teachers <u>maintain</u> there is currently <u>insufficient academic material</u> for students to engage with, especially <u>in relation to</u> English and <u>Mathematics</u>. As a result, the level of first-year <u>university</u> students <u>is lower than in the past</u>. Therefore, there is no time for driving lessons in the school curriculum.

<u>A more appropriate way</u> to teach children how to drive is for their <u>parents</u> or professional instructors to do so after school.

One <u>compromise</u> might be to <u>devote</u> a few of hours a term at school to the discussion of some of <u>the dangers of driving</u>, in particular: speeding and drunk-driving, which <u>are a grave concern in this country</u>. (148 words)

Speech

The woman: 'I don't agree with you, Marko. You see, while driving's kind of a useful skill, kids at school've really got lots of other things to study....

Dunno. The last two years of school are pretty full on. But I've still heard teachers going on about there not being enough serious stuff, like English and Maths. They say the level of kids at uni now just isn't what it used to be....

Well, we certainly could do with more defensive driving, and...and less drunk-driving. That's a massive problem here....

Only, don't you think it's better for mums and dads to show their kids how to drive after school, or to get them professional driving lessons?...

How about we meet half way? Maybe school kids could spend a few hours a term on the dos and don'ts of driving, especially on speeding and drunk-driving. They don't need a full-on course.'

Vocabulary with similar meaning

YOUR TURN   *Here is a list of the spoken and written language above. Can you complete it?*

I don't agree	→	I do not believe
You see,	t	(a filler)
kind of	t	(a filler)
kids at school	t	school children
've got (have got)	→	_____
lots of	→	_____
last	→	final
pretty	→	particularly
full on (common slang)	→	_____
go on about*	→	_____
not enough serious stuff	→	_____
like	→	in relation to
Maths (abbreviation)	→	Mathematics
uni (abbreviation)	→	_____
isn't what it used to be	→	_____
Well,	→	_____
a massive problem here	→	_____
spend (time) on	→	devote (time) to
Only,	→	_____
it's better for	→	_____
mums and dads	→	parents
get	→	(The whole sentence is rewritten.)
meet half way	→	_____
the dos and don'ts of (idiom)	→	the dangers of

*A phrase like *go on about,* above, doesn't exactly mean *maintain.* It is closer to *complain,* but that's too negative for the essay.

From the list above, it's clear there are a lot of differences in vocabulary between speaking and writing. The tone is more formal and more neutral in the essay. Idioms and phrasal verbs are used throughout the speaking, but less so in the writing.

While some words and phrases change in writing, others are left out. Repetition is tolerated more in speaking than in writing. Some new vocabulary is also added to the essay for clarity or interest.

The grammar in the writing differs from the speaking in one major way: the length of sentences. This is because there are a large number of compound and complex sentences in the essay. One sentence contains 37 words, whereas the longest spoken sentence has just 20.

Now, take notes on what the man says.

Play Audio **PLAY RECORDING 34 again.**

_____

_____

_____

_____

_____

_____

Use your notes to write a 150-word Task 2 answer from the man's point of view.

_____

_____

_____

_____

_____

_____

_____

_____

_____

_____

_____

_____

_____

_____

_____

✓ **Checklist:**

___ Have you removed the man's repetition of ideas?

___ Are you using nominalisation (noun phrases instead of subject+verb phrases)?

___ Is your vocabulary more formal?

___ Have you changed phrasal verbs into single long verbs?

___ Have you changed 'get' into other verbs?

___ Do you mostly have compound and complex sentences?

___ Are your linkers more academic and more varied?

___ Is your spelling correct?

IF YOU WANT A SEVEN

Read the Task 2 paragraph below. It is another IELTS Nine answer.

A new word has recently been coined for travelling and volunteering as part of the same holiday – voluntourism. One typical example of this is a woman who goes to Nepal to trek in the mountains for two weeks, then spends a week teaching English at an orphanage in the capital Kathmandu. As a volunteer, she is not paid for her efforts, and in fact, it is likely she pays a tour company or the orphanage for the privilege of being there. In this essay, I shall discuss the benefits and drawbacks of this kind of tourism. Overall, I think it is detrimental to the very community it is trying to support. It is mere vanity for the traveller, who believes she is doing good, when in reality she is disturbing the children, providing little genuine tuition, and possibly encouraging corruption with her 'donation'. Principally, she is indulging herself in a feel-good photo opportunity. (153 words)

The writer is now speaking on this topic in Part 3 of the Speaking test.

Listen to the recording as many times as you like until you have found the differences between the spoken and written versions. There is no script for you to compare.

Play Audio **PLAY RECORDING 35.**

1 <u>Contractions</u>: Eg: *I've,* _____

2 <u>Phrasal verbs</u>: Eg: *go on* and _____

3 <u>Informal vocabulary</u>: Eg: *kind of,* _____

4 <u>Exaggerated / emotive language</u> (less neutral than in the writing – although the writing is persuasive): Eg: *about a million photos* and _____

_____

5 <u>A highly personal example</u> from the writer's *n* __ __ __ __ __ __ __ __.

6 <u>Some irrelevant details</u>: *Kathmandu is a dump* and _____

7 The order isn't as *l* __ __ __ __ __ __ __ as in the writing.

Excellent vocabulary

What are two excellent adjectives the speaker uses in Recording 35 to describe the effect on the orphans of the visit, and her final opinion of the trip?

d __ __ __ __ __ __ __ __ __   and **s** __ __ __ **-in** __ __ __ __ __ __ __

The opposing viewpoint

Listen to another candidate giving the opposing viewpoint.

Play Audio **PLAY RECORDING 36.**

Take notes on what the man says.

_____

_____

_____

_____

_____

_____

Use your notes to write a 150-word Task 2 answer.

_____

_____

_____

_____

_____

_____

_____

_____

_____

_____

_____

_____

_____

_____

Look back at the checklist on page 211.
Read the recording script and model answer on page 392.

Summary of vocabulary and grammar

What are the missing words? Write the letters to complete each one. There is an example.

In this section, we've (eg) *learnt* that IELTS Speaking and Writing require rather

dif _ _ _ _ _ _ _ grammar and vocabulary. In both cases, accuracy,

varie _ _, and precision are necessary. However, spoken English has more

sh _ _ _ sentences, more phrasal verbs, and more **emo** _ _ _ _ language.

Pronunciation

The last Speaking criterion is Pronunciation, which is often called Pron.
You may need a dictionary for this section as there are some technical words.
Good pronunciation means a candidate can speak without the negative effects of his or her first language. This is done by:

1 producing English sounds, or *phonemes*, correctly;
2 using *word and sentence stress*;
3 understanding *intonation*; and,
4 having *connected speech*.

First language interference

Read the text below. Then answer the questions that follow.

<u>Only up until the age of about **thirteen** can a person learn different languages and pronounce them perfectly</u>. IELTS does not penalise adult candidates for their accents. However, if the sounds and stress patterns of a candidate's first language are very strong, and English pronunciation is weak or unintelligible, then a candidate can't expect more than a Five for Pron. For example: in Arabic, there is no /p/ sound, so an IELTS Four candidate might say: 'I had a bicnic in the bark'. Likewise, Russian doesn't have as many short vowels as English, so a candidate may say: 'I leave in Moscow' instead of: 'I live in Moscow'.

English has consonant clusters – two or more consonants together – as in the word '<u>strength</u>'. These present problems for many speakers who separate them by adding vowels because this is what happens in their languages. For a Korean, 'bridge' doesn't sound right, so a speaker may add / iː/ to say 'brid-gee'. A city like 'Sydney' may become 'Syderney' for a Spanish or Japanese speaker.

In Cantonese, words are generally shorter than in English. Some Cantonese speakers forget to say the ends of English words clearly, especially those with /s/ or /z/. The final sounds /k/, /t/, and /d/ are also problematic. In contrast, Mandarin speakers say '-ng' /ŋ/ far too strongly, so that it sounds like /n/ and /g/.

Many languages, like Turkish, have different word stress from English. A Turk may not hear the difference between the words 'important' and 'impotent'. The first has the stress on the second syllable: 'im-POR-tant', whereas the second has the stress on the first syllable: 'IM-po-tent'. 'My grandfather was an impotent man' may not be what a speaker intended to say.

Other languages, like French, do not have word stress at all – each syllable is said about the same length, pitch, and loudness – and speakers who do not learn English patterns may sound too French for an examiner to award a Seven.

Intonation – the rising and falling of speech to create meaning – is different in each language. Some IELTS Fives may be too flat, or monotonous, in English. Others may rise and fall like a bouncing ball. This is often the case with speakers of Indian languages, and they can be annoying to listen to.

Basically, to get a Six, a candidate needs to work hard to limit the effects of his or her first language on English pronunciation. To get a Seven, a candidate has almost totally got rid of first language interference.

YOUR TURN *The following statements refer to the text that you have just read. Mark each one as True (T), False (F), or Not Given (NG). Underline your evidence in the text. There is an example.*

Eg A sixteen-year-old who learns another language can pronounce it perfectly. _F_

1 In IELTS, an adult candidate can have an accent as long as it is not too strong. ___

2 Consonant clusters don't usually cause speakers problems. ___

3 Chinese speakers generally have good English pronunciation. ___

4 Strange phoneme or word stress patterns can lead to a different word being said in English, which may be embarrassing. ___

5 English intonation is similar to that of Indian languages. ___

Phonemes

Here's one of the most important tables in this book: the International Phonetic Alphabet (IPA). Most speakers of other languages have around half of the same sounds as English in their language. A language close to English, like Dutch, has more similar sounds (as well as grammar and vocabulary) than a language further away, like Arabic or Thai.

Vowel sounds cause particular problems as no other language has as many as English. A Seven is familiar with all these symbols, and tries hard to reproduce them.

THE INTERNATIONAL PHONETIC ALPHABET (IPA)

Vowel sounds				Consonant sounds			
Monophthongs		Diphthongs					
/iː/	m**ea**t	/eɪ/	w**ay**	/p/	**p**art	/s/	**s**eem
/ɪ/	s**i**t	/ɔɪ/	b**oy**	/b/	**b**est	/z/	rai**s**e
/ʊ/	p**u**t	/aɪ/	f**i**ve	/t/	**t**own	/ʃ/	**sh**ow
/uː/	**u**se	/ɪə/	f**ear**	/d/	**d**ay	/ʒ/	plea**s**ure
/e/	m**e**n	/ʊə/	p**ure**	/tʃ/	**ch**at	/h/	**h**elp
/ə/ **a**fraid; c**o**mput**er**; **e**vent; r**e**turn		/eə/	**air**	/dʒ/	**j**ust	/m/	**m**any
/ɜː/	t**ur**n	/əʊ/	**go**	/k/	**c**are	/n/	**n**o
/ɔː/	t**a**ll	/aʊ/	n**ow**	/g/	**g**reen	/ŋ/	si**ng**
/æ/	s**a**t			/f/	**f**irst	/l/	**l**ive
/ʌ/	**u**p			/v/	**v**ery	/r/	**r**ight
/aː/	c**a**r	ˈ	Stress mark	/θ/	**th**ink	/j/	**y**et
/ɒ/	h**o**t			/ð/	**th**e	/w/	**w**ant

There are 44 phonemes in English – 24 consonant and 20 vowel sounds. Some of them correspond to letters of the alphabet. Within vowels, there are twelve single sounds (on the left of the table). Some of these are short, like /æ/ in 'back', and others are long, like / iː/ in 'beak'. There are eight vowel sounds called diphthongs. A diphthong, like /eɪ/ in 'bake' or /aɪ/ in 'bike', is one vowel sound moving into another but taking the same time to say as a long vowel. Can you say 'back', 'beak', 'bark', 'bake', and 'bike' easily?

The shaded consonant sounds in the table are unvoiced or voiceless. This means when a speaker makes these sounds his or her vocal chords in the larynx do *not* vibrate so much. It's as though the sound stays inside the speaker's mouth. In voiced phonemes, the chords vibrate much more, and the air is pushed out of the mouth. Say 'Sue' and 'zoo', or 'thin' and 'this', or 'photo' and 'vote'. Can you hear and feel that the first words in these pairs are unvoiced?

Since this book is written for candidates who speak different languages, we'll analyse a few common problems with phonemes. For specific problems related to your language, consult a good book or a reliable website. Remember, to get more than a Five for Pronunciation, you've got to master the phonemes!

For many people, pronunciation is not such a big deal, although getting a Seven is hard because, frankly, most candidates don't know exactly what pronunciation involves. For some people, particularly those from Thailand, Cambodia, Hong Kong, Nepal, or Bangladesh, pronunciation is a major obstacle. A Vietnamese speaker may get three Sevens for Fluency and Coherence, for Grammar, and for Vocabulary, but just can't manage a Seven for Pronunciation even after taking the IELTS exam several times. If you're in this category, you need special help like private lessons from a person who really understands pronunciation.

YOUR TURN   *Listen to pairs of candidates. Their grammar and vocabulary are correct. The phonemes, or problems to focus on, are shown on the right. Who has better pronunciation: A or B? Which word or words does the other speaker pronounce wrongly? There is an example.*

 PLAY RECORDING 37.

CONSONANT SOUNDS

	A	B	Phonemes to listen for		A	B	Phonemes / Problems to listen for
Eg	x	✓	/p/ *party*	**5**			/ʒ/
1			/tʃ/	**6**			/ŋ/
2			/w/	**7**			/j/
3			/θ/	**8**			*Consonant clusters and the ends of words are not said.*
4			/ʃ/	**9**			*Extra vowel sounds are added*

Now, practise saying the correct sentences after each speaker.

 PLAY RECORDING 38.

Listen to some more candidates. Who has better pronunciation: A or B?

 PLAY RECORDING 39.

VOWEL SOUNDS

	A	B	Phonemes to listen for		A	B	Phonemes to listen for
1			/iː/	6			/ɑː/
2			/e/	7			/eɪ/
3			/ɜː/	8			/eə/
4			/ɔː/	9			/əʊ/
5			/ʌ/	10			/ɔɪə/

Practise saying the correct sentences after each speaker.

PLAY RECORDING 40.

Single-syllable words that IELTS candidates find hard to say

While it's good to link words together for fluency, and elide or assimilate sounds, it's important to say the ends of words, particularly when they're plural nouns or regular verbs in the past.

Furthermore, there are quite a few words of one syllable in English that candidates turn into two. The words 'ask', 'asks', and 'asked' are all one syllable with different endings.

Other single-syllable words have vowel sounds that cause problems.

YOUR TURN   *What are the missing letters in the words below? Write them in the spaces provided. There is an example.*

Eg 'At the weekend I **as_ked_** my neighbour for some advice.'

1 'The Minister for the Environment has recently **blo __ __ __ __** several mining applications.'

2 'I was **ca __ __ __ __** Lydia because my parents met in Turkey.'

3 'My grandfather **clai __ __ __** he'd met the boxer Mohammed Ali.'

4 'I hope the Millennium Development Goals will **cl __ __ __** the gap between rich and poor countries.'

5 'I don't wear formal **cl __ __ __ __ __** very often.'

6 'It gets pretty **c __ __ __** in my city. We had minus forty this winter.'

7 'I believe **dre __ __ __** can tell us something.'

8 'People have **floc __ __ __** to the city from the countryside.'*

9 'Recent **fl __ __ __ __** in the south of China left thousands of people homeless.'

10 'The road toll is **qu __ __ __** high in my country.'

_____

*Check the meaning of *to flock*.

11 'While I was travelling in Laos, I badly **scra** __ __ __ __ __ my leg, and it still hasn't healed.'

12 'The standard of living has **sli** __ __ __ __ because the currency is worth less.'

13 'My father **spla** __ __ __ __ out for my sister's wedding. I think there were 400 guests.'

14 'I get **str** __ __ __ __ __ out by working and looking after three children at the same time.'

15 'The exam prep course I did was excellent. It really **stret** __ __ __ __ me.'

Look up any new vocabulary.

Practise saying the sentences after each speaker.

PLAY RECORDING 41.

Here are some more single-syllable words that an IELTS Five should know. All of them are hard to say.

SINGLE-SYLLABLE WORDS THAT ARE HARD TO SAY

bags	blood *and* flood	bring *and* brought	changed	comes
depth	judged	laughs	law	lunch
months	played	proved	risks	sew
sixth	split	strange	strength	switched
think	through	view	works	worst

Practise saying the words after the speakers.

PLAY RECORDING 42.

Go to the IELTS Speaking Log on page 445 to add any other words like these that you need to practise.

Stress

There are two main ideas behind stress:

- word stress
- sentence or contrastive stress

Word stress

In the example on page 213, with 'IMpotent' and 'imPORtant', we can see that words in English have stress. One syllable is said longer, a little higher, and more loudly than the others. Single-syllable words, like 'France', may be stressed within a sentence, but they don't have word stress.

Most IELTS candidates don't worry about word stress. However, every time a speaker puts the wrong stress on a word, a listener gets a small electric shock – really, that's what it's like. As a result, the listener doesn't pay attention to the speaker's content. To get a Seven, word stress has to be right.

YOUR TURN Here are some countries and their word stress patterns. 'Poland' has two syllables with stress on the first syllable: 'POland (Oo); but 'Ukraine' has second-syllable stress: 'uKRAINE' (oO). Stress is usually shown in a dictionary with a little mark: 'Poland, or U'kraine

Put each country in the box into the table where it belongs. Write the country names in the spaces provided.

Argentina	Brazil	Cambodia	Italy	Jordan
Morocco	Pakistan	Spain	Vietnam	

	Oo most common	**Ooo** most common	**oO**	**oOo**
France	China	Canada	_____	Korea
_____	_____	_____	Japan	_____
	Poland	_____	Ukraine	New Zealand (*not* Newsy Land)

oOoo		**ooO** least common	**ooOo**	
Australia			_____	
_____		Cameroon	Indonesia	
South Africa				

Some word stress rules

The majority of two- and three-syllable English nouns, adjectives, and adverbs are stressed on the first syllable.

All '-en' verbs have first syllable stress, like 'FRIGHTen' and 'HAPpen'. There are quite a few verbs with second-syllable stress, like 'beLIEVE', 'conVINCE', 'deLAY', 'forGET', 'proDUCE', and 'reTURN'. Remember: 'enterTAIN'.

Sometimes stress tells us which part of speech a word is. 'REcord' is a noun, but 'reCORD' is a verb. The noun 'CONtent' has different stress from the adjective 'conTENT'.

For longer words – three or more syllables – count back three syllables from the end of the word to find the stress. It's easy to understand this visually.

O	ri	gin	**o**rigin
3	*2*	*1*	

o	**RI**	gi	nal	o**ri**ginal

	PHO	to	graph	**pho**tograph

pho	**TO**	gra	phy	pho**to**graphy

res	**PON**	si	ble	res**pon**sible

res	pon	si	**BI**	li	ty	responsi**bi**lity

	U	ni	verse	**u**niverse

u	ni	**VER**	si	ty	uni**ver**sity (but uni**ver**sal)

	VA	ri	ous	**va**rious

va	**RI**	e	ty	va**ri**ety

Of course, this doesn't always work. Consider 'adVANtage' and 'advanTAgeous'.

Prefixes and suffixes are rarely stressed in English. Note: 'LIKEly' and 'unLIKEly'; 'POSsible' and 'imPOSsible'. However, we do stress the 'ee', in 'employEE', 'eer' in 'enginEER', and 'ese' in 'JapanESE'. Otherwise, final-syllable stress is uncommon.

There is always stress on the syllable before the sound /ʃɪn/, so 'pronunciAtion', or 'muSIcian', and almost always preceding '-al', as in 'fiNANcial'. The syllable before '-ic' in adjectives is usually stressed, like 'ecoNOmic', but '**A**rabic' is an exception, and has first-syllable stress.

Words (nearly all nouns) that are compounds generally have first-word stress. (A compound is two words that over time have joined to become one word or are separate but regarded as a chunk.) Note: *birthday cake* is 'BIRTHday cake'; *grandmother* is 'GRAND-mother'; and, *post office* is 'POST office'. To get a Six in Pron, you need your compounds correct.

Easy words often wrongly stressed by IELTS candidates that prevent them from getting a Seven

Put the words in the box into the table where they belong. Write them in the spaces provided.

WORDS WITH FIRST-SYLLABLE STRESS

Arabic fashionable fortunate grandmother natural organised peacekeeper quiet* studying supermarket teenager various

Oo	Ooo	Oooo
_____	_____	*interesting*
_____	*carrier*	*motivated*
	conference	*temperature*
	_____	_____
	festival	
	_____	
	_____	
	_____	
	_____	
	_____	
	restaurant	
	_____	

 PLAY RECORDING 43 to check your answers.

Practise saying these words after each speaker.

---

*'Qui-et' has two syllables; the adverb 'quite' has one. IELTS Fours and Fives often confuse these words in Speaking and Writing.

WORDS WITH SECOND-SYLLABLE STRESS

career	computer	convenient	disorganised	hotel	illegal	obese
	prefer	pronounced	success	unfortunate	unique	

oO	oOo	oOoo
Chinese	*achievement*	_____
_____	_____	_____
mature	_____	*economy*
_____	_____	*obesity*
_____	*romantic*	_____
_____		
report, succeed		
_____		
_____		

 PLAY RECORDING 44 to check your answers.

Practise saying these words after each speaker.

WORDS WITH THIRD- OR FOURTH-SYLLABLE STRESS

accidental	disadvantage	enthusiastic	motivation	opportunity	politician	volunteer

ooO	oooO	ooOoo	oooOo
impolite	_____	_____	_____
_____	_____		*pronunciation*
	individual		
	_____		
	_____		

 PLAY RECORDING 45 to check your answers.

Practise saying these words after each speaker.

Sentence stress

Sentence stress is also called contrastive stress. One word in each utterance (sentence, clause or phrase) is stressed more than others to change the meaning of the sentence. For example: 'I was born in India.' could be stressed four different ways.

1 '*I* was born in India.' But my *brother* was born in another country.
2 'I *was* born in India.' I really was! I'll show you my passport.
3 'I was *born* in India.' But I *grew up* elsewhere.
4 'I was born in *India*.' Which has over a billion people.

Here's another example which shows why this is called contrastive stress. Let's say an examiner asks in Part 1 of the Speaking test: 'What are some different sports you enjoy in different seasons?' A candidate might answer: 'In **summer** I play *tennis*; but in **winter**, I prefer *football*.' We can see visually (in **bold** and *italics*) the contrasts here.

As we saw in Fluency and Coherence, words that are stressed in each sentence are content words: nouns, verbs, adjectives, and adverbs.

YOUR TURN	*Read the Speaking Part 1 script below. The **bold** words are stressed.*
Examiner	What do you like doing on **Friday night**?
Candidate	I **usually** go out with my **mates**, but **sometimes**, like **recently** for **IELTS**, I've been at **home**, **studying**.

Listen to the Part 1 questions and answers below, and mark the stressed words as you hear them.

Play Audio | **PLAY RECORDING 46.**

Examiner	What do you think is the best part of the weekend?
Candidate	Sunday afternoon because I'm at home relaxing. It's a custom in our family to have friends and relatives over for a big lunch.
Examiner	Do you think weekends are long enough?
Candidate	Yes, I do. I think work is the most important part of a person's life, and it's immature to want holidays all the time.

Pitch and intonation

YOUR TURN *Match the items in the boxes with the numbered blanks in the text below. Write the numbers in the spaces provided. There is an example.*

				eg				
bored	emotion	enthusiasm	fall	high	important	New Zealand	song	unfinished

If you think of a word as a note in music, then its pitch is how –eg– it is. Usually, in English, when people lie, their pitch rises. When speaking normally, only the most –1– word in an utterance will be a higher pitch than the others around it. 'Best' and 'weekend' are higher pitched in the dialogue above.

Intonation is how the voice rises and falls to add meaning, often to show a speaker's –2–.

Intonation is a little different in each English-speaking country. If you've learnt English in –3– or Queensland in Australia, and lived there for a while, but you take the IELTS test in the UK, you may be in trouble. You see, rising intonation at the end of a sentence is common in NZ and Queensland, and doesn't have any negative meaning, but in the UK or US it means your answer is –4–, or you're unsure of it. Therefore it's better to use English intonation that's acceptable everywhere when you take the IELTS test.

If you're an Indian or a Scandinavian, then you've got to work on intonation because your English might sound like a –5– to an examiner if your voice rises and falls too much. By contrast, some northern Chinese speakers are too flat in English, which means they sound –6–. They need more music in their speech.

There are many intonation patterns in English, but some of them are unnecessary for IELTS as candidates don't ask questions or make offers to the examiner.

Five intonation patterns are:

1   Rise (at the end of an utterance) = for an unfinished answer
2   –7– = for something complete or definite
3   Fall-rise = for uncertainty
4   Rise-fall = for –8–
5   Level = for a lack of interest / a neutral statement (A candidate will score below a Six in Pron if he or she sounds bored.)

Identifying good and bad pronunciation

Now, let's listen to some candidates. All these speakers have accents, but only one of them has such a strong accent it's hard for a listener to understand.

YOUR TURN   *In each group of three speakers, who has the best pronunciation: A, B, or C? For this exercise, the candidates have perfect grammar and vocabulary. Fluency, however, is sometimes strange.*

Play Audio **PLAY RECORDING 47.**

	A	B	C
Eg	✓		
1			
2			
3			

Can you hear why the speakers below have these pron problems, marked with a cross?

Play Audio **PLAY RECORDING 48.**

Candidate	Phonemes	Word stress	Sentence stress	Intonation	Chunking and Rhythm
Eg: B	x			x	
Eg: C	x			x	x
1A	X	X		X	X
1C	X		X		X

IF YOU WANT A SEVEN

Now, you mark the pronunciation of two candidates. Put a cross where there are problems.

 PLAY RECORDING 49.

Candidate	Phonemes	Word stress	Sentence stress	Intonation	Chunking and Rhythm
2A					
2B					

Pronunciation in Speaking Part 2

Can you remember what happens in Part 2 of the Speaking test? Cross out the wrong answer. There is an example.

In Part 2: **eg** ~~The candidate~~ / The examiner chooses the topic.

 i The candidate has 30 / 60 seconds to prepare an answer.

 ii The candidate speaks for at least two / three minutes.

 iii The candidate says around 250 / 350 words.

 iv The examiner may ask one or two questions in the middle / at the end.

 v The candidate talks about a personal experience / more general ideas.

Gutted Part 2 answers

YOUR TURN The verb 'to gut' means to remove the parts of a fish that you can't eat. A gutted house has been destroyed by a storm or a fire, or by builders about to rebuild it. A gutted text has all the main ideas (content words), but none of the grammar.

Probably readers of this book don't know about Army Day in Australia (in fact, it's called ANZAC Day), so this is a realistic exercise. You've got to use ALL the words in the gutted text in your reconstructed Part 2 answer.

The topic is: 'Talk about a national holiday in your country: what happens; its importance; and, how the event has changed recently.'

Gutted text (i)

Army Day – April 25th – start 5 AM religious service in city – cold and dark – crowds – singing – candles – flowers – school children and veterans – midday big veterans march + current army, navy, air force – afternoon tv programmes different wars and peacekeeping now more than fighting – evening barbecues

Past = unpopular; now = serious, very popular especially with schools. Maybe change because veterans very old or dead from WWI and II. National identity – history – memories – honouring dead. Even if against war, still emotional day.

Don't write this out because written English is different from spoken English. Understand the gutted text, and record your speaking onto your phone or computer. You need to speak for two minutes.

Remember: clear phonemes, word and sentence stress, chunking, weak forms, contractions, pauses in the right places, and falling intonation at the end of sentences.

The topic is: 'Talk about a present you received as a child: what it was; who gave it to you; and, what you particularly liked about it.'

Gutted text (ii)

Dolls' house – four years old - parents – Christmas – magical: mother set it up waiting for me.

Large house = 4 rooms + roof lift off. Upstairs = kitchen, parents' bedroom + bathroom. Downstairs = living room + kids' bedroom.

Favourite room = kitchen – white wooden table with top painted red + dresser, fridge, stove. Cute plastic food – jelly + roast chicken. Also frying pan + two fried eggs + tiny kettle + red lid.

Four dolls like our family + maid = larger wooden doll – others made of pipe cleaners and felt. Maid = Russian Nina – no idea why Russian. Nina = favourite doll.

Family = similar mine. Mother + piano. Father + newspaper. Parents busy. Children fight. Aunt Alice = peg doll, couldn't stand up, so leant against wall = dissatisfied with life. How does 4-yr-old know that about woman's life?

Played for hours and hours – all weekend. Occasionally new items = grandfather clock + baby doll when brother born.

Record your answer. Listen to a possible answer.

 PLAY RECORDING 50.

Note that the speaker doesn't say what she particularly liked about her present. The bullet points on the speaking page are a guide for candidates only. As long as you've answered the main question – a present you received as a child – you'll be fine.

Pronunciation in Speaking Part 3

In Part 3, where questions are more complex, many candidates begin to lose control of their Fluency. In particular, they pause too often while thinking of vocabulary. Under pressure, they may revert to poor pronunciation.

IF YOU WANT A SEVEN

Listen to a Speaking Part 3 answer. Don't worry about the fluency, grammar, or vocabulary. Can you see why the examiner has made the following assessment?

 PLAY RECORDING 51.

Candidate A			
Phonemes			
Vowel sounds	All correct	Some incorrect ✓ Eg: /e/ 'celery' instead of 'salary'	Many incorrect
Consonant sounds	All correct	Some incorrect ✓ Eg: /ʒ/ is not said in 'usually'; she says 'uwally'	Many incorrect
Ends of words	Clear where necessary	Sometimes unclear ✓ Eg: /st/, /ts/, and /ps/ endings: 'balance' instead of 'balanced'; 'subjeck' instead of 'subject' or 'subjects'; 'limit' instead of 'limits' and 'stop' instead of 'stops'.	Often unclear
Extra vowel sounds added	Never ✓	Occasionally	Often

Stress

Word stress	Yes	Sometimes stress on the wrong syllable ✓ Eg: she should say: 'SUB-ject', but she says 'sub-JECK'; she should say: 'PRI-mary', but she says 'pri-MARY'; she should say: 'MO-ti-va-ted', but she says 'mo-ti-VA-ted'. 'Average' and 'History' are usually two syllables, but she makes them three.
Sentence stress	Yes ✓	Sometimes stress on the wrong word

Connected speech

Chunking, contractions, and weak forms Her chunking and weak forms are inconsistent. She only sometimes has weak forms of 'to be'. She contracts 'don't' twice, but not at some other possible times.	Yes	Sometimes ✓	Almost none

Intonation

Rising and falling of the voice to add meaning	Mostly fine ✓	Voice is too flat	Voice is sing-songy

Pronunciation bands

The following are examiners' reports for pronunciation. Mark each one according to whether it matches a Five, a Seven, or an Eight. The example is a Six.
What do you think the speaker in the previous recording is?

___ This speaker can be understood almost all the time. Very occasionally his or her accent prevents understanding. Only one or two words are stressed wrongly, or have mispronounced phonemes. Connected speech is used throughout. Intonation is well managed.

___ This speaker can be easily understood the whole time. He or she uses a wide range of phonological features to add meaning. He or she has an accent, but this has very little effect on anyone listening. There is almost no extra pausing, hesitation, or self-correction. Connected speech and good intonation are used throughout.

___ This speaker can pronounce some English well. However, there are words which a listener can't understand. Connected speech is occasional. Intonation may be flat or too up and down.

__6__ This speaker can generally be understood. There are a few brief moments when mispronunciation of phonemes or strange stress causes confusion for a listener. Connected speech is used, but not always.

What can I do to improve my Pronunciation?

Get talking!

Fill out the Speaking Log on page 445.

Listen carefully to English speakers on TV. Pay attention to their phonemes, stress, connected speech, and intonation.

Make a conscious effort to change bad habits. Buy a book or find a website with diagrams of the mouth to show how each phoneme is pronounced. Always contract and chunk.

Take private lessons if pronunciation is your weakness.

Summary of Pronunciation

Listen to the recording, and complete the missing words. There is an example.

Play Audio **PLAY RECORDING 52.**

In this section, we've learnt that Pronunciation is how well a candidate produces English sounds or (eg) _phonemes_. Among the vowel sounds, diphthongs may be **h** __ __ __ to say, and need practice. Two common problems with consonant sounds are: adding vowels in **clus** __ __ __ __; and, not saying the **en** __ __ of words. Word stress, or saying one **sy** __ __ __ __ __ __ louder than the others, is a fundamental part of good English pronunciation. Sentence **str** __ __ __, giving some content words in each sentence extra importance, is also essential.

Connected **s** __ __ __ __ __, or saying words in chunks, is part of Pronunciation as well as Fluency. Without this, a speaker sounds **unna** __ __ __ __ __.

Although any adult learner of English will have an **a** __ __ __ __ __ from his or her first language, minimising the effect of this improves a candidate's IELTS score.

Speaking – Putting it all together

We've looked at the four marking criteria for Speaking: Fluency and Coherence, Grammar, Vocabulary, and Pronunciation. They are equally important. Each candidate, however, will have strengths and weaknesses.

We've seen how F&C and Pron are connected, and that they're both complex.

Spoken grammar is less complex than written, but a candidate needs to be accurate. A wide variety of vocabulary is important. Spoken vocabulary may be harder than written because precise yet less informal language is needed – often including phrasal verbs.

Assessing candidates

YOUR TURN   *Listen to four candidates: A, B, C, and D. Mark your answers in the spaces provided.*

Play Audio **PLAY RECORDING 53.**

1   Overall, who's the best speaker? ____

2   Who's the worst? ____

3   Which candidate has very good vocabulary and grammar, but trouble with fluency? ____

4   Which speaker has patches of speaking that are hard to understand either because they are incoherent or the vocabulary is strange? ____

Strategies for improvement

Match the strategies below with the speakers above. Write the letters in the spaces provided.

_B_ : You're half way to being a good speaker. Don't give up now. Continue to work hard at the IPA, using weak forms, chunks, and contractions. Your intonation is like a song, and quite hard to listen to. You need falling intonation at the end of most of your sentences. Reading is the key to learning vocabulary. Filling out the Reading Log each week will certainly help you. Every time you read something interesting, tell a friend about it in English. Although you may have been studying English for a long time, you still need some work on quite basic grammar. There are lots of free grammar materials online. If you can afford it, take an intensive grammar course.

____ : You've reached a point where you may be satisfied with your level, or you may need to develop to live and work abroad. It's much harder to go up a band from where you are than it was to reach this point. You've got some very good grammar and vocabulary, but your fluency has let you down. Until you fix this (perhaps by taking private lessons), you won't get a Seven. Consistent work on contractions should be your short-term goal. Perhaps with more confidence, you'll hesitate less.

____ : Why not take some intensive English classes or pay a private teacher to help you. You really do need to learn the IPA – I know you haven't! Understand what problems your first language is causing. Go online to find diagrams for how your mouth should look when producing certain phonemes. If you're in an English-speaking country, spend less time with people who speak your language, and more time with good English speakers. Spend money on a good dictionary and a good grammar book. Read for ten minutes in English every day. If you've been learning English for a short time, be realistic about your future plans. You won't be doing a Master's degree in English for at least three years.

____ : Although you may already be living and working in an English-speaking environment, you may not become a native speaker without attention to detail. Ask a trusted friend or colleague to give you feedback on one or two persistent errors particularly in grammar. Reading highbrow magazines (*New Scientist*, *National Geographic*, *The Economist* etc), newspapers (*The Guardian*, *The New York Times*), and novels (any Booker Prize winner) is the best way to extend your vocabulary.

Advice from an examiner

Which of the following do you think examiners like?

Candidates who:

1 are on time or before time. ___

2 wear clothes for a party or disco. ___

3 tell them they've taken the exam three times already. ___

4 haven't cleaned their teeth recently. ___

5 have chosen an English name like Purple or Season or Beer or Quicky or Liquid Snake or David Beckham or Sonic Boom or Pavarotti. ___

6 answer questions fully and with enthusiasm. ___

7 smile. ___

8 give memorised speeches. ___

9 keep their real true strong opinions to themselves, and instead present milder opinions in the exam. ___

10 give mainly short answers. ___

11 say they need a Seven. ___

12 leave the exam building immediately after the Speaking test. ___

Spelling clearly shows a candidate's level. It relates to how much a person reads.

There are many spelling rules in English, which you can research. If you read a lot, you don't need to know the rules because you have a visual memory.

Most IELTS books pay little attention to spelling. In the Listening test, however, spelling is important. If you look at the table of IELTS bands on page 7, you can see that a candidate who misspells just three words goes down half a band. Furthermore, in the Writing test, a candidate may be limited to a Five due to poor spelling.

YOUR TURN *Read the information below about IELTS Writing bands. What are the missing words? Write the letters to complete each one. There is an example.*

Eg Spelling is *marked* as part of Vocabulary in *Writing*.

1   To get a Seven in Vocabulary, a candidate can only have a *f* __ __ spelling mistakes

in each task – let's say six in *a* __ __ his or her writing. These are generally more

c __ __ __ __ __*x* words. Perhaps *phenomenon* is misspelt with an initial *f* or a

final *m*.

2   A *S* __ __ will have some mistakes – *t* __ __ __ __ as many as a Seven – but these

do not *a* __ __ __ __ __ communication. They will be errors like the spelling of

relevant as *relevent*.

3   A Five will have noticeable spelling mistakes that *cau* __ __ some difficulty for a reader.

Words may be written as they *sou* __ __, like *nolidge* for *knowledge*. Letters may be

mixed up, like *precent* **ins** __ __ __ __ of *percent*. Similar-looking words might be used,

like *low* for *law*.

4   A Four will have such **fre** __ __ __ __ __ errors that it is **ha** __ __ and annoying

to read his or her writing. Almost every *s* __ __ __ __ __ __ __ has spelling

mistakes.

Writing Task 1

YOUR TURN *Read the model answers on the next page. They are perfect except for spelling. What do you think the questions were? A number at the end of a line shows how many spelling mistakes there are in that line. Correct all 35 of them.*

	cycle	
The life ~~sicle~~ of frogs		eg (1)
Frogs live part of there lives in the water, and part of their lives out of it.		(1)
After matting in spring, a female frog lays more then 2000 eggs in water, usually in a		(2)
small pond. These eggs are coverd with jelly for food and protection; they float near		(1)
the surface of the water. Befor the end of three weeks, tadpoles hatch from the eggs.		(1)
They look like tainy fish with tales for swimming. Also like fish, they have gills, wich		(3)
extract oxygen from water so the tadpoles can breath. Over the next three months, the		(1)
creetures develope front legs, back legs, and lungs; their tails shrink. Finally, they		(2)
look like frogs. They are called froglets untill they reach machurity, which takes three		(2)
years. Froglets spend most of their time in the water, but gradualy start to live on land.		(1)
A frog can live up to ten years although in the wild their lives are short as they have		(0)
numrous enemies. (159 words)		(1)

Dear Nadia,		(0)
I'm writting to congratulate your daughter on wining a scholarship to the Univercity		(3)
of Sydney next year. Well done!		(0)
As you know, I've been living in this beutiful city for the past forteen years, and there		(2)
are a few things I'd like to tell Ksenia.		(0)
Firstly, the coast of living is high, and accomodation is particularly expensive. It's		(2)
likely Ksenia will need a part-time job just to servive. Secondly, the city is safer than		(1)
St Petersburg, but there are some arias to avoid after dark. I'll point those out when		(1)
she arrives. This is a multi-cultural city, so initialy Ksenia may be surprised by all the		(1)
nationalities here, but she'll soon find that everyone gets along. The climat is		(1)
wonderfull although summer is to hot – over 40 in February, and extremly humid.		(3)
Ksenia won't need to bring her winter gare since it never snows in Sydney. Winter		(1)
nights can be cool, but mainly becouse houses don't have descent heating.		(2)
In fact, I don't think Ksenia need bring anything spacial with her – everything is		(1)
availible here.		(1)
I'm really exited about seeing Ksenia soon.		(1)
Your friend,		(0)
Luda (185 words)		

Writing Task 2

YOUR TURN   *Read the Task 2 answer below about learning a musical instrument. It is perfect except for its spelling. What do you think the question was?*

A number at the end of a line shows how many spelling mistakes there are in that line. Correct all 20 of them.

In this essay I would like to discus the advantages and disadvantages of a child	(1)
learning a musical insturment. In general, I consider this not to be a terribly usefull	(2)
skill.	(0)
Increasing numbers of parents in my country are encourageing their children to learn	(1)
musical instruments: the piano, gitar, and clarinet are popular. A major reason for	(1)
this is the parents' desire to seem wealthy enough to do so as tution is expensive, and	(1)
the instruments themselfs are also costly. A secondary reason might be that parents	(1)
hope to keep their children out of trouble by filing their spear time with musical	(2)
activities. Lastly, the pleasure the children recieve from accomplishment and from	(1)
learning another language – for music is a language – might relacks them, and assist	(1)
them with other pursuits later in life.	(0)
However, the benifit for the child learning the instrument might be slight. It could be	(1)
a cause of anxiety to the learner that he or she is actually neither talented nor able to	(1)
work hard at the instrument. Perhaps the child does not like the teacher, but is afraid	(0)
to say so, awear of the money his or her parents are spending. It might be a berden	(2)
that while others are playing with one another or enjoing free time alone, this child is	(1)
forst to practise or attend classes. In an ever-more competive world, very few people	(2)
make a living as professional musicians, and those that do probably weren't	(0)
compeled by their parents to learn an instrument, but took it up spontanously	(2)
themselves. (256 words)	(0)

Spelling and Pronunciation

Spelling and pronunciation can be improved together by learning words according to the phoneme in their stressed syllable. Refer to the IPA chart on page 214 if necessary.

YOUR TURN   *Play the recordings listed below. Use each recording to fill in the accompanying tables. Each table has examples. For Recordings 54-61, do one a day.*

Play Audio **PLAY RECORDING 54.**

/ iː /			
Oo	**Ooo**	**oO**	**oOo**
decent _____	_____	belief _____ _____ routine	_____

/ ɪ /			
Oo	**Ooo**	**oO**	**oOo**
_____	typical _____	_____	specific

Play Audio **PLAY RECORDING 55.**

/ uː /			
Oo	**Ooo**	**oO**	**ooOoo**
losing _____	_____	_____	_____

/ e /		
Oo	**Ooo**	**oOoo**
decade _____ _____	_____ _____ negative _____	_____

/ ɔː /			
Oo	**Ooo**	**oOo**	**oOoo**
_____	organise	_____	co-ordinate unfortunate

Play Audio **PLAY RECORDING 56.**

/æ/

Oo	Ooo	oOo	ooOoo
_____	analyse (US analyze) _____ _____	_____	nationality

/aː/

oO	Ooo	oOo
_____	_____	_____

/ɒ/

Oo	oO	oOoo	ooOoo
promise _____ _____	_____	_____	_____

Play Audio **PLAY RECORDING 57.**

/eɪ/

Oo	oOo	oOoo	oooOo
daily _____ _____ _____	_____	advantageous	_____

/ɔɪ/

Oo	Ooo	oOo
noisy	loyalty _____	_____

/aɪ/

Oo	Ooo	oO	oOoo
_____	library primary	decide	anxiety _____ _____

Play Audio **PLAY RECORDING 58.**

/ɪə/	
oOoo	**ooO**
ideally	_____
	_____

/eə/			
Oo	**Ooo**	**oO**	**oOoo**
_____	area	aware	_____
rarely	_____	_____	

Play Audio **PLAY RECORDING 59.**

/əʊ/		
Oo	**oO**	**oOo**
showing	_____	_____
_____		_____

/aʊ/	
oO	**oOo**
amount	_____
_____	_____

Play Audio **PLAY RECORDING 60.**

/aɪə/				
Oo	**Ooo**	**Oooo**	**oOo**	**oOoo**
fire			_____	entirely
_____	_____	hierarchy	inspire	enquiry
_____			_____	_____

Play Audio **PLAY RECORDING 61.**

Words with the schwa /ə/ or /ɪ/ in the **unstressed** syllable.		
Oo	**oO**	**Ooo**
	advise	
_____	_____	
_____	_____	
_____	review	_____
driver		
local	_____	

IF YOU WANT A SEVEN

Each sentence has one spelling mistake. Can you fix it? Write the correct spelling.

1 Unfortunately, some people in the countryside are still ilitrate.
2 The local government has taken the inishative and begun saving energy.
3 It is a right, not a priviledge, to undertake higher education.
4 There has been an enthusastic response to the anti-litter campaign.
5 In every comunity there are elderly people who need assistance.
6 Professional athleets are paid extraordinary sums of money.
7 I believe the emfasis should be on prevention of disease.
8 There has been an imense improvement in longevity since the 1970s.
9 The competition for jobs is intence.
10 Many reputible companies suffered during the economic crisis.
11 I feel there has been an apalling lack of concern for the marine environment.
12 With more forsight, the problem could have been averted.
13 Composit cars are popular in my country.
14 There is less optamism about the future than there used to be.
15 Learning vocabulary is not easy, but if you perseveer it can be done.

 PLAY RECORDING 62 and say the words after the speakers.

Single-syllable words often misspelt

The missing words all have just one syllable. What are they? Write the letters to complete each word. There is an example.

Eg Students learn effectively <u>*through*</u> concentrated reading.

1 A business may **lo** __ __ customers when it moves to another location.

2 The **len** __ __ __ of women's clothing reflects the economic climate in inverse proportion.

3 What is **mea** __ __ by acceptable behaviour may change over time.

4 Dear Sue, I know we haven't **cau** __ __ __ up for ages, but I'd love to see you.

5 One recent **la** __ in my country is the banning of smoking in restaurants.

6 Playing a musical instrument **do** __ __ take dedication.

7 These days it is a challenge to **ra** __ __ __ children.

8 To get a Seven, a candidate needs **flai** __.

9 Water is becoming **sca** __ __ __.

10 The **dr** __ __ __ __ __ in Sydney lasted for eight years.

Many candidates find the missing words in sentences 4, 5, and 10 hard to pronounce. What does the missing word in sentence 8 mean?

 PLAY RECORDING 63 and say the words after the speakers.

The length of vowel sounds and spelling

Cross out the misspelt words below. Which phoneme is the stressed vowel? Is it short, long, or a diphthong? What happens to the consonant that follows: is it single or double? There is an example.

Eg I am <u>writing</u> / ~~writting~~ to you about a purchase I made at your shop.

/aɪ/ <u>*diphthong, therefore single t*</u>

1 <u>Waiting</u> / <u>Waitting</u> for public transport can be tiresome.

/　/ ＿＿＿＿＿＿＿＿

2 We are <u>hoping</u> / <u>hopping</u> to visit Nepal in summer.

/　/ ＿＿＿＿＿＿＿＿

3 An elderly person who is not <u>feeling</u> / <u>felling</u> well should be looked after at home by relatives.

/　/ ＿＿＿＿＿＿＿＿

4 <u>Fiting in</u> / <u>Fitting in</u> at primary school can be difficult for only children.

/　/ ＿＿＿＿＿＿＿＿

5 My cousin's <u>wedding</u> / <u>weeding</u> was lovely.

/　/ ＿＿＿＿＿＿＿＿

6 Japanese homes often have grass <u>mating</u> / <u>matting</u> on the floor.

/　/ ＿＿＿＿＿＿＿＿

7 There are a lot of <u>unplaned</u> / <u>unplanned</u> pregnancies in my country.

/　/ ＿＿＿＿＿＿＿＿

The following spelling rules have missing words. Write the letters to complete each one. There is an example.

If a **<u>word</u>** has a **l** __ __ __ vowel sound, like /iː/ in se*at*ing, or a diphthong, like /aɪ/ in *rid*ing, then it usually has a **s** __ __ __ __ __ consonant. If a word has a short

v __ __ __ __, like /ɒ/ in sho*pp*ed, then it has a **d** __ __ __ __ __ consonant.

Common words with the sounds /dʒ/, /g/, or /ʒ/

Put the words into three groups as you listen. Write the letters dg, g, gg, or j for the sounds shown at the top of each column. There are examples.

Play Audio PLAY RECORDING 64.

/dʒ/	/g/	/ʒ/
exa**gg**erate	a**g**ainst	bei**ge**
_____	_____	_____
gender	be**gg**ar	(This is a very small group.)
_____	**gh**ost	
January	_____	
_____	_____	
ma**j**ority		
_____		
pre**j**udice		
_____		
_____		
tra**g**ic		

Add one word with two /dʒ/ sounds and another with one /dʒ/ sound.

_____

_____

Add one more.

_____

Common words with the sound /k/

Write c, cc, ch, ck, or k in the gaps.

a___ustomed   a___e   authenti___   ___areer   ___emistry
___offee   flu___tuate   pani___ing   psy___ologi___al
re___less   sho___ing   South ___orea   stoma___

Common words with the sound /f/

Write f, ff, gh, or ph in the gaps.

a___ectionate   al___abet   con___use   em___asis   enou___
___atal   ___ossil   ___uel   ___inance   gra___   o___icial
___iloso___y   tele___one   ___enomenon   ___otogra___er
pre___er   re___ugee   rou___   tra___ic

Common words with the sound /ʃ/

*Write **ch, ci, sh, ss**, or **ti** in the gaps.*

a___amed   ___ic   emo___on   fa___ion   ini___ally

ma___ine   mi___ion   poten___al   ru___ hour   ___opaholic

so___al   vi___ous

Check any new vocabulary.

Spelling and remembering what you see

As mentioned previously, spelling is visual. A keen reader is a good speller.

The order of letters

Some IELTS candidates, especially those who do not use the Roman alphabet in their own language, have problems with the order of letters. If a word should be written *their*, a person may write *thier* instead.

Find one or two words in each sentence that are misspelt like this, and fix them.

1 Some people think having tow children is enough.

2 It is ture more people live to eighty than in the past.

3 Hunger and poverty still exits in many countries.

4 To slove this problem, driving skills could be taught at school.

5 In Europe, quiet a few cities have bicycle lanes.

6 These days, morden apartments in Lagos have many appliances.

7 Some people prefer to study online instade of attending a course in person.

8 Fristly, fathers spend less time with their families if they work aboard.

9 In 1900, people ate one hunderd grams of protien a week; now, it is seven times that amount.

10 Thirty precent of food has colour or perservative added according to the table.

Missing letters

Some candidates do not put all the letters into a word even when they're pronounced as in sentences 5-8 below.

In each sentence below there is a word or words missing one or more letters. Find the words and fix them by adding the missing letters. There is an example.

      ageing
Eg An ~~aging~~ population means a smaller tax base.

1 Befor refrigeration, people hung food in trees or kept it in water.

2 The theatre is opposit the railway station.

3 Crime is rising in my city. Therefor more police should be employed.

4 The average daily temprature in winter is minus ten in Moscow.

5 A large propotion of revenue goes to the army in my country.

6 More people are studing hydrology now because of the water crisis.

7 Over a quater of respondents said their favrit sport was fishing.

8 In my opion, cars are more conveint than bicycles.

Silent letters

There are quite a few words in English with silent letters.

Each word below is missing one letter. Put the letters back in. There is an example.

ca**l**m   casle   climer   cuboard
Chrismas   dout   fasinated
haf (½)   hansome   onest   iland
nowledge   lisen   musle
sychology   receit   samon
sience   sin   wich

IF YOU WANT A SEVEN

campai**g**n   det   have (verb from '½')
morgage   poinant   senery
sofen   sutle   tom   reckage

 PLAY RECORDING 65 and say the words after the speakers.

Missing syllables

How do you say the word 'interesting'? If a speaker says 'in-ter-es-ting', making it four syllables, then he or she is probably *not* interested, and possibly angry. Normally, speakers say 'in-tres-ting' as though the first e were missing. Saying this correctly will improve Fluency and Pronunciation in Speaking.

*In each word below, cross out one letter to show how the word is pronounced with a reduced syllable. The **bold** words need two letters removed. (Don't cross out any letters at the beginning or end of words.) There are examples.*

average, **basically**, business, camera, (un)**comfortable**, (in)definite, different, (un)**fashionable**, **favourite** (US favorite), general, (un)generous, interest, literature, reference, **restaurant**, separate (adj only – the verb has 3 syllables), temperature, valuable, vegetable, **Wednesday**

IF YOU WANT A SEVEN

category, desperate, **extraordinary**, (dis)**honourable**, **originally**, preferable

 PLAY RECORDING 66 and say the words after the speakers.

Confusing vowels: *ie* or *ei*?

- *ie:* In general, there are more *ie* words in English than *ei*. The letters *ie* are pronounced in different ways. The most common way is /iː/ as in 'achieve'. When the syllable with *ie* is unstressed, the sound is a schwa or /ɪ/ as in 'patient'. In 'audience' the *i* and *e* are separate sounds.

- *ei:* There are several ways *ei* are pronounced: /eɪ/ for 'eight', or /iː/ for 'ceiling' are the most common.

PLAY RECORDING 67.

Write the words in the columns below depending on whether they are spelt with ie or ei.

ie	*ei*
achieve	ceiling
audience	_____
_____	freight
brief	_____
_____	_____
_____	neighbour (US neighbor)
efficient	neither
_____	_____
_____	_____
ingredient	weight
_____	weird
_____	
piece	
_____	

IF YOU WANT A SEVEN

*Write **ie** or **ei** in the gaps.*

ag___ng   caff ___ ne   consc___nce   gr___vance,
h___rarchy   hyg___ne   (in)suffic___nt   med___val
perc___ve   r___gn,   r___nforce   r___nstate   s___ze

Double letters

The letters *a, h, i, j, k, q, u, v, w, x,* and *y* are almost never doubled in English.
Common doubles are: *bb, cc, dd, ee, ff, gg, ll, mm, nn, oo, pp, rr, ss,* and *tt.*
The vowel sound before double consonants is usually short or unstressed.

Words with double consonants

Which letters are missing from the groups of words below? Write the letters in each gap. Add another word to each group. There is an example.

Eg   banning, beginning, running   winning

1   dile____a, i____igration, reco____end   _____

2   a____ident, a____omplish, a____urate   _____

3   di____atisfy, nece____ity, proce____   _____

4   exce____ent, i____egal, vi____age   _____

5   cu____ency, i____elevant, ma____iage   _____

6   a____ropriate, o____ortunity, o____osite   _____

Now, there are two or three double consonants missing. Put them back in.

a____identa____y, a____o____odation, a____re____,
a____re____ive, a____ua____y, co____i____ed, emba____a____,
mi____e____ium, o____u____ence, po____e____ion,
su____e____fu____y, u____ece____ary

Can you think of another word like those above?   _____

Suffixes

A suffix is a letter or letters at the end of a word which add grammatical information. For example: the letters *-ment* are for abstract nouns; *-able* are for adjectives; and, *-ly* are for regular adverbs.

Regular adverbs

There are only a few irregular adverbs in English like *fast*, as in, 'My brother drives fast.' (not 'fastly'), or *hard* as in 'Yesterday I worked hard.' (not 'hardly'). The three regular adverbial endings are: *-ally*, *-ily*, and *-ly*.

● The first ending is for adjectives that end in *-ic*, for example: *basic* ➝ *basically*.

● The second ending is for adjectives ending in *-y*, eg: *happy* ➝ *happily*.

● The last one is the largest group, for all others. If an adjective ends in *l*, it keeps that *l* in the adverb, eg: *careful* ➝ *carefully*. Note: *extremely* and *immediately* keep their *es*, but *possibly* doesn't keep its *y*.

Change the adjectives in the box into adverbs. Put them into groups in the columns below. Write them on the lines provided.

day	dramatic	economic	~~funny~~	gradual	private
probable	~~rapid~~	rare	~~typical~~	wonderful	

-ly

_____

_____

_____

rapidly

_____

typically

_____

-ily

_____

funnily

-ally

_____

_____

IF YOU WANT A SEVEN

annual	approximate	drastic	economic	imperceptible	magic
	noisy	public*	~~remote~~	sincere	

-ly

_____

_____

_____

remotely

_____

-ily

_____

-ally

_____

_____

*An exception.

Common adjective and noun endings

-ful

Remember: these adjectives have only one *l*.

awful, beautiful, careful, grateful, harmful, respectful, successful, stressful, wasteful

Add two more: _____ and _____

Which two above have opposites with the suffix *-less*?

_____ and _____

Which three have opposites with the prefix *un-*?

_____, _____, and _____

Which one has an opposite with the prefix *dis-*? _____

-ent or -ant?

These suffixes are unstressed, and their sound is: /ɪnt/. Because they sound the same, *-ent* and *-ant* are often misspelt. However, *-ent* is far more common than *-ant*.
  The nouns for these adjectives end in *-ence* or *-ance*.
  Usually a word has both an adjective and a noun, like *adolescent* and *adolescence*; occasionally the adjective is a participle, like *maintained* or *maintaining*. The adjective *appar**e**nt* goes with the noun *appe**a**rance* – watch out for their spelling.

*Put **e** or **a** into the adjectives and nouns below.*

brilli_nt, (un)confid_nt, (in)conveni_nt, excell_nt, experi_nce,

ignor_nt, (in)depend_nt, (un)intellig_nt, perform_nce,

(im)perman_nt, refer_nce, (non-)viol_nce.

IF YOU WANT A SEVEN

acquaint_nce, (in)compet_nt, (non-)exist_nt, interfer_nce,

(ir)relev_nt, occurr_nce, persever_nce, (in)signific_nt.

-able or -ible (adj)? -ability or -ibility (n)?

*In this first group, the opposite prefix is un-. Which letter is missing in the adjectives: **a** or **i** ? Write the missing letters.*

accept_ble, avail_ble, chang**e**_ble, desir_ble, lik_ble,

manag**e**_ble, notic**e**_ble, reli_ble

and: cap_ble and hospit_ble (with in- as their opposite prefix).

*This second group has im-, in-, or ir- as opposite prefixes. Which letter is missing: **a** or **i** ? Write the missing letters.*

compat_ble,   cred_ble,   elig_ble,   flex_ble,   poss_ble,   respons_ble,

sens_ble,   vis_ble.

These adjectives do <u>not</u> have -ity as their noun suffix. What are their nouns?

horrible ➡   <u>   horror (n)   </u>   preferable ➡   _____

terrible ➡   _____   valuable ➡   _____

-ment

*All the **verbs** below have -ment as their noun suffix. What happens to the letter before -ment? Add the suffix and write each word correctly. There are examples.*

achieve ➡   <u>achiev**e**ment</u> (*keep the* **e**)   advertise ➡   _____

arg**ue** ➡   <u>argument</u> (*drop the* **e**)   commit ➡   <u>commi**t**ment</u> (*single* **t**)

develop ➡   _____   embarra**ss** ➡   _____

encourag**e** ➡   _____   entertai**n** ➡   _____

equip ➡   _____   fulfi**l** ➡   _____

Add two more verbs that have -ment as their noun suffix.

_____ and _____

The sound /ʃɪn/

*There are several different ways to spell the sound /ʃɪn/. The most common way is -tion as in accommoda**tion** or rela**tion**ship. What is another possibility?* _____

Change the verbs into nouns which end in -tion, -sion, or -ssion. Write the new words correctly. Notice which other letters are different in the verbs and nouns.

accommodat**e** ➡   <u>*accommodation*</u>   add ➡   _____

compet**e** ➡   _____   comprehen**d** ➡   <u>*comprehension*</u>

creat**e** ➡   _____   depress ➡   _____

distribut**e** ➡   _____   permi**t** ➡   _____

pollut**e** ➡   _____   prepar**e** ➡   _____

pron**ou**nce ➡   _____   solv**e** ➡   _____

Other possibilities:

What are the missing words? Write the letters to complete each one.

The Atlantic and the Pacific are two vast **o** __ __ __ __ __.

A resident of Moscow is likely to be a **R** __ __ __ __ __ __.

Someone who makes a living from playing music is a **m** __ __ __ __ __ __ __.

A person who represents others in politics is a **p** __ __ __ __ __ __ __ __ __.

The sound /ʒɪn/

The verb *confuse* becomes the noun *confusion*.

Change each verb below to a noun in the same way.

decide ➡ _____   revise ➡ _____

Can you add one more to this group? _____ ➡ _____

Confusing words

There are many words in English that look or sound similar. Some of them are related to each other, like *advice* and *advise* – the noun and the verb in the same family. Others are unrelated, but sound the same or similar. Think about *sight* and *site*, or *celery* and *salary*.

Read the example below.

Eg *decent* and *descent*		
Do these words sound the same?	~~Yes~~ / No	<u>IPA</u>: /ˈdiːsɪnt/ /dɪˈsent/
Are they related to each other?	~~Yes~~ / No	
What do they mean?		
decent (adj) = very good or moral		
descent (n; from verb descend) = the act of going down (slightly formal)		
Used in sentences:		
'I'd like a <u>decent</u> job after I graduate,' Mariella said, 'not just working as a shop assistant as I am now.'		
The climbers made a sudden <u>descent</u> into the cave.		
Which one do you think is more common?		*decent*

Before you complete the next page, make five copies of it.
    *Fill in the information for three sets of confusing words that are **new for you**.*

Words to choose from:

A	accept, except; affect, effect; all ready, already; angel, angle
B	bases, basis; borrow, burrow; bowl, bowel; brake, break; breath, breathe
C	carton, cartoon; celery, salary; censor, sensor; cent, scent, sent; cereal, serial; choose, chose; cite, sight, site; collage, college; complement, compliment; currant, current
D	discus, discuss; does, dose
E	envelop, envelope; especially, specially; every one, everyone; excited, exited
F	fair, fare, fire; floor, flour, flower
G & H	grate, great; heroin, heroine; human, humane
I & L	it's, its; lead, led; loose, lose
P & Q	peace, piece; passed, past; personal, personnel; precede, proceed; prescribe, proscribe; principal, principle; quiet, quit, quite
S	sever, severe; sew, so, sue; spacious, specious; summary, summery
T	than, then; their, there, they're; to, too; tour, tower; tow, two
V, W, & Y	vary, very; wander, wonder; weak, week; weather, whether; your, you're

1

Do these words sound the same?	Yes / No	IPA:
Are they related to each other?	Yes / No	

What do they mean?

Used in sentences:

Which one do you think is more common?	

2

Do these words sound the same?	Yes / No	IPA:
Are they related to each other?	Yes / No	

What do they mean?

Used in sentences:

Which one do you think is more common?	

3

Do these words sound the same?	Yes / No	IPA:
Are they related to each other?	Yes / No	

What do they mean?

Used in sentences:

Which one do you think is more common?	

CHAPTER **7** IELTS Vocabulary and Grammar

Introduction to Vocabulary

Without consulting a dictionary or writing names, can you think of six English words that have ten or more letters?

_____ and _____

_____ and _____

_____ and _____

One measure of a candidate's level is the number of long words that he or she uses accurately.

Put three of the words above into sentences of around 20 words each.

1 _____

_____

2 _____

_____

3 _____

_____

IF YOU WANT A SEVEN

Choose one sentence above, and rewrite it so that its meaning stays the same but its vocabulary and grammar change.

4 _____

_____

YOUR TURN   *Put the information below about English vocabulary in order by numbering the strips from 1 to 7. Two items have been done for you.*

	English is mainly comprised of French, but also Latin, something like German, and even Scandinavian languages. From its imperial past, it contains words from hundreds of other tongues.
	IELTS candidates make almost five times as many errors with vocabulary than with grammar. This means extra study of vocabulary is essential, or reading sophisticated texts for 15 minutes in English every day to increase exposure to new language.
	Ancient Greek influenced English. Many items related to science originate in this language. As a result of this huge lexical influx, English has an enormous number of words of similar meaning, but contrary to popular belief very few that mean exactly the same thing.
1	English vocabulary is large – in fact, the largest of any language. The complicated history of what is now the United Kingdom – being invaded many times and later building its own empire – contributed to this size and richness.
4	To score highly in IELTS, vocabulary needs to be precise, varied, idiomatic, and appropriate to writing or speaking, to formal or informal contexts.
	An educated English speaker will have a vocabulary exceeding 25,000 words whereas an IELTS Six has just a few thousand, most of which will be passive, meaning he or she can recognise and understand a word or phrase in context, but seldom or never produce it.
	By contrast, active vocabulary is language a person uses accurately and frequently. IELTS Writing and Speaking test active knowledge.

IF YOU WANT A SEVEN

In number seven above, the little-known fact about errors is extremely important. Once again:

what is the ratio between lexical and grammatical error? _____ : _____

Knowing this statistic, a candidate is wise to devote a significant amount of IELTS preparation time to vocabulary.

Precision, idiom, and appropriateness

These are three concepts related to vocabulary that IELTS examiners consider when awarding bands.

Precision means using the exact word.

Choose the correct item of the three possibilities below.

1   'I was trying to take something off the wall last night. I couldn't find a screwdriver / secateurs / stapler, so I ended up using a knife.'

2   'I caught a fleeting / momentary / narrow glimpse of the Duchess of Cambridge when she was on a royal tour.'

3   'I'll never forget being castigated / conjugated / coruscated by my Latin teacher for the mispronunciation of a poem.'

An **idiom** is a word or phrase that takes on a meaning separate from its original literal one.

Choose the correct item of the three possibilities below.

1   'I'm bogged down / rained out / snowed in at work at the moment.'

2 'The Island of Khizhi is <u>out of my league / out of my mind / out of this world</u>. Its old buildings are so beautiful.'

3 'I'd like to go to New Zealand, but I'm <u>put down / put off / put out</u> by the long flight.'

See pages 278-281 for more on idiom.

There are two aspects to **appropriateness**.

- It can mean using vocabulary suitable to speaking (and not to writing) or to writing (and not to speaking).

- It can also mean using formal or informal language.

Choose the more appropriate item in each pair.

1 (In Speaking Part 2) 'I think I can pick up new ideas pretty fast.' / 'I think I have the ability to acquire knowledge with great speed.'

2 (In Writing Task 2) *A large number of immigrants to my city have made it culturally a more interesting place. / Immigration has contributed to greater cultural diversity in my city.*

3 (In GT Writing Task 1 – a formal letter) *I look forward to hearing from you. Yours sincerely, Thomas Nielsen / Thanking you in advance. Best wishes, Tom*

Go to page 397 for the answers.

The Academic Word List (AWL)

In recent years, there has been an attempt to determine which words are frequently used in academic writing. One such list of words is called the Academic Word List, and its subsets can be found online. In general, academic words are long and Latinate. IELTS Academic Reading tests include many words from the AWL as does Section 4 of the Listening Test. Academic candidates should use them in both writing tasks; GT candidates may use them in Task 2.

Paraphrasing

This is saying the same thing in a slightly different way. It involves using synonyms, other parts of speech, and alternative grammatical structures. It is not an easy skill to master, but it is indispensable in keeping a reader's or listener's interest. IELTS examiners keenly look out for good paraphrasing, and it is a key concept in the criterion of Vocabulary.

YOUR TURN   Below are three attempts to paraphrase a Writing Task 2 question. There are no mistakes with grammar.

Here is the question: *In some countries, health care is free, paid for by the state. In other countries, payment is divided between the state and people themselves.*

Discuss both systems, and say which one is better.

Which candidate is the best? ___

A *The hot button topic of whether the government or the population should pay for medical nurture is a fascinating question.*

B *Health care is free in some countries, where it is paid for by the state. In other places, the state and people divide the payment.*

C *Free or state-financed health care is available in some countries while in other parts of the world payment is made by the state and the rest by people themselves.*

Who is the worst? ___   Why?

Circumlocution

This is saying something in a longer way because a candidate has forgotten the exact word or doesn't know it. It is generally a spoken skill.

If you're an Eight, you don't rely on circumlocution because you always use precise vocabulary. If you're a Five, you rarely attempt it. For a Six who wants to show that he or she could be a Seven, circumlocution is helpful because it proves the candidate knows a variety of language, and it keeps the communication going, which contributes to Fluency.

YOUR TURN   Here are three speakers. They've all started with: 'I was trying to take something off the wall last night ...'

Who has successfully used circumlocution? ___

A   'I couldn't find the right thing to use. I wanted one of those sticks with a pointer that rotates and releases pins.'

B   'I couldn't find the right tool. You know, the one with a sharp point in the shape of a cross which turns and pulls out little metal things that are similar to nails.'

C   'I couldn't find the right instrument. I wanted a blade that eradicates scores.'

Who has not given an accurate description of the missing word? ___

Who has confused the listener more? ___

Here are three more speakers. Each one has used circumlocution effectively. What were the words they intended to say but had <u>forgotten</u>?

D   'I was meant to play squash last night, but I decided <u>to schedule the match at a later date</u> because I wanted a good sleep before this exam.'

<u>Intended word:</u> **p** __ __ __ __ __   or   **p** __ __ __ __ __ __ __ __

E   'The Persians had the first large kingdom, I mean, it was <u>more than a kingdom</u> because the land they took after winning several wars stretched for a very long way, and the rulers in these places didn't give up all their power, but instead paid taxes to the Persians in their capital.'

<u>Intended word:</u> **e** __ __ __ __ __

F   'My son's six, and he used to be a gentle little guy, but I'm quite shocked at some of the behaviour he's come home with from school. He wants to fight physically with his older brother at every opportunity, and he shouts when he wants anything, or comes up and starts hitting me.'

<u>Intended word:</u> **agg** __ __ __ __ __ __ __   (an opposite of 'gentle')

How can I improve my vocabulary?

- By reading. (This is about five times more effective than listening.)

- By reading at every opportunity you get. (At home. On the bus. Waiting for the doctor...)

- By reading different genres – that is, different styles of writing: academic articles; newspaper or magazine articles; encyclopaedia entries; short stories or novels; and, biographies.

- By devising a system of recording vocabulary.

- By testing yourself regularly.

- By using new words and phrases in writing and speaking.

YOUR TURN   Here is part of the back page of a magazine that the Australian Red Cross publishes.

This text is useful for an IELTS candidate because it contains numerous abstract nouns and longer more formal Latinate verbs, both found in the Reading test.

The seven principles of the organisation are described in paragraphs A to G below. Match the paragraphs with the missing principles in the box. There is an example.

| ~~Humanity~~   Impartiality   Independence   Neutrality   Unity |
| Universality   Voluntary service |

'In all activities, Red Cross staff members and volunteers are guided by the following fundamental principles.

A = *Humanity*: The International Red Cross and Red Crescent Movement, born of a desire to bring assistance without discrimination to the wounded on the battlefield, endeavours, in its international and national capacity, to prevent and alleviate human suffering wherever it may be found. Its purpose is to protect life and health, and ensure respect for the human being. It promotes mutual understanding, friendship, co-operation, and lasting peace among all people.

B = _____: It makes no discrimination as to nationality, race, religious beliefs, class, or political opinions. It endeavours to relieve the suffering of individuals, being guided solely by their needs, and to give priority to the most urgent cases of distress.

C = _____: In order to continue to enjoy the confidence of all, the Movement may not take sides in hostilities or engage at any time in controversies of a political, racial, religious, or ideological nature.

D = _____: The Movement is independent. The national Societies, while auxiliaries in the humanitarian services of their governments and subject to the laws of their respective countries, must always maintain their autonomy so that they may be able at all times to act in accordance with the principles of the Movement.

E = _____: It is a voluntary relief movement not prompted in any manner by desire for gain.

F = _____: There can be only one Red Cross or Red Crescent Society in any one country. It must be open to all. It must carry out its humanitarian work throughout its territory.

G = _____: The International Red Cross and Red Crescent Movement, in which all Societies have equal status and share equal responsibilities and duties in helping each other, is worldwide.'*

The table below lists the nouns and verbs from the text about the Red Cross. Go down each column, and mark those that you know. Now is the time to learn the others.

Abstract nouns			Latinate verbs
assistance	health	respect	alleviate
autonomy	humanity	status	endeavour
capacity	impartiality	suffering	engage
co-operation	independence	understanding	ensure
desire	life	unity	maintain
discrimination	nature	universality	prevent
distress	neutrality	voluntary service	prompt
friendship	peace	work	protect
gain			relieve

See 'Nominalisation' on pages 152-154 for more about nouns and their importance in Writing Task 2.

---

* Copyright © The Australian Red Cross, 2011.

Word families

A word family is words with the same root, related to each other.
In the word family for 'family', there are:

Common noun	Abstract noun (+ preposition)	Regular reflexive verb (+ preposition)	Adjective (+ preposition)
family (sing) families (pl)	familiarity (with)	familiarise myself (with)	familiar (with)

Other parts of speech, like the adverb, are extremely rare.
In the word family for 'related' there are the same number of parts, but more examples:

Common nouns	Regular verb (+ preposition)	True and participial adjectives (+ preposition)	Adverb
relative; relation; relationship	relate (to)	relative (to); (un)related (to)	relatively

In writing and speaking, candidates need to manipulate different parts of speech within a word family with confidence.

In the Reading test, there is also one question type which relies on a knowledge of word families. This is a summary completion question. (See page 31.) It has a list of choices in which synonyms for words in the passage and slightly different parts of speech are used. For example, the passage may mention: 'The anthropologists know the town well.' The summary question is: 'The anthropologists have a certain...with the town.' The answer is: 'familiarity'.

While it may be easy to learn tables of words, as above, putting words into the right context can be tricky. For example, 'a related question' and 'a relative question' mean different things. Check their meanings in a good dictionary.

As we have already learnt, IELTS reading and writing use academic language, so it is a good idea to learn word families related to an academic word list.

Use the IELTS Vocabulary Log on page 446 to collect new word families.

YOUR TURN   The words in the tables on the following pages are from the Academic Word List.
What are the missing people, verbs, and adjectives?

A

Common and abstract nouns	Person who does this thing	Regular verbs	True and participial adjectives
administration	_ _ _ _ _ _ _ _ _ _ _ _ _	administer	administrative
analysis	_ _ _ _ _ _ _	_ _ _ _ _ _ _	analytical
approach	(No person)	_ _ _ _ _ _ _ _	(un) approachable

1 'I'm not quite sure what my mother does, but she's an _____ assistant at a university.'

2 'My former boss was completely _____. Even at work parties, people were too scared to chat to him for very long.'

3 *For literature to succeed, it needs to be _____ as well as descriptive.*

Here are some more.

B

Common and abstract nouns	Person who does this thing	Regular verbs	True and participial adjectives
benefit	beneficiary (of)	_ _ _ _ _ _ _ (from)	benefitted
contract	contractor	_ _ _ _ _ _ _ _	contractual
definition	(No person)	_ _ _ _ _ _	definitive / (un)defined
distribution	_ _ _ _ _ _ _ _ _ _ _	distribute	distributed

1 'I really _____ from extra Maths tuition when I was at secondary school.'

2 'One _____ of adulthood that I like is: "If you've bought a couch, you're an adult.'

3 According to the information in the second chart, the market for paintings from the 19th century _____ since 1980.

4 In New Zealand, wireless subscribers are evenly _____ across the country; in Laos, they are almost all in cities.

Here is the final lot.

C

Common and abstract nouns	Person who does this thing	Regular verbs	True and participial adjectives
environment	environmentalist	(No verb)	_ _ _ _ _ _ _ _ _ _ _
evidence	(No person)	(No verb)	_ _ _ _ _ _
export	_ _ _ _ _ _ _	export	exportable / exported
factor	(No person)	_ _ _ _ _ _ in (phrasal verb)	(No adjective)
function	functionary (rare)	_ _ _ _ _ _	(dys)functional

1 'To tell you the truth, I grew up in a pretty _____ family. My parents were separated, and my older sister had run away from home.'

2 It appears _____ degradation has occurred along the Amazon.

3 Papua New Guinea _____ gold and gas.

4 From the data, it is _____ that smokers' lives are shorter than non-smokers'.

5 Once accommodation costs are _____ in, workers in Darwin and Cairns have similar amounts of money left to spend.

Make similar tables yourself with academic words you encounter.
One way to learn vocabulary more quickly is to personalise it. Start your sentences with:
'The last time I...' or 'In my opinion, . . .' or 'My father used to say that . . .'

Reference and substitution

YOUR TURN   *Unscramble the words below. There is an example.*

Reference is the (eg) (*mert*) *term* used when a word, like a pronoun, refers back or (*drafwo*) _____ to another idea. Substitution is when a word like 'another', 'mine', 'one' or 'own' is used (*desaint*) _____ of repeating a noun or noun phrase.

Because reference and substitution (*dovia*) _____ repetition, they speed up speech or text improving (*eneChorec*) _____. Knowing the right word to use as a substitute or referent shows good Vocabulary.

An IELTS Five or Six uses reference and substitution to some (*nettex*) _____. A Seven has almost mastered them.

Research has shown there is one particular referent, with its own name: replacive one, that is a clear (*ridointca*)_____of a Seven.

Identifying reference and substitution

Read the following paragraph about artists.

All artists synthesise the new ideas of <u>others</u> with <u>their own</u> and with the traditions of their chosen medium; a great artist produces distinctive yet recognisable work <u>which</u> the public agrees towers above other creations in <u>its</u> field.

The underlined words refer to or substitute for ideas in the text or outside it.

'others' substitutes for other artists (inferred)

'their' refers back to 'artists' and forward to 'own'; 'own' substitutes for artists' own ideas

'which' refers back to 'work'

'creations' is a synonym or substitute for works

'its' refers back to 'work' and forward to 'field'

YOUR TURN   A less skilful writer might have written the same paragraph in this way:

All artists synthesise the new ideas of other artists with their own ideas and with the traditions of their chosen medium; a great artist produces distinctive yet recognizable work. The public agrees this work towers above other works in its field.

Which three nouns, above, are repeated unnecessarily?

i _____   ii _____   iii _____

The paragraph below follows the initial one about artists. Fill each blank with a word from the box.

he	him	himself	his	one	that	this	who

Astor Piazzolla, the late Argentinean musician and composer, was _____ such man. Although _____ died more than 20 years ago, _____ 1000+ compositions are still performed regularly. His particular genre, known as World Music, blended Argentinean tango with Western classical forms and American jazz.

Born in Argentina in 1921, Piazzolla showed early promise as a player of the bandoneón, making his first record at the tender age of nine. At 16, he met the renowned pianist Arthur Rubenstein, _____ encouraged _____ in his study of classical piano. Piazzolla did _____ under the Hungarian, Bela Wilda, who instilled in him a love of baroque music, particularly _____ of Bach. Later, Piazzolla became a pupil of local composer Alberto Ginastera, and in 1950, he began serious composition _____ with a film soundtrack.

Pronouns

From the text about Astor Piazzolla, it is clear that while English nouns do not change their endings for masculine or feminine, or for subject or object, English pronouns do.

There are five different forms of a pronoun, described in slightly different ways in different grammar books. Consider 'she' and 'they'.

Subject pronoun	Object pronoun (direct or indirect)	Reflexive pronoun	Possessive pronoun	Possessive adjective
she	her / to her (as an indirect object placed after a direct object)	herself	hers	her (before a noun)
She lives in Los Angeles.	The manager likes her. / I gave her a present. / I gave a present to her. (The first one is more natural.)	She can change a tyre by herself.	'Whose coat is this?' 'It's Anna's.' / 'It's hers.' / 'Where's her car?' 'It's the red one* on the left.' / 'Hers is the red one on the left.' / One of her brothers is the mayor. / A brother of hers is the mayor.	She lent me her umbrella.
they	them / to them	themselves	theirs	their
They work hard.	I don't always agree with them. / I used to send them money. / I used to send money to them.	My parents built up their business themselves.	If I think back to my grandparents' youth, theirs was a hard life.	I try to take their advice.

* 'One' is replacive one, replacing 'car'.

YOUR TURN   *All the sentences below, from the Speaking test, have one mistake connected to the word 'I'. Fix the mistakes. There is an example.*

> *My father and I*
> **Eg** 'I and my father sometimes go fishing.'

1 'My mother gave to me her old car.'

2 'Me and my friend often go clubbing at the weekend.'

3 'A relative of me won an Olympic medal for rowing about 40 years ago.'

4 'My parents sent my sister and I to boarding school. It wasn't a great experience.'

5 'My boss and myself were the only ones who stayed to clean up the mess after the recent floods.'

6 'I was thrilled when my university sent a letter me announcing I'd won a scholarship.'

7 'Unfortunately, the car belonging to me was stolen last week.'

8 'Grandparents live quite far away, so I rarely see them.'

9 Examiner (as the candidate is leaving the room): 'Is this your pen?'
    Candidate: 'Yes, thanks. It's my pen.'

10 'I can only blame me for being overweight – I almost never exercise.'

She or he?

This problem is a spoken one. It occurs with speakers whose first language, like Mandarin, does not have male or female pronouns; or, with speakers whose language has them, like Indonesian, but the male pronoun starts with the sound /s/, causing confusion with the English equivalent. A speaker with this she-or-he problem receives a Four or a Five in Speaking because the examiner becomes too confused.

YOUR TURN   *All the sentences below have **two** mistakes related to 'he' or 'she'. What are they? Write the corrections.*

1 'My uncle has own business. She sells electronic goods.'

2 'My sister was the best student at she school. Now he's studying Medicine.'

3 'I saw a ballet performance on TV. One of the dancers was fantastic. Body was so muscular, and she could lift female dancers very easily.'

4 'My father grew up on a farm. She could ride a horse, and milk a cow. Now, she's a lawyer in the city.'

Its or it's?

These words sound the same, but the former is a possessive adjective, like 'her' or 'their', while the latter is a contraction for 'it is', and is restricted to IELTS Speaking.

YOUR TURN   *All of the sentences below contain apostrophes, but only one apostrophe is needed. Cross out the four that are incorrect.*

1   The koala bear is a symbol of Australia, but recently it's habitat has become so small it is now endangered.

2   I think it's a good idea to put efficiency ratings on appliances.

3   California is famous for it's beaches and forests, it's heavy industries, and Hollywood and Disneyland.

4   The Airpod is a new kind of vehicle. It's engine runs on compressed air.

Demonstrative, reflexive, and relative pronouns

Consult a good grammar book or website for information about these types of pronouns.

YOUR TURN   *The items below in italics come from the Writing test. Those in quotation marks are from Speaking. Each item has one mistake related to the pronouns above. Fix the mistakes. There are examples.*

                                                                 , which

Eg   *One of the largest organs in the human body ~~which~~ is the skin. ~~It~~ is made up of two layers of tissue.*

                                these days

Eg   'It's hard not to be a consumer ~~in this day~~.'

1   'For our class party, we prepared a barbecue ourself.'

2   'It took my grandfather two hours to walk to work. In them days, almost no one had a car, and there wasn't much public transport either.'

3   'It's easy enough to learn yourself how to swim.'

4   'My cousin who lives in Addis Ababa she has her own chain of hairdressing shops.'

5   'I don't think children should be left at home by theirselfs until they're twelve.'

6   'People which park their cars in my space really annoy me.'

7   *The epidermis which is mainly fat and makes the skin waterproof.*

8   *The dermis which is beneath the epidermis. It contains blood vessels, nerves, muscles, oil, sweat glands, and hair roots.*

9   *As well as protecting the body from injury, infection and burns, the skin's main function, which is to regulate body temperature.*

10   *In China everyone knows what companies cause water pollution.*

11   *I believe this companies should be fined heavily.*

12   *It is the president who's responsibility it is to guide the country.*

Reference and substitution in Speaking Part 2

YOUR TURN   *Here is an answer to a Speaking Part 2 topic. What are the missing words? Complete each one by writing the letters in the spaces provided.*

'My favourite teacher was the **o** __ __ we had for English in Year 9, and **w** __ __ probably encouraged __ __ the most. I really stretched **m** __ __ __ __ __ in her class. In fact, I won an English prize **t** __ __ __ year.

My teacher's name is Mrs McCafferty, but __ __ all called her Mrs Mick. __ __ __ 's separated with three daughters, one of **w** __ __ __ was our school captain. She's Canadian, but her parents were from Lebanon and Germany, and __ __ __ can speak five languages. __ __ __ favourite food is chocolate despite **i** __ __ high fat content. Mrs Mick sincerely believes that because chocolate contains the chemical theobromine, __ __ makes **t** __ __ __ __ who eat it feel as though __ __ __ __ 're in love, so putting on a few grams here and there doesn't really matter.

I enjoyed __ __ __ classes since **t** __ __ __ seemed to be about life rather than just English. For __ __, the personality of my teacher matters as much as what __ __ or she teaches.'

How might you answer this question about your favourite teacher?

Reported speech

IF YOU WANT A SEVEN

Remember, pronouns change in reported speech. (Consult a good grammar book or website.)

Fix the underlined mistakes in the candidate's speaking below. They are connected to pronouns as well as other language around reported speech. Write the corrections.

---

1 Examiner   What experiences in early life do you think change a person forever?

   Candidate   I think suffering. For example, my uncle told me <u>I have seen</u> some terrible things during the civil war. <u>My</u> family was killed and <u>my</u> village was destroyed.

2 Examiner   Did you receive good advice from any of your school teachers?

   Candidate   Yes. My maths teacher in particular. You see, I wasn't a very good student, but I wanted to become an engineer. My teacher said <u>to me you have</u> to understand <u>this maths</u> because <u>it's</u> the foundation for engineering at university.

3 Examiner   What about any advice connected to your personal life?

   Candidate   We were lucky that our history teacher was a sympathetic woman. She asked us almost every week what <u>is your aim in life</u>, what <u>do you want</u> from relationships with other people.

Replacive one

IF YOU WANT A SEVEN

The following passages are taken from the practice reading tests in this book. They all contain examples of replacive one. In each case, what does 'one' or 'ones' replace? There is an example.

Eg Dr Molveldt moved from Pietermaritzburg, a small **city**, to Durban, a larger, more cosmo-politan **one**. *'one' replaces 'city'*

1 If a product featured in a person's early life in one place, then, as a migrant, he or she is likely to buy that same product even though it is more expensive than an otherwise identical locally-produced **one**. *'one' replaces '   ' (singular)*

2 Passengers or passers-by might have concerns about explosions with such pressure, but, in the rare event of **one**, the thermoplastic tanks split to release air, rather than shattering and exploding. *'one' replaces '   ' (make this noun singular)*

3 What are some of the difficulties mature-aged students face? The most glaring **one** is the visual fact that they're not as attractive or energetic as all those young things lounging on quadrangle lawns. *'one' replaces '   ' (make this noun singular)*

4 The supermarkets may no longer be stocked with big sweet yellow cultivars but with tiny purple, pink, red, or green-and-white striped **ones** that currently exist in the depths of the forest and will not be cheap to domesticate. *'ones' replaces '   ' (plural)*

Here are some passages from the Writing test. In each one, the candidate has repeated an idea instead of using replacive one. Correct the writing. There is an example.

Eg I believe it is wasteful that after only four years many people change their car for a new ~~car~~. *one*

1 There are several differences between the way men and women deal with conflict. In my opinion, the most notable difference is that women tend to avoid it more.

2 To some extent people learn from failure. Sometimes holidays where things go wrong become the most memorable holidays.

3 Natural disasters seem to be occurring more frequently recently. Although there is consid-erable media coverage of these, I am not convinced that, in the event of a disaster, people in my city would be able to cope.

4 Every country has its own iconic structures. In China, the most famous structure is the Great Wall, which extends many thousands of kilometres.

Collocation

Collocation is the unchangeable partnership of two or more words (eg: verb + noun; adjective + noun; adjective + preposition etc).

YOUR TURN   *Put a word from the box into each blank in the text below. There is an example.*

| ~~can't~~ | dialects | from | instead | must | one | preposition |
| random | seven | varies | widely | | | |

In English, we say: 'I make a mistake', and 'I do my homework'. 'Make' collocates with 'mistake'; 'do' with 'homework'. I (eg) <u>can't</u> 'do a mistake', or 'make my homework'. In French, there is _____ verb for both these situations. In German, I can describe a man as being 'long'; in English, he _____ be 'tall'. A person, a building, or a tree in English is 'tall'. A mountain, however, is 'high'.

Some IELTS candidates find collocations with adjective + _____ particularly diffi-cult. It is correct to say: 'My cousin is married to a Czech.'; I can't say: 'She is married with a Czech.'

A candidate needs to read _____ to be exposed to collocation. Research suggests that reading one collocation in at least _____ different texts is likely to fix it in the memory.

As with article use, collocation is a _____ part of English. There is no reason connected to meaning that the preposition 'to' should follow 'married' _____ of 'with'.

Collocation _____ slightly among English-speaking countries. An Australian is more likely to say: 'Sydney is different to Beijing', whereas an English person might say 'differ-ent from', and an American 'different than'. In IELTS, candidates should use collocations _____ the country where they are taking the test. However, nowhere in the English-speaking world will an examiner accept 'I did a mistake', or 'I made my homework'. The vast majority of collocations are fixed across _____ as well.

Which word collocates?

Below is a writing question and an IELTS Nine answer. Which collocation is correct in each pair? There are examples.

The world now has a (eg) <u>huge</u> / ~~very great~~ population.
Many countries encourage (eg) ~~little~~ / <u>small</u> families.
What do you think are the advantages (eg) <u>of</u> / ~~with~~ having only one or two children in each family?

Around seven billion people are living at present, and the prediction is (1) *for / of* another billion by the end of the 21st century. This is an unbelievable population for a (2) *final / finite* resource: Earth. Some countries, (3) such as/like New Zealand, give (4) _financial / money_ incentives, for example, tax breaks to smaller families. Clearly people there believe that slowing the growth of the global population is a worthy goal.

Life is expensive now: food is harder to grow due to climate change; housing is (5) _little / scarce_ and pricey, especially in mega-cities; and, education, in most places, is no (6) _longer / more_ free. If a person is to succeed (7) _at / in_ life, he or she needs decent food, shelter, and education. If there are a lot of children in a family, it may be very difficult or impossible (8) _for / to_ parents, or the state, to provide these. Both parents work in many families these days, or families have a(n) (9) _only / single_ parent. This means that children are often (10) _by / on_ their own, or looked after at childcare (11) _facilities / utilities_. This can lead to badly-behaved or depressed children. When there are only one or two children in a family, it is less likely that both parents have to work fulltime, making for emotionably stabler children with better (12) _chances / opportunities_ for the future.

On a more serious note: if there is over-population as well as a strain (13) _of / on_ resources, there is a(n) (14) _increased / more_ likelihood of war. Why not send soldiers to die when there are so many young men, and when the country (15) _neighbouring / next door_ has a water supply while yours no longer does? Yemen is a country where half the population is (16) _beneath / under_ fifteen, and it is predicted to double to 50 million within a decade. It has very large families and (17) _dwindling / reducing_ resources. Already, it is endangering the region. Pakistan, Bangladesh, and Afghanistan are countries with (18) _like / similar_ profiles.

(19) _In / To_ conclude, I believe it is essential to reduce the global population any way that states can in order to prevent (20) _enormous / massive_ wars and the further degradation of our environment.

Collocations from the essay above have been put into the table below.

adjective + noun	adjective + preposition
• dwindling / finite resource • enormous building / difficulty • financial incentive / system • increased likelihood (_always singular_) • little brother / sister • massive war / debt • neighbouring country • only child / son / daughter • similar profile / story • single / solo parent • small family	• difficult / impossible for someone to do something

noun + verb	noun + adjective	verb + preposition
• country / factory produces • family has	• commodity (abstract idea) is scarce • gold is scarce • housing is scarce	• succeed at something
noun + adverbial	**compound nouns**	**adverbials**
• chance for the future • country next door (door = *always singular*) • prediction is for ... • strain (*always singular*) on resources	• childcare facility • climate change (*always singular*) • job / rare opportunity • public utility (water, gas, or electricity supply)	• below / under 15 • beneath the table • by oneself • in conclusion • in life • on a more serious note • on one's own • to conclude
noun + of + noun	**quantifiers**	**adverb + adjective**
• alteration of clothing / plans • advantage / disadvantage of having	• a little less / more likely • a little bit of something • little + uncountable noun; eg: little money / patience	• no longer free

How do I learn collocations?

Almost any text has collocations. Here are: an ad for a bank, and information from a bicycle manual. Collocations are **in bold**.

I am a global Latin American. Vika Munz. The ninth artist to **participate in** *MoMA's Artist's Choice series.*

'When I was 21, I decided to leave my country and **immigrate to** *the United States. I didn't speak English, so I* **learned** *the language* **by** *attending* **cooking and carpentry classes.** *That's when I began* **my career as an artist,** *and today my work is* **featured in galleries** *and museums* **around the world.** *My goal is to create art that's as fascinating as Latin America, my continent. My name is Vika Munz. I'm a global Latin American. And Atrium is the global Latin American bank.'*

This text has:

Eg two compound nouns ➡ *cooking classes* and *carpentry classes*

1 three verbs + prepositions ➡ _____, _____,

 and _____

2 a noun + an adverbial ➡ _____

3 a verb + an adverbial ➡ _____

4 an adverbial phrase ➡ _____

*Many states require specific **safety devices**. It is your responsibility to **familiarise yourself with** the laws of the state where you ride, and to **comply with** all **applicable laws**, including **properly equipping** yourself and your bike **as the law requires**.*

This text has:

Eg a compound noun ➝ <u>*safety devices*</u>

6 a verb + preposition ➝ _____

7 a reflexive verb + preposition ➝ _____

8 an adjective + a noun ➝ _____

9 an adverb + a present participle ➝ _____

10 an adverbial phrase ➝ _____

YOUR TURN *Complete each sentence with a true statement about your own life. There is an example.*

Your life

Eg 'Recently, I <u>participated in</u> a chess championship.'

1 'I'd like to <u>immigrate to</u> _____,'

2 'I <u>learnt</u> _____ <u>by</u> _____,'

3 'I began <u>my career as a(n)</u> _____ in _____
_____,'

4 'My favourite actor is _____, who <u>featured in</u> _____,'

5 'A newcomer to my city could <u>familiarise</u> himself <u>by</u> _____,'

6 'I don't think enough companies <u>comply with</u> _____,'

7 'When I went _____ing, I <u>properly equipped</u> myself by _____
_____,'

8 'Too few people _____ <u>as the law requires</u>.'

Vocabulary in Speaking Part 1 – Personal information and mini topics

Part 1 of the Speaking test deals with familiar topics. The first set of questions is about where a candidate lives, or what a candidate does.

Where I live

Put the vocabulary in the box on the following page into two groups. Accommodation has 15 items. There are examples.

| 1990s building | balcony | commercial | a large complex |

1990s building ~~balcony~~ ~~commercial~~ *a large complex*
a good place to bring up children *good local facilities*
three-bedroom *north-facing/south-facing* *on the ground/21st/top floor*
parking *rented* *residential*
spacious *sunny* *well-equipped (a/c, kitchen, laundry, etc)*

Accommodation	Neighbourhood
1990s building	commercial

My home town

Read the answer below. Choose what's true for your home town from the alternatives.

My home town is _____, in the north / south /east / west / centre of _____. (Choose between:) It's quite small with only 50 / 100 / 250 thousand people. (Or:) It's quite large with one / two / five / ten million people, and its main industries are: (Choose two from:) agriculture / manufacturing / mining / tourism / services. It's growing steadily, and... (Or:) It's about the same size as it was ten years ago, and... (Or:) It's shrinking, but it's generally a decent place to live.

IF YOU WANT A SEVEN

Are these adjectives positive or negative? One of them could be either. Place each one in the correct box. There are examples.

~~accessible~~ *ample (facilities/parks/public transport/shopping)* ~~congested~~
deprived *diverse* *dull* *dynamic* *limited (facilities etc)*
over-developed *over-priced* *pleasant* *run-down* *semi-industrial*
thriving *undergoing gentrification* *up-market (UK)/upscale (US)*

Positive	Negative
accessible	congested

What I do

Here are some sentences about jobs and work. Cross out the part which is wrong. There is an example.

Eg I'm ~~teach.~~ / a teacher.

  1 I'm an accountant / a counter.

  2 I'm an electronic / electronics engineer.

  3 I'm a medical specialist. / I'm specialise in medicine.

  4 I'm doing / I've got my own business.

  5 I'm work / I'm working part-time in a . . .

  6 I work as / in IT.

  7 I work / I'm a worker for X (company name).

  8 I'm doing a / some research into . . .

  9 I'm just graduate / I've just graduated with a / an (degree acronym, eg: BA/BSc/MBA), and I'm looking for work.

 10 I'm a mother with young children. / I work in home looking after my children.

How I describe my job

*Which verb – **has got** / **involves** / **is** / **requires** – is used with the following? Are the ideas positive, negative, or either depending on intonation? There are examples.*

Eg My job ~~has~~ / 's a long commute away. *negative*

Eg My job involves / ~~'s~~ quite a lot of overtime. *either*

  1 My job 's got / 's challenging. _____

  2 My job involves / 's ideal for me. _____

  3 My job involves / 's a lot of responsibility. _____

  4 My job hasn't / isn't really what I want to do. _____

  5 My job has / requires good people skills. _____

  6 My job hasn't / isn't so well paid. _____

  7 My job 's got / requires the potential for management experience. _____

  8 My job has / 's quite repetitive. _____

  9 My job has / 's tiring. _____

 10 My job involves / 's travelling. _____

What I'm studying

Below are an examiner's questions in italics, and some answers. Cross out the wrong words or phrases. There is an example.

What qualification will you get when you complete your course?

A Bachelor of (eg) ~~Architect.~~ / Architecture.

A / An MA.

A Diploma in Early Childhood Study. / Studies.

A Certificate in / of Property Services, part of a Diploma in Real Estate.

Which part of your course do you think will help you most in your future job?

I think <u>Course 210B on Applied Dietetics / both the theoretical and practical parts</u> will be helpful.

That's a little hard to say, but probably some of the assignments using <u>statistic / statistical</u> programs.

Who do you find more helpful: the teachers on your course, or the other students?

Actually, <u>I'm finding / I find</u> both of them helpful.

I found the lecturers excellent. They knew their <u>stuff / topics</u>, and were always <u>available / ready</u> for consultation.

What are the missing words in the following text? Complete each one by writing the letters in the spaces provided.

Learn what your job or course is, and how to ***pro*** __ __ __ __ __ __ it. Don't ***for*** __ __ __ 'a' or 'an' before your job or your qualification. Also, we say: 'I work as' + a job, but 'I work __ __' + an ***indu*** __ __ __ __, and 'I work __ __ __' + a company / organisation / institution.

The present simple shows something that is ongoing, eg: 'I work as a doctor'; the ***cont*** __ __ __ __ __ __ is for something short-term, eg: 'I'm working two nights a week at a clinic because I've got an 18-month-old baby; my husband looks after her while I'm at work.' Make sure you ***fo*** __ __ the continuous correctly: subject (*I*) + auxiliary ('*m*) + ***part*** __ __ __ __ __ __ (*working*).

The verb 'to be' (' *'s*) goes before ***adj*** __ __ __ __ __ __ __; 'to have', or a verb like 'to involve' or 'to require', goes before nouns or gerunds.

Avoid being too specific: 'Course 210B'. Try to use idioms, like: 'The lecturers knew their __ __ __ __ __.'

Mini topics

The second part of Part 1 has two mini topics, unconnected to each other. They could be: Dancing and How you organise your time; or, Flowers and Clothes; or, Public holidays and A place where there is a lot of water.

The order of the four questions within each mini topic goes from what you think / feel / have experienced, to what other people, in general, believe.

YOUR TURN   *The table on the next page shows answers containing mainly information words from four candidates. A Nine has been given as the example. Who, from A, B, and C, is a Five, a Six, or a Seven, based on their vocabulary?*
The questions were:

1   How do you organise your time?
2   Who taught you to organise your time?
3   What would you do with more free time?
4   What are the benefits of being well-organised?

Nine	A = _____
1 Calendar update throughout the day. Set aside 15 minutes note down tasks of following day. Prioritise. 18-month wall-planner fill in. Set goals: personal, financial, work-related.	1 Diary write in every day. Time at the end of the day... write about what to do tomorrow. Set personal goals or goals related to money and work.
2 No one in particular. Mother extremely organised...brought up kids... studying...working. It beats me how she did it. Brother quite successful. Learnt some tricks from him. I don't do too badly.	2 No one but mother...very organised... looked after kids... studying...working. Brother successful... learnt from him. I do fine.
3 Take up singing...choir. Close relationships formed with other choristers. Consider voluntary work... after-school care carpentry for kids.	3 Singing again...choir. Friendly with other people in choir. Possibly voluntary work. Teaching kids at after-school care some skills.
4 Quite simply: people achieve more in a shorter time.	4 I think people do more with their lives.

B = _____	C = _____
1 Write list every day on mobile. Some personal or work goals.	1 Calendar update daily. 15 mins...write tasks for tomorrow. Wall-planner write in. Set goals: personal, financial, and about work.
2 No one but mother...very organised...looked after kids...studying...working.	2 No one really. Mother very organised...looked after kids...studying...working. Brother successful. Learnt from him. I do fine.
3 Singing again. Friendly with other people in group. Maybe also teaching kids some skills.	3 Take up singing...choir. Close friendships formed with other members of choir. Possibly voluntary work. After-school care...making things with kids.
4 In a nutshell: people do more.	4 I believe people achieve more.

Comparison of the Nine and the Seven

Nine 'Calendar update throughout the day. *Set aside* 15 minutes *note down* tasks of following day. Prioritise. 18-month wall-planner *fill in*. Set goals: personal, financial, *work-related*.'

Seven 'Calendar update daily. 15 mins *write* tasks for tomorrow. Wall-planner *write in*. Set goals: personal, financial, and *about work*.'

They have some vocabulary in common. However, the Nine uses far more phrasal verbs, eg: 'set aside', 'note down', 'fill in'. The Seven only has: 'write in'. 'Work-related' is the adjective meaning 'about work', which is more sophisticated being a compound. The Nine also adds: 'prioritise' and '18-month'.

In the rest of the Nine's answers, there are rarer items of vocabulary like: 'choristers', and idioms like: 'It beats me how she did it!'. The candidate also uses: 'I'm not doing too badly.', which is a gentler way of saying he or she is doing well. The other candidates are more boastful with: 'I do fine.'

Comparison of the Six and the Five

Six 'Singing again...*choir*. Friendly with other people in choir. *Possibly voluntary work*. Teaching kids at *after-school care* some skills.'

Five 'Singing again. Friendly with other *people in group. Maybe* also teaching kids some skills.'

They have some vocabulary in common. However, the Six uses: 'choir' for a group of singers; and prefers the less common: 'possibly' to 'maybe'. The Six adds: 'voluntary work' and 'after-school care'.

Only the Five uses inappropriate language like: 'In a nutshell'.

In reality, the Five and Six also both use words that don't exist in English, or do exist, but are used in the wrong context. They may also include language that is used in writing, perhaps saying 'in addition' instead of 'also'.

Phrasal verbs

Phrasal verbs are very common in English, especially in speaking. The vast majority of phrasal verbs have multiple meanings, many of which are idiomatic. Consider the following:

1 'All the rubbish in our local park <u>was picked up</u> on Clean Up Australia Day.'
2 'Where's the dry cleaning?' 'I <u>haven't picked</u> it <u>up</u> yet.'
3 'Watch out for older men in museums who try <u>to pick</u> young women <u>up</u>.'
4 'I <u>didn't pick up</u> much German while I was working in Zurich.'
5 'We'll need two days of <u>pickups</u> to finish the film,' said the director.

Only sentence 1 is literal: 'pick' (choose) + 'up' (from the ground) can be understood separately.

There are near equivalents of many phrasal verbs in long verbs, mostly from Latin. An official for Clean Up Australia Day may write: *Rubbish was collected from many public parks.* 'Pick up' and the Latinate 'collect' are synonyms here. 'Collect' could be used in sentence 2 although it sounds unnatural. 'Collect' cannot be used in sentences 3-5. In sentence 3, 'pick up' = 'chat to, hoping to start a sexual relationship'. In sentence 4, 'pick up' = 'learn without studying at a school'. In sentence 5, 'a pickup' = 'filming something that has been missed out or done badly'; it is a noun made from a phrasal verb.

Some IELTS candidates are scared of phrasal verbs with their multiple meanings and complicated grammar – 'it' goes in the middle of 'pick up' as in sentence 2. However, one difference between a Six and a Seven is that a Seven uses more phrasal verbs in speaking.

Ways to learn phrasal verbs

YOUR TURN *Number the following in order. Two have been done for you.*

1 Some people learn phrasal verbs by verb (eg: those with 'pick');
___ A third group learns phrasal verbs in a context
___ others concentrate on the particles (eg: 'up').
7 because the grammar is embedded in the sentence,
5 There is no correct way to learn,
___ but research has shown that the third way could be the most effective
4 (eg: in a short text on one topic: like sport).
___ and the meaning may be clearer.

Focusing on the verb

Which verb goes into each group below? Write it in the space provided. Make sure you choose the correct form of the verb. There is an example.

Eg a. 'That wall looks so big and white. Why don't you <u>break</u> it <u>up</u> with some pictures or tall pot plants?'

    b. 'America <u>broke</u> <u>away</u>* from Britain in the War of Independence that ended in 1783.'

    c. 'Japan <u>has</u> just <u>broken</u> off relations with North Korea again over the issue of nuclear testing.'

1 a. '_____ <u>up</u> on Thursday for lunch would suit me.'

    b. 'It took me a while _____ <u>on</u> that Anne and Omar were an item.'

    c. 'We _____ <u>out</u> when the financial crisis struck, and our pension fund went under.'

2 a. 'Why did you and Pham split up?'

    'Actually, I'd rather not _____ <u>into</u> it.'

    b. 'I keep _____ <u>over</u> the accident in my head.'

    c. 'House prices _____ <u>up</u> steadily.'

3 a. 'We've had three freezing days in a row. I think winter _____ <u>in</u>.'

    b. 'The next _____ <u>down</u> is Kent Street,' said the shuttle bus driver.

    c. 'After the renovation, we _____ <u>about</u> replanting the lawn that the builders had ruined.'

Focusing on the particle

Which particle goes into each group below? Write it in the space provided. There is an example.

Eg a. 'Igor was caught shoplifting in Hong Kong, but the department store <u>let</u> him <u>off</u>.'

    b. 'I don't know dhow Dalia <u>pulls</u> <u>off</u> those real estate deals.'

    c. 'I find it a real <u>turnoff</u> if a woman I'm dating makes comments about her ex.'

1 a. 'The sharp _____ <u>turn</u> in stocks has meant investors are putting their money back into gold.'

    b. 'I <u>drove</u> _____ to Karachi for this exam.'

    c. 'I hope Suzy <u>holds</u> _____ this job. The last three she's left after only a week.'

2 a. 'It seems to me you always <u>fall</u> _____ with your husband's plans no matter how inconvenient they may be.'

    b. 'After the hugely exorbitant Olympic Games, the government had <u>to rein</u> _____ spending.'

    c. 'I <u>traded</u> _____ my old car.'

---

*In formal writing this would be: America *seceded* from Britain...

3 **a.** 'There's been an _____ break of malaria in the south.'

   b. 'I think multinational oil companies should pull _____ of the Niger Delta because they're polluting it.'

   c. 'I'm going to send _____ for lunch.'

4 **a.** 'I wouldn't worry about the fight you had with Jo. I'm sure things will blow

   _____.'

   b. 'My mother comes _____ every Monday and Wednesday to look after my daughter while I'm at uni.'

   c. 'Rio Centro has just made another take _____ bid for Xenthos.'

5 **a.** 'I'm tired of doing other people's work around here.'

   'Why don't you bring it _____ at the next meeting?'

   b. 'I hope this rain clears _____ because I'm off to the opera tonight.'

   c. 'Ikea was set _____ in the 1970s in Sweden, and has spread around the world.'

Phrasal verbs in a context

Films and TV programmes are full of phrasal verbs. Listen out for them.

Popular magazines and newspapers are a good source as well, especially sporting or horoscope pages. Naturally, interviews contain them. More reputable newspapers, however, have far fewer phrasal verbs, preferring Latinate language.

Unscramble this headline: **out the of bear woods**

Read the article below. Underline the phrasal verbs and one noun which is made from a phrasal verb.

Star golfer Bear Woods has notched up his first top-10 finish since last spring. He shot a final-round 65 at Royal Course, which is set in the rolling green hills of Canterbury. He's provided fans with hope that his old form is coming back. Nick Watson took out the honours, making it to the clubhouse in 15 under par. Jesse van Burgh shook up spectators with some ill-judged comments caught on the mobile phone of a nearby fan. It seems he's convinced Woods' confession about the breakdown of his marriage is a stunt to divert attention from the Big Bear's game.

Draw arrows to match the phrases on the left with those on the right.

a breakdown	to disturb
to come back	to return
to notch up	to score
to shake up	to win the prize
to take out the honours (idiom)	when something stops working

IF YOU WANT A SEVEN

Of course, it's not so easy to spot a phrasal verb: a preposition or an adverb that follows a verb may not belong to it. 'Set in', above, is not a phrasal verb. 'Set' is a single verb; 'in' is a preposition and part of the adverbial phrase: 'in the rolling green hills'. In the sentence: 'The rain set in.', 'set in' *is* a phrasal verb. 'Caught on', above, is also not a phrasal verb. 'Caught' is a single verb', and 'on' belongs to 'on the mobile phone'. In: 'It took me a while to catch on that Jan and Tony were married.' 'catch on' is a phrasal verb.

'Provide', above, is a verb with a dependent preposition 'with'; it is not a phrasal verb. Neither is 'divert from', because 'divert' can stand on its own. Consider: 'The water is going to be diverted.' We don't need to know where from. But, in: 'I was well <u>brought up</u> by my grand-mother.', or: 'I was well <u>brought up</u>.', we need the adverb 'up', so this must be a phrasal verb. Admittedly, a language learner may not be able to work these details out, so consulting a dictionary is useful.

The grammar of phrasal verbs

There is a lot to learn about phrasal verbs. Working through a good grammar book will certainly help.

Typical IELTS errors are:

1   confusing the verb.
2   confusing the particle.
3   forgetting the particle, especially of a three-part phrasal verb.
4   forgetting a dependent preposition.
5   forgetting the pronoun object.
6   putting the pronoun object in the wrong place. (Is the verb separable or inseparable?)
7   adding an unnecessary pronoun object.
8   making a verb passive that can't be passive. (Is the verb transitive or intransitive?)
9   making a verb phrasal when it isn't.

Two of the sentences below are correct. Mark each correct sentence with a checkmark (✓). Fix the others, bearing in mind the list above. There are examples.

Eg	✗	'I don't have time now, but let's go ~~into~~ *over* the accounts tomorrow.'
Eg	✗	'When I was a girl, my aunty often looked after_∧ *me*.'
Eg	✓	'You'll need to slow right down. I know this road, and it's treacherous.'
1		'Don't forget to look up me when you're in Ankara.'
2		'Why did you tell the whole world my phone number?' 'I didn't. I swear, I didn't give out.'
3		'I was having a great time playing with my brother's new puppy, but suddenly she turned me on.'
4		'I wonder if you could drop the cakes off two hours before the party.'
5		'My parents are going to be in town for the long weekend. Do you think we can put them down?'
6		'Our teacher was grown up in Abu Dhabi.'
7		'3-D printing sounds like a technological breakout.'
8		'Thankfully, the case against my father threw out of court.'

9   'Ursula's always making out she's poor, but once you see her family home, you know that's not the case.'

10   'You should cut down dairy food unless you eat low-fat products.'

One of these sentences below, from the IELTS Writing test, is correct. Which is it? Fix the others.

11 *China is made of provinces. However, there are also Special Economic and Special Administrative Zones.*

12 *I look forward hearing from you.*

13 *In the past two decades, pollution has spread out dramatically.*

14 *The breakup of Yugoslavia was a traumatic process.*

15 *The number of tourists to Machu Pichu rose up between 1990 and 2000.*

Using too many Latinate verbs

In speaking, many candidates overuse Latinate verbs. This may be because their first language is a Romance language, or they've learnt English mainly from reading.

If you have too many Latinate verbs in IELTS Speaking, your tone is too formal. If you mix them carelessly, your tone may be uneven, so you go down in Task Fulfilment. By the same token, too many phrasal verbs detract from IELTS Writing.

YOUR TURN *Here is a Speaking Part 2 answer from an older man. His topic is: Tell me about a very good friend.*

For this exercise, his only problem is with phrasal verbs.

Ten more mistakes are underlined. Fix them. Write the correct words on the lines below. There are examples.

I suppose my wife is also my best friend. (eg) I've <u>known of</u> her for 20 years, and we still get along famously.

I (eg) <u>went out</u> Cecilia for six years before we got married. We had to (1) <u>save</u> our money (2) <u>to pay</u> the wedding and (eg) <u>to establish</u> our new home. By the time (3) we <u>went along</u> the aisle, we were in our thirties, but we knew each other extremely well. I think that's the secret of an enduring relationship. Even now, we almost never argue, and if we do, (4) we <u>make it up</u> quickly.

We're both very proud of our children, who, fortunately, (5) <u>resemble</u> Cecilia more than me. Admittedly, while I was busy with my career, (6) their <u>bringingup</u> was left almost entirely to her. I think she did a fantastic job.

Now that I'm semi-retired, (7) we're <u>compensating</u> by enjoying life more. We travel a lot, especially in Argentina, where Cecilia's family (8) <u>originates</u>. (9) And we <u>expect</u> many happy years together.

I think we're the ideal couple.

Really, (10) I <u>didn't fabricate anything</u>.*

Eg I've known of her ➝ *I've known her*
Eg I went out Cecilia ➝ *I went out* **with** *Cecilia*
Eg to establish ➝ *to set up*

---

* Adapted from p. 117, *Grammar for English Language Teachers*, Parrot, M., Cambridge University Press, 2001. Reprinted with the permission of Cambridge University Press.

1 to save our money ➔ _____

2 to pay the wedding ➔ _____

3 we went along the aisle ➔ _____

4 we make it up quickly ➔ _____

5 resemble ➔ _____

6 their bringingup ➔ _____

7 we're compensating for ➔ _____

8 originates ➔ _____

9 expect ➔ _____

10 I didn't fabricate any of it. ➔ _____

Here is a written version of some of the speech above. What are the missing words? Complete them by writing the letters in the spaces provided.

These days, some young people **da_ _** *for a long time before* **mar __ __ __ __ __** *in order to save money for wedding expenses and the establishment of a home. This means, at marriage they know each other extremely well, which* **co __ __ __** *be the secret of an enduring relationship. Disagreement is rare, and when arguments do occur, they are speedily* **resol __ __ __.**

Perhaps, while **purs __ __ __ __** *his career, a husband leaves the childrearing to his wife. However, on* **reti __ __ __ __ __ __,** *the couple may compensate for lost time by travelling together.*

Note: The meaning is virtually the same between the written 'establish', 'resemble', 'compensate', and 'originate' and their spoken phrasal equivalents. However, 'fabricate' does *not* equal 'make up' here. 'Fabricate' is generally used in a legal context to suggest deliberate lying, as in: 'It would appear that the witness has fabricated her entire testimony.'

Complete each sentence with a true statement about your own life. There is an example.

Your life

Eg 'I wish I could <u>give up</u> *biting my nails*.'

1 'Right now, I'<u>m looking forward</u> to _____.'

2 'I'm trying <u>to save up</u> for _____.'

3 'I <u>take after</u> my _____ because I have _____.'

4 'Sometimes I find it hard <u>to put up with</u> _____.'

5 'Fingers crossed, my car/computer <u>hasn't broken down</u> since _____

_____.'

6 'I used to be a fan of _____, but I'<u>ve gone off</u> him/her because _____

_____.'

7 'Recently I had to <u>fill out</u> _____,'

8 'The _____ was <u>pulled down</u>, which I think is _____,'

9 'I <u>went through</u> a rough patch when _____,'

10 'As a child, I loved <u>helping</u> _____ <u>out</u> by _____,'

How to pronounce phrasal verbs

IF YOU WANT A SEVEN

Consider the following words that a beginner says: 'stick…broken…two.' From this amount of information, a listener can understand what's happening, and fill in the grammar, thus: 'The stick was broken into two.' But with 'car…broken…twice.' Does the speaker mean: 'My car was broken into twice.', or 'My car's broken down twice.'? This shows that the particle of a phrasal verb contains more meaning than an ordinary preposition or adverb, and so should be given pronunciation importance. In fact, the particle is pronounced as a strong form, and has more sentence stress than the verb.

Consider the following: 'The movie's **set** in Cuba.' and 'The rain's set **in** for today.' In the first sentence, the verb is stressed and the preposition 'in' is weak: /n/; while in the second, the particle is stressed and is therefore strong: /ɪn/. Likewise: 'The stick was **broken** into /ˈɪntə/ two.' but 'My car's been broken **into** /ˈɪntuː/ twice.'

In a noun or adjective created from a phrasal verb, the first part is stressed like: '**break**through', '**take**over', '**turn**off', and '**up**bringing'.

Phrasal verbs in Speaking Part 2

YOUR TURN   **A** *Here is a Speaking Part 2 topic:* Tell me about a day you really enjoyed travelling with some friends.

Put the phrases on the right back into the IELTS Nine answer. There are examples.

I really (eg) <u>get on</u> well with my friend Larissa. We both enjoy travelling, eating, and

learning about new cultures. I (1) _____ with her and her husband, Martin,

recently. She'd been working in Qianzhou while I'd been studying in Beijing. Martin (2)

_____ from Prague.

Together we spent a delightful day at the Great Wall at a place called Simitai. We

joined a group of other tourists at a youth hostel in the south of Beijing, and we

(3) _____ at nine AM in an old bus. It took about three hours to get to the

wall. The bus drove through the city, the suburbs, and the countryside, and we

(4) _____ other travellers on the way. While the view was interesting –

farms, orchards, quaint villages – the journey was spoilt by the bus making loud

grumbling noises most of the way, and I was worried it might (5) _____.

break down

caught up

~~get on~~

had just flown in

picked up

set off

Suddenly, through the bare branches of trees, we could see the Great Wall and its towers along the top of a high ridge: it was most impressive. We paid for our tickets, which were somewhat over-priced, and we (eg) *split up*.

Larissa and Martin are far fitter than I am, so they climbed the wall quickly, and went as far as they could. I ambled along, taking photos and enjoying the breath-taking views. The wall is mostly safe, but it's steep and (6) _____ in places, and you do need to be careful.

As soon as we reached the city, we (7) _____ for dinner, which was tasty and good value. Then, we were lucky enough to get seats for an acrobatic performance. I (8) _____ to this ever since I'd arrived in China. The show was certainly colourful, and the acrobats twisted their bodies in all sorts of ways. However, in my opinion, it was slightly tacky when the women twirled plates of champagne glasses on top of swords stuck into their stomachs.

Around midnight, I (9) _____ a taxi and (10) _____ to my hotel.

How might you talk about the same topic?

B *Here is another Speaking Part 2 topic:* Tell me about a job you would like to do.
Put the phrases on the right back into the IELTS Nine answer. There is an example.

As I've already mentioned, I'm an accountant. However, I think being a teacher would (eg) *make for* an interesting job, and I'm probably quite suited to teaching because I'm patient and even-tempered.

My main reason for wanting to be a teacher is that teachers can stay youthful all their lives due to their contact with young people. In other jobs, you're stuck with people around your own age. Young people are generally enthusiastic and (1) _____. They (2) _____ by adult responsibilities and disappointments. They're also a lot of fun: they (3) _____ all sorts of mischief. They're often very creative; they (4) _____ some terrific ideas when they (5) _____ assignments.

Teaching is a bit like being a gardener: you can watch the students in your class growing and flowering, like plants. It must be rewarding to think that you (6) _____ in that process. Unlike plants, however, students form strong bonds with their teachers, and often (7) _____ them. I think I'd enjoy that respect.

If I were a teacher who also had children, I'd be able to spend more time with them while they (8) _____ because our holidays would coincide. That doesn't happen in many other jobs.

Lastly, being a teacher's quite stable. Even when there's an economic (9) _____, it's possible (10) _____ work.

---

got into

had been looking forward

split up

went back

went out

worn out

---

come up with

downturn

forward-looking

get up to

have taken part

haven't been beaten down

look up to

make for

to pick up

were growing up

work on

How might you talk about the same topic?

C *Here is a third Speaking Part 2 topic:* Tell me about a series of educational TV programmes that you enjoyed.

Put the phrases on the right back into the IELTS Nine answer. There is an example.

When I saw this question, my heart sank because I really don't spend much time watching TV, and I didn't think I'd have enough (eg) *to talk about*.

Then, I remembered an amazing series I saw a couple of years ago. I think it was presented by David Attenborough, and called 'Life in the Freezer'.

This series is about Antarctica, and the plants, animals, and humans who live there. There are two things that have stuck in my mind. Firstly, there's a seal called a leopard seal, which is about four metres long, and is the most vicious killer on the continent. It (1) _____ six medium-sized penguins in one hour.

There was one brilliant sequence where the seals were filmed under the water as well as on the ice. In the water, they (2) _____ the penguins they've caught like a cat does a mouse; on the ice, they just lie and (3) _____ unsuspecting birds (4) _____ out of the water and practically into their mouths.

There were several sequences on the Emperor Penguin, which is a remarkable creature.

The female lays an egg, but transfers it to the male. If she drops the egg, or if it (5) _____ on the ice for two minutes, it'll freeze, and the chick inside will die. After the female has given the male the egg, she (6) _____ to feed. Then, the male (7) _____ the egg and later the chick throughout the long winter. He (8) _____ his young for over 100 days, including 34 in total darkness when temperatures (9) _____ to minus seventy. On the female's return, the male – almost dead from starvation – goes to sea (10) _____ food for himself.

How might you talk about the same topic?

feasts on

go down

goes off

is left out

looks after

play with

takes care of

to jump up

to look for

~~to talk about~~

wait for

Other idiomatic language a Seven uses

YOUR TURN   *The text, below, about idioms, is missing eight items. Match each item from the box with one of the numbered blanks. Write the item in the blank. There is an example.*

An idiom has to be understood as a chunk = ____
An idiom or idiomatic phrase has lost its original, literal meaning = **eg**
but only be a few native English speakers could tell you = ____
Each English-language speaking country has its own particular idioms = ____
Idiomatic language is very common in speaking = ____
one sentence should never contain two similar-sounding idioms = ____
Phrasal verbs have both literal and idiomatic meanings = ____
the natural and confident use of idiomatic language is necessary = ____
There are fashions in idioms = ____

Eg   <u>An idiom or idiomatic phrase has lost its original, literal, meaning</u>. For example, in the sentence 'I made a titanic effort to prepare for my final medical exams.', you can guess that 'titanic' means 'enormous', (**1**) _____

_____ that this adjective derives from the noun 'Titan', and in classical Greek mythology, the Titans were giants who inhabited the earth before gods and then humans. An idiom like 'to give someone the green light' originated more recently with traffic control. It means 'to authorise a person to start a project'. A film director may say; 'I'd had the script for some time before the producer gave me the green light.'

2   _____. Looking up each word in a dictionary is generally unhelpful. To think of a person actually being 'given' a 'light' that is 'green' is baffling.

3   _____. Take the verb 'look at', which means 'to use your eyes to see something' (its literal meaning), and 'consider' (its idiomatic meaning). A verb like 'pick up' has at least five common idiomatic meanings.

4   _____. It does occur in academic writing, but its use is judicious.
In the IELTS Speaking test, a golden rule (another idiom) is that (**5**) _____

_____ as in: 'I <u>was green with envy</u> that my cousin <u>was born with a silver spoon in his mouth</u>.' On hearing this, any examiner will 'keep a straight face' while thinking: 'Is this guy for real?'

6   _____. Some do not 'last the distance' whereas others remain 'trusty friends.' Yet others 'hang around like a bad smell' to become clichés (overused phrases). IELTS candidates who write 'Every coin has two sides' (which is not an English idiom), or say 'it was raining cats and dogs' (which is out of fashion) are unlikely to score a Seven.

7   _____. However, the ones on pages 280-281 are known universally. It's certainly useful and entertaining to learn local idioms, but the IELTS exam may not be the place for some of the more colourful ones.
That said (an idiom meaning, 'despite all that has been said previously'), to get a

Seven, (**8**) _____.

Realistic examples of idiomatic language in the Speaking test

As mentioned earlier, idiom is common in speaking, but a candidate's speech is not 'peppered' with it. (It does not occur too often.) Below is the right frequency.

Put a word from the box into the blanks in each candidate's speech.

feet   made   of   off   run   show   took   under   welcome   wing

Part 1

Examiner   Tell me about your first week at your new job?

Candidate   Well, my first week was pretty grueling. I mean – there was so much to do that I was _____ _____ my _____. At the same time, I was thrilled to have a job after so many years of being a student, and I was really lucky that one of my colleagues who comes from the same town as I do _____ me _____ her _____.

Examiner   What do you like most about your job?

Candidate   At first, I admit, the money was _____, but now I'm enjoying being able to _____ what I'm _____ _____. Already my boss has given me a degree of responsibility.

figures   for   head   in   moon   over   sums   sunny   touch   up

Part 2

Examiner   I'd like you to describe a member of your family you get on well with.

Candidate   I'd like to tell you about my older sister, Vartika. First of all, her name means 'light', and that _____ her _____ – she's got a very _____ disposition. But there's a serious side to her as well. She's a chartered accountant. I'd have to say she's got a better _____ _____ _____ than me.

She got married last year, and she's having a baby in about three months' time. My mother's _____ the _____.

Unfortunately, we don't see much of Vartika now because she moved to Canada, but we keep _____ _____ with phone calls.

amount   at   away   face   look   on   race   rat   ridiculous   slave

Part 3

Examiner   Do you think life is easier or more difficult for young people these days?

Candidate   _____ the _____ of it it's easier with more technology and less social control, but in reality it's a _____ _____ in China. There are so many people competing for jobs now, and when you do finally get one, you _____ _____ to keep it or get promoted. Also, women have different expectations of men. I'd like to get married, but it seems I'll have to save a _____ _____ of money before a girl will even _____ _____ me.

Thirty-three idioms which are safe to use in the Speaking test

The idioms below are grouped by positive, neutral, or negative connotation. What are the first 15 missing words? Complete each one by writing the letters in the spaces provided.

Positive connotations

1 Since we moved here, my daughter has **gone from strength to str __ __ __ __ __.** = *She's progressing rapidly.*

2 My aunt **has a fl __ __ __ for** languages, and speaks seven. = *She has a special ability.*

3 Unfortunately, I don't **have a h __ __ __ for figures**. = *I'm (not) very good with numbers.*

4 My neighbour often **lends a h __ __ __.** = *She often helps other people.*

5 My nephew's a real **live w __ __ __.** *He's full of energy and new ideas.*

6 I'm lucky, my supervisor and I are **on the s __ __ __ wavelength.** = *We see the world the same way.*

7 My sister's got **a su __ __ __ disposition.** = *She's always happy.*

8 My husband and I are **on tr __ __ __** to buy a house this year. = *We planned to buy one, and we shall.*

9 Some people think the driving test is **a piece of ca __ __**, but I understand the pass rate is one in three for people under 20. = *They think it's very easy.*

10 Leading this new project at work means I'm able to **show what I'm m__ __ __ of.** = *I can prove to others how capable I am.*

11 I was quite unhappy at boarding school until another boarder **took me under her w __ __ __.** = *She looked after me and showed me how to do all the new things.*

No connotations

12 I'd say **a ballp __ __ __ figure** for renovating a bathroom is $20,000. = *An approximate figure for renovation is $20,000.*

13 There used to be free **cradle to gr __ __ __** medical care, but now everyone has to pay something towards it. = *There used to be free care throughout one's whole life.*

14 In some places like Congo, aid is **a drop in the o __ __ __ __.** There are so many children suffering from disease or displacement. = *No matter how much aid is given, it will never be enough.*

15 I felt like **a f __ __ __ out of water** when I first came here, but two years later, I'm completely at home. = *I felt very strange because I was not used to things.*

16 It took me a while to **get my head around** triple bottom line accounting. = *It took me a while to understand it completely.*

17 I don't know if my café will **get off the ground**. My first two business plans have been **pooh-poohed** by my accountant. = *I don't know if my café will become a reality. My accountant was very negative about my business plans.*

18 I've got **my hands full** at the moment with a nine-month-old baby, a part-time job, and my MA course two nights a week. = *I'm extremely busy.*

19 It's becoming **harder and harder** to **make ends meet**. Food, electricity, and petrol prices have all gone up recently. = *It's becoming progressively more difficult to find enough money for necessities.*

20 I thought my boss was **kidding** when she offered me a promotion because I'd only been working two weeks. = *I didn't think she was serious.*

21 **Off the top of my head**, I don't know what the unemployment rate is in Korea, but it's higher than it is here. = *I don't know the exact figures, but I can guess…*

22 My grandmother had always been very healthy, but, **out of the blue**, she got cancer, and died within six months. = *She suddenly got cancer.*

23 I think older people prefer to maintain **the status quo**. = *They like things to stay the same.*

Negative connotations

24 Some changes seem to happen **at a snail's pace**. = *They happen extremely slowly.*

25 Our company was **caught off guard** when it lost a government tender. = *Our company did not expect the loss.*

26 There are certainly people who can't cope and **fall by the wayside**. = *They lose their place in society, their job, their home, or their social position, which results in poverty and depression.*

27 It's **a rat race** in Brazil, which is why so many young people are leaving. = *It's extremely competitive now.*

28 There's so much **red tape** in my country, and it's very hard to set up one's own business. = *There is far too much official regulation.*

29 I've just spent **a ridiculous amount** of money on a new vacuum cleaner. = *I've spent a very large amount.*

30 I've been **slaving away** at my doctoral thesis for three years, and I'm still far from finished. = *I've been working extremely hard.*

31 Child abuse is a problem in my country, but most people still **turn a blind eye to it**. = *Most people know it happens, but don't want to face it.*

32 The relationship between Cambodia and Laos has **turned sour** because of a dam Laos is building that'll reduce the flow of water into Cambodia. = *The relationship is now poor.*

33 Of course doing an MBA and then working as a manager are **a whole different ball game**. = *Doing an MBA and then working as a manager are two very different things, and the latter is more difficult.*

Multi-choice test for vocabulary, grammar, and spelling 1

The questions below test vocabulary, grammar, and spelling. A Five will know some of the answers; a Six should know most of them. Sentences in quotation marks come from Speaking tests; those in italics are from Writing.

To fill each gap, choose the correct letter: a, b, c, or d. Read the examples carefully.

Eg 'My _____ to work takes over an hour each morning.'
    a journey   **b** tour   **c** travel   **d** trip
The answer is choice **a**.

    'Tour' is used for a short, guided walk around a museum or factory, or for longer travel with a group of tourists to another city or country. 'Travel', as a noun, contains the idea of a holiday, and is rare. 'Trip' describes something pleasant but irregular like: 'My trip to Spain was fantastic.' Going to work, however, is habitual. There is also a sense of something long and difficult about a journey. It is idiomatic here, since it is normally used with ships.

Eg *There has been a _____ change in the way banks are supervised by the government.*
    a grate   **b** large   **c** major   **d** serious
The answer is choice **c**.

    'Great change' would be possible, but the spelling, above, is incorrect. ('Grate' is a verb meaning to cut something very small, usually cheese or carrot, with a metal grater.) 'Large' and 'serious' do not collocate with 'change', so the answer is 'major'.

1i *Shenzhen is quite _____ city.*
    a a developing   **b** an exiting   **c** a morden   **d** a new

ii *_____ being expensive, smoking causes health problems.*
    a As well   **b** Beside   **c** Besides   **d** Except for

iii 'I _____ a housewarming party just last week.'
    a did   **b** had   **c** made   **d** presented

iv '_____ in the mountains is relaxing.'
    a Life   **b** Lifestyle   **c** The life   **d** The living

2i 'I like my bedroom because it's painted _____ colours.'
    a bright   **b** glossy   **c** strong   **d** vivid

ii *The cinema _____ the beach has been converted into a shoe shop.*
    a beside   **b** near   **c** next to   **d** opposite

iii 'I _____ this idea.'
    a agree   **b** agree with   **c** am agree   **d** am agree with

iv *There is a _____ towards smaller families.*
    a tendancy   **b** trend   **c** trendency   **d** trendy

3i 'I've just spent $300 on a _____ jacket.'
    a beautiful green silk Thai   **b** beautiful green Thai silk   **c** green beautiful silk Thai
    d green beautiful Thai silk

ii 'I seem to work best _____ morning.'
    a at   **b** at the   **c** in   **d** in the

iii 'I use Skype to _____ with my friends and family.'
    a connect   **b** enjoy   **c** keep in touch   **d** speak

iv 'One of my favourite _____ is birds singing in the early morning.'
    a hearings   **b** musics   **c** noises   **d** sounds

4i 'I often read _____ books.'
    a historic   **b** historical   **c** history   **d** hysterical

ii 'Canada is a little different _____ the United States.'
    a from   **b** of   **c** then   **d** with

iii 'I get up at six thirty, and _____ my computer straight away.'
    a open   **b** open up   **c** turn on   **d** turn up

iv 'My sister has a forceful _____.'
    a character   **b** mind   **c** personality   **d** temper

5i 'My cousin was in a _____ car accident.'
    a big   **b** grave   **c** very serious   **d** very terrible

ii '_____ there's a lot of noise from the ring road near my home.'
    a Honestly   **b** In fact   **c** To be frank   **d** Unfortunately

iii 'My grandmother _____ when I was a teenager.'
    a dead   **b** died   **c** is dead   **d** was died

iv *These days, very few people wear national _____ in my country.*
    a clothes   **b** cloths   **c** costume   **d** custom

6i 'My grandfather was very _____.'
    a kind   **b** kindly   **c** kind-hearted   **d** large-hearted

ii *There is _____ smog in the city these days.*
    a much   **b** so terrible   **c** such a terrible   **d** such terrible

iii *The literacy level has been _____ in the countryside.*
    a improving   **b** raising   **c** rising up   **d** uprising

iv *The role of women in _____ is rather different from what it was a generation ago.*
    a nowadays society   **b** nowaday's society   **c** todays society   **d** today's society

7i 'My best friend at school was _____.'
   a not so short   **b** not so tall   **c** short   **d** stunted
ii *A violin is made _____ wood.*
   a by   **b** from   **c** of   **d** with
iii 'My aunt _____ her company from nothing.'
   a built   **b** built up   **c** grew   **d** grew up
iv *Some children have _____ to learn musical instruments.*
   a chance   **b** the chance   **c** the oportunity   **d** the possibility

8i *I am _____ that appearance matters.*
   a conceived   **b** confessed   **c** convicted   **d** convinced
ii 'I'm not much good _____ the guitar, but I enjoy it.'
   a at play   **b** at playing   **c** in play   **d** in playing
iii *It is hard to ___ the pollution in Beijing.*
   a adjust with   **b** bare   **c** get used   **d** put up with
iv *Some people become _____ because they do not believe in eating animal products.*
   a veegans   **b** vegetarians   **c** virginians   **d** virgins

9i 'Working at night doesn't _____ me.'
   a suit   **b** suitable   **c** suit to   **d** suit with
ii '_____ are good friends.'
   a I and my brother   **b** Me and my brother   **c** My brother and I   **d** My brother and me
iii *I think it is important to _____ other cultures.*
   a get some knowledge of   **b** have some knowledge about   **c** know about
   d know of
iv 'People go to the mountains near here to enjoy the _____.'
   a lands   **b** landscape   **c** scenery   **d** scenes

10i 'I had _____ holiday in Cameroon.'
   a an impressionable   **b** an impressive   **c** a memorable   **d** an unforgetable
ii *_____ young people from my village have moved to the city.*
   a Almost the   **b** Most of   **c** Most of the   **d** The most
iii 'Four hundred people _____ my brother's wedding.'
   a attended   **b** came in   **c** participated in   **d** took part in
iv *Spending reached a _____ in 2008.*
   a peak   **b** peek   **c** summit   **d** top

11i *More than fifty _____ watched the concert on TV.*
   a million people   **b** million persons   **c** millions viewers   **d** millions viewer's
ii '_____ my quite well-paid job, I just can't save any money.'
   a Although   **b** Even though   **c** Despite   **d** In spite
iii *The population of Istanbul has _____ since 1900.*
   a climbed   **b** grown   **c** inclined   **d** trippled
iv *On leaving Iran, some tourists buy small carpets as _____.*
   a memorials   **b** memories   **c** remembrance   **d** souvenirs

12i *The _____ outlook is quite good.*
   a economic   **b** economical   **c** economise   **d** economist
ii 'After this exam, I'm going _____.'
   a home straight away   **b** straight away home   **c** straight to home
   d to home straight away
iii 'I don't think it's necessary to keep _____ every tradition.'
   a on   **b** on with   **c** up   **d** up with
iv 'Recently, one of our customers has been _____.'
   a causing problem   **b** causing trouble   **c** making problems   **d** making troubles

If you got more **i** answers wrong, you need to work on your adjectives. Find a good grammar book or website.

If you got more **iii** answers wrong, you need to work on your verbs.

If you got more **iv** answers wrong, you need to work on your nouns.

Number **ii**s test the little words: adverbs, determiners, linkers, and prepositions.

Multi-choice test for vocabulary, grammar, and spelling 2

Many of the questions below have two gaps to fill. Choose the correct letter: a, b, c, or d. Circle the letter of your choice. (An IELTS 6.5 should score 15/20.)

1   'I think it's _____ going to the casino, but my father _____.'
  a fun; doesn't   **b** fun; isn't   **c** funny; doesn't   **d** funny; isn't

2   'Many students who study _____ do not _____ home.'
  a aboard; go back   **b** aboard; return to   **c** abroad; go back   **d** abroad; return to

3   'At primary school we had to _____ a lot of poetry. I can still _____ it.'
  a memorise; remember   **b** memorise; remind   **c** remember; memorise
  d remember; remind

4   'As a child, I _____ of _____.'
  a had fear; dark   **b** had fear; the dark   **c** was afraid; dark
  d was afraid; the dark

5   '_____ I didn't like the deserted streets _____ in Christchurch.'
  a At first; at night   **b** At first; in the night   **c** In the beginning; at night
  d In the beginning; in the night

6   'I _____ my friend some money after he was _____.'
  a borrowed; burgled   **b** borrowed; stolen   **c** lent; burgled   **d** lent; stolen

7   In _____ years, factories have _____ in my city.
  a recent; closed   **b** recent; closed down   **c** the last; closed
  d the last; closed down

8   _____ *children should start school at four.*
  a According to me   **b** According to my opinion   **c** From my point of view
  d In my opinion

9   'Since I'm a student, I can't _____ new _____.'
  a afford; furniture   **b** afford; furnitures   **c** pay; furniture   **d** pay; furnitures

10 'I don't really like _____ music. I find it _____ slow.'
  a classic; so   **b** classic; too   **c** classical; so   **d** classical; too

11 'When I broke _____ leg, I was in hospital _____ six weeks.'
  a my; during   **b** my; for   **c** the; during   **d** the; for

12 'My boyfriend always _____.'
  a happily seems   **b** seems happily   **c** seems happy   **d** seems like happy

13 'I saw a terrific film _____ days _____.'
  a a few; ago   **b** a few; before   **c** few; ago   **d** few; before

14 *I would _____ if you could resolve this _____.*
   a be grateful; matter   **b** be greatful; problem   **c** grateful; matter
   d greatful; problem

15 *'If you're not too _____, there's part-time _____ available.'*
   a careful; job   **b** careful; work   **c** fussy; job   **d** fussy; work

16 *'My brother and I are very _____. We even have the same _____ in women.'*
   a alike; preferences   **b** alike; taste   **c** like; preferences   **d** like; taste

17 *One _____ of lead pollution is reduced intellectual capacity in children living close
   to the _____.*
   a affect; sauce   **b** affect; source   **c** effect; sauce   **d** effect; source

18 *The _____ of converting all vehicles to unleaded petrol is expensive but
   worth it _____.*
   a cost; in long term   **b** cost; in the long run   **c** price; in long term
   d price; in the long run

19 *'I saw a cyclist _____ by a car recently. I wanted to help the woman, but I was _____
   I might hurt her, so I waited for the ambulance.'*
   a knocked down; anxious   **b** knocked down; nervous   **c** knocked out; anxious
   d knocked out; nervous

20 *There are so many different _____ available _____ the market.*
   a makes; in   **b** makes; on   **c** marks; in   **d** marks; on

Sentence types

English has simple, compound, complex, and compound-complex sentences, or short
answers. To get a Seven, you need a mix of these. Short answers are appropriate in the
Speaking test only.

A **short answer** does not have a subject or a complete verb.

Here are some examples:

● 'At a private college.'   'Not really.'   'Playing computer games.'

A **simple** sentence has a subject and a complete verb.

Here are some examples:

● 'I've made some great new friends.'

● Until recently, only nation states and their agencies, like NASA or the ESA, were capable of
   sending satellites and astronauts into space. (*This is a long sentence, but it only has one
   subject: 'nation states and their agencies', and one complete verb: 'were'.*)

A **compound** sentence is two simple sentences (now called clauses) joined together by a
semi-colon (;), or by conjunctions like: 'and', 'because', 'but', 'if', 'or', 'so', 'while', etc. The
two parts are equally important.

Here are some examples:

● 'The bride was gorgeous, and the food was great.'

● These two feats were achieved at a fraction of the cost of competitors while high safety
   standards were still maintained.

In a **complex** sentence, there are two clauses. One is more important than the other and is
called the main clause. It usually opens the sentence. The subordinate clause which starts

with a relative pronoun or a participle – if the clause is reduced – is less important, and is embedded in, or follows, the main clause.

To get a Six, you need some complex sentences.

Here are some examples:

* **The person** <u>leading this session</u> **thinks PowerPoint is overused**. (***Bold*** *for the main clause;* <u>*underlining*</u> *for the subordinate clause, which is reduced because its longer form would be: 'who is leading this session'.*)

* 'In second class, **I made a lion mask** for a play that <u>we put on</u>.'

* '**My father took us** to the site where <u>the archaeologists were working</u>.' (*'To the site' is an adverbial phrase.*)

A **compound-complex** sentence is two or more complex sentences joined together, or a compound and a complex sentence joined together.

Passage 3 in Academic Reading contains several compound-complex sentences, so it is harder to read than Passage 1 or 2, where there are only a few.

An IELTS Six or a Seven writes compound-complex structures, but with varying accuracy, while an Eight's compound-complex structures are completely accurate. A Five does not attempt them.

Here is an example:

* 'I'm staying at Blackheath, which is in the mountains, with my cousin, and I've been taking the train to Camperdown, where the hospital is that I work at, but the commute is really tough, so I'll probably move down into the city soon.'

YOUR TURN   *Read the sentences below from a Task 2 essay.*
Are they simple, compound, complex, or compound-complex? There are examples.

Eg	In the developed world, some advanced and wealthy nations are finding that the number of secondary or high school children taking science subjects is declining. *Compound-complex (It has three clauses, two subordinate.)*
1	With fewer students studying science, there will be fewer science graduates, a lessening of scientific knowledge, less research, fewer scientific breakthroughs, and ultimately a decline in economic superiority. _____
2	Every day, we cook, go to the doctor, grow or buy vegetables, use electricity, log on to a computer, and gaze at the stars. _____
3	Science is an integral part of our lives. _____
Eg	If students were made aware of scientific connections with everyday life, perhaps more would develop a love for science enough to make it a career. *Compound (Two independent clauses are joined by 'if'. 'Enough to make it a career' is a complement to the second clause, not an independent clause.)*
4	Although arts subjects are essential for students to develop a rounded approach to life, science subjects will provide them with intellectual challenges which could result in new discoveries. _____
5	While there are science fairs to encourage ideas, above all, children need exciting and innovative teachers. _____

Complete this sentence:

From above, it is clear that in IELTS writing, most sentences are (**6**) _____ .

PART III

IELTS PRACTICE TESTS

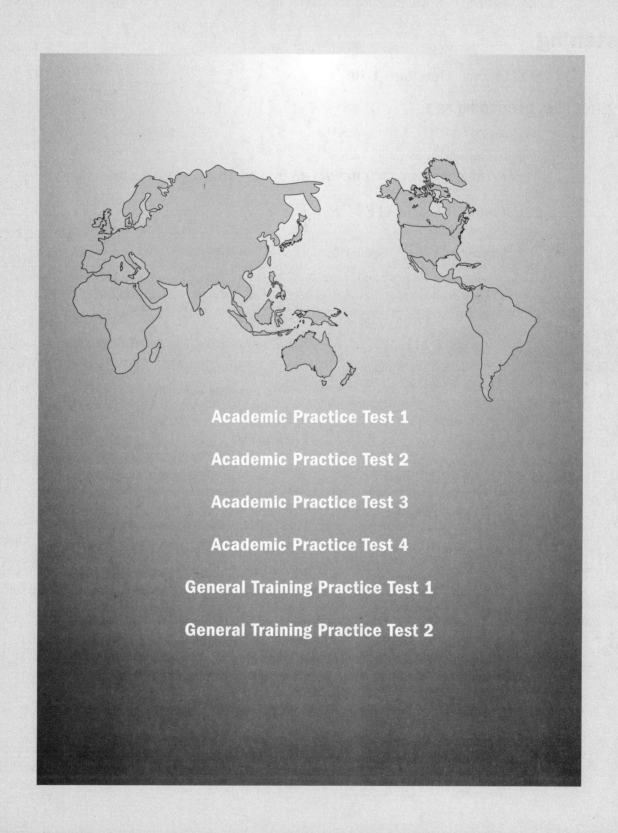

Academic Practice Test 1

Academic Practice Test 2

Academic Practice Test 3

Academic Practice Test 4

General Training Practice Test 1

General Training Practice Test 2

ACADEMIC PRACTICE TEST 1

There are four parts to this test: Listening; Reading; Writing; and Speaking. If you do all four parts together, they will take you about three hours.

Listening

SECTION 1   Questions 1-10

 PLAY RECORDING 68-1.

Questions 1-5
Complete the notes below.
*Write **NO MORE THAN TWO WORDS AND / A NUMBER** for each answer.*

CHOOSING FLATMATES

Mauro	Spring	Katia	Aziza
Comes from Mexico.	Comes from Hong Kong.		Comes from eg *Turkey*.
	Probably cannot 2 ...*cook/afford*...	Is studying Environmental 3 ...*Engenbing*... Won a prize at university for a(n) 4 ...*model*... she made.	Shared a house in Istanbul for 1 ...*2 years*...
Works as a security guard 5 ...*at night*...			Works as a telephone counsellor.

Questions 6-10

Complete the sentences below.

*Write **ONE WORD** for each answer.*

6   Alexander is unsure about Katia because she seems ......*shy*...... .

7   Julie didn't like Lucy coming .....*late*............. to view the flat.

8   Julie and Alexander are both glad that Tina has ...*gone*............. .

9   Two drawbacks of the flat are: it is far from the .....*city*............. ; and in an old building.

10   By the end of the conversation, Julie and Alexander have decided their flatmates should be Aziza and ...*Lucy*............. .

LISTENING
READING
WRITING
SPEAKING

| | SECTION 1 | SECTION 2 | SECTION 3 | SECTION 4 |

SECTION 2 Questions 11-20

 PLAY RECORDING 68-2.

Questions 11-14

Complete the sentences below.

*Write **ONE WORD** for each answer.*

DESIGNING A VERANDA GARDEN

11   The speaker believes veranda gardens help city residents feel at ......Peace........... .

12   She also suggests a veranda garden adds ...& Value........ to a property an owner may soon wish to sell.

13   No matter which .... you're on, a veranda garden still works.

14   This particular garden design is high ...maintanance..in the first year, but easier after that.

Questions 15-20

Look at the diagram below.

Choose the appropriate letter from the diagram for each item.

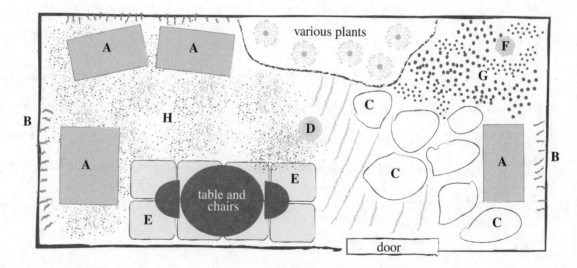

15   A drain = F

16   Irregular stones = E

17   Sand = H

18   Bamboo screens = B

19   A maple tree = ~~A~~ D/A

20   A stone lantern = C

LISTENING | SECTION 1 | SECTION 2 | SECTION 3 | SECTION 4
READING
WRITING
SPEAKING

SECTION 3 Questions 21-30

PLAY RECORDING 68-3.

Questions 21-25

ARCHITECTURE ESSAY

Classify the following statements according to whether they are related to

   A   *Napier*

   B   *Bandung*

   C   *Napier and Bandung*

Write the correct letter, **A**, **B**, *or* **C** *on your answer sheet.*

Here:

21   The Art Deco architectural style still survives. *A*

22   Architects used elements from native culture. *B*

23   Art Deco was chosen after an earthquake. *A*

24   Buildings associated with the government were Art Deco. *C*

25   Art Deco was aided by local tourism. *C*

Questions 26-30

Complete the summary below.

Write **ONE WORD OR A NUMBER** *for each answer.*

Art Deco was influenced by the Paris Expo of **26** *decorative arts* . It differed from the

previous architectural **27** .... , called Art Nouveau. It no longer idealised nature

but the **28** *fluent* .... age. New materials like **29** *concrete* ...... , steel, and glass were

used in Art Deco buildings. Now, many people love Art Deco, but in the past, it was

30 *Somewhat* ...... low-class.

LISTENING   SECTION 1   SECTION 2   SECTION 3   SECTION 4

READING
WRITING
SPEAKING

SECTION 4   Questions 31-40

Play
Audio **PLAY RECORDING 68-4.**

Questions 31-35

Choose the correct letter: A, B, or C.

WETSUITS

31   The speaker thinks all designers must overcome difficulties with

A   materials and production.

B   rapid technological change.

C   material and labour costs.

32   The main problem with early wetsuits was that they

A   were only available in France.

B   tore easily.

C   were made from synthetic materials.

33   The nitrogen gas inside neoprene conducts heat

A   poorly.

B   as well as a liquid.

C   well.

34   The speaker thinks .... invented the wetsuit.

A   Bradner

B   the Meistrell brothers

C   it is unimportant who

35   The speaker suggests wetsuits sold well because

A   people had more leisure time for sport after 1945.

B   the O'Neill company had an effective marketing strategy.

C   diving and surfing were popular in the US in the 1950s.

Questions 36-40

*Write **ONE WORD** for each answer.*

36   Most wetsuits are made of two materials: neoprene for ...*gluing*... ; and lycra for backing.

37   By the early 1980s, ...*Blind*... stitching was being used to sew sections of wetsuit together without the neoprene inside being touched.

38   The lecturer believes designers should develop products that are distinctive yet ...*affordable*... to a large number of people.

39   Since wetsuits increase warmth and buoyancy, swimmers who wear them break more ...*records*... .

40   These days, wetsuits are only allowed in ...*short*... swimming events.

| LISTENING |
| READING |
| WRITING |
| SPEAKING |

| PASSAGE 1 | PASSAGE 2 | PASSAGE 3 |

Reading

You have one hour for this test.

READING PASSAGE 1

*You should spend about 20 minutes on **Questions 1-13**, which are based on Reading Passage 1 on the following pages.*

THE STRESS OF RELOCATION

For some people, there is little in life more stressful than moving house; for others, there is a definite excitement in relocation since the belief that the grass is greener on the other side holds sway.

However, for Dr Jill Molveldt, a psychotherapist in Durban, South Africa, Relocation Stress Syndrome, or RSS, which she has been researching for a decade, is a matter of professional concern. Dr Molveldt began her career as a medical doctor in 1999, but turned to therapy when she doubted the efficacy of some medication. Time and again, patients presented at her surgery who – to all intents and purposes – had little physically wrong, but were not functioning optimally. Usually, such people with anxiety-related disorders are prescribed drugs, but Dr Molveldt observed that many seemed to improve just as readily through talking to her. Therefore, from 2006-2008, she underwent extensive training in the United States in a number of techniques used in therapy.

On return to South Africa, Dr Molveldt moved her family and her burgeoning practice – now devoted entirely to therapy – from Pietermaritzburg, a small city, to Durban, a larger, more cosmopolitan one. Immediately following this move, Dr Molveldt herself fell ill. Medical testing for vague symptoms like headaches, skin rashes, and insomnia brought neither relief nor diagnosis. At the time, she could not possibly have imagined that she, herself, had any psychological problems. Her only recent difficulty had been relocating to Durban due to her children's maladjustment to their third school in three years, and to the irritation caused by a protracted renovation. All the same, she far preferred the beachside lifestyle of Durban to that of conservative inland Pietermaritzburg.

Quite by chance, in the summer of 2010, Dr Molveldt ran into a neighbour from her old city who had also moved to Durban. This woman seemed uncharacteristically depressed, and had experienced mood swings and weight gain since her arrival. As the neighbour recounted her complicated tale of moving, Dr Molveldt suddenly realised that her acquaintance – like herself – was suffering from RSS.

Upon this discovery, Dr Molveldt began sifting through medical and psychological literature to learn more about her syndrome, only to find precious little written about it. Conferences she attended in Greece and Argentina in which stress featured as a topic for keynote speakers did little to enlighten her. Therefore, Dr Molveldt felt she had no option but to collect her own patient data from medical practice and Emergency Room records in Durban and Cape Town in order to ascertain the extent of the problem. Over four years, she surveyed people with non-specific health problems as well as those who had had minor accidents.

In Durban and Cape Town, it might be expected in the general population that 1% of people have moved within a month, and 5% within six months. Yet nearly 3% of patients seen by GPs in Dr Molveldt's study had moved within one month, and 9% within six. Minor accident patients had also moved recently, and some of them had had more than two residential addresses in one year.

Dr Molveldt then examined records of more serious accidents from a nationwide database, and, with the aid of a research grant, conducted interviews with 600 people. Admittedly, alcohol played a part in serious accident rates, but many interviewees said they had been drinking in response to circumstances – one of which was moving house. People who had had serious accidents, however, had not moved more frequently than those with non-specific ailments.

So just how stressful is moving? After all, stress is part of life – think about exams, a new job, marriage, having a child, divorce, illness, or the death of a loved one. Where does RSS fit in relation to these? Dr Molveldt puts it above exams (including for medical school), and somewhere between being newly married and bearing a child. (Newlyweds and young mothers also visit doctors' surgeries and Emergency Rooms more than they should statistically.)

Interestingly, subjects in several of Dr Molveldt's tests rated moving less highly than she did, putting it about equal to sitting a tough exam.

As a side issue, Dr Molveldt found that the number of relationships that broke down around the time of moving was elevated. She considers the link between breakdown and RSS to be tenuous, suggesting instead that couples who are already struggling move house in the hope of resuscitating their relationship. Invariably, this does not happen. Moreover, it is the children in these cases who suffer most: not only has upheaval meant the loss of their old school and friends, but it also signals adjustment to occupation of their new home while one absent parent resides in another.

If Dr Molveldt's research is anything to go by, next time you yearn to live elsewhere, think twice. Moving may be more stressful than you imagine, and the only papers you get to say you've done it are a fee from your doctor and a heap of mail from the previous inhabitants of your dwelling.

Questions 1-6

*Choose the correct letter: **A**, **B**, **C**, or **D**.*

Write the correct letter in boxes 1-6 on your answer sheet.

1   RSS stands for
    A   Relationship Stress Syndrome
    B   Relocation Sickness Syndrome
    C   Relocation Stress Symptoms
    D   Relocation Stress Syndrome

2   When Dr Molveldt fell ill in 2009,
    A   she was worried she had psychological problems.
    B   no one could work out what was wrong with her.
    C   she thought she missed Pietermaritzburg.
    D   she realised she had RSS.

3   As part of her RSS, Dr Molveldt's old neighbour
    A   had backache.
    B   had headaches.
    C   had skin problems.
    D   was happy one day but sad the next.

294 PART III IELTS Academic Practice Test 1

LISTENING
READING
WRITING
SPEAKING

PASSAGE 1   PASSAGE 2   PASSAGE 3

4   Initially, Dr Molveldt's data came from

    A   patients of medical practices and hospital emergency departments.

    B   hospital emergency department patients only.

    C   patients of medical practices only.

    D   other research.

5   In Dr Molveldt's study, the relationship between the number of people who move house in the general population and those who also visit a doctor within one month of relocation is

    A   twice as many.

    B   three times as many.

    C   half as many.

    D   two-thirds as many.

6   Some of Dr Molveldt's data on serious accidents came from

    A   a Pietermaritzburg database.

    B   Durban and Cape Town databases.

    C   a database for all South Africa.

    D   international databases.

Questions 7-13

Complete each sentence with the correct ending, A-J, below.

Write the correct letter, A-J, in boxes 7-13 on your answer sheet.

7   Some people who had had accidents due to alcohol

8   Serious accident rates and relocation rates

9   Dr Molveldt thinks moving house is more stressful

10   Test subjects and Dr Molveldt

11   According to Dr Molveldt, relationship breakdown

12   Children suffer most when moving if

13   Both the writer and Dr Molveldt suggest

A	was one result of relocation.
B	had also recently moved house.
C	was unlikely to be caused by moving.
D	than having a baby.
E	their family is also split up at the same time.
F	disagreed about the stress caused by moving.
G	than getting married.
H	were no higher than other categories.
I	they go to new schools.
J	people should consider moving very carefully.

READING PASSAGE 2

*You should spend about 20 minutes on **Questions 14-27**, which are based on Reading Passage 2 on the following pages.*

TERRIFIC TUPPERWARE

A Throw open anyone's kitchen cupboards from Andorra to Zimbabwe, and you'll find colourful plastic products for the preparation, serving, and storage of food. Chances are, some of these are Tupperware.

B For many people in developed countries, Tupperware is redolent of the 1950s when grandma and her friends bought and sold it at 'Tupperware parties'. Some would even say Tupperware became a cultural icon in that decade. However, these days, while parties are still popular, online sales are challenging the model. Indeed, since 2000, more Tupperware franchises have opened in China than anywhere else.

C Take the Hundred Benefits shop in Hangzhou, one of China's fastest-growing cities. Located in a chic part of town, it's full of twenty-somethings who haven't yet had a child but are building a nest. They've got plenty of expendable income, and they're picking out items to reflect their new-found optimism. China is undergoing a home-decorating revolution after years of dull, unreliable products. Furthermore, the average size of living space for urban Chinese has almost doubled recently, so there's room for lots of stuff. But why choose Tupperware? It's functional as well as fun. It's sealable, stackable, durable, microwave-and-freezable, dishwasher-friendly, and culturally sensitive: four-layer traditional Chinese lunch-boxes, revamped in bright sexy colours, grace the shelves of the Hundred Benefits shop.

D What is the Tupperware story? The special plastic used in it was invented in 1938 by an American called Earl Tupper. The famous seals, which keep the air out and freshness in, came later. Tupper's company was established in 1946, and for more than 40 years boasted every success, but, recently, Tupperware Brands Corporation has been sold several times, and its parent company, Illinois Tool Works, has announced that declining American prospects may mean resale.

E Until the 1990s, Tupperware relied totally on a pyramid sales model. In this, a person buys products from a person above him or her, rather than from a wholesale company or retail shop, and after sale of the new product to a third party, gives a small percentage of the money to the person from whom he or she originally bought. In turn, when the person on the lowest level recruits more vendors, those people return percentages to the person above. Initially, Tupperware operated like this because it was not available in shops. A more direct line between the manufacturer and the buyer results in cheaper products, and, as Tupperware is largely sold in the home, women suddenly have an independent income. A disadvantage might be that since people typically buy from and sell to friends, there are pressures at ordinary social gatherings to do deals, which some people may consider unethical. This raises the question: am I going for a pleasant dinner at Alison's; or am I expected to buy a set of measuring cups from her as I leave? This pyramid model is prohibited in China, and has lost favour in many countries like Britain, Germany, Australia, and New Zealand, where once it was all-pervasive. At present, most US sales are still on the party plan, but online and franchise sales are catching up.

F Tupperware became fashionable after World War II. During the war, large numbers of women were in paid employment outside the home while their men were away fighting. When the men

296   PART III   **IELTS Academic Practice Test 1**

LISTENING
READING
WRITING
SPEAKING

PASSAGE 1   PASSAGE 2   PASSAGE 3

returned, the women mostly resumed their household duties. There are widely divergent views about Tupperware's role at this time. Some feminists propose that the company promulgated an image of women confined to the kitchen, making the female pursuit of a career less likely. Others say that the pyramid sales model allowed women to earn, promoting autonomy and prosperity. In particular, those who were pregnant and at home could enjoy some extra cash.

G Effective rebranding of Tupperware has taken place in the East, but what about in America? Well, the Tupperware website there has developed a 'Chain of Confidence' programme to improve sales. In this, women reinforce the notion of female solidarity by purchasing Tupperware and swapping true stories. Over a million dollars from this programme has also been donated to a girls' charity.

H What the future holds for the pretty plastic product is uncertain. Will Tupperware become a relic of the past like cane baskets and wooden tea chests, or will online social programmes and avid Chinese consumers save the company?

• •

Questions 14-17

The text has eight paragraphs: **A-H**.

*Which paragraph, **A-H**, has the following information?*

*Write the correct letter, **A-H**, in boxes 14-17 on your answer sheet.*

14   The benefits of Tupperware in the kitchen.

15   Opposing views on Tupperware and the position of women.

16   A sales model which might spoil friendship.

17   Worldwide availability of Tupperware.

Questions 18-22

Look at questions 18-22 and the list of countries below.

Match each statement with a country.

*Write the letters, **A-D**, in boxes 18-22 on your answer sheet.*

18   Consumers here are now less keen on the pyramid sales model

19   Tupperware buyers in this country give money to help others

20   Young women here lead the way in the purchase of Tupperware

21   The writer uses this to represent many countries

22   Just after World War II, Tupperware was established here

List of countries
(A) Andorra
(B) China
(C) Germany
(D) US

Questions 23-27

Do the following statements agree with the claims of the writer in Reading Passage 2?

In boxes 23-27 on your answer sheet, write:

YES	*if the statement agrees with the claims of the writer*
NO	*if the statement contradicts the claims of the writer*
NOT GIVEN	*if it is impossible to say what the writer thinks about this*

23 Keeping food fresh is something Tupperware does well.

24 Tupperware was responsible for a negative image of women in the 1950s.

25 Rebranding in China has been unsuccessful.

26 Tupperware containers are good for the environment.

27 The future of Tupperware Brands Corporation is assured.

READING PASSAGE 3

*You should spend about 20 minutes on **Questions 28-40**, which are based on Reading Passage 3 on the following pages.*

MARVELLOUS MONTICELLO

Thomas Jefferson is renowned for many accomplishments, among which he was the principal author of the American Declaration of Independence and the third president of the United States, during which time America grew significantly in size and stature.

Jefferson also designed his own three-storeyed, 33-roomed mansion, called Monticello, familiar to every American from the nickel, or 5-cent coin, on which can be seen a simple domed building with a four-columned portico.

Influenced by classical European design, and emulated across the land, Monticello took more than 40 years to build. Numerous labour-saving devices inside, invented by Jefferson himself, and gardens the envy of agronomists represent the scientific spirit of a new age.

Modelled on Andrea Palladio's 16th-century Italian villas, Monticello is a tribute to the man and style that Jefferson idolised. As Palladio considered the position of a building to be of the utmost importance, Jefferson had Monticello built on a mountain with splendid views. According to Palladio, a building should be symmetrical since mathematical order bestows harmony upon its inhabitants. Thus Monticello boasts a colonnaded entrance and a central room with a dome.

But who was the man who created Monticello? Thomas Jefferson was born at Shadwell, Virginia, on the east coast of America in 1743. On his father's death, he inherited a large property where Monticello was subsequently constructed. Jefferson, both a lawyer and politician, was elected to the House of Burgesses in 1768, and in 1775 to the Continental Congress, where he revised the laws of Virginia. Two of his famous pieces of legislation include: the Virginia Statute for Religious Freedom; and the Bill for the More General Diffusion of Knowledge.

Throughout Jefferson's early adulthood, America had been fighting Britain in the War of Independence. In 1776, Jefferson, who was never a combatant, wrote the Declaration of Independence, and although the conflict did not end until 1783, Americans consider the birth of their nation came with that declaration. As well as proclaiming America's freedom, the declaration outlines universal human rights, stating that all men are equal regardless of birth, wealth, or status, and, furthermore, that government is the servant, not the master, of the people. Although Jefferson's work was based on the ideas of John Locke, an Englishman, and on a body of French philosophy, it remains a uniquely American document.

After the war, Jefferson took up the post of Governor of Virginia, before returning to Congress. He then served five years in France as a US trade representative and minister. He was American Vice-President between 1797-1801 and President for the following eight years. As president, he

298　PART III　**IELTS Academic Practice Test 1**

LISTENING
READING
WRITING
SPEAKING

PASSAGE 1　　PASSAGE 2　　PASSAGE 3

organised the purchase of a vast tract of land from the French, who were embattled in Europe and strapped for cash. This land, called the Louisiana Territory, doubled the size of America. Jefferson was also responsible for financing Lewis and Clark – two explorers who undertook a momentous journey along the Ohio River to survey nature and appraise land for settlement.

In retirement, Jefferson remained active. His huge library, donated to the nation, and known as the Library of Congress, is still one of the world's most reputable. He founded the University of Virginia, designed most of its early buildings, defined its curriculum, and became its first rector or chancellor. When he died, on the fourth of July 1826, America had lost a truly great man.

Monticello, his home for most of his life, is on the UNESCO World Heritage List partly because Jefferson lived there, but mainly because it brought classicism – the style of Palladio – to the New World. It was Jefferson's belief that if America were to assume the mantle of a powerful nation, it needed to draw on the best of the European past as well as creating its own style.

Monticello is not a very large building: it is 1022 square metres (11,000 square feet) – these days, a football player or film star has a house as big.

Monticello was not all built at once since Jefferson's finances were seldom secure. Furthermore, his ideas about building changed during his sojourn in France. In 1768, the mountaintop where Monticello would sit was leveled. Bricks were manufactured over a two-year period by Jefferson's slaves – he owned about 200. Wood was sourced from trees on Jefferson's land; stone and limestone were quarried on his property; and – in keeping with his concept of elegance – the window glass and furniture were imported from Europe. Jefferson moved into the South Pavilion in 1770. Around 1772, the Dining Room in the north wing was built. The first house was mostly complete in 1782, the year Jefferson's wife died. On return from France in 1796, Jefferson had the upper storey demolished, and the whole structure remodelled, which took eleven years. In 1800, the dome was fitted. A North Pavilion was added from 1806-8. Extensive gardens – both ornamental and productive – were created since Jefferson believed in pursuing agriculture in a scientific manner.

As mentioned previously, Jefferson was an inventor. Since Virginian summers can be hot, he designed special fans and blinds. Blocks of ice were stored in the cellar all year round – a rarity at the time. For the cold winters, Monticello has numerous fireplaces and stoves. In the late 1790s, Jefferson altered the fireplaces to apply some modern fuel-saving principles. He introduced skylights – another unusual feature – and he designed tables that could be turned easily and doors that opened automatically. He even had a shaft-and-pulley system between floors for hoisting food. However, not until 1822, was the roof covered with durable material. Just four years later, Jefferson died.

Jefferson is remembered as a statesman, philosopher, educationalist, and architect. Fiercely American, he drew on a European heritage. He was optimistic, far-sighted, and creative, and Monticello remains a monument to the man as much as his age.

Questions 28-32

Do the following statements agree with the information in the text on the following page?

In boxes 28-32 on your answer sheet, write:

TRUE	*if the statement agrees with the information*
FALSE	*if the statement contradicts the information*
NOT GIVEN	*if there is no information on this*

28   Monticello was inspired by Italian architecture.

29   Jefferson fought in the War of Independence.

30   During Jefferson's presidency, the French bought some American land, greatly reducing the size of the country.

31   Jefferson taught at the University of Virginia.

32   By today's standards, Monticello appears quite a small house for a famous person.

Questions 33-39

Complete the table below.

Write **NO MORE THAN TWO WORDS OR A DATE** *for each answer.*

Time or period	Important event(s)
1768	The mountaintop **33** .... to prepare for the building of Monticello.
1768-1770	**34** .... were made by Jefferson's slaves. Wood and stone also came from Jefferson's land.
1770	Jefferson began to live in the **35** ....
36 ....-1807	Monticello was remodelled. Some of Jefferson's own inventions include: fans, blinds, special fireplaces, skylights, automatic **37** .... , and delivery systems.
1822	The **38** .... was covered with long-lasting material.
39	The death of Jefferson.

Question 40

Which plan shows the stages in which Monticello was built?

A	B	C

Dining Room

N

N

Dining Room

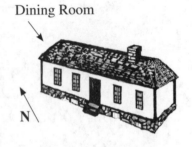

N

To be demolished

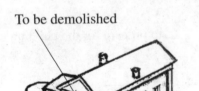

N

To be demolished

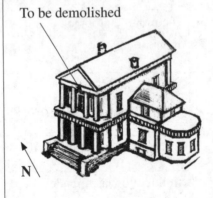

N

N

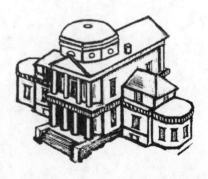

Writing

You have one hour for this test.

Task 1

Spend about 20 minutes on this task.

The diagram shows how sports shoes are made.
Write a summary of the information. Select and report the main features.
Write at least 150 words.

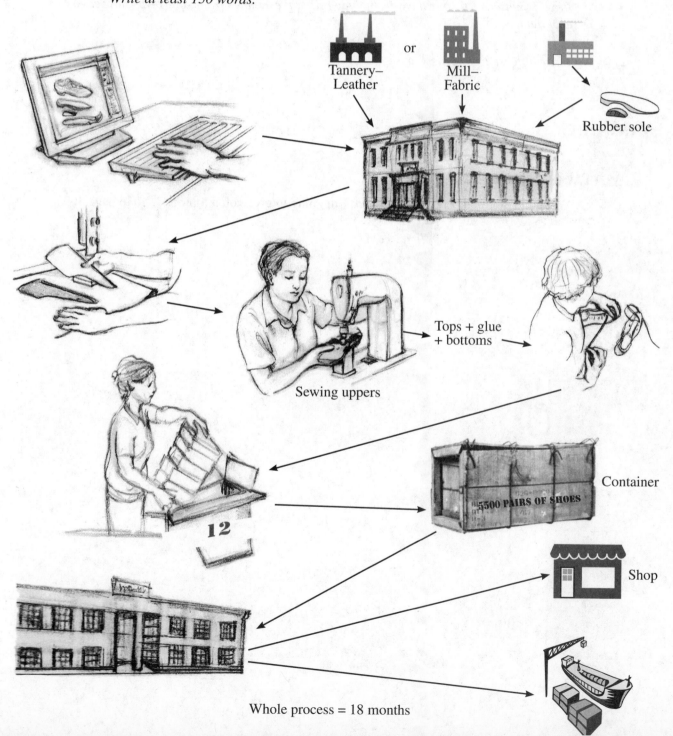

Tannery–
Leather

or

Mill–
Fabric

Rubber sole

Tops + glue
+ bottoms

Sewing uppers

12

Container

5500 PAIRS OF SHOES

Shop

Whole process = 18 months

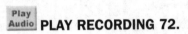

Task 2

Spend about 40 minutes on this task.

Write about the following topic:

These days many countries help other countries by giving free food, medical, or other aid.

What are the benefits and drawbacks of this for countries that give and receive?

Provide reasons for your answer. Include relevant examples from your own knowledge or experience.

Write at least 250 words.

Speaking

PLAY RECORDING 72.

When the examiner says: 'In this part, I'm going to give you a topic...', go to page 409.

LISTENING	SECTION 1	SECTION 2	SECTION 3	SECTION 4
READING				
WRITING				
SPEAKING				

ACADEMIC PRACTICE TEST 2

There are four parts to this test: Listening; Reading; Writing; and Speaking. If you do all four parts together, they will take you about three hours.

Listening

SECTION 1 Questions 1-10

 **PLAY RECORDING 70-1.**

Questions 1-4

Complete the notes below.

Write ONE WORD AND / OR A NUMBER for each answer.

JOINING UP

Example: *Library* application form	
Name:	Paulo de Mello
Identification:	Brazilian passport
Occupation:	1 .an.accountant
Address:	2 ...19.................. Wood Street
Email:	3 .paulo.880...........@hotmail.com
Other family member(s) using this card:	Yes, his 4 ....wife...........

LISTENING
READING
WRITING
SPEAKING

| **SECTION 1** | **SECTION 2** | **SECTION 3** | **SECTION 4** |

Questions 5-8

Complete the plan below.

Write **NO MORE THAN TWO WORDS** *for each answer.*

8 _Events_............ Room	Teens Room	
		7 ...Non Fiction...
Computers		
5 ...Notice Board...	Chute	Entrance
		6 ...Newspaper & Magazines...

Questions 9-10

Answer the questions below.

Write NO MORE THAN TWO WORDS *for each answer.*

9　How many items can members borrow at a time? ...up to 10...

10　When is the library open at the weekend? ...Saturday mornings

LISTENING   SECTION 1   SECTION 2   SECTION 3   SECTION 4
READING
WRITING
SPEAKING

SECTION 2 Questions 11-20

Play
Audio **PLAY RECORDING 70-2.**

Questions 11-14

CLIMBING THE SYDNEY HARBOUR BRIDGE

Complete the sentences below.

*Write **ONE WORD OR A NUMBER** for each answer.*

11   The company takes climbers up the Sydney Harbour Bridge ......363............... days
a year.

12   The colour of the overall climbers wear is ....grey................ .

13   The top of the arch of the bridge is ......134............... metres above sea level.

14   If a climber suffers from a fear of ......hights........... *heights* , he or she is put at the front of
a climbing group.

Questions 15-20

Complete the sentences below.

*Write **NO MORE THAN TWO WORDS OR A NUMBER** for each answer.*

15   The guide shows the climbers items of clothing, and items related to ......safety........... .

16   The climbers are going to be on the bridge in time for ...sunrise............ .

17   All climbers wear sliders that attach them to a(n) .....chain.......... on the bridge.

18   The climb is ......more than 3........ hours long.

19   At the top of the arch, the guide will take a(n) ....photo........... of the climbers.

20   The climbers aren't allowed to carry their own belongings in case they drop them into
the ....trafic........... below.

LISTENING   **SECTION 1   SECTION 2   SECTION 3   SECTION 4**
READING
WRITING
SPEAKING

SECTION 3 Questions 21-30

PLAY RECORDING 70-3.

Questions 21-25

Complete the sentences below.

*Write **ONE WORD** for each answer.*

WATER FOR PEACE PRESENTATION

21   Water For Peace (WFP) started in ....

22   Beatrice doesn't want some of Cathy's photos in their presentation because she thinks
they do not ...~~relate~~............ to their topic.

23   One of Cathy's photos is of women getting water from a(n) ...~~wave/whale~~............ .

24   WFP is involved with .... projects, education, and cross-border relations.

25   Antonio and Cathy think most of their presentation should be ...~~analyze~~............ and
not just descriptive.

Questions 26-30

Classify the following by person:
   A   *for the man, Antonio*
   B   *for the woman, Beatrice*
   C   *for the woman, Cathy*
*Write the correct letter, **A**, **B**, or **C** on your answer sheet.*

This person:

~~C~~ **26**   will talk about the historical context in their presentation.

~~C~~ **27**   will illustrate their presentation with maps of towns and villages involved in the project.

~~A~~ **28**   admires Mr Koussa, who founded WFP.

~~B~~ **29**   will discuss international legal frameworks in their presentation.

~~A~~ **30**   prefers the grassroots approach to community projects.

LISTENING SECTION 1 SECTION 2 SECTION 3 SECTION 4

READING

WRITING

SPEAKING

SECTION 4 Questions 31-40

Play Audio **PLAY RECORDING 70-4.**

Questions 31-35

Complete the sentences below.

*Write **ONE WORD OR A NUMBER** for each answer.*

LEARNING STYLES

31 The lecturer begins by asking the question: what helps students ...learn...?

32 How students relate to their teachers and the classroom ...Environment... influence educational success.

33 Early learning-style theories put learners into ...four... personality types.

34 Fleming divided learners into ...., Auditory, Reading-Writing, and Kinesthetic Learners.

35 Fleming's ...Mark... Model was used all over the world.

Questions 36-40

*Choose the correct letter: **A**, **B**, or **C**.*

36 Jackson, a researcher, used .... to deduce that Fleming's model didn't work.

    A results from teaching experiments

    B evidence from brain scans

    C interviews with learners

37 Jackson believed that to learn the following is / are necessary:

    A building models and going on excursions.

    B deciding what the final achievement will be.

    C setting goals, working hard, and reading deeply.

38 A major disadvantage of Fleming's model is that

    A it is time consuming for teachers and learners.

    B children need to absorb more than in the past.

    C exams have renounced reading and writing skills.

39 Recent experiments using VARK showed that students learnt .... with traditional teaching methods.

    A better

    B worse

    C just as well

40 Overall, the lecturer considers Fleming's system to be

    A interesting but outdated.

    B an experiment we were better off without.

    C a valid learning methodology with some limitations.

Reading

You have one hour for this test.

READING PASSAGE 1

*You should spend about 20 minutes on **Questions 1-13**, which are based on Reading Passage 1 on the following pages.*

Questions 1-4

*Reading Passage 1 has five sections: **A-E**.*

*Choose the correct heading for sections **B-E** from the list of headings below.*

*Write the correct number, **i-vii**, in boxes 1-4 on your answer sheet.*

List of Headings

   i SpaceX remains pragmatic

 ii A fashion that may not last

iii SpaceX's achievements

 iv Accidents will happen

   v Challenging the status quo

 vi NASA leads the pack

vii Not as easy as it looks

Example	Answer
Section A	*v*

THE PRIVATE-SECTOR SPACE RACE

Section A

Until recently, only nation states and their agencies, like NASA or the European Space Agency, were capable of sending satellites and astronauts into space. A colony on Mars set up by a private company was the stuff of science fiction. However, since the late 1990s, a number of private firms has entered the space race. Questions about their intentions have inevitably been raised. Will they engage effectively in tourism in sub-orbital space as they claim? Will they be robust enough to send missions into orbit beyond Earth? Or are they mere manifestations of hubris?

Section B

In the latter part of the 20th century, a handful of super-rich men decided to purchase football clubs – the ultimate in toys for the boys. These days, owning a company involved in space tourism may be an early 21st-century equivalent, given it is the provenance of billionaires like Jeff Bezos, Richard Branson, John Carmack, and Elon Musk. Bezos was the man behind Amazon, the online retailer. Branson owns transport companies. Carmack brought the world the video games *Doom* and *Quake*. And Elon Musk sold PayPal to eBay for $1.5 billion before he founded SpaceX. From these backgrounds, you may construe that some space-company owners are more at home in the virtual world than that of highly complex engineering. They may also be keener to promote a pie-in-the-sky tourist industry than to engage in really useful science.

Their space-tourism companies – Armadillo Aerospace, Blue Origin, Virgin Galactic, SpaceX, Starchaser, and XCOR Aerospace – were all in existence in 2010, and all boasted that very soon they'd be propelling paying passengers to the edge of Earth's atmosphere. By 2016, however, one company had ceased trading; three had scaled down operations or revised launch dates significantly; and only two were actively developing new products. Space tourism had taken a backseat to other more profitable areas of the space industry.

Section C

Furthermore, safety concerns and the customer base have been queried. In order for the US Federal Aviation Administration to license craft that carry passengers, test missions have to be completed at full speed and at an altitude of 100 kilometres (62 miles). To date, only two companies have been able to do this, and only with unmanned craft. Meanwhile, tests with manned scale models have been fraught, as evidenced by the crash in the Mojave Desert in California of a Virgin Galactic craft.

Then, there is the conundrum that people wealthy enough to afford a $200,000, three-minute thrust into the great blue yonder may not pass a medical. Space travel isn't the same as jetting off on holiday to Tahiti, where all you need is a passport and sunscreen. The British company Starchaser, which has diversified into space education, is one of the few to offer passenger training, even though there is now no date set for its own first space journey. Starchaser provides a two-week preparatory course that includes: vehicle familiarity and space-travel scenarios; parachute, decompression, and centrifuge training; an introduction to safety systems; first aid and survival training; and protocols for radio use. All the same, this is greatly removed from what professional astronauts receive.

Section D

Of the few major companies still active in the private-sector space race, SpaceX may be the most well known. Established in 2002, it is the brainchild of the South African entrepreneur Elon Musk, now resident in California.

Musk has been passionate about the future since his student days, and he is certain his own children will live on other planets, as this is the only way for humans to prevent self-destruction or save themselves from a catastrophe like the impact of a large meteorite.

He also set up SpaceX because he believed NASA to be inefficient. To prove his hypothesis, one of SpaceX's earliest endeavours was the construction of the Merlin engine, which, while elegant and powerful, runs on kerosene – half the price of conventional rocket fuel. Later, SpaceX produced reusable rocket parts, which is an industry innovation, and it designed craft with fewer stages in their transformation. That is: there are fewer times a rocket separates into smaller parts as it journeys onward. These two feats were achieved at a fraction of the cost of competitors, while high safety standards were still maintained.

Indeed, the list of SpaceX's successes is long. Within seven years of establishment, it had sent a satellite into space. By 2010, it had produced the Falcon 9 launcher, and the shuttle *Dragon*. Subsequently, it was contracted by NASA to provide an unmanned service to the International Space Station (ISS), with *Dragon* completing more than a dozen trips in a decade. It had achieved both take-offs and landings for its rockets both near the terrestrial test site and near beacons in the ocean. More recently, SpaceX has been working with NASA in the Commercial Crew Development programme, in which manned spacecraft are sent to the ISS.

Section E

Although Musk still supports the colonising of space, it would seem that space tourism, even for SpaceX, is on the back burner. Instead, the company raises funds by subcontracting to NASA, aiding humanity's efforts to go beyond Earth mainly by providing glorified taxis to the ISS.

Questions 5-8

*Choose **NO MORE THAN TWO WORDS AND / OR A NUMBER** from the passage for each answer.*

Write your answers in boxes 5-8 on your answer sheet.

5   Musk raised money to start SpaceX from the ....-dollar sale of PayPal.

6   Although space-tourism companies started out optimistically, by .... many of their predictions had not come true.

7   A regulatory authority in the US insists passenger spacecraft must be able to reach an altitude of ....

8   Starchaser's short courses are substantially different from those that .... would undertake.

Questions 9-13

Do the following statements agree with the information in Passage 1?

In boxes 9-13 on your answer sheet, write:

> **TRUE**   *if the statement agrees with the information*
> **FALSE**   *if the statement contradicts the information*
> **NOT GIVEN**   *if there is no information on this*

9   Musk believes his children could live on Mars.

10   Musk founded SpaceX to prove that NASA wasted resources.

11   The shuttle *Dragon* takes astronauts to the ISS.

12   SpaceX partners with NASA on some projects.

13   SpaceX will probably send tourists into space soon.

READING PASSAGE 2

*You should spend about 20 minutes on **Questions 14-26**, which are based on Reading Passage 2 on the following pages.*

BRAND LOYALTY RUNS DEEP

At almost any supermarket in Sydney, Australia, food from all over the world fills the shelves. Perhaps you fancy some Tick Tock Rooibos tea made in South Africa, or some Maharaja's Choice Rogan Josh sauce from India. Alongside local Foster's beer, Chinese Tsingtao and Indonesian Bintang are both to be found. For homesick Britons, the confectionary aisle is stocked with Mars Bars and Bountys, while for pining Poles sweets manufactured by firms like Wawel or Solidarposc are available. Restaurants in Sydney range from Afghan to Zambian, catering for different ethnic groups as well as the rest of the curious general public.

All of this variety is a result of population movement and changes in global trade, and, to a lesser extent, reduced production and transportation costs. While Australia can claim around 40% of its population as first generation, other countries, like Switzerland, may have fewer international migrants, but still have people who move from city to city in search of work. Even since the 1990s, taxes or tariffs on imported goods have decreased dramatically. The World Trade Organisation, for example, has promulgated the idea of zero tariffs, which has been adopted into legislation by many member states. It is estimated that within a century, agriculture worldwide has increased its efficiency five-fold. Faster and better integrated road and rail services, containerisation, and the ubiquitous aeroplane have sped up transport immeasurably.

Even with this rise in the availability of non-local products, recent studies suggest that supermarkets should do more to increase their number to match more closely the proportion of shoppers from those countries or regions. Thus, if 10% of a supermarket's customers originate in Vietnam, there ought to be 10% Vietnamese products in store. If Americans from southern states dominate in one northern neighbourhood, southern brands should also be conspicuous. Admittedly, there are already specialist shops that cater to minority groups, but minorities do frequent supermarkets.

Two separate studies by Americans Bart Bronnenberg and David Atkin have found that brand loyalty (choosing Maharaja's Choice over Patak's, or Cadbury's over Nestlé) is not only determined by advertising, but also by a consumer's past. If a product featured in a person's early life in one place, then, as a migrant, he or she is likely to buy that same product even though it is more expensive than an otherwise identical locally-produced one.

In the US context, between 2006 and 2008, Bronnenberg analysed data from 38,000 families who had bought 238 different kinds of packaged goods. Although the same brands could be found across America, there were clear differences in what people purchased. In general, there were two leading brands in each kind of packaged good, but there were smaller brands that assumed a greater proportion of consumers' purchases than was statistically likely. One explanation for this is that 16% of people surveyed came from interstate, and these people preferred products from their home states. Over time, they did buy more products from their adopted state, but, surprisingly, it took two decades for their brand loyalty to halve. Even people who had moved interstate 50 years previously maintained a preference for home-state brands. It seems the habits of food buying change more slowly than we think.

Bronnenberg's findings were confirmed by Atkin's in India although there was something more unexpected that Atkin discovered. Firstly, during the period of his survey, the cost of all consumables rose considerably in India. As a result, families reduced their spending on food, and their calorific intake fell accordingly. It is also worth noting that although India is one country, states impose tariffs or taxes on products from other Indian states, ensuring that locally-produced goods remain cheaper. As in the US, internal migrants bought food from their native place even when it was considerably more expensive than local alternatives, and at a time when you might expect families to be economising. This element made the brand-loyalty theory even more convincing.

There is one downside to these findings. In relatively closed economies, such as India's, people develop tastes that they take with them wherever they go; in a more globalised economy, such as America's, what people eat may be more varied, but still dependent on early exposure to brands. Therefore, according to both researchers, more advertising may now be directed at minors since brand loyalty is established in childhood and lasts a lifetime. In a media-driven world where children are already bombarded with information their parents may not consider appropriate yet more advertising is hardly welcome.

For supermarkets, this means that wherever there are large communities of expatriates or immigrants, it is essential to calculate the demographic carefully in order to supply those shoppers with their favourite brands, as in light of Atkin and Bronnenberg's research, advertising and price are not the sole motivating factors for purchase as was previously thought.

~~~~~~

Questions 14-18

*Choose the correct letter: **A**, **B**, **C**, or **D**.*

Write the correct letter in boxes 14-18 on your answer sheet.

14   In this article, the writer refers to food products that are sold

    A   at markets.

    B   wholesale.

    C   online.

    D   retail.

15   In Sydney, shoppers can buy beer from

    A   China and Indonesia.

    B   India and South Africa.

    C   Poland.

    D   Vietnam.

16   The greater variety of goods and brands now available is mainly due to:

    A   cheaper production and more migration.

    B   changes in migration and international trade.

    C   cheaper production and transport.

    D   changes in migration and transport.

17   The writer thinks supermarkets .... should change their products slightly.

    A   in Australia

    B   in India and the US

    C   in Switzerland

    D   worldwide

18   The writer suggests that:

    A   the quality of products at specialist shops will always be better than at supermarkets.

    B   specialist shops will close down because supermarkets will be cheaper.

    C   specialist shops already supply minority groups, so supermarkets shouldn't bother.

    D   specialist shops already supply minority groups, yet supermarkets should compete with them.

LISTENING
READING
WRITING
SPEAKING

| PASSAGE 1 | PASSAGE 2 | PASSAGE 3 |

Question 19

Which chart below – *A*, *B*, or *C* – best describes the relationship between shoppers at one Sydney supermarket, and what research suggests that same supermarket should sell?

Write your answer in box 19 on your answer sheet.

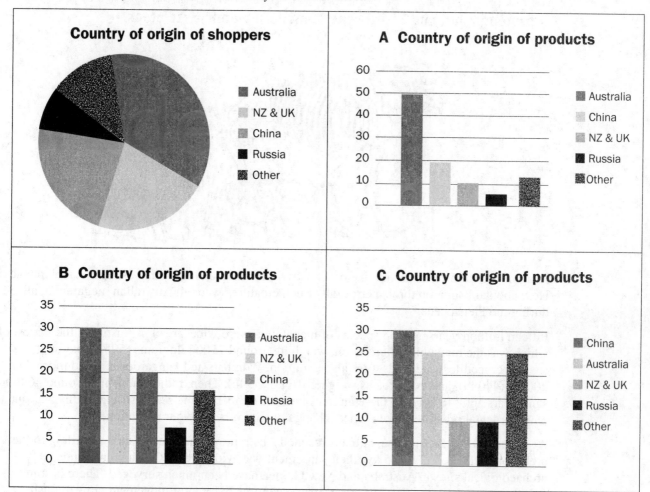

Questions 20-26

Which study/studies do the following statements relate to?

In boxes 20-26 on your answer sheet, write:

    A   if the information relates only to Atkin's study

    B   if the information relates only to Bronnenberg's study

    C   if the information relates to both Atkin's and Bronnenberg's studies

20   There was a correlation between brands a shopper used in childhood, and his or her preferences as an adult.

21   One reason for the popularity of smaller brands was that many people surveyed came from another state where those brands were bigger.

22   Even living in a new state for a very long time did not mean that shoppers chose new brands.

23   In general, food became more expensive during the time of the study. Despite this, families bought favourite brands and ate less.

24   Taxes on products from other states also increased the cost of food. This did not stop migrants from buying what they were used to.

25   Children may be the target of more food advertising now.

26   Advertising and price were once thought to be the main reasons for buying products. This theory has been modified now.

READING PASSAGE 3

You should spend about 20 minutes on Questions 27-40, which are based on Reading Passage 3 below.

Diprotodon, human, Pleistocene & modern wombat skeletons

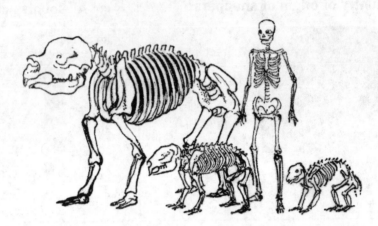

Imagine a bird three times the size of an ostrich, or a burrowing animal as big as an elephant. How about a kangaroo three metres tall? Such creatures were all Australian megafauna, alive during the Pleistocene.[1]

Fifteen million years ago, 55 species of megafauna were widespread in Australia, the largest of which was the marsupial[2] diprotodon, weighing around 2700 kilograms (5952 lb). Giant snakes, crocodiles, and birds were also common. Wombats and kangaroos reached more than 200 kg (440 lb), and even koalas weighed 16 kg (35 lb). Then, rather suddenly, around 46 thousand years ago (46 kyr), all these animals became extinct. Some scientists claim this was due to environmental pressures, like climate change or fire; others favour predation.[3]

At the end of the Pleistocene, humans reached Australia via Indonesia, and, according to the archaeological record, by 45 kyr their settlement was widespread. One hundred and sixty archaeological sites in Australia and New Guinea have been much surveyed. There is some disagreement about the dates of these sites; meantime, a forceful movement aims to push human settlement back before 45 kyr.

Dating the rare bones of megafauna was highly controversial until 20 years ago, when a technique called optically stimulated luminescence (OSL) was developed. With OSL, the age of minerals up to 200 kyr can be established with +/- 10% accuracy.

The largest OSL dating of megafauna was carried out in 2001 by Roberts, who put the extinction date for megafauna at around 46 kyr, very early on in the time of human habitation.

Megafaunal bones are rare enough, but, at archaeological sites with human habitation, they are extremely rare with fewer than 10% of the 160 sites containing them. Bones that show cutting, burning, or deliberate breaking by humans are virtually non-existent, and thus far, not one megafaunal skeleton shows conclusively an animal was killed by humans. There are no 'kill

---

[1] A period 2.6 million-10,000 years ago.
[2] This mammal, like a kangaroo, keeps its very young baby in a pouch.
[3] The killing of a group or groups of animals by another group.

LISTENING
READING
WRITING
SPEAKING

| PASSAGE 1 | PASSAGE 2 | PASSAGE 3 |

sites' either whereas in New Zealand, where the giant moa bird became extinct in the 18th century due to hunting, there are sites with hundreds of slaughtered creatures. As a result, many scientists still believe that humans were not responsible for megafaunal extinction – especially as the weapons of Australian Aborigines at 45 kyr were only wooden clubs and spears.

There is, perhaps, a cultural record of megafauna in Aboriginal myths. The Adnyamathanha people of South Australia tell of the Yamuti, something like a diprotodon. An ancient rock painting in Arnhem Land shows an extinct giant echidna. But this record is small and open to interpretation.

If the Aborigines were not technologically advanced enough to kill them, what else might have destroyed megafauna? One theory has been climate change – perhaps there was a relatively hot, dry period between 60-40 kyr. Research suggests otherwise. Indeed, at 40 kyr, the climate was moderate, and Lake Eyre, in central Australia, grew. If there was desertification, scientists would expect megafauna to have moved towards the coast, looking for food and water, but instead, the fossil record details an equal distribution of the dead inland and on the coast.

In addition, changes in specific vegetation occurred *after* the extinction of the megafauna. Trees that relied on large animals to eat their fruit and disperse their seed covered far smaller areas of Australia post 40 kyr. These plants were not threatened by climate change; rather, they died off because their megafaunal partners had already gone.

Typically, climate change affects almost all species in an area. Yet, around 46 kyr, only the megafauna died. Previously, there had been many species of kangaroo, some as heavy as 200 kg (440 lb), but, after, the heaviest weighed only 32 kg (70 lb). This phenomenon is known as dwarfing, and it occurred with many animals in the Pleistocene.

Dwarfing has been studied extensively. In 2001, Law published research related to fish farming. Despite excellent food and no predators, farmed fish become smaller as generations continue. This adaptation may be a response to their being commercially useless at a smaller size, meaning they hope to survive harvest.

Of the dwarf marsupials, the most notable development over the giants was their longer reproductive lives, which produced more young. They were better runners as well, or, those that were slow-moving retreated to the mountainous forest, beyond the reach of humans.

If climate change isn't a credible factor in extinction, what about fire? Fire is caused naturally by lightning strikes as well as by humans with torches. Surprisingly, the charcoal record for many thousands of years does not show a marked increase in fire after human habitation of Australia – there is only a slow increase over time. Besides, it could be argued that forest fires aid megafauna since grass, their favoured food, invariably replaces burnt vegetation.

Johnson, an archaeologist, has proposed that the Aborigines could have wiped out all 55 megafaunal species in just a few thousand years. He believes that the 45 kyr human settlement date will be pushed back to make this extinction fit, and he also maintains that 700 years are enough to make one species extinct without large-scale hunting or sophisticated weapons. Johnson used computer modelling on a population of only 1000 animals to demonstrate this. If just 30 animals are killed a year, then the species becomes extinct after 520-700 years. Human populations in Australia were small at 45 kyr – only 150 people occupied the same 500 square kilometres as 1000 animals. However, at a rate of killing just two animals a year by each group of ten people, extinction is highly likely.

A recent study on the albatross has shown the bird has almost disappeared due to females' occasionally being hooked on fishing lines. A large number of animals do not need to be killed to effect extinction especially if an animal breeds late and infrequently like the albatross and like megafauna.

With Johnson's model, it is easy to see that the archaeological record need not be filled with tonnes of bones. Megafaunal skeletons are not visible because hunting them was a minor activity, or because they are yet to be found.

The mystery of the rapid extinction of Australian megafauna may be over. These animals probably became extinct because they were large, slow, easy victims whose birth rates never exceeded their death rates. Their disappearance is consistent with predation rather than environmental change. Although hard evidence of hunting is lacking, it remains the simplest explanation.

Questions 27-30

*Complete each sentence with the correct ending, **A-G**, below.*

*Write the correct letter, **A-G**, in boxes 27-30 on your answer sheet.*

27   Many animals in the Pleistocene were

28   Australian megafauna became extinct

29   The figure 45 kyr refers to

30   OSL represented

A	surprisingly swiftly.
B	optically stimulated luminescence.
C	over a long period of time.
D	considerably larger than their modern equivalents.
E	the date of megafaunal disappearance.
F	human habitation of Australia.
G	a breakthrough in dating technology.

Questions 31-34

*Choose **NO MORE THAN TWO WORDS** from the passage for each answer.*

Write your answers in boxes 31-34 on your answer sheet.

31   'Kill sites' for moas have been found in .... , but no equivalents have been found for megafauna in Australia.

32   It seems unlikely megafaunal extinction was caused by ....

33   Modern kangaroo species bear more .... than megafaunal species.

34   Johnson does not think it is strange that megafaunal .... with proof of hunting have not yet been found.

LISTENING
READING
WRITING
SPEAKING

PASSAGE 1   PASSAGE 2   PASSAGE 3

Questions 35-39

Look at questions 35-39 and the list of people below.

Match each statement with a person or group of people.

Write the letters in boxes 35-39 on your answer sheet.

35	This scientist used reliable dating techniques to propose a likely extinction date for megafauna.	
36	These people have a mythical description of a creature like the diprotodon.	**List of people**
37	This scientist drew on data from fish farming to understand dwarfing.	**(A)** The Adnyamathanha
38	This person believes dates will be revised so that the period between human settlement in Australia and the extinction of megafauna is longer.	**(B)** Johnson **(C)** Law **(D)** Roberts
39	This scientist developed a theory that even with basic weapons, Aborigines made megafauna extinct.	

Question 40

Choose the correct letter: A, B, C, D, or E.

Write the correct letter in box 40 on your answer sheet.

Which of the following is the most suitable title for Reading Passage 3?

A   The rise and fall of giant mammals in Australia

B   Is a koala still cute at 16 kilograms?

C   Climate change: killer of Australian megafauna

D   Modern research techniques solve an archaeological puzzle

E   Invisible hunters caused mass extinctions

Writing

Task 1

Spend about 20 minutes on this task.

The following show the main sources of rubbish collected during a public clean-up day in one city and the main sources of rubbish collected from three locations within that city.

Write a summary of the information. Select and report the main features, and make comparisons where relevant.

Write at least 150 words.

Rubbish collected during a public clean-up day in one city

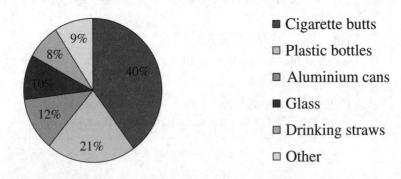

- ■ Cigarette butts
- □ Plastic bottles
- ▨ Aluminium cans
- ■ Glass
- ▨ Drinking straws
- □ Other

Location	Top three items & weight in kilograms (kg)						Total weight of top three items in kg
Arden Park	Glass	33	Aluminium cans	24	Cigarette butts	9	66
Diego Beach	Tyres	563	Cigarette butts	161	Plastic bottles	79	803
Memorial Park	Cigarette butts	214	Plastic bottles	108	Aluminium cans	66	378

Task 2

Spend about 40 minutes on this task.

Write about the following topic:

In some rich countries, the number of children at secondary or high school who are taking science subjects is declining.

What effect might this have on the children's and their countries' futures? How can children be encouraged to study science?

Provide reasons for your answer. Include relevant examples from your own knowledge or experience.

Write at least 250 words.

Speaking

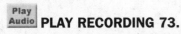 **PLAY RECORDING 73.**

When the examiner says 'In this part, I'm going to give you a topic…', go to page 417.

ACADEMIC PRACTICE TEST 3

There are four parts to this test: Listening; Reading; Writing; and Speaking. If you do all four parts together, they will take you about three hours.

Listening

SECTION 1 Questions 1-10

PLAY RECORDING 72-1.

Questions 1-4

Complete the sentences below.

*Write **ONE WORD** for each answer.*

CURRICULUM VITAE (CV)

| Eg | Jun Hee does not think she will hear *back* from an employer she rang. |

1   So far, Jun Hee has not had one ....Job...Interview....

2   Jun Hee thinks she isn't getting work because she lacks ....experience.... .

3   When she worked for her uncle, Jun Hee wasn't very good at ....typing............ .

4   Harry offers to ....change............ Jun Hee's CV.

Questions 5-10

Classify the following things that Harry thinks Jun Hee should

    A   *add to her CV*

    B   *remove or reduce from her CV*

    C   *keep in her CV*

*Write the correct letter, **A**, **B**, or **C**, on your answer sheet.*

  C **5**   some colours

  B **6**   some fonts

  B **7**   her marital status

  C **8**   her sports

  A **9**   her current studies

  A **10** the languages she speaks

SECTION 2 Questions 11-20

Play Audio PLAY RECORDING 72-2.

Questions 11-14

Complete the sentences below.

*Write **ONE WORD** for each answer.*

COPPER SCULPTURE

11 Very soon, the artist is exhibiting in ......*LA*................. .

12 Michelle's artwork continues ...*date back*...... that began in ancient Greece.

13 Michelle became interested in her theme when she learnt how a(n)
...*Presance*........ can speed up the healing process.

14 Michelle has been asked to make a statue by a local ...*Counsile*......... .

Questions 15-20

Complete the table below.

*Write **ONE WORD OR A NUMBER** for each answer.*

Stage	Producing copper sculpture for commission
i	Selection of artist and artwork
ii	**15** ...*modelling*.... in clay of sculpture
iii	Creation of **16** ...*wax*............... copy
iv	Building up of cast with stucco and ceramic granules
v	Firing of cast at **17** ...*high*........... temperature
vi	Preparation of **18** ...*three*........ elements – mainly molten copper
vii	Pouring of metal into cast
viii	**19** ...*Settling*.... of metal over several hours
ix	Removal of cast
x	Polishing of sculpture
xi	Approval by commissioning authority
xii	**20** ...*City Square*..... in building or public place

SECTION 3 Questions 21-30

PLAY RECORDING 72-3.

Questions 21-26

Complete the sentences below.

Write ONE WORD OR A NUMBER for each answer.

UNIVERSITY COUNSELLING SESSION

21   Although she is ready for her ....presentation... Rachel has yet to start work on her other assignments.

22   To date, Rachel has not been following her .... plan.

23   Rachel's essay for Criminal Law is .... words.

24   If Rachel does not take time to write her long essay, she is likely to receive a(n) .... mark.

25   Rachel feels bothered by the demands of her flatmate and her ...assignment...

26   Last week Rachel did ....12.................. hours' overtime at the supermarket.

Questions 27-30

Complete the sentences below.

Write ONE WORD for each answer.

27   The counsellor suggests Rachel keep her ex-boyfriend at a(n) .....distance... .

28   Rachel admits that as she has not been to enough tutorials she does not understand the ......basics........... legal arguments needed in her essay.

29   Rachel considers her situation to be ...awful............ , but the counsellor disagrees.

30   The counsellor advises Rachel to ....Reduce........ contact with unhelpful people.

SECTION 4 Questions 31-40

Play Audio PLAY RECORDING 72-4.

Questions 31-35

Choose the correct letter: A, B, or C.

RATIONAL-EMOTIVE THERAPY (RET)

31 Rational-Emotive Therapy is a treatment that
  A   uses thinking and talking.
  B   relies on medication.
  C   goes back to the first century.

32 One idea behind RET is that people cannot control unfortunate circumstances,
  A   and feeling angry about them is natural.
  B   and they may never recover from them.
  C   but they can control their feelings about them.

33 The lecturer gives the example of a woman who fails to get money back from her sister to show
  A   how the language people use reflects their beliefs.
  B   how RET may help solve family problems.
  C   different ways people treat each other.

34 Albert Ellis uses 'awfulise' to mean many people
  A   generally feel life is awful.
  B   believe depression is caused by awful experiences.
  C   make things seem far worse than they are.

35 In Albert Ellis' ABCD-scheme, D stands for:
  A   Depression can be overcome.
  B   Distinguishing between healthy and unhealthy beliefs.
  C   Distinction is everyone's goal.

Questions 36-40

*Write **ONE WORD** in the sentences below.*

36 Albert Ellis' theories have also been applied to refugees. It seems those who were badly affected by trauma ......choose........ to be so.

37 After a bad experience, an RET therapist helps a person understand that a healthy reaction is to be ....upset............ rather than angry.

38 In RET, patients reduce their anxiety by .... their fears.

39 RET differs from other treatments as it does not focus on a patient's ....

40 Opponents of RET say that it avoids ....Everyday.... problems, so it doesn't cure patients.

Reading

You have one hour for this test.

READING PASSAGE 1

*You should spend about 20 minutes on **Questions 1-13**, which are based on Reading Passage 1 on the following pages.*

━━ ━ ━ ━ ━ ━ ━ ━ ━ ━ ━ ━ ━ ━ ━ ━ ━ ━ ━ ━

DRIVING ON AIR

No matter how costly, hazardous, or polluting they are, nor how tedious it is to be stuck in traffic jams, cars are here to stay. In fact, the global car industry is worth a massive two trillion dollars a year.

Recently, Guy Negre, a French engineer on Renault's Formula One engines, designed and produced the Airpod – a vehicle which runs on air, is lightweight and compact, and capable of reaching moderate speeds.

Since the transport sector constitutes one seventh of all air pollution, Negre spent 15 years developing the Airpod, hoping to significantly reduce greenhouse-gas emissions. Petrol-electric hybrids, already on the market, are touted as being environmentally friendly, yet he says they are barely less polluting than combustion-engine vehicles. The Airpod, on the other hand, produces just 10% of the carbon monoxide of other cars.

Major manufacturers are now considering hydrogen as a power source for vehicles, but this technology may be decades away. Meantime, according to Negre, electric vehicles remain impractical: batteries are expensive, and need replacement within five years; recharging takes several hours.

Negre's secondary aim in creating the Airpod was to bring cars within reach of consumers in the developing world. To date, his most impressive deal has been with an Indian car manufacturer which predicts the Airpod will retail for the price of an average motorcycle.

Currently, only three-wheeled Airpods are available, but Negre has a four-wheeled, five-door family saloon, plus vans, buses, taxis, boats, and aircraft on the drawing board.

So what is an Airpod? This small vehicle resembles an ordinary car except that it is made mostly from fiberglass – ten times as strong as steel but very light – meaning an Airpod weighs just 220 kilograms (484 lb). It has glass windows and an aluminium engine. However, it uses a joystick instead of a steering wheel, and it has backward-facing passenger seats and a front-opening door.

The 180cc engine of an Airpod allows it to reach a speed of around 70 kilometres per hour (kph) (43 mph), and it can drive for about 220 kilometres (137 miles) before refilling is necessary. It takes as little as 90 seconds to pump air into an Airpod from a high-speed compressor at a gas station, with air costing a mere 50 cents for a 220-kilometre journey. An on-board pump can refill the tank at home overnight.

How does an Airpod work? Quite simply: air is released through pistons in the engine, which drive the wheels. Compressed air tanks store up to 175 litres (46 gallons) of air at about 180 times the pressure of an average car tyre. Passengers and passers-by might have concerns about explosions with such pressure, but, in the rare event of one, the thermoplastic tanks split to release air, rather than shattering and exploding. In fact, the same tanks are already installed on natural-gas buses.

324 PART III **IELTS Academic Practice Test 3**

LISTENING
READING
WRITING
SPEAKING

PASSAGE 1 PASSAGE 2 PASSAGE 3

For longer journeys, there is a battery-assisted hybrid Airpod, which Negre maintains is capable of reaching 80 kph (50 mph) and travelling around 1500 kilometres (930 miles) on four litres of petrol, although this version has yet to be manufactured or tested.

Still in its infancy, the Airpod has both supporters and critics. Marcus Waardenberg, the organiser of an Airpod trial at a major Dutch airport, was impressed. 'The Airpods went over 40 kph (25 mph), were quiet and manoeuverable. Refilling was fast and straightforward.' As a result, his company is replacing its fleet of electric service vehicles with Airpods.

Perhaps more significantly, AK Jagadeesh, from the Indian conglomerate, Tata, signed a $60-million deal. 'We're going to use Airpod technology in Tata's Nano car,' he said.

Ulf Bossel, a sustainable energy consultant, commented that the Airpod easily reaches speeds of over 50 kph (31 mph). 'Initially, it could capture the second-car market. Then, there are those older people who can no longer afford conventional cars.' Both Europe and North America have ageing populations.

Bill Robertson, a motoring journalist, noted that the Airpod would suit large numbers of people who make two or three trips a day of fewer than ten kilometers, or who live in distant suburbs of big cities where public transport is poor. If the Airpod looked a little sexier, there would be the potential for it to make inroads into the golf buggy sector, which currently uses electric vehicles.

Among the detractors of the Airpod is the former champion racer, Martella Valentina, who would prefer a vehicle with a more robust engine. 'There are so many aggressive drivers out there,' she said. 'As a woman, I don't feel safe in an Airpod.' She added, 'Refilling overnight is a drag.'

The automotive engineer, Hamid Khan, concurs, expressing skepticism about sufficient energy storage under reasonable pressure to drive the car any distance, let alone the alleged 220 kilometres (135 miles) before refill. He insists this is unconfirmed by independent tests. Stopping and starting in typical city conditions would also lower the range even further, and more distressingly, safety data is lacking for crash testing. 'Negre claims fibreglass is stronger than steel, but the Airpod looks as though it would crumple under the wheels of a normal saloon,' commented Khan.

Nevertheless, Negre has signed deals to manufacture his car in the US, Latin America, India, and several European countries. Compressed air may no longer take a back seat to other power sources, and it is even conceivable that one day we may be flying in aircraft that fly on air.

LISTENING
READING
WRITING
SPEAKING

PASSAGE 1   PASSAGE 2   PASSAGE 3

Questions 1-8

*Complete the summary using the list of words, **A-O**, below:*

*Write the correct letter, **A-O**, in boxes 1-8 on your answer sheet.*

The **1** .... of combustion-engine cars continues **2** .... there being problems with them. According to Negre, an automotive engineer and inventor, a(n) **3** .... , a petrol-electric car, is really not much less **4** .... Negre believes his Airpod is far cleaner and cheaper, and will **5** .... drivers in the developing world in particular.

An Airpod is lighter than other cars at only **6** .... kilograms. The highest confirmed speed it can reach is around **7** .... kph. It can be refilled fast at a service station or more slowly at home. Some people may be worried about the high-pressure gas stored on board an Airpod, but its tanks are safe and already in **8** .... on public buses.

A exist	**B** popular	**C** polluting
D 80	**E** benefit	**F** although
G 70	**H** polluted	**I** alternate
J alternative	**K** 220	**L** use
M popularity	**N** 180	**O** despite

Questions 9-13

Look at the following statements and the list of people below.

*Match each statement with the correct person: **A, B, C,** or **D.***

*Write the correct letter, **A, B, C,** or **D**, in boxes 9-13 on your answer sheet.*

9   He claims the hybrid Airpod can travel 1500 kilometres on four litres of petrol.

10   He imagines the Airpod will appeal to the elderly.

11   He doesn't think the Airpod will compete with golf buggies unless it changes its appearance.

12   He doesn't believe the Airpod can drive as far as its creator maintains.

13   He has agreed to the manufacture of the Airpod in a number of countries.

List of people
A   Bill Robertson
B   Guy Negre
C   Hamid Khan
D   Ulf Bossel

READING PASSAGE 2

*You should spend about 20 minutes on **Questions 14-27**, which are based on Reading Passage 2 on the following pages.*

Questions 14-19

*Reading Passage 2 has seven sections: **A-G**.*

*Choose the correct heading for sections **B-G** from the list of headings below.*

*Write the correct number, **i-ix**, in boxes 14-19 on your answer sheet.*

List of Headings
i Middle-aged bliss
ii Some new definitions of happiness
iii Overall and temporary measures
iv Children bring pleasure and pain
v Culture and contentment
vi How wealth and age relate to happiness
vii Acceptance affects happiness
viii The benefits of an ageing population
ix Countries that use happiness measures

Example	Answer
Section A	*ii*

Section A

We're probably all aware of measures economists use to ascertain the wealth of a country and its people. Income generated annually is measured by a figure called the Gross Domestic Product or the Gross National Income. In the past, it was assumed that the richer a country was, the happier its citizens were. More recently, economists have rated countries according to additional criteria, such as: how livable its cities are, what access people have to education and green space, and how safe people feel.

The Human Development Index (HDI) is considered the most reliable of these new expanded economic indicators, but a more focused measure of well-being is the Human Happiness Index (HHI). In this, people from 156 countries rate their country's level of social support; their life expectancy; their freedom to make choices; the generosity of other inhabitants; and the trust they have in the state or private enterprise, as indicated by an absence of corruption.

Section B

This interest in quantifiable gladness came about because, in 2008, Bhutan, a small Asian country, developed a happiness index to assist with policy-making. If people indicated one of their concerns was rising fuel costs, the government attempted to subsidize fuel, not only because it hoped to retain power, but also because if this anxiety were allayed, its citizens would be happier and more productive. Another worry of the Bhutanese was the quality of primary education. Once alerted to this, the state commenced investment. Also in 2008, the economists Amartya Sen and Joseph Stiglitz were invited to France to devise a happiness index for that country. Finally, in 2011, the General Assembly of the United Nations passed a resolution asking member states to measure contentment.

Section C

There are two common measures of happiness: a global measure and a hedonic measure. The former appraises life in general; the latter a person's emotional feeling just yesterday. Two

LISTENING   PASSAGE 1   PASSAGE 2   PASSAGE 3
READING
WRITING
SPEAKING

measures are considered necessary because altered circumstances produce different results. As any parent can attest, having children makes people happier overall, especially as the children mature and start their own families, yet, on a day-to-day basis, when the children are young, raising them can be difficult: parents may experience stress, anger, and even misery. Globally, parents are glad they have family; hedonically, they may be going through a bad patch. Likewise employment: a secure enjoyable job contributes greatly to happiness, but being temporarily unemployed can have a deleterious effect.

Section D

Using both these measures – the global and hedonic – some surprising data have come to light. Firstly, wealthier is indeed happier, but there are still some miserable rich people. Danes and Hong Kong Chinese have almost identical purchasing power. Yet, on a scale of one to ten, Hong Kongers consistently rate their well-being as 5.5 whereas Danes - usually the world's happiest people - give theirs as 7.5. Likewise, incomes in Latin America vary little from those in countries of the former Soviet Union, like Ukraine or Kazakhstan, but Latinos are far healthier, longer-lived, and more cheerful.

The second significant finding is that the level of happiness increases with age. Despite the body's decay and fewer financial resources, older people are more stable, less anxious, and less angry. It is now universally agreed that suicide rates worldwide peak in the early forties for women and the early fifties for men. Of 72 countries in one recent poll, the average age was 46 after which life became easier. Ukrainians bucked this trend, not finding happiness until after 62, while the Swiss were fortunate for their discontent to decline from 35.

Section E

Some common beliefs have been confirmed by the happiness data, for instance that introverted cultures produce more unhappy people. Asians all identified themselves as being unhappier than Western Europeans (with the exception of the Portuguese and the Greeks). In 2017, Japan rated highly on the HDI, but near the middle of the HHI. Still, Japan has the world's longest-living women – 83 years is their average life expectancy – so, if people are generally happier as they age, Japanese women do have longer than women elsewhere in which to get happy!

Section F

What are the reasons for happiness after middle age? Basically, people understand where they fit in the world. Their ambitions have settled to realistic levels – they accept what they can and cannot do. For example, I won't be able to win the Nobel Prize in Literature, but I could conceivably take first place in a local short-story competition.

Section G

It is good news that people become happier as they grow older because populations in most developed countries age, and projections are for many developing countries to have more people over 50 after 2020. Governments have had some concern about the burden on younger taxpayers of this greying population, but perhaps they should reconsider the data: older people, being happier, are potentially more capable than younger ones. Loss of memory and poorer physical skills are counterbalanced by cheerfulness. Therefore, the retirement age could be extended without concerns about productivity.

Personally, I'd rather have a smiling, competent, grey-haired colleague than a pretty twenty-something who pretends to know it all but, underneath, is a seething mass of discontent.

Questions 20-25

Choose **ONE WORD OR A NUMBER** *from the passage for each answer.*

Write your answers in boxes 20-25 on your answer sheet.

20 There are many different ways to gauge a country's success. Recent indices concentrate on .... in particular.

21 A hedonic measure shows a person's emotional condition ....

22 Despite being financially well off, people in Hong Kong did not seem happy. They rated themselves as only .... out of ten.

23 The international average age for people becoming happier was ....

24 People from less outgoing .... rated themselves as unhappier.

25 Middle-aged happiness is probably due to a(n) .... understanding of a person's place in the world.

Questions 26-27

Choose the correct letter: **A, B, C,** *or* **D.**

Write the correct letter in boxes 26-27 on your answer sheet.

26 Which of the following does the writer think is true of older people?

   A   Government spending on them will always outweigh their productivity.

   B   They should retire earlier.

   C   Their life expectancy relates to their level of happiness.

   D   Because they are more cheerful, they make better employees.

27 Which of the following is the most suitable title for Reading Passage 2?

   A   Happiness surveys give oldies plenty to smile about

   B   Gender affects happiness in curious ways

   C   We're richer and happier now than ever before

   D   Novel ways to measure happiness

READING PASSAGE 3

*You should spend about 20 minutes on **Questions 28-40**, which are based on Reading Passage 3 on the following pages.*

SPACE-BASED SOLAR POWER

In an energy-hungry world, new safe ways to generate electricity are constantly being sought.

Space-based solar power, or SBSP, is not yet up and running, but several space agencies and commercial companies are pursuing it. Simultaneously, its critics view it as little more than a fantasy.

SBSP is a system that would harness sunlight in space, convert it into electrical energy, and beam this, via a microwave or laser transmitter, to receivers in Earth's equatorial zone. SBSP satellites would probably be in low orbit, 1100 kilometres (684 miles) above earth.

Advantages

To date, solar energy has been collected on the ground, but it is estimated there is 144% more solar power available in space as Earth's atmosphere absorbs light. Furthermore, since the planet rotates, energy can only be collected during daylight. It is possible at the poles to collect light almost continuously in summer, but in winter such plants cannot operate due to snow, ice, and darkness. In space, however, solar power collection could occur around the clock.

A further benefit may be that the energy produced could be directed to multiple locations whereas terrestrial power plants are limited to sending power one way into a grid.

Design

Most prototypes of SBSP structures look like a giant tent hanging in space. Its light, hollow equilateral triangular frame is 336 metres (1103 feet) long while its depth is 303 metres (994 feet). Down two sides are solar collectors, called arrays; on the floor of the 'tent' sit a solar converter and a transmitting antenna. The antenna sends microwaves to earth. These waves are at a frequency of 2.45-5.8 gigahertz, or somewhere between infrared and radio signals. They pass through Earth's atmosphere easily with only minor energy loss. On earth, the invisible column of microwave energy – perhaps two to three kilometres (a mile or two) wide – is received by a large 'rectenna' – a new word combining 'rectifying' + 'antenna'. A pilot beam, also on earth, ensures the satellite stays in position in space.

Two major technical obstacles remain before SBSP becomes a reality. The first is launching satellites into orbit. While most scientists favour low orbit, others believe a higher orbit like 36,050 kilometres (22,400 miles), or about one tenth of the distance between Earth and the Moon, would harness more sunlight. However, no agency or company has any experience of launching and controlling a satellite in high orbit. Even with low-orbit satellites that agencies or companies recognize, anywhere up to 150 launches would be needed to construct a single SBSP system. Launch costs are currently around $320 billion, which would be prohibitive. Furthermore, the impact of emissions from 150 launches on Earth's atmosphere would be considerable. The second stumbling block is wireless power transmission. In 2009, American and Japanese researchers successfully sent microwave energy between two islands in Hawaii that are 145 km (90 miles) apart – equidistant to Earth's atmosphere. In 2015, Mitsubishi Heavy Industries beamed 10 kilowatts to a receiver 500 metres (1640 feet) away. Still, it is unknown whether these efforts can be reproduced in space.

330   **PART III**   **IELTS Academic Practice Test 3**

LISTENING	PASSAGE 1	PASSAGE 2	PASSAGE 3
READING			
WRITING			
SPEAKING			

History

SBSP is not a new idea. Dr Peter Glaser designed a system in the late 1960s, and was granted a US patent in 1973. The US Department of Energy in conjunction with NASA conducted feasibility studies in the 1970s, but a conservative administration in the 1980s discontinued investment. Only in 1997 did the US reconsider the idea.

In 2015, a proposal for a US SBSP system won the prestigious D3 (Diplomacy, Development, Defence) competition. Meanwhile, the China Academy for Space Technology unveiled a design for a one-gigawatt system by 2050 at a recent International Space Development conference.

Japanese initiatives

It seems the Japanese are closest to producing a reliable system. Since 1998, JAXA (the Japanese space agency) has been involved in all aspects of SBSP, and its forecast puts its first satellite in orbit by 2030. Among private companies, Mitsubishi and IHI Corporation fund research.

There are six broad areas that JAXA is working on. These are: (1) general configuration; (2) assembly work and operation; (3) solar array; (4) transmitting antenna; (5) power transmission and reception system; and (6) testing methods. The first of these is the most developed. The solar array and transmitting antenna are second in terms of development. Testing methods are relatively unsolved. Assembly work and operation, and power transmission and reception system remain far from being solved.

Disadvantages

SBSP has numerous detractors. There are those who imagine the microwave beam to be something like a science-fiction death ray. Physicists reassure the public it is a non-ionising wave, like a radio wave or x-ray. It cannot displace electrons from atoms to charge particles, so it does not damage DNA. The waves may be slightly warm, but they present no danger to wildlife or humans. Still, the waves must be carefully guided by the rectennas.

Other opponents of SBSP say that while there is neither corrosion nor damage from plants or animals in space, background radiation could harm the satellite. There is the very real danger of collision with space junk, as recently happened at the International Space Station, or with small meteors hitting it. Repairing an unmanned structure so far from Earth would be extremely difficult.

Solar power via the Moon is an option which some scientists say can be in operation in ten years at a fraction of the cost. Most tellingly, companies already involved in the space-power race have not been successful. In the early 2000s, three US firms predicted they would be contributing electricity to the national grid with SBSP within fifteen years. None of them is even close, and one company has withdrawn from the race altogether.

The vast majority of those opposed to SBSP consider it expensive and unnecessary, given that many other forms of renewable energy on earth are operating successfully. Terrestrial solar power is relatively underdeveloped; the Arizona Desert in the US and deserts across North Africa provide easily-accessible locations for new systems that would be five times more cost-effective than SBSP.

Viability

Nevertheless, as energy requirements accelerate, as unrest in oil-producing regions and nuclear accidents make alternative energy more attractive, space-based solar power may have a future after all.

Question 28

Which map below – *A*, *B*, or *C* – best illustrates the most effective zone for Space-based Solar Power (SBSP) receivers?

Write your answer in box 28 on your answer sheet.

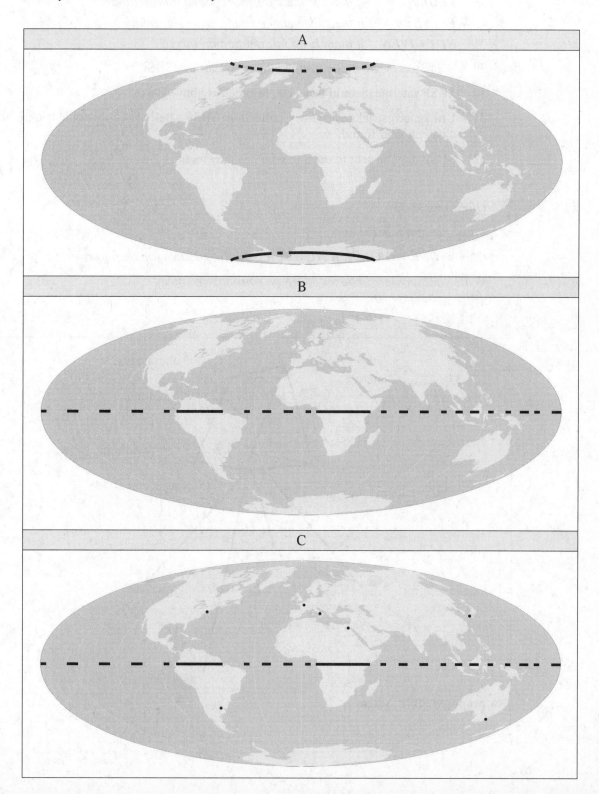

332   PART III   IELTS Academic Practice Test 3

LISTENING
READING
WRITING
SPEAKING

| PASSAGE 1   PASSAGE 2   PASSAGE 3 |

Questions 29-32

What are the following statements according to information in the passage?

In boxes 29-32 on your answer sheet, write:

> **TRUE**   *if the statement agrees with the information*
> **FALSE**   *if the statement contradicts the information*
> **NOT GIVEN**   *if there is no information on this*

29   Solar energy would be beamed down to Earth in SBSP.

30   SBSP satellites would orbit 100 kilometres above Earth.

31   Unlike terrestrial solar power collection, SBSP satellites could collect sunlight 24 hours a day all year round.

32   SBSP may be sent to anyone who has a rectenna.

Questions 33-35

Label the diagram below.

*Choose **ONE WORD OR A NUMBER** from the passage for each answer.*

Write your answers in boxes 33-35 on your answer sheet.

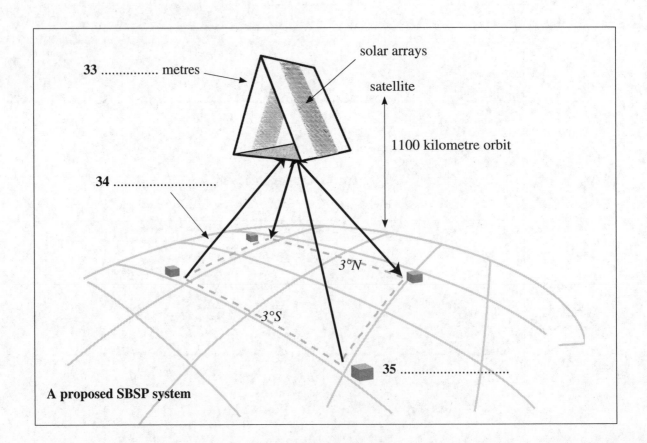

A proposed SBSP system

Questions 36-39

Complete the table below.

*Choose **TWO WORDS OR A NUMBER** from the passage for each answer.*

Write your answers in boxes 36-39 on your answer sheet.

JAXA and SBSP	
Predicted launch date: **36**	
Degree of Achievement	
37	Mostly solved
Assembly work and operation	Almost entirely unsolved
38	Solved to some degree
Transmitting antenna	Solved to some degree
Power transmission and reception system	Almost entirely unsolved
Testing methods	**39** ....

Question 40

*Choose the correct letter: **A**, **B**, **C**, or **D**.*

Write the correct letter in box 40 on your answer sheet.

Which represents the view of most critics of SBSP?

A   It is a fantasy of physicists, and impossible to build.

B   Dangers in space mean satellites could easily be destroyed.

C   It is better to concentrate on clean energy production on earth.

D   Oil and nuclear energy are cheaper in the short term.

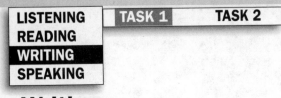

Writing

You have one hour for this test.

Task 1

Spend about 20 minutes on this task.

The plans below show a building before and after remodelling.

Write a summary of the information. Select and report the main features, and make comparisons where relevant.

Write at least 150 words.

COMMUNITY ART CENTRE

Gallery 1	Gallery 2	Parking	
Art Studio		Kitchen	Toilets

COMMUNITY ART AND AUDIO CENTRE (after remodelling)

Recording Studio (To rent)	Gallery 2	Gallery 1	(No parking)
Art Studio (To rent)		Café	Outdoor Exhibition Space
		Toilets	

Key
* = Plant
⊕ = Table and chairs

LISTENING
READING
WRITING
SPEAKING

TASK 1   TASK 2

Task 2

Spend about 40 minutes on this task.

Write about the following topic:

More and more information about the lives of celebrities is found in newspapers, magazines, and online.

Why is this happening? What are the disadvantages for the reading public?

Provide reasons for your answer. Include relevant examples from your own knowledge or experience.

Write at least 250 words.

Speaking

Play Audio PLAY RECORDING 74.

When the examiner says: 'In this part, I'm going to give you a topic...', go to page 425.

ACADEMIC PRACTICE TEST 4

There are four parts to this test: Listening; Reading; Writing; and Speaking. If you do all four parts together, they will take you about three hours.

Listening

SECTION 1 Questions 1-10

 **PLAY RECORDING 74-1.**

Questions 1-6

Complete the sentences below.

*Write **ONE WORD OR A NUMBER** for each answer.*

PHONE SERVICES

eg	Ann would like to get the *Internet* at home.

1   Ann wants wireless and ....*mobile phone*.... services combined.

2   The salesman says that soon any customer who signs a(n) ....*18*....-month contract will receive a new smartphone.

3   Ann wants a basic phone so an employer can contact her for relief ....*teaching*.... .

4   Ann believes it is expensive to replace the glass ....*screen*.... of a fancy phone.

5   Each year, Ann spends about $....*3,000*.... on phone bills.

6   The salesman suggests Ann buy ....*insurance*.... in case of damage or theft.

Questions 7-10

Classify the following descriptions as relating to:

    A   *a 6-month contract*

    B   *a 12-month contract*

    C   *a 24-month contract*

*Write the correct letter, **A**, **B**, or **C** on your answer sheet.*

This contract:

C **7** requires photo ID, a financial statement, and proof of address.

C **8** has a $200 penalty if the service is cancelled early.

B **9** is no longer available.

A **10** does not come with a modem.

SECTION 2   Questions 11-20

 **PLAY RECORDING 74-2.**

Questions 11-15

Write ONE WORD OR A NUMBER for each answer.

RUNNING A SMALL BUSINESS

According to John Lim:

11   both looking after children and running a business need clear priorities and excellent time
      ...management...

12   the town he moved to was changing – farming and mining were being replaced by
      ...Agriculture... industries.

13   the national figure for small businesses that fail within two years of setting up is around
      ...40... percent.

14   a small business needs a good ...time... as well as capital.

15   a small business benefits from both ...Five year plan... and day-by-day plans.

Questions 16-19

Choose the correct letter: A, B, or C.

16   John Lim's survey found that .... of people who work at home were inefficient.
      (A)   40%
      B   50%
      C   60%

17   In addition, ... them put in more hours than their office counterparts.
      (A)   40%
      B   50%
      C   60%

18   John Lim suggests that since humans are social creatures, those who work alone at home miss
      (A)   being with other people.
      B   the office gossip.
      C   the company of an animal.

19   People who go bankrupt ought to
      A   find a good accountant.
      (B)   take a long holiday.
      C   shoulder the burden of their failure.

Question 20

Which sequence best illustrates the history of John Lim's business?

*Write **i**, **ii**, or **iii** in box 20 on your answer sheet.*

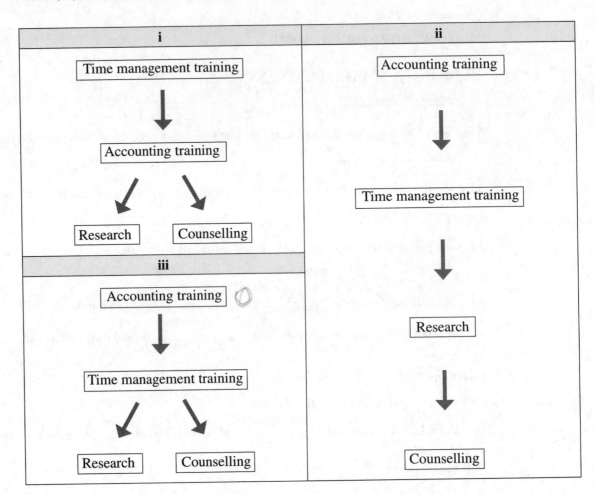

SECTION 3   Questions 21–30

PLAY RECORDING 74-3.

Questions 21–26

ESSAY-WRITING SKILLS

Complete the summary below.

*Write **ONE WORD OR A NUMBER** for each answer.*

The students need to write **21** ....2500.......... words for their essays. Sue, however, has

written many more as she is extremely **22** ...knowledge...... in the Human Development

Index.

Sue thinks Isaaq should expand his introduction to show which **23** .... he supports. He should include more **24** .... while avoiding plagiarism, which is **25** .... another writer's ideas. At university, students are expected to have more sophisticated ideas than **26** .... students.

Questions 27-30

Which of the following does Sue suggest Isaaq do?

Write the answers in boxes 27 to 30 on your answer sheet.

A Summarise his topic more clearly.

B Paraphrase his long quote.

C Provide an in-text reference for his quote.

D Acknowledge using the Oxford System.

E Read his worksheet on referencing from the first tutorial.

F Write a new bibliography.

G Read the articles written by Sword and Newcombe.

H Email her his extra paragraphs later that night.

SECTION 4 Questions 31-40

 PLAY RECORDING 74-4.

Questions 31-32

Choose the correct letter: A, B, or C.

DESALINATION

31 Desalination is the process of

    A recycling salty water.

    B taking minerals out of seawater.

    C separating salt from water.

32 Critics of desalination say

    A it is inefficient and dirty.

    B there are simpler alternatives.

    C it may not work in future.

Questions 33-35

Label the diagram below.

Write **ONE WORD** for each answer.

DESALINATION BY REVERSE OSMOSIS

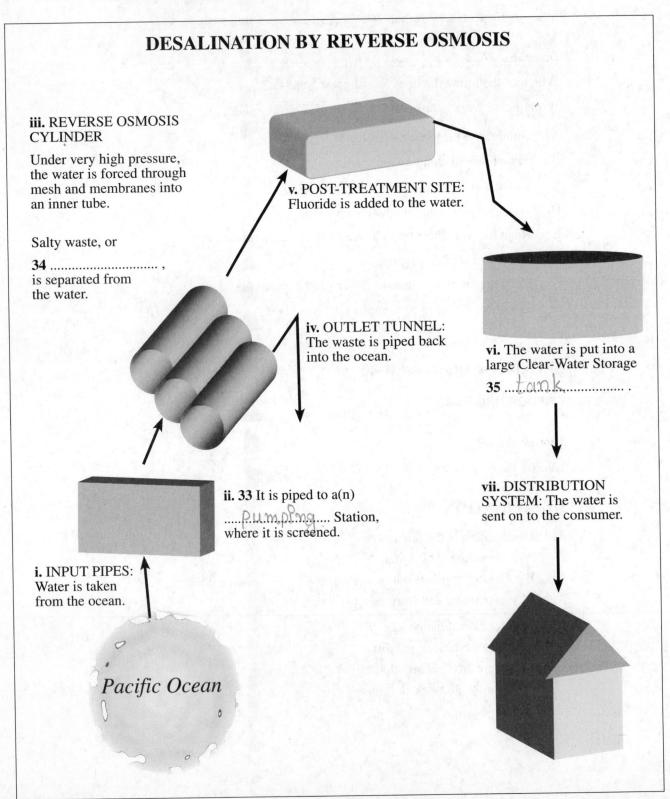

iii. REVERSE OSMOSIS CYLINDER

Under very high pressure, the water is forced through mesh and membranes into an inner tube.

Salty waste, or

34 .... , is separated from the water.

v. POST-TREATMENT SITE: Fluoride is added to the water.

iv. OUTLET TUNNEL: The waste is piped back into the ocean.

vi. The water is put into a large Clear-Water Storage

35 ......*tank*............... .

ii. 33 It is piped to a(n)

......*pumping*..... Station, where it is screened.

vii. DISTRIBUTION SYSTEM: The water is sent on to the consumer.

i. INPUT PIPES: Water is taken from the ocean.

Pacific Ocean

Questions 36-40

Complete the sentences below.

Write **ONE WORD OR A NUMBER** *for each answer.*

36   Desalination is ...Cost 5........ times more costly than any other method of extracting potable water.

37   If ....2........... percent of water were recycled in Sydney, it would equal the amount produced by one desalination plant in a year.

38   Through education and restriction, the city of Sydney used ....20.......... percent less water than previously.

39   Desalination causes pollution. One Sydney plant pumps ......1.5............ billion litres of waste into the ocean every day.

40   Governments choose desalination because it is too hard to get ...3.0..MAPOW..of residents to use recycling systems.

342   PART III   **IELTS Academic Practice Test 4**

LISTENING	**PASSAGE 1**	PASSAGE 2	PASSAGE 3
READING			
WRITING			
SPEAKING			

Reading

You have one hour for this test.

READING PASSAGE 1

*You should spend about 20 minutes on **Questions 1-13**, which are based on Reading Passage 1 on this and the following page.*

THE BATTLE OF TOWTON

March 29th, 1461, in tiny Towton was one of the bloodiest days in English history, yet only recently have a small number of soldiers' bodies undergone exhumation and examination. Several thousand still lie buried in mass graves on the battlefield. Early analysis of the remains has led to a reassessment of medieval warfare.

Towton, a village in the north of England, between York and Leeds, is unknown to many English people. History taught at school largely ignores the mid-15th century. Towton itself has neither museum nor large memorial, merely a roadside cross to mark where the battle took place.

In 1996, a building nearby called Towton Hall was being renovated when labourers unearthed skeletons in its grounds and beneath its floor. Twenty-eight of these were complete; another 20 or so were partial. What shocked archaeologists was the violent way in which the men had met their deaths and the callous manner of their burial. We are all familiar with the gory wars of the 20th century, and might assume that technology and politics have become more destructive over time. However, it could be the case that humans have long been vicious – only now is the evidence coming to light.

So what was the Battle of Towton? It was one clash of many between two powerful families – the Lancastrians and the Yorkists – who each wanted their king to rule England. The Lancastrians believed the current King of England, Henry VI, was incapable if not insane, whereas the Yorkists, led by Richard Plantagenet, supported Henry since he had chosen Richard as the next king. When Richard was killed in 1460, his son Edward, only 18, vowed to assume the throne in his father's place. Needless to say, the Lancastrians disputed this. Effectively, the Battle of Towton would legitimate Edward's reign.

Prior to Towton, military encounters in England had been small-scale: battles were fought with hundreds or at most a few thousand men, and no army was professional. In so-called peace time, private armies consisted of men – ranging in age from 15 to 50 – whose levels of fitness were variable, and whose training and equipment were poor. This meant that when fighting did erupt, it seldom lasted long – perhaps just a few days. Nor were many men killed. In fact, there is evidence that more men died from their wounds or other illnesses *after* combat. Towton it seems was different, for here was a battle in which both sides assembled large armies, and there were terrible casualties in the field.

The number of soldiers killed at Towton is a matter of speculation as few records have come down to us, and those that do survive may have exaggerated the victory of King Edward IV, as Edward became, in order to intimidate his enemies. One estimate of the dead is 28,000 out of the 75,000 soldiers who took part. These 75,000 represent 10% of all fighting-age men in England at the time – the total population being just three million. Twenty-eight thousand dead on one day is, therefore, a staggering number.

As injuries show on the skeletons of soldiers already studied, those men were hacked to death, shot by arrows, or trampled by horses. Some of the first bullets used in England were fired that

LISTENING
READING
WRITING
SPEAKING

PASSAGE 1   **PASSAGE 2**   **PASSAGE 3**

day. Lead-composite shot has been dug up on the battlefield, and one archaeologist claims to have found part of a handgun, but there are no obvious deaths from guns, and it is hard to say how they were used. The most effective weapon was the poleaxe – a long, heavy iron weapon with a sharp tip, a small axe blade on one side and, on the other, a large sharp head like a Philips-head screwdriver. It was used to kill soldiers who were running away as battle lines broke up, and it is thought this is how most of the Lancastrians buried at Towton Hall died.

It is not known why the death rate in this battle was so high, nor why the bodies of soldiers were so disfigured. Skeletal evidence indicates that often a dozen blows were given to a man who would have been killed by the initial two or three. Archaeologists are uncertain when these additional blows were made – on the battlefield or in the burial process – but such savagery suggests the emergence of a new concept of an opponent as not merely someone to kill but someone whose identity should be utterly effaced. After death, in a ritual never before seen in English warfare, soldiers were stripped of their clothes and tossed into mass graves to further dehumanise them.

It is easy to forget that in medieval England burial was sacred, and people believed ascent to Heaven only took place when the body of the dead was whole. In all Europe, there is only one other known mass grave on the scale of Towton from around the same time – that is in Sweden from 1361. There, however, soldiers from the Battle of Wisby were buried whole in their armour.

It appears that the savagery of the Yorkists did effect submission since Edward remained king for the next 22 years.

Today, at Towton, work continues on excavation and analysis of the medieval skeletons. Theories about a new kind of violent warfare and the purpose of mass graves abound. It seems that organised brutality is no recent phenomenon; it existed 550 years ago.

Questions 1–5

Complete the summary below.

*Choose **ONE WORD OR A NUMBER** from the passage for each answer.*

Write your answers in boxes 1–5 on your answer sheet.

The battlefield at Towton in northern England has only recently been surveyed and excavated. Archaeologists are now looking at medieval **1** .... in a new way. Although a major battle took place at Towton, this is not popular knowledge for English people as the battle is not studied at **2** ....

In 1996, soldiers' skeletons were found under a building near Towton. **3** .... of these had all their bones. This meant archaeologists could accurately determine how the soldiers had died. The archaeologists were very surprised by the **4** .... means of death, and the uncaring method of **5** ....

Questions 6-9

What are the following statements according to information in the passage?

In boxes 6-9 on your answer sheet, write:

> **TRUE**   *if the statement agrees with the information*
>
> **FALSE**   *if the statement contradicts the information*
>
> **NOT GIVEN**   *if there is no information on this*

6   The Battle of Towton was part of a war between two families seeking control over England.

7   Soldiers who fought at Towton were better trained than in the past.

8   Ten percent of all soldiers in England died at Towton.

9   Guns killed many soldiers at Towton.

Questions 10-13

Choose the correct letter: A, B, C, or D.

Write the correct letter in boxes 10-13 on your answer sheet.

10   Most Lancastrians were killed

    A   fleeing the Yorkists.

    B   at Towton Hall.

    C   in prison.

    D   fighting in lines on the battlefield.

11   At Towton, it is likely soldiers' bodies were cut up and buried in mass graves

    A   as this was common practice at the time.

    B   because King Edward IV was against religion.

    C   since Yorkists hated Lancastrians.

    D   so opponents of King Edward IV would live in fear.

12   Soldiers who died in a Swedish battle in 1361

    A   were also killed with poleaxes.

    B   went to Heaven.

    C   were buried in individual graves.

    D   were buried more respectfully.

13   A suitable title for this passage would be:

    A   Towton: a forgotten battle in English history

    B   The horrors of warfare in an age before guns

    C   Modern savagery in medieval Towton

    D   Towton: a turning point in military techniques

LISTENING | PASSAGE 1 | PASSAGE 2 | PASSAGE 3
READING
WRITING
SPEAKING

READING PASSAGE 2

*You should spend about 20 minutes on **Questions 14-27**, which are based on Reading Passage 2 on the following pages.*

• •

HARD-PASTE PORCELAIN

Definition and origin

The term porcelain refers to ceramics made from similar materials and baked at high temperatures which are light, durable, and vitreous.* Porcelain combines the positive qualities of glass and clay – glass is smooth and translucent while clay retains its shape when moulded. However, due to the addition of a few more minerals, porcelain is stronger than either glass or clay. It is also extremely beautiful and valuable: Chinese Ming Dynasty (1368-1644 AD) bowls can fetch a million dollars on the international art market.

For around fifteen hundred years, porcelain has been employed as tableware and decoration, but its more recent applications include: dental crowns and electrical insulators.

Porcelain was first made in China. During the Tang Dynasty (618-907 AD), small amounts were used by the court and the very rich. High-quality porcelain, like that manufactured today, was not widely available until the Yuan Dynasty (1279-1368 AD).

Chinese porcelain was traded with kingdoms in Central, Southeast Asia, and the Middle East from the seventh century. By the Middle Ages, it had reached Europe.

European obsession

Porcelain was consumed in enormous quantities by European royal families, nobles, and the church, all of whom tried desperately to discover its chemical composition. The English word, 'porcelain', derives from the Portuguese name for a sea creature, the nautilus, which has a spiral orange vitreous shell from which it was believed at one time that porcelain was made. Other more astute Europeans contended the ceramic contained crushed glass or bone.

Early experiments in the production of porcelain included adding ground glass to clay. The result is called 'soft-paste' as it is weaker than true porcelain.

So great was the frenzy for possessing Chinese porcelain, or attempting to recreate their own hard-paste, that a number of European principalities endangered themselves financially, spending as much of their budgets on pursuing porcelain as on their armies. Frederick II of Prussia (now in Germany) was one such fanatic. Fortunately, for Prussia, two scientists – Johann Böttger and Ehrenfried von Tschimhaus – in the monarch's service, solved the porcelain puzzle. Their discovery, made in 1707, combined clay with ground feldspar – a mineral containing aluminium silicate.

Meanwhile, in England, the recipe was a little different: ash, from cattle bones, was mixed with clay, feldspar, and quartz. This became known as 'bone china', and is still manufactured. Although not true porcelain, it remains popular in the US and the UK because it is harder than porcelain.

Constituents

The raw materials from which porcelain is made are abundant. They are: white clay (china clay or ball clay), feldspar, or perhaps flint, and silica – all of which are noted for their small

---

*Having a glassy appearance

particles. Feldspar and flint are used as fluxes, which reduce the temperature needed for firing, and bind the glass, silica, and clay granules. Porcelain may also contain other ingredients like alumina or steatite.

Manufacture

To produce porcelain, the raw materials are selected and weighed. Then, they are crushed in a two-stage process. Jaw crushers work first; mullers or hammer mills subsequently reduce particles to 0.25 cms (0.1 inch) or less in diameter. A third crushing, using ball mills, takes place for the finest porcelain. During purification, which follows, granules that are not of uniform size are screened out. Magnetic filtration then removes iron, commonly found in clay, because this prevents porcelain from forming correctly. The fifth stage, preparatory to firing, is formation. There are several types of formation by hand or machine. After formation, the ware undergoes its initial firing in a kiln – a special oven.

A glaze is a glassy liquid similar in composition to porcelain. If a porcelain object is painted, a glaze covers the paint, or its decoration may just be the glaze. Glaze is applied by painting or dipping, and takes place after the first firing. Not only are porcelain wares gorgeous, but their decoration and glazing are also of great interest.

In making porcelain, the temperature in the kiln is critical – high enough to reconstitute the elements, yet low enough to vaporise contaminants and minimise shrinkage. A typical temperature is 1454° Celsius (2650° Fahrenheit).

During the firing process, a number of chemical reactions occur. Carbon-based impurities burn out at 100-200°C (215-395°F). As the kiln is heated, carbonates and sulfates decompose. When heated to 700-1100°C (1295-2015°F), the fluxes react with the decomposing minerals to form liquid glass. After a certain density is reached, at around 1200°C (2195°F), the ware is cooled, causing the liquid glass to solidify.

Pause for thought

So, next time you dine from fine porcelain, take a moment to reflect on the complicated history and sophisticated manufacture of this exquisite product.

• •

Questions 14-18

For which places are the following statements about porcelain true?

In boxes 14-18 on your answer sheet, write:

    A   *China*
    B   *Europe*
    C   *Both China and Europe*

14   Here, dishes have sold for very high prices.

15   It was first invented here.

16   Its English name comes from here.

17   Military and porcelain expenditure were equal in some places here.

18   Here 'bone china' was produced.

LISTENING
READING
WRITING
SPEAKING

PASSAGE 1   PASSAGE 2   PASSAGE 3

Questions 19-23

Label the stages in the process below.

*Choose **NO MORE THAN TWO WORDS OR A NUMBER** from the passage for each answer.*

Write your answers in boxes 19-23 on your answer sheet.

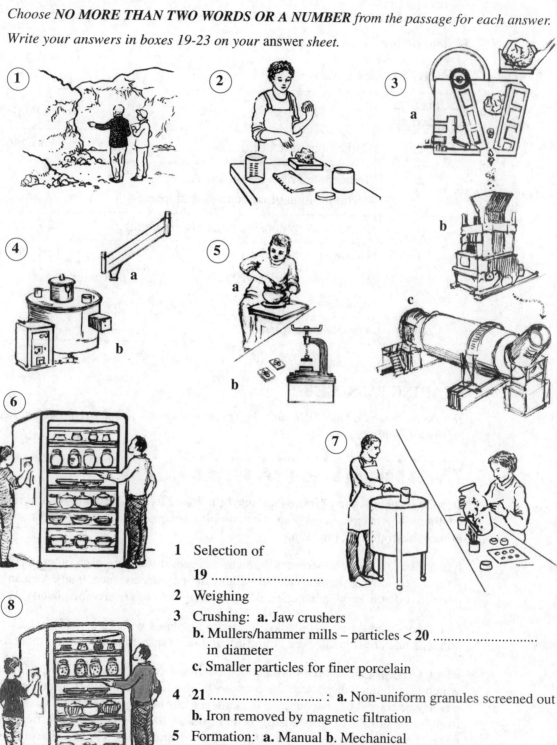

1 Selection of
   19 ....
2 Weighing
3 Crushing: **a.** Jaw crushers
   b. Mullers/hammer mills – particles < **20** ....
   in diameter
   c. Smaller particles for finer porcelain

4 **21** .... : **a.** Non-uniform granules screened out
   b. Iron removed by magnetic filtration
5 Formation: **a.** Manual **b.** Mechanical

6 **22** .... : Wares placed in kiln and baked

7 Decoration: **23** .... and/or painting
8 Second firing

LISTENING
READING
WRITING
SPEAKING

PASSAGE 1   PASSAGE 2   PASSAGE 3

Questions 24-27

Complete the notes below.

*Choose **ONE WORD OR A NUMBER** from the passage for each answer.*

Write your answers in boxes 24-27 on your answer sheet.

FIRING PORCELAIN

Chemical reaction	Event	Temperature range
1	Carbon-based impurities **24** .... out	100-200° C
2	Temperature rises inside **25** .... → decomposition of carbonates & sulphates	
3	Fluxes + decomposing minerals → liquid glass	**26** ....-1100° C
4	Density reached: Liquid glass begins to **27** .... ; porcelain complete	c 1200-1454° C
Cooling	Porcelain complete	c 1454-15° C

READING PASSAGE 3

*You should spend about 20 minutes on **Questions 28-40**, which are based on Reading Passage 3 on the following pages.*

IS AID HURTING AFRICA?

Despite its population of more than one billion and its rich land and natural resources, the continent of Africa remains poor. The combined economies of its 54 states approximate that of France, at around $2.4 trillion.

It is difficult to speak of Africa as a unit as its states differ from each other in culture, climate, size, and political systems. Since mid-20th-century independence, many African states have pursued different economic policies. Yet, none of them has overcome poverty. Why might this be?

One theory says Africa is unlucky. Sparsely populated with diverse language and culture, it contains numerous landlocked countries, and it is far from international markets.

Dambisa Moyo, a Zambian-born economist, has another theory. In her 2009 book, *Dead Aid*, which is still much discussed, she proposes that international aid is largely to blame for African poverty because it has encouraged dependence and corruption, and has diverted talented people from business. One of her statistics is that from 1970-98, when aid to Africa was highest, poverty rose from eleven to 66%. If aid were cut, she believes Africans would utilise their resources more creatively.

When a state lacks the capacity to care for its people, international non-governmental organisations (NGOs), like Oxfam or the Red Cross, assume this role. While NGOs distribute food or

LISTENING
READING
WRITING
SPEAKING

PASSAGE 1　PASSAGE 2　PASSAGE 3

medical supplies, Moyo argues they reduce the ability of the state to provide. Furthermore, during this process, those in government and the military siphon off aid goods and money themselves. Transparency International, an organisation that surveys corruption, rates the majority of African states poorly.

Moyo provides another example. Maybe a Hollywood star donates American-made mosquito nets. Certainly, this benefits malaria-prone areas, but it also draws business away from local African traders who supply nets. More consultation is needed between do-gooder foreigners and local communities.

In order to increase their wealth, Moyo proposes African nations increase their investment in bonds or their co-operation with China.

The presidents of Rwanda and Senegal are strong supporters of Moyo, but critics say her theories are simplistic. The international aid community is not responsible for geography, nor has it anything to do with military takeover, corruption, or legislation that hampers trade. Africans have had half a century of self-government and economic control, yet, as the population of the continent has doubled, its GDP has risen only 60%. In the same period, Malaysia and Vietnam threw off colonialism and surged ahead economically by investing in education, health, and infrastructure; by lowering taxes on international trade; and by being fortunate to be surrounded by other successful nations.

The economist Paul Collier has speculated that if aid were cut, African governments would not find alternative sources of income, nor would they reduce corruption. Another economist, Jeffrey Sachs, has calculated that twice the amount of aid currently given is needed to prevent suffering on a grand scale.

In *Dead Aid*, Moyo presents her case through a fictitious country called 'Dongo', but nowhere does she provide examples of real aid organisations causing actual problems. Her approach may be entertaining, but it is hardly academic.

Other scholars point out that Africa is dominated by tribal societies with military-government elites. Joining the army, rather than doing business, is often the easiest route to personal wealth and power. Unsurprisingly, military takeovers have occurred in almost every African country. In the 1960s and 70s, European colonials were replaced by African 'colonials' – African generals and their families. Meantime, the very small, educated bourgeoisie has moved abroad. All over Africa, strongmen leaders have ruled for a long time, or one unstable regime has succeeded another. As a result, business separate from military government is rare, and international investment limited.

Post-secondary education rates are low in Africa. Communications and transportation remain basic, although mobile phones are having an impact. The distances farmers must travel to market are vast due to poor roads. High cross-border taxes and long bureaucratic delays are par for the course. African rural populations exceed those elsewhere in the world. Without decent infrastructure or an educated urbanised workforce, business cannot prosper. Recent World Bank statistics show that in southern Africa, the number of companies using the internet for business is 20% as opposed to 40% in South America or 80% in the US. There are 37 days each year without water, whereas there is less than one day in Europe. The average cost of sending one container to the US is $7600, but only $3900 from East Asia or the Pacific. All these problems are the result of poor state planning.

Great ethnic and linguistic diversity within African countries has led to tribal favouritism. Governments are often controlled by one tribe or allied tribes; civil war is usually tribal. It is

350   PART III   **IELTS Academic Practice Test 4**

LISTENING
READING
WRITING
SPEAKING

PASSAGE 1   PASSAGE 2   PASSAGE 3

estimated each civil war costs a country roughly $64 billion. Southern Africa had 48 such conflicts from 1940-2015 while South Asia, the next-affected region, had only 27 in the same period. To this day, a number of bloody conflicts continue.

Other opponents of Moyo add that her focus on market investment and more business with China is shortsighted. The 2008 financial crisis meant that countries with market investments lost money. Secondly, China's real intentions in Africa are unknown, but everyone can see China is buying up African farmland and securing cheap oil supplies.

All over Africa, there are untapped resources, but distance, diversity, and low population density contribute to poverty. Where there is no TV, infrequent electricity, and bad roads, there still seems to be money for automatic weapons just the right size for 12-year-old boys to use. Blaming the West for assisting with aid fails to address the issues of continuous conflict, ineffective government, and little infrastructure. Nor does it prevent terrible suffering.

Has aid caused problems for Africa, or is Africa's strife of its own making or due to geography? Whatever you think, Dambisa Moyo's book has generated lively discussion, which is fruitful for Africa.

• •

Questions 28-38

Complete the chart on the following page.

*Choose **ONE WORD OR A NUMBER** from the passage for each answer.*

PART III **IELTS Academic Practice Test 4** 351

LISTENING
READING
WRITING
SPEAKING

PASSAGE 1   PASSAGE 2   PASSAGE 3

AFRICA'S PROBLEMS

Africa has a lot of people, **28** .... , and natural resources.

Yet it is still **29** ....

Moyo's theory	Other scholars' theories
International **30** .... is largely responsible. States now depend on it, and are corrupt as a result. Talented people have been drawn away from **31** .... by working for NGOs. If foreigners help, they ought to involve local **32** .... more. African states should buy into bond markets, and have a closer relationship with **33**	This is because Africa is unfortunate due to its **34** .... It is a long way from international markets. It is also culturally and politically diverse. However, corrupt military-government elites control most of the economy. Many African business-people have left. There is little international **35** .... **36** .... , communications, and transportation remain under-developed. Numerous civil wars, mostly tribal, have been costly. From 1940-2015, there were **37** .... of these.

Without international aid:

Moyo's theory	Other scholars' theories
Africa would use its resources more creatively.	Africans would experience enormous **38** ....

Questions 39-40

*Choose **TWO** letters: A-E.*

Which of the statements does the writer of Passage 3 support?

    A   Moyo is right that international aid is causing Africa's problems.

    B   Moyo has ignored the role of geography in Africa.

    C   Convincing evidence is lacking in Moyo's theory.

    D   Most political leaders in Africa agree with Moyo's analysis.

    E   Useful discussion about Africa has resulted from Moyo's book.

TASK 1   TASK 2

Writing

You have one hour for this test.

Task 1

Spend about 20 minutes on this task.

The tables show population in 2010 and 2100.

Write a summary of the information. Select and report the main features, and make comparisons where relevant.

Write at least 150 words.

TOP TEN COUNTRIES WITH POPULATION IN MILLIONS

2010	
China	1341
India	1225
USA	310
Indonesia	240
Brazil	195
Pakistan	174
Nigeria	158
Bangladesh	149
Russia	143
Japan	127

2100 projection	
India	1551
China	941
Nigeria	730
USA	478
Tanzania	316
Pakistan	261
Indonesia	254
Democratic Republic of Congo	212
Philippines	178
Brazil	177

Task 2

Spend about 40 minutes on this task.

Write about the following topic:

In some countries, health care is free, paid for by the state. In other countries, payment is divided between the state and people themselves.

Discuss both systems, and say which one is better.

Provide reasons for your answer. Include relevant examples from your own knowledge or experience.

Write at least 250 words.

Speaking

PLAY RECORDING 75.

When the examiner says: 'In this part, I'm going to give you a topic...', go to page 425.

GENERAL TRAINING PRACTICE TEST 1

There are four parts to this test: Listening; Reading; Writing; and Speaking. If you do all four parts together, they will take you about three hours.

The Listening and Speaking tests are the same for General Training and Academic.

Listening

Go to page 288.

Reading

You have one hour for this test.

SECTION 1 *Questions 1-14*

Read the text below, and answer questions 1-7.

CHANGES TO RECYCLING

The information below was sent to all residents.

GETTING SORTED
From 1 July, curbside recycling is changing.
One big bin: Your new bin is bigger than your old bin. Now you must put paper products inside your bin with all other recyclables, not on the pavement in plastic bags or cardboard boxes.

WHAT CAN GO IN THE BIN?		
Aluminium cans **Cardboard** **Egg cartons** **Empty aerosols**	**Envelopes & junk mail** **Glass bottles, jars + lids** **Magazines & newspapers** **Paper**	**Plastic bottles, containers + lids** **Tetra Pak cartons** **Tin cans + lids**

WHAT CAN'T GO IN THE BIN?	
Batteries **Building waste** **Chemicals, oil, or paint** **Clothing, shoes, or textiles** **Electrical or electronic waste** **Food or garden waste** **Glass** from frames, mirrors, or windows	**Hazardous waste** **Light bulbs** (Leave at participating retailers.) **Medical waste** **Nappies** [Diapers] **Plastic bags** – These get trapped in sorting machinery, causing breakdowns. (Leave at participating retailers.) **Polystyrene packaging**

WHEN DOES THE BIN GO OUT?
On weekdays: As currently, before 6:30 AM. **On public holidays:** As currently, put your bin out the day after a holiday. When there is a two-day holiday, put your bin out on the second day of the holiday. This is a new service.
Suburban: Fortnightly collection: Your new bin is labelled with your suburb, its collection day, and fortnight (A or B).
CBD: Daily or weekly collection: Your new bin is labelled with your zone. Daily collection continues in Zone 1, but extends into Zone 2. Friday collection continues in Zone 3.

LISTENING
READING
WRITING
SPEAKING

SECTION 1   SECTION 2   SECTION 3

WHAT HAPPENS TO THE OLD BIN?
You can keep it or put it out for collection in July.
Further Information
For a list of places where you can leave these items, go to: **Drop_while_you_shop.com**. For all other information, go to: **RecycleWell.org.nz**.

Questions 1-7

Do the following statements agree with the information given in Section 1?

In boxes 1-7 on your answer sheet, write:

TRUE	*if the statement agrees with the information*
FALSE	*if the statement contradicts the information*
NOT GIVEN	*if there is no information on this*

1 From 1 July, residents must put paper and non-paper recyclables into separate containers.

2 It will still not be possible for all glass to be recycled.

3 Plastic bags damage mechanical equipment, so they cannot be recycled.

4 There is the same number of collection days each year under the new scheme.

5 The local council charges fees to collect some recyclables.

6 Residents do not need to return their old recycling bins.

7 Drop While You Shop buys non-recyclables left at retailers.

WORM FARMING

Read the text below, and answer questions 8-14.

The big picture

While it is true that food and garden waste is less destructive than inorganic matter, its disposal is still problematic, especially when buried in vast amounts, as happens in metropolitan areas. Since land is at a premium, landfill facilities almost invariably mechanically compact organic waste, causing acidic reactions in the airless environment belowground. This means methane is released into the atmosphere, and impurities leach into groundwater, which would otherwise be potable.

The farm

Even if householders are unaware of the dangers of landfill, some dispose of food scraps in worm[*] farms, an innovation from the 1990s, because, as well as speedily breaking down material, the animals produce nutrient-rich castings – shed skin and other excreta – that can be used as fertilizer.

---

[*]A worm is a small, pink or brown animal with no legs or bones that lives in soil.

LISTENING
READING
WRITING
SPEAKING

SECTION 1   SECTION 2   SECTION 3

For apartment-dwellers, a worm farm 40 cm in diameter and 50 cm in height can sit on a balcony; for people with gardens, a larger farm one metre by one metre is suitable.

There are two layers to a worm farm, although as the number of worms grows, more layers can be added. The top layer, a deep plastic tray with tiny holes in the bottom, contains the scraps and the worms. The bottom tray traps the castings, which can be scooped out for use as is or diluted into liquid fertilizer.

The little creatures

Worms consume waste so fast that five kilograms will be broken down within eight weeks.

Essentially, worms eat anything that was once living. Favourites include:

- Fruit and vegetable scraps
- Teabags and leaves; coffee grounds
- Torn-up newspaper, egg or pizza cartons
- Eggshells (to restore the pH balance)
- Dust from dustpans or vacuum cleaners
- Hair and nail clippings

To fatten worms, flour or milk powder can be added to the farm from time to time.

NB: Worms will eat meat and cheese, but only when no other food is available. Most citrus peel and tomatoes are too acidic for worms, so they are best avoided.

Questions 8-11

Label the items below.

Write the correct letter, A-F, next to questions 8-11.

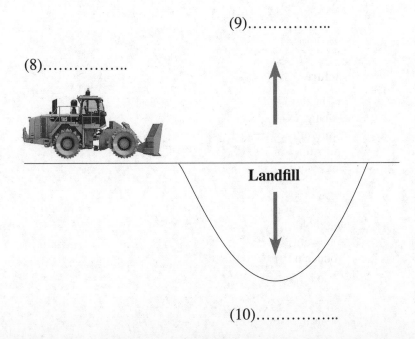

(9)……………..

(8)……………..

Landfill

(10)……………..

(11)................ →

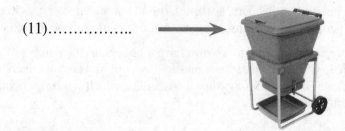

| **A** | Castings tray | **B** | Clean groundwater | **C** | Compactor |
| **D** | Food-and-worm tray | **E** | Greenhouse gas | **F** | Polluted groundwater |

Questions 12-14

Answer the questions below.

Write **NO MORE THAN THREE WORDS OR A NUMBER** *for each answer.*

Write your answers in boxes 12-14 on your answer sheet.

12 How many kilograms of waste can worms break down within eight weeks?

    ....……

13 Which food may improve the worms' pH balance?

    ....……

14 Which two kinds of food will worms eat as a last resort?

    ....……

LISTENING
READING
WRITING
SPEAKING

| SECTION 1 | SECTION 2 | SECTION 3 |

SECTION 2 *Questions 15-27*

Read the text below and answer questions 15-27.

PROFESSIONAL DEVELOPMENT WORKSHOPS

English Language Centre, South Western University – 20-22 May

	AM Session	**PM Session**
May 20th	**(A) Plenary – Great Hall** Dr Carlee Smith will open the three-day workshop. Dr Hans Dykstra will report on a conference he recently attended in Brazil. Ms Adela Xu will update staff on the joint ventures. (Those interested in working in China may email her their CV.) Lunch provided in the Buttery.	**(B) Individual – Computer Lab A** <u>Pronunciation</u>: • Using the IPA (International Phonetic Alphabet) • Raising awareness about fluency • Analysing the features of talkback radio and TV panel discussions ✓ • Recording on SoundCloud • Providing feedback
May 21st	**(C) Individual – Room 204** <u>Essay-writing skills</u>: • Writing elegantly • Writing convincingly • Hedging • Describing data • Drawing on multiple sources • Paraphrasing and quoting • Bibliographic conventions • Using footnote and endnote programs	**(D) Individual – Room 207** <u>Group discussion skills</u>: • Showing enthusiasm and understanding • Turn-taking • Clarifying • Disagreeing politely • Interrupting • Reaching consensus • Chairing or moderating <u>Presentation skills</u>: • Establishing rapport with an audience • Reducing dependence on PowerPoint slides • Providing analysis rather than only description
May 22nd	**(E) Individual – Basement Café** <u>Sam Sleepyhead and Tina Tiara?</u> • Strategies for dealing with the unmotivated	**(F) Individual – Room 213** <u>Creative ideas for the last ten minutes of class time</u>: • Drawing each other in pairs • Summarising YouTube clips
(G) Other information		
• Presenters will receive a certificate of appreciation and a gift voucher. • Submission of papers is welcomed by the online journal *Tertiary English Today*, edited by Dr Dykstra. • Attendees doing the Diploma of Tertiary Teaching may wish to complete a workshop journal for credit towards Module 40010.		
NB: In order for casual or part-time staff to be paid for these days when they would otherwise not be working, they must email proof of session attendance to Payroll.		

Questions 15-21

The reading above has seven sections: **A-G**.

Which section contains the following information?

Write the correct letter, A-G, in boxes 15-21 on your answer sheet.

> **NB**   *You may use any letter more than once.*

15 This session is in the morning on May 21ˢᵗ.

16 Teachers keen to work in China should attend this session.

17 In this session, managing conversation is discussed.

18 Teachers having difficulty with lazy students should attend this session.

19 With proof of attendance, all staff will be paid for this professional development.

20 In this session, teachers are encouraged to incorporate art in their practice.

21 It is likely that the person leading this session thinks PowerPoint is overused.

Read the text below, and answer questions 22-27.

VOLUNTEERING IN AUCKLAND

It is estimated that volunteers constitute ten percent of the New Zealand workforce. As the population ages and immigration rises, their number grows.

Recently, Myra Khan, from *The Star*, caught up with four volunteers. 'Let's start with Hikitea Po since you're an old hand.' 'Indeed. Over the years, I've done all kinds of volunteering, as any mother has. I did the school fair, and drove sports teams around. But since I retired, I've taken on more challenges. Now, I plant trees on Rangitoto Island, assist with Save Our Rivers, and foster dogs. I guess I'm a volunteer junkie.'

'Or a sucker,' put in Sara Rustaqi, whose own experience had not been so rosy. 'I was a teacher in Argentina, so, while waiting for local registration, I volunteered to teach Spanish at a primary school in the eastern suburbs. To be honest, the kids were spoilt. They couldn't believe I'd be doing it for nothing.'

'I know how you feel,' said Terry Wilkinson. 'I was in education for 20 years. Even after I quit, I spent a whole year depressed. Finally, a mate of mine told me about Restorative Justice, or RJ.' 'What's that?' asked Myra. 'Basically, it's when victims and perpetrators of crime meet each other informally. Let's say a house is burgled, and the police catch the guy. He's charged, and a date for his court appearance is set. Beforehand, he's asked if he wants to meet the people who live in the house, perhaps to say sorry. If he does, his sentence may be reduced.' 'And what do you do, Terry?' 'I facilitate the meetings. I've seen some incredible moments. Perpetrators meet real people, and see how their actions have affected them; victims feel considerable relief at an apology. Recently, I became a paid, full-time member of the RJ team. I couldn't be happier.'

Innocent Jonas adds, 'My story's similar. I was an obstetrician in Ethiopia, but I didn't want to undergo the rigorous registration process here. However, I've been volunteering as an aide at North Shore Hospital, and I've been so impressed I'm going to retrain as a nurse. My manager has even promised me paid work while I study. Volunteering has really opened doors for me.'

Questions 22-27

Look at the following statements and the list of people below.

*Match each statement with the correct person: **A**, **B**, **C**, or **D**.*

*Write the correct letter, **A**, **B**, **C**, or **D**, in boxes 22-27 on your answer sheet.*

22   This volunteer feels privileged to have witnessed emotional scenes.

23   Volunteering has meant this person could pursue medicine again.

24   This person's current voluntary experience revolves around nature.

25   After a mid-life crisis, volunteering led to a rewarding new career for this person.

26   Volunteering was not a positive experience for this person.

27   This person compares volunteering to parenthood.

List of people
A   Hikitea Po
B   Sara Rustaqi
C   Terry Wilkinson
D   Innocent Jonas

SECTION 3   *Questions 28-40*

Read the text below and answer questions 28-40.

• •

SECRETS AND LIES IN THE DIGITAL AGE

You're at a work lunch when your boss's smartphone rings, but she doesn't take the call. Ten seconds later, her phone's receiving a text; still, no response. Finally, after several loud buzzes for incoming email, your boss excuses herself. Returning to the table a few minutes later, she's all smiles and insists you order dessert with your coffee, even though this has never happened at a work do before. You wonder if your boss has just had some really good news or some really bad. If it were the former, she'd probably announce it, whereas the latter is generally skated over or concealed altogether. Perhaps, it is only your boss's sudden desire for dessert that alerts you to anything amiss.

As psychologists well know, people trying to keep secrets, or pass off lies, devote considerable effort to maintaining relationships with those they hope to deceive. Of course, at work, you don't need to know who's pursuing your boss, but let's imagine you were enjoying a romantic dinner with your new love interest; certainly, you'd be keen to find out who was on the phone. Admittedly, there'd be occasions when your date and the caller had legitimate urgent business; and, even if your date told a white lie about the call, you may not be upset. However, it would be a red flag if, while your love interest were paying the bill, the phone buzzed again, and there on the screen was illuminated: 'C U soon'. And when you queried this, your date gave you an elaborately plausible explanation. Later, as no one had done in years, on passing a street vendor, your date spontaneously bought you a gorgeous bouquet.

The fact remains that most of us are unable to detect white lies, let alone the darker, more sinister variety; and many of us are oblivious to deceivers turning a situation to their own advantage.

Indeed, there are even a few innocents who remain unaware of the physical traits of liars: that they blink more often than normal, and raise the pitch of their voices infinitesimally when uttering untruths. But what of a liar's email habits?

Firstly, there's the issue of who's actually writing, since anyone can set up an account with an assumed identity: males can become females; an adolescent can pass herself off as a twenty-something. Even a LinkedIn profile may be mostly a work of fiction.

Recently, Dr Yla Tausczik from the University of Maryland recruited volunteers who had kept a significant secret for the last seven years in order to analyse the language and frequency of their email sent both to people they were aiming to dupe and in whom they intended to confide.

A significant number of studies into behaviour involve a surprisingly small number of participants, largely because recruitment is problematic. In Dr Tausczik's case, persuading keepers of secrets to reveal their pretence, even for scientific purposes, was more awkward. Thus, to allay the fears of those involved, real emails accessed by Dr Tausczik had various identifying features, like names, dates, and places, removed. Still, around 2400 people expressed initial interest, of whom 1133 completed a questionnaire to determine suitability, and 61 from all walks of life were eventually chosen. Sixty-one is a sufficient number to gather meaningful data, particularly when emails came from a six-month period, and participants each generated a minimum of 415 and a maximum of 1278.

The seven-year-old secrets that participants had been keeping mostly involved romantic relationships or their own sexual orientation. In a minority of cases, they concerned medical conditions that could adversely affect employment or educational prospects. People from whom the information was kept were spouses, family members, or colleagues. Confidants were usually best friends, although, in the digital age, a handful of these were people the secret-keepers had met solely online.

Dr Tausczik's findings differed from traditional literature on deceivers that suggests they restrict or shun social contact. She discovered secret-keepers had a wide social network and emailed those they were deceiving continually. In fact, if their secret was one of sexual infidelity or addiction, they were more likely to send multiple emails soon after the behaviour had occurred. Additionally, these were not just one-liners but two or three paragraphs discussing all kinds of topics, often incorporating the deception itself, albeit in a more harmless form, or making a tangential allusion.

Dr Tausczik also found that in replies secret-keepers used similar or identical language to their confidants to simulate intimacy – possibly because the friends may otherwise have been less sympathetic towards any deceptive behaviour – or merely to ensure confidants were sucked into the soap opera and would be available for the next installment.

Dr David Markowitz from Stanford University has studied academic research papers retracted from conferences or publications due to scientific misconduct, usually in the form of entirely fake studies or partially faked results. He discovered a tendency towards a high number of references, in general higher than papers that cited genuine data.

A third researcher in this field of fraudulence, Dr Norah Dunbar from the University of California, posits that computer programs could be developed to trawl email. Meantime, she is analysing the actual language cheats use in email, although, as yet, she has not discerned recognizable linguistic patterns.

It would seem Dr Tausczik's research indicates that extra attention to the deceived in terms of length of email was significant, while both Dr Tausczik and Dr Markowitz found that frequency or number could suggest wrongdoing. However, the jury is still out on the actual content.

As we all know, liars and secret-keepers have been getting away with it their whole lives long. If they're reading this, maybe they'll now modify their email with those they plan to keep in the dark. Meantime, the best you can hope for in the company of the fraudulent is a piece of cake or a blushing rose; and remember, not every email you read contains the whole truth and nothing but the truth.

• •

Questions 28–34

Complete the sentences below.

*Choose **NO MORE THAN TWO WORDS OR A NUMBER** from the text for each answer.*

Write your answers in boxes 28–34 on your answer sheet.

28   The writer suggests people usually announce ....

29   Psychologists believe secret-keepers and liars try very hard to .... with those they deceive.

30   When people do notice ...., they generally do not mind them.

31   Liars can be detected by listening carefully to the higher .... of their voices.

32   An email account or online profile can easily be set up with a fake ....

33   Participants in Dr Tausczik's study had kept their major secrets for the last .... years.

34   Dr Tausczik finally selected .... secret-keepers for her study.

Questions 35–40

*Choose the correct letter, **A**, **B**, **C**, or **D**.*

Write the correct letter in boxes 35–40 on your answer sheet.

35   Many of the secrets participants kept concerned
   A   financial problems.
   B   love affairs.
   C   serious illness.
   D   misconduct at work.

36   In the past, researchers thought secret-keepers
   A   would not mention their secrets online.
   B   were far more promiscuous.
   C   limited their socializing.
   D   felt guilty about their secrets.

362   PART III   **IELTS General Training Practice Test 1**

LISTENING
READING
WRITING
SPEAKING

SECTION 1   SECTION 2   SECTION 3

37   Dr Tausczik found that secret-keepers sent their deceivers

    A   relatively infrequent email.

    B   more emails after a deception.

    C   numerous one-line emails.

    D   explicit accounts of deception.

38   Secret-keepers maintained closeness with their confidants by

    A   sympathizing with them.

    B   mirroring their language.

    C   regularly updating them.

    D   taking them out to dinner.

39   Dr Markowitz discovered that some retracted academic papers

    A   were rejected by publications due to invalid research methods.

    B   contained references that did not support the data.

    C   had a tendency towards questionable data.

    D   included more references than those with legitimate research.

40   Dr Tausczik and Dr Markowitz's research suggests that fraud could be detected by

    A   the length or number of items.

    B   the length or language of items.

    C   the number or language of items.

    D   computer programs.

LISTENING
READING
WRITING
SPEAKING

| TASK 1 | TASK 2 |

Writing

You have one hour for this test.

Task 1

Spend about 20 minutes on this task.

Your old friend has invited you to his / her child's wedding, but you cannot go.

Write a letter to your friend. In your letter:
• **Thank your friend.**
• **Explain why you would like to but cannot go.**
• **Say that you are sending a present.**

Write at least 150 words.

You do NOT need to write any addresses.

Start your letter with:

Dear _____,

Task 2

Spend about 40 minutes on this task.

Write about the following topic.

In some countries, health care is free, paid for by the state. In other countries, payment is divided between the state and the people themselves. Discuss both systems, and say which one is better.

Provide reasons for your answer. Included relevant examples from your own knowledge or experience.

Write at least 250 words.

Speaking

 PLAY RECORDING 72.

When the examiner says, 'In this part, I'm going to give you a topic…', go to page 409.

GENERAL TRAINING PRACTICE TEST 2

There are four parts to this test: Listening; Reading; Writing; and Speaking. If you do all four parts together, they will take you about three hours.

The Listening and Speaking tests are the same for General Training and Academic.

Listening

Go to page 303.

Reading

You have one hour for this test.

SECTION 1 Questions 1-14

Read the text below, and answer questions 1-7.

GREAT BARRIER ISLAND TRANSPORT

Great Barrier Island is near the city of Auckland in New Zealand. It has only 850 permanent residents, but it is a popular tourist destination.

Ferries				
To Great Barrier Island		**To Auckland**		
Monday-Friday	Weekends & Public holidays	Monday-Friday	Weekends & Public holidays	
First ferry: 0530	0630	0800	0900	
Ferries leave on the hour every hour throughout the day				
Last ferry: 1800	1800	2030	2030	
Fares		**One way**	**Return**	
Adult:		$75	$120	
Student/Pensioner:		$50	$80	
Child (5-15; young children travel free):		$25	$40	
Family (2 adults + 2 or more children):		$180	$300	
Pet (Dogs must be on a lead; cats are forbidden):		$10	$15	
Booking				
By phone: 846 1305.	In person: Tickets may be purchased at Wharf 4.			

Other information
There is a restaurant on board.
The journey lasts 2½ hours in calm seas.
Ferries do not operate in thick fog, severe storms, or on Christmas Day.

Car hire on Great Barrier Island		
Rates are for sedans; four-wheel drives are an additional $30 per day.		
Half day (1-4 hours)	1-4 days	4 days +
$40	$70	$65 a day

Bicycle hire		
Rates are for mountain bikes.		
Half day (1-4 hours)	1-4 days	4 days +
$20	$35	$30

Questions 1-7

Answer the questions below.

*Write **NO MORE THAN TWO WORDS AND/OR A NUMBER** for each answer.*

Write your answers in boxes 1-7 on your answer sheet.

1   How many people live on Great Barrier Island?

    ....

2   When does the first ferry leave Great Barrier Island for Auckland on a weekday?

    ....

3   How much does a return ticket to Great Barrier cost for a family?

    ....

4   Which animals are not allowed on Great Barrier?

    ....

5   How long does a normal ferry trip to Great Barrier take?

    ....

6   What is one reason, connected to weather, that ferries do not run?

    ....

7   How much does it cost to hire a 4-wheel drive for one day on Great Barrier?

    ....

DISCOVERING GREAT BARRIER ISLAND

Read the text below, and answer questions 8-14.

What can tourists do on Great Barrier Island?

Walking	Mountain Biking
There are ten walking tracks that go through native forest or around beaches. Hiking times and degree of difficulty vary from 30 minutes and very easy to five hours and quite demanding. Views are stunning.	Recent track development by the Department of Conservation makes biking exciting on Great Barrier. It is New Zealand law to wear a helmet when riding. Watch out for walkers as they share tracks.
Surfing and Swimming	**Kayaking and Diving**
There are several famous surf beaches with big waves. Inland, there are hot springs. Bring plenty of sunscreen because the UV rays are extremely dangerous. Burn times in mid-summer are as low as ten minutes, and you still burn in the water.	There are two hire companies operating on Great Barrier for all the gear you need. Kayaking is done on the sheltered western side of the island. Snorkeling and scuba diving are popular everywhere. The wreck of the Wiltshire, off the south coast, provides extra interest.
Fishing and a Seafood Festival	**Learning About Local History**
Eating seafood is a must. Indulge in fish caught by locals, or try your luck at some popular fishing spots. January sees the Mussel Festival. Shellfish is cooked up in every way imaginable, accompanied by musical performances.	The hardwood forests on Great Barrier Island were exploited for over 100 years by loggers. Walking around, you will see ruins from this industry. Most trees are protected these days. There are some old wooden houses from the 19th century that make for excellent photographs.

Questions 8-14

*Choose the correct letter **A**, **B**, **C**, or **D**.*

Write the correct letter in boxes 8-14 on your answer sheet.

8 Walks along easy tracks on Great Barrier take about

    A 15 minutes.

    B half an hour.

    C 45 minutes.

    D one hour.

9 The views on Great Barrier are

    A extraordinary.

    B pleasant.

    C famous.

    D passable.

10 Walkers and bikers

A   take great photos.

B   have to wear helmets.

C   use some of the same tracks.

D   use different tracks.

11 One disadvantage of swimming in New Zealand is

A   sharks.

B   dangerous waves.

C   dangerous sun.

D   cold water.

12 It is better to kayak on the _____ side of the island.

A   northern

B   southern

C   eastern

D   western

13 The Mussel Festival takes place each year in

A   January.

B   February.

C   March.

D   April.

14 In the past, Great Barrier was noted for

A   tourism.

B   photography.

C   fishing.

D   logging.

LISTENING
READING
WRITING
SPEAKING

SECTION 1   SECTION 2   SECTION 3

SECTION 2 Questions 15-27

Read the information below, and answer questions 15-21.

A
Building Trades
(Including: Bricklaying, Building, Carpentry, Fire Protection, Floor & Wall Tiling, and Plumbing)
Building:
Part-time: 12 hours per week
Duration: 2 years
This course is for people wanting to acquire building skills for the residential construction industry.
You will study the social, environmental, and legal aspects of residential construction projects. Special focus will be on: quantities of materials, site safety, and computing.
This course, along with Carpentry and Bricklaying, will give you the technical qualifications for a Builder's Licence.

B
Child Studies
(Including: Children's Services, Early Childhood Education & Care, and a Traineeship)
Diploma of Early Childhood Education & Care:
Part-time: 21 hours per week (3 days)
Duration: 18 months
This course is for people wanting to become qualified childcare workers in day care centres.
You will develop the skills, knowledge, and attitudes relevant to meet the intellectual, physical, and emotional needs of children in day care. Special focus will be on: occupational health and safety, ethical work practices, and legal issues.
On completion of this diploma, graduates may apply for advanced standing at universities that offer Early Childhood courses.
Note: A police check will be carried out before applications are accepted. A criminal record involving violence or abuse seriously affects career prospects.

C
Real Estate
(Including: Agency Management, Marketing, and Property Services)
Property Services:
Full time: 35 hours per week
Duration: 4 months
This certificate, which is recognised nationally, provides learners with the skills and knowledge needed to market, sell, lease, and manage property within an agency. It is a pre-requisite for the diploma.

LISTENING
READING
WRITING
SPEAKING

SECTION 1   SECTION 2   SECTION 3

D
Screen & Digital Media
(Including: Film & TV Production, Interactive Digital Media, & Network Administration)
<u>Film & TV Production:</u>
Part-time: 21 hours per week (3 days)
Duration: 4 months
This certificate, a pre-requisite for the Diploma of Screen & Digital Media, introduces learners to the film and television industry.
You will learn how to write a script, plan and produce a short pre-recorded programme segment, and work effectively as a production crewmember.

E
Outreach
A variety of courses chosen by learners from all Certificate I-II courses on offer at the college, as well as compulsory: Introductory Computing, First Aid, and English Language.
Flexible delivery options.
Outreach aims to remove barriers for people wanting to return to education. These barriers could be: income level, English-language ability, little previous education, geographic isolation, disability, or family commitments.

Questions 15-21

The text above has five sections: A-E.

Which section, A-E, has the following information?

Write the correct letter, A-E, in boxes 15-21 on your answer sheet.

This course:

15   is fulltime.

16   lasts the longest.

17   takes the fewest hours to complete.

18   leads to a licence.

19   helps people who are disadvantaged.

20   is related to the entertainment industry.

21   once completed, can go towards a university course.

LISTING
READING
WRITING
SPEAKING

SECTION 1   SECTION 2   SECTION 3

Questions 22-27

The passage below has seven paragraphs: A-G.

Choose the correct heading for paragraphs B-G from the list of headings below.

Write the correct number, i-ix, in boxes 22-27 on your answer sheet.

List of Headings	MATERIALS

List of Headings

i   Older students sometimes resent the young

ii   Worth the effort

iii   More mature-aged students in developed countries

iv   High academic achievement

v   The dangers of unfinished studies

vi   Why they exist

vii   Oldies find friendship harder at university

viii   Problems at home

ix   Mature-aged students are great organisers

Example	Answer
Paragraph A	iii

MATURE-AGED STUDENTS

A Only a generation ago, there were few tertiary students who had begun their studies when they were over the age of 21. It was virtually unheard of for people to start courses in their forties or fifties. These days, in all developed countries, not only are there large numbers of online learners who are mature-aged, but, on campus, mums and dads with their laptops and library books are also making an appearance. In some countries, China for example, university study still remains the preserve of the young. Population pressure means that providing education for those aged 18-24 is difficult enough. Only English-language and IT opportunities exist at private colleges for older people.

B There are four main reasons for this rise in mature-aged students. Firstly, universities have changed entry requirements as more courses have become fee-paying. If students can afford to pay, and meet the academic level, then it doesn't matter how old they are. Secondly, the concept of a job for life is a thing of the past. Many people now have several careers. Life expectancy has reached 80 in at least 20 countries; retirement ages have risen accordingly. Therefore, retraining for longer working lives is essential. Lastly, there has been a general expansion of the education sector as the workforce needs to be better trained for a more competitive knowledge-based world.

C Clearly there are advantages to undertaking study later in life. There is the increased likelihood of a higher salary after study, and enhanced self-esteem. But what are some of the difficulties mature-aged students face? The most glaring one is the visual fact that they're not as attractive or energetic as all those young things lounging on quadrangle lawns. It's unlikely that they will socialise with people the same age as their sons or daughters, and that could make university life rather lonely. Befriending other mature-aged students is a possibility, but perhaps they also seem too old.

D In lectures and tutorials, older learners may get tired more quickly, but research has proven they focus on their studies. They work harder, and generally perform better than younger students. Their life experiences and analytical powers are good study aids. When there are group assignments, older students may become annoyed, feeling they do all of the work while the youngsters are out partying or working at part-time jobs. Furthermore, younger students often feel the pressure of their peers more acutely. They may be scared to participate in tutorials, worried what those their own age think of them. This means older students contribute more to discussion. While tutors are certainly grateful for their efforts, the mature-aged students themselves may occasionally wish they were not in the spotlight so often.

E For most mature-aged students, juggling work, family, and other commitments is a tricky business. Their organisational skills are admirable. However, their children, partners, or work-mates may resent the absence or distraction of the older student. The student may win a qualification, but he or she may have to fight other battles on the home front.

F Then there are the greatly discouraged mature-aged drop-outs. These people already feel they failed at the end of their schooling by not going on to university, and being unable to complete their studies a second time can cause considerable anxiety. Fortunately, statistics show there are not very many of these people. Completion rates for undergraduate and post-graduate courses, for mature-aged students, are high.

G It takes courage, determination, personal and financial sacrifice to complete studies at university. Despite these difficulties, large numbers of mature-aged men and women all over the world are succeeding.

SECTION 3

Read the text below and answer questions 28-40.

THE HUMBLE BANANA

As the world's most eaten fruit, it is hard to believe that the banana has only become widely available in the last one hundred years. Nor can most people imagine a world without bananas. However, disease is threatening the existence of popular varieties, and while the banana itself is unlikely to die out, what consumers call a banana could change dramatically since new disease-resistant strains may differ in taste, texture, size, and colour from fruit currently on offer.

History

A native of tropical South and Southeast Asia, it is thought bananas were first cultivated in today's Papua New Guinea around 10,000 years ago. Spreading to Madagascar, Africa, and then the Islamic world, bananas reached Europe in the 15th century. The word 'banana' entered English via Portuguese from Wolof – a West African language. Only in 1872 did the French writer Jules Verne describe bananas to his readers in some detail as they were so exotic, and it was another 30 years before plantation-grown produce from Central America would flood the global market.

Botanical data

Most modern edible bananas come from the wild species *Musa acuminata*, *Musa balbisiana*, or their hybrids. Two common varieties today are the larger more curved Cavendish and the smaller straighter Lady Finger both of which turn yellow when ripe.

Bananas are herbs, not trees, although they can reach more than seven metres (24 ft). Their stem, not trunk, is a soft fibrous shoot from an underground corm, or bulb. After fruiting, the whole stem dies, and the plant regenerates from the corm, one of which may last 25 years.

Normally, each banana stem produces one very large purple heart inside of which the fruit develops from female flowers, and hangs in a cluster weighing 30-50 kilograms (66-110 lb) and containing hundreds of bananas.

Domesticated bananas no longer have seeds, so their propagation must occur through the removal and transplantation of part of the corm, or through tissue culture in a laboratory, the latter being a complicated procedure that can lead to plant contamination.

Uses and benefits

As bananas grow all year round, they have become a vital crop. They are easy to eat (just peel) and easy to transport (no packaging needed).

Banana fruit, skin, heart, and stem are all edible, and alcohol can also be made from the plant.

The world's greatest banana-eaters are in East Africa, where the average Ugandan devours 150 kilograms (330.6 lb) a year, and receives 30% of calories this way. This habit is healthy since a single 100-gram (3.5 oz) banana contains 371 kilojoules (89 kcal) of energy, and protein represents 1.09% of its weight – 25 times more than that of an apple.

In daily requirements for an adult, one banana provides: 2% of Vitamin B1, 5% of B2, 4% of B3, 7% of B5, 28% of B6, 5% of B9; 15% of Vitamin C; 1% of calcium; 2% of iron; 7% of magnesium; 3% of phosphorous; 8% of potassium; and, 1% of zinc.

A further health benefit is a lower risk of breast, bowel, or liver cancer, and some psychiatrists recommend bananas as they increase dopamine levels in the brain, thus improving mood.

Aside from food and drink, bananas have other uses. Their large flexible leaves become recyclable plates or food containers in Asia. Traditionally, the Japanese boiled banana shoots in lye until their fibres softened and separated. Fine cloth was woven from this fibre. Paper is made from banana stems, and more recently, skins have been employed to clean up polluted rivers as their absorption of heavy metals is high.

In several religions, bananas feature prominently. Tamils believe the banana is one of three holy fruits. Buddhists often decorate trays with bananas to offer to the Buddha. Moslems eat copious quantities during the holy month of Ramadan during which time global trade in the fruit spikes.

Threats to bananas

Between 1820 and 1950, a banana called the Gros Michel was the most common commercial variety. Suddenly, this was attacked by a fungus called Panama disease, and worldwide, the Gros Michel was almost wiped out. Its commercial replacement, the Cavendish, considered less delicious by gourmands, may now suffer the same fate as its predecessor. All Cavendish bananas are genetically identical, making them susceptible to disease. While the original Panama disease was controlled, it mutated into Tropical Race 4 (TR4), which has destroyed banana crops in Southeast Asia, and for which there is no known defence except genetic modification.

Black Sigatoka is another deadly disease. In Uganda – once a world-leader in banana production – it reduced crops by 40% in the 1970s. The treatment for Black Sigatoka is as controversial as it is expensive ($1000 per hectare per annum) since chemical spray contaminates soil and water supplies. Banana cultivars resistant to Black Sigatoka do exist, but none has been accepted by major supermarket buyers because their taste and texture differ greatly from bananas that shoppers are used to.

In 2010, East Africa was hit by another plague – Banana Xanthomonas wilt. The Ugandan economy lost more than $500 million due to this, and thousands of small farmers abandoned bananas as a crop, leading to widespread financial hardship and a far poorer diet.

Scientists, however, have not given up hope, and the National Banana Research Programme in Uganda has been adding a sweet pepper gene, disease-resistant in a number of vegetables, to bananas. Yet genetically modified crops remain banned in Uganda, and other scientists believe identifying and domesticating disease-free wild bananas rather than adopting expensive and largely unproven gene technology would be more prudent.

Human civilization has a long and critical relationship with bananas. If this is to continue, it may be time to reconsider what a banana is. The supermarkets may no longer be stocked with big sweet yellow cultivars but with tiny purple, pink, red, or green-and-white striped ones that currently exist in the depths of the forest and will not be cheap to domesticate.

~~~~~~

Questions 28-33

Choose **ONE WORD OR A NUMBER** *from the passage for each answer.*

Write your answers in boxes 28-33 on your answer sheet.

28   Only since the turn of the 20th century have bananas become readily ....

29   Farmers in what is now Papua New Guinea first started growing bananas about .... years ago.

30   Banana plants do not have a trunk but a(n) ....

31 An adult can receive ....% of his or her daily vitamin C requirements from an average banana.

32 The Japanese used to make .... from banana fibre.

33 During the Muslim holy month of Ramadan, international .... in bananas increases dramatically.

Questions 34-39

Complete each sentence with the correct ending, A-I, below.

Write the correct letter, A-I, in boxes 34-39 on your answer sheet.

34 The popular banana, the Gros Michel, was

35 Since Cavendish bananas lack genetic diversity,

36 Scientists and farmers fought Panama disease, but it was not eradicated. Instead, it

37 Large numbers of Ugandan farmers

38 Vegetables with additional sweet pepper genes

39 Food security worldwide is partly dependent on

A	are no longer growing bananas. ✓
B	there are enough bananas.
C	they may also be destroyed by disease. ✓
D	are keen to try GM banana strains.
E	almost made extinct by a fungus. ✓
F	have successfully withstood disease. ✓
G	a continuous supply of bananas.
H	became Black Sigatoka disease.
I	transformed itself into TR4. ✓

Question 40

*Choose **TWO** of the following letters: **A**, **B**, **C**, **D**, or **E**.*

Write the correct letters in box 40 on your answer sheet.

Which TWO of the following does the writer believe about bananas on sale in supermarkets of the future?

    A They will not come from Africa.

    B They will be multicoloured.

    C They will taste better.

    D They will be less expensive.

    E They will be a variety of banana that is wild now.

LISTENING
READING
WRITING
SPEAKING

| TASK 1 | TASK 2 |

Writing

You have one hour for this test.

Task 1

Spend about 20 minutes on this task.

You are studying for a qualification, and you would like some time off work to complete it.

Write a letter to your manager. In your letter:
• **Ask for some time off to complete a qualification.**
• **Suggest what you will do later at work if you have time off.**
• **Say how the qualification helps your job or company.**

Write at least 150 words.

You do NOT need to write any addresses.

Start your letter with:

Dear Mr/Ms _____,

Task 2

Spend about 40 minutes on this task.

Write about the following topic:

In some countries, fathers are playing a greater role in raising their children.

Why is this happening? What are the benefits of it?

Provide reasons for your answer. Include relevant examples from your own knowledge or experience.

Write at least 250 words.

Speaking

 **PLAY RECORDING 73.**

When the examiner says: 'In this part, I'm going to give you a topic...', go to page 417.

Answers to Parts I and II

Chapter 1. Introducing IELTS

<u>What does all this mean?</u> 1. answers; 2. accent; 3. going; 4. assuming; 5. Operational; 6. residency; 7. Mandarin.

Chapter 2. IELTS Listening

<u>Introduction to the Listening test</u>: 1. NG; 2. T; 'Any answer that can't be read easily, however, is marked wrong.'; 3. F; 'The Listening test takes 30 minutes.'; 4. T; Sections last 'between five and six minutes'; 5. NG; 6. T; 'There are never more than ten MCQs in a test.'; 7. F; 'No answer in IELTS Listening is more than three words.'; 8. T; 'Listening questions are all in order.'.

<u>What are the four different sections of the Listening test</u>? <u>What is tested</u>? 1. talking about; 2. programme; 3. academic; 4. challenging; 5. refute; 6. global; 7. attitude; 8. 700; 9. spelling; 10. not.

<u>How the Listening test is marked</u>: 1. lose; 2. score; 3. several; 4. guesses; 5. twice; 6. vast; 7. back.

<u>How to fill out the Listening and Reading answer sheets</u>:

	Candidate's answers	Problem	Solution
Eg	*quater*	**Sp**	**quarter / ¼**
Eg	*to expensive*	**V**	**too expensive**
Eg	*B / D*	**U**	*Which one?*
1	*new acommodation*	**Sp**	new accommodation
2	*high buildings*	**V**	tall buildings
3	*studing in groups*	**Sp**	studying in groups
4	*differents nationalities*	**G**	different nationalities
5	*ivi*	**U**	iv // v // vi *Which one?*
6	*spreaded throughout Asia*	**G**	spread throughout Asia
7	*150,00$*	**U**	$150.00 // $150,000 *Which one?*

32	*Mz Masters*	**Sp**	Ms Masters *(Ms – pronounced Miz – is the female equivalent of Mr.)*
33	*school principle*	**V**	school principal *(Check the different meanings of 'principal' and 'principle'.)*
35	*obey traffic rules & regulations*	**T**	*One of these will be correct*: obey traffic rules / obey rules / rules & regulations
36	*local goverment*	**Sp**	local government
37	*due to late*	**G**	due to lateness *('due to being late' is grammatically correct, but four words.)*

38	*barbecue* ~~*barbicue*~~ *with neighbours*	√
39		*Never leave a blank. Guess. You might be right.*
40	*comunity* *sense of* ~~*community*~~	*A correct answer that is replaced with an incorrect one is marked wrong.*

If you want a Seven

	Candidate's answers	Problem	Solution
1	writting a journal	Sp	**writing** *Remember: a single consonant 't' for a long vowel sound /aɪ/.*
2	a six-pages story	G	**six-page** *There are no plural adjectives in English.*
3	𝒯	U	*The letters T and F need to be clear, or they are marked wrong.*
4	footbreak	Sp	**foot brake**
5	adjust review mirror	V	**rearview / rear-vision**
6	discover in 1955	G	**discovered**
7	*Di 6 ohy*	U	*Handwriting needs to be clear, or the answer is marked wrong.*
8	opposing thumbs	V	**opposable** *Check the differences in meaning of: 'opposable', 'opposing / opposed', and 'opposite' in your dictionary.*
9	gorillas, orangutans, chimps, humans	T	*One of these is not needed.*
10	Made some researches	V & G	**did some research / did research** *The noun 'research' needs the verb 'do' before it. 'Research' is an uncountable noun, so is singular.*
11	Three millions people	G	*'Hundred', 'thousand', and 'million' are adjectives in English, so they are never plural.*
12	endangered specious	V	**species** *Check the meaning of 'specious'.*

The Reading answer sheet: wrong; few; summary; accidentally; transfer; within; first; careful; mark; back.

Listening Strategies: The hardest set: Set II would be the hardest to answer because candidates need to write up to three words for the answers. Some of the words are hard to spell. One answer, #5, is a negative: 'shouldn't'. Negatives are tricky. Set I, which is easier, is still harder than Set III because the questions take longer to read. Set III is about the level of an IELTS set for Section 1.

Recording 1: The first part of Section 1: Set I: 1. B; 2. C; 3. A and D (*must have both letters to get one mark*); 4. Four/4/4PM/4 o'clock/1600; 5. glad; Set II: 1. Majestic (*capital optional*); 2. ordinary; 3. on the inside; 4. Sally McPherson (*capitals optional*); 5. 6-6:30PM ('*Six to half past' is wrong because it's four words*); Set III: 1. C; 2. Gordon (*capital optional*); 3. this afternoon; 4. 9841 3628; 5. Sally (*This is testing your pronunciation as the sound 'æ' is written 'a' in English, and a short vowel has a double consonant after it like 'll'.*)

Recording 2: The second part of Section 1: The harder set: Sets IV and V are equally difficult.

If you want a Seven: 1. Because Sally's family name, McPherson, is too hard to spell, and it isn't spelt out. 2. Question #1 because 'Majestic' is too hard to spell. 3. This question could be in Section 3 or Section 4. 4. Because they're asking candidates to listen for complex ideas. The multiple matching question type of Set IV causes candidates to panic because they're unfamiliar with it, but it's only focusing on half of the script. Set V questions are focusing on all of the script. There's also more to read in the questions in Set V.

Always listen for evidence: In the script on pages 23-24, the **bold** writing shows answers for Set IV questions; the *italic* writing shows answers for Set V questions. In the script below, **bold** words are those candidates write as their answers. Underlined words show why an answer is correct.

Man	Majestic Theatre. How may I help you?
Woman	Good afternoon. My name's Emma **Gordon**. I'm ringing to find out if anyone handed in a raincoat last night. I think I left mine in the bar.
Man	Yes, I believe someone did. In fact, I've got two coats and two umbrellas here. Perhaps you could describe your coat for me, Ms Garden?
Woman	Gordon. Emma Gordon.
Man	Right.
Woman	It's quite an ordinary coat, really. You see, it was pouring when I left home to go to the theatre last night, but lovely and fine after the performance. I suppose I just walked out –

Man	As I said, I've got two coats here. What's yours like?
Woman	It's green, **shortish**, and waterproof. I don't know what the material is – maybe Gore-Tex? It's brand new.
Man	<u>Does it have a hood?</u>
Woman	<u>Yes it does.</u> You can roll it up and hide it in the collar.
Man	<u>Any pockets?</u>
Woman	<u>Two – but they're</u> on the inside. <u>And a long zipper.</u>
Man	You're in luck, Ms Gordon. That sounds just like one I've got.
Woman	Great. <u>Could I come and pick it up some time this **evening**</u>?
Man	No problem. One thing though – my shift's over soon, so <u>Sally</u>'ll be in the box office, not me.
Woman	<u>**Sally**</u>?
Man	My colleague <u>Sally McPherson</u>. I'll put a note on the coat with your details. How do you spell your name?
Woman	Emma – E. double M. A. – **Gordon. G.O.R.D.O.N.**
Man	<u>And a contact phone number</u>?
Woman	**Nine eight four one; three six two eight.**
Man	Thanks. <u>Sally's</u> here from four to eleven PM. She's got a break from six to half past, so avoid coming then. Anyway, I'm glad we've sorted things out with your coat.

<u>Set IV</u>: 6. B; 7. A; 8. A; 9. B; 10. C; <u>Set V</u>: 6. C; 7. C; 8. B; 9. 21/11 *or* Nov 21 *or* 21 Nov *or* November 21st *or* 21st November *(Many Chinese candidates write November 21th and do **not** get a mark.)*; 10. credit card.

<u>Set IV</u>: 7. 'A Christmas Carol' opens towards the end of November because we're told that 'A Doll's House' is on 'the 21st of November', and 'A Christmas Carol' is the next show (lines 11 and 14). 8. 'A Christmas Carol' might make audiences laugh because we're told (line 14) that 'it's a comedy'. 9. 'A Doll's House' has no seats left next week because we're told (line 18) that 'it's completely booked out'.; <u>Set V</u>: 7. Emma can either exchange her ticket for another one, or get her money back because we're told (line 7) that a 'Z' ticket is 'exchangeable or refundable'. 8. 'A Christmas Carol' is not the kind of production Emma likes because we're told (line 16) that it's 'not [her] cup of tea'. This is an idiom for not really liking something. 9. 21/11 *or* Nov 21 *or* 21 Nov *or* November 21st *or* 21st November.

The **grey** text shows the answers for Set IV questions. The **bold** text shows answers for Set V questions.

Woman	Before I forget. I've got a ticket for a play **'A Doll's House' in November, but I won't be able to use it. I have to go to a conference abroad.** I wonder if I could exchange it, or get a refund?
Man	Do you have the ticket there with you?
Woman	Yes, I do.
Man	In the top right-hand corner of the ticket there's a letter: X, Y, or Z. Which letter do you have?
Woman	Um…**I've got Z.**
Man	**That means your ticket is exchangeable or refundable.** So, which would you like: another date for the same show; another show; or, your money back?
Woman	**The critics have been raving about your production of 'A Doll's House'.** I'd love to see it. **What's the last date it's on?**
Man	**The twenty-first of November.**
Woman	That's no good. I'll still be at the conference – that might even be the day of my presentation. **What show's next?**
Man	**'A Christmas Carol'.** I'm sure you know it. However, it's been updated, and **it's more of a comedy than the original.**
Woman	**I'm afraid that's not my cup of tea.** What about **next week**? Is there a performance of **'A Doll's House' then**, before I go away?
Man	Yes, there is, **but it's completely booked out**.
Woman	Could I use my ticket for another play next year? Aren't you doing **'Romeo and Juliet'**?

Man	**That's scheduled for February – opening on Valentine's Day. Unfortunately, we only exchange tickets within the same season, so you'd have to buy another ticket if you wanted to see that.**
Woman	It looks like a refund is my only option.
Man	Would you like me **to put the money into your credit card account directly**?
Woman	If you can, that'd be lovely.

Timing: minutes; pauses; SECONDS; ignore; transfer; five.

Strategies for each question type (i): answer; list; graphics; completion; maps; short; multiple.

Recording 3: Set VI: 11. a decade // 10 / ten years; 12. 70%/seventy percent (*not percentage*); 13. year (round); 14. cooling; 15. 150 m(etres); 16. 24/twenty-four; 17. reversing; 18. raised; 19. hot-water (*accepted as two words, but not as one without a hyphen*); 20. pressure.

Set VII: 11. C; 12. B; 13. A; 14. C; 15. B; 16. under ground (*accepted as one word*); 17. reversing; 18. temperature; 19. pressure; 20. evaporator.

Salesman: Good evening. I'm here for Heat Smart Solutions, a company that provides inexpensive air conditioning for commercial space. We're also about to enter the domestic market with a scaled-down version. Not only will your business significantly reduce its energy bill with geothermal A/C, but your carbon footprint will also be smaller. These days, companies need to be globally responsible as well as financially viable.

Big-name stores in Europe, the Arabian Gulf, and North America have been using geothermal technology for at least a **decade** because of its efficiency and cost-effectiveness. Figures from the International Ground Source Heat Pump Association show that your investment is recovered within four years of installation. Pretty quick, huh? From the fourth year on, you'll reduce your energy bill by a whopping **seventy** percent.

So how do geothermal heat pumps work? Basically, water is piped under ground where the temperature is **constant** and moderate, and brought back up to heat or **cool** your store. Water inside the underground loop absorbs heat in winter and releases it in summer. The temperature of the water returning to your building is between two to **twenty-four** degrees Celsius, a much narrower temperature range than that of outdoor air used in traditional air conditioning.

Pipes are usually put down below an existing car park. **One hundred and fifty metres** is a normal depth. A big supermarket might need fifty of these pipes.

…Let's look at a diagram of the system inside your building.

There are seven parts to the system. As in a refrigerator, the first thing that happens is an **evaporator** (i *in the diagram*) transfers the heat from the underground loops to a refrigerant fluid. Since the liquid is already at a **moderate** temperature – between two and **twenty-four** degrees – there's not a lot of energy to be transferred.

From the evaporator, the liquid travels to the reversing valve – that thing that looks like a fork (ii). This controls the direction of the liquid. If the liquid is too cold, as in winter, it is sent to the compressor (iii), where its temperature is **raised** with pressure. Liquid that is the right temperature for your building is sent from the reversing valve directly to the fan (iv). In summer, there may be excess heat coming off the compressor, so the de-superheater (v) sends it into a **hot-water** cylinder (vi). Oh, I've forgotten the expansion valve at the bottom of the diagram (vii). Here the **pressure** of the fluid is lowered, so it heads back towards the **evaporator** to start the cycle again.

In an era of global warming, we all want to live, work, and shop in comfort. Smart Heat Solutions and its geothermal pumps are a safe bet for keeping your customers cool while cutting your energy costs.

Strategies for each question type (ii): sentence; summary; flowcharts; maps; diagrams.

Recording 4: The alphabet etc.:

/iː/	/uː/	/e/	/aː/	/eɪ/	/aɪ/	/əʊ/
B	Q	F	R	A	I	O
C	U	L		H	Y	
D	W	M		J		
E		N		K		
G		S				
P		X				
T		Z				
V						

Commonly confused letters: 1. i. P; ii. T; iii. N; 2. i. S; ii. E; iii. V; iv. G; v. U, W.

Recording 5:

1	Name:	Simon *Johnston*
	Address:	Unit 4, *22 Harris* St
	Phone #:	492 0557
	Email:	*STJ2010*@hotmail.com

2	Name:	Kirsten *Muller*
	Nationality:	*German*
	Passport #:	*D7000868B*
	Date of Birth:	06 May 1991
	Place of Birth:	*Ulm*

Recording 6: <u>The time</u>: 1. 11:50 AM; 2. 2:15 PM; 3. A is correct; 4. B should say 'ten forty-five' or 'a quarter to eleven'.

Recording 7: <u>Money</u>: 1. $390; 2. €600; 3. ¥50,000; 4. £12; 5. 72c.

Recording 8: <u>Amazing facts</u>: 1. Mauna Kea; 10,200; 2. HD1566668B; 80; 3. 660; 4. half; 762 grams/gms; 5. Serbia; 5,450; 46 days.

1. Approximately a **third** of the countries have coal-fired power stations. 2. Over **a** quarter of international students have scholarships. 3. My grandparents have just had their **fiftieth** wedding anniversary. 4. ✓.

<u>Percent or percentage?</u> 1. Only two **percent** walk to work. 2. **The** percentage of walkers is low.

<u>Numbers that are quantifiers</u>: 1. ✓ 2. People have been living in caves on the Tigris for thousands **of** years. 3. **Millions** of dollars were spent on security when Oprah Winfrey visited. 4. An inexpensive vaccine would save millions of **lives**.

<u>Writing numbers in the writing test</u>: twelve; numeral; start; larger; inside. 1. ✓ 2. **Seventy percent** had stayed for two weeks. 3. ✓ 4. Of the 300 people surveyed, only **three** had not enjoyed their holiday at all.

<u>Compound adjectives</u>: 1. My husband has just signed **a** three-year contract to teach in Abu Dhabi. 2. ✓ 3. ✓ 4. Taipei has lots of hundred-storey **buildings**. 5. A 50-**cent** vaccine could end meningitis in Africa.

<u>If you are from China or India</u>: languages; Five; ten thousand; likely.

Chapter 3. IELTS Reading

<u>What happens in the Reading test</u>: 1. 60; 2. 2700; 3. Answers; 4. no; 5. as; 6. wrong; 7. dictionaries; 8. missing: 9. questions; 10. title; 11. once; 12. F; 13. NG; 14. T; 15. F; 16. T; 17. F; 18. T; 19. T; 20. NG.

<u>Missing words 1</u>: three; 1000; between; general; <u>Missing words 2</u>: specific; views; skimming; data; lower; <u>Missing words 3</u>: lose; scores; designed; guesses; twice; not.

<u>Missing words</u>: sentence; undergraduate; 1000; 20; 16; syllables; underestimated; infer; another.

<u>Reading strategies</u>: 1. a; 2. a; 3. a; 4. b; 5. b; 6. b; 7. a; 8. a; 9. a; 10. a; 11. b; 12. a; 13. a; 14. b; 15. a; 16. a; 17. b; 18. b; 19. b; 20. b; 21. b.

<u>Missing words</u>: <u>Matching **headings**</u>: bother; main; correct; synonyms; examples; symbols; stop. <u>Matching sentence **endings**</u>: Eliminate; own.

<u>Choosing the correct proper noun from a list of answers</u>: Scan; means; Infer.

<u>Answering True/False/Not Given questions</u>: underline; text; not; negative. <u>Answering Yes/No/Not Given questions</u>: opinions; agrees; evidence; key; skim.

<u>Choosing the correct word from a list of answers for summary questions</u>: without; connections; collocates; nouns. <u>Choosing the correct word from the text for summary questions</u>: scan; Mark; sense; thoroughly; order; around; speech; number; Copy.

<u>Choosing the correct title</u>: general; similar.

<u>Extra flowchart practice</u>: 14. performed; 15. serious problems; 16. volunteers; 17. side effects; 18. placebo; 19. 3/three; 20. cheaper; 21. state; 22. warning; 23. B; 24. A; 25. D; 26. C; 27. A and E / E and A.

<u>Extra diagram practice</u>: <u>Fluorescent microscopy</u>: 15. Chemistry (*capital optional*); 16. light; 17. detail; 18. Objective (*capital optional*); 19. filters; 20. reconstruction; 21. fluorochromes/dyes; 22. Laser (*capital optional*); 23. Specimen/Target (*capital optional*); 24. Mirror (*capital optional*); 25. Emission (*capital optional*); 26. Photons; 27. D and E / E and D (*both letters necessary*).

<u>Special information about the GT Reading Test</u>: 1. 40; 2. up to 2500; 3. at least 5/five; 4. scanning; 5. work or training; 6. a deeper understanding; 7. higher scores; 8. manage their time; 9. 30; 10. 30.

Chapter 4. IELTS Writing

<u>What happens in the Academic Writing test?</u>: higher; precise; formal; diagram; times; clear; reasons.

<u>Task 2 inputs</u>: i. A; ii. O; iii. P-S; iv. P-S; v. A.

<u>What happens in the GT Writing test?</u>: bullet; request; complaint; more.

How is the Writing test marked? 1. Coherence and Cohesion; 2. Task Fulfilment; 3. Grammar; 4. Vocabulary

Reconstructing visual inputs for Academic Writing Task 1:

Main hobby for people in New Zealand

	Men	Women
Art and craft	10	13
Cooking	21	24
DIY	16	8
Gaming	21	5
Gardening	12	12
Reading	20	38

Missing words: one; not; easier; sophisticated; limit; variety.

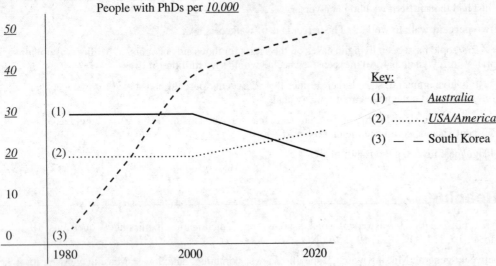

People with PhDs per 10,000

Key:
(1) ———— Australia
(2) ········· USA/America
(3) — — South Korea

Describing a procedural diagram: (1) Well; (4) White water; (5) Grey water; (6) Black water; ⌃ Upflow filter; ♠ Optional on-site treatment system.

Writing about a single table: Missing words: logical; differences; copying; speech; pronoun.

Model answer: The two countries shown are similar in size and one language spoken. Otherwise, they are quite different.

Luxembourg is slightly larger than Comoros: 2586 to 2170 square kilometres. In both countries, three languages are spoken, one of which is French. Arabic and Comoran are also spoken in Comoros; Luxembourgish and German are spoken in Luxembourg.

Of the many differences, Comoros became independent in 1975 while Luxembourg formed in 1867. Comoros, off the East African coast, is an island nation with three main islands and a number of much smaller ones. Luxembourg, however, is a landlocked plateau in Western Europe. Despite having a smaller area, Comoros has almost twice the population of Luxembourg: 800,000 people to 470,000. Its economy, reliant on the export of vanilla and cloves, is much weaker than Luxembourg's. It is also the recipient of international aid. Luxembourg, meantime, is a banking and service centre, home to various European Union institutions. (*153 words*)

Assessing Academic Writing Task 1: Order of model paragraphs: 2, 1, 3.

Does the candidate:

1) Mention every shop? *No – the pet shop is omitted. Will the candidate be penalised for this omission? No, because it is minor, and the word limit has already been reached.*

2) Give an overview of changes? *Yes – to get 6 and above this is* <u>essential</u>*. It makes the material easy for the reader to understand. If there is no overview, the reader has too much to work out him/herself.*

3) Describe where the shops are located? *No – only a lower-level candidate would do this to reach the word limit.*

4) Detail changes from left to right along the road? *No – only a lower-level candidate would do this.*

5) Say which shops changed their size? *Yes – because there are noticeable changes.*

6) Group together similar kinds of shops? *Yes – this is the most logical thing to do, and makes understanding easy for the reader.*

7) Provide a reason for the changes? *No – description of the data is all that is required in Task 1. Task 2 expects analysis.*

8) Say which shops he or she likes the best? *No – this is irrelevant.*

9) Mention the transport changes? *Yes – and the candidate notes they are 'significant'. Would he or she be penalised if she had not mentioned them? Yes. They are noticeably different.*

10) Have a conclusion? *No – the low number of words in Task 1 means a conclusion is unnecessary.*

<u>Ranking answers</u>: A = 4th; B = 3rd; C = 1st; D = 2nd.

<u>Examiner's reports</u>: 1 = D; 2 = C.

<u>Highlighted text from script F</u>: Grey: because all these nouns need articles before them, or the wrong kind of article is used; <u>Underlined</u>: because these verbs should be past participles; <u>B and W</u>: because all these vocabulary items are wrong.

<u>Assessing candidates for GT Writing Task 1: Analysis of Letter B (the best letter)</u>: 1. Yes; 2. Yes; 3. Yes; 4. No; 5. No; 6. Yes; 7. Yes; 8. Yes; 9. Yes; 10. No; 11. Yes; 12. Yes; 13. Yes.

<u>Examiner's report on Letters A and C</u>: 1. TF; C; 2. Gra; A; 3. Voc; A; 4. TF; A; 5. Voc; C; 6. Gra; C; 7. C and C; A; 8. C and C; C.

<u>Missing words</u>: letters; strengths; score; same.

<u>Understanding Task Fulfilment</u>: <u>Retirement homes</u>: A is a Six; B is a Nine. <u>Circle the correct answer about A</u>: 1. The young; 2. The elderly; 3. Yes, in (iii) 'good medical care' is not the same as 'around-the-clock medical care'; 4. Yes, in (vi); 5. No, see (v); 6. Yes, (vii). <u>Other differences</u>: Paragraph B has longer, more complex sentences than A. (B has 82 words in four sentences; A has 94 words in seven sentences.) There is no redundancy in B, like 'with a more and more competitive society' or 'it is well known that'. B avoids 'in addition' and 'furthermore'. B's language is neutral – no 'delicious', 'luckily', or 'really'. B uses the modals 'could' and 'might'. Reference is effective in B with 'they', 'this', 'it', 'these', and 'others'. There is an example of ellipsis: there is no subject before the verb 'opt'. B restricts discussion to reasons. Drawbacks, like the expense of retirement homes, mentioned in A, will be in a separate paragraph in B's essay.

<u>Persuasive techniques: Missing letters</u>: persuade; others; Restrict; probably; extreme; Never; vague; language; But; childish.

<u>Clichés: Missing letters</u>: 1. dogs; 2. leap; 3. playing; 4. woods.

<u>Inversion</u>: 1. Never has the time been more opportune to consider alternative energy sources. 2. Seldom are there occasions when volunteers are recognised publically. 3. Rarely do we see such convincing acting in Bollywood films. 4. Never did people even venture beyond their village.

<u>Concession</u>: Despite the expense and well-documented health problems, people continue to smoke cigarettes.

<u>An even tone is created by</u>: 1. vi; 2. i; 3. vii; 4. viii; 5. ix; 6. v.

<u>The tone is strange/perfect</u>: 1. iv, vii; 2. ix; 3. viii; 4. ✓; 5. vi; 6. viii; 7. ✓.

<u>Improved sentences</u>:

Eg. Although many people support road-widening, I believe it has significant disadvantages.

1. I think overpopulation presents a grave threat. Therefore reducing human numbers is essential.

2. While higher income is assured, the thought of dealing with patients' mouths is rather unappealing.

3. It is deeply disturbing to many people that soon there will be eight billion people on Earth. One solution to prevent war and famine would be for international laws to be passed that limit family size, especially in places like the Gulf, where the number of births per female is high.

4. *(The tone is perfect.)*

5. There is the possibility that students consider Dentistry takes longer to study than Accountancy or Marketing.

6. Despite opposition to video games, their harm has not clearly been established. I believe they provide entertainment to millions of people.

7. *(The tone is perfect.)*

<u>The introduction in Task 2</u>: The writer's position is still unclear, and 40% of the essay has been wasted in the introduction.

<u>Model introduction</u>: *In this essay, I shall discuss having the Internet at home. In my opinion, its benefits far outweigh its drawbacks.*

<u>Introduction about art, craft and music at school</u>: 1. Yes; 2. Yes; 3. No; 4. No.

<u>Five introductions</u>: A = 3rd, comment ii; B = 1st, comment iv; C = 5th, comment iii; D = 2nd, comment i; E = 4th, comment v.

<u>Topic and Supporting sentences in Writing Task 2</u>: <u>Missing words</u>: relevant; main; opens; developed; examples.

<u>Missing topic sentences – Art, craft and music at school</u>: 2, eg, 5, 3, 4, 1, 6.

Drawing, painting, film, design, woodwork, metalwork, and all kinds of music from classical to hip hop (eg) <u>are part of a universal cultural heritage</u>. Learning a song from another country, possibly in another language, introduces children to something beautiful and mysterious. It reminds us that we are all part of one human family.

Indeed, (1) <u>national identity is formed not only through momentous events, but also through music and art</u>. How often have you heard a tune on the radio and nearly cried because it has reminded you of your country?

However, in my opinion, the greatest value of teaching these subjects is that (2) they develop lateral thinking, which is extremely useful for a tertiary student, a researcher, or even an employee. Lateral thinking is when a person solves a problem by looking at it from different angles. Significantly, art and music activate different parts of the brain from language or chemistry, so they encourage problem-solving.

Activities like building a theatre set or playing in an orchestra (3) develop discipline and teamwork, also useful in later life. These more complex skills are more easily learnt at secondary school.

(4) Through art, craft and music, students learn to relax, which will improve their capacity for study.

Today the world is full of products; it is nice to be able to appreciate good design, or to decorate one's own home tastefully after (5) exposure to different aesthetics at school.

(6) A talented few might even pursue careers as artists or musicians as a result of studies at school. Since these continued to secondary level, students received a solid foundation.

The conclusion in Task 2: Essay 1 = a, b, e; Essay 2 = c, f, i; Essay 3 = d, g, h.

Understanding C and C: Missing words: 1. topic; 2. But; 3. slow down; last; avoid; 4. instead; 5. refer.

Identifying paragraphs: 2nd paragraph: between 'seven or eight' and 'Supporters'; 3rd paragraph: between 'study at all' and 'However'; final paragraph: between 'parents' prestige' and 'In my view'.

C and C in a Task 2 model: Eg. This essay is coherent because there is a logical order, and each paragraph contains a clear idea. 1. If the essay were cut up into sentences, it would be easy to put back together again. 2. It is also cohesive. For linking, the writer uses conjunctions, referents, clear punctuation, and sophisticated sentence structure to knit the essay together. 3. Note: there are no words or phrases like 'firstly', 'in addition', or 'in conclusion' to start sentences. 4. A writer who is a Seven or above can avoid such mechanical items.

If You Want a Seven: Missing words: Since; meantime; also; who; many; This; well; From; her; they; and; this.

Linkers: Using correct linkers: 1. and; moreover; 2. Although; view; 3. certainly; 4. however; 5. While; except for; 6. whether; since.

A question of style: 1. Known reserves of oil rose by 6.6 billion barrels in 2010 because major discoveries were made in Brazil, India, and Russia. 2. More than 50% of the world's oil reserves are in the Middle East. Therefore / As a result, this region has become important politically. 3. If China pumps out oil at its current rate, its reserves will be exhausted within ten years. / Its reserves will be exhausted within ten years if China pumps out oil at its current rate. // Since / As China does not have much oil, its reserves will be exhausted within ten years. 4. Although Saudi Arabia pumped more oil in 2010 than Venezuela, it has one third the reserves of Venezuela. (The subject is Saudi Arabia, so 'it' refers back to Saudi Arabia.) // Although Saudi Arabia pumped more oil in 2010 than Venezuela, Venezuela has three times the reserves of Saudi. 5. Nigeria and Canada each pumped out about 40 billion barrels in 2010. However, Nigeria has 42.4 years' worth of reserves; Canada has only 26.3.

If you want a Seven: paragraphs B and C.

Punctuation:

Dear Mr Brown,

My name is Joseph Denka, and I am taking a six-week intensive course at the School of Commerce. My company is paying for my tuition, and I am using my summer vacation to study. It is expected I will pass an international actuarial exam as a result, and be transferred abroad. Therefore, it is rather important to me that I am able to study in the best environment.

I am staying in West Hostel on campus. While my room is pleasant and the facilities are very good, the hostel is extremely noisy. When I organised my accommodation, I was assured I would be staying only with post-graduate or intensive-course students. However, most of the people in this hostel are doing summer-school courses due to academic failure, and they are all under 25. It seems to me they are enjoying one long party: certainly no one observes lights out or turns down music despite being asked to.

I wonder if I may be moved to a hostel which is more conducive to serious study, or I may use the remainder of my accommodation fee to go towards payment for a hotel.

I look forward to hearing from you.

Yours sincerely,
Joseph Denka (197 words)

If you want a Seven: Missing words: adjective; proper; joined; seasons; end; always; joined; comma; Unnecessary; apostrophe; twelve; example; separate; clause; phrase.

Handwriting: 1. T/True; 2. NG/Not Given; 3. NG/Not Given; 4. T/True; 5. F/False; 6. F/False; 7. F/False; 8. F/False; 9. T/True; 10. NG/Not Given.

Understanding Vocabulary in Task 2: A is a Five; B is a Six.

Here is an IELTS Nine answer:

People enjoy shopping malls because the vast supermarkets provide all the necessities, and discounts are frequently offered. Malls are clean and air-conditioned. When I lived in Krakow, Poland, I far preferred shopping at the mall to trudging through the cold, snowy, slippery streets.

Here is the second Nine's answer:

In my view, the behaviour of drivers is mostly to blame for accidents. Certainly, some may be inexperienced, and unsure how to handle problems, but a large number go on the road in a state unfit to drive – drunk, drugged, or exhausted. They speed, disobey other road rules, and appear not to notice any other road-user. Imposing high fines and taking licences away from repeat offenders do influence behaviour to some extent.

<u>Describing graphs and charts</u>: <u>Two currencies</u>: 1. T; 2. F (only the AUD reached one USD); 3. T; 4. T; 5. F (the NZD is more volatile because it has risen less smoothly).

<u>Collocation</u>: **Adjective + noun**: the strongest currency // the weakest currency. **Adverbs about equality**: They were on par with the dollar / They were worth the same. Time expressions: the entire time // over the period. **Downward trend**: It declined considerably. / It experienced a fall. / It fell from its peak. / It plummeted to… / Its lowest point was… **Stability**: It plateaued at… / It remained fairly stable. / It fluctuated at around… **Upward trend**: It strengthened slightly. / It tripled in value. / It rose dramatically. / It peaked at…

<u>Changes</u>: (1) *an insignificant change* (2) *a minor change* (3) *a major change* (4) *a marked change* (5) *a dramatic change* (6) *a complete change*

<u>True information from the graph</u>: 1. Overall, sales *~~fell~~ / fluctuated*. 2. They reached a peak in *July / ~~August~~*. 3. In August, sales fell to the lowest point of *~~1000~~ / 2000*. 4. Between September and October there was a *modest / ~~rapid~~* decline.

<u>Cook Islanders</u>: 5. A reasonable number of Cook Islanders play sport. 6. A small minority of Cook Islanders hold post-graduate qualifications. 7. The vast majority of Cook Islanders live in New Zealand.

<u>Bird numbers in Wollai Park</u>: decline; marked; maintained; experienced; around; plunged; low; made; survive; at.

<u>Approximate language</u>: <u>Advice</u>: 150; data; kinds; add; subcategories; in; approximate.

<u>Approximate language</u>: roughly; mainly; similar; about; almost; just over; a fraction of; perhaps; approximately.

<u>Nominalisation</u>: <u>Missing headings</u>: 1. v; 2. iii; 3. i; 4. iv; 5. ii.

<u>Two topics</u>: 1. HS; 2. LE; 3. LE; 4. HS; 5. LE.

<u>Understanding Grammar</u>: A is a Five; B is a Four.

<u>Here is an IELTS Nine answer</u>: *This table and map show the involvement of seventeen countries in Antarctica. The vast majority of them have scientific bases there, and seven have territorial claims. With the exception of four countries, which did so in the 1980s, all the countries signed the Antarctic Treaty in either 1960 or 1961.*

1. b; 2. b; 3. a; 4. a (There is no comma after 'who' because this is a defining relative clause. We are only talking about / We have defined one group of older readers; there is probably another group of readers who enjoy reading about celebrities.); 5. b; 6. a; 7. b; 8. a; 9. a; 10. a.

<u>Grammar and Vocabulary Test 1</u>:

While the total size of the property and the building remains the same, the configuration and use of space, both internal and external, are substantially different.

With regard to the outdoors, after remodelling, the yard is still a rectangle, but its length is longer than its width. There is no parking allowed, and since there is now an indoor café, there are tables and chairs outside. There are also plants, and the possibility of exhibitions being held in the yard.

Inside, after remodelling, the centre is rectangular rather than L-shaped. There are six spaces instead of five, the largest of which – Gallery 2 and the Art Studio – have maintained their original size and location. Gallery 2 is roughly the middle third of the building, with the Art Studio, now for rent, occupying one corner.

Gallery 1 and the toilets still exist, in slightly smaller form and different locations. The kitchen has disappeared altogether; there is now a café between Gallery 1 and the toilets.

The function of one space has altered considerably: what was once Gallery 1 is now a recording studio, also for rent, meaning the name of the centre has been changed accordingly. (*195 words*)

<u>Grammar and Vocabulary Test 2</u>:

Dear Khuloud and Abdulwahid,

I'm writing to thank you for the lovely time I had staying in your gorgeous house in Bab Touma while I was studying Arabic last summer.

As you know, I'd never been to the Middle East when I arrived in Damascus, and I was thrilled to find so many wonderful people and amazing archaeological sites. I really had no idea about Syria's rich heritage. Almost all the stereotypes we have in Norway of Syria were soon proven wrong. I met many people whose worldview is pretty much the same as my own. I've certainly told everyone back home about the fascinating and generous community of Bab Touma.

My most memorable experience was celebrating Easter with you – that incredible Palm Sunday parade and those bonfires, as well as the Easter Mass in four languages. I'm so grateful you shared those things with me.

Please accept a small token of my gratitude, enclosed, and remember, if you're ever in Oslo, I'd be delighted to put you up, and show you around.

Your friend,
Hege (*176 words*)

<u>Grammar and Vocabulary Test 3</u>: *See answer for Task 1 of GT Writing Taster Test on page 387.*

<u>GT Task 1 Formal letters</u>: 1. I can hardly believe that Michael is getting married. 2. My sister has invited quite a few guests to her party. I would like some information on spring semester courses. 3. I expect you will be tired on arrival. 4. I need not describe all the details now. 5. The changes won't affect many people. 6. Yours sincerely, Abdulwahab Alkurdi.

<u>Model GT Task 1 Formal request</u>: Dear Mr Mukherjee,

My name is Ashoke Gupta. My family and I own flat 26B in the Forest Lake Complex. We have been living here for twelve years.

I am writing to you with regard to an extension I would like to make to my flat now that we have three children. I intend to add three square metres to the western side of my ground floor, and create a terrace on the roof of this addition. At present, there is a service lane on the western side, which is virtually unused. My addition would not restrict access to this lane, nor would it cause my neighbours to lose any light as there is already a high wall around our complex which darkens this aspect.

I would like to begin work on this addition as soon as possible. I hope the body corporate will agree to my plan.

I look forward to hearing from you.

Yours sincerely,
Mr Ashoke Gupta. (*160 words*)

<u>Model GT Task 1 Formal complaint</u>: Dear Sir,

My name is Mrs Penny Wu. *I have been a resident of* Smithfield Avenue, Coogee, for several years.

I am writing to you *in reference to* the changed parking conditions in Coogee that *came into effect from* the first of October last year. *I believe these are an inconvenience to residents, and should be reconsidered.*

In the past, I was always able to park my car on the street outside my house without any *difficulty*. When metered parking *was introduced to* my suburb, particularly near the beach, some visitors started parking their vehicles further away from the beach *in order to avoid payment*. My street *appears to be* the perfect place for these people: it is not too far from Coogee Beach, and the parking is still free. Between October and December, I occasionally found it hard to park, but when summer finally *arrived*, there were two days a week when I *was forced to* park hundreds of metres away from my home. On public holidays, I *resorted to* metered parking myself.

I understand the local council *hopes to benefit financially* from metered parking, or perhaps to encourage people to use public transport. Nevertheless, residents like myself are inconvenienced by this system. I suggest either residents be allowed to park free in metered zones which *extend a greater distance* or metering cover a smaller area, and ticket prices be raised. *Additional* bus services would also reduce congestion.

I look forward to hearing from you.

Yours faithfully,
Mrs Penny Wu

<u>Model GT Task 1 Formal offer</u>: Dear Sir,

I am writing to City Evening College **in** reference **to** an advertisement I saw in *The Echo* **on** July 12th **for** language teachers **at** your college.

I am interested **in** teaching Korean and Korean Cookery. I have seen that your guide **for** last term does not include these courses, but I understand there are now large numbers **of** second- and third-generation Koreans living in this part **of** the city who may be keen to learn more about their language and culture.

I have a Bachelor of Science degree and a teaching diploma. I hold special qualifications **in** language teaching and cookery. I was a science teacher in Korea, but moved **to** Los Angeles **in** 2002. There, I taught Korean **for** Beginners and Korean Cookery **at** two community colleges. The language course assumed students had no prior knowledge **of** Korean. It gave them simple everyday language, as well as recognition of the alphabet. The cookery course focused **on** easy meal preparation and the art **of** pickling, or *kim chi*.

In Vancouver, I could teach the same courses as previously, or we could devise new ones, depending **on** what the college considered its market to be.

I look forward **to** hearing **from** you.

Yours faithfully,
Mrs Won-Kyong Stevenson (*203 words*)

Model GT Task 1 Semi-formal view: Line #: 4. *M*; dividing **it** in; sold **up** at; 5. *OK*; 6. *M*; barriers **do** little 7. *M*; lanes **is** a; 8. *OK*; 9. *NN*; be **returned** back 10. *NN*; when **the** people; 11. *M*; should **be** developing; 12. *NN*; far **distance** from; 13. *NN*; would ~~very~~ support; 14. *M*; tramway **if** any; 15. *M*; space **that / which** will; 16. *OK*; 17. *M*; imagine **so**, but; 18. *OK*; 19. *NN*; can ~~to~~ promote; 20. *M*; publicise **the** campaign.

Writing Taster Tests: Academic Task 1:

Student enrolments at the University of Westchester changed greatly over a period of 150 years.

The most noticeable changes were the number of students and the kind of students. From 1875-1899, when data was first collected, there were only one thousand male students. By 2024, there will be a total of 51,000 students, and these are in four categories: male, female, mature-aged, and international students.

The growth rate of all four groups was dramatic and constant, with the single exception of male students, whose enrolments dropped slightly in the last period. There were no international students before 1950, yet it is predicted they will reach 12,000 by 2024, representing just over a quarter of all students. Women and students over the age of 25 did not enrol at Westchester University until 1900. In the period 2000-2024, the former became the largest student group at 15,000; the latter were the smallest group at 10,000. (*153 words*)

Academic and GT Task 2

For each human being, there are different stages of life, experienced in different ways. In my view, for men the most challenging stage is young adulthood, whereas for women it is middle age. Men are more affected by the acquisition of money and status, which is best done as a young person, while women are more susceptible to the loss of physical beauty, which happens after the age of 30. In many cultures, there is pressure on men to succeed – to drive the latest model car, to own their own home, to have sufficient money to raise a family. This means studying and working hard, and choosing careers and friends carefully. If a man fails to establish his wealth and social status young, he is left behind. It is well known that suicides among men are highest when they are under 30. Also, the high incidence of drinking and drug use, especially in Anglo-Celtic culture, shows that young males are vulnerable. Women are less likely to pursue challenging careers or to focus on becoming rich, but if they do not marry, or if they are separated or divorced, then their lives are particularly difficult from middle age onwards. Financially and socially they become almost invisible in society.

What are the solutions? Strong familial relationships and strong communities mean that men who fail have somewhere to go, and help to find. Or, men do not fail in the first place because they have support. Of course, in an age when so many people move for work or are refugees, this is hard to achieve. Education for life is another possibility. That is: school education that prepares people not just academically but also psychologically or philosophically for life's changes. If both men and women seek further qualifications as they age, they increase the likelihood of continued employment when jobs are lost or become extremely competitive. Lastly, believing in life, in all its splendour, and not merely focusing on money, status, or looks will make change easier to accept for both men and women. (*343 words*)

GT Task 1

To the Editor,

My name is Warawan Chattaporn – a resident of Burtonville for two years. My family moved here due to its affordability and proximity to the city. We also enjoy several small parks in which our sons and their friends play. One of these parks is Davis Park, on Bellingham Street. It is not large, but it is well-used, clean, and safe.

Recently, I learnt that Burtonville Council has decided to sell this public amenity for development. The land has already been rezoned residential, so I assume as many dwellings as possible – perhaps even fifty apartments – could be built here.

While I am not a lawyer, and do not know by which legal process this land could be sold, as a resident, I was neither informed nor consulted about it. All my neighbours say the same thing. We have petitioned the council, and I hope this letter reaches a wider public.

Our website, SaveDavisPark.com, lists a number of protest activities in which we hope your readers may join us.

Too few green and tranquil public spaces remain in this over-developed city. Save Davis Park before it is too late.

Warawan Chattaporn (*187 words*)

Writing – Putting it all together: Strategies for improvement: 1 = C; 2 = A; 3 = B.

Chapter 5. IELTS Speaking

<u>What happens in the Speaking test</u>: 1. 25; 2. unfriendly; 3. personal; 4. two; 5. abstract; 6. functions; 7. change; 8. followed; 9. judge; 10. will.

<u>How is the Speaking test is marked</u>? 1. Vocabulary; 2. Fluency and Coherence; 3. Fluency and Coherence; 4. Grammar; 5. Pronunciation; 6. Grammar; 7. Vocabulary

<u>Detailed information about the criteria</u>: <u>Missing words</u>: hesitation, overuse; modal, complex; precise, style; own, chunking

<u>Fluency and Coherence</u>: <u>The main features</u>: 1. down; 2. radio; 3. connected; 4. rhythm; 5. groups; 6. linking; 7. going; 8. pauses.

1. iii; 2. i; 3. iv; 4. v; 5. ii.

C: 'The maths because I didn't do a lot of maths at school. Also, I've got a part-time job, so I don't have a lot of time to study.'

D: *The candidate doesn't answer the question, which is about difficulty. She talks about what's nice or easy. Remember: Answer the question even if it's not true.* 'The hospital's <u>far</u> from my home, and the doctors <u>aren't</u> so nice. Although I like to make people happy and healthy, sometimes the patients cause problems.' *Or:* 'Although the hospital's close to my home and the doctors are really nice, I work quite long hours, and I'm often tired at the end of a shift.'

<u>Examiner's report</u>: 1. chatting; 2. Barbie; 3. memorised; 4. contradicts; 5. targeted advertising; 6. irrelevant; 7. discourse markers; 8. fillers; 9. contractions; 10. Five.

1. F; 2. NG; 3. F; 4. T; 5. T; 6. T.

<u>Contractions</u>: 1. she's; 2. I've; 3. they've; 4. he'll; 5. I'd; 6. it'd; 7. haven't; 8. don't; 9. won't; 10. wouldn't

Examiner	First of all, I'd like to ask you a few questions about yourself. At the moment, are you working or studying?
Candidate	I'm a student.
Examiner	Where are you studying?
Candidate	At a college. (*What's its name? Where is it?*)
Examiner	Why did you choose this college?
Candidate	I didn't. (*So, who did?*)
Examiner	What do you like about your college?
Candidate	I have some new friends. ('<u>I've made</u> some new friends' is better.)
Examiner	Do many people from your country choose the same subject that you're studying?
Candidate	Yes.
Examiner	Why?
Candidate	I have no idea. (*Do you really want a Five?*)
Examiner	Now I'd like to talk about music. Do you like music?
Candidate	Yes, I do.
Examiner	Why?
Candidate	It's relaxing *and sometimes exciting. I really like dancing.*
	<u>Or</u>: It's relaxing. *I listen to my Ipod on the way to work, which makes the journey faster.*
Examiner	Did you study music at school?
Candidate	No, *I didn't.*
Examiner	Do you think every child should learn to play a musical instrument?
Candidate	No, I don't.
Examiner	Why not?
Candidate	Because not everyone's interested, *and these days children have a lot more important things to study.*

(Extended answers are shown in *italics*.)

To get a Seven you need to know the IPA.

Recordings 17-18: <u>Exact speech</u>

Examiner	Now let's talk about making things by hand. Tell me about some things you made by hand at primary school.
Candidate	I didn't make many things, but there are two I remember well. In second class, I made a lion mask for a play that we put on.

Recordings 19-20:

Candidate	Then, in sixth class, I was part of a group that made a model of an ancient city. It was pretty good. My father took us to the site where the archaeologists were working, so we could imagine what our model would be like.
Examiner	What about at secondary school?
Candidate	I don't think I made anything by hand there, unless you count paper darts that we threw at the Biology teacher.
Examiner	Hmm. What do you think are the benefits of primary-school children making things by hand?
Candidate	They learn to follow instructions. They may understand a topic better if they make a model or draw diagrams. And, they have a chance to have fun.

Recording 21: <u>Weak forms: 'the'</u>:

1. 'I listen to my iPod on the (W) way to work, which makes the (W) journey go faster.'
2. 'The (S) only thing I like about my college is the (W) friends I've made.'

Recording 22: <u>Weak forms: prepositions</u>:

1. 'Where do you come <u>from</u> (S)? // 'I'm <u>from the</u> (W) south of China.'
2. 'Zhenzhou is famous <u>for its</u> (W) tea.' (Remember: 'Famous Fritz'.)
3. 'I made a lion mask <u>for a</u> (W) play that we put on.' (Remember: 'Fra'.)
4. 'What are you looking <u>at</u> (S)?'
5. 'I'm studying <u>at a</u> (W) college in the city.'
6. 'I listen <u>to</u> (W) my Ipod on the way to (W) work.'
7. 'I'd like <u>to</u> (S) apply <u>for</u> (W) another job.' (Remember: 'Fra-nother'.)

Recording 23: <u>Strong or weak forms: 'to be'</u>:

1. 'Do you think children these days are (W) better educated than 20 years ago?
   'Yes, I think they are.' (S)
2. 'I didn't make many things, but there are (W) two I remember well.'
3. 'I was (W) part of a group that made a model of an ancient city.'
4. 'My father took us to the site where the archaeologists were (W) working.'

Recording 24: <u>Strong or weak forms: 'going to'</u>:

1. 'I'm going to (W) be a radiographer. I've done my first two years of study.'
2. 'My brother's going to organise my graduation party.' (W or S)
3. 'My sister's going to (W) have a baby in two weeks' time. I'm really excited.'
4. 'My parents are going to Europe for a holiday.' (S) This is 'going' + 'to' as a preposition. 'Europe' starts with /j/, which is a consonant sound.
5. 'My uncle who's a banker says there's going to (W) be another financial crash.'

Recording 25: <u>Chunking</u>: 1. A; 2. B; 3. B; 4. A.

Recording 26: <u>Natural or Unnatural?</u> 1. U: No contraction; no weak forms of 'from' or 'the'; 2. N; 3. U: Strange chunking – pauses in the wrong places, after 'children', 'lot', 'important'; self-correction 'childs-children'; 4. U: All said as separate words – no chunking; no word stress – could be a French speaker; 5. N; 6. N; 7. U: Hesitation: 'my-my', 'which-which'; long pauses after 'in' and 'and'. Very slow speech; 8. N.

Recording 27: 'My city's famous for its mountains.'

'In second class, I made a lion mask for a play that we put on.'

'My father took us to the site where the archaeologists were working.'

'It's the biggest city in the country with a lot of modern buildings.'

Recording 28: 'I'm from the south of China.'

'These days, children have a lot more important things to study.'

'I didn't make many things, but there are two I remember well.'

'It's my own space, which no one's allowed in except my friends and my mum.'

Recording 29: <u>Modelling longer Part 1 answers</u>: Weak forms are in **bold**.

Examiner	Now, I'd like to ask you about sport. D'you like sport?
Candidate	No, I don't really. I sometimes watch football on TV <u>with my</u> friends, <u>but</u> that's about all.
Examiner	<u>Have you</u> ever played sport?
Candidate	At school we did PE <u>and</u> basketball. I joined <u>a</u> gym <u>a</u> month ago, so I've <u>been</u> doing <u>some</u> weight training. I've also tried yoga, <u>but</u> I'm not very good.

Recording 30: **Weak forms are in bold.**

Examiner	Let's move on <u>to</u> talk about <u>the</u> sea. When <u>was the</u> last time you <u>were at the</u> sea?
Candidate	Actually, I'm living near Long Bay. I go down there almost every day.
Examiner	What <u>do</u> people like about <u>the</u> sea?
Candidate	<u>The</u> sea's got different moods. One day it's grey <u>and</u> stormy; <u>the</u> next, it's calm <u>and</u> bright blue. Perhaps people identify <u>with the</u> sea.
Examiner	What problems <u>can the</u> sea cause?
Candidate	Flooding, mostly. There've <u>been some</u> terrible tsunamis recently.

Recording 31: <u>Fluency in Speaking Part 2</u>: *Here is one possible Part 2 answer. The ten contractions are underlined. There are now six (numbered) sentences which are compound, complex, or compound-complex.*

Candidate	'<u>I'm</u> going to tell you about something I had to save money to buy. (1) <u>It's</u> a car. This car is an old VW (that/which) I bought from a classmate. (2) <u>It's</u> about fifty years old, but I love it. <u>It's</u> quite reliable, and it <u>doesn't</u> use too much gas. Plus I think the design is nice. (3) <u>It's</u> turquoise, and <u>it's</u> got a soft top, which you can roll down when <u>it's</u> a fine day.
	I went for a trip with my classmate in this car, and I loved it. (4) A few months later, he had to go back to Egypt, where he comes from, and he desperately needed some money. (5) <u>I couldn't</u> afford to buy the car, so he left it with his uncle who I paid each week until it was enough. (6) At one point, the uncle got mad, and asked for all the rest of the money, so I had to work overtime at my job as well as study full time to find the money. <u>That's</u> not easy. Anyway, it was worth it in the end. My girlfriend loves the car. In fact, I think all girls do.'

Recording 32: The woman = C, a Six. A = a Five; B = a Seven.

Recording 32: <u>Assessing candidates</u>:

Examiner	We've been talking about a favourite teacher, and now I'd like to discuss some more general questions about education. Firstly, do you think China has a good system of primary education?
Candidate	These days, yes. Everywhere primary education is available. The curriculum is balance – children learn a lot of different subject – and most of… most of children are mo-ti-va-ted. But the average class size in my city is 40 student, which I think is too big. In addition, teachers do not get a high celery, so sometimes take other job in the evening, and are tired at school or don't care.
Examiner	How well does primary education prepare students for secondary school?
Candidate	In most subject it prepares them well, but I think for girls not so well, especially maths. I mean, the teaching is fast and boys understand, but uwally girls do not. As a result, they have low marks and maybe not go to university. Also, they choose easy subject like English or history, and I think that stop them, that limit what job they can get.
Examiner	What improvements do you think could be made to primary education in China?
Candidate	As I mentioned, decreasing class size. Also… increasing pay for teachers.

Recording 33: <u>Summary</u>: 1. going; 2. long; 3. chunking; 4. groups; 5. content; 6. weak; 7. Contractions; 8. kind; 9. logical; 10. markers.

<u>Vocabulary in spoken and written English</u>: 1. F; Contractions are necessary in IELTS Speaking for chunking (good fluency); they should <u>not</u> be used in IELTS Writing. 2. T; 3. F; Phrasal verbs are more common in speaking. 4. T; 5. T; Many longer, more formal words used in writing have come from the languages Latin or Greek into English; 6. T; These words are informal speaking words. Slang like 'cool' is commonly understood, so it's acceptable. Abbreviations are only all right if common, like 'uni' for 'university'. 7. F; Short answers are sometimes required in IELTS Speaking. They are unacceptable in writing. 8. T; 9. T; 10. T; 11. F; In spoken English, it's acceptable to end a sentence with a preposition. Eg: 'Imports are something we all depend on.' In writing, this becomes *All countries are dependent on imports.*; 12. F.

<u>Collocation</u>: 1. b; 2. a; 3. b; 4. b; 5. b; 6. a; 7. a; 8. a; 9. a; 10. a.

<u>Idiomatic language</u>: 1. b; 2. a; 3. a; 4. a; 5. b; 6. b; 7. a; 8. a; 9. b; 10. b.

Common vocabulary problems in Speaking: Low-level mistakes (i): 1. tore; upset/embarrassed; 2. had; thrilled; 3. turns off; 4. tall; cook; 5. go; 6. the education system; improved; 7. get along.

Low-level mistakes (ii): 8. below; poverty; 9. 's got; courtyard; also; undercover; 10. memorable; recall/remember; 11. a little over-weight; 12. 500,000; a state called Uttar Pradesh.

6+ mistakes (i): 1. chance/opportunity; 2. hazardous; 3. put down; run over; 4. touristy; 5. tacky; 6. broke/split up; young; live; different.

6+ mistakes (ii): 7. bottom; 8. extinction; 9. handwriting; illegible; 10. (auto)biographies; inspiring; 11. insidious; pester/pressure/hassle; 12. large male breasts; tight swimming costumes.

Verb forms: 1. b; 2. a; 3. b; 4. a; 5. c; 6. c; 7. b; 8. a; 9. c; 10. c.

Functions: A = vi and vii; B = iii; C = i; D = ii or v; E = x; 1 = E; 2 = D; 3 = C; 4 = A; 5 = B.

Delaying tactics: dangerous; fluency. The one-minute preparation time before Part 2: topic; notes; level; anything.

Comparing the vocabulary and grammar of six Speaking candidates: 1. A; iv; 2. E; ii; 3. D; vi; 4. F; v; 5. C; i; 6. B; iii.

Vocabulary with similar meaning:

I don't agree	→	I do not believe
You see,	→	(a filler)
kind of	→	(a filler)
kids at school	→	school children
've got (have got)	→	have
lots of	→	a considerable number of
last	→	final
pretty	→	particularly
full on (common slang)	→	intense
go on about	→	maintain
not enough serious stuff	→	insufficient academic material
like	→	in relation to
Maths (abbreviation)	→	Mathematics
uni (abbreviation)	→	university
isn't what it used to be	→	is lower than in the past
Well,	→	(a filler)
a massive problem here	→	a grave concern in this country
spend (time) on	→	devote (time) to
Only,	→	(a filler)
it's better for	→	a more appropriate way
mums and dads	→	parents
get	→	(The whole sentence is rewritten.)
meet half way	→	compromise
the dos and don'ts of (idiom)	→	the dangers of

Model answer: *Teaching driving at school*

I fully support the idea of driving being taught at school. In order to accommodate it as a subject, some other things could be removed from the curriculum. After all, is the analysis of twentieth-century poetry more useful to a seventeen-year-old than the avoidance of car accidents?

While some children may be fortunate enough to be taught to drive by relatives, or to be given professional driving lessons, others are unable to afford this. Therefore, schools should assume this responsibility.

Moreover, if every school-leaver – both male and female – had a driver's licence, not only would this raise their confidence, but also assist them in finding employment.

Recording 35: <u>Converting spoken English into written English</u>

1   <u>Contractions</u>: 'I've', 'should've', 'can't', 'it's' etc

2   <u>Phrasal verbs</u>: 'go on', 'come back'

3   <u>Informal vocabulary</u>: 'kind of', 'dump', 'kids', 'stuff', 'cute' etc

4   <u>Exaggerated / emotive language</u> (less neutral than in the writing – although the writing is persuasive): 'about a million photos', 'the kids bawled their eyes out'

5   <u>A highly personal example from the writer's **neighbour**</u>

6   <u>Some irrelevant details</u> – that Kathmandu is 'a dump'; that her neighbour works for an insurance company.

7   <u>The order isn't as **logical** as in the writing.</u>

Disruptive and *self-indulgent* = 2 missing adjectives.

Recording 36: <u>Voluntourism</u>: 'Next year, I'm gonna do a short course in how to teach English before heading off to Nepal for a month. There's a great package – part of this new thing called voluntourism – where you're taken trekking for a fortnight, then you teach at an orphanage in Kathmandu. I reckon this is perfect for me because it's short and sweet. I mean, if I had to volunteer for longer, I mightn't be able to afford it. With the English course behind me, I'll do a decent job. Of course, I'm not a qualified teacher, but I'll make up for that in enthusiasm.

I've thought about the fact that just one week there might disrupt the kids, but if I like what I see, I might go back. I'm sure I'll tell my friends and family about them, and that could lead to sponsorship in the future.

I'm sure living at the orphanage will deepen my understanding of Nepal, which wouldn't happen if I just stayed at a hotel. I like the idea of giving my money to a charity as well. I think learning and lending a helping hand are as important as having a good time, these days, when we're all global citizens.'

<u>Model answer</u>: *The benefits of voluntourism*

Voluntourism is a recent trend in tourism where people holiday and then volunteer for a short time. I believe this is a good way to travel because the volunteer deepens his or her understanding of a culture while assisting locals. One voluntourism package, in Nepal, offers a two-week trek followed by a week-long teaching placement in an orphanage in Kathmandu.

Some people have reservations about the quality of teaching that a volunteer might provide, but many volunteers prepare by doing short courses before they leave home, or they transfer skills they already have. It is likely their enthusiasm compensates for their lack of qualifications. Other people maintain that one week is insufficient time to benefit the orphans. However, I consider this is to be an affordable taster experience: many serious people return for longer stints, or contribute financially after they have left. The degree of disruption to the children need not be great if they are fully aware of what is happening.

Voluntourists also prefer that their money go towards charities than to hotel chains. Their live-in experience adds to their cultural sensitivity.

In my view, travel is no longer just about having a good time, but also about taking global responsibility. (202 words)

<u>Summary</u>: different; variety; short; emotive.

<u>Pronunciation</u>: <u>First language interference</u>: 1. T; 2. F; 3. NG; 4. T; 5. F.

Recording 37: <u>Consonant sounds</u>: 1. A; cheese; 2. A; when; 3. B; Thursday; 4. B; shopping; 5. A; usually; 6. B; singer; 7. A; yesterday; 8. A; 9. B.

<u>Vowel sounds</u>: 1. B; feelings; 2. B; red; 3. A; work; 4. A; law; 5. B; company; 6. A; heart; 7. A; pay; 8. B; fair; 9. B; don't and smokers; 10. A; employers.

<u>Single-syllable words that are hard to say</u>: 1. blocked; 2. called; 3. claimed; 4. close; 5. clothes; 6. cold; 7. dreams; 8. flocked; 9. floods; 10. quite; 11. scratched; 12. slipped; 13. splashed; 14. stressed; 15. stretched.

<u>Word stress for countries</u>:

No word stress because only one syllable	Oo	Ooo	oO	oOo
France, Spain	China, Jordan, Poland	Canada, Italy, Pakistan, Vietnam	Brazil, Japan, Ukraine	Korea, Morocco, New Zealand

oOoo	ooO	ooOo
Australia, Cambodia, South Africa	Cameroon	Argentina, Indonesia

Recordings 43-5: <u>Word stress patterns</u>:

Oo	Ooo	Oooo	oO	oOo	oOoo
conference, natural, quiet, restaurant	Arabic, carrier, fashionable, festival, fortunate, grandmother, interesting, organised, peacekeeper, studying, teenager, temperature, various	motivated, supermarket	Chinese, hotel, mature, obese, prefer, pronounced, report, succeed, success, unique	achievement, career, computer, illegal, romantic,	convenient, disorganised, economy, obesity, unfortunate

	ooO		ooOo		ooOoo	oooOo
	impolite, volunteer		accidental, disadvantage, individual, motivation, politician		opportunity	enthusiastic, pronunciation

Recording 46: <u>Sentence stress</u>:

Examiner	What do you think is the **best** part of the **weekend**?
Candidate	**Sunday afternoon** because I'm at **home relaxing**. It's a **custom** in **our family** to have friends and relatives over for a **big lunch**.
Examiner	Do you think weekends are **long enough**?
Candidate	Yes, **I do**. I think **work** is the most important part of a person's **life**, and it's **immature** to want holidays all the time.

<u>Pitch and Intonation</u>: 1. important; 2. emotion; 3. New Zealand; 4. unfinished; 5. song; 6. bored; 7. Fall; 8. enthusiasm.

Recording 47: <u>Identifying good and bad pronunciation</u>: 1. B; 2. C; 3. B.

Recording 49: <u>If you want a Seven</u>:

Candidate	Phonemes	Word stress	Sentence stress	Intonation	Chunking and Rhythm
2A	✗ 'Would', 'have', 'walking', 'work', and 'singing' are mispronounced. 'Would', 'to', and 'when' should be weak.	Acceptable	✗ Almost *every* word is given equal stress	✗ This is too up and down.	✗ All words are said separately.
2B	*Perfect*	Acceptable	✗ Most words are given equal stress.	Acceptable	✗ All words are said separately.

<u>Pronunciation in Speaking Part 2</u>: i. 60; ii. two; iii. 350; iv. at the end; v. a personal experience.

<u>Pronunciation bands</u>: 7, 8, 5, 6.

Recording 52: <u>Summary</u>: 1. hard; 2. clusters; 3. ends; 4. syllable; 5. stress; 6. speech; 7. unnatural; 8. accent.

Recording 53: <u>Assessing Candidates</u>: 1. D; 2. C; 3. A; 4. B. Strategies for improvement: B, A, C, D.

<u>Advice from an Examiner</u>: 1, 6, 7, 9, 12.

Chapter 6. IELTS Spelling

1. few, all, complex; 2. Six, twice, affect; 3. cause, sound, instead; 4. frequent, hard, sentence.

Writing Task 1 models: The life **cycle** of frogs

Frogs live part of **their** lives in the water, and part of their lives out of it.

After **mating** in spring, a female frog lays more **than** 2000 eggs in water, usually in a small pond. These eggs are **covered** with jelly for food and protection; they float near the surface of the water. **Before** the end of three weeks, tadpoles hatch from the eggs. They look like **tiny** fish with **tails** for swimming. Also like fish, they have gills, **which** extract oxygen from water so the tadpoles can **breathe**. Over the next three months, the **creatures develop** front legs, back legs, and lungs; their tails shrink. Finally, they look like frogs. They are called froglets **until** they reach **maturity**, which takes three years. Froglets spend most of their time in the water, but **gradually** start to live on land. A frog can live up to ten years although in the wild their lives are usually short as they have **numerous** enemies.

GT Writing Task 1

Dear Nadia,

I'm **writing** to congratulate your daughter on **winning** a scholarship to the **University** of Sydney next year. Well done!

As you know, I've been living in this **beautiful** city for the past **fourteen** years, and there are a few things I'd like to tell Ksenia.

Firstly, the **cost** of living is high, and **accommodation** is particularly expensive. It's likely Ksenia will need a part-time job just to **survive**. Secondly, the city is safer than St Petersburg, but there are some **areas** to avoid after dark. I'll point those out when she arrives. This is a multi-cultural city, so **initially** Ksenia may be surprised by all the nationalities here, but she'll soon find that everyone gets along. The **climate** is **wonderful** although summer is **too** hot – over 40 in February, and **extremely** humid. Ksenia won't need to bring her winter **gear** since it never snows in Sydney. Winter nights can be cool, but mainly **because** houses don't have **decent** heating.

In fact, I don't think Ksenia needs to bring anything **special** with her – everything is **available** here.

I'm really **excited** about seeing Ksenia soon.

Your friend, Luda

GT Writing Task 2

In this essay I would like to **discuss** the advantages and disadvantages of a child learning a musical **instrument**. In general, I consider this not to be a terribly **useful** skill.

Increasing numbers of parents in my country are **encouraging** their children to learn musical instruments: the piano, **guitar**, and clarinet are popular. A major reason for this is the parents' desire to seem wealthy enough to do so as **tuition** is expensive, and the instruments **themselves** are also costly. A secondary reason might be that parents hope to keep their children out of trouble by **filling** their **spare** time with musical activities. Lastly, the pleasure the children **receive** from accomplishment and from learning another language – for music is a language – might **relax** them, and assist them with other pursuits later in life.

However, the **benefit** for the child learning the instrument might be slight. It could be a cause of **anxiety** to the learner that he or she is actually neither talented nor able to work hard at the instrument. Perhaps the child does not like the teacher, but is afraid to say so, **aware** of the money his or her parents are spending. It might be a **burden** that while others are playing with one another or **enjoying** free time alone, this child is **forced** to practise or attend classes. In an ever-more **competitive** world, very few people make a living as professional musicians, and those that do probably weren't **compelled** by their parents to learn an instrument, but took it up **spontaneously** themselves. (257 words)

Recordings 54-61

/iː/			
Oo	**Ooo**	**oO**	**oOo**
decent, sequence, skiing	previous	belief, disease, obese, routine	achievement

/ɪ/			
Oo	**Ooo**	**oO**	**oOo**
women, written	discipline, typical, vitamin	fulfil	religion, specific

/uː/			
Oo	**Ooo**	**oO**	**ooOoo**
losing, truly	beautiful	pursue	opportunity

/e/			
Oo	**Ooo**	**oOoo**	
decade, pleasant, schedule	exercise, medicine, negative, recipe	development	

/ɔː/			
Oo	**Ooo**	**oOo**	**oOoo**
quarter	organise (US organize)	exhausted	co-ordinate, unfortunate

/æː/			
Oo	**Ooo**	**oOo**	**ooOoo**
planning	analyse (US analyze), practical, strategy	dynamic,	nationality

/aː/			
oO	**Ooo**	**oOo**	
guitar	architect	departure	

/ɒ/			
Oo	**oO**	**oOoo**	**ooOoo**
promise, toxic, wallet	across	apologise (US apologize)	cosmopolitan

/eɪ/			
Oo	**oOo**	**ooOo**	**oooOo**
daily, paying, safety, spacious	behaviour	advantageous	congratulations

/ɔɪ/			
Oo	**Ooo**	**oOo**	
noisy	loyalty, poisonous	employer	

/aɪ/			
Oo	**Ooo**	**oO**	**oOoo**
trying	library, primary	decide	anxiety, reliable, variety

/ɪə/			
oOoo		**ooO**	
ideally		interfere, volunteer	

/eə/			
Oo	**Ooo**	**oO**	**oOoo**
careless, rarely	area, various	aware, repair	librarian

/əʊ/			
Oo	**oO**	**oOo**	
showing, social	although	exposure, proposal	

/aʊ/	
oO	oOo
amount, pronounce	accountant, allowance

/aɪə/				
Oo	Ooo	Oooo	oOo	oOoo
fire, prior, via	wireless	hierarchy	admire, inspire, supplier	entirely, enquiry / inquiry, inspiring

Unstressed syllables as /ə/or /ɪ/		
Oo	oO	Ooo
climate, desert, donor, driver, local	advise, event, offend, review, support, survive	opposite

Recording 62: <u>If you want a Seven</u>: 1. illiterate; 2. initiative; 3. privilege; 4. enthusiastic; 5. community; 6. athletes; 7. emphasis; 8. immense; 9. intense; 10. reputable; 11. appalling; 12. foresight; 13. composite; 14. optimism; 15. persevere.

Recording 63: <u>Single-syllable words often misspelt</u>: Eg. through; 1. lose; 2. length; 3. meant; 4. caught; 5. law; 6. does; 7. raise; 8. flair; 9. scarce; 10. drought.

<u>The length of vowel sounds and spelling</u>: Eg. *writing*, /aɪ/, diphthong, therefore single *t*; 1. *waiting*, /eɪ/, diphthong, therefore single *t*; 2. *hoping*, /əʊ/, diphthong, therefore single *p*; 3. *feeling*, /iː/, long vowel, therefore single *l*; 4. *fitting*, /ɪ/, short vowel, therefore double *t*; 5. *wedding*, /e/, short vowel, therefore double *d*; 6. *matting*, /æ/, short vowel, therefore double *t*; 7. *unplanned*, /æ/, short vowel, therefore double *n*.

If a <u>*word*</u> has a <u>*long*</u> vowel sound, like /iː/, in *seating*, or a diphthong, like /aɪ/ in *riding*, then it usually has a <u>single</u> consonant. If a word has a short <u>*vowel*</u>, like /ɒ/ in *shopped*, then it has a <u>double</u> consonant.

Recording 64: <u>Words with the letters *dg, g, gg,* or *j*</u>:

/dʒ/	/g/	/ʒ/
exaggerate, garage, gender, gym, January, knowledge, majority, marriage, prejudice, reject, suggest, tragic	against, aggressive, beggar, ghost, govern, guarantee	beige, mirage (The second 'g' in 'garage' can also be said /ʒ/.)
+	+	
judge, village	girl	

<u>/k/-sounding words</u>: accustomed, ache, authentic, career, chemistry, coffee, fluctuate, panicking (panic n), psychological, reckless, shocking, South Korea, stomach.

<u>/f/-sounding words</u>: affectionate, alphabet, confuse, emphasis, enough, fatal, fossil fuel, finance, graph, official, philosophy, telephone, phenomenon, photographer, prefer, refugee, rough, traffic.

<u>/ʃ/-sounding words</u>: ashamed, chic, emotion, fashion, initially, machine, mission, potential, rush hour, shopaholic, social, vicious.

<u>The order of letters</u>: 1. two; 2. true; 3. exist; 4. solve; 5. quite; 6. modern; 7. instead; 8. firstly, abroad; 9. hundred, protein; 10. percent, preservative.

<u>Missing letters</u>: 1. before; 2. opposite; 3. therefore; 4. temperature; 5. proportion; 6. studying; 7. quarter, favourite (US favorite); 8. opinion, convenient.

Recording 65: <u>Silent letters</u>: calm, castle, climber, cupboard, Christmas, doubt, fascinated, half, handsome, honest, island, knowledge, listen, muscle, psychology, receipt, salmon, science, sign, which or witch.

<u>If you want a Seven</u>: campaign, debt, halve, mortgage, poignant, scenery, soften, subtle, tomb, wreckage.

<u>Reduced syllables</u>: average, basically, business, camera, (un)comfortable, (in)definite, different, (un)fashionable, favourite (US favorite), general, (un)generous, interest, literature, reference, restaurant, separate, temperature, valuable, vegetable, Wednesday.

Recording 66: <u>If you want a Seven</u>: category, desperate, extraordinary, (dis)honourable, originally, preferable.

Recording 67: <u>*ie* or *ei* words</u>: *ie*: achieve, audience, believe, brief, chief, convenient, efficient, experience, friend, ingredient, niece; patient, piece, species; *ei*: ceiling, foreign, freight, height, leisure, neighbour (US neighbor), neither, protein, receive, weight, weird.

<u>If you want a Seven</u>: ageing (US aging), caffeine, conscience, grievance, hierarchy, hygiene, insufficient, medieval, perceive, reign, reinforce, reinstate, seize.

<u>Double consonants</u>: 1. mm; common; 2. cc; accent; 3. ss; Russian; 4. ll; illogical; 5. rr; arrange; 6. pp; apply.

accidentally, accommodation, address, aggressive, annually, committed, embarrass, millennium, occurrence, possession, successfully, unnecessary.

<u>Adverbial endings</u>: -*ly*: gradually, privately, probably, rapidly, rarely, typically, wonderfully; -*ily*: daily, funnily; -*ally*: dramatically, magically.

<u>If you want a Seven</u>: -*ly*: annually, approximately, imperceptibly, publicly (exception), remotely, sincerely; -*ily*: noisily; -*ally*: drastically, economically.

<u>Common adjective and noun endings</u>: -*ful*: + delightful and tasteful; careless and harmless; ungrateful, unsuccessful, unstressful; disrespectful.

-*ant* or *ent*? brilliant, (un)confident, (in)convenient, excellent, experience, ignorant, (in)dependent, (un)intelligent, performance, (im)permanent, reference, (non-)violence.

<u>If you want a Seven</u>: acquaintance, (in)competent, (non-)existent, interference, (ir)relevant, occurrence, perseverance, (in)significant.

(These following have participial adjectives: *acquainted* (not *acquaintant*); *interfering* (not *interferent*); *occurring* (but *recurrent*); *performed/ing*; *persevering*; and, *referred/ing*.)

-*able/-ible* etc: acceptable, available, changeable, desirable, likable (*likeable* is also accepted), manageable, noticeable, reliable; capable, hospitable, compatible, credible, eligible, flexible, possible, responsible, sensible, visible.

horrible, horror; preferable, preference; terrible, terror; valuable, value.

-*ment*: achieve, achievement; advertise, advertisement; argue, argument; commit, commitment; develop, development; embarrass, embarrassment; encourage, encouragement; entertain, entertainment; equip, equipment; fulfil, fulfilment; + govern, government; and, judge, judgement or judgment.

/ʃɪn/: accommodate, accommodation; add, addition; compete, competition; comprehend, comprehension; create, creation; depress, depression; distribute, distribution; permit, permission; pollute, pollution; prepare, preparation; pronounce, pronunciation; solve, solution.

oceans; Russian; musician; politician.

/ʒɪn/: decide, decision; revise, revision; televise, television.

Chapter 7. IELTS Vocabulary and Grammar

<u>Introduction to Vocabulary</u>: <u>Ordering</u>: 2731456; <u>The ratio between lexical and grammatical error</u>: 5:1.

<u>Precision</u>: 1. screwdriver; 2. fleeting; 3. castigated. <u>Idiom</u>: 1. bogged down; 2. out of this world; 3. put off. <u>Appropriateness</u>: 1. 'I think I can pick up new ideas pretty fast.'; 2. *Immigration has contributed to greater cultural diversity in my city.* (See Nominalisation.); 3. *I look forward to hearing from you. Yours sincerely, Thomas Nielsen.*

<u>Paraphrasing</u>: C is the best; A is the worst because no IELTS topic is a 'hot button' or 'controversial' topic, and the substituted words 'government', 'population', 'medical', and 'nurture' do not mean the same as the originals in the question; B has used too many of the same words as the question, merely changing their order, but B is still much better than A.

<u>Circumlocution</u>: B is correct; A has wrongly described the tool; C has confused the listener more; D: intended words: 'put off / postpone'; E: intended word: 'empire'; F: intended word: 'aggressive'.

<u>How to improve vocabulary</u>: <u>Principles of the Red Cross</u>: B = Impartiality; C = Neutrality; D = Independence; E = Voluntary service; F = Unity; G = Universality.

<u>Word families</u>: A: <u>Table</u>: administrator; analyse (US analyze); analyst; approach. <u>Sentences</u>: 1. administrative; 2. unapproachable; 3. analytical.

B: <u>Table</u>: benefit (from); contract; define; distributor. <u>Sentences</u>: 1. benefitted; 2. definition; 3. contracted; 4. distributed.

C: <u>Table</u>: environmental; evident; exporter; factor (in); function. <u>Sentences</u>: 1. dysfunctional; 2. environmental; 3. exports; 4. evident; 5. factored.

<u>Reference and Substitution: Scrambled words</u>: forward; instead; avoid; Coherence; extent; indicator.

<u>Identifying reference and substitution</u>: i. artists; ii. ideas; iii. work (in any order). <u>Astor Piazzolla</u>: one; he; his; who; him; this; that; himself.

<u>Words connected to 'I'</u>: 1. 'My mother gave ~~to~~ me her old car.' / 'My mother gave her old car **to me**.' 2. **My friend and I** often go clubbing at the weekend.' 3. '**A relative of mine** won an Olympic medal for rowing about 40 years ago.' / '**One of my relatives** won an Olympic medal for rowing about 40 years ago.' 4. 'My parents sent my sister and **me** to boarding school. It wasn't a great experience.' 5. 'My boss and **I** were the only ones who stayed to clean up the mess after the recent floods.' 6. 'I was thrilled when my university sent **me a letter** announcing I'd won a scholarship.' / 'I was thrilled when my university sent **a letter to me** announcing I'd won a scholarship.' 7. 'Unfortunately, **my car** was stolen last week.' 8. '**My** grandparents live quite far away, so I rarely see them.' 9. Examiner (as the candidate is leaving the room): 'Is this your pen?' Candidate: 'Yes, thanks. It's **mine**.' 10. 'I can only blame **myself** for being overweight – I almost never exercise.'

<u>She or he?</u> 1. 'My uncle has **his** own business. **He** sells electronic goods.' 2. 'My sister was the best student at **her** school. Now **she's** studying Medicine.' 3. 'I saw a ballet performance on TV. One of the dancers was fantastic. **His** body was so muscular, and **he** could lift female dancers very easily.' 4. 'My father grew up on a farm. **He** could ride a horse, and milk a cow. Now, **he's** a lawyer in the city.'

<u>It's or its?</u> 1. its; 2. it's; 3. its; its; 4. Its. (Only #2 has an apostrophe.)

<u>Demonstrative, reflexive, and relative pronouns</u>: 1. 'For our class party, we prepared a barbecue **ourselves**.' 2. 'It took my grandfather two hours to walk to work. In **those** days, almost no one had a car, and there wasn't much public transport either.' 3. 'It's easy enough to **teach yourself** how to swim.' / 'It's easy enough to learn ~~yourself~~ how to swim.' 4. 'My cousin who lives in Addis Ababa ~~she~~ has her own chain of hairdressing shops.' 5. 'I don't think children should be left at home by **themselves** until they're twelve.' 6. 'People **who / that** park their cars in my space really annoy me.' 7. *The epidermis ~~which~~ is mainly fat, and makes the skin waterproof.* (Add comma after 'fat'.) 8. *The dermis, which is beneath the epidermis, ~~It~~ contains blood vessels, nerves, muscles, oil, sweat glands, and hair roots.* (Add comma after 'dermis'; change full stop to comma after 'epidermis'.) 9. *As well as protecting the body from injury, infection and burns, the skin's main function ~~which~~ is to regulate body temperature.* (No comma after 'function'.) 10. *In China everyone knows **which** companies cause water pollution.* 11. *I believe **these** companies should be fined heavily.* 12. *It is the president **whose** responsibility it is to guide the country.*

<u>Reference and substitution in Speaking Part 2</u>: 'My favourite teacher was the **one** we had for English in Year 9, and **who** probably encouraged **me** the most. I really stretched **myself** in her class. In fact, I won an English prize **that** year.

My teacher's name is Mrs McCafferty, but **we** all called her Mrs Mick. **She**'s separated with three daughters, one of **whom** was our school captain. She's Canadian, but her parents were from Lebanon and Germany, and **she** can speak five languages. **Her** favourite food is chocolate despite **its** high fat content. Mrs Mick sincerely believes that because chocolate contains the chemical theobromine, **it** makes **those** who eat it feel as though **they**'re in love, so putting on a few grams here and there doesn't really matter.

I enjoyed **her** classes since **they** seemed to be about life rather than just English. For **me**, the personality of my teacher matters as much as what **he** or she teaches.'

<u>Reported speech</u>: 1. Candidate: I think suffering. For example, my uncle told me **he'd** seen some terrible things during the civil war. **His** family was / had been killed and **his** village (was) destroyed. 2. Candidate: Yes. My Maths teacher in particular. You see, I wasn't a very good student, but I wanted to become an engineer. My teacher said **I had** to understand **the maths we were studying** because it **was** the foundation for engineering at university. 3. We were lucky that our History teacher was a sympathetic woman. She asked us almost every week **what our aim in life was**, what **we wanted** from relationships with other people.

<u>Replacive one: From reading</u>: 1. product; 2. explosion; 3. difficulty; 4. cultivars.

<u>From writing</u>: 1. There are several differences between the way men and women deal with conflict. In my opinion, the most notable **one** is that women tend to avoid it more. 2. To some extent people learn from failure. Sometimes holidays where things go wrong become the most memorable **ones**. 3. Natural disasters seem to be occurring more frequently recently. Although there is considerable media coverage of these, I am not convinced that, in the event of **one**, people in my city would be able to cope. 4. Every country has its own iconic structures. In China, the most famous **one** is the Great Wall, which extends many thousands of kilometres.

<u>Collocation</u>: can't; one; must; preposition; widely; seven; random; instead; varies; from; dialects.

<u>Which word?</u>: 1. for; 2. finite; 3. such as; 4. financial; 5. scarce; 6. longer; 7. in; 8. for; 9. single; 10. on; 11. facilities; 12. chances; 13. on; 14. increased; 15. next door; 16. under; 17. dwindling; 18. similar; 19. To; 20. massive.

<u>How do I learn collocations? An ad for a bank</u>: 1. participate in; immigrate to; learn by; 2. my career as an artist; 3. featured in galleries; 4. around the world; <u>A bicycle safety manual</u>; 6. comply with; 7. familiarise yourself with; 8. applicable laws; 9. properly equipping; 10. as the law requires.

Vocabulary for Speaking Part 1: Where I live:

Accommodation	Neighbourhood
1990s building; balcony *a large complex* *three-bedroom* *north- / south-facing* *on the ground / 21st / top floor* *parking; rented* *spacious* *sunny; well-equipped*	*commercial* *a good place to bring up children* *good local facilities* *residential*

If you want a Seven:

Positive	Negative
accessible *ample (facilities / parks / public transport / shopping)* *diverse; dynamic* *pleasant; thriving* *undergoing gentrification (this could be negative)* *up-market (UK) / upscale (US)*	*congested* *deprived* *dull* *limited (facilities / parks / public transport / shopping)* *over-developed* *over-priced* *run-down; semi-industrial*

What I do: 1. I'm an accountant. 2. I'm an electronic engineer. 3. I'm a medical specialist. 4. I've got my own business. 5. I'm working part-time in a… 6. I work in IT. 7. I work for X company. 8. I'm doing some research into… 9. I've just graduated… 10. I'm a mother with young children.

Describing my job: 1. 's; either; 2. 's; positive; 3. involves; positive; 4. isn't; negative; 5. requires; positive; 6. isn't; negative; 7. 's got; positive; 8. 's; negative; 9. 's; negative; 10. involves; positive.

What I'm studying: An MA; A Diploma in Early Childhood Studies; A Certificate in Property Services, part of a Diploma in Real Estate; I think both the theoretical and practical parts will be helpful.; That's a little hard to say, but probably some of the assignments using statistical programs. Actually, I find both of them helpful.; I found the lecturers excellent. They knew their stuff, and were always available for consultation.

Missing letters: pronounce; forget; in; industry; for; continuous; form; participle; adjectives; stuff.

4 candidates in a table: A = 6; B = 5; C = 7.

A Nine's answer fleshed out: The **bold** language is natural and sophisticated.

How do you organise your time?

I've got a **calendar** on my mobile phone, which I **update throughout the day**. I **set aside** fifteen minutes at the end of each working day to **note down the tasks of the following day**. I also **prioritise** them. I've got an **18-month wall-planner** that I **fill in**. I try to set **goals: personal, financial, and work-related** every few months.

Who taught you to organise your time?

No one in particular although my mother was **extremely** organised. She **brought up** three kids while doing a Master's degree and a part-time job. **It beats me how she did it!** My brother's also quite successful, and I've **learnt some tricks** from him. For example, he only **checks** his email once a day for 20 minutes. He gets up at 5:30 to go running, and to do his **household budgeting**. I'm **not as committed as** that, but I suppose **I don't do too badly**.

What would you do with more free time?

I'd almost certainly **take up** singing again. I used to be in a choir at university, and I really miss that – the music and **the close relationships formed** with other **choristers**. I'd **consider doing** some **voluntary work**, perhaps teaching kids in **after-school care** something like **carpentry**, which I'm good at.

What are the benefits of being well-organised?

Quite simply: people **achieve** more in a shorter time.

Phrasal verbs: Ways to learn phrasal verbs: 1327 5648. 'Some people learn phrasal verbs by verb (eg: those with 'pick'); others concentrate on the particles (eg: 'up'). A third group learns phrasal verbs in a context (eg: in a short text on one topic like sport).

There is no correct way to learn, but research has shown that the third way could be the most effective because the grammar is embedded in the sentence, and the meaning may be clearer.'

<u>Focusing on the verb</u>: 1a. Catching; b. to catch; c. were caught; 2a. go; b. going; c. have been going; 3a. has set; b. setdown; c. set.

<u>Focusing on the particle</u>: 1. down; 2. in; 3. out; 4. over; 5. up.

<u>Phrasal verbs in a context</u>: <u>Headline</u>: *Bear out of the woods*

<u>Article</u>: Star golfer Bear Woods **has notched up** his first top-ten finish since last spring. He shot a final-round 65 at Royal Course, which **is set in** the rolling green hills of Canterbury. He's provided fans with hope that his old form is **coming back**. Nick Watson **took out the honours**, making it to the clubhouse in 15 under par. Jess van Burgh **shook up** spectators with some ill-judged comments caught on the mobile phone of a nearby fan. It seems he's convinced Woods' confession about the **breakdown** of his marriage is a stunt to divert attention from the Big Bear's game.

<u>Matching</u>: A breakdown = when something stops working; to come back = to return; to notch up = to score; to shake up = to disturb; to take out the honours = to win the prize.

<u>The grammar of phrasal verbs</u>: 1. 'Don't forget to **look me up** when you're in Ankara.' 2. 'Why did you tell the world my phone number?' 'I swear, I didn't **give it out**.' 3. 'I was having a great time playing with my brother's new puppy, but suddenly she **turned on me**.' 4. ✓ 5. 'My parents are going to be in town for the long weekend. Do you think we can **put them up**?' 6. 'Our teacher **was brought up / grew up** in Abu Dhabi.' 7. '3-D printing sounds like a technological **breakthrough**.' 8. 'Thankfully, the case against my father **was thrown out** of court.' 9. ✓ 10. 'You should **cut down on** dairy food unless you eat low-fat products.' 11. *China is made up of provinces. Within these, there are Special Economic and Special Administrative Zones.* 12. *I look forward to hearing from you.* 13. *In the past two decades, pollution has spread ~~out~~ dramatically.* 14. ✓ 15. *The number of tourists to Machu Pichu rose ~~up~~ / went up between 1990 and 2000.*

<u>Speaking Part 2 answer from an older man</u>: 1. to save up our money; 2. to pay for the wedding; 3. we went down the aisle (to go down the aisle = to get married); 4. we make ~~it~~ up quickly; 5. take after; 6. upbringing; 7. we're making up for; 8. comes from; 9. look forward to; 10. I didn't make anything up. / I didn't make up anything.

<u>Missing letters</u>: date; marriage/marrying; could; resolved; pursuing; retirement.

<u>Phrasal verbs for Speaking Part 2</u>: A: 1. caught up; 2. had just flown in; 3. set off; 4. picked up: 5. break down; 6. worn out; 7. went out; 8. had been looking forward; 9. got into; 10. went back.

B: 1. forward-looking; 2. haven't been beaten down; 3. get up to; 4. come up with; 5. work on; 6. have taken part; 7. look up to; 8. were growing up; 9. downturn; 10. to pick up.

C: 1. feasts on; 2. play with; 3. wait for; 4. to jump up; 5. is left out; 6. goes off; 7 and 8. (interchangeable): looks after and takes care of; 9. go down; 10. to look for.

<u>Other idiomatic language a Seven uses</u>: <u>Missing items</u>: An idiom has to be understood as a chunk. = **2**; but there would only be a few native English speakers who could tell you = **1**; Each English-language speaking country has its own particular idioms. = **7**; Idiomatic language is very common in speaking. = **4**; one sentence should never contain two similar-sounding idioms = **5**; Phrasal verbs have both literal and idiomatic meanings. = **3**; the natural and confident use of idiomatic language is necessary. = **8**; There are fashions in idioms. = **6**.

<u>Realistic examples of idiomatic language in the Speaking test</u>: <u>Part 1</u>: run off; feet; took; under; wing; welcome; show; made of. <u>Part 2</u>: sums; up; sunny; head for figures; over; moon; in touch. <u>Part 3</u>: On; face; rat race; slave away; ridiculous amount; look at.

<u>33 idioms which are safe to use in the Speaking test</u>: 1. strength; 2. flair; 3. head; 4. hand; 5. wire; 6. same; 7. sunny; 8. track; 9. cake; 10. made; 11. wing; 12. ballpark; 13. grave; 14. ocean; 15. fish.

<u>MCQ test for vocabulary, grammar, and spelling 1 (for an IELTS Six)</u>:

Set	1	2	3	4	5	6	7	8	9	10	11	12
i	d	a	b	c	c	a	b	d	a	c	a	a
ii	c	b	d	a	d	d	b	b	c	c	c	a
iii	b	b	c	c	b	a	b	d	c	a	b	c
iv	a	b	d	c	c	d	b	b	c	a	d	b

<u>MCQ test for vocabulary, grammar, and spelling 2 (for an IELTS 6.5)</u>: 1. a; 2. c; 3. a; 4. d; 5. a; 6. c; 7. b; 8. d; 9. a; 10. d; 11. b; 12. c; 13. a; 14. a; 15. d; 16. b; 17. d; 18. b; 19. a; 20. b.

Sentence types: 1. With fewer students (who are) studying science, there will be fewer science graduates, a lessening of scientific knowledge, less research, fewer scientific breakthroughs, and ultimately a decline in economic superiority. (*Compound-complex*); 2. Every day, we cook, go to the doctor, grow or buy vegetables, use electricity, log on to a computer, and gaze at the stars. (*Compound: This is a list of subject + verb without subordination*) 3. Science is an integral part of our lives. (*Simple*); 4. Although arts subjects are essential for students to develop a rounded approach to life, science subjects will provide them with intellectual challenges which could result in new discoveries. (*Compound-complex*); 5. While there are science fairs to encourage ideas, above all, children need exciting and innovative teachers (*Compound: Two clauses joined by 'while'*); 6. compound.

Speaking Taster (Buzzer) Test — Part 2 Topic

I'd like you to tell me about a long holiday you enjoyed as a child.

• *Where did you go?*

• *Who did you go with?*

• *What did you particularly enjoy?*

Answers to Part III

Academic Practice Test 1

<u>LISTENING</u>: **Answers and Script** with highlighted evidence for answers

<u>Section 1</u>: 1. 2/two years; 2. cook; 3. Engineering (*capital optional*); 4. model; 5. at night; 6. shy; 7. late; 8. gone; 9. city; 10. Lucy (*capital optional*). <u>Section 2</u>: 11. peace; 12. value; 13. floor; 14. maintenance; 15. F; 16. C; 17. H; 18. B; 19. D; 20. G. <u>Section 3</u>: 21. C; 22. C; 23. A; 24. B; 25. B; 26. 1925; 27. style; 28. machine; 29. concrete; 30. considered. <u>Section 4</u>: 31. A; 32. B; 33. A; 34. C; 35. A; 36. insulation; 37. blind; 38. affordable; 39. records; 40. long-distance (*hyphen necessary*).

Narrator	Recording Sixty-eight. Practice Listening Test One. Section One. Choosing Flatmates.
Julie	OK Alex, let's make a decision now. I've got to head off to my parents' place for the weekend, and we'll need our two new flatmates to move in soon. Who do we have again?
Alex	Mauro, Spring, Katia, Lucy, and that lovely girl from Turkey (eg). What was her name?
Julie	Aziza. I think she's my first choice; she seemed very mature.
Alex	She did, didn't she?
Julie	She also said she'd shared a house in Istanbul for **two years** before she came here (1), so she knows what flatting is all about.
Alex	That's true. While you were on the phone, I had a talk to her about her part-time job as a telephone counsellor for the Turkish community. It sounds quite steady and well enough paid, so she won't have any problems with the rent unlike our old flatmate, Tina.
Julie	Who would you choose next?
Alex	How about a guy?
Julie	I don't know. Neither of them was that impressive. I mean – Mauro, from Mexico – was a party animal. Remember, he only found our place because he knew there was a certain nightclub nearby, and Spring seemed spoilt to me. He told me that his father in Hong Kong paid all his parking and speeding fines, and he ate out at restaurants almost every night. I doubt he's got any idea how to **cook** (2).
Alex	That leaves us with Katia and Lucy then, and I found Katia rather **shy** (6). We hardly know anything about her.
Julie	I think she's the strong silent type, but while you were showing Mauro around, I had a chat to her. She's in her third year of Environmental **Engineering** (3).
Alex	Really? She's going to be an engineer?
Julie	Yes, in fact, she won a prize at university last year for a **model** she made (4).
Alex	That does sound interesting.
	But what about Mauro? We could do with someone social. I'm sure he'd be keen on our Sunday get-togethers. He promised me he knew how to barbecue. Plus he's working as a security guard **at night** (5), so he'll be around during the day. It's not a bad idea having someone in the flat while we're all out.
Julie	I don't know. If he works night shift (5), he might sleep during the day. This year, I'll need to practise the piano here in the mornings for my performance course. It's likely my music would disturb him.
Alex	That's a fair point.
Julie	What's wrong with three women living here, Alex? I think Katia would be fine. She won't be so **shy** once she gets to know us (6).
Alex	You know, Julie, I can't give a rational explanation for why I didn't take to Katia. I'd just prefer someone else. Why don't we reconsider Lucy? I know you were annoyed because she came an hour **late** (7), but I rather liked her.
Julie	She's doing a Master's in Public Health, isn't she?
Alex	Yes. I think she's quite a serious person, and since she's been a nurse, you'd hope she'd be clean.
Julie	Yes, you would.
	Didn't Lucy mention she had a boyfriend?
Alex	I don't think so.

Julie	I don't want anyone with a boyfriend. Remember Tina?
Alex	How could I ever forget her! She really did have us wrapped around her little finger.
Julie	She certainly did. I'm so glad she's **gone** (8). Yes, Lucy seemed nice and normal, and she'd probably get on with Aziza. I think they're the same age.
Alex	I've just had a thought: we need to choose three people. Someone we like may have found another place. I love our flat, but it's some distance from the **city**, and not everyone likes an old building (9).
Julie	So, who should we have?
Alex	How about Aziza and **Lucy** (10), and Mauro as reserve?
Julie	I agree with your top two (10), but I think Katia should be back-up.
Alex	I'll call Aziza and Lucy, and if one of them has made another commitment, we'll think again.

Narrator	Section Two. Designing a Veranda Garden.
Female speaker	Welcome back to the workshop. In this part, we're going to look at making a veranda garden.

These days few people can afford to live in a house with a garden, but we can all create a tranquil space on a balcony or veranda.

It has long been my belief that a veranda garden softens the sharp lines of the urban environment. Greenery, blossom, and fruit, which attract birds and insects, bring us closer to nature. If well designed, its mood changes with each season, and it may reflect Japanese spiritual traditions that help us feel at **peace** (11).

Of course, everyone's needs are different. Perhaps you'd like more privacy, or to conceal an unsightly building next door. Perhaps there's too much glare from the setting sun. In these instances, fast-growing plants in strategic places will be your main ambition. One client of mine whose husband was blind chose scented plants for their veranda garden. He sat out there every night, delighting in the fragrances. Another client of mine opted for an area of raked gravel with one large ornamental rock, reminiscent of a famous temple garden in Kyoto.

From a more practical perspective, a low-maintenance veranda garden will increase the **value** of your property (12). You may be surprised to know that around the world there's a movement in big cities for roof, terrace, and veranda gardens, so buyers won't be put off by your creativity at all.

But on to our design. I'm assuming your veranda is about one point eight metres deep, and four point five metres wide. If it's larger than this, all the better. If it's smaller, you'll need to plan more carefully, foregoing some features. It doesn't matter which **floor** of the building you're on (13), but if you've got a view, you might consider how tall particular plants grow. The handout I've given you details a range of plant characteristics. For example: a loquat tree grows to six metres, but an azalea bush only reaches three. Loquats bear fruit as well, which you might like to eat, or you might find a chore to pick up and dispose of. In my design, I've chosen a Japanese maple as the centerpiece (19) since I love the way its foliage changes colour in autumn. In a large pot, a maple will grow to about four metres.

The garden design I'm going to show you is quite high **maintenance** at the start (14) – I'd say you'd have to spend three hours a week tending it – but after a year or so, it virtually takes care of itself.

…

So, let's get started.

Your veranda probably has a concrete floor and a low brick or concrete wall around it. It's more than likely you've got a drain in the top right corner (15).

The floor of the veranda garden is the first priority. In my design, I've chosen four different surfaces to create a sense of space, and because they react in different ways to light and rain. In a small area, you want to maximise texture. I've chosen practical square concrete pavers for the area under the table and chairs, and elsewhere large irregular stones (16), sourced from a river, and small round stones not much bigger than pebbles. There's also an area of sand, which is marked with the letter 'H' in your diagram (17). You'll find this might be popular with your pet if you have one.

After laying the floor, most people construct a wooden or aluminium frame over the concrete wall. Onto this, bamboo is attached for plants to climb up (18). In front of the bamboo, wooden planters or boxes may be positioned. The choice of plants in these is up to you, but, again, think about height, shape, loss of leaves, fruit, scent, and cost. Although maples are expensive, they're beautiful, and I've put one in the centre (19).

After you've planted, you'll probably want to buy a really nice set of outdoor furniture. Stackable plastic chairs are a no-no as, in my view, they're part of the ugly mass-produced culture we're trying to escape. I also discourage people from putting a barbecue on their veranda because they're so seldom used, and they take up such a lot of space. Some people do add features like a small pond or birdbath or a stone lantern to their newly landscaped area (20).

So, happy designing. Any questions?

Narrator	Section Three. Architecture Essay
Maria	Hi, Helen. How are you?
Helen	I'm actually pretty excited about the research I've been doing. I've found out heaps about Art Deco architecture in New Zealand.
	While all the major cities there have pockets of Art Deco, it seems that Napier, a small city on the east coast of the North Island, is considered one of the world's purest Art Deco enclaves (21) – there are so many examples of the style still visible today.
Maria	Really? I've been concentrating on Bandung, which is in central Java in Indonesia. It is also a major Art Deco city (21). Unfortunately, it hasn't been preserved so well, and, in the race to modernise, many marvellous buildings have gone under the wrecker's ball.
Helen	How do you think we should structure our essay? Should we write about New Zealand first or Indonesia?
Maria	Art Deco appeared in Bandung in the 1920s, but from what I've read, it didn't make it to Napier until much later. If we choose a chronological scheme, then Indonesia would go first, but I'm in favour of writing our essay using thematic similarities and differences.
Helen	That's a good idea. Let's identify what the two cities have in common. From what I've discovered, in both places, Art Deco architects combined a new European aesthetic with native elements (22).
Maria	Yes, they did.
Helen	In New Zealand, Maori motifs were used as decoration. The Maoris are the indigenous people who lived in New Zealand before it became a British colony (22). There's a sort of spiral symbol called a *koru*, and there are zigzags, like patterns from Maori weaving, both of which were incorporated into Art Deco buildings. There's a bank in the middle of the city and an old headquarters for a tobacco company both with gorgeous carved stucco facades that utilise these motifs.
Maria	Indonesia was also a colony – a Dutch colony. I understand almost all of the architects in the Art Deco period were Dutch, and as you said, they were influenced by a new aesthetic in Europe, but they were also affected by native architectural styles. At ITB – the famous technical institute in Bandung – there are Art Deco roofs that imitate traditional Javanese mosque or temple roofs (22).
Helen	That's interesting.
	I know that the city of Napier was rebuilt in 1931 after a massive earthquake (23), and since people wanted the town to feel like an optimistic new place, they chose Art Deco for many of their buildings. But I've no idea why Bandung has so much of the style.
Maria	I was quite puzzled about the prevalence of Art Deco myself. After fossicking in the library in some old journals, I learnt that there was a plan that never eventuated to move the capital from Jakarta to Bandung, so lots of public buildings were commissioned around the same time (24) – the early 1920s.
Helen	That's curious. I thought the majority of the famous Art Deco buildings in Bandung were large hotels (25) or private houses.
Maria	I think the split is 50-50 – private and public. Certainly the campus of ITB was enlarged then. College education for the rich expanded in the 1920s. And the local tourist industry was taking off as well (25).
Helen	You're right we've got tourism to thank for the grand Art Deco hotels like the Savoy and the Praenger, built in the late 20s and the early 30s. Photos of the foyer and ballroom of the Praenger are so romantic.
	…
Helen	OK. Let's have a paragraph on the historical reasons for these two cities' featuring Art Deco; then, another on what Art Deco actually is.
Maria	It's a French term, isn't it?
Helen	Yes. One influence was the **1925** Paris International Expo of Decorative Arts (26). But Art Deco was chiefly a reaction against the previous **style** of Art Nouveau (27), which had held sway from the end of the 19th century. That was all about nature and fluid forms whereas Art Deco celebrated the **machine** age and the geometric (28).
Maria	There are lots of influences, aren't there?
Helen	Should we include anything on building materials?
Maria	Definitely. They were different from the past. More **concrete** was used, more steel, more glass (29). These days, people rave about Art Deco, but at the time, it was **considered** somewhat low-class (30) because the materials are quite inexpensive, and fabrication was rapid. These concepts were in stark contrast with some of the previous notions of craftsmanship in building. Yes, we'll certainly need a paragraph on materials.

Narrator	Section Four. Wetsuits.
Lecturer	Welcome to the Monday Design Forum. Today's item is the wetsuit, used by water-sport enthusiasts, by surfers, divers, canoeists, and long-distance swimmers. Long-distance, mind. I'll tell you about the great swimsuit debate a little later (40).

The reason I chose the wetsuit for a case study is that it exemplifies two design themes: the importance of materials; and, reliable production techniques (31).

I may not look the sporty type, but I've been diving for 20 years. In that time, I've had eight wetsuits. Like much else after 1945, technology has just kept on changing.

My first wetsuit was French, and very expensive. It was made entirely from sponge rubber. It looked great, but it was horrible to get into and out of, and it weighed a tonne. In general, first-generation wetsuits were liable to rip when being removed, and were rather heavy (32). Pretty soon, I swapped my Pêche-Sport suit for a lighter neoprene version.

So what's neoprene? It's a synthetic material considerably lighter than rubber. It's still spongy because it contains tiny bubbles of nitrogen gas. Since gases have lower thermal conductivity than liquids or solids – that is: they don't transport heat well – the body heat of a person wearing neoprene escapes only very slowly through the material (33). This means that a diver in a neoprene suit stays warmer longer than one in a suit made from rubber.

Wetsuits are a recent innovation, and were invented in the US, but there's no real agreement by whom or when. Hugh Bradner tried to patent a design in 1951. However, he was unsuccessful. The Meistrell brothers and the O'Neills from California were all making and selling neoprene suits to the burgeoning diving and surfing community by 1953. In my view, it's irrelevant who the inventor of the wetsuit was (34). What is significant is that post-war prosperity brought more free time and a boom in sporting goods (35).

But back to my collection of wetsuits. Since neoprene is fragile with all those gas bubbles, it's hard to join pieces of it together. Any hole, however tiny, just grows and grows. This means sewing with needle and thread is all but impossible. Therefore, early wetsuits were made by gluing or taping their seams.

My first neoprene suit was black with yellow tape. I thought this yellow tape was to make me more visible under water, but in fact, it joined the body-hugging sections together without letting water in. While neoprene itself was warmer and lighter than rubber, the taped seams proved to be a weakness, and I tore three of my suits!

Suit number five was much stronger. Aside from being bright blue, my new suit came with lycra backing, which was a technological breakthrough. This meant my suit was a bit like a sandwich. There was lycra on the outside and inside – so putting on and taking off were easier, and there was neoprene in the middle for **insulation** (36).

By the early 1980s, there'd been a revolution in wetsuit production – no glue, no tape, but a new kind of stitching. In fact, a technique called **blind** stitching had been developed (37). With this, a curved needle, in a sophisticated sewing machine, is used. The stitching dips into the lycra backing – the top bread of the sandwich – but doesn't pierce the neoprene filling inside. Remember neoprene is susceptible to tearing, so covering it with lycra was a smart idea. Suddenly, wetsuits were warm, light, and durable.

This revolution is important for Design students because without this sewing technique, wetsuits would've continued to rip, and remained the preserve of the rich. In design, you want a product that's unique, reliable, and **affordable** (38).

I admit I'm still wearing my neoprene suit from three years ago, but I've heard there are now models on the market with inbuilt heating panels, and yet others made from a mix of fibres that include merino wool and titanium.

At the start of this lecture, I mentioned there'd been a swimsuit controversy. Essentially, a wetsuit not only keeps a person warm, but also provides a swimmer with a lift in the water. Unsurprisingly, swimmers wearing wetsuits break more **records** (39), so the International Olympic Committee has declared that only **long-distance** swimmers can use wetsuits (40). In short events, they're banned.

That's all from me. I'm off to the beach.

READING: Passage 1: 1. D; 2. B; 3. D; 4. A; 5. B; 6. C; 7. B; 8. H; 9. G; 10. F; 11. C; 12. E; 13. J. Passage 2: 14. C; 15. F; 16. E; 17. A; 18. C; 19. D; 20. B; 21. A; 22. D; 23. Y/Yes; 24. NG/Not Given; 25. N/No; 26. NG/Not Given; 27. N/No. Passage 3: 28. T/True; 29. F/False; 30. F/False; 31. NG/Not Given; 32. T/True; 33. was level(l)ed; 34. bricks; 35. South Pavilion (*capitals optional*); 36. 1796; 37. doors; 38. roof; 39. 1826; 40. A.

> The highlighted text below is evidence for the answers above.
> If there is a question where 'Not given' is the answer, no evidence can be found, so there is no highlighted text.

Passage 1: The stress of relocation

For some people, there is little in life more stressful than moving house; for others, there is a definite excitement in relocation since the belief that the grass is greener on the other side holds sway.

However, for Dr Jill Molveldt, a psychotherapist in Durban, South Africa, (1) Relocation Stress Syndrome, or RSS, which she has been researching for a decade, is a matter of professional concern. Dr Molveldt began her career as a medical doctor in 1999, but turned to therapy when she doubted the efficacy of some medication. Time and again, patients presented at her surgery who – to all intents and purposes – had little physically wrong, but were not functioning optimally. Usually, such people with anxiety-related disorders are prescribed drugs, but Dr Molveldt observed that many seemed to improve just as readily through talking to her. Therefore, from (2) 2006-2008, she underwent extensive training in the United States in a number of techniques used in therapy.

On return to South Africa, Dr Molveldt moved her family and her burgeoning practice – now devoted entirely to therapy – from Pietermaritzburg, a small city, to Durban, a larger, more cosmopolitan one. (2) Immediately following this move, Dr Molveldt herself fell ill. Medical testing for vague symptoms like headaches, skin rashes, and insomnia (2) brought neither relief nor diagnosis. At the time, she could not possibly have imagined that she, herself, had any psychological problems. Her only recent difficulty had been relocating to Durban due to her children's maladjustment to their third school in three years, and to the irritation caused by a protracted renovation. All the same, she far preferred the beachside lifestyle of Durban to that of conservative inland Pietermaritzburg.

Quite by chance, in the summer of 2010, (3) Dr Molveldt ran into a neighbour from her old city who had also moved to Durban. This woman (3) seemed uncharacteristically depressed, and had experienced mood swings and weight gain since her arrival. As the neighbour recounted her complicated tale of moving, Dr Molveldt suddenly realised that her acquaintance – like herself – was suffering from RSS.

Upon this discovery, Dr Molveldt began sifting through medical and psychological literature to learn more about her syndrome, only to find precious little written about it. Conferences she attended in Greece and Argentina in which stress featured as a topic for keynote speakers did little to enlighten her. Therefore, (4) Dr Molveldt felt she had no option but to collect her own patient data from medical practice and Emergency Room records in Durban and Cape Town in order to ascertain the extent of the problem. Over four years, she surveyed people with non-specific health problems as well as those who had had minor accidents.

In Durban and Cape Town, (5) it might be expected in the general population that **1%** of people have moved within a month, and 5% within six months. (5) Yet nearly **3%** of patients seen by GPs in Dr Molveldt's study had moved within one month, and 9% within six. Minor accident patients had also moved recently, and some of them had had more than two residential addresses in one year.

(6) Dr Molveldt then examined records of more serious accidents from a nationwide database, and, with the aid of a research grant, conducted interviews with 600 people. Admittedly, (7) alcohol played a part in serious accident rates, but many interviewees said they had been drinking in response to circumstances – one of which was moving house. (8) People who had had serious accidents, however, had not moved more frequently than those with non-specific ailments.

So just how stressful is moving? After all, stress is part of life – think about exams, a new job, marriage, having a child, divorce, illness, or the death of a loved one. Where does RSS fit in relation to these? (9) Dr Molveldt puts it above exams (including for medical school), and somewhere between being newly married and bearing a child. (Newlyweds and young mothers also visit doctors' surgeries and Emergency Rooms more than they should statistically.)

(10) Interestingly, subjects in several of Dr Molveldt's tests rated moving less highly than she did, putting it about equal to sitting a tough exam.

As a side issue, (11) Dr Molveldt found that the number of relationships that broke down around the time of moving was elevated. She considers the link between breakdown and RSS to be tenuous, suggesting instead that couples who are already struggling move house in the hope of resuscitating their relationship. Invariably, this does not happen. Moreover, it is (12) the children in these cases who suffer most: not only has upheaval meant the loss of their old school and friends, but it also signals adjustment to occupation of their new home while one absent parent resides in another.

(13) If Dr Molveldt's research is anything to go by, next time you yearn to live elsewhere, think twice. Moving may be more stressful than you imagine, and the only papers you get to say you've done it are a fee from your doctor and a heap of mail from the previous inhabitants of your dwelling.

Passage 2: Terrific Tupperware

A Throw open anyone's kitchen cupboards (17) from Andorra (and 21) to Zimbabwe, and you'll find colourful plastic products for the preparation, serving, and storage of food. Chances are, some of these are Tupperware.

B For many people in developed countries, Tupperware is redolent of the 1950s when grandma and her friends bought and sold it at 'Tupperware parties'. Some would even say Tupperware became a cultural icon in that decade. However, these days, while parties are still popular, online sales are challenging the model. Indeed, since 2000, (20) more Tupperware franchises have opened in China than anywhere else.

C Take the Hundred Benefits shop in Hangzhou, one of China's fastest-growing cities. Located in a chic part of town, it's full of twenty-somethings who haven't yet had a child but are building a nest. They've got plenty of expendable income, and they're picking out items to reflect their new-found optimism. China is undergoing a home-decorating revolution after years of dull, unreliable products. Furthermore, the average size of living space for urban Chinese has almost doubled recently, so there's room for lots of stuff. (14) But why choose Tupperware? It's functional as well as fun. It's sealable, stackable, durable, microwave-and-freezable, dishwasher-friendly, and culturally sensitive: four-layer traditional Chinese lunch-boxes, revamped in bright sexy colours, grace the shelves of the Hundred Benefits shop.

D What is the Tupperware story? The special plastic used in (22) it was invented in 1938 by an American called Earl Tupper. (23) The famous seals, which keep the air out and freshness in, came later. (22) Tupper's company was established in 1946, and for more than forty years boasted every success, but, recently, Tupperware Brands Corporation has been sold several times, and its parent company, Illinois Tool Works, has announced that declining American prospects may mean resale.

E Until the 1990s, Tupperware relied totally on a pyramid sales model. In this, a person buys products from a person above them, rather than from a wholesale company or retail shop, and after sale of the new product to a third party, gives a small percentage of the money to the person from whom they originally bought. In turn, when the person on the lowest level recruits more vendors, those people return percentages to the person above. Initially, Tupperware operated like this because it was not available in shops. A more direct line between the manufacturer and the buyer results in cheaper products, and, as Tupperware is largely sold in the home, women suddenly have an independent income. (16) A disadvantage might be that since people typically buy from and sell to friends, there are pressures at ordinary social gatherings to do deals, which some people may consider unethical. This raises the question: am I going for a pleasant dinner at Alison's, or am I expected to buy a set of measuring cups from her as I leave? (18) This pyramid model is prohibited in China, and (18) has lost favour in many countries like Britain, **Germany**, Australia, and New Zealand, where once it was all-pervasive. At present, most US sales are still on the party plan, but online and franchise sales are catching up.

F Tupperware became fashionable after World War II. During the war, large numbers of women were in paid employment outside the home while their men were away fighting. When the men returned, the women mostly resumed their household duties. There are widely divergent views about Tupperware's role at this time. (15) Some feminists propose that the company promulgated an image of women confined to the kitchen, making the female pursuit of a career less likely. Others say that the pyramid sales model allowed women to earn, promoting autonomy and prosperity. In particular, those who were pregnant and at home could enjoy some extra cash.

G (25) Effective rebranding of Tupperware has taken place in the east, but what about (19) in America? Well, the Tupperware website there has developed a 'Chain of Confidence' programme to improve sales. In this, women reinforce the notion of female solidarity by purchasing Tupperware and swapping true stories. (19) Over a million dollars from this programme has also been donated to a girls' charity.

H (27) What the future holds for the pretty plastic product is uncertain. Will Tupperware become a relic of the past like cane baskets and wooden tea chests, or will online social programmes and avid Chinese consumers save the company?

Passage 3: Marvellous Monticello

Thomas Jefferson is renowned for many accomplishments, among which he was the principal author of the American Declaration of Independence and the third president of the United States, during which time America grew significantly in size and stature.

Jefferson also designed his own three-storeyed, 33-roomed mansion, called Monticello, familiar to every American from the nickel, or 5-cent coin, on which can be seen a simple domed building with a four-columned portico.

(28) Influenced by classical European design, and emulated across the land, Monticello took more than 40 years to build. Numerous labour-saving devices inside, invented by Jefferson himself, and gardens the envy of agronomists represent the scientific spirit of a new age.

(28) Modelled on Andrea Palladio's 16th-century Italian villas, Monticello is a tribute to the man and style that Jefferson idolised. As Palladio considered the position of a building to be of the utmost importance, Jefferson had Monticello built on a mountain with splendid views. According to Palladio, a building should be symmetrical since mathematical order bestows harmony upon its inhabitants. Thus Monticello boasts a colonnaded entrance and a central room with a dome.

But who was the man who created Monticello? Thomas Jefferson was born at Shadwell, Virginia, on the east coast of America in 1743. On his father's death, he inherited a large property where Monticello was subsequently constructed. Jefferson, both a lawyer and politician, was elected to the House of Burgesses in 1768, and in 1775 to the Continental Congress, where he revised the laws of Virginia. Two of his famous pieces of legislation include: the Virginia Statute for Religious Freedom, and the Bill for the More General Diffusion of Knowledge.

Throughout Jefferson's early adulthood, (29) America had been fighting Britain in the War of Independence. In 1776, Jefferson, who was never a combatant, wrote the Declaration of Independence, and although the conflict did not end until 1783, Americans consider the birth of their nation came with that declaration. As well as proclaiming America's freedom, the declaration outlines universal human rights, stating that all men are equal regardless of birth, wealth, or status, and, furthermore, that government is the servant, not the master, of the people. Although Jefferson's work was based on the ideas of John Locke, an Englishman, and on a body of French philosophy, it remains a uniquely American document.

After the war, Jefferson took up the post of Governor of Virginia, before returning to Congress. He then served five years in France as a US trade representative and minister. He was American Vice-President between 1797-1801 and President for the following eight years. As president, (30) he organised the purchase of a vast tract of land from the French, who were embattled in Europe and strapped for cash. This land, called the Louisiana Territory, doubled the size of America. Jefferson was also responsible for financing Lewis and Clark – two explorers who undertook a momentous journey along the Ohio River to survey nature and appraise land for settlement.

In retirement, Jefferson remained active. His huge library, donated to the nation, and known as the Library of Congress, is still one of the world's most reputable. He founded the University of Virginia, designed most of its early buildings, defined its curriculum, and became its first rector or chancellor. When he died, on the fourth of July 1826, America had lost a truly great man.

Monticello, his home for most of his life, is on the UNESCO World Heritage List partly because Jefferson lived there, but mainly because it brought classicism – the style of Palladio – to the New World. It was Jefferson's belief that if America were to assume the mantle of a powerful nation, it needed to draw on the best of the European past as well as creating its own style.

(32) Monticello is not a very large building: it is 1022 square metres (11,000 square feet) – these days, a football player or film star has a house as big.

Monticello was not all built at once since Jefferson's finances were seldom secure. Furthermore, his ideas about building changed during his sojourn in France. (33) In 1768, the mountaintop where Monticello would sit was leveled. (34) Bricks were manufactured over a two-year period by Jefferson's slaves – he owned about 200. Wood was sourced from trees on Jefferson's land; stone and limestone were quarried on his property; and – in keeping with his concept of elegance – the window glass and furniture were imported from Europe. (35 and 40) Jefferson moved into the South Pavilion in 1770. Around 1772, the Dining Room in the north wing was built. The first house was mostly complete in 1782, the year Jefferson's wife died. (36 and 40) On return from France in 1796, Jefferson had the upper storey demolished, and the whole structure remodelled, which took eleven years. (40) In 1800, the dome was fitted. A North Pavilion was added from 1806-8. Extensive gardens – both ornamental and productive – were created since Jefferson believed in pursuing agriculture in a scientific manner.

As mentioned previously, Jefferson was an inventor. Since Virginian summers can be hot, he designed special fans and blinds. Blocks of ice were stored in the cellar all year round – a rarity at the time. For the cold winters, Monticello has numerous fireplaces and stoves. In the late 1790s, Jefferson altered the fireplaces to apply some modern fuel-saving principles. He introduced skylights – another unusual feature – and (37) he designed tables that could be turned easily and doors that opened automatically. He even had a shaft-and-pulley system between floors for hoisting food. (38) However, not until 1822 was the roof covered with durable material. (39) Just four years later, Jefferson died.

Jefferson is remembered as a statesman, philosopher, educationalist, and architect. Fiercely American, he drew on a European heritage. He was optimistic, far-sighted, and creative, and Monticello remains a monument to the man as much as his age.

WRITING: Task 1

From design to display in a retail outlet, the process of making a sports shoe takes 18 months. Numbers of different people are involved in several locations.

Firstly, a shoe is designed on a computer.

Then, three basic shoe parts are collected by a factory. The leather has already been ordered from a tannery or the fabric from a textile mill. The rubber has been sourced from elsewhere, and two pieces pressed together into a sole.

Inside the factory, the leather is cut, and the uppers are sewn. The tops and bottoms are glued together and sent for lacing. Pairs of shoes are then put into boxes; 12 boxes go into one carton. The cartons are moved to a warehouse.

From the warehouse, the finished product is sent either directly to a shop for sale or onto a container ship for export. One container can hold up to 5500 pairs of shoes. (152 words)

Task 2

International aid has grown considerably in the last 50 years. It aims to reduce the gap between rich and poor countries. While there are some drawbacks, I believe both recipients and donors benefit greatly from this.

Countries receive aid in many forms: the donation of free food, of medical or building supplies; and, the transfer of expertise. Sometimes, large infrastructural projects are subsidised by donors. There is a trend towards providing in-country education and training. These days, there are also some more novel ideas like direct cash handouts to the poor instead of free supplies.

As well as assisting by doing, there are efforts to persuade impoverished countries not to do. That is, to create national parks in wilderness regions instead of fishing, mining, logging, or clearing the land. Norway has recently paid Guyana in South America several billion dollars on condition that it protect large rainforests. Norway argues that the whole world will benefit from lower carbon levels due to rainforest retention. Furthermore, Norway's wealth has come from oil, one of the causes of global warming, so perhaps Norwegians feel they are compensating for their own destructive behaviour. An additional benefit to donors is international stability since severely impoverished countries often go to war with neighbours or experience destructive civil wars.

Disadvantages of international aid include: patronising attitudes of donors towards recipients; the diversion of talented individuals into highly-paid aid jobs instead of their building up local businesses or institutions; and, the corruption of officials who receive aid. Moreover, in donor countries there are still disparities between rich and poor that need to be addressed.

In conclusion, I consider the disadvantages of international aid are far outweighed by the advantages. For a stable, more prosperous world, aid should be increased. (291 words)

Recording 72: <u>SPEAKING:</u> There are no answers for any practice test.

<u>Practice Speaking Test 1 – Part 2 topic</u>

I'd like you to tell me about something you had that got broken.

• *What was it?*

• *How did you break it?*

• *What did you do afterwards?*

Academic Practice Test 2

Plan of the library

8 Events Room	Teens Room	Storeroom

Fiction	**7 Non-fiction**

Computers		Items in Languages Other Than English

Librarians' Desk	**6 Newspapers & Magazines**

5 Notice Board	Chute	Entrance

<u>Section 1</u>: 1. accountant; 2. 19; 3. Paulo2020; 4. wife; 5. Notice Board (*accepted as one word; capitals optional*); 6. Newspapers, Magazines (*in any order; capitals optional; must be plural*); 7. Non-fiction (Books/Section/Collection) (*capitals optional; hyphen necessary*); 8. Events (*capital optional; must be plural*); 9. 10/ten; 10. Saturday morning(s) (*capital necessary*). <u>Section 2</u>: 11. 363; 12. grey/gray; 13. 134; 14. heights; 15. safety; 16. sunrise; 17. static line; 18. 3/three; 19. photo(graph); 20. traffic. <u>Section 3</u>: 21. Jordan (*capital optional*); 22. relate; 23. well; 24. water-saving (*hyphen necessary*); 25. analytical; 26. C; 27. A; 28. A; 29. B; 30. A. <u>Section 4</u>: 31. learn; 32. environment; 33. four; 34. Visual (*capital optional*); 35. VARK (*capitals optional*); 36. B; 37. C; 38. A; 39. C; 40. B.

Narrator	Recording 70.
	Practice Listening Test 2.
	Section 1. Joining Up.
Paulo	Good afternoon. I'd like to join the library (eg).
Librarian	Take a seat. I'm Tanya Porter, a librarian here.
Paulo	Nice to meet you, Tanya. I'm Paulo de Mello.
Librarian	The application process is quite short and involves filling in a form and a tour of the library. In order to become a member, Paulo, I'll need some photo ID.
Paulo	Actually, I've brought my passport.
Librarian	Lovely. You'll also need to prove that you live or work nearby.
Paulo	My office is just around the corner in Belmore Road. Here's my business card. Will that be enough proof?
Librarian	Yes, I think so. Thanks. So, you're an **accountant** (1)?
Paulo	That's right.
Librarian	I'll write 'accountant' on the application form (1).
	What's your residential address, Paulo?
Paulo	My wife and I live at number **19** Wood Street (2).

Librarian	And your email address?
Paulo	It's Paulo2020@hotmail.com. (3)
Librarian	**P-A-U-L-O-two zero two zero** (3)?
Paulo	Yes.
Librarian	If you don't mind, I'll just scan your passport.
	I see you're from Brazil. We've got a section for languages other than English, but I'm afraid we don't have many Portuguese items. I'd be grateful if you could recommend any must-see movies.
Paulo	I'd be delighted.
	By the way, does my **wife** need to join as well, or can she use my card (4)?
Librarian	She's welcome to use yours, but if she brings anything back late, you'll have to pay the fine.
	…
	Let's go outside now, Paulo, to see the returns chute. You can put your returns in it at any time. In fact, I'm told this complex is open 24 hours, and there's always a security guard on duty. Next to the chute is the **notice board** (5), where we advertise library events and community events.
Paulo	My wife might like to join a book club.
Librarian	Why not? Our book clubs have proven very popular. We've got three different ones running at present. The majority of our events are free, but I would recommend booking since we only seat 20 people in the Events Room.
	Back inside, here's my desk, and opposite, on the right, an area for **newspapers** and **magazines** (6). That's always a popular spot. Behind the papers is the foreign-language section I was referring to before.
	Here's the main part of the library with our fiction collection. It's one of the biggest in the country. **Non-fiction**, however, is not so large (7).
Paulo	What can I see through that glass wall?
Librarian	Our Teens Room, for teenagers; the **Events** Room, for clubs and talks; and, a small storeroom on the right (8). When we had all that rain over the new year, the Teens Room was flooded, so while it's being renovated, we're using the Events Room instead.
Paulo	I'm impressed. Do you also have a computer room?
Librarian	There's no dedicated one. Our six computers are behind my desk. You'll find the library catalogue is all online, and we subscribe to a number of databases that are excellent for research.
Paulo	By the way, how many items can I borrow at a time?
Librarian	Up to **ten** for one month (9). You can renew everything except for DVDs for a fortnight. There's no renewal allowed on DVDs. And you can renew by phone, by text message, or online.
Paulo	Thanks a lot, Tanya. I imagine I'll drop in to the library on the way back from work in the evenings. I see you're open quite late.
Librarian	Yes, six PM Monday, Tuesday, and Friday, and nine PM Wednesday and Thursday.
Paulo	But your hours are limited at weekends.
Librarian	I'm afraid that's true. Just **Saturday mornings** (10). We're still seeking permission from the council to open on Sundays, and we'll probably get that before the end of the year.
	Any more questions, Paulo?
Narrator	Section Two. Sydney Harbour Bridge Climb.
Kevin Peters	Hi everyone. I'm Kevin Peters, your guide today. I know it's dark and rainy, and you're probably wondering what you're doing here at four thirty AM, but let me assure you it's often the most exciting experience to climb the Sydney Harbour Bridge in wild wet weather. Our company operates **363** days a year (11). We have Christmas off, and about once a year an electrical storm prevents climbing.
	Before I go any further, I hope you've all signed the Bridge Climb Declaration form, which is a legal requirement. It just ensures there's no one here who shouldn't be – any woman who's more than 24 weeks pregnant, any child under 10, or anyone with broken bones. It might sound like common sense to you that these people are forbidden from climbing, but, in my experience, common sense is not that common.
	Now, I can see a couple of you starting to shiver. Don't worry about not having enough clothing; we've got everything you'll need.
	OK. Gather round, so you can see what's on the table in front of me. You'll get these items from the dressing room later.

Clothing first: rubber-soled shoes; a jacket; a woollen hat; and, an overall. We've got shoes, jackets, and overalls in every conceivable adult size, but the hats are one size fits all. You put the overall on over everything else partly to keep warm and dry, and partly to make us feel we're a group. You'll notice the overall's **grey** (12). This way when we climb the bridge, also painted grey, we won't distract the drivers below. The traffic's crazy enough down there, and it'll be peak hour when we reach the top of the arch. Yes, today we're going right to the top, folks: **134 metres above sea level** (13).

By the way, if there's anyone who suffers from a fear of **heights** (14), you'll be leading the group. Research has shown this is the best way to overcome your phobia. Anyhow, we'll all be attached to a static line, so falling isn't a concern (17).

…

Righto, ladies and gents: the next lot of items to look at are for **safety** (15). Firstly, a headset for commentary and communication. While we're climbing, I'll be filling you in on some lesser-known details about the bridge – like the fact that about six million rivets were used to put it together, or from 1932 till 1967, it was the tallest structure in Australia. But back to your headset. This button on the left can be used if you need to speak to me – if your static line gets caught, or you're in any other difficulty. Please keep your headset switched on at all times.

Secondly, there's a chain for your glasses. I see two of you are wearing prescription glasses. The views up on the bridge are spectacular, especially at **sunrise** (16), which we'll see, but if you want to enjoy them, keep your glasses attached with the chain. Also, our company will lose its licence if anyone drops anything into the traffic.

Next, a light, which attaches to the headset. Check yours is working, won't you, because the batteries do run out. The first 20 minutes of our climb are in the dark, and we've got 200 metal stairs to go up, so you might need the light. There are also some narrow mesh catwalks to crawl along, and some girders to squeeze past.

The last safety item, and by far the most important, is the slider. As I said before, we're all clipped to a **static line** while we climb (17). That line is permanently attached to the bridge, and this slider connects us to it.

It's a comforting thought that we're all attached, but some of you might be thinking: doesn't that mean I won't go so far, or see so much? Our climb lasts more than **three** hours (18), and this bridge is the fourth-longest steel-arch bridge in the world at one point one five kilometres. Two US bridges and one in Shanghai do outdo it for length, but not for height. After sunrise, we can see the whole of Sydney harbour and up to 80 kilometres north, south, and west.

One last warning. Please leave your personal items in the dressing room. You can't take your wallet or camera, or even a bar of chocolate. I'll take a **photo** of the group at the top of the arch (19), and send it to your email address. As I think I've already mentioned, our licence is granted on condition our customers abide by all our regulations. You're forbidden from carrying things for two reasons: one – you might drop them and cause an accident in the **traffic** below (20); and, two – you need both hands free to balance, or to hold on to the static line (17). We're going up high, remember: 134 metres above sea level (13).

Narrator	Section Three. Water For Peace Presentation.
Beatrice	So, how are we going to do this? Shall I go first, or you, Cathy?
Cathy	It might be better if I start the presentation, Beatrice, since I used to live in the Middle East.
Antonio	Did you? Whereabouts?
Cathy	In **Jordan**, where Water For Peace was set up (21). I've got quite a few photos we could use.
Antonio	What are they of?
Cathy	The ancient city of Petra, camels, and me at the Dead Sea.
Beatrice	Hmm. I don't think they **relate** to our topic (22).
Cathy	I do have some from a village where women still draw their water from a **well** (23). In the countryside this is a common phenomenon. In fact, our concept of a constant supply of clean piped water is unheard of in many parts of Jordan or Palestine. If people don't get water from a well (23), they might have it trucked in by large tanker, which is expensive as well as inconvenient.
Antonio	And I've got photos off the WFP website of the director, Mr Koussa, and a map of the region. The map shows all the towns and villages involved in this **water-saving** project (24 and 27).
Beatrice	That sounds better.
Cathy	Antonio, did you find any pictures of people from Jordan, Israel, and Palestine attending WFP workshops together?
Antonio	Unfortunately, no.

Cathy	In my opinion, that's what this project's about – improving cross-border relations. I mean, where the population is so dense, and where there's been such a long history of conflict, it's terrific that people are now coming together to learn from each other about ways to save water, as well as ways to distribute it more equitably.
Antonio	I agree. I find WFP very inspiring.
Cathy	What's the focus of our presentation?
Beatrice	To describe the research we've done?
Antonio	I think it's to analyse our research, or reach a conclusion.
Cathy	That's how I feel as well. I mean, we can summarise all the information we've collected, but we need to synthesise it. At Master's level we're expected to be **analytical** (25).
	…
Antonio	What are you going to say, Cathy, in your introduction?
Cathy	I'll show my photos of Petra while I talk about the history of the region (26). Then, I'll use an up-to-date regional map to show fresh water sources – rivers, lakes, aquifers, reservoirs, and the like – and major concentrations of population. That'll help our audience understand the current water issues facing the three countries, and lead on to Antonio's map of individual towns and villages involved in the project (27). Lastly, I've got some statistics from 2010 about how much water is used in agriculture, in industry, and domestically. I'll cut and paste these into the photo of women getting water from the well (23) that I mentioned earlier.
Beatrice	Don't forget to emphasise the importance of the Jordan River, Cathy, and how WFP has saved it.
Antonio	Yes, that's amazing isn't it? And all thanks to one man, really, Mr Koussa (28). Maybe I should follow Cathy since my research is on WFP itself. Whereas, Beatrice, you're more interested in international law and the role of the United Nations, aren't you (29)?
Beatrice	Yes. I've found all the development goals that WFP is aiming towards. According to the World Health Organisation, the right to water is linked to other rights enshrined in various United Nations treaties, such as the rights to food, livelihood, and housing.
Cathy	That may be so, but not all three countries in this project are bound by the same international law. Frankly, on paper, governments may be signatories to treaties and conventions, but, on the ground, they've failed in their efforts to ensure those rights, or to protect the environment.
Antonio	In my country, the Philippines, we've tried to get international money and support for big government-led projects, but they're often ineffective. WFP is working from the grassroots up, which I think is preferable (30). What do you think, Beatrice?
Beatrice	I'm not sure. The wider context *is* important. We need the UN to provide a legal framework and to set standards.
Antonio	Perhaps. D'you think we've got time tomorrow to practise our presentation?

Narrator	Section Four. Learning Styles.
Lecturer	Good afternoon. Today we're going to ask the question: what helps students **learn** (31)?

We've all been students from an early age, and we all remember teachers and schools we loved. Considerable research has been done into factors that contribute to learning, and there's certainly a connection between how we feel about our teachers, and how well we do in education. A teacher's own knowledge and passion for a subject is instantly communicated to his or her students, and this translates into successful learning outcomes. The teacher's personal qualities of warmth, humour, fairness, and dedication are also significant. Some educators believe the rapport between the teacher and the student is the single most important factor in learning. Research has also shown that the classroom **environment** affects performance (32). Children in classes with a small number of students, and those in clean, warm, spacious, and pleasantly decorated classrooms score consistently higher on aptitude tests.

But in the 1970s, another idea swept through education like wildfire: millions of teachers, including me, were trained in this method. Basically, it maintained that students learn best when they use one particular learning style.

The first famous learning-style theory was proposed by Kolb. He divided learners into **four** personality types (33). Two of these tended towards abstract conceptualisation, while the other two favoured concrete experience. He claimed if teachers devised activities related to personality type, learners would be more likely to retain information.

Later, Fleming developed a similar theory, which was the one taken up by education ministries around the world. His model is known as the VARK Model: or the **Visual**, Auditory, Reading-Writing, and Kinesthetic learning styles model (34). Fleming said visual learners benefit from material being presented in diagrammatic form or in photographs. Boys are often considered more visual learners than girls. Auditory learners prefer to pick up new concepts from listening either to their teacher or another source. Class discussions or debates often suit them. Reading-Writing learners do fine with the traditional methods which rely heavily on these skills. Kinesthetic or tactile learners learn faster through experience, for example if they build models, conduct experiments, act out plays, or go on excursions.

Fleming believed that less than half of students benefit from reading and writing alone, and that others should be taught according to their preferences for visual, sound-based, or movement-based activities (34).

Let's fast forward to the 1990s. Chris Jackson is a neuropsychologist. He's interested in changes in the brain as a result of learning. Using MRI scans, Jackson declared that Fleming's VARK Model was inadequate (36). He concluded that four *other* factors influence learning. These are: goal-setting; diligence; concentrated reading; and, being emotionally intelligent (37). In 2007, Siadaty supported Jackson. She added that considering what a student's *achievement* will be is by far *the most effective* way to learn. Making a child understand what he or she will be able to do makes it easier for the steps along the way to be learnt.

But let's go back to Fleming's **VARK** model (35) for a moment, and consider it from a teaching perspective. Deciding which students are visual, and which like moving around takes time (38). Developing specific activities is even more laborious. Furthermore, children these days need to learn rather more than children only 30 years ago. The world is a more complex and competitive place. Besides which, most exams, national and international, have little interest in the visual or kinesthetic, preferring answers that are written or spoken.

Recent experiments with VARK, in ideal situations, have produced results no better than using traditional teaching methods (39).

So, back to the question I posed at the beginning: what helps students learn (31)? It appears the significant factors remain: the classroom environment (32), the teacher's personal qualities, the student's relationship with the teacher, and, above all, each student's long-term goals, or belief in achievement. In my view, VARK has burdened teachers with extra preparation, pigeon-holed many learners, and been a diversion from the main game (40).

READING: Passage 1: 1. Section B: ii; 2. Section C: vii; 3. Section D: iii; 4. Section E: i; 5. 1.5 billion/bn; 6. 2016; 7. 100 kilometres/km // 62 miles/mi; 8. professional astronauts; 9. Not Given/NG; 10. True/T; 11. False/F; 12. True/T; 13. False/F.

> The highlighted text below is evidence for the answers above.
>
> If there is a question where 'Not given' is the answer, no evidence can be found, so there is no highlighted text.

Passage 1: The private-sector space race

Section A

Until recently, only nation states and their agencies, like NASA or the European Space Agency, were capable of sending satellites and astronauts into space. A colony on Mars set up by a private company was the stuff of science fiction. However, since the late 1990s, a number of private firms has entered the space race. Questions about their intentions have inevitably been raised. Will they engage effectively in tourism in sub-orbital space as they claim? Will they be robust enough to send missions into orbit beyond Earth? Or are they mere manifestations of hubris?

Section B

(1) In the latter part of the 20th century, a handful of superrich men decided to purchase football clubs – the ultimate in toys for the boys. These days, owning a company involved in space tourism may be an early 21st-century equivalent, given it is the provenance of billionaires like Jeff Bezos, Richard Branson, John Carmack, and Elon Musk. Bezos was the man behind Amazon, the online retailer. Branson owns transport companies. Carmack brought the world the video games *Doom* and *Quake*. And Elon Musk sold PayPal to eBay for $ (5) 1.5 billion before he founded SpaceX. From these backgrounds, you may construe that some space-company owners are more at home in the virtual world than that of highly complex engineering. They may also be keener to promote a pie-in-the-sky tourist industry than to engage in really useful science.

Their space-tourism companies – Armadillo Aerospace, Blue Origin, Virgin Galactic, SpaceX, Starchaser, and XCOR Aerospace – were all in existence in 2010, and all boasted that very soon they'd be propelling paying passengers to the edge of Earth's atmosphere. By (6) 2016, however, one company had ceased trading; three had scaled down operations or revised launch dates significantly; and only two were actively developing new products. (1) Space tourism had taken a back seat to other more profitable areas of the space industry.

Section C

(2) Furthermore, safety concerns and the customer base have been queried. In order for the US Federal Aviation Administration to license craft that carry passengers, test missions have to be completed at full speed and at an altitude of (7) 100 kilometres (62 miles). (2) To date, only two companies have been able to do this, but and only with unmanned craft. Meanwhile, tests with manned scale models have been fraught, as evidenced by the crash in the Mojave Desert in California of a Virgin Galactic craft.

Then, there is the conundrum that people wealthy enough to afford a $200,000, three-minute thrust into the great blue yonder may not pass a medical. (2) Space travel isn't the same as jetting off on holiday to Tahiti, where all you need is a passport and sunscreen. The British company, Starchaser, which has diversified into space education, is one of the few to offer passenger training, even though there is now no date set for its own first space journey. Starchaser provides a two-week preparatory course that includes: vehicle familiarity and space-travel scenarios; parachute, decompression, and centrifuge training; an introduction to safety systems; first aid, and survival training; and protocols for radio use. All the same, this is greatly removed from what (8) professional astronauts receive.

Section D

Of the few major companies still active in the private-sector space race, SpaceX may be the most well known. Established in 2002, it is the brainchild of the South African entrepreneur, Elon Musk, now resident in California.

Musk has been passionate about the future since his student days, and he is certain his own children will live on other planets, as this is the only way for humans to prevent self-destruction or save themselves from a catastrophe like the impact of a large meteorite.

(10) He also set up SpaceX because he believed NASA to be inefficient. To prove his hypothesis, one of SpaceX's earliest endeavours was the construction of the Merlin engine, which, while elegant and powerful, runs on kerosene – half the price of conventional rocket fuel. Later, SpaceX produced reusable rocket parts, which is an industry innovation, and it designed craft with fewer stages in their transformation. That is: there are fewer times a rocket separates into smaller parts as it journeys onward. (3) These two feats were achieved at a fraction of the cost of competitors, while high safety standards were still maintained.

(3) Indeed, the list of SpaceX's successes is long. Within seven years of establishment, it had sent a satellite into space. By 2010, it had produced the Falcon 9 launcher, and the shuttle Dragon. (11) Subsequently, it was contracted by NASA to provide an **unmanned** service to the International Space Station (ISS), with Dragon completing more than a dozen trips in a decade. It had achieved both take-offs and landings for its rockets both near the terrestrial test site and near beacons in the ocean. (12) More recently, SpaceX has been working with NASA in the Commercial Crew Development programme, in which manned spacecraft are sent to the ISS.

Section E

Although Musk still supports the colonising of space, (12) it would seem that space tourism, even for SpaceX, is **on the back burner**. (4) Instead, the company raises funds by subcontracting to NASA, aiding humanity's efforts to go beyond Earth mainly by providing glorified taxis to the ISS.

Passage 2: 14. D; 15. A; 16. B; 17. D; 18. D; 19. B; 20. C; 21. C; 22. B; 23. A; 24. A; 25. C; 26. C.

Passage 2: Brand loyalty runs deep

At almost any (14) supermarket in Sydney, Australia, food from all over the world fills the shelves. Perhaps you fancy some Tick Tock Rooibos tea made in South Africa, or some Maharaja's Choice Rogan Josh sauce from India. (15) Alongside local Foster's beer, Chinese Tsingtao and Indonesian Bintang are both to be found. For homesick Britons, the confectionary aisle is stocked with Mars Bars and Bountys, while for pining Poles sweets manufactured by firms like Wawel or Solidarposc are available. Restaurants in Sydney range from Afghan to Zambian, catering for different ethnic groups as well as the rest of the curious general public.

(17) All of this variety is a result of population movement and changes in global trade, and to a lesser extent, reduced production and transportation costs. While Australia can claim around 40% of its population as first generation, other countries, like Switzerland, may have fewer international migrants, but still have people who move from city to city in search of work. Even since the 1990s, taxes or tariffs on imported goods have decreased dramatically. The World Trade Organisation, for example, has promulgated the idea of zero tariffs, which has been adopted into legislation by many member states. It is estimated that within a century, agriculture worldwide has increased its efficiency five-fold. Faster and better integrated road and rail services, containerisation, and the ubiquitous aeroplane have sped up transport immeasurably.

(17) (*This is inferred – not stated.*) Even with this rise in the availability of non-local products, recent studies suggest that supermarkets should do more to increase their number to match more closely the proportion of shoppers from those countries or regions. (19) (*This is inferred – not stated.*) Thus, if 10% of a supermarket's customers originate in Vietnam, there ought to be 10% Vietnamese products in store. If Americans from southern states dominate in one northern neighbourhood, southern brands should also be conspicuous. (18) Admittedly, there are already specialist shops that cater to minority groups, but minorities do frequent supermarkets.

(20) Two separate studies by Americans Bart Bronnenberg and David Atkin have found that brand loyalty (choosing Maharaja's Choice over Patak's or Cadbury's over Nestlé) is not only determined by advertising, but also by a consumer's past. If a product featured in a person's early life in one place, then, as a migrant, he or she is likely to buy that same product even though it is more expensive than an otherwise identical locally-produced one.

In the US context, between 2006 and 2008, Bronnenberg analysed data from 38,000 families who had bought 238 different kinds of packaged goods. Although the same brands could be found across America, there were clear differences in what people purchased. In general, there were two leading brands in each kind of packaged good, but there were smaller brands that assumed a greater proportion of consumers' purchases than was statistically likely. (21) One explanation for this is that 16% of people surveyed came from interstate, and these people preferred products from their home states. Over time, they did buy more products from their adopted state, but, surprisingly, it took two decades for their brand loyalty to halve. (22) Even people who had moved interstate 50 years previously maintained a preference for home-state brands. It seems the habits of food buying change more slowly than we think.

Bronnenberg's findings were confirmed by Atkin's in India although there was something more unexpected that Atkin discovered. Firstly, (23) during the period of his survey, the cost of all consumables rose considerably in India. As a result, families reduced their spending on food, and their calorific intake fell accordingly. It is also worth noting that (24) although India is one country, states impose tariffs or taxes on products from other Indian states, ensuring that locally-produced goods remain cheaper. (21) As in the US, internal migrants bought food from their native place even when it was considerably more expensive than local alternatives, and at a time when you might expect families to be economising. This element made the brand-loyalty theory even more convincing.

There is one downside to these findings. In relatively closed economies, such as India's, people develop tastes that they take with them wherever they go; in a more globalised economy, such as America's, what people eat may be more varied, but still dependent on early exposure to brands. (25) Therefore, according to both researchers, more advertising may now be directed at minors since brand loyalty is established in childhood and lasts a lifetime. In a media-driven world where children are already bombarded with information their parents may not consider appropriate yet more advertising is hardly welcome.

For supermarkets, this means that wherever there are large communities of expatriates or immigrants, (26) it is essential to calculate the demographic carefully in order to supply those shoppers with their favourite brands, as in light of Atkin and Bronnenberg's research, advertising and price are not the sole motivating factors for purchase as was previously thought.

Passage 3: 27. D; 28. A; 29. F; 30. G; 31. New Zealand (*capitals optional*); 32. climate change/environmental pressures; 33. young; 34. bones/skeletons; 35. D; 36. A; 37. C; 38. B; 39. B; 40. E.

Passage 3

(27) Imagine a bird three times the size of an ostrich, or a burrowing animal as big as an elephant. How about a kangaroo three metres tall? Such creatures were all Australian megafauna, alive during the Pleistocene.

Fifteen million years ago, 55 species of megafauna were widespread in Australia, the largest of which was the marsupial diprotodon, weighing around 2,700 kilograms (5,952 lb). Giant snakes, crocodiles, and birds were also common. Wombats and kangaroos reached more than 200 kg, and even koalas weighed 16 kg. (28) Then, rather suddenly, around 46 thousand years ago (46 kyr), all these animals became extinct. (32) Some scientists claim this was due to **environmental pressures**, like climate change or fire; others favour predation.

At the end of the Pleistocene, (29) humans reached Australia via Indonesia, and, according to the archaeological record, by 45 kyr their settlement was widespread. One hundred and sixty archaeological sites in Australia and New Guinea have been much surveyed. There is some disagreement about the dates of these sites; meantime, a forceful movement aims to push human settlement back before 45 kyr.

(30) Dating the rare bones of megafauna was highly controversial until 20 years ago, when a technique called optically stimulated luminescence (OSL) was developed. With OSL, the age of minerals up to 200 kyr can be established with +/- 10% accuracy.

The largest OSL dating of megafauna was carried out in 2001 by (35) Roberts, who put the extinction date for megafauna at around 46 kyr, very early on in the time of human habitation.

Megafaunal bones are rare enough, but, at archaeological sites with human habitation, they are extremely rare with fewer than 10% of the 160 sites containing them. Bones that show cutting, burning, or deliberate breaking by humans are virtually non-existent, and thus far, not one megafaunal skeleton shows conclusively an animal was killed by humans. (31) There are no 'kill sites' either whereas in **New Zealand**, where the giant moa bird became extinct in the 18th century due to hunting, there are sites with hundreds of slaughtered creatures. As a result, many scientists still believe that humans were not responsible for megafaunal extinction – especially as the weapons of Australian Aborigines at 45 kyr were only wooden clubs and spears.

(36) There is, perhaps, a cultural record of megafauna in Aboriginal myths. The Adnyamathanha people of South Australia tell of the Yamuti, something like a diprotodon. An ancient rock painting in Arnhem Land shows an extinct giant echidna. But this record is small and open to interpretation.

If the Aborigines were not technologically advanced enough to kill them, what else might have destroyed megafauna? (32) One theory has been **environmental pressures** such as **climate change** – perhaps there was a relatively hot, dry period between 60-40 kyr. Research suggests otherwise. Indeed, at 40 kyr, the climate was moderate, and Lake Eyre, in central Australia, grew. If there was desertification, scientists would expect megafauna to have moved towards the coast, looking for food and water, but instead, the fossil record details an equal distribution of the dead inland and on the coast.

In addition, changes in specific vegetation occurred *after* the extinction of the megafauna. Trees that relied on large animals to eat their fruit and disperse their seed covered far smaller areas of Australia post 40 kyr. These plants were not threatened by climate change; rather, they died off because their megafaunal partners had already gone.

Typically, climate change affects almost all species in an area. Yet, around 46 kyr, only the megafauna died. Previously, there had been many species of kangaroo, some as heavy as 200 kg, but, after, the heaviest weighed only 32 kg. This phenomenon is known as dwarfing, and it occurred with many animals in the Pleistocene.

(37) Dwarfing has been studied extensively. In 2001, Law published research related to fish farming. Despite excellent food and no predators, farmed fish become smaller as generations continue. This adaptation may be a response to their being commercially useless at a smaller size, meaning they hope to survive harvest.

(33) Of the dwarf marsupials, the most notable development over the giants was their longer reproductive lives, which produced more **young**. They were better runners as well, or, those that were slow-moving retreated to the mountainous forest, beyond the reach of humans.

If climate change isn't a credible factor in extinction, what about fire? Fire is caused naturally by lightning strikes as well as by humans with torches. Surprisingly, the charcoal record for many thousands of years does not show a marked increase in fire after human habitation of Australia – there is only a slow increase over time. Besides, it could be argued that forest fires aid megafauna since grass, their favoured food, invariably replaces burnt vegetation.

(38 and 39) Johnson, an archaeologist, has proposed that the Aborigines could have wiped out all 55 megafaunal species in just a few thousand years. He believes that the 45 kyr human settlement date will be pushed back to make this extinction fit, and he also maintains that 700 years are enough to make one species extinct without large-scale hunting or sophisticated weapons. Johnson used computer modelling on a population of only 1000 animals to demonstrate this. If just 30 animals are killed a year, then the species becomes

extinct after 520-700 years. Human populations in Australia were small at 45 kyr – only 150 people occupied the same 500 square kilometres as 1000 animals. However, at a rate of killing just two animals a year by each group of ten people, extinction is highly likely.

A recent study on the albatross has shown the bird has almost disappeared due to females' occasionally being hooked on fishing lines. A large number of animals do not need to be killed to effect extinction especially if an animal breeds late and infrequently like the albatross and like megafauna.

(34) With Johnson's model, it is easy to see that the archaeological record need not be filled with tonnes of **bones**. Megafaunal **skeletons** are not visible because hunting them was a minor activity, or because they are yet to be found.

The mystery of the rapid extinction of Australian megafauna may be over. These animals probably became extinct because they were large, slow, easy victims whose birth rates never exceeded their death rates. (40) Their disappearance is consistent with predation rather than environmental change. Although hard evidence of hunting is lacking, it remains the simplest explanation.

WRITING: Task 1

During a public clean-up day in one city, large amounts of rubbish were collected.

Of the top five types of rubbish, cigarette butts were the main constituent at 40 percent, followed by plastic bottles at 21 percent, and aluminium cans at 12 percent.

Of the three specific sites, Memorial Park was the only one whose top three items corresponded to those of the city in type and weight, although, at Diego Beach, the second-most common form of rubbish was cigarette butts, and they were twice as heavy as plastic bottles, as was the case in the city. At Diego Beach, however, tyres weighed 563 kilograms, almost five times that of cigarette butts. Rubbish items collected at Arden Park, although the lowest in weight, did not correspond in type or proportion to the city's top three. Instead, glass made up half of the park's total 66 kilograms, followed by aluminium cans at 24 kilograms, and cigarette butts at nine.

Since there are no figures for total weight at any of the three sites, it is hard to know which one was the most polluted. It is likely that this was Diego Beach, whose top three types of rubbish amounted to 803 kilograms, while Memorial Park, which was next, had only 378 kilograms. (208 words)

Note: This is a tricky task because you have to do some maths to work out if the rubbish at the three sites corresponds to that of the city. Remember, when there are two inputs, their relationship needs to be described.

Task 2

In the developed world, some advanced and wealthy nations are finding that the number of secondary or high school children taking science subjects is declining. With fewer students studying science, there will be fewer science graduates, a lessening of scientific knowledge, less research, fewer scientific breakthroughs, and ultimately, a decline in economic superiority.

Science is an integral part of our lives. Everyday we cook, go to the doctor, grow or buy vegetables, use electricity, log on to a computer, and gaze at the stars. Seldom do we think that these involve chemistry, biology, botany, physics, engineering, astronomy, and mathematics. If students were made aware of the scientific connections with everyday life, perhaps more would develop a love for science enough to make it a career.

Not studying science in any depth will not only disadvantage children's futures, but also the future of their nations. Although arts subjects are essential for students to develop a rounded approach to life, science subjects will provide them with intellectual challenges which could result in new discoveries. With these discoveries the business world will flourish, and a natural follow-on is that their countries will flourish economically.

So how are we going to attract these reluctant learners to the world of science? First, introduce them to science at a very young age, even at the preschool-level through games. Then let them make predictions about certain actions. Get them to keep a worm farm, and subsequently use the fertiliser to feed a small garden. Have them play counting games with adding and subtracting. Make it fun.

At primary-school level, children's interests need to be catered to, and the approach may be more mysterious, or more personal. Depending on the age group, investigating the family gene pool may be of interest. For example, the colour of eyes and hair, or special family characteristics could be tabled over three generations and the results discussed. Children need visual representations, simple graphs, pattern recognition, and games.

At secondary and highschool level, general science and maths are a must, but again, students need to be kept involved. They need to have a passion for an area of science that will stay with them. They might be asked to find out about genetically modified genes, about how to end aging, about a disease-free world, about artificial intelligence, about electricity from plant life, or about driving on air. While there are science fairs to encourage ideas, above all, children need exciting and innovative teachers.

Hopefully, then, students will take science subjects at tertiary level, and thereby continue to keep their nations at the scientific and economic forefront. (433 words)

Recording 73:

> ### Practice Speaking Test 2 – Part 2 topic
> *I'd like you to tell me about a small company you know that has been successful.*
> * *What is the company called?*
> * *What does it do?*
> * *Why has it been successful?*

Academic Practice Test 3

LISTENING: Answers and Script with highlighted evidence for answers

Section 1: 1. interview; 2. experience; 3. typing; 4. redesign; 5. C; 6. B; 7. B; 8. B; 9. A; 10. A. Section 2: 11. Italy/Venice (*capital optional*); 12. traditions; 13. pet; 14. council; 15. model(l)ing; 16. wax; 17. high; 18. 3/three; 19. setting; 20. installation. Section 3: 21. presentation; 22. study; 23. 3000; 24. low; 25. boss; 26. 12/twelve; 27. distance; 28. complex; 29. awful; 30. reduce. Section 4: 31. A; 32. C; 33. A; 34. C; 35. B; 36. chose; 37. upset; 38. confronting/facing; 39. past; 40. underlying.

Narrator	Recording Seventy-two. Practice Listening Test Three. Section One. Curriculum Vitae or CV.
Harry	What's up, Jun Hee? You don't look happy.
Jun Hee	I rang about three jobs, today, Harry. Two of them had already gone. The last employer asked for my CV, which I sent off straight away, but I know he won't call **back** (eg).
Harry	Oh dear. Would you like a cup of tea?
Jun Hee	Thanks a lot. What I'd really like is some advice. I haven't had a single job **interview** in the entire month I've been looking for work (1), and if I don't find something soon, I'll have to borrow money from my parents again to continue my studies. I really don't want to do that.
Harry	I saw your friend, Fumiko, today. Why don't you get a job with her in the café?
Jun Hee	I'd love to, but I've never worked in hospitality in any capacity. In fact, that's one of my problems: I don't have much **experience** at anything (2). I've only been a nanny for a summer in Paris just before I started my under-graduate degree.
Harry	Didn't you work for your uncle in Seoul?
Jun Hee	I worked for a fortnight when his office assistant was away, but I wouldn't call that a job.
Harry	What did you do?
Jun Hee	Photocopying and typing mostly. I'm not very good at **typing** (3).
Harry	Is that job on your CV?
Jun Hee	No. I was too ashamed to include it. Besides, what would happen if anyone actually gave me a typing test – I'd fail miserably (3).
Harry	I've got an idea: show me your CV, and I'll help you **redesign** it (4).
Jun Hee	Would you, Harry? I'd really appreciate that.
	…
Harry	Looking at your CV, I do like the colours you've chosen; I'd certainly keep them (5). Do you know what I mean by the word 'font'?
Jun Hee	The style of the letters: whether they're Times New Roman or Arial?
Harry	Yes. You've got about ten different fonts.
Jun Hee	I thought that'd show I had creative flair. It's fun to use a variety, isn't it?
Harry	Fun for a party invitation. Stick to two fonts is my advice (6).
Jun Hee	All right. What about the content? You're a local lad – I expect you can give me some pointers about the content.
Harry	Your education in Korea is fine, and so is being a nanny. In Britain, people don't usually mention whether they're single or married (7). It's unnecessary to include your hobbies, especially if they're dangerous (8).
Jun Hee	Are you sure about that? Doesn't snow boarding make me sound more interesting, like a person who's looking for a challenge?
Harry	No. Employers might think you won't find their job exciting enough.
Jun Hee	It seems we should cross off both my marital status and my sports (7 and 8).
Harry	I can't see here that you're a Master's student, or that you've got a driving licence.
Jun Hee	No. I didn't want to say I was doing a post-grad course because an employer might wonder why I'm applying for such a lowly job. I didn't mention being able to drive because almost everyone here my age can. Do I really need to spell that out?
Harry	Yes (9). And you're fluent in Mandarin, right (10)?

Jun Hee	Right. I studied in Nanjing for almost two years as part of an exchange programme. My spoken Mandarin is pretty good, and if necessary, I could brush up my writing. I used to know about 2000 characters.
	I picked up some French while I was nannying in Paris, but I'm hardly fluent, and I doubt it would be useful to an employer here.
Harry	So, let's add Driver's Licence and three languages as your skills (10). We'll forget about your being single (7) and the snow boarding (8). Let's keep the blue (5), put all the text on the left, and reduce the fonts (6).
Jun Hee	Thanks, Harry. That's much better.
Narrator	Section Two. Copper Sculpture.
Interviewer	And now on 'Art Today', I've got Michelle Blanche.
Michelle Blanche	Good morning.
Interviewer	So you're off to **Italy** tomorrow (11)?
Michelle Blanche	Yes. I'm taking part in a major international art exhibition, called the **Venice** Biennale (11).
Interviewer	Congratulations. What work are you taking?
Michelle Blanche	Ten small copper sculptures that I'm just putting the finishing touches to. They're on the theme of people and pets.
Interviewer	That's kind of a strange theme for a contemporary art show, isn't it?
Michelle Blanche	Perhaps, but I follow **traditions** that date back to ancient Greece (12). I believe in highly developed craft as well as accessibility to the viewer. Frankly, I find a lot of modern art has alienated the public both with its form and content. I'm trying to create something that people can easily respond to.
Interviewer	So why people and pets?
Michelle Blanche	You're not the first person to have asked me that question. Actually, I've never owned a pet myself, but last year, I saw an amazing TV programme about a general hospital in Calgary. Volunteers take dogs onto wards there during visiting hours, and the presence of the animals has been found to improve patients' health significantly. Raising the spirit does wonders for the body. It seems that people heal faster if they can be around an animal or if they have their own **pet** (13), so I decided to explore this in my artwork.
Interviewer	Interesting. Who buys your sculptures?
Michelle Blanche	I've sold to both private art collectors and public museums. All of about 20 of my small works have been purchased by individuals. The Lightfoot Building downtown has one of my early copper pieces in its foyer – you can see it through the window from Brook Street – and two regional museums have bought large bronze sculptures that I made in 2011.
Interviewer	And you've just been asked by the mayor to produce a statue, right?
Michelle Blanche	Not the mayor, himself, but a local **council** (14). The council had a competition for a work based on local history (14), which I won. I'm making a sculpture for a square downtown. It's my first major outdoor commission, so I'm very excited.
Interviewer	Anything to do with animals?
Michelle Blanche	Yes, it honours a dog that saved a girl in the river. Everyone in the city knows this story – it's practically a legend– but there's not one memorial to this incredible act of devotion.
	…
Interviewer	So, Michelle, tell our listeners about the process of making a large copper sculpture.
Michelle Blanche	For me, the process is as remarkable and as enjoyable as the finished product. Its physically quite tough, which I think accounts for not many women pursuing metal-based sculpture.
	Generally, I submit a portfolio of work to a client. After being chosen for a commission, I spend around two weeks **modelling** (15) the sculpture in clay. Then, I make a perfect wax copy, coated in a slurry of stucco, and ducted with ceramic granules –.
Interviewer	Hang on a minute. That's too technical for me.
Michelle Blanche	OK. Basically, I make a clay model; then, I make a copy in **wax**. I use wax because (16), ultimately, this will be melted and replaced with copper. The wax model is painted with a special liquid, which is called stucco. It's a kind of soft plaster. Then the stucco is sprayed with tiny grains of ceramic to make a hard shell or cast.
Interviewer	What's next?

Michelle Blanche	The cast is fired – heated to a very **high** temperature – in an industrial furnace (17). My studio is in a disused boiler-making factory, and I'm very fortunate to have this furnace. The firing process is a little dangerous, so I employ two assistants. While they're firing the cast, I prepare the metal.
Interviewer	The copper?
Michelle Blanche	Yes. In fact, a copper sculpture is not one hundred percent copper. It consists of **three** elements: ninety-five percent copper, four percent silicon, and one percent manganese (18). The trace elements strengthen the copper without altering its other qualities.
Interviewer	Uh huh.
Michelle Blanche	After the cast is made, the molten metal is poured in, and left to set. **Setting** takes several hours, depending on the size of the work (19). When the cast is removed, the sculpture is polished. This also takes time, but is quite thrilling since you see the brightly shining metal emerge beneath your hands. As I said before, the process is quite physically demanding, but the end result is gorgeous.
Interviewer	Indeed.
Michelle Blanche	Finally, it's approved by the commissioning authority, and installed in its permanent place – in this case the city square.
Interviewer	When is the **installation** date (20)?
Michelle Blanche	The third of June, which marks the centenary of the girl's rescue.

Narrator	Section Three. University Counselling Session.
Counsellor	So, Rachel, how have things been going?
Rachel	All right, I suppose.
Counsellor	Are you ready for your **presentation** tomorrow (21)?
Rachel	I think so.
Counsellor	Great. What about the rest of the **study** plan we made (22)? Have you been sticking to it?
Rachel	Well…That's why I came back to you. I did manage to get everything done for my presentation, but now I'm way behind with my other assignments (21), and I'm starting to panic.
Counsellor	You've got the **3000**-word essay for Criminal Law, haven't you (23), and one on Taxation?
Rachel	That's right.
Counsellor	What seems to be preventing you from doing them?
Rachel	My own indecision is one factor. You see, we were given two choices for the Criminal Law essay, and I seem to change my mind daily about which one to do.
	I remember in our last session that you said I might be using procrastination to obscure some other inadequacy – perhaps not understanding the legal topic as well as I ought to. If I get a **low** mark, I can just say, 'Well, I did that essay in such a rush' instead of admitting that I don't have a grasp of the subject (24). Intellectually, I understand what you've told me, but I'm afraid it hasn't made a difference to my starting the essay.
	Another thing that's affecting me is the demands of other people (25).
Counsellor	Like what?
Rachel	Take my flatmate, Teresa, who's a nursing student (25). We've been sharing a flat for over a year, and we used to get along really well. But recently, she's been pestering me to help her with her assignments.
Counsellor	You might suggest your flatmate get help from her college with her studies.
Rachel	I've done that, and she claims she's been going to the Student Learning Centre on campus. Meantime, if I don't help her at home, she calls me selfish, or arrogant, or unfriendly, and then starts sulking. The atmosphere in our place is poisonous.
	What can I do about my **boss** (25)? Last week, I worked **twelve** hours' overtime (26). I'm exhausted! I felt obliged to accept the work because right now he's making decisions about who to keep on over the summer, and if I turn down extra shifts, he may not consider me. I certainly can't afford to lose my summer job.
Counsellor	Remember, Rachel, your goals and priorities. Is your long-term goal to work in a supermarket, or to be a lawyer?
Rachel	Of course to be a lawyer. I know I've got to concentrate on that.
	As I think I've said, I can see everything clearly when I'm here in the office with you, but I waver as soon as I leave.

...

Counsellor	You wanted to talk about your ex-boyfriend, Dan.
Rachel	Yes. Dan. Hmmm. I know we went through all this in the last session as well, but he's been bugging me again.
Counsellor	What does he want?
Rachel	To get back together.
Counsellor	Do you want that?
Rachel	Yes. No. I mean... I ended the relationship. Dan's a great person and I'll always think of him fondly, but we somehow brought out the worst in each other.
Counsellor	All right. Keep Dan at a **distance** (27) while you focus on your studies. Politely tell him that you want to remain apart. Let's make another study plan, now, with your starting work on your 3000-word essay tomorrow (22 and 23). That's due on the ninth, isn't it?
Rachel	Yes, just ten days away. I can't possibly do it by then. Even if I settle on a topic, the reading list is as long as my arm. And I've another confession to make: I've barely attended a single tutorial for that course, so I don't even understand the basics. With the state I'm in, I won't be able to absorb any of the **complex** arguments, let alone critique them (28). Really, my situation's **awful** (29). Do you think I could get an extension?
Counsellor	Rachel, your situation is difficult, not awful (29), and all of these things, we can solve. Remember: **reduce contact with people who don't help you (30)**, and reduce your hours at the supermarket. Focus on your essays and your future goal.

Narrator	Section Four. Rational-Emotive Therapy or RET.
Lecturer	Good afternoon. Last week, we discussed why people seek therapy. This week, we're going to look at one kind of psychotherapy called Rational-Emotive Therapy or RET (31). But before we get started, I'd like to quote a first-century philosopher, called Marcus Aurelius, whose words I think are apposite to this discussion. He wrote something like: 'The universe is about change; life is what thinking makes it.' RET is also about accepting the world while changing thought patterns. RET was created by an American, Albert Ellis, in the 1950s. The main aim of RET is to develop healthy emotional responses to cope with unfortunate circumstances (32). Anger, anxiety, or depression is replaced with upset, followed by acceptance, then by moving on. Let's take the example of a person who is involved in a car accident. Of course, your physical injuries are your primary concern, and satisfactory medical assistance in hospital is critical, but how fast you heal after that assistance is not only determined by the kind of medical care you have received, but also by your attitude. You probably had no control over the accident, but you *can* control how you feel about it afterwards. Anxiety, guilt, and even rage at others involved are all mental states that you can overcome. Here's another scenario: your sister borrowed some money from you a year or so ago, and hasn't made any effort to give it back. A well-balanced person thinks: 'Oh dear, never mind', but an unbalanced one says: 'My sister *should* give me my money back'; 'She *mustn't* do this to me'. Or, 'She's *always* been so selfish'; 'She *never* treats me well'. Now, people, including your sister, are both good and bad, and they *do* change. Imagining how awful your circumstances are doesn't help. You're far more likely to get your money back if your sister knows you don't judge her, and you avoid words like 'should', 'must', 'always', and 'never' (33). One of Albert Ellis' fundamental beliefs was that too many people these days 'awfulise'. Yes, he even coined the term to awfulise. He considered that people make things seem awful that really aren't. They disable themselves through anxiety, rather than accepting the challenges there are in modern life (34). To introduce his ideas to the world, Ellis came up with the ABC scheme. In this, 'A' stands for 'adversity' – something out of the ordinary that causes difficulty. Ellis was convinced that when A struck, it was B – a person's 'beliefs' – that often affected them more than A itself. This leads to C, or 'consequences'. Some of these could be relatively minor, like headaches or skin disorders, but others could be serious and debilitating like long-term mental illness. Ellis added 'D' to his ABC scheme. This means a person 'distinguishes' between 'awfulising' and healthy beliefs (35). During this process of distinguishing, a person's mental worldview undergoes a significant change, and as a result, he or she makes a genuine recovery.

Albert Ellis set up his practice in the cosseted world of New York City, where the majority of his patients could afford superior medical care, and probably hadn't really experienced any great trauma.

So what if something really awful does happen? How would RET be effective with those sufferers?

Quite a lot of research has been done on refugees from major conflicts. They appear to fall almost equally into two groups: one, the badly affected, and, two, the largely unaffected. All the refugees lived through the same war, but they *chose* to be happy, or they *chose* to be sad (36).

So, how does RET work? Initially, therapists and patients target specific problems, and set daily and weekly goals. Exercises are connected to everyday life. There are links on my website to some of these if you're interested. As I mentioned earlier, replacing anger with **upset** is the first phase of treatment (37). Anger can be as threatening to the body as the original trauma.

Confronting the very thing a patient is afraid of is another approach (38). If a person has a phobia of cars after an accident, he or she is put right back behind the wheel.

Critics of RET say the treatment is too short and too unkind, and its rehabilitation rate of around 40% is not very high.

Because it focuses on mental states in the present, and it completely ignores a patient's **past** (39), detractors believe it fails to address **underlying** issues. Other, more conventional methods of therapy, explore the past in some detail (40).

Nevertheless, Ellis and RET have reintroduced rationalist philosophical notions into everyday treatment. I'll leave it up to you to evaluate their success.

READING: Passage 1: 1. M; 2. O; 3. J; 4. C; 5. E; 6. K; 7. G; 8. L; 9. B; 10. D; 11. A; 12. C; 13. B. Passage 2: 14. Section B: ix; 15. Section C: iii; 16. Section D: vi; 17. Section E: v; 18. Section F: vii; 19. Section G: viii; 20. happiness; 21. yesterday; 22. 5.5 (*point not comma*); 23. 46/forty-six; 24. cultures; 25. realistic; 26. D; 27. A. Passage 3: 28. B; 29. F/False; 30. F/False; 31. T/True; 32. NG/Not Given; 33. 336; 34. converter; 35. microwaves; 36. 2030; 37. General configuration (*capital optional*); 38. Solar array (*capital optional*); 39. Relatively unsolved; 40. C.

Passage 1: Driving on air

(1 and 2) No matter how costly, hazardous, or polluting they are, nor how tedious it is to be stuck in traffic jams, cars are here to stay. In fact, the global car industry is worth a massive two trillion dollars a year.

Recently, Guy Negre, a French engineer on Renault's Formula One engines, designed and produced the Airpod – a vehicle which runs on air, is lightweight and compact, and capable of reaching moderate speeds.

Since the transport sector constitutes one seventh of all air pollution, (4) Negre spent 15 years developing the Airpod, hoping to significantly reduce greenhouse-gas emissions. (3) Petrol-electric hybrids, already on the market, are touted as being environmentally friendly, (4) yet he says they are barely less polluting than combustion-engine vehicles. The Airpod, on the other hand, produces just 10% of the carbon monoxide of other cars.

Major manufacturers are now considering hydrogen as a power source for vehicles, but this technology may be decades away. Meantime, according to Negre, electric vehicles remain impractical: batteries are expensive, and need replacement within five years; recharging takes several hours.

(5) Negre's secondary aim in creating the Airpod was to bring cars within reach of consumers in the developing world. To date, his most impressive deal has been with an Indian car manufacturer which predicts the Airpod will retail for the price of an average motorcycle.

Currently, only three-wheeled Airpods are available, but Negre has a four-wheeled, five-door family saloon, plus vans, buses, taxis, boats, and aircraft on the drawing board.

So what is (6) an Airpod? This small vehicle resembles an ordinary car except that it is made mostly from fiberglass – ten times as strong as steel (6) but very light – meaning an Airpod weighs just 220 kilograms (484 lb). It has glass windows and an aluminium engine. However, it uses a joystick instead of a steering wheel, and it has backward-facing passenger seats and a front-opening door.

(7) The 180cc engine of an Airpod allows it to reach a speed of around 70 kilometres per hour (kph) (43 mph), and it can drive for about 220 kilometres (137 miles) before refilling is necessary. It takes as little as 90 seconds to pump air into an Airpod from a high-speed compressor at a gas station, with air costing a mere 50 cents for a 220-kilometre journey. An on-board pump can refill the tank at home overnight.

How does an Airpod work? Quite simply: air is released through pistons in the engine, which drive the wheels. Compressed air tanks store up to 175 litres (46 gallons) of air at about 180 times the pressure of an average car tyre. (8) Passengers and passers-by might have concerns about explosions with such pressure, but, in the rare event of one, the thermoplastic tanks split to release air, rather than shattering and exploding. In fact, the same tanks are already installed on natural-gas buses.

For longer journeys, there is a battery-assisted hybrid Airpod, which (9) Negre maintains is capable of reaching 80 kph and travelling around 1500 kilometres on four litres of petrol, although this version has yet to be manufactured or tested.

Still in its infancy, the Airpod has both supporters and critics. Marcus Waardenberg, the organiser of an Airpod trial at a major Dutch airport, was impressed. 'The Airpods went over 40 kph, were quiet and manoeuverable. Refilling was fast and straightforward.' As a result, his company is replacing its fleet of electric service vehicles with Airpods.

Perhaps more significantly, AK Jagadeesh, from the Indian conglomerate, Tata, signed a $60 million deal. 'We're going to use Airpod technology in Tata's Nano car,' he said.

(10) Ulf Bossel, a sustainable energy consultant, commented that the Airpod easily reaches speeds of over 50 kph. 'Initially, it could capture the second-car market. Then, there are those older people who can no longer afford conventional cars.' Both Europe and North America have ageing populations.

(11) Bill Robertson, a motoring journalist, noted that the Airpod would suit large numbers of people who make two or three trips a day of fewer than ten kilometers, or who live in distant suburbs of big cities where public transport is poor. (11) If the Airpod looked a little sexier, there would be the potential for it to make inroads into the golf buggy sector, which currently uses electric vehicles.

Among the detractors of the Airpod is the former champion racer, Martella Valentina, who would prefer a vehicle with a more robust engine. 'There are so many aggressive drivers out there,' she said. 'As a woman, I don't feel safe in an Airpod.' She added, 'Refilling overnight is a drag.'

The automotive engineer, (12) Hamid Khan, concurs, expressing skepticism about sufficient energy storage under reasonable pressure to drive the car any distance, let alone the alleged 220 kilometres before refill. He insists this is unconfirmed by independent tests. Stopping and starting in typical city conditions would also lower the range even further, and more distressingly, safety data is lacking for crash testing. 'Negre claims fibreglass is stronger than steel, but the Airpod looks as though it would crumple under the wheels of a normal saloon,' commented Khan.

Nevertheless, (13) Negre has signed deals to manufacture his car in the US, Latin America, India, and several European countries. Compressed air may no longer take a back seat to other power sources, and it is even conceivable that one day we may be flying in aircraft that fly on air.

Passage 2

Section A: We're probably all aware of measures economists use to ascertain the wealth of a country and its people. Income generated annually is measured by a figure called the Gross Domestic Product or the Gross National Income. In the past, it was assumed that the richer a country was, the happier its citizens were. More recently, economists have rated countries according to additional criteria, such as: how livable its cities are, what access people have to education and green space, and how safe people feel.

The Human Development Index (HDI) is considered (20) the most reliable of these new expanded economic indicators, but a more focused measure of well-being is the Human Happiness Index (HHI). In this, people from 156 countries rate their country's level of social support; their life expectancy; their freedom to make choices; the generosity of other inhabitants; and the trust they have in the state or private enterprise, as indicated by an absence of corruption.

Section B: This interest in quantifiable gladness came about because, in 2008, (14) Bhutan, a small Asian country, developed a happiness index to assist with policy-making. If people indicated one of their concerns was rising fuel costs, the government attempted to subsidize fuel, not only because it hoped to retain power, but also because if this anxiety were allayed, its citizens would be happier and more productive. Another worry of the Bhutanese was the quality of primary education. Once alerted to this, the state commenced investment. Also in 2008, the economists Amartya Sen and Joseph Stiglitz were invited to (14) France to devise a happiness index for that country. Finally, in 2011, the General Assembly of the United Nations passed a resolution asking (14) member states to measure contentment.

Section C: (15 & 21) There are two common measures of happiness: a global, and a hedonic one. The former appraises life in general; the latter a person's emotional feeling just yesterday. Two measures are considered necessary because altered circumstances produce different results. As any parent can attest, having children makes people happier overall, especially as the children mature and start their own families, yet, on a day-to-day basis, when the children are young, raising them can be difficult: parents may experience stress, anger, and even misery. Globally, parents are glad they have family; hedonically, they may be going through a bad patch. Likewise employment: a secure enjoyable job contributes greatly to happiness, but being temporarily unemployed can have a deleterious effect.

Section D: Using both these measures – the global and hedonic – some surprising data have come to light. (16) Firstly, wealthier is indeed happier, but there are still some miserable rich people. Danes and Hong Kong Chinese have almost identical purchasing power. (22) Yet, on a scale of one to ten, Hong Kongers consistently rate their well-being as 5.5 whereas Danes – usually the world's happiest people – give theirs as 7.5. Likewise, incomes in Latin America vary little from those in countries of the former Soviet Union, like Ukraine or Kazakhstan, but Latinos are far healthier, longer-lived, and more cheerful.

(16) The second significant finding is that the level of happiness increases with age. Despite the body's decay and fewer financial resources, older people are more stable, less anxious, and less angry. It is now universally agreed that suicide rates worldwide peak in the early forties for women and the early fifties for men. Of 72 countries in one recent poll, (23) the average age was **46** after which life became easier. Ukrainians bucked this trend, not finding happiness until after 62, while the Swiss were fortunate for their discontent to decline from 35.

Section E: (17 & 24) Some common beliefs have been confirmed by the happiness data, for instance that introverted **cultures** produce more unhappy people. Asians all identified themselves as being unhappier than Western Europeans (with the exception of the Portuguese and the Greeks). In 2017, Japan rated highly on the HDI, but near the middle of the HHI. Still, Japan has the world's longest-living women – 83 years is their average life expectancy – so, if people are generally happier as they age, Japanese women do have longer than women elsewhere in which to get happy!

Section F: (18 & 25) What are the reasons for happiness after middle age? Basically, people understand where they fit in the world. Their ambitions have settled to **realistic** levels – they accept what they can and cannot do. For example, I won't be able to win the Nobel Prize in Literature, but I could conceivably take first place in a local short-story competition.

Section G: (27) It is good news that people become happier as they grow older because populations in most developed countries age, and projections are for many developing countries to have more people over 50 after 2020. Governments have had some concern about the burden on younger taxpayers of this greying population, but perhaps they should reconsider the data: (19) older people, being happier, are potentially more capable than younger ones. Loss of memory and poorer physical skills are counterbalanced by cheerfulness. Therefore, the retirement age could be extended without concerns about productivity.

(26) Personally, I'd rather have a smiling, competent, grey-haired colleague than a pretty twenty-something who pretends to know it all but, underneath, is a seething mass of discontent.

Passage 3: Space-based solar power

In an energy-hungry world, new safe ways to generate electricity are constantly being sought.

Space-based solar power, or SBSP, is not yet up and running, but several space agencies and commercial companies are pursuing it. Simultaneously, its critics view it as little more than a fantasy.

(28) SBSP is a system that would harness sunlight in space, (29) convert it into **electrical** energy, and beam this, via a microwave or laser transmitter, to receivers in Earth's equatorial zone. (30) SBSP satellites would probably be in low orbit, **1100** kilometres (684 miles) above earth.

Advantages

To date, solar energy has been collected on the ground, but it is estimated there is 144% more solar power available in space as Earth's atmosphere absorbs light. Furthermore, since the planet rotates, energy can only be collected during daylight. It is possible at the poles to collect light almost continuously in summer, but in winter such plants cannot operate due to snow, ice, and darkness. (31) In space, however, solar power collection could occur around the clock.

A further benefit may be that the energy produced could be directed to multiple locations whereas terrestrial power plants are limited to sending power one way into a grid.

Design

Most prototypes of SBSP structures look like a giant tent hanging in space. (33) Its light, hollow equilateral triangular frame is **336** metres (1103 feet) long while its depth is 303 metres (994 feet). Down two sides are solar collectors, called arrays; on the floor of the 'tent' sit a solar converter and a transmitting antenna. (34) The antenna sends **microwaves** to Earth. These waves are at a frequency of 2.45-5.8 gigahertz, or somewhere between infrared and radio signals. They pass through Earth's atmosphere easily with only minor energy loss. (35) On Earth, the invisible column of microwave energy – perhaps two to three kilometres (a mile or two) wide – is received by a large **'rectenna'** – a new word combining 'rectifying' + 'antenna'. A pilot beam, also on earth, ensures the satellite stays in position in space.

Two major technical obstacles remain before SBSP becomes a reality. The first is launching satellites into orbit. While most scientists favour low orbit, others believe a higher orbit, like 36,050 kilometres (22,400 miles), or about one tenth of the distance between Earth and the Moon, would harness more sunlight. However, no agency or company has any experience of launching and controlling a satellite in high orbit. Even with low-orbit satellites that agencies or companies recognize, anywhere up to 150 launches would be needed to construct a single SBSP system. Launch costs are currently around $320 billion, which would be prohibitive. Furthermore, the impact of emissions from 150 launches on Earth's atmosphere would be considerable. The second stumbling block is wireless power transmission. In 2009, American and Japanese researchers successfully sent microwave energy between two islands in Hawaii that are 145 km (90 miles) apart – equidistant to Earth's atmosphere. In 2015, Mitsubishi Heavy Industries beamed 10 kilowatts to a receiver 500 metres (1640 feet) away. Still, it is unknown whether these efforts can be reproduced in space.

History

SBSP is not a new idea. Dr Peter Glaser designed a system in the late 1960s, and was granted a US patent in 1973. The US Department of Energy in conjunction with NASA conducted feasibility studies in the 1970s, but a conservative administration in the 1980s discontinued investment. Only in 1997, did the US reconsider the idea. In 2015, a proposal for a US SBSP system won the prestigious D3 (Diplomacy, Development, Defence) competition. Meanwhile, the China Academy for Space Technology unveiled a design for a one-gigawatt system by 2050 at a recent International Space Development conference.

Japanese initiatives

It seems the Japanese are closest to producing a reliable system. Since 1998, (36) JAXA (the Japanese space agency) has been involved in all aspects of SBSP, and its forecast puts its first satellite in orbit by **2030**. Among private companies, Mitsubishi and IHI Corporation fund research.

There are six broad areas that JAXA is working on. These are: (1) (37) general configuration; (2) assembly work & operation; (3) (38) solar array; (4) transmitting antenna; (5) power transmission & reception system; and (6) testing methods. The first of these is the most developed. The (38) solar array and transmitting antenna are second in terms of development. Testing methods are (39) relatively unsolved. Assembly work & operation, and power transmission & reception system remain far from being solved.

Disadvantages

SBSP has numerous detractors. There are those who imagine the microwave beam to be something like a science-fiction death ray. Physicists reassure the public it is a non-ionising wave, like a radio wave or x-ray. It cannot displace electrons from atoms to charge particles, so it does not damage DNA. The waves may be slightly warm, but they present no danger to wildlife or humans. Still, the waves must be carefully guided by the rectennas.

Other opponents of SBSP say that while there is neither corrosion nor damage from plants or animals in space, background radiation could harm the satellite. There is the very real danger of collision with space junk, as recently happened at the International Space Station, or with small meteors' hitting it. Repairing an unmanned structure so far from Earth would be extremely difficult.

Solar power via the Moon is an option that some scientists say can be in operation in ten years at a fraction of the cost.

Most tellingly, companies already involved in the space-power race have not been successful. In the early 2000s, three US firms predicted they would be contributing electricity to the national grid with SBSP within fifteen years. None of them is even close, and one company has withdrawn from the race altogether.

(40) The vast majority of those opposed to SBSP consider it expensive and unnecessary, given that many other forms of renewable energy on earth are operating successfully. Terrestrial solar power is relatively underdeveloped; the Arizona Desert in the US and deserts across North Africa provide easily-accessible locations for new systems that would be five times more cost-effective than SBSP.

Viability

Nevertheless, as energy requirements accelerate, as unrest in oil-producing regions and nuclear accidents make alternative energy more attractive, space-based solar power may have a future after all.

WRITING: For Task 1, go to Grammar and Vocabulary Test 1 on page 385. For Task 2, there are some ideas on pages 155-157.

Recording 74:

> **Practice Speaking Test 3 – Part 2 topic**
>
> *I'd like you to tell me about a photograph of yourself that you like very much.*
> • *Who took the photograph?*
> • *What were you doing when the photograph was taken?*
> • *Why do you like the photograph so much?*

Academic Practice Test 4

LISTENING: **Answers and Script** with: highlighted evidence for answers

Section 1: 1. mobile/phone; 2. 18/eighteen; 3. teaching; 4. screen; 5. 300; 6. insurance; 7. C; 8. C; 9. B; 10. A. Section 2: 11. management; 12. cleaner/lighter/service; 13. 40/forty; 14. product; 15. 5-year/five-year (*must be singular; must have a hyphen and not be written as two separate words*); 16. C; 17. B; 18. A; 19. A; 20. iii. Section 3: 21. 2,500 (*comma optional*); 22. interested; 23. argument; 24. sources; 25. stealing; 26. school/secondary; 27-30. (*in any order*): B, C, F, G. Section 4: 31. B; 32. A; 33. Pumping (*capital optional*); 34. concentrate; 35. Tank (*capital optional*); 36. 5/five; 37. 20/twenty; 38. 10/ten; 39. 1.5 (*must be a point and not a comma*); 40. millions (*must be plural*).

Narrator	Recording Seventy-four. Practice Listening Test Four. Section One. Phone Services.
Salesman	Good morning, may I help you, ma'am?
Ann	I'm reading one of your brochures on wireless services since I'd like to get the **internet** at home (eg). I wonder if you could you tell me about some different deals.
Salesman	Certainly.
Ann	First of all, do you have any packages that are wireless and **mobile/phone** combined (1)?

Salesman	I'm afraid we don't.
Ann	That's a pity.
Salesman	You may like to know that from next week, we're starting a deal whereby anyone who signs a phone contract for 18 months gets a brand new smartphone (2). That way, the internet is with you all the time, on your phone, and not just at home on your computer. How does that sound?
Ann	I'm sure lots of people will jump at it, but I don't want the internet with me all the time. I don't need a fancy phone. I need to be contactable for work – I'm a post-grad student, and I support myself with relief **teaching** (3). I need to send a few texts and make a couple of calls a day, but that's all. A basic phone and pre-paid monthly vouchers suit me.
Salesman	As you please.
Ann	Also, my friend bought a smartphone recently, dropped it, and shattered the glass **screen** (4). To get the screen replaced, she's going to spend $300. Well, **$300** is almost my annual phone budget (5).
Salesman	Yes, you do have to be careful with smartphones. However, for just a few dollars a week, we also offer **insurance** (6) against damage or theft. That might be worth considering.
Ann	Thank you for the offer, but I'm sticking to my cheap phone that I've dropped a dozen times but still keeps working.

…

Let's get back to wireless services at home. I've brought my laptop, and I'd like to see if your modems are compatible. |
| Salesman | We've got a comprehensive range of modems, so I'm sure we'll find something.

What operating system do you have? |
Ann	OSX twelve point five. I'll just check that. Sorry, it's OSX twelve point nine.
Salesman	Yes, several of our modems will work with that.
Ann	If I choose a deal now, is there any chance I can get my computer set up right away?
Salesman	Absolutely. You can be online in 15 minutes.
Ann	Really?

I know I said I didn't want a long-term plan for my phone, but for wireless, your 24-month plan looks the best. |
Salesman	I think it's excellent, ma'am: $80 a month for ten gigabytes and a modem.
Ann	If I opt for this contract, what would you need from me now other than the cash?
Salesman	Proof of identification, financial details, and an official letter with your address (7).
Ann	Pardon me?
Salesman	Proof of ID, a bank statement, and a letter like a gas bill or pay slip sent to where you live.
Ann	I'll see what I've got in my purse. Here's my student card. I do online banking now, so no statements. Here's an electricity bill I paid yesterday.
Salesman	I'm sorry to say, ma'am, but those things aren't enough. You can't sign a long contract without showing your passport or driver's licence, and something from your bank (7).

Have you thought about the pre-paid one-month internet deal similar to the one you already have for your phone? |
Ann	According to your brochure, it's a lot dearer – about 50% dearer – than the two-year contract.
Salesman	Yes, pre-paid is always more expensive, but it has fewer obligations.
Ann	What do you mean?
Salesman	Well, on the 24-month plan, there's also a $200 cancellation fee if you end the service by leaving the country permanently (8).
Ann	Goodness. I had no idea such things existed!
Salesman	I'm afraid so.
Ann	How about one-year contracts? I couldn't see any one-year contracts advertised. D'you have them?
Salesman	They've just been discontinued (9) – there wasn't enough demand – but a six-month pre-paid is possible.
Ann	Do I need lots of ID for that?
Salesman	No.
Ann	What about the modem – is it still included?

Salesman	With pre-paid, customers supply their own modems (10). I do, however, have one here for only $110.
Ann	A hundred-and-ten!
	I think I'll need some time to think things over.
Salesman	Not a problem.
Narrator	Section Two. Running a Small Business.
Interviewer	Let's welcome John Lim, owner of Business Training, to today's show.
John Lim	Nice to join you.
Interviewer	First of all, I've heard you've got triplets, John, as well as a growing business.
John	That's right. Two boys and a girl. They're six years old. I tell people running a business is like looking after children. Apart from being flexible, and expecting the unexpected, you need clear priorities and excellent time **management** (11). In a way, I owe my business success to my children. Like so many young families who struggle with the high cost of living, we couldn't afford to stay in the city any longer, so we moved to Casterbridge, which, at the time, met all our requirements. It was really flourishing, particularly because its **cleaner** industries, like light engineering and servicing, were replacing agriculture and mining (12). So it seemed a desirable place for people to set up small businesses.
Interviewer	What's it like now?
John	Unfortunately, the last three years have been pretty tough due to the downturn in the economy. A third of the new companies in Casterbridge have gone bust. Still, the national figure for the failure of small businesses within two years of establishment is around **40**%, so maybe a third isn't too bad (13).
Interviewer	Forty percent (13)! Why so high?
John	Let's consider success for a moment. To be successful in a small business you need to know your customers – who's going to want your product. You need to lower expenses – not by putting off staff – but rather by cutting out unnecessary luxuries. And most importantly, you need to tailor your product to a niche market. In the case of my company, I had a good **product** – training (14). Initially, we provided basic accounting training for non-accountants. Later, we provided business management skills seminars (20). For a company to stay alive, it needs a good product, followed by another good product.
Interviewer	You diversified, right?
John	Yes, I did. After providing overall management skills techniques, I moved into the more specialised area of time management (20). I gave workshops on how to manage time to businesses in Casterbridge and surrounding areas. You see, even if a company has capital – the money to get it up and running – many business people don't manage their time well, or plan well. Time management is easy if you stick to the rules, which are: schedule large and small tasks; keep to your time limits; keep focused; learn to delegate; set goals; and, learn to rest. That 40% failure rate I mentioned earlier is mostly the result of poor planning.
Interviewer	I see.
John	To be successful you've got to operate on two levels. First, you need a **five-year** plan – where your business is headed and what its core activities are. And second, you need a day-by-day plan – a list of daily tasks in order of importance (15).
	…
Interviewer	When I spoke to you before the show, you said you were branching out once more.
John	That's right. I've recently sold the management and training parts of my business, and now I'm into research and counselling (20). In fact, I've just completed a major survey on working from home for the government.
Interviewer	Working from home is my dream.
John	Really? Wait till you hear the statistics. Six out of ten respondents to our survey said their efficiency was lower at home than in an office (16). Five out of ten people we surveyed worked many more hours each week than they would in a conventional office (17). It's all too easy to check your emails after dinner, rather than scheduling them into acceptable working hours. And four out of ten people in our survey suffered from loneliness.
Interviewer	Loneliness?
John	Perhaps they miss the office gossip, or haven't got a pet to talk to. Seriously though, many of us need to socialise because, on the whole, humans are gregarious creatures (18).
Interviewer	Tell me about your counselling work.
John	I'm helping people who've gone bankrupt. As you probably know, this is a dreadful experience, both financially and emotionally. It's one time when you really do need a good accountant (19), so you come out with something.
Interviewer	Indeed.

John	Also, here's a tip. It may sound odd, but, if your business does go bankrupt, take a holiday – have a week in Bali. Or if you can't afford that, head off to a lake, a beach, or a national park. And then, shrug your shoulders, and go on. Life goes on.
Interviewer	Yes, it does. Many thanks for your insights, John.
Narrator	Section Three. Essay-Writing Skills.
Isaaq	How's it going, Sue?
Sue	Pretty well, except that I'm almost asleep on my feet. I was up until 2 AM finishing my essay.
Isaaq	Me too. However, I've still only written 1800 words, and we're meant to hand in **2500** (21). I've no idea where I'm going to get another 700 from.
Sue	Oh dear. I've got the opposite problem – my essay's nearly 4000 words long, so I'll need to be quite brutal with editing.
Isaaq	How ever did you manage that?
Sue	I'm really **interested** in the topic (22), so I did lots of independent research. I've got a pretty thorough knowledge of the HDI now.
Isaaq	The HDI?
Sue	The Human Development Index. You know, the list of indicators for health, income, sustainability--
Isaaq	Yeah yeah.
Sue	What statistics did you draw on for your discussion of poverty?
Isaaq	Don't ask. The graphs and charts I found I didn't know how to describe, so in the end I cut and pasted a table and a paragraph from my friend Abdul's essay. He took this course last year. I don't really understand any of the stuff I copied from him either, but he passed, which is all that counts.
Sue	I see.
Isaaq	Before we meet our tutor, Sue, I wonder if you could do me a favour. When I had my consultation with him last week, he crossed out so much of my first draft that I had to start all over again.
Sue	OK. Show me your first page. Well, you might add a sentence to your introduction – it's not clear to me which **argument** you support (23), or is that in the conclusion?
Isaaq	But if I add one sentence to the introduction that's only another 20 words.
Sue	True. Skimming through this, it seems you've used two **sources** for research, whereas our lecturer insisted that we have at least five (24). This quote on the second page is really long. It is relevant, but I hope you realise quotes aren't counted in the word limit.
Isaaq	So, now I don't even have 1800 words? How about I take away the quotation marks, so it'll look like my own writing?
Sue	I don't think that'll work. In fact, it's plagiarism – **stealing** from another writer (25). Our essays are put through a computer program to check what's copied from elsewhere.
Isaaq	I don't get why people care about plagiarism. In my country, that's how we learn.
Sue	At secondary **school** here, some students do copy, but, at university, we should develop our own ideas (26).
Isaaq	What if I don't have any ideas?
Sue	Then, it's time to get some!
	…
Isaaq	What shall I do about this long quote, Sue?
Sue	You can paraphrase or summarise it (27A). You'll need a reference as well.
Isaaq	A reference?
Sue	An in-text citation (28C), like the Harvard System. You need to acknowledge where the information came from.
Isaaq	Whoa!

Sue	We were given a worksheet on the Harvard System in the first tutorial. Have a look at my essay, now, to see what you need to do.
Isaaq	Are these names and dates in brackets a reference?
Sue	Yes. They refer to the bibliography on my last page. That reminds me, you don't seem to have attached your bibliography. Do you have it floating around in your bag?
Isaaq	Yes, here is it. Have a look.
Sue	Is this your bibliography or Abdul's?
Isaaq	What do you mean?
Sue	Well, I'd say it was Abdul's because there are seven sources, and none of them is either on our reading list or referred to in your essay. Our tutor wasn't born yesterday (29F)!
Isaaq	I can sort the bibliography out later. That's the least of my worries. We still haven't solved how I'm going to write another 700 words in fewer than 24 hours.
Sue	You'll need to do some more research today. I found Newcombe really helpful and also Sword. Why don't you read them (30G)?
Isaaq	I would if I had time, but I'm working tonight. In fact, I start at two o'clock and go through till nine thirty.
Sue	Read the articles at work, then. They're not very long. I found both of them offered convincing arguments for redefining poverty, and their alternative indicators for failed states are also interesting.
Isaaq	But I'm running out of time, and I can't walk around the Menswear Department reading scraps of paper. Look, let me make a suggestion. Why don't you write the extra paragraphs, Sue? I bet you'd be able to do them in about half an hour. You could email them to me tonight – I'll check my email the minute I get home. In return, I'll give you a gift voucher from my department store.
Sue	Nice try! Firstly, I've got to work tonight as well. Remember, I told you about editing my essay. Secondly, the tutor will spot my writing style. And lastly, believe it or not, I'm that rare breed of female who doesn't like shopping.

Narrator	Section Four. Desalination.
Lecturer	In an era of climate change, many countries no longer have the rainfall they used to have. Furthermore, with population increase, the already depleted groundwater supplies are running out. Therefore, worldwide, governments, cities, industries, and ocean-going ships have opted for desalination.
	There are various methods of desalination used in the world today – there's solar desalination, geothermal desalination, multi-stage distillation, and salt-water reverse osmosis desalination.
	In this lecture, I shall describe salt-water reverse osmosis desalination, with particular reference to the supply of fresh drinking water. I shall also outline its drawbacks.
	Desalination is the process of removing salt and other minerals from water molecules, making it potable, or ready for drinking (31).
	In reverse osmosis desalination, seawater is purified by being forced, at very high pressure, through a membrane – a kind of skin. The solid waste and bilge are separated out, and the water sent on to the consumer.
	There are seven stages to the process. Follow me on the diagram while I explain. In the top left-hand corner, you can see the word 'intake', which means filling a pipe in the ocean. This water goes to the **Pumping** Station (33). Here come two objections to desalination – there are lots of pipes, causing leakage or evaporation, so we lose the very water we're trying to catch. Secondly, pumping requires energy – massive amounts of energy – which produces greenhouse gases (32).
	Back to the diagram. At the Pumping Station, the water is screened (33): sand, shells, and rubbish are removed. Next, the water is forced into a revolving cylinder. Inside this cylinder there's mesh and a sandwich of membranes through which the impurities are spun out. The **concentrate** – brackish, salty waste – is pumped back into the sea. That's number 34 on your diagram (34).
	After desalination, fluoride is added. Then, the water goes into a huge Clear-Water Storage **Tank** (35) before entering the city's existent water network.
	Desalination produces fresh water, but at what cost? In fact, in the US, the organisation *Food and Water Watch* found desalinated water to be the most expensive form of fresh water available, costing **five** times as much to harvest as other sources (36).
	The price tag on one plant in Sydney was more than two billion Australian dollars.

Another objection is that cheaper alternatives exist. Take recycling. Currently, in Sydney, about 2% of the total amount of water used is recycled. However, if rainwater were captured in tanks on the roofs of buildings, then it'd be easy to recycle up to **20%** a year, roughly the amount of fresh water a desalination plant produces in the same time (37).

Recently, there's been a campaign to educate Australians about water use. There've also been restrictions in place, like when you can water your garden or fill your swimming pool. With just these two things – education and restriction – Sydney residents used **10%** less water in the past five years than in the five preceding (38).

As I've said, desalination plants require excessive energy, but there's another problem: they flood the ocean with waste. In Sydney, up to **1.5** billion litres (39) of concentrate (34) go into the Pacific Ocean daily. And perhaps even more alarmingly, there's a problem at the intake end too. Marine biologist Sylvia Earle has commented on the hidden environmental cost of desalination, by claiming that ocean water is filled with living creatures, and most of them are lost in the process of desalination.

You might be asking: why were desalination plants built in the first place? Probably because water could be even scarcer in future; and, it's easier to build big projects than to persuade **millions** of homeowners to recycle (40).

READING: Passage 1: 1. warfare; 2. school; 3. 28/Twenty-eight (*capital optional*); 4. violent; 5. burial; 6. T/True; 7. NG/Not Given; 8. F/False; 9. F/False; 10. A; 11. D; 12. D; 13. C. Passage 2: 14. C; 15. A; 16. B; 17. B; 18. B; 19. Raw materials (*capital optional*); 20. 0.25cm/0.1inch (*zero and point are both necessary. This cannot be written with a comma*); 21. Purification (*capital optional*); 22. First/Initial firing (*capital optional*); 23. glazing; 24. burn; 25. kiln; 26. 700; 27. solidify. Passage 3: 28. land; 29. poor; 30. aid; 31. business/traders; 32. communities; 33. China (*capital optional*); 34. geography; 35. investment; 36. education; 37. 34/thirty-four; 38. suffering; 39–40. C and E/E and C.

Passage 1

March 29th, 1461, in tiny Towton was one of the bloodiest days in English history, yet only recently have a small number of soldiers' bodies undergone exhumation and examination. Several thousand still lie buried in mass graves on the battlefield. (1) Early analysis of the remains has led to a reassessment of medieval **warfare**.

Towton, a village in the north of England, between York and Leeds, is unknown to many English people. (2) History taught at **school** largely ignores the mid-15th century. Towton itself has neither museum nor large memorial, merely a roadside cross to mark where the battle took place.

In 1996, a building nearby called Towton Hall was being renovated when labourers unearthed skeletons in its grounds and beneath its floor. (3) **Twenty-eight** of these were complete; another 20 or so were partial. (4) What shocked archaeologists was the **violent** way in which the men had met their deaths and the callous manner of their (5) **burial**. We are all familiar with the gory wars of the 20th century, and might assume that technology and politics have become more destructive over time. However, it could be the case that humans have long been vicious – only now is the evidence coming to light.

(6) So what was the Battle of Towton? It was one clash of many between two powerful families – the Lancastrians and the Yorkists – who each wanted their king to rule England. The Lancastrians believed the current King of England, Henry VI, was incapable if not insane, whereas the Yorkists, led by Richard Plantagenet, supported Henry since he had chosen Richard as the next king. When Richard was killed in 1460, his son Edward, only 18, vowed to assume the throne in his father's place. Needless to say, the Lancastrians disputed this. Effectively, the Battle of Towton would legitimate Edward's reign.

Prior to Towton, military encounters in England had been small-scale: battles were fought with hundreds or at most a few thousand men, and no army was professional. In so-called peace time, private armies consisted of men – ranging in age from 15 to 50 – whose levels of fitness were variable, and whose training and equipment were poor. This meant that when fighting did erupt, it seldom lasted long – perhaps just a few days. Nor were many men killed. In fact, there is evidence that more men died from their wounds or other illnesses *after* combat. Towton it seems was different, for here was a battle in which both sides assembled large armies, and there were terrible casualties in the field.

The number of soldiers killed at Towton is a matter of speculation as few records have come down to us, and those that do survive may have exaggerated the victory of King Edward IV, as Edward became, in order to intimidate his enemies. (8) One estimate of the dead is 28,000 out of the 75,000 soldiers who took part. These 75,000 represent 10% of all fighting-age men in England at the time – the total population being just three million. Twenty-eight thousand dead on one day is, therefore, a staggering number.

As injuries show on the skeletons of soldiers already studied, those men were hacked to death, shot by arrows, or trampled by horses. Some of the first bullets used in England were fired that day. Lead-composite shot has been dug up on the battlefield, and one archaeologist claims to have found part of a handgun, (9) but there are no obvious deaths from guns, and it is hard to say how they were used. The most effective weapon was the poleaxe – a long, heavy iron weapon with a sharp tip, a small axe blade on one side and, on the other, a large sharp head like a Philips-head screwdriver. (10) It was used to kill soldiers who were running away as battle lines broke up, and it is thought this is how most of the Lancastrians buried at Towton Hall died.

It is not known why the death rate in this battle was so high, nor why the bodies of soldiers were so disfigured. Skeletal evidence indicates that often a dozen blows were given to a man who would have been killed by the initial two or three. Archaeologists are uncertain when these additional blows were made – on the battlefield or in the burial process – but such savagery suggests the emergence of a new concept of an opponent as not merely someone to kill but someone whose identity should be utterly effaced. After death, in a ritual never before seen in English warfare, soldiers were stripped of their clothes and tossed into mass graves to further dehumanise them.

It is easy to forget that in medieval England burial was sacred, and people believed ascent to Heaven only took place when the body of the dead was whole. In all Europe, there is only one other known mass grave on the scale of Towton from around the same time – that is in Sweden from 1361. (12) There, however, soldiers from the Battle of Wisby were buried whole in their armour.

It appears that the savagery of the Yorkists did effect submission since Edward remained king for the next 22 years.

Today, at Towton, work continues on excavation and analysis of the medieval skeletons. Theories about a new kind of violent warfare and the purpose of mass graves abound. (13) It seems that organised brutality is no recent phenomenon; it existed 550 years ago.

Passage 2: Hard-paste porcelain

Definition and origin

The term porcelain refers to ceramics made from similar materials and baked at high temperatures which are light, durable, and vitreous. Porcelain combines the positive qualities of glass and clay – glass is smooth and translucent while clay retains its shape when moulded. However, due to the addition of a few more minerals, porcelain is stronger than either glass or clay. It is also extremely beautiful and valuable: Chinese Ming Dynasty (1368-1644 AD) (14) bowls can fetch a million dollars on the international art market.

For around fifteen hundred years, porcelain has been employed as tableware and decoration, but its more recent applications include: dental crowns and electrical insulators.

(15) Porcelain was first made in China. During the Tang Dynasty (618-907 AD), small amounts were used by the court and the very rich. High-quality porcelain, like that manufactured today, was not widely available until the Yuan Dynasty (1279-1368 AD).

Chinese porcelain was traded with kingdoms in Central, Southeast Asia, and the Middle East from the seventh century. By the Middle Ages, it had reached Europe.

European obsession

Porcelain was consumed in enormous quantities by European royal families, nobles, and the church, all of whom tried desperately to discover its chemical composition. (16) The English word, 'porcelain', derives from the Portuguese name for a sea creature, the nautilus, which has a spiral orange vitreous shell from which it was believed at one time that porcelain was made. Other more astute Europeans contended the ceramic contained crushed glass or bone.

Early experiments in the production of porcelain included adding ground glass to clay. The result is called 'soft-paste' as it is weaker than true porcelain.

(17) So great was the frenzy for possessing Chinese porcelain, or attempting to recreate their own hard-paste, that a number of European principalities endangered themselves financially, spending as much of their budgets on pursuing porcelain as on their armies. Frederick II of Prussia (now in Germany) was one such fanatic. Fortunately, for Prussia, two scientists – Johann Böttger and Ehrenfried von Tschimhaus – in the monarch's service, solved the porcelain puzzle. Their discovery, made in 1707, combined clay with ground feldspar – a mineral containing aluminium silicate.

Meanwhile, in England, the recipe was a little different: ash, from cattle bones, was mixed with clay, feldspar, and quartz. (18) This became known as 'bone china', and is still manufactured. Although not true porcelain, it remains popular in the US and the UK because it is harder than porcelain.

Constituents

(19) The **raw materials** from which porcelain is made are abundant. They are: white clay (china clay or ball clay), feldspar, or perhaps flint, and silica – all of which are noted for their small particles. Feldspar and flint are used as fluxes, which reduce the temperature needed for firing, and bind the glass, silica, and clay granules. Porcelain may also contain other ingredients like alumina or steatite.

Manufacture

To produce porcelain, the raw materials are selected and weighed. Then, they are crushed in a two-stage process. Jaw crushers work first; (20) mullers or hammer mills subsequently reduce particles to **0.25 cms (0.1 inch)** or less in diameter. A third crushing, using ball mills, takes place for the finest porcelain. (21) During **purification**, which follows, granules that are not of uniform size are screened out. Magnetic filtration then removes iron, commonly found in clay, because this prevents porcelain from forming correctly. The fifth stage, preparatory to firing, is formation. There are several types of formation by hand or machine. (22) After formation, the ware undergoes its initial firing in a kiln – a special oven.

A glaze is a glassy liquid similar in composition to porcelain. If a porcelain object is painted, a glaze covers the paint, or its decoration may just be the glaze. (23) Glaze is applied by painting or dipping, and takes place after the first firing. Not only are porcelain wares gorgeous, but their decoration and **glazing** are also of great interest.

In making porcelain, the temperature in the kiln is critical – high enough to reconstitute the elements, yet low enough to vaporise contaminants and minimise shrinkage. A typical temperature is 1,454° Celsius (2,650° Fahrenheit).

During the firing process, a number of chemical reactions occur. (24) Carbon-based impurities **burn** out at 100-200°C (215-395°F). (25) As the **kiln** is heated, carbonates and sulfates decompose. (26) When heated to **700**-1100°C (1295-2015°F), the fluxes react with the decomposing minerals to form liquid glass. (27) After a certain density is reached, at around 1200°C (2195°F), the ware is cooled, causing the liquid glass to **solidify**.

Pause for thought

So, next time you dine from fine porcelain, take a moment to reflect on the complicated history and sophisticated manufacture of this exquisite product.

Passage 3: Is aid hurting Africa?

(28 and 29) Despite its population of more than one billion and its rich **land** and natural resources, the continent of Africa remains **poor**. The combined economies of its 54 states equal that of one European country: the Netherlands.

It is difficult to speak of Africa as a unit as its states differ from each other in culture, climate, size, and political systems. Since mid-20th-century independence, many African states have pursued different economic policies. Yet, none of them has overcome poverty. Why might this be?

One theory says Africa is unlucky. Sparsely populated with diverse language and culture, it contains numerous landlocked countries, and it is far from international markets.

Dambisa Moyo, a Zambian-born economist has another theory. In her 2009 book, *Dead Aid*, which is still much discussed, (30) she proposes that international **aid** is largely to blame for African poverty because it has encouraged dependence and corruption, and (31) has diverted talented people from **business**. One of her statistics is that from 1970-1998, when aid to Africa was highest, poverty rose from eleven to 66%. If aid were cut, she believes Africans would utilise their resources more creatively.

When a state lacks the capacity to care for its people, international non-governmental organisations (NGOs), like Oxfam or the Red Cross, assume this role. While NGOs distribute food or medical supplies, Moyo argues they reduce the ability of the state to provide. Furthermore, during this process, those in government and the military siphon off aid goods and money themselves. Transparency International, an organisation that surveys corruption, rates the majority of African states poorly.

Moyo provides another example. Maybe a Hollywood star donates American-made mosquito nets. Certainly, this benefits malaria-prone areas, but it also draws business away from local African traders who supply nets. (32) More consultation is needed between do-gooder foreigners and local **communities**.

In order to increase their wealth, (33) Moyo proposes African nations increase their investment in bonds or their co-operation with **China**.

The presidents of Rwanda and Senegal are strong supporters of Moyo, but (34) critics say her theories are simplistic. The international aid community is not responsible for **geography**, nor has it anything to do with military takeover, corruption, or legislation that hampers trade. Africans have had half a century of self-government and economic control, yet, as the population of the continent has doubled, its GDP has risen only 60%. In the same period, Malaysia and Vietnam threw off colonialism and surged ahead economically by investing in education, health, and infrastructure; by lowering taxes on international trade; and, by being fortunate to be surrounded by other successful nations.

The economist Paul Collier has speculated that if aid were cut, African governments would not find alternative sources of income, nor would they reduce corruption. Another economist, Jeffrey Sachs, has calculated that twice the amount of aid currently given is needed to prevent suffering on a grand scale.

(39 and 40C) In *Dead Aid*, Moyo presents her case through a fictitious country called 'Dongo', but nowhere does she provide examples of real aid organisations causing actual problems. Her approach may be entertaining, but it is hardly academic.

Other scholars point out that Africa is dominated by tribal societies with military-government elites. Joining the army, rather than doing business, is often the easiest route to personal wealth and power. Unsurprisingly, military takeovers have occurred in almost every African country. In the 1960s and 70s, European colonials were replaced by African 'colonials' – African generals and their families. Meantime, the very small, educated bourgeoisie has moved abroad. All over Africa, strongmen leaders have ruled for a long time, or one unstable regime has succeeded another. (35) As a result, business separate from military government is rare, and international **investment** limited.

(36) Post-secondary **education** rates are low in Africa. Communications and transportation remain basic, although mobile phones are having an impact. The distances farmers must travel to market are vast due to poor roads. High cross-border taxes and long bureaucratic delays are par for the course. African rural populations exceed those elsewhere in the world. Without decent infrastructure or an educated urbanised workforce, business cannot prosper. Recent World Bank statistics show that in southern Africa, the number of companies using the internet for business is 20% as opposed to 40% in South America or 80% in the US. There are 37 days each year without water, whereas there is less than one day in Europe. The average cost of sending one container to the US is $7600, but only $3900 from East Asia or the Pacific. All these problems are the result of poor state planning.

Great ethnic and linguistic diversity within African countries has led to tribal favouritism. Governments are often controlled by one tribe or allied tribes; civil war is usually tribal. It is estimated each civil war costs a country roughly $64 billion. (37) Southern Africa had **48** such conflicts from 1940-2015 while South Asia, the next-affected region, had only 27 in the same period. To this day, a number of bloody conflicts continue.

Other opponents of Moyo add that her focus on market investment and more business with China is shortsighted. The 2008 financial crisis meant that countries with market investments lost money. Secondly, China's real intentions in Africa are unknown, but everyone can see China is buying up African farmland and securing cheap oil supplies.

All over Africa, there are untapped resources, but distance, diversity, and low population density contribute to poverty. Where there is no TV, infrequent electricity, and bad roads, there still seems to be money for automatic weapons just the right size for 12-year-old boys to use. (38) Blaming the West for assisting with aid fails to address the issues of continuous conflict, ineffective government, and little infrastructure. Nor does it prevent terrible **suffering**.

Has aid caused problems for Africa, or is Africa's strife of its own making or due to geography? (39 and 40) Whatever you think, Dambisa Moyo's book has generated lively discussion, which is fruitful for Africa.

WRITING: Task 1

The table compares the population of the world's top ten countries in 2010 with projected numbers in 2100.

In 2010, China had the highest population of 1,341 million, with India second on 1,225 million. However, by 2100, India is projected to have the highest population of 1,551 million with China second on 941 million – down 400 million since 2010.

Although the USA is projected to increase its population from 310 million to 478 million, it steps down from third to fourth place, being overtaken by Nigeria, which moves up from seventh place with 158 million, to a total of 730 million, representing a massive increase of 572 million. Brazil drops from fifth place in 2010 with 195 million, down to tenth in 2100 on 177 million – a decrease of 18 million.

Some countries such as Bangladesh, Russia, and Japan do not appear on the 2100 list. Instead, they are superseded by Tanzania, the Democratic Republic of Congo, and the Philippines.

Except for China and Brazil, all other projections show an increase between 2010 and 2100, but there is a significant shuffling of position by some countries, the elimination of others, and the introduction of new contenders for a top-ten placing. (200 words)

Note: The overall statement comes at the end of this model.

Task 2

Health care in most countries is a major social concern. Healthy people live longer, work better, and are generally happier than those who suffer from illness and disease. But since medical care is very costly, just how to finance health care is a worldwide problem. Should the government pay for all health care, or should the people contribute? Should there be a combination of both? Of the many systems of health care, I shall discuss two in this essay: free health care, and a combination of state and personal payment.

Free health care, that is, all medical payments from doctors' visits to prescriptions to hospital care and convalescence, has long been an ideal of welfare states. It takes away the worry of where money is to come from when medical attention is needed, and it usually means that people seek medical advice before a symptom develops into something worse.

But free health care must be funded by very high taxes. In Denmark, this system has worked well for 40 years. The health of the nation is excellent, the standard of living is high, and people are happy. However, in Great Britain, free health care seems to have got out of hand. Medical rooms are always full, and patients get less quality time with a doctor. Also, patients go to the doctor for minor complaints, which eventually heal of their own accord. Because it is free, people take advantage. Moreover, free health care is a drain on the country's revenue. However, for all that, under free health care, people get the medical attention they need, without being financially disadvantaged.

Another way of providing health care is for payment to be divided between the state and the people themselves. This system is used where taxes are not too high. For example, in New Zealand, once a welfare state, taxes are no longer high and health care is no longer free, except for hospital care for permanent residents. Otherwise, the state pays a proportion of a doctor's fees, while the patient pays the rest – almost half and half. Prescriptions are also subsidized. Due to the relatively high payment for doctors' visits, many people have private medical insurance to cover costs. Whatever the method of payment, people pay through taxes, medical insurance, and out of pocket. As a result, those in the low socio-economic sector are often reluctant to seek medical help, and are far less healthy than those who can afford to pay.

There seems to be no perfect way to provide health care. Quality free health care means very high taxes. However, the overall health of the nation is usually very good because medical needs are attended to quickly. Conversely, where the government pays a proportion of health care and the public the rest, poorer citizens are medically and financially worse off. Therefore, in the interests of fairness and overall national well-being, health care paid for by the state seems preferable to that of a combined system. (495 words)

Recording 75:

> **Practice Speaking Test 4 – Part 2 topic**
>
> *I'd like you to tell me about the oldest person you know.*
>
> • *Who is this person?*
> • *What is interesting about his or her life?*
> • *What kind of life does this person have now?*

GENERAL TRAINING PRACTICE TEST 1

LISTENING: See Academic Practice Test 1 on page 403.

READING: Section 1: 1. False/F; 2. True/T; 3. True/T; 4. False/F; 5. Not Given/NG; 6. True/T; 7. Not Given/NG; 8. C; 9. E; 10. F; 11. D; 12. 5/Five; 13. Egg shells; 14. Meat and cheese. Section 2: 15. C; 16. A; 17. D; 18. E; 19. G; 20. F; 21. D; 22. C; 23. D; 24. A; 25. C; 26. B; 27. A. Section 3: 28. good news; 29. maintain relationships; 30. white lies; 31. pitch; 32. identity; 33. 7/seven; 34. 61/sixty-one; 35. B; 36. C; 37. B; 38. B; 39. D; 40. A.

Section 1: Changes to recycling

The information below was sent to all residents.

GETTING SORTED
(1) From 1 July, curbside recycling is changing.
One big bin: Your new bin is bigger than your old bin. Now (1) you must put paper products inside your bin with all other recyclables, not on the pavement in plastic bags or cardboard boxes.

WHAT CAN GO IN THE BIN?		
Aluminium cans Cardboard Egg cartons Empty aerosols	Envelopes & junk mail (2) Glass bottles, jars + lids Magazines & newspapers Paper	Plastic bottles, containers + lids Tetra Pak cartons Tin cans + lids

WHAT CAN'T GO IN THE BIN?	
Batteries Building waste Chemicals, oil, or paint Clothing, shoes, or textiles Electrical or electronic waste Food or garden waste (2) Glass from frames, mirrors, or windows	Hazardous waste Light bulbs (Leave at participating retailers.) Medical waste Nappies [Diapers] (3) Plastic bags – These get trapped in sorting machinery, causing breakdowns. (Leave at participating retailers.) Polystyrene packaging

WHEN DOES THE BIN GO OUT?
On weekdays: As currently, before 6:30 AM. **On public holidays:** As currently, put your bin out the day after a holiday. (4) When there is a two-day holiday, put your bin out on the second day of the holiday. This is a new service.
Suburban: Fortnightly collection: Your new bin is labelled with your suburb, its collection day, and fortnight (A or B). **CBD: Daily or weekly collection:** Your new bin is labelled with your zone. (4) Daily collection continues in Zone 1, but extends into Zone 2. Friday collection continues in Zone 3.

(6) WHAT HAPPENS TO THE OLD BIN?
You can keep it, or put it out for collection in July.

Further Information
For a list of places where you can leave these items, go to: **Drop_while_you_shop.com.** For all other information, go to: **RecycleWell.org.nz.**

Worm farming

The big picture

While it is true that food and garden waste is less destructive than inorganic matter, its disposal is still problematic, especially when buried in vast amounts, as happens in metropolitan areas. Since land is at a premium, (8) landfill facilities almost invariably mechanically compact organic waste, causing acidic reactions in the airless environment below ground. (9) This means methane is released into the atmosphere, and (10) impurities leach into groundwater, which would otherwise be potable.

The farm

Even if householders are unaware of the dangers of landfill, some dispose of food scraps in worm farms, an innovation from the 1990s, because, as well as speedily breaking down material, the animals produce nutrient-rich castings – shed skin and other excreta – that can be used as fertilizer.

For apartment-dwellers, a worm farm 40 cm in diameter and 50 cm in height can sit on a balcony; for people with gardens, a larger farm one metre by one metre is suitable.

(11) There are two layers to a worm farm, although as the number of worms grows, more layers can be added. (11) The top layer, a deep plastic tray with tiny holes in the bottom, contains the scraps and the worms. The bottom tray traps the castings, which can be scooped out for use as is, or diluted into liquid fertilizer.

The little creatures

Worms consume waste so fast that (12) five kilograms will be broken down within eight weeks. Essentially, worms eat anything that was once living. Favourites include:

- Fruit and vegetable scraps
- Teabags and leaves; coffee grounds
- Torn-up newspaper, egg or pizza cartons
- (13) Eggshells (to restore the pH balance)
- Dust from dustpans or vacuum cleaners
- Hair and nail clippings

To fatten worms, flour or milk powder can be added to the farm from time to time.

NB: Worms will eat (14) meat and cheese, but only when no other food is available. Most citrus peel and tomatoes are too acidic for worms, so they are best avoided.

Section 2: Professional development workshops

English Language Centre, South Western University – 20-22 May

	(15) **AM Session**	**PM Session**
May 20th	**(A) Plenary – Great Hall** Dr Carlee Smith will open the three-day workshop. Dr Hans Dykstra will report on a conference he recently attended in Brazil. Ms Adela Xu will update staff on the joint ventures. (16) (Those interested in working in China may email her their CV.) Lunch provided in the Buttery.	**(B) Individual – Computer Lab A** Pronunciation: • Using the IPA (International Phonetic Alphabet) • Raising awareness about fluency • Analysing the features of talkback radio and TV panel discussions • Recording on SoundCloud • Providing feedback
(15) **May 21st**	**(C) Individual – Room 204** Essay-writing skills: • Writing elegantly • Writing convincingly • Hedging • Describing data • Drawing on multiple sources • Paraphrasing and quoting • Bibliographic conventions • Using footnote and endnote programs	**(D) Individual – Room 207** Group discussion skills: • Showing enthusiasm and understanding • (17) Turn-taking • Clarifying • Disagreeing politely • Interrupting • Reaching consensus • (17) Chairing or moderating Presentation skills: • Establishing rapport with an audience • (21) Reducing dependence on PowerPoint slides • Providing analysis rather than only description
May 22nd	**(E) Individual – Basement Café** Sam Sleepyhead and Tina Tiara? • (18) Strategies for dealing with the unmotivated	**(F) Individual – Room 213** Creative ideas for the last ten minutes of class time: • (20) Drawing each other in pairs • Summarising YouTube clips
(G) Other information		
• Presenters will receive a certificate of appreciation and a gift voucher. • Submission of papers is welcomed by the online journal *Tertiary English Today*, edited by Dr Dykstra. • Attendees doing the Diploma of Tertiary Teaching may wish to complete a workshop journal for credit towards Module 40010.		

NB: (19) In order for casual or part-time staff to be paid for these days when they would otherwise not be working, they must email proof of session attendance to Payroll.

Volunteering in Auckland

It is estimated that volunteers constitute 10 percent of the New Zealand workforce. As the population ages and immigration rises, their number grows.

Recently, Myra Khan, from *The Star*, caught up with four volunteers. 'Let's start with Hikitea Po since you're an old hand.' 'Indeed. Over the years, (27) I've done all kinds of volunteering, as any mother has. I did the school fair, and drove sports teams around. But since I retired, I've taken on more challenges. Now, (24) I plant trees on Rangitoto Island, assist with Save Our Rivers, and foster dogs. I guess I'm a volunteer junkie.'

'Or a sucker,' put in (26) Sara Rustaqi, whose own experience had not been so rosy. 'I was a teacher in Argentina, so, while waiting for local registration, I volunteered to teach Spanish at a primary school in the eastern suburbs. (26) To be honest, the kids were spoilt. They couldn't believe I'd be doing it for nothing.'

'I know how you feel,' said Terry Wilkinson. 'I was in education for 20 years. (25) Even after I quit, I spent a whole year depressed. Finally, a mate of mine told me about Restorative Justice, or RJ.' 'What's that?' asked Myra. 'Basically, it's when victims and perpetrators of crime meet each other informally. Let's say a house is burgled, and the police catch the guy. He's charged, and a date for his court appearance is set. Beforehand, he's asked if he wants to meet the people who live in the house, perhaps to say sorry. If he does, his sentence may be reduced.' 'And what do you do, Terry?' 'I facilitate the meetings. (22) I've seen some incredible moments. Perpetrators meet real people, and see how their actions have affected them; victims feel considerable relief at an apology. (25) Recently, I became a paid, full-time member of the RJ team. I couldn't be happier.'

Innocent Jonas adds, 'My story's similar. (23) I was an obstetrician in Ethiopia, but I didn't want to undergo the rigorous registration process here. However, (23) I've been volunteering as an aide at North Shore Hospital, and I've been so impressed I'm going to retrain as a nurse. My manager has even promised me paid work while I study. Volunteering has really opened doors for me.'

Section 3: Secrets and lies in the digital age

You're at a work lunch when your boss's smartphone rings, but she doesn't take the call. Ten seconds later, her phone's receiving a text; still, no response. Finally, after several loud buzzes for incoming email, your boss excuses herself. Returning to the table a few minutes later, she's all smiles, and insists you order dessert with your coffee, even though this has never happened at a work do before. You wonder if your boss has just had some really (28) good news or some really bad. If it were the former, she'd probably announce it, whereas the latter is generally skated over or concealed altogether. Perhaps, it is only your boss's sudden desire for dessert that alerts you to anything amiss.

As psychologists well know, people trying to keep secrets, or pass off lies, devote considerable effort to (29) maintaining relationships with those they hope to deceive. Of course, at work, you don't need to know who's pursuing your boss, but let's imagine you were enjoying a romantic dinner with your new love interest; certainly, you'd be keen to find out who was on the phone. Admittedly, there'd be occasions when your date and the caller had legitimate urgent business; and, even if your date told a white lie about the call, you may not be upset. However, it would be a red flag if, while your love interest were paying the bill, the phone buzzed again, and there on the screen was illuminated: 'C U soon'. And when you queried this, your date gave you an elaborately plausible explanation. Later, as no one had done in years, on passing a street vendor, your date spontaneously bought you a gorgeous bouquet.

The fact remains that most of us are unable to detect (30) white lies, let alone the darker, more sinister variety; and many of us are oblivious to deceivers' turning a situation to their own advantage. Indeed, there are even a few innocents who remain unaware of the physical traits of liars: that they blink more often than normal, and raise the (31) pitch of their voices infinitesimally when uttering untruths. But what of a liar's email habits?

Firstly, there's the issue of who's actually writing, since anyone can set up an account with an assumed (32) identity: males can become females; an adolescent can pass herself off as a twenty-something. Even a LinkedIn profile may be mostly a work of fiction.

Recently, Dr Yla Tausczik from the University of Maryland recruited volunteers who had kept a significant secret for the last (33) seven years in order to analyse the language and frequency of their email sent both to people they were aiming to dupe and in whom they intended to confide.

A significant number of studies into behaviour involve a surprisingly small number of participants, largely because recruitment is problematic. In Dr Tausczik's case, persuading keepers of secrets to reveal their pretence, even for scientific purposes, was more awkward. Thus, to allay the fears of those involved, real emails accessed by Dr Tausczik had various identifying features, like names, dates, and places, removed. Still, around 2400 people expressed initial interest, of whom 1133 completed a questionnaire to determine suitability, and (34) 61 from all walks of life were eventually chosen. (34) Sixty-one is a sufficient number to gather meaningful data, particularly when emails came from a six-month period, and participants each generated a minimum of 415 and a maximum of 1278.

(35) The seven-year-old secrets that participants had been keeping mostly involved romantic relationships or their own sexual orientation. In a minority of cases, they concerned medical conditions that could adversely affect employment or educational prospects. People from whom the information was kept were spouses, family members, or colleagues. Confidants were usually best friends, although, in the digital age, a handful of these were people the secret-keepers had met solely online.

(36) Dr Tausczik's findings differed from traditional literature on deceivers that suggests they restrict or shun social contact. She discovered secret-keepers had a wide social network and emailed those they were deceiving continually. In fact, if their secret was one of sexual infidelity or addiction, (37) they were more likely to send multiple emails soon after the behaviour had occurred. Additionally, these were not just one-liners but two or three paragraphs discussing all kinds of topics, often incorporating the deception itself, albeit in a more harmless form, or making a tangential allusion.

(38) Dr Tausczik also found that in replies secret-keepers used similar or identical language to their confidants to simulate intimacy – possibly because the friends may otherwise have been less sympathetic towards any deceptive behaviour – or merely to ensure confidants were sucked into the soap opera and would be available for the next installment.

Dr David Markowitz from Stanford University has studied academic research papers retracted from conferences or publications due to scientific misconduct, usually in the form of entirely fake studies or partially faked results. (39) He discovered a tendency towards a high number of references, in general higher than papers that cited genuine data.

A third researcher in this field of fraudulence, Dr Norah Dunbar from the University of California, posits that computer programs could be developed to trawl email. Meantime, she is analysing the actual language cheats use in email, although, as yet, she has not discerned recognizable linguistic patterns.

It would seem (40) Dr Tausczik's research indicates that extra attention to the deceived in terms of length of email was significant, while both (40) Dr Tausczik and Dr Markowitz found that frequency or number could suggest wrongdoing. However, the jury is still out on the actual content.

As we all know, liars and secret-keepers have been getting away with it their whole lives long. If they're reading this, maybe they'll now modify their email with those they plan to keep in the dark. Meantime, the best you can hope for in the company of the fraudulent is a piece of cake or a blushing rose; and remember, not every email you read contains the whole truth and nothing but the truth.

Writing: Task 1

Dear Bernadette,

I was thrilled to receive your lovely printed invitation to Chloe's wedding. It's sitting on my desk as I type. I can't believe she and Tomas are tying the knot. It seems like yesterday that they were both at school. I'm sure Chloe will make a beautiful bride, and a fine wife and mother. As for Tomas, you must be glad to have such an accomplished son-in-law who is also a thoroughly decent person. I've only met him once, but he drove me back to my hotel from a picnic when it was quite out of his way.

Unfortunately, I won't be able to go to the wedding since I have a work commitment abroad that I can't change, much as I'd like to. I'll be in snowy Istanbul while you're in sunny Nelson.

As a small token of my affection for Chloe and Tom, and of course, for our many years of friendship, I'd like to send some money to the happy couple, and I wonder if you could send me bank account details. I'll also post a little something from Turkey.

Yours sincerely,

Anna (188 words)

Task 2: Go to page 433.

General Training Practice Test 2

LISTENING: See Academic Practice Test 2 on page 410.

READING: Section 1: 1. 850; 2. 0800; 3. $300; 4. cats; 5. 2½ hours; 6. thick fog/severe storms; 7. $100; (*Remember to add the additional rate of $30 for a 4-wheel drive to the one-day rate for sedans of $70, so your answer = $100*). 8. B; 9. A; 10. C; 11. C; 12. D; 13. A; 14. D. Section 2: 15. C; 16. A; 17. D; 18. A; 19. E; 20. D; 21. B; 22. Section B: vi; 23. Section C: vii; 24. Section D: i; 25. Section E: viii; 26. Section F: v; 27. Section G: ii. Section 3: 28. available; 29. 10,000; 30. stem; 31. 15/fifteen; 32. cloth; 33. trade; 34. E; 35. C; 36. I; 37. A; 38. F; 39. G; 40. B and E/E and B.

Section 1: Great Barrier Island

Great Barrier Island is near the city of Auckland in New Zealand. (1) It has only **850** permanent residents, but it is a popular tourist destination.

Ferries			
To Great Barrier Island		**To Auckland**	
Monday-Friday	Weekends & Public holidays	Monday-Friday	Weekends & Public holidays
First ferry: 0530	0630	(2) **0800**	0900
Ferries leave on the hour every hour throughout the day			
Last ferry: 1800	1800	2030	2030
Fares		**One way**	**Return**
Adult:		$75	$120
Student/Pensioner:		$50	$80
Child (5-15; young children travel free):		$25	$40
(3) Family (2 adults + 2 or more children):		$180	**$300**
Pet (Dogs must be on a lead); (4) cats are forbidden:		$10	$15
Booking			
By phone: 846 1305.	In person: Tickets may be purchased at Wharf 4.		

Other information
There is a restaurant on board. (5) The journey lasts **2½** hours in calm seas. (6) Ferries do not operate in **thick fog**, **severe storms**, or on Christmas Day.

Car hire on Great Barrier Island			
Rates are for sedans; (7) *four-wheel drives are an additional $30 per day.*			
Half day (1-4 hours)	1-4 days		4 days +
$40	(7) **$70**		$65 a day
Bicycle hire			
Rates are for mountain bikes.			
Half day (1-4 hours)	1-4 days		4 days +
$20	$35		$30

What can tourists do on Great Barrier Island?

Walking	Mountain Biking
There are ten walking tracks that go through native forest or around beaches. (8) Hiking times and degree of difficulty vary from 30 minutes and very easy to five hours and quite demanding. (9) Views are stunning.	Recent track development by the Department of Conservation makes biking exciting on Great Barrier. It is New Zealand law to wear a helmet when riding. (10) Watch out for walkers as they share tracks.
Surfing and Swimming	**Kayaking and Diving**
There are several famous surf beaches with big waves. Inland, there are hot springs. (11) Bring plenty of sunscreen because the UV rays are extremely dangerous. Burn times in mid-summer are as low as ten minutes, and you still burn in the water.	There are two hire companies operating on Great Barrier for all the gear you need. (12) Kayaking is done on the sheltered western side of the island. Snorkeling and scuba diving are popular everywhere. The wreck of the Wiltshire, off the south coast, provides extra interest.
Fishing and a Seafood Festival	**Learning About Local History**
Eating seafood is a must. Indulge in fish caught by locals, or try your luck at some popular fishing spots. (13) January sees the Mussel Festival. Shellfish is cooked up in every way imaginable, accompanied by musical performances.	(14) The hardwood forests on Great Barrier Island were exploited for over 100 years by loggers. Walking around, you will see ruins from this industry. Most trees are protected these days. There are some old wooden houses from the 19th century that make for excellent photographs.

Section 2: Courses

A
Building Trades (Including: Bricklaying, Building, Carpentry, Fire Protection, Floor and Wall Tiling, and Plumbing) Building: Part-time: 12 hours per week (16) Duration: 2 years This course is for people wanting to acquire building skills for the residential construction industry. You will study the social, environmental, and legal aspects of residential construction projects. Special focus will be on: quantities of materials, site safety, and computing. (18) This course, along with Carpentry and Bricklaying, will give you the technical qualifications for a Builder's Licence.

B
Child Studies (Including: Children's Services, Early Childhood Education and Care, and a Traineeship) Diploma of Early Childhood Education and Care: Part-time: 21 hours per week (3 days) Duration: 18 months This course is for people wanting to become qualified childcare workers in day care centres. You will develop the skills, knowledge, and attitudes relevant to meet the intellectual, physical, and emotional needs of children in day care. Special focus will be on: occupational health and safety, ethical work practices, and legal issues. (21) On completion of this diploma, graduates may apply for advanced standing at universities that offer Early Childhood courses. Note: A police check will be carried out before applications are accepted. A criminal record involving violence or abuse seriously affects career prospects.

C
Real Estate (Including: Agency Management, Marketing, and Property Services) Property Services: (15) Full time: 35 hours per week Duration: 4 months This certificate, which is recognised nationally, provides learners with the skills and knowledge needed to market, sell, lease, and manage property within an agency. It is a pre-requisite for the diploma.

D
(20) **Screen and Digital Media** (Including: Film and TV Production, Interactive Digital Media, and Network Administration) Film and TV Production: (17) Part-time: 21 hours per week (3 days) Duration: 4 months This certificate, a pre-requisite for the Diploma of Screen and Digital Media, introduces learners to the film and television industry. You will learn how to write a script, plan and produce a short pre-recorded programme segment, and work effectively as a production crewmember.

E
Outreach A variety of courses chosen by learners from all Certificate I-II courses on offer at the college, as well as compulsory: Introductory Computing, First Aid, and English Language. Flexible delivery options. (19) *Outreach* aims to remove barriers for people wanting to return to education. These barriers could be: income level, English-language ability, little previous education, geographic isolation, disability, or family commitments.

Mature-aged students

A Only a generation ago, there were few tertiary students who had begun their studies when they were over the age of 21. It was virtually unheard of for people to start courses in their forties or fifties. These days, in all developed countries, not only are there large numbers of online learners who are mature-aged, but, on campus, mums and dads with their laptops and library books are also making an appearance. In some countries, China for example, university study still remains the preserve of the young. Population pressure means that providing education for those aged 18-24 is difficult enough. Only English-language and IT opportunities exist at private colleges for older people.

B (22) There are four main reasons for this rise in mature-aged students. Firstly, universities have changed entry requirements as more courses have become fee-paying. If students can afford to pay, and meet the academic level, then it doesn't matter how old they are. Secondly, the concept of a job for life is a thing of the past. Many people now have several careers. Life expectancy has reached 80 in at least 20 countries; retirement ages have risen accordingly. Therefore, retraining for longer working lives is essential. Lastly, there has been a general expansion of the education sector as the workforce needs to be better trained for a more competitive knowledge-based world.

C Clearly there are advantages to undertaking study later in life. There is the increased likelihood of a higher salary after study, and enhanced self-esteem. But what are some of the difficulties mature-aged students face? The most glaring one is the visual fact that they're not as attractive or energetic as all those young things lounging on quadrangle lawns. (23) It's unlikely that they will socialise with people the same age as their sons or daughters, and that could make university life rather lonely. Befriending other mature-aged students is a possibility, but perhaps they also seem too old.

D In lectures and tutorials, older learners may get tired more quickly, but research has proven they focus on their studies. They work harder, and generally perform better than younger students. Their life experiences and analytical powers are good study aids. (24) When there are group assignments, older students may become annoyed, feeling they do all of the work while the youngsters are out partying or working at part-time jobs. Furthermore, younger students often feel the pressure of their peers more acutely. They may be scared to participate in tutorials, worried what those their own age think of them. This means older students contribute more to discussion. While tutors are certainly grateful for their efforts, the mature-aged students themselves may occasionally wish they were not in the spotlight so often.

E For most mature-aged students, juggling work, family, and other commitments is a tricky business. Their organisational skills are admirable. (25) However, their children, partners, or workmates may resent the absence or distraction of the older student. The student may win a qualification, but he or she may have to fight other battles on the home front.

F (26) Then there are the greatly discouraged mature-aged drop-outs. These people already feel they failed at the end of their schooling by not going on to university, and being unable to complete their studies a second time can cause considerable anxiety. Fortunately, statistics show there are not very many of these people. Completion rates for undergraduate and post-graduate courses, for mature-aged students, are high.

G It takes courage, determination, personal and financial sacrifice to complete studies at university. (27) Despite these difficulties, large numbers of mature-aged men and women all over the world are succeeding.

Section 3: The humble banana

(28) As the world's most eaten fruit, it is hard to believe that the banana has only become widely **available** in the last 100 years. Nor can most people imagine a world without bananas. However, disease is threatening the existence of popular varieties, and while the banana itself is unlikely to die out, what consumers call a banana could change dramatically since new disease-resistant strains may differ in taste, texture, size, and colour from fruit currently on offer.

History

A native of tropical South and Southeast Asia, it is thought (29) bananas were first cultivated in today's Papua New Guinea around **10,000** years ago. Spreading to Madagascar, Africa, and then the Islamic world, bananas reached Europe in the 15th century. The word 'banana' entered English via Portuguese from Wolof – a West African language. Only in 1872 did the French writer Jules Verne describe bananas to his readers in some detail as they were so exotic, and it was another 30 years before plantation-grown produce from Central America would flood the global market.

Botanical data

Most modern edible bananas come from the wild species *Musa acuminata*, *Musa balbisiana*, or their hybrids. Two common varieties today are the larger more curved Cavendish and the smaller straighter Lady Finger both of which turn yellow when ripe.

Bananas are herbs, not trees, although they can reach more than seven metres (24 ft). (30) Their **stem**, not trunk, is a soft fibrous shoot from an underground corm, or bulb. After fruiting, the whole stem dies, and the plant regenerates from the corm, one of which may last 25 years.

Normally, each banana stem produces one very large purple heart inside of which the fruit develops from female flowers, and hangs in a cluster weighing 30-50 kilograms (66-110 lb) and containing hundreds of bananas.

Domesticated bananas no longer have seeds, so their propagation must occur through the removal and transplantation of part of the corm, or through tissue culture in a laboratory, the latter being a complicated procedure that can lead to plant contamination.

Uses and benefits

As bananas grow all year round, they have become a vital crop. They are easy to eat (just peel) and easy to transport (no packaging needed).

Banana fruit, skin, heart, and stem are all edible, and alcohol can also be made from the plant.

The world's greatest banana-eaters are in East Africa, where the average Ugandan devours 150 kilograms (330.6 lb) a year, and receives 30% of calories this way. This habit is healthy since a single 100-gram (3.5 oz) banana contains 371 kilojoules (89 kcal) of energy, and protein represents 1.09% of its weight – 25 times more than that of an apple.

(31) In daily requirements for an adult, one banana provides: 2% of Vitamin B1, 5% of B2, 4% of B3, 7% of B5, 28% of B6, 5% of B9; (31) 15% of Vitamin C; 1% of calcium; 2% of iron; 7% of magnesium; 3% of phosphorous; 8% of potassium; and, 1% of zinc.

A further health benefit is a lower risk of breast, bowel, or liver cancer, and some psychiatrists recommend bananas as they increase dopamine levels in the brain, thus improving mood.

Aside from food and drink, bananas have other uses. Their large flexible leaves become recyclable plates or food containers in Asia. (32) Traditionally, the Japanese boiled banana shoots in lye until their fibres softened and separated. Fine **cloth** was woven from this fibre. Paper is made from banana stems, and more recently, skins have been employed to clean up polluted rivers as their absorption of heavy metals is high.

In several religions, bananas feature prominently. Tamils believe the banana is one of three holy fruits. Buddhists often decorate trays with bananas to offer to the Buddha. Moslems eat copious quantities (33) during the holy month of Ramadan during which time global **trade** in the fruit spikes.

Threats to bananas

Between 1820 and 1950, a banana called the Gros Michel was the most common commercial variety. (34) Suddenly, this was attacked by a fungus called Panama disease, and worldwide, the Gros Michel was almost wiped out. Its commercial replacement, the Cavendish, considered less delicious by gourmands, may now suffer the same fate as its predecessor. (35) All Cavendish bananas are genetically identical, making them susceptible to disease. (36) While the original Panama disease was controlled, it mutated into Tropical Race 4 (TR4), which has destroyed banana crops in Southeast Asia, and for which there is no known defence except genetic modification.

Black Sigatoka is another deadly disease. In Uganda – once a world-leader in banana production – it reduced crops by 40% in the 1970s. The treatment for Black Sigatoka is as controversial as it is expensive ($1000 per hectare per annum) since chemical spray contaminates soil and water supplies. Banana cultivars resistant to Black Sigatoka do exist, but none has been accepted by major supermarket buyers because their taste and texture differ greatly from bananas that shoppers are used to.

In 2010, East Africa was hit by another plague – Banana Xanthomonas wilt. (37) The Ugandan economy lost more than $500 million due to this, and thousands of small farmers abandoned bananas as a crop, leading to widespread financial hardship and a far poorer diet.

(38) Scientists, however, have not given up hope, and the National Banana Research Programme in Uganda has been adding a sweet pepper gene, disease-resistant in a number of vegetables, to bananas. Yet genetically modified crops remain banned in Uganda, and other scientists believe identifying and domesticating disease-free wild bananas rather than adopting expensive and largely unproven gene technology would be more prudent.

(39) Human civilization has a long and critical relationship with bananas. If this is to continue, it may be time to reconsider what a banana is. (40B) The supermarkets may no longer be stocked with big sweet yellow cultivars but with tiny purple, pink, red, or green-and-white striped ones (40E) that currently exist in the depths of the forest and will not be cheap to domesticate.

WRITING: Task 1

Dear Mr Habibi,

I am writing to you about the possibility of taking a fortnight off work in order to complete my Master's degree in Engineering. I am almost finished writing my thesis, which must be submitted to my university by June 30th. Unfortunately, all my annual leave has been used up. Any time I took off would naturally be unpaid; I would also check my email daily, and be available for emergency phone calls. On return, I would endeavour to come into the office earlier than usual and work Saturdays in order to catch up on anything I had missed. I have already spoken about my situation to my colleagues Mr Grunewald and Ms Tak, who are both willing to assume my responsibilities for two weeks.

I realise my temporary absence could be an inconvenience to you and the rest of the team, but in the long term, our company will benefit from my research. As you may be aware, I have been investigating 3-D printing for some time, and my thesis compares three printers already on the market with two designs pending patent and production. Since our company is considering developing software for these printers, my expertise will help give us a competitive edge.

I look forward to hearing from you.

Yours sincerely,
Edwin Bambang Soesanto (219 words)

Task 2: Go to 'If you want a Seven', on page 133.

Appendices

IELTS Log: READING

Copy the next page <u>before</u> you write on it.

Read in English every day.

Read in your first language every day.

Read different kinds of texts.

Share texts you have enjoyed with other candidates.

What is your **PB** each week? (PB = Personal Best, sports vocabulary)

Title of the text I read	Where it came from	Summary of the text	Style Journalistic / Academic / Technical / Literary (a poem or short story)	What the writer's purpose is & who will read the text	Three new words / phrases from the text (3 are enough each time)	Number of words in the text	Time it took me to read it
eg Date palms of Nizwa	*Oman Observer*	Compares different varieties of dates grown in Nizwa; suggests Khalas variety is most valuable and popular	Journalistic semi-formal, some technical words	Provide information to general public, especially tourists to Oman	staggering variety; demand outstrips supply; oval-shaped	c700	30 mins
1							
2							
3							
4							
5							
6							

PERSONAL BEST: Total time spent reading this week = _____. Total number of words read this week = _____.

IELTS Log: SPEAKING – Fluency & Coherence; Pronunciation

Copy this page before you write on it.
Speak in English every day – aloud to yourself, recording yourself, or to other people.
Talk about anything that interests you. Ask people to correct you (nicely).

Who I talked to / What I recorded	What I talked about	What feature(s) I tried to improve Eg: keep on going, speed, chunking, weak forms, contractions, pausing for meaning, phonemes, word or sentence stress, intonation etc	Corrections other people made	Time I spent talking
eg My classmate from Brazil on the bus	The weather; shopping; transport	Contractions	'I'll' instead of 'I will'; 'gonna' for 'going to'	12 mins
eg My cousin in the US on the phone	My studies; her studies; her cat; her city, Cleveland	Keeping on going; correcting myself	None (but her English is vg, so it was nice to listen)	7 mins
eg Recording on my computer	Part 2 topic (a present)	Everything!	I listened later, and could hear too many words were separate – not in chunks. There was lots of hesitation.	2 mins (It's really a long time!!)
1				
2				
3				
4				
5				

Pronunciation that I need to master

Phonemes	Odd words	Consonant clusters	Word stress	Other
eg /iː/ in teach, feeling, & release	whales; New South Wales	sprained	ca-RE-er; COU-ri-er	Intrusion – too /w/ early
1	float & flout	express		
2				
3				
4				

Pronunciation research

Books / CDs I listened to / read	Websites I used

PERSONAL BEST: Total time spent speaking English this week = _____.

IELTS Log: VOCABULARY – Word families

Copy this page before you write on it.
Collect families for new words, not ones you already know!
Ask people to correct you (nicely) if you use the wrong part of speech.

Noun (countable or uncountable?)	Person (if there is one) or thing	Verb (regular or irregular?)	Adjective (true or participial?)	Adverb
extension (c) After the extension, the house was 300 square metres. extent (only singular) I agree to some extent. The extent of the damage was great after the floods.	extender Fish pies are not made with fish but with food extenders – wheat, glucose, and fish flavouring mostly.	extend (reg) I extended my visa.	extensive; extendable; extended My aunt had extensive plastic surgery after she was burnt in an accident. This table is extendable for when we have more guests. Extended families are less common now.	-ly **eg**
				1
				2
				3
				4
				5

Checklists for practice and real tests

Copy these pages four times. Read them before each practice test, and fill them in honestly afterwards.

During a Listening test:	Yes	No	Comments
1 I concentrate hard the whole time because I know the recording is only played once. I never daydream.			
2 In each section, during the pauses, I either read the questions ahead or check my answers. I listen, read the questions, and write the answers at the same time where I can.			
3 Because I've practised all question types, I can deal with each one. **I do not panic.**			
4 To keep up with the recording, I let words go that I do not know.			
5 I answer questions in the same order as the audio.			
6 I only mark **key** words in the question booklet to help me. I don't mark too many.			
7 I follow all the instructions carefully. In particular, I never write more than three words for an answer.			
8 Where there are examples, I analyse them. I don't skip them.			
9 Sections 1 and 2 are quite easy, so I make sure I get them right. (Each section has 10 questions; each of the 40 questions is worth one mark.)			
10 As there is no pause in the middle of the recording in Section 4, I read only MCQ question stems, and skim all other questions.			

During a Listening test:		Yes	No	Comments
11	I look for relationships between questions, so I can answer more than one at a time.			
12	I predict answers.			
13	I analyse the grammar of questions, especially the summary or sentence completion questions. I decide whether my answer should be a noun, a verb, a gerund, an adjective etc.			
14	If two answers are needed for a question, I write both, eg: *A, E*. I never put two answers where there should be one. In Section 3 or 4, if asked to fill gaps with *ONE WORD ONLY*, that's what I do.			
15	I write all my answers neatly, especially *T / F*, letters, or numbers. I'm careful with: *i, ii, iii, iv, v, vi, vii, viii, ix, & x*. If I cross out or erase, my final answer is clear.			
16	I transfer my answers in 6 minutes, and check for 4. I always check my spelling.			
17	I only change an answer if I've transferred or spelt it wrongly, or if I'm **100%** sure it should be changed.			
18	I check that my answers are sensible even if I'm not sure they're correct.			
19	I answer every question even if I have to guess.			
20	If I'm a strong candidate, I might double-check my answers randomly, or from 40 backwards.			
Anything else I need to be careful about:				

Note: *If I find Section 4 hard, and I've guessed most of it, I realise I'm unlikely to get more than 5.5.*

CHECKLIST   *Copy these pages four times. Read them before each practice test, and fill them in honestly afterwards.*

During a Reading test:	Yes	No	Comments
1	I concentrate for the whole hour although I may have a sip of water or stretch my body.			
2	Because I've practised all question types, I can deal with each one. **I do not panic.**			
3	I read the questions and write the answers onto the answer sheet as I go since there's no time to transfer.			
4	To help with checking later, I mark my answer sheet after questions 13 or 14, and 26 or 27 to show where the three passages are. (These divisions are a little different in each test.)			
5	I follow all the instructions carefully. In particular, I never write more than three words for an answer.			
6	I always read the questions **before** each passage even when they're printed after.			
7	I use graphics, titles, and headings to give me clues about the text.			
8	Where there are examples, I analyse them. I don't skip them.			
9	I aim to read and answer **Passage 1 in 15** minutes; **Passage 2 in 18** minutes; **Passage 3 in 22** minutes; so I have at least **five minutes to check**.			
10	I leave difficult questions for later. I return to these questions near the end of the test.			
11	I mark **key** words in the question booklet to help me. I may use a code: underlining, circling, and zigzagging.			
12	Where there are T / F / NG questions I **always** mark the evidence in the text. If I'm unsure about an answer, NG may be my best choice.			
13	Since I know Yes / No / NG questions are about the opinion of the writer, or other writers mentioned, I look for evidence as with T / F / NG questions, but I also look carefully for words with positive or negative connotations.			
14	If two answers are needed for a question, I write both (eg: *library & bookshop*).			

During a Reading test:		Yes	No	Comments
15	I never put two answers where there should only be one.			
16	In the Reading passages, I skim for general ideas. I scan for details, especially numbers and names.			
17	At all times, I work quickly. I read the text word by word **only** in Passage 3, or when I check at the end.			
18	I look for relationships between questions. I try to answer two or more questions at a time.			
19	I predict answers.			
20	I analyse the grammar of questions, especially the summary, sentence completion, and labelling questions. I decide whether my answer should be a verb, a gerund, an adjective etc.			
21	On the answer sheet, I write all my answers neatly, especially *T/F*, letters, or numbers. I'm careful with: *i, ii, iii, iv, v, vi, vii, viii, ix, & x*. When I cross out or erase, my final answer is clear.			
22	When I answer with words taken from a reading passage or a question box, I make sure I copy them correctly. When I supply words, myself, again I check my spelling, and also my grammar.			
23	If a question asks for an answer from a passage or a box, I don't use synonyms. Even if they're right, I will lose a mark.			
24	I only change an answer if I've transferred or spelt it wrongly, or if I'm **100%** sure it should be changed.			
25	I check that my answers are sensible even if I'm not sure they're correct.			
26	I answer every question even if I have to guess.			
27	If I'm a strong candidate, I might double-check my answers randomly, or from 40 backwards.			
Anything else I need to be careful about:				

Note: *If I find Passage/Section 3 hard, and I've guessed most of it, I realise I'm unlikely to get more than 5.5.*

CHECKLIST   *Copy these pages four times. Read them before each practice test, and fill them in honestly afterwards.*

During a Writing test:	Yes	No	Comments
1 I concentrate for the whole hour although I may have a sip of water or stretch my body.			
2a I remember: **A, W, C**. (**ANALYSE, WRITE, CHECK**.) Task 1 is worth around 40%. A good way to spend my time is: **3 minutes** to **analyse** the Task 1 inputs;			
2b **15 minutes** to **write** Task 1;			
2c **2 minutes** to **check** Task 1; (Total time = 20 minutes).			
3a Task 2 is worth around 60%. A good way to spend my time is: **5 minutes** to **analyse** and write a **plan** for the Task 2 question;			
3b **30 minutes** to **write** Task 2;			
3c **5 minutes** to **check** Task 2; (Total time = 40 minutes). (Be honest here – **ALWAYS CHECK!**)			
4 Because I've practised all question types, I can deal with each one. **I do not panic.**			
5 I mark only **key** words in the inputs and essay questions to help me. I don't mark too many.			
6a In Task 1 of the Academic module, my first paragraph is one or two sentences saying what the inputs are.			
6b My second paragraph gives an **overall** statement. That is, I decide what the most noticeable feature of the inputs is. It's unlikely I'll score more than 6 without this.			
6c Then, I compare and contrast the material if it is a graph or a table; or, I logically describe a plan, diagram, or process.			
7 In Task 1, I don't give my opinion on the inputs, but I do in Task 2 essays.			
8 I choose vocabulary appropriate to academic writing. This means there are a lot of noun phrases. I avoid contractions, spoken language (many phrasal verbs), slang, or texting. I may need the passive to describe a process.			

During a Writing test:	Yes	No	Comments
9 If I take the General Training test, where I need to write a letter in Task 1, I include all the information in the bullet points. (There are usually three.)			
10 In GT, I might use an informal or semi-formal style if the letter is to a friend.			
11 In both the Academic and GT tests, I join phrases, sentences, and paragraphs naturally. I don't use too many linkers.			
12 I demonstrate a range of grammatical structures, including compound and complex sentences. I'm aware that Task 1 often tests tenses, so I know my irregular verbs.			
13 I use a range of vocabulary, and I avoid repetition.			
14 In the Academic test, I don't need to describe everything in the inputs as there is a 150-word limit. However, in both Academic and GT, I must write at least 145 words or I'll lose marks.			
15 I may answer Task 2 first or second.			
16 I don't copy the question exactly in Task 2; I write it in another way. If I copy it, I'll lose marks.			
17 In Task 2 of both the Academic and GT tests, I must analyse the question well. If there are two parts to it, I discuss both of them.			
18 I only write what is **relevant** to the question, and I never write about a similar or a different topic. The examiner will notice this, and I'll get a 5 or less.			
19 For Task 2, I make a plan on my answer booklet. I don't just put: 'Introduction, Body, Conclusion' – I note arguments and examples with the strongest first.			
20 In my essay, I include a topic sentence in each paragraph, and then give clear examples. If I don't have topic sentences, if my examples are weak, or I don't have paragraphs, I'll get a 5 or less.			
21 If the essay is about advantages and disadvantages, I need to state clearly in the introduction or conclusion which I think there are more of. In my body, I always have an uneven number of arguments – either more advantages, or more disadvantages.			
22 My Task 2 essays must have at least 250 words. With fewer words, I'll lose marks.			

During a Writing test:		Yes	No	Comments
23	I write my essays neatly in my answer booklet. Bad handwriting usually means a low score.			
24	When I cross out or erase, I make sure my final answer is clear. If I want to add anything, I show clearly where the insert goes.			
25	In the last 5 minutes of the test, I check my grammar (articles, prepositions, auxiliary verbs – most of Task 2 can be written in the present tense). I check my vocabulary (precise and interesting words); and ways to link ideas. I check my spelling and punctuation. If an examiner sees there are no changes on my answer sheet, he or she realises I haven't checked anything. Without checking, I'm unlikely to get more than 5.5.			
26	I remember this is an exam, so I should show what I know.			
27	If I'm a strong candidate, and I hope to get a 7 or above, I must have flair.			
Anything else I need to be careful about:				

Note: *If I can't finish the test or I write short essays, I realise I'm unlikely to get more than 5.5. Mostly, it's hard for me to know what band I'll score.*

CHECKLIST   *Copy this checklist before a real IELTS test. Read it carefully before the test, and fill it in honestly afterwards.*

During a Speaking test:	Yes	No	Comments
1 I clean my teeth before my test, or have a peppermint.			
2 Since this is an exam, the examiner probably may not speak to me before the recording starts, and will expect me to leave the room as soon as the interview has finished.			
3 I concentrate for the whole 11-14 minutes.			
4 Throughout the Speaking, I'm friendly and interested even if I think some questions are silly. I maintain eye contact.			
5 Because I've practised all question types, I can deal with each one. **I do not panic.**			
6 I avoid giving memorised answers. Most examiners will either ignore these, or stop me.			
7 If I don't understand something, I say to the examiner, 'Could you say that again, please?' or 'Could you say that in another way?' or 'What does x mean?' I don't say, 'Repeat!' or 'What means x?'			
8 In Part 1, I can give short answers, but my examiner will probably ask me to extend my answers by adding a 'why' question.			
9 I analyse the grammar of each question and, where possible, reflect it. If the examiner asks, 'Which foreign country **would** you like to visit?', I say, 'I**'d** like to go to Spain because...' The important verb in the question is 'would', which shows a future wish that may not come true. I can't answer with, 'I went to Spain last year,' because this is about the past, and it happened. I can't say, 'I like to visit Canada,' either, because the present simple shows a regular event, meaning, I probably visit Canada every year. I need to understand the functions of verbs.			
10 In Part 2, when I'm asked to talk on a topic for 'one to two minutes', actually, this means I need to talk **for two minutes**, and say at least 350 words. If my answer lasts for only a minute or less, I'm unlikely to get more than 5.			

During a Speaking test:	Yes	No	Comments
11 I have a minute to think about my Part 2 topic, and can make some notes. I use all of this minute, and I do not daydream. Nor do I write the notes in my own language. The examiner will see this.			
12 It's fine to correct my own mistakes. This shows I know they're wrong.			
13 I don't try to get more thinking time by saying, 'That's an interesting question', or 'I've never thought about that', as suggested in some IELTS books or websites. Most examiners consider these delaying tactics to mean that my fluency is poor.			
14 I never say I don't have an opinion because it shows I am not fluent; I make up an answer.			
15 I remember to soften any strong opinions or negative ideas by prefacing them with statements like: 'It might seem', or 'In my opinion'. I should concede when I can: putting the opposite idea first, then adding my own.			
16 I avoid giving opinions that might annoy the examiner. For example, I don't talk about race, religion, or sexuality, and I try to make balanced statements about politics. I know that if a candidate says, 'I hate gay people' – and the examiner doesn't share those views – then he or she will naturally take a dislike to that candidate and give lower marks.			
17 I never tell the examiner which score I need, or ask him / her how I've done. Most examiners find this annoying.			
18 I remember this is an exam, so I should show what I know.			
19 If I'm a strong candidate, and I hope to get a 7 or above, I must have flair.			

Anything else I need to be careful about:

Note: *Speaking examiners are usually friendly; they're also trained to ask questions at my level. Therefore, I may think my exam went well because my examiner smiled a lot, or I talked all the time. In fact, it's hard for me to know what band I'll score.*

Answer sheet

Copy this page twice for each practice test. It is the same for Listening and Reading.

Practice Test #____   **Listening / Reading**

1		21	
2		22	
3		23	
4		24	
5		25	
6		26	
7		27	
8		28	
9		29	
10		30	
11		31	
12		32	
13		33	
14		34	
15		35	
16		36	
17		37	
18		38	
19		39	
20		40	

Total ____ / 40